S

ON REFERRING IN LITERATURE

ON REFERRING IN LITERATURE

EDITED BY

ANNA WHITESIDE

AND

MICHAEL ISSACHAROFF

INDIANA UNIVERSITY PRESS
BLOOMINGTON AND INDIANAPOLIS

Manufactured in the United States of America

Library of Congress Cataloging-in-Publication Data
On referring in literature.
Bibliography: p.
Includes index.
Contents: Metafictional implications for novelistic
reference / Linda Hutcheon—The double bind: self-
referring poetry / Anna Whiteside—Bad references /
Gerald Prince—[etc.]
1. Literature—Philosophy. 2. Reference (Philosophy)
3. Reference (Linguistics) I. Whiteside, Anna.
II. Issacharoff, Michael.
PN49.05   1987   801   86–45748
ISBN 0–253–34262–7
ISBN 0–253–20437–2 (pbk.)
1 2 3 4 5 91 90 89 88 87

CONTENTS

PREFACE

The purpose of this volume is to show how reference is an integral part of (literary) interpretation. While much has been made, quite justifiably, of Jakobson's Theory of Communication, of speech-act theory, and of the sign in recent critical and theoretical works, the question of reference in literature remains a relatively unexplored domain. Those who have ventured to speak of it all too often equate it with mere reference to "real world" existents. But even then the issue is not as simple as it might appear; for what, one must ask, is this literary "real" world? Is it not, in fact, an artificial construct? If so, how is referential illusion created? This volume explores these problems and goes on to deal with other types of literary reference, showing what it is and how it works. Reference lies at the crossroads of reality and fiction, perception and interpretation being contingent on the way the referent and reference are construed.

Up till now, discussion of reference has been primarily philosophical and linguistic, with little contact between the Anglo-Saxon and European schools of thought. Although Ogden and Richards, as early as 1923 in *The Meaning of Meaning*, propounded their theory of the tripartite sign (Symbol/Thought/Referent), and though recent interest in Peirce, Austin, Searle, and Strawson has continued to underscore the validity of the referent as an indispensable third dimension of the sign, literary applications have been few. The European school, on the other hand, under the influence of Saussurian linguistics, has hitherto considered the sign as a binary entity (Signifier/Signified), while the referent was all but overlooked. Literary semiotics has tended to apply to its analyses the abstract Saussurian construct rather than the empirical Anglo-Saxon model. Yet the latter is, in fact, better suited to the specifics of literary interpretation.

These essays collectively pave the way to a marriage of the two schools and provide a series of essentially empirical applications of different aspects of the theory of reference (and hence of semiotics and linguistics) to a wide spectrum of major modern literary texts, comprising samples of drama, fiction, and poetry. We thus offer the reader a volume of practical semiotics focussing on the referent and reference in varied literary situations. The conclusion provides the theoretical backcloth for discussing and honing the multi-faceted concept of literary and, by definition, linguistic reference. It is our hope that these collected essays, given their empirical slant, will serve as the basis for similar applications in virtually any domain in world literature, in any genre, and thereby extend reference theory through the examination of literary praxis.

All the essays in this volume touch on types, ways, and modes of referring, as well as referentially determined meaning. The order in which they are presented is especially designed to reflect the ever-widening referential contexts they imply. For the way referring expressions and their referents (thus reference and ultimately meaning) are construed depends first and foremost on contexts and their interplay. The latter inevitably imply mode and mode-mixing (of "serious" and make-believe discourse, for example), help define types of reference (definite or indefinite, direct or opaque, unique or ambiguous), and obviously play an essential role in referential dynamics. For as anaphoric and cataphoric chains of reference evolve, they inter-relate and so propel reference and coreference between contexts in a continually expanding and protean cross-referential network.

Accordingly, the first essay, by Linda Hutcheon, presents an overview of the four contextual spheres or levels: metatextual, intratextual, intertextual, and extra-textual. Since her topic is "Metafictional Implications for Novelistic Reference" she arranges the levels according to their self-referential bias. Thus the "autore-presentational" or metatextual level is linked with the intertextual, since both are self-reflexive, while the extratextual and the intratextual are not. The essays that follow first elaborate reference within one contextual level, gradually widening to two, then three contexts, comparing and contrasting contextual interplay, and finally (in the last three chapters) embrace all contexts viewed in an ever-expanding frame-work of complementary contexts, reaching beyond them, opening up new referential horizons.

The second essay, by Anna Whiteside, limits itself to the metatextual context in self-referring poetry, discussing signs which are not only their own referents but also refer to their own process of reference and, thereby, of generating sense. Next Gerald Prince explores "bad reference" (in a Robbe-Grillet novel) which never succeeds in being extratextual or even intertextual, but remains intratextual and, in a sense, self-referential, since these apparently non-referring expressions ultimately refer to themselves as what they are: pure fiction. Jean Alter's "Waiting for the Referent: Waiting for Godot?" contrasts the virtual text as an intratextual entity and the performed text as an extratextual, ideological statement—one amongst a host of possible others, and so referring to the particular ideology it mirrors. In "Topological Poetics: Eluard's 'La Victoire de Guernica,' " Jean-Jacques Thomas also explores the opposition between intratextual and extratextual reference. He sees the extratextual evidence of the massacre of Guernica as a way of enhancing the irony underscored by this poem's internal system of opposition: victory versus the catastrophe the very name Guernica evokes. In the same vein, dealing with fiction, playscripts, and poetry, Françoise Meltzer, Michael Issacharoff, and Ross Chambers all develop the discussion of proper names: their status when, in literature, they refer extratextually to known existents such as Napoleon, Lenin, and Paris, and the altered status their intratextual use confers. Thus Napoleon is used to make fiction "realistic," Paris to trip the reader and so make him aware that in fact intertextuality (and not extratextual reference as it at first appears) is Baudelaire's dominant context, since his Parisian pictures refer first and foremost to other Parisian *pictures*. Michael Issacharoff uses reference within a play to Lenin and the quotation of one of his letters to show how different types of speech-act and the mixing of serious and non-serious modes determine reference, while at the same time con-trasting extratextual and intertextual reference. Ultimately, as in the case of Guernica and Napoleon, it is the intratextual context which prevails. Michael Issacharoff goes on to contrast this intratextuality, prevalent in dramatic dialogue, with the play-script's "serious" extratextual instructions to real people (actors) about how to perform.

Intertextuality is explored by Bruce Morrissette in his analysis of Robbe-Grillet's device of slipping into and out of juxtaposed texts so that reference which initially seemed extratextual is only intertextually operative. It forms a series of intertextual mirrors and coreferential linkings. Recognizing these intertextual chains, and the codes to which they refer, is all part of a complex interpretational strategy.

Patrice Pavis, in "Production, Reception, and the Social Context," also focusses on interpretational strategies. In examining play productions as extratextually ideo-logical statements (as do Jean Alter and Michael Issacharoff), he links interpretation to the intratextual whole, whose signs *mean* precisely through their internal reference and interplay. This intratextual level then affords a comparative intertextual inter-pretation and, finally, an ideological extratextual one as it incorporates superimposed levels of different ideologies. Wladimir Krysinski adds to these three contexts a metatextual one, thereby reminding us of the metatextual perspective of the first essay. But the focus is different, for what interests him is not so much the metatext mirroring the text (though inevitably it does) as texts which mirror their own creative process, and, whilst playing on extratextual and intratextual reference, point to their own process of becoming; that is, they refer autotelically. The final essay by Thomas Lewis on "The Referential Act" picks up this process and explores reference as an *act*. He opens the door to the ideological becomings of the text by showing how its ideology mirrors both those of other texts and the extratextual ideological pro-jections of successive generations of readers. So reference, and the ideological interpretations it engenders, expands in ever-widening circles from the moment of a text's inception to the last syllable of its recorded readings.

Our warm thanks are due to all our contributors for their cooperation and patience; to Margot Dalingwater, to Manon Ames and McMaster University, and to Kitty Letsch and Johns Hopkins University for their help in preparing the typescript.

I.

METAFICTIONAL IMPLICATIONS FOR NOVELISTIC REFERENCE

Linda Hutcheon

The critical acceptance, not to say canonization, of contemporary metafiction—postmodernist, neobaroque,[1] or whatever it is eventually to be named—has led to a rethinking of many of the traditional assumptions about the novel as a mimetic genre. In other words, the actual forms of the fictions themselves have brought about a challenging of the theories that purport to explain them. For example, a self-reflexive form of fiction, one which in effect constitutes its own first critical commentary, has disturbing implications for concepts of novelistic reference. While the realist novel of the last century has usually provided the data base from which Marxist theories of reference[2] have developed, metafiction's *auto*-referential dimension complicates any attempt to conceive of fictional reference only in intra-textual and extratextual terms. The major worry is probably that perhaps what metafiction has really done is to make explicit what is a truism of *all* fiction: the overdetermination of novelistic reference.

Of all the literary genres, the novel has had the most difficulty in escaping from naïve referential theories. Poetry was rescued from the myth of the instrumentality of language by the Symbolists, the New Critics, and a host of others. Part of the novel's problem is no doubt the result of the extended length of the genre. New Critical methods are not totally successful with larger verbal structures, partly because of the limitations of human memory: a novel is never one coherent spatio-temporal unit in the reader's mind, as a lyric poem might be. Critics, in discussing its language, must therefore decide whether they will isolate passages as subtexts for commentary, trace linguistic threads through a work, or use some other method.[3] Metafiction, in one sense, resolves this particular critical dilemma by bringing the formal language issue into the foreground of the fiction itself.

This kind of linguistic self-reflexiveness[4] can be overtly thematized in a text. Of course, the powers and limitations of language in both experiential and literary contexts are themes that are not the exclusive property of contemporary fiction. *Tristram Shandy*, not to mention *Don Quijote*, had raised the same questions about linguistic functioning in their narratives. What does seem to be more uniquely modern is the actualized or concretized version of these insights into language and the increased stress on the role of the reader. If words have the power to create worlds, for novelist and for reader, then novels can perhaps be generated from word play. Jean Ricardou, following the lead of Raymond Roussel, is only one of those who have investigated this possibility.

I.

If metafiction in general calls attention, overtly or covertly, to the fact that it is *text* first and foremost, that it is a human construct made up of and by words, then the traditional mimetic assumptions of novel criticism are explicitly being contested by the fiction itself. The "referential fallacy," when applied to this kind of fiction, becomes in a sense short-circuited. It is no longer, in Michael Riffaterre's formulation,[5] both the central obstacle to and the first step towards the reader's reaching the significance (semiosis) of the text. Instead, the fiction itself points to the fallacy as a fallacy, thereby preempting much of its status as necessity by presuming it as a given. What is immediately postulated as axiomatic in such fiction is the fictiveness of the referents of the text's language.

The clearest paradigm for this postulation is fantasy literature: here new, nonexistent worlds must be created by using only the language of *this* world. But, of course, *all* novelists must convince the reader of the "existence" of their fictive universes, at least *during* the act of reading, and they must do so through language alone. Fantastic fiction, it might be argued, demands an increased effort on the writer's part because of the axiomatic imaginary character of its world. But perhaps the opposite is really true; that is, perhaps the reader's expectations as he reads a fantasy novel facilitate the task by also making axiomatic the fictiveness of the referents of the language. No one seems to demand that Tolkien's Middle Earth be a counter to our empirical world, just that it be an intratextually coherent universe. Tolkien himself wrote that the successful story-maker creates "a Secondary World which your mind can enter. Inside it, what he relates is 'true': it accords with the laws of that world. You therefore believe it, while you are, as it were, inside."[6] This would be true of even more radical fantasy worlds such as that of Ambrose Bierce's "The Damned Thing," where there are colours human eyes cannot see and sounds human ears cannot hear, or in David Lindsay's land of Tormance (in *A Voyage to Arcturus*) where Maskull, the human hero, has to grow non-human organs to cope with the geographical and emotional peculiarities of each region.

Fantasy literature manages to evade the demand for extratextual reference that plagues more traditional, especially realist, narrative. The self-conscious thematization of this very issue in metafiction acts as a marker of fictionality (like "once upon a time") and suggests that the referent of the language of *all* fiction is likely not the same as that of non-literary language. Prose may also be the form of our newspapers and our letters, but there is one important difference in context between my letter to my parents and that of Richardson's Pamela to hers. My letter will be judged by informational or expressive criteria (the accuracy and interest of its details, my sincerity as writer), but both the details and the form of Pamela's letter have an intratextual structural function in the plot and character motivation of the novel, *Pamela*. They have, in addition, no necessary reference at all to any extratextual reality.

Jean Ricardou feels that the main problem of the kind of realist poetics that would deny this last statement arises from a naïveté about extralinguistic reference that results in a confusing of the signified of a literary sign and its referent: "I think of all those people who, when reflecting on a novel, say: if I had been that character I would have done something different. . . . Well, one could say that those people are transposing a character from the domain of the signified to that of the referent."[7] But, despite the convenience of this distinction, it is not quite accurate. Surely, in strictly linguistic terms, the signified of a word in my letter and of the same word in Pamela's would be the same, that is, if they were taken in isolation. Their different contexts, however, would demand different referents. Therefore one could say that it is the nature of the referent itself that changes when a fictive universe is posited.

This kind of thinking underlies much of the recent work in pragmatics, semantics, and logic[8] on alternate or possible worlds, especially theories derived from Frege's distinction between sense and reference (or, in Ricardou's Saussurian terms, signified and referent).[9] Frege argued that in ordinary language usage a sign could have a sense and yet no reference if the latter did not "demonstrably" exist in our empirical world. In *literary* discourse, however, this idea of truth-value reference ceases to have much value or meaning, and Frege's own solution is not very satisfying. In an epic poem, he argues, "we are only interested in the sense of the sentences and the images and feelings thereby aroused. The question of truth would cause us to abandon aesthetic delight for an attitude of scientific investigation." If literary texts do not denote but only seem to denote, as Frege claims, then perhaps the notion of reference has to be expanded—not denied—to include such pseudo-denotative processes by which readers create fictive worlds. Recently pragmatic theories of "fictionality," as the regulative principle dominating all semantic operations in literary communication, have offered one way of opening up the concept of novelistic reference to make room for the implications of metafiction that explicitly or implicitly teaches its reader how to create its universe out of words, how to actualize a possible world through the act of reading. The fictions of Robert Coover, John Barth, Julio Cortazar, John Fowles, and others encode the fictiveness of their worlds directly into their texts, thereby implicating both the agent (the reader) and his or her world model in the creation of a new world.

These novels all suggest that what would be useful would be an expanded notion of referentiality that would make possible distinctions between real and fictive referents. One such theory was offered by Georges Lavis in response to a Frege-like claim that literary texts lacked referents.[10] At the level of *langue*, Lavis claims (using Saussure's definition of reference), there can be real referents which are either physical ("table," "forehead") or non-physical ("honesty"). There can only be fictive referents which are physical ("unicorn") or non-physical ("ubiquity"). At this level of *langue*, fictive referents are not real because they are nonexistent in empirical reality. On the level of *parole*,[11] the issue is more complex and more relevant to our discussion of literature. Referents can again be real, as in most ordinary language usage, or fictive (physical or not). Here, however, they are fictive either because they are lies (false referents) or because the objects are imagined. Obviously this latter case is of interest here, for two reasons. First, the denigration of fiction in earlier periods as "lies" can be seen to have its root in this question of false and fictive referents. Second, in the literary text, one could argue that there are no such things as real referents for the *reader* at least: *all* are fictive—"table," "forehead," "unicorn," "honesty," "ubiquity"—because their context would be an imagined world. Readers accept this as a given when they accept the fact that what they are reading is a fiction, that is, an imagined construct.

This acceptance is what Norman Mailer plays upon in *The Armies of the Night* when he divides his book into two parts: the novel as history, and history as a novel. Genres are more than mere classificatory devices for literary critics; they also enable readers to orient themselves and to understand the context in which they must situate the referent. "In the novel," wrote Maurice Blanchot, "the act of reading is unchanged, but the attitude of the person reading makes it different."[12] It is very relevant to the reading experience whether or not the referent is believed to be real or fictive, that is, whether one is reading about the real world or one is creating an imaginary possible world oneself. This is not to deny referentiality, as we shall see, but rather to reconsider its dimensions.

Metafiction today challenges that reification which made what is essentially a temporally limited period-concept of realism into a definition of the entire novel genre. The result of this realist imperialism had been the implied positing of the referent of fiction as *real*, with the underlying assertion (and apologia for the novel) that if something "really happened," or could be made to seem to, it was therefore its own justification and verification.[13] But this referential illusion could be said to destroy the integrity of the sign, almost cancelling out the signified by presuming direct collusion between referent and signifier. This establishes a kind of incomplete denotation (sign/referent becomes signifier/referent) in order to create what Barthes called an "*effet* de réel."

Yet even early and traditionally realistic novels have thematized this effect as mere effect. Don Quijote and Emma Bovary are literary examples of what happens when the referent of fiction is presumed to be real and operative. Emma is the most serious of realists, for she truly believes that art, even the romantic literature she reads, is a vehicle for experiences which really exist or can be made to exist in her own world. Her belief raises the question of how both ordinary and literary language can ever correspond to the precise nature of non-verbal realities. It is not that Emma reads the wrong books, as some have suggested, but that, like Don Quijote, she reads believing the referents to be real.

It is now an accepted truism of much contemporary criticism that literature cannot lay claim to truth value in a philosophical sense, and that in effect it derives its autonomous ontological status and value from this very fact. We can now see that the linguistic reason for this autonomy is that a truth claim would demand a real referent, not a fictive one. At the level of *parole*, lies and imaginary objects lack real referents. It is the fictiveness of the language's referents that effects the freeing of the reader from what Georges Poulet has called his "usual sense of incompatibility between [his] consciousness and its objects.''[14] It is the *objects*, which he or she now creates, that have changed their level of reference. Fictive referents[15] project a fictional universe, one which is aware always of its verbal reality.

One warning ought to be issued at this point: in fiction, the fictive referent and the signified ought never to be confused, in the sense that the former lies outside the Saussurian linguistic sign. Its focus is the imagination of the reader: hence Ricardou's refusal to acknowledge the different kinds of reference. Within his structuralist critical framework, the referent is, in fact, irrelevant. In the act of reading a novel, however, especially a metafictional one, it is too relevant to ignore. This is not in any way to place the referent above the sign itself in importance for textual analyses. Two signs may have the same referent ("mutt" and "dog") but, since the signified marks the distinctive features of the sign, the pejorative connotations of "mutt" are revealed through it and not through the referent that both signs share. In cancelling out this important role of the signified, realist dogma implicitly postulates a common real referent that all readers share, despite individual ideolects. In doing so, one could argue, a realist poetics actually mitigates the possibility of a "vivid" imagining of the text's universe.

II.

When a reader first picks up a novel and begins to read, one could say that at this early stage s/he can *only* read in such a way as to refer words to his/her own linguistic and experiential knowledge (which, since it includes his/her past reading experience as well, is in no way limited to his/her actual practical experience).[16] This is the realm of the Peircean "secondness," of "object," which exists prior to the sign. It is that with which the reader and author must presuppose an acquaintance in order for communication to take place at all. Gradually the words read by the reader take on their own unity of reference and create a self-contained world that is its own validity through its own contextual ideolect. Although this created world is total and complete, novel reference itself is never so. This is the difference between a novel and a film. In other words, the reader busily fills in the gaps in reference, guided by the text's encoded instructions,[17] actualizing a new possible world but doing so, at first, by means of his/her linguistic and empirical knowledge of his/her own world. The metafictions of Jorge Luis Borges, for one, stand as allegories of this, the reading (as well as writing) side of *poiesis*. The fictive referents gradually accumulate during the act of reading, thereby constructing a "heterocosm"—another cosmos, a second ordered referential system. This fictional universe is obviously not an object of perception, but an effect to be experienced by the readers, in the sense that it is something created by them and in them. Yet here *is* a link to real life.

Criticism today accepts that the novel is not a copy of the real world; nor does it stand in opposition to it. It seems to be less generally acknowledged, however, that the novel is, in fact, related to life experience in a very real way *for the reader*: that is, the novel is a continuation of that ordering, decoding, naming, fiction-making *process* that is part of the reader's normal coming-to-terms with experience in the real world. And it is this fact that theories of novelistic reference ultimately have to take into account, given the self-conscious narrative and linguistic thematization of it in metafiction itself.

For instance, in John Barth's novel, *The End of the Road*, the mythic world-creating or story-telling capacity of the mind is thematized overtly as the basis of what in the novel is called "mythotherapy." In life, as the doctor explains to the hero, Jacob Horner, "there are no essentially major or minor characters. To that extent, all fiction and biography, and most historiography, are a lie. Everyone is necessarily the hero of his own life story . . . we're the ones who conceive the story, and give other people the essences of minor characters."[18] For Barth, the narrative "heterocosmic" impulse is related to human choice and existential freedom. "So in a sense," continues the doctor, "fiction isn't a lie at all, but a true representation of the distortion that everyone makes of life."

Jacob, who is a teacher of the English language—the means by which he creates his fictions—is in the grip of a Pirandellian relativity paradox. To turn experience into linguistic speech, he reflects,

> —that is, to classify, to categorize, to conceptualize, to grammarize, to syntactify it—is always a betrayal of experience, a falsification of it; but only so betrayed can it be dealt with at all, and only in so dealing with it did I ever feel a man, alive and kicking. It is therefore that, when I had cause to think about it at all, I responded to this precise falsification, this adroit, careful *myth-making*, with all the upsetting exhilaration of any *artist at his work*. When my mythoplastic razors were sharply honed, it was unparalleled sport to lay about with them, to have at reality. (pp. 112–113; italics mine)

Jacob perceives two important things here: that language, by its creative power, is the key to this myth-making, and that, by its structures, language is the means to the only lucidity one can ever know. *Metafictions such as this which show a character looking at—that is, creating through words—the novelistic world, mime the mind's ordering and naming processes of coding and decoding, ciphering and deciphering.* And the essence of literary language lies not in its conforming to the kind of statement found in factual studies, but in its ability to create something new, a coherent, motivated "heterocosm." Svevo's hero in *La coscienza di Zeno*, thinking that he can be the novelist of his own life, learns that to recapture the past is to structure it, to falsify it; in short, to invent it as if it belonged to someone else. Later, in "Il vecchione," the only part of the past that Zeno actually can recall as real is what he wrote down, which is in part invented due to his linguistic limitations. A native Triestine-speaker, Zeno can only relate in Italian, and in writing, those parts of his world for which he has sufficient vocabulary.

This idea of a linguistic "heterocosm" of fictive referents that the reader and the writer co-create is not merely a concept of just *another*, possible world. The *cosmos* is "the world or universe as an *ordered* and *harmonious* system" (*O.E.D.*). Even in classical mimetic theory, mirrors are seen to create worlds even as they imitate (as Plato explains in the *Republic* X). In most metafiction today, literature remains a self-sufficient aesthetic system of internal relations among parts that aim at an Aristotelian harmony which the reader actualizes. But along with coming to terms with the ordered and self-informing characteristics of the novelistic universe (as created in the act of reading), the reader must also come to terms with that fictiveness which we have been examining. Since fiction is not a way of viewing reality, but a "reality" in its own right, the fictive "heterocosm" will have its own rules or codes of which the reader becomes gradually aware as he proceeds.

As well as being ordered and fictional, the "heterocosm" is, as we have seen, constructed in and through language, and both author and reader share the responsibility for this creation. Literature has a particular context created by relationships between words which are activated by the reader. Furthermore, the actual referents of those words are not real in the context of empirical reality. The result of this dual removal from the real is the liberation of the reader from the world he knows only through the senses. This does not deny a mimetic referentiality in the sense of a semantic, pragmatic, or psychological accumulation of reference, but it does relegate it to second place. The fictiveness of the referents of the novel's signs is responsible for this freeing of language from being just a counter to any reality outside fiction. It would be simplistic to claim, as indeed some have, that detective stories are "unrealistic" because, although full of murders, no one really dies. Surely, this is true of all fiction: no one fictional event is more or less real than any other.

In a very basic sense, all reading, whether of literature, history, or science, is an escape, for it involves a temporary transference of the reader's mind from his empirical surroundings to things imagined rather than perceived. The bridge from the real world to the other one of fiction is often explicitly provided by the narrator. For the reader, the narrator's living in that world is simultaneous with his writing of it: "as long as I live or write (which in my case means the same thing)," comments Tristram Shandy. The narrating "historian" of Gabriel García Márquez's Macondo, in *Cien años de soledad*, presents to the reader real, that is historical, events (the Colombian civil wars) as if lived for the first time in his fictive world where fantastic things occur equally logically. Time and space have no meaning (certainly no reference, in Frege's sense) outside the text itself.

It is thus only by the gradual cumulative constructing of the "heterocosm" through its (acknowledged) fictive referents that readers can be said to share in the creation of a text or a possible world. Though in actual fact the novel has no ultimate responsibility to the real, there are still retired cavalry officers who write to Claude Simon that they lived the events of his *La Route des Flandres*, the novel Ricardou claims is not at all representational. When this question arose at Cerisy in 1971, Ricardou's reply was typically dismissive because to him, and possibly to Simon, such real, personal reader experience is irrelevant: "What Simon gives are the referents of fiction: in no way does this mean that the fiction obtained by the text is the equivalent of the 'documentary' referent."[19]

This consciousness of the possible tension in the reading experience between real and fictive referents is perhaps most clearly seen in the novelist's use of real place names in novelistic settings, as many critics have pointed out. Robbe-Grillet admits that he has used Hong Kong and New York as explicit locations for the action of his fiction, but he perhaps rather naïvely adds: "I knew, though, that it could no longer be a question of representation, and I could name a real city while still producing a perfectly imaginary city by my own text."[20] Lest this appear to be a new and radical stand, it is worth recalling Kafka's vision of Prague. In his Preface to *Roderick Hudson*, Henry James even wrote that he actually felt that the naming of a real place in the novel, instead of being economical and realistic as intended, was limiting and unnecessary.

The autonomy of the referents of literary signs in relation to real referents is, therefore, not a modern radical realization of recent *criticism*. And even modern, self-informing, self-reflexive metafiction merely points self-consciously to what is a reality of the novel genre, a reality that has also been singled out indirectly by linguistic philosophers of this century, who worked to end the confusing of the meaning of a name with the bearer of a name, and to suggest that the final interpretation of art is justified by its internal, not external, relations. All language is experience, and not merely a store of easily extractable meaning. Yet there does seem to be a difference in the reader's imaginative process, an increase in the active element of that experience, if the referents are acknowledged as fictive—by the word "novel" on the book's cover, or even more overtly and textually, through metafictional thematization.

In summary, these fictive referents form an increasingly complete "heterocosm" of fictively referential totalities by means of a process of semantic accumulation. Nothing is in these referents that has not been expressed, explicitly or implicitly, in the text itself (or in the reader's filling in of gaps guided by the text). Therefore both the ontological and epistemological natures[21] of the "heterocosm" (of its characters, events, and so on) are in this sense fundamentally different both from those of the real world and from those of other texts. No matter how "prosaic" the language, no matter how close to banal reality the story, the language of fiction is transformed because it invites the reader, in Blanchot's words, "to make the words themselves render an understanding of what is happening in the world being proposed and whose reality is to be the object of a tale."[22]

It is the reader's genre expectations and his imaginative creating of the fictional universe through the referents of the language, and *not* the subject matter or any supposedly real referents, that determine the validity and even the status of the novel's world. In John Fowles's novel, *The French Lieutenant's Woman*, Sarah's "true story" is revealed to be fictional, and it is through the very realization of both that fictiveness and its validity that Sarah can free Charles at the end of the novel—in a *mise en abyme* of the liberation of the reader by the novelist.

III.

Metafictions such as Fowles's, which acknowledge their fictiveness textually and thematically, do not represent the death of the novel as some critics and reviewers insist. Rather, like fantasy fiction, they become emblematic of what begins to look like a literary reality of the novelistic form. All fiction retains the representational orientation of words, largely because this remains outside its control—that is, in the reader. But fiction also creates a new "heterocosm" through those words because the representation is of fictive referents, as the reader soon realizes. A second system comes into being, one which increasingly predominates in his act of reading. Although we move beyond the purely mimetic in reading, we never manage to eradicate it completely. A house in a novel can exist because it exists in the real world, or rather in our perceptual and linguistic experience of the real world. But this is never the point at which the reader stops. The theories of possible worlds and fictive referents permit a broadening of the concept of reference in reading fictive texts. They do so by allowing room for the positing of distinctions, distinctions that bring to light what is really an overdetermination of novelistic reference.

In fact, at least four separate but complementary levels of reference can be isolated in metafiction. Two of these, the most commonly overlapping, have already been discussed in detail: the inner (intratextual) reference is to the "heterocosm" in all its coherence and fictiveness, and the necessary outer mimetic reference is to the world outside the novel, in the sense of that first and inevitable presupposed knowledge that makes the "heterocosm" possible. It is crucial to keep in mind that we are still dealing on this level with fictive referents and that even if the author of a determinedly naturalistic novel should choose (for reasons of economy) to draw upon his/her reader's knowledge of extraliterary realities, he/she can do so in the sense of his/her text's having an "analagon"[23] to the world outside it. One could argue that such a relationship is, strictly speaking, almost metaphoric rather than referential, especially if by referential we mean, with Frege, having a real referent. The inner reference is also to fictive referents, of course. Here fantasy literature is the paradigm, for one hopes that vampires, unicorns, and hobbits only exist in words. Only language can conceive of the absent, the unreal, the supernatural.[24]

There are, however, at least two other levels of reference that metafiction specifically displays: an autorepresentational (the text as text) and an intertextual reference.[25] Certain current theories argue that intertextuality is a modality of perception in literature in that, through recognition of it, the reader identifies the structures which actually make the text a work of art. In Michael Riffaterre's terminology, it is in the "intertext" that this process operates. The loose and flexible limits of the "intertext" are those of the corpus of texts which a reader can legitimately connect with the text s/he is reading. (The legitimacy is determined by Riffaterre by the restriction that the connections must be made between variants of the same structure.)

Without disputing these complex and convincing theories, we should note the simple fact that metafiction again makes overt the intertextual reference of perhaps all fiction. Sometimes a particular text (or set of texts) is backgrounded (intended intertext) as is the Victorian novel, for example, in Fowles's *The French Lieutenant's Woman*. The modern novel here consists of a conscious superimposition of the new and the old. It incorporates the techniques and structures of fiction as written by George Eliot or Thomas Hardy, but there remains a critical distancing between the backgrounded and the foregrounded texts that still allows us to call this device parody, although the judgment is not always at the expense of the so-called parodied text.[26] Sometimes in metafiction it is not a text but a set of literary conventions, such as the journal or epistolary novel, that is the object of intertextual reference. At other times a particular stereotyped narrative structure will be used. One of the most common of these employed by metafiction is that of the detective or mystery novel, itself a self-reflexive variation of the puzzle or enigma form. Highly codified, the detective novel actually possesses *as conventions* overt and covert modes of self-consciousness: there is often a writer of detective stories embedded within the fiction, just as there is inevitably a discussion about the novel's events happening as if in fiction, not life. On a more covert level, the detective plot itself, the following of clues by the detective, is a hermeneutic allegory of the reader's act.

The ready adaptability of this particular narrative form to metafictional intertextual reference is probably a result of these latter autorepresentational traits. The fact that a text can refer to itself as a text, as language, is not particularly new, but perhaps what is new, as suggested earlier, is the textual level at which it can do so.[27] Furthermore, what metafiction's autoreferentiality appears to do is *not* what one might expect it to, that is, to divert readers from making other references and to limit them to a narcissistic textual formalism. Instead, autoreference and intertextual reference actually combine to direct readers back to an outer reference; in fact, they direct the readers outside the text, by reminding them (paradoxically) that, although what they are reading is only a literary fiction which they themselves are creating through language, this act itself is really a paradigm or an allegory of the ordering, naming processes that are part of their daily experience of coming to terms with reality. Instead of there being a textual dialectic between fiction and reality, as Robert Alter has suggested,[28] there is a conflating of the two poles by the over-determined reference demanded by the act of reading metafiction. The two most self-reflexive modes of reference point directly towards the least so and, from there, outside the text's boundaries. It is true that the extratextual level reached here is one of *process*, the process of reading, and not one of an "analagon" with external reality as a *product* (as fictive referents or represented objects). But the reified notion of mimesis as product representation is one of those nineteenth-century novelistic throwbacks (admittedly one aided by Auerbach, Watt, and other important novel critics) that metafiction challenges.

The overt encoding of the ᵈ   der in these texts forces open the Jakobsonian concept of the self-focussing message in its "poetic" function and demands that the addressee enter as *part* of that self-focussing process, not as part of an additional function (conative). Literary discourse then becomes, in Ricoeur's terms, an *event*.[29] The frequent metafictional use of detective plots and journal and epistolary conventions points to the importance of the event of reading as having a role in literary creation, a role as significant as that of writing. It is the metafiction reader's perception of these superimposed levels of reference that directs him/her into, through, and *out of* the text, the text as language. In other words, in metafiction, the only way to make any mimetic connection to *real* referents, as I have defined them here, would be on the level of *process*, that is, of the act of reading as an act of ordering and creating. The encoding within the text itself of the decoder and his/her role acts as a set of instructions to the *reader who exists in the real world* and who, though implicated directly by the existence of this narratee or surrogate addressee *within* the text, is actually an existing being, an interpreting, deciphering being, outside the work of art. The reader can read (or actualize or bring to life) the "heterocosm" of fictive referents only through an act that is the *same* as, and not the "analagon" of, the decoding process s/he engages in constantly in coming to terms with experience of all kinds. If we insist on wanting to speak of fiction's real referents, which by Frege's definition must exist in the real world, metafiction teaches us that it is going to have to be on another level: the *process* may indeed turn out to be "referential" in this sense, and in a way that the *products* can not be.

NOTES

1. The postmodernist label has recently been given the sanction of John Barth himself in "The Literature of Replenishment: Postmodernist Fiction," *The Atlantic* (January 1980), pp. 65–71. "Neobaroque" is the term used to describe the particular version of this phenomenon that arises in Latin America out of the Spanish tradition. See Severo Sarduy, "El barroco y el neobarroco" in César Fernandez Moreno, ed., *America Latina en su Literatura* (1972; 2nd ed., Buenos Aires: Siglo XXI, 1974), pp. 167–84.

2. See Thomas E. Lewis's interesting attempt to combine Marxist and semiotic approaches to the referent in his "Notes Toward a Theory of the Referent," *PMLA* 94, 3 (May 1979), 459–75.

3. See, for example, Ian Watt, "The First Paragraph of *The Ambassadors*," *Essays in Criticism* 10 (1960), 250–74; David Lodge, *Language of Fiction* (New York: Columbia University Press, 1966), p. x; Roger Fowler and Peter Mercer, "Criticism and the Language of Literature," *Style* 3 (1969), 45–72.

4. There is also a narrative or diegetic form of this. See Linda Hutcheon, "Modes et formes du narcissisme littéraire," *Poétique* 29 (février 1977), 90–106.

5. In his course on "The Semiotics of Poetry" at the International Summer Institute for Semiotic and Structural Studies, University of Toronto, June 1980.

6. J.R.R. Tolkien, "On Fairy-Stories," *The Tolkien Reader* (New York: Ballantine, 1966), p. 37.

7. "Je songe à tous ces gens qui pensent à propos de tel roman: moi, à la place de tel personnage, j'aurais fait autre chose . . . Eh bien, ces gens font en quelque sorte passer un personnage du domaine du signifié à celui du référent." In *Nouveau Roman: hier, aujourd'hui*, II, ed. J. Ricardou et F. van Rossum-Guyon (Paris: U.G.E. 10/18, 1972), p. 43.

8. For example, in the volume edited by Teun A. van Dijk, *Pragmatics of Language and Literature* (Amsterdam and Oxford: North-Holland Publishing Co., 1976), the following articles are of interest: Teun A. van Dijk, "Pragmatics and Poetics," pp. 23–57; David Harrah, "Formal Message Theory and Non-formal Discourse," especially p. 72; S.-Y. Kuroda, "Reflections on the Foundations of Narrative Theory from a Linguistic Point of View," pp. 107–140; and Siegfried J. Schmidt, "Towards a Pragmatic Interpretation of 'Fictionality,' " pp. 161–78.

9. See Frege's "On Sense and Reference" in *Translations from the Philosophical Writings of Gottlob Frege* (Oxford: Blackwell, 1952), pp. 56–78. For the signified/referent par-

allel, see the argument of Oswald Ducrot in O. Ducrot and T. Todorov, *Dictionnaire encyclopédique des sciences du langage* (Paris: Seuil, 1972), pp. 319–20; translation, *Encyclopedic Dictionary of the Sciences of Language* (Baltimore: Johns Hopkins University Press, 1979), pp. 249–50.

10. Georges Lavis, "Le Texte littéraire, le référent, le réel, le vrai," *Cahiers d'analyse textuelle*, No. 13 (1971), 7–22; his attack is upon Arrivé's article in *Langue Française*, No. 3 (septembre 1969).

11. Frege does not make this crucial *langue/parole* distinction.

12. "Dans le roman, l'acte de lire n'est pas changé, mais l'attitude de celui qui lit le rend différent." In "Le Langage de la fiction," in *La Part du feu* (Paris: Gallimard, 1949), p. 82.

13. See Roland Barthes, "L'Effet de réel," *Communications*, No. 11 (1968), 88: "The *having-been-there* of things is a sufficient principle of words" ("*l'avoir-été-là* des choses est un principe suffisant de la parole").

14. "Phenomenology of Reading," *New Literary History* I (Autumn 1969), 55. Poulet, of course, attributes this change to different causes entirely.

15. Paul Ricoeur calls these referents "non-ostensive" ones, but retains a similar definition. See his "The Model of the Text: Meaningful Action Considered as a Text," in *Social Research* 38 (1971), 536. Ricoeur links the concept further to Heidegger and Wilhelm von Humboldt.

16. See Maurice-Jean Lefèbve, *Structure du discours et du récit* (Neuchâtel: La Baconnière, 1971), p. 108, on this point, although his final signified/referent distinction is not in accord with the one presented in this paper.

17. See Wolfgang Iser's *The Act of Reading* (Baltimore: Johns Hopkins University Press, 1978), pp. 135–59.

18. (1958; Garden City, N.Y.: Doubleday, 1967), p. 83. All further references will be to this edition and page numbers will appear in parentheses in the text.

19. "Ce qui est donné par Simon, ce sont les référents de la fiction: cela ne veut nullement dire que la fiction obtenue par le texte est l'équivalent du référent donné à titre documentaire." In *Nouveau Roman: hier, aujourd'hui*, I, p. 30. Note the contradiction to the remark quoted above to the effect that this involved instead a signified/referent confusion. Here he seems to have slipped outside the rigid linguistic structure.

20. "Je savais désormais qu'il ne pouvait plus être question de représentation, et je pouvais nommer une ville réelle tout en produisant par mon propre texte une ville parfaitement imaginaire." *Nouveau Roman: hier, aujourd'hui*, II, p. 166.

21. See Lubomír Doležel, *Narrative Modes in Czech Literature* (Toronto: University of Toronto Press, 1973), pp. 5–6.

22. "Réaliser sur les mots eux-mêmes la compréhension de ce qui se passe dans le monde qu'on lui propose et dont toute la réalité est d'être l'objet d'un récit." In "*Le langage de la fiction*," p. 84.

23. See Claude Duchet, "Une écriture de la socialité," *Poétique* 16 (1973), 450. See also, however, Paul Ricoeur's hermeneutic perspective on this level of reference in "Writing as a Problem for Literary Criticism and Philosophical Hermeneutics," in *Philosophical Exchange* 2 (1977), 10: ". . . to understand a text is to interpolate among the predicates of our situation all the significations which make a *Welt* out of our *Umwelt*. It is this enlarging of our horizon of existence which permits us to speak of the references opened up by the referential claims of most texts."

24. See Tzvetan Todorov, *Introduction à la littérature fantastique* (Paris: Seuil, 1970), p. 87. Trans. R. Howard: *The Fantastic; a Structural Approach to a Literary Genre* (Cleveland: Press of Case Western Reserve University, 1973), p.82.

25. See the early theory of Julia Kristeva in *Semeiotiké: recherches pour une sémanalyse* (Paris: Seuil, 1969), p. 255, and also more importantly, Michael Riffaterre, "The Semiotics of Poetry" course at the I.S.I.S.S.S.,1980.

26. See Linda Hutcheon, "Parody Without Ridicule: Observations on Modern Literary

Parody," *Canadian Review of Comparative Literature* 5, 2 (Spring 1978), 201–211, and also "Ironie et parodie: structure et stratégie," *Poétique* 36 (novembre 1978), 367–77.

27. This is the implication of Ricardou's interdimensional (i.e., fiction/narration) distinction between "autoreprésentation *expressive*" (pejorative) and "autoreprésentation productive" (modern and acceptable) in "La Population des miroirs," *Poétique* 22 (1975), 212.

28. *Partial Magic: The Novel as a Self-conscious Genre* (Berkeley: University of California Press, 1975).

29. "Biblical Hermeneutics," *Semeia* 4 (1975), 29–148; and "Structure, mot, événement" in *Le Conflit des interprétations* (Paris: Seuil, 1969) or the English translation "Structure, Word, Event" in *The Conflict of Interpretations*, ed. Don Ihde (Evanston: Northwestern University Press, 1974).

II.

THE DOUBLE BIND
SELF-REFERRING POETRY

Anna Whiteside

The purported prototype of self-referring expressions is Epimenides' Cretan paradox: "All Cretans are liars," said the Cretan. Since then, many others have also tried their hand. Quine's English rendition of Gödel's[1] mathematical homage to Epimenides is probably one of the best known: " 'Yields falsehood when appended to its quotation' yields falsehood when appended to its quotation." Other examples abound: "The sentence on the other side is true"; the other side of the page says "the sentence on the other side is false." Recently a similar round paradox appeared[2] (see fig. 1). Then there is "This sentence no verb," referring to that very lack by omission, and David Moser's story:

> *This Is the Title of This Story, Which Is Also*
> *Found Several Times in the Story Itself.*
> This is the first sentence of this story. . . . This sentence regretfully states that up to this point the self-referential mode of narrative has had a paralyzing effect on the actual progress of the story itself, that is, these sentences have been so concerned with analyzing themselves and their role in the story that they have failed by and large to perform their function as communicators of events and ideas that one hopes coalesce into a plot, character development, etc., in short, the very *raisons d'être* of any respectable, hardworking sentence in the midst of a piece of compelling prose fiction.[3]

Logicians are not alone in their fascination with self-reference. In the arts the very characteristics of the aesthetic function of an art form are this same ambiguity and self-reflexiveness of the message.[4] A host of examples springs to mind: Bach's and Hindemith's fugal and mirror writing,[5] Magritte's and Escher's art, literature's delight in *mise en abyme* and metacommentary, figures of speech such as palindromes,[6] chiasmas, paragrams, or hypograms,[7] and, most obviously perhaps, concrete poetry and its related forms. Although it is the latter which particularly interests us here, all poetry has a self-referential tendency. For poetic discourse (including the subversive prose-poem) goes beyond diegetic representation, beyond mimesis

Figure 1

too, and in fact, as Michael Riffaterre argues in his *Semiotics of Poetry*, represents nothing but itself.

The types of poetry we will be considering fall into three categories. The first is the ideogramme, the second concrete poetry, the third what I will call, for want of a better term, the sound icon. There also exist various permutations which take up and interweave the perennial loose ends of all three.

The ideogramme, stemming from the Hellenistic *technopagnia*, appears initially to refer extratextually. Apollinaire's "Il pleut" ("It's Raining," figs. 2a, 2b), with rain dripping down the page, or his "La Colombe poignardée et le jet d'eau" ("The Stabbed Dove and the Fountain," figs. 3a, 3b),[8] who flutters (or rather does not) above the fountain's spray of words, are typographical mimetic representations of the rain, in the first case, and a bird and fountain in the second. In "Il pleut" the streaming rain is metaphorically converted into bonds or chains falling away, so that although the title provides context to endow the vertical signifers with a sig-nified, they refer not so much to rain as to themselves as a semiosical chain of semantic polyvalence. The dove and the fountain are referentially more equivocal because the proper names inscribed in the wings of the dove refer (proper names being the truest of referring expressions) to women Apollinaire knew. The fountain's stream of names of his male friends likewise corroborates an impression of extra-textual reference. But here again reference is primarily intratextual, as is obvious from the typically Apollinairian female (dove) and male (fountain) symbols[9] and their visually suggested relationship to one another. It becomes clear that, though the names indeed refer to existents, their function as mentions is not so much that of a definite referring expression to this woman or that man ("individuals," ac-cording to Strawson) as to the two classes "women and men Apollinaire has known," and thus to representative women and men. The two groups refer, as do their symbols here, to their relationship to each other, and the ambiguous lips with the round circle in the middle reiterates the essentially reciprocal nature of the two signs foregrounded by the title and commented on by the labial epigraph. Here, then, the icons of the dove and the fountain cannot seriously be deemed to refer to any particular dove or fountain. If reference there is, it seems rather to collide with

Il Pleut

It's Raining

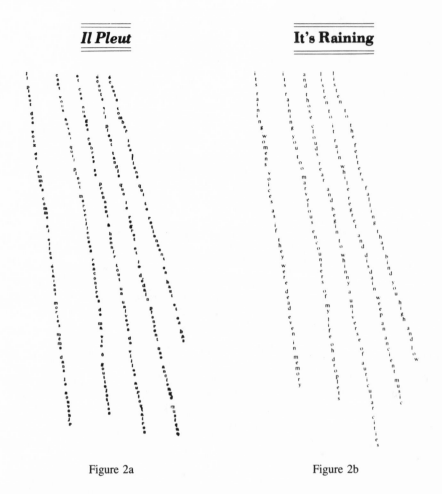

Figure 2a   Figure 2b

the poetic (or aesthetic) function as a visible demonstration of implied ambiguity and intratextual reference.

Concrete poetry is far less preoccupied with any pretence of mimetic extratextual reference for the simple reason that it is much more obviously self-referential. Called variously *"lettrisme,"* "typewriter poems," *"spatialisme,"* "physical poetry," or "thing-poetry," it fulfills what Ezra Pound advocated when he called for a visual poetry akin to ideographic writing in which we seem "to be watching *things* work out their fate."[10] Hiro Kamimura's "Water and Ice" (fig. 4)[11] shows both Pound's "haecceity"[12] and visible dynamics admirably. Here the "things" are the very signs themselves, and their opposition (forty-eight "ices" to one "water" completing the seven-line diamond square) is visually stated in terms analogous to their semantic relation to one another. Just as ice is water in an altered state, and *vice versa*, so the square's presentation is altered to a diamond and this diamond ensconced in the outer framing square. The single water character is surrounded by

La Colombe Poignardée
et le Jet d'Eau

The Bleeding-Heart Dove
and the Fountain

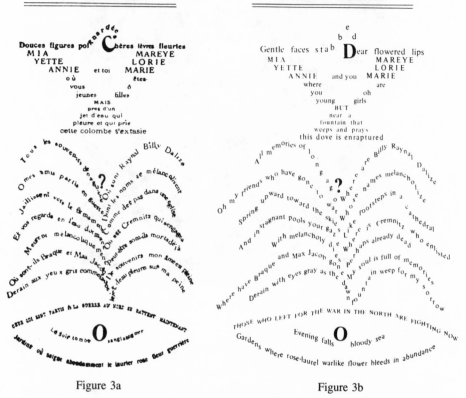

Figure 3a

Figure 3b

"ice" and, beyond, by what might be construed as the water's missing dot multiplied in the four corners of the non-ice non-water field, which thus refers to the marker of the difference between the conflicting signs and concepts, whilst reminding us that, apart from this dot, they are the same. Sameness and difference are stated in white on a dark field—two more concepts represented physically as mutually defining and so mimetically referring to the complementary contradiction of the difference.

In a reversal of concrete poetry's usual letter- or type-centered compositions, Henri Chopin's "Il manque toujours l'y" ("The y is always missing," fig. 5)[13] appears to "refer" to absence. It does this in several ways. The title "refers" to what is not there (and indeed it is not, since the row of y's is missing); but immediately after the two incomplete alphabets and the statement that the y is always missing, there follows an isolated row of them. So, though it is missing in the alphabetical system represented here in assorted typefaces, it is present outside the system. It is there (y means "there" in French) in more senses than one. It is visible not as a printed letter, but as a space all through the alphabet—once back to front—a

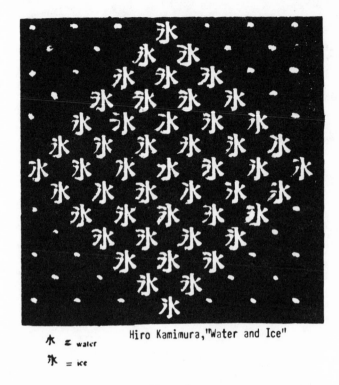

Hiro Kamimura,"Water and Ice"

水 = water

氷 = ice

Figure 4

mirror image of the reader's enlarged why (and "y," since it is conspicuously *not* "there") and, once more, in fragmented form. These fragments could be construed as *y*'s absence being about *y* since the upper left fragment can be seen as an inverted *i* with a long dot, which, in turn, could be a fragment of a distorted capital iota (⌐: doubly distorted because not only is it fragmented, but the angles of this z-like letter should be oblique and not acute). In this case the pivotal dot-cum-iota fragment refers to and relates the two forms of iota, the "*i grec*" (French for *y*), neither standing up straight, and both upside down in relation to each other—perhaps corresponding to the righthand *y*'s inversion.

Indeed switching around, ambiguity, and being left out are the historical fate of this letter. Used in Latin to transcribe the Greek *upsilon*, it was an abused *iota*, as the lexicalized interpretation of *S* and *U* (Chopin's only upper case letters in this otherwise lower case alphabet) corroborate, by asking "est-ce *U*" (pronounced as the letters *s u* are in French)—is it *U*? The ambiguous answer to the doubts raised by this switching around: "Quelle importance" ("what does it matter" or "what importance," since there is no question mark), merely echoes the ambiguity of this letter in French: both yod and *i*, it is half vowel, half consonant; it is both letter and word. As a word (which appeared in French in 842) or, more precisely, as a pronoun, it can refer to many words left out or places not seen; as a letter, it is all

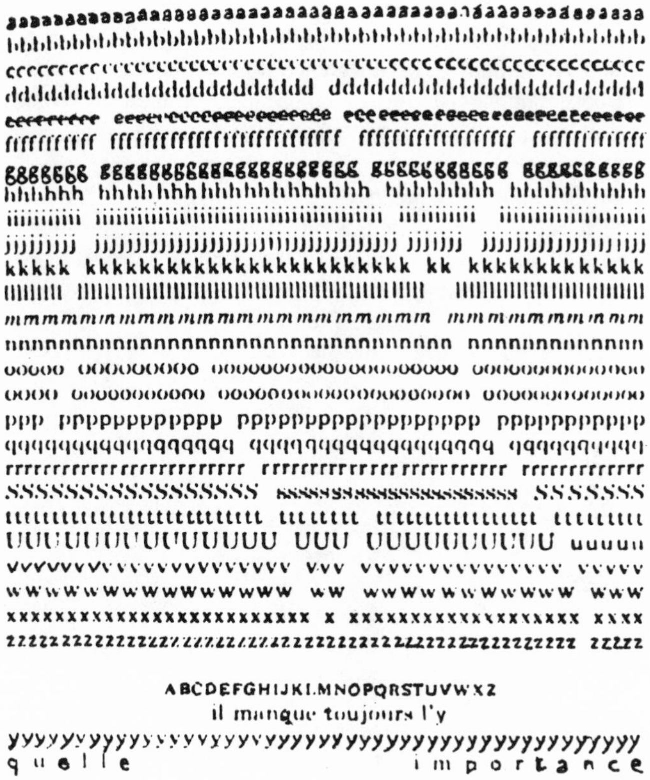

aaaaaaaaaaaaaaaaaaaaaaaaaaaaaaaaaaaaaaaaaaaaaaaaaaaaaa
bbbbbbbbbbbbbbbbbbbbbbbbbbbbbbbbbbbbbbbbbbbbbbbbbbbbbb
ccccccccccccccccccccccccccccccccccccccccccccccccccccccc
ddddddddddddddddddddddddd ddddddddddddddddddddddddddd
eeeeeeeee eeeeeeeeeeeeeeee eeeeeeeeeeeeeeeeeeeeeeeee
fffffffff fffffffffffffffff ffffffffffffffff fffffffffffff
ggggggg gggggggggggggggggg gggggggggg gggggggggg
hhhhhh hhhhh hhhh hhhhhhhhhhhhhh hhhhhhhhh hhhhhhhhhh
iiiiiiiii iiiiiiiiiiiiiiiiiiiiiiiiiiiiiiiii iiiiiiiiii iiiiiiiiiiiiiiiiiii
jjjjjjjj jjjjjjjjjjjjjjjjjjjjjjjjjjjjjjjjj jjjjjjj jjjjjjjjjjjjjjjjjj
kkkkk kkkkkkkkkkkkkkkkkkkkkkkkk kk kkkkkkkkkkkkk
lllllll llllllllllllllllllllllllllllllllllllllll llllllllllllllllllllllll
mmmmmmm mmm mm mm mm mm mm mm m mm m mm mm m m m
nnnnnnnnnnnnnnnnnnnnnnnnnnnnnnnnn nnnnnnnnnnnnnn
ooooo ooooooooo oooooooooooooooooooo oooooooooooooo
oooo oooooooooo oooooooooooooooooo ooooooooooooo
ppp pppppppppppp ppppppppppppppppppp ppppppppppp
qqqqqqqqqqqqqqqqq qqqqqqqqqqqqqqqqqqq qqqqqqqqqq
rrrrrrrrrrrrrrrrrrrrrrrr rrrrrrrrrrrrrrrrrrrrrr rrrrrrrrrrrr
ssssssssssssssssss sssssssssssssssssssssssss ssssss
ttttttttttttttttttttttttttt tttttttt tttttttttttttttttt ttttttttt
uuuuuuuuuuuuuuuuu uuu uuuuuuuuuuuu uuuuu
vvvvvvvvvv vvvvvvvvvvvvvv vvv vvvvvvvvvvvvvvv vvvvv
wwwwwwwwwwwwww ww wwwwwwwwwwwwww www
xxxxxxxxxxxxxxxxxxxxxxxxx x xxxxxxxxxxxxxxxxxx xxxx
zzzzzzzzzzzzzzzzzzzzzzzzzzzzzzzzzzzzzzzzzzzzzz zzzzz

ABCDEFGHIJKLMNOPQRSTUVWXZ
il manque toujours l'y
yyyyyyyyyyyyyyyyyyyyyyyyyyyyyyyyyyyyyyyyyyyyyyyyyyy
q u e l l e   i m p o r t a n c e

Figure 5

but left out of the French alphabet since with the exception of "y," all lexical items beginning in *y* are not French.[14]

So, what at first seemed to be a concrete poem not so much about letters as the spaces between them, is, in fact, about one particular letter referring to others, the better to refer to itself and its own ambivalence. Again, as in "Water and Ice," referring expressions (the signs singled out and their associated parts) and their referents a) are mutually referring, and thus entirely intratextual, b) create the dynamics of reference from opposition and ambiguity contained within themselves.

This creating or recreating of the pure referent, divesting it of all its fixed connotations, this attempt to "de-cliché" and thus resuscitate it, is and ever has been the aim of literature and, *a fortiori*, of poetry, which, unlike fiction and drama, has little or no representational pretensions, or preoccupation with "*l'effet de réel*." Since clichés arise from ossifying repetition in stereotyped contexts, let us see how concrete poetry, though restricted by its epigrammatic economy, liberates these frozen fossils. In a sense "Water and Ice" does this by setting one in opposition to the other. A similar example is Michael Gibbs's thirty-three identical reiterations of the three-in-one-word line ("treestreetree") where the word "tree," or its plural, is repeated in a long column down the page (fig. 6).[15] This monotony of tripled repetitions is suddenly broken at the bottom by "AVENUE"—different in meaning, appearance, and typography. The difference refers contrastively to the monotony of the rest, whose sameness is further emphasized both by the coalescing of the usually discrete lexeme "tree" into "treestreetree" and by the numerically suggested phonetic resemblance between threes lazily pronounced "trees" ("treetree" or 3, 3, that is, 33). Thus "treestreetree" could be vague enough to have *no* precise meaning since it could be construed as an ambiguous acoustic image of "trees" or of numbers. With the surprise contrast of "AVENUE" sameness evanesces, and

treestreetree
treestreetree
treestreetree
treestreetree
treestreetree
treestreetree
treestreetree
treestreetree
treestreetree
treestreetree
treestreetree
treestreetree
treestreetree
treestreetree
treestreetree
treestreetree
treestreetree
treestreetree
treestreetree
treestreetree
treestreetree
treestreetree
treestreetree
treestreetree
treestreetree
treestreetree
treestreetree
treestreetree
treestreetree
treestreetree
treestreetree
treestreetree
treestreetree

AVENUE

Figure 6

meaning is reborn as a "street," lined with trees on both sides, springs to life, reminding us that this is no longer a mere street, but a distinctive type whose arboreal difference is marked by its very name "avenue." Paradoxically it is still a type of street, but it now seems quite different as the eye oscillates between the two readings of the lines: unmarked clichés juxtaposed with marked non-clichés differentiated and rejuvenated. Thus "AVENUE" triggers a vertical reading (aligned "street" betwixt two rows of trees) which is projected on and transforms the hitherto undifferentiated horizontal one, as first the micro-referring expressions (tree, street, tree), then the macro-referring expression (the overall image) refer to their own representation of difference.

In poetry which uses sound icons, clichés are also unmarked and rejuvenated. Unfortunately the best examples I have encountered are virtually untranslatable. However, since the phenomenon shows language referring to empty language, that is, a mere sound signifying nothing—or anything, practically—a minimal commentary should suffice. Robert Desnos's "Rrose sélavy, etc." (figs. 7a, 7b)[16] refers to Ronsard's oft-quoted seductive *Carpe diem* ploy used in his poems to the various ladies whose charms he sought to exploit. The usual formulation involved the ephemeral rose to be plucked quickly ere tomorrow it wither and fade. As everyone knows, this rose is life. Now Desnos's title is a lexically distorted and contracted "clichéified" version of "rose c'est la vie" ("rose, that's life"). By its very (meaningless) form it refers to itself as an empty sign, referring in turn to the cliché as an equally empty sign. However, the rest of the poem refers . . . to the title—the title which, as an empty cliché, can be used to mean anything that corresponds to the same sounds. So that each line refers phonetically both to the title and to each and every other line, with a syncopated reiteration at the end:

> Rrose est-ce aile, est-ce elle?
> Est celle
> AVIS

Like a needle stuck on a record, it reminds us that this could go on indefinitely— as its co-referent *etc.* in the title has already indicated. The variation—the added *e* or "et" ("and") in lines 5 and 9–12, which splits the cliché into two, each half joined by an "and" or its approximate phonetic equivalent, merely reinforces the cliché's emptiness—it seems each half of the cliché can be used as two equally empty wholes. But the hole is not so wholly empty as at first appears, for in fact these self-referring expressions show the cliché for what it is and at the same time rekindle its erotic meaning in a new anti-context within, as it were, the old shell: a new context where the thing (the rose and the cliché symbol) is converted into a proper name, one which refers indefinitely, that is, atypically, not so much, one feels, to a particular Rose[17] as to a class—to any Rose, to Rose being Rose being Rose.

Desnos's *Langage Cuit* (literally "cooked," that is, dead language) abounds in reference to clichés of all sorts and in particular to ordinary discourse's idiomatic

Rrose Selavy, etc.

Rose aisselle a vit.
Rr'ose, essaie là, vit.
Rôts et sel à vie.
Rose, S, L, have I.
Rosée, c'est la vie.
Rrose scella vît.
Rrose sella vît.
Rrose sait la vie.
Rose, est-ce, hélas, vie?
Rrose aise héla vît.
Rrose est-ce aile, est-ce elle?
        Est celle
            AVIS

Figure 7a

[Rrose Zatslyffe, etc.

Rose armpit has prick.
Rr'dare, try there, it lives.
Roast and salt for life.
Rose it is, she, have I.
Rosy, dew, that's life.
Rrose clasped tightly to have seen.
Rrose astraddle to have lived.
Rrose now knows life.
Rose, is that, alas, life?
Rrose happy, hailed it, the better to live.
Rrose is it a wing, is it?
        It is
            WARNING]
                              (Approximate literal translation)

Figure 7b

expressions. On the one hand words are reduced to mere empty sounds and referred to as such by their de-lexicalisation; words become mere letters which, when spoken, are acoustic icons of the words: mutually referring symbols *qua* symbols.

Aime haine	[Love hate
Et n'aime	And loves not
haine aime	hate loves
aimai ne	I loved not]
M N	
N M	
N M	
M N[18]	

A more colourful example is his "Langage Cuit I." Ruth Amossy[19] has called this non-referring discourse, and it is true that, like most surrealist and nonsense writings, it very obviously makes no attempt to refer extratextually, nor even to represent any recognisable situation. But in fact it does refer. By blocking our usual representational interpretation strategies, discourse becomes self-referring and immediately opens up a new reading strategy: one of constant cross-reference to a cliché-ridden palimpsest.

Langage Cuit
I
Ce vieillard encore violet ou orangé ou rose
porte un pantalon en trompe d'éléphant.

Mon amour jette-moi ce regard chaud
où se lisent de blancs desseins!

Portrait au rallongé de nos âmes
parlerons-nous à coeur fermé
et ce coeur sur le pied?
Ou jouerons-nous toute la nuit à la main froide?

[*Cooked Language* I
This old man still purple or amber or pink
is wearing elephant-trunk-trick (lit. in the shape of an
elephant's trunk) pants.

My love throw me over that hot look
in which one reads white scheming!

Toe-nail (lit. "long") sketch of our souls
Shall we talk closed-heartedly
and wear this heart on our knees (lit. "foot")?
Or shall we play all night long at hands off
(lit. "cold hands"—a play on the game hot cockles)?][20]

Youth is normally suggested by "green" but the substitution of *violet* points to the strangeness of the literal image of green men, a strangeness enhanced by the alternative colours. Flared trouser legs are cut "en patte d'éléphant" ("like an elephant's leg") but here the trunk ousts the leg, making us laugh at an expression whose elephantine arbitrariness we accepted unthinkingly till now. In the fourth line the cliché "black" or "dark" scheming is evoked by its harmless white opposite—harmless indeed since read in a lover's eyes. This bifocal reading next opposes the "long sketch" to the standard abridged one ("portrait au rallongé," here rendered as a toe-nail sketch to evoke the usual thumbnail one). The closed heart (l. 6) should be open, for in French one speaks "with an open heart" and one wears one's heart on one's hand ("avoir le coeur sur la main") instead of the English sleeve, whereas here it's on the foot; in French lovers traditionally play

hot cockles all night ("jouer à la main chaude") with hot hands and not with
Desnos's cold ones. So here language, cooked and otherwise, refers to language,
and its bizarre referring expressions which were almost empty of meaning refer to
their bizarrerie in a contrapuntal way as reference is established between the cliché
distorted and the distorting cliché, as well as to language as a string of clichés;
"cooked" language indeed—no longer the instrument of communication, but the
overdone product of impoverished phatic intercourse.

The creation and destruction of meaning is obviously not just a culinary matter;
it depends on context as does the referential function. In Michel Leiris's *Glossaire
(Glossary)*, words, apparently without context, are referred to as words—an as-
sembling of letters—by a "definition" which reinforces this quality:

h-o-m-m-e: à chaud aime et meut[21]

[m-a-n: in heat loves and moves]

Unfortunately the translation is incapable of rendering the phonetic effect of the
definition's exact echo of the letter sounds in this example of what Genette calls
"lexicalized spelling." In this case the lexeme's insertion in a glossary suggests
semantic context, whilst the way the lexical items are listed (each letter separated
from the next) suggests the more mechanical context of their graphic and phonetic
codes of representation—the letters and sounds that compose them. So that this
Glossary's entries refer to the role of context in deciding what the referent is: a
seme, a series of letters, or a series of sounds. Once again, an essentially bifocal
perception is in order (since the mediating graphic elements are subsequently subordinated to their phonetic equivalents): the referent is not one or the other, but
both. Reference obtains on the one hand between the two halves of each expression:
1) *homme* + definition, and 2) the sounds of the letters h-o-m-m-e and their lex-
icalization. On the other hand, co-reference obtains between both versions, one
jousting with and at the same time enhancing the other, as language's "double
articulation"[22] is brought to the fore. Coincidentally, reference is circular, since
each half of both versions may be seen as glossematic referring expression *and*
referent.

This use of different contexts to create contrapuntal polyvalence is best seen if
we return to concrete poetry. Ian Hamilton Finlay's sails and waves (fig. 8)[23] show
at a glance the effect of contextual anchors (verbal here) and their role in perception.[24] At the same time *Sails/Waves* suggests graphically a continuum of undifferentiated, that is, non-discrete signs which only cultural conditioning allows us
to "read" discretely.[25] Here then is written language referring to itself as a signifying system, with its own rules for encoding and decoding within a cultural
context, and another quasi-representational language (the curves) referring to its
own polysemic possibilities.

Finlay elaborates this bilingually in *Vague* (fig. 9)[26] as two codes of graphic
symbols interplay—alphabetical and proof-correcting symbols—whilst at the same
time interchanging French ("*vague*"; "wave") and English ("vague") codes and
cultural contexts,[27] so that wave and vague become confused—a fact attested to

Figure 8

Figure 9

by the wavy misspellings. This polysemy is enhanced by the physical context of the concrete wall bearing the inscription set against the curving cobblestone pattern beneath it, and also by the title of Finlay's subsequent postcard photograph of the inscription: "The Battle of the Atlantic." This title foregrounds the less evident French code (given that the site, Livingston New Town, is not by the sea)—though the ∿, enhanced by the generous curve of the *g*, is in itself a sufficiently obvious representation of waves and counter-waves. Double meanings here serve to enhance

Figure 10

a duplicitous concrete referent which is vague both in its form (the wavy line gropes its way back through the misspellings) and in our perception of it (which oscillates between contexts and codes), so that both come to refer to one another and these distinctive self-referents seem, paradoxically, to merge.

Frames and titles constitute another sort of context, as René Magritte eloquently shows in his "Ceci n'est pas une pipe" (fig. 10).[28] Here the fact that the words are within an ornate painted frame, and so part of the picture rather than outside it, ironically refers to the painting as painting—to this pipe's representational but *non-referential* status and, perhaps equally ironically, to perceptual and interpretive conventions: particularly that of equating the signifier (the painting here) with its referent (an actual pipe, an existent).

Paul de Vree's "Eros" (fig. 11)[29] provides an excellent example of similar play on frame and title. For the title is very literally the frame of reference, but this frame is divided into its two parts *er-* and *-os*, and the reader must couple *er-* printed outside all four sides of the text and *-os* printed in the centre along four axes so that each is opposite and linked with one *er-*. Each signifier or half-signifier points to its other half, as mythological (intratextual) reference is completed by the reader. At the same time the reader finds himself in a central labyrinth, constituted by the four geometrically shaped *o*'s and *s*'s of *-os*, which provides the mythological context needed to identify recognisable (though sometimes distorted) referring expressions: five proper names—Er*os*, Daidal*os*, Knoss*os*, Icar*os*, Min*os*, and, given the mythological context these establish, one definite description—taur*os*, the Minotaur. Thus the final *-os* completes recognition of the referring expressions and, by relating them, reference—both intratextual and intertextual. But, more important,

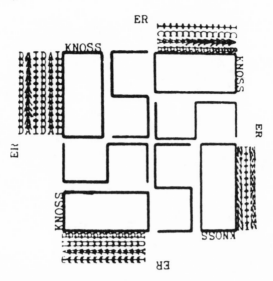

Figure 11

this -*os* relates these five referring expressions to and in Eros, lying as they do between its two parts, and to the a-mazing complexities we associate with these characters and their errings in these places (Minos's mother Europa and his wife Pasiphae both having been seduced by a bull, for example). The coupling of Eros from within and without—for the frame is both on the outside and on the inside— activates what might be considered a second frame of reference: a gnostic one derived from the coupling of Knoss-os (also spelt Gnossus, Cnossus, and Knosos), and so to the process of gaining knowledge: knowledge in its primal, Biblical sense, knowledge as a holistic linking of parts. What is particularly interesting in de Vree's dynamic linkings is that he shows how literary titles and proper names can sometimes share a similarly ambiguous role, both being simultaneously referring expressions *and* referents in a dynamic dipole which ultimately creates the text—for the title is indeed an integral part of the text.

Emmett Williams's "Thomas Stearns Eliot" (fig. 12)[30] plays entirely on a single proper name which is title, text, and context. It too is segmented, but here seg- mentation isolates not syllables but letters, each letter of the name-title constituting an immutable grid as the exact position of each letter of the extratextual referring expression's syntagm is reproduced in its vertical paradigmatic development. Thus, by the very act of reading, we activate the poetic function (defined by Jakobson as the projection of the paradigmatic axis on the syntagmatic axis[31]) as we read first the syntagm, then the paradigm, and, in the process, refer back to the syntagm of the name-title. Echoing this self-referential movement (name referring to name *qua* name) the text refers semantically not so much to the person as to the literary *persona* adduced from his texts' effect and religious connotations. But though one moves from an initial suggestion of extratextual proper-name reference through

thomas stearns eliot

Figure 12

intertextual reference, here again the dominant referential level is intratextual. De-spite an apparently static form, the act of reading paradoxically shows reference to be dynamic by activating the recreation of a poetic function, whose two axes our reading brings together—a process that the change in direction and axis of "alas" (written left to right, right to left and diagonally rather than horizontally) seems to emphasize just before the eye returns to the title.

That the poetic and referential functions merge in the examples shown—and most obviously in this last one—is hardly surprising, given the self-referring overstate-ment of this type of text. Their merging echoes that of the signifier and referent (be they graphic, linguistic, or acoustic) in these examples of indisputably triadic signs. In fact, contrary to Ogden and Richards's representation, the link between signifier and referent is stronger than those between signified and signifier or signifed and referent. Beyond these two aspects of concrete, ideogrammatic, and iconic sound poetry's self-reference lies a third: reference itself. For in fact these self-referring texts refer also, and, I suggest, above all, to reference as an act, an act of linking—refer, that is, to the dynamics of reference itself in which the act of reading functions as shifter—and thus brings out the parallels between graphic creation and interpretive (re)creation.

Emmett Williams's chiasma-like reversal in "sound sense"[32] emphasizes this co-reference (and cross-reference):

```
SENSE SOUND
SONSE SEUND
SOUSE SENND
SOUNE SENSD
SOUND SENSE
```

Here he plays on the principle of Lewis Carroll's "doublets" in which one word is transformed into another by letter substitution, so turning "head" into "tail":

```
HEAD
heal
teal
tell
tall
TAIL
```

or, as when he introduces Walrus to Carpenter, by syllable substitution:

```
WALRUS
peruse
harper
CARPENTER[33]
```

In the process of William's reversal, sound sense is itself transformed into a more literal sound sense as we hear the different sounds and see different senses or "non-senses."

One of the most economic (self-referring) expressions of the dynamics of the process of reference in process is Pierre Garnier's five-letter poem:[34]

```
                o

     m t            m t
```

In this ball-game one "word" or "*mot*" creates another as the *o* is tossed backwards and forwards—coincidentally referring to the process of writing (and reading) as words generate more words, one word leading to another and back again as the text's co-referring expressions link up anaphorically and cataphorically. This movement is graphically expressed by the *o*'s position: not central but either nearing or leaving the empty "*m-t*"—moving between the two, linking these co-referring and self-referring images, and caught in the very act of reference to itself as an act.

In fact, if we reconsider any of the examples given, we realize that beyond their obvious self-referring anamorphosis (a referring expression as pure form referring to form)[35] lies self-reference, shown for what it is: an act in process, a dynamic linking. "Il pleut" shows the act of raining, referring to the act of literary semiosis, whilst the present action ("it *is* raining") refers to becoming as it suffers a rain-change into its own metaphoric metamorphoses (voices communicating, chain

fetters, links). "Water and Ice" refers to the act of becoming and the tenuous-
ness of ice versus water—to the imminent and immanent becoming, the transformation of either state into the other. "Il manque toujours l'y"—in appearance as
static as "Thomas Stearns Eliot"—is also referring to its act of referring, in a three-
dimensional way, as we look everywhere and then find it magnified in the spaces,
its reversed and inverted images graphically recounting the dynamics of its diachronic metamorphoses. For here y refers to itself in the act of referring to its other
symbols as it leads the eye through its transformations: from y to i to $\diagdown\!\!\!\_$ to U.

The dynamics of *self*-reference as an act is also reinforced, as in y, by reading
strategies (quite physically) in, say, *Vague*, where the letters led us from right to
left and the $\sim$ from left to right, both colliding, or rather eliding, as they move
towards one another. Reference moves in a mysterious way—forwards and backwards—as we know from reading any text. "Eros" forces us to read around the
square by turning it (or ourselves), and it takes us with it through its own labyrinthian
co-referential linking.

Even the sound icons force us to read in two different ways (in the case of
lexicalized spellings and "Langage Cuit"), and in many ways in "Rrose Sélavy."
In the latter many anamorphoses force us to undo the new-found segmenting and
hear it as the original form, this form itself hiding another (the Ronsardian prototype). From there we juggle contrapuntally, unleashing a grand stretto, as we play
them all together.

So a double bind does indeed exist. On the one hand, these three types of poetry
exaggerate literary discourse's tendency to refer to itself within itself; on the other,
literary discourse is at the same time referring to itself referring to itself. The paradox
(returning to Epimenides) is that whilst these examples refer to their process of
becoming, they are themselves in the process of becoming, for we the readers are
(re)creating them.

NOTES

1. The English paraphrase of which has been translated thus: "All consistent axiomatic
formulations of number theory include undecidable propositions." Douglas R. Hofstadter,
Gödel, Escher, Bach: an Eternal Golden Braid (Hassocks, Sussex: Harvester Press, 1979),
p. 17.
2. See the letter from L. N. Godbole in "Letters," *The Economist*, vol. 282, no. 7224
(Feb. 13, 1982), p. 6.
3. In Douglas R. Hofstadter, "Metamagical Themas," *Scientific American*, Jan. 1982,
12–16. This article reproduces two other interesting examples of self-reference. The first,
by Beverly Rowe, describes an *Errata* page in a hypothetical book, which reads thus:

(vi)

Errata

Page (vi): For "Errata" read "Erratum."

The second, which appears in D. R. Hofstadter's "Metamagical Themas," *Scientific American*, Jan. 1981, 34–41, is slightly more complex: "This sentance has three errors."

4. Cf. Umberto Eco's statement: "Les caractéristiques de l'image esthétique d'une langue sont l'ambiguité et l'autoréflexivité des messages." In "Langage artistique, segmentation du contenu et référent," *Degrés* 3 (juillet 1973).

5. Perhaps the most striking example is in Hindemith's *Ludus Tonalis*. Here the "Praeludium" and the "Postludium" are mirror images of each other, not only on a horizontal axis—the "Postludium" being a complete reversal of the "Praeludium"—but also vertically, so that the "Postludium" is the "Praeludium" both back to front and upside down.

6. Sometimes called Sotadics after Sotades. One of the most familiar examples in Greek is "nipon anomemata me monan opsn" (wash my transgressions, not only my face), often found inscribed in monastery or church fonts. There is another variety of palindrome in which each component word is also a palindrome: "Odo tenet mulum, madidam mappam tenet Anna, Anna tenet mappam madidam, mulum tenet Odo."

7. The distinction being that the paragram's matrix is lexical or graphematic, and derived from fragments of the key words scattered along the sentence, each embedded in the body of a word. The hypogram, as Riffaterre explains, "appears quite visibly in the shape of words embedded in sentences whose organisation reflects the presuppositions of the matrix's nuclear word." *Semiotics of Poetry* (Bloomington and London: Indiana University Press, 1978), p. 168. The example quoted is: Tibi vero gratias agam quo *clamore*? Amore more ore re (My emphasis).

8. *Calligrammes* in *Oeuvres poétiques* (Paris: Gallimard, 1965), pp. 203 and 213, respectively. Trans. Anne Hyde Greet: *Calligrammes* (Los Angeles and London: University of California Press, Berkeley, 1980), p. 123.

9. See particularly the *Poèmes à Lou* which may be seen as a key to the erotic nature of many of Guillaume Apollinaire's poems—particularly *Calligrammes*. See also my article "Poèmes de guerre et d'amour . . . ou la double chevauchée d'Apollinaire." *French Review*, vol. 54, no. 6 (May 1982), 147–172.

10. Ernest Fenollosa, *The Chinese Written Character as a Medium for Poetry*, ed. Ezra Pound (San Francisco: City Lights Books, 1936), p. 9.

11. Reprinted from *Speaking Pictures*, ed. Milton Klonsky (New York: Harmony Books 1975), p. 279.

12. This is C. S. Peirce's term which he uses (when explaining his three categories) to describe the second, the idea of "brute and obstinate existence . . . something *there*, a datum, a singular *this*." See David Savan, *An Introduction to C. S. Peirce's Semiotics*, Part I (Toronto: Toronto Semiotic Circle, 1976), p. 7. His "object" (our referent) is related to this class further on in the elaboration of his evolving triadic system.

13. Reprinted from *An Anthology of Concrete Poetry*, ed. Emmett Williams (West Glover, Vermont: Something Else Press, 1967), no pagination.

14. "Yeuse" (ilex) is from the old Provençal.

15. *Connotations* (Cardiff: Second Aeon Publications, 1973). No pagination.

16. *L'Aumonyme* in *Corps et biens* (Paris: Gallimard, 1953), p. 67.

17. Later in *Rrose Sélavy* (also in *Corps et biens*, a collection of epigrammatic phonetic echoes), Rrose Sélavy is a character who, despite the author's note (p. 31) is an Everyman's Everywoman cast again in a context of lexicalised sounds and whose definite reference is subordinated to semantico-phonetic games.

18. "Élégant cantique de Salomé Salomon," *Langage cuit*, in *Corps et biens*, p. 77.

19. Ruth Amossy et Elisheva Rosen, *Le Discours du cliché* (Paris: SEDES, 1982); see in particular the last chapter.

20. *Langage Cuit*, p. 72.

21. *Glossaire j'y serre mes gloses* in *Mots sans mémoire* (Paris: Gallimard, 1969), p. 93.

22. André Martinet, "La double articulation linguistique," *Travaux du Cercle Linguistique de Copenhague* 5 (30–37).

23. Reprinted from Groupe μ (Jacques Dubois *et al.*): *Documents de Travail et pré-publications: Trois fragments d'une rhétorique de l'image*. (Urbino: Università di Urbino, Centro Internazionale di Semiotica e di Linguistica, serie F, nos. 82–83, March-April, 1979), p. 42.

24. For a discussion on the vital role of contextual anchoring and how the latter determines interpretation, i.e., perception, see E. H. Gombrich, *Art and Illusion: A Study in the Psychology of Pictorial Representation* (Princeton: Princeton University Press, 2nd ed., 1969), in particular his discussion in the first chapter of the ambiguous cartoon (which had also fascinated Wittgenstein) of a shape we can interpret as either a duck's or a rabbit's head. Charles Chastain discusses aspects of the same problem in relation to primary and secondary reference in "Reference and Context," *Language, Mind and Knowledge*, ed. K. Gunderson, *Minnesota Studies in the Philosophy of Science*, no. vii (Minneapolis, 1975).

25. See Jean Piaget, *Les Mécanismes perceptifs* (Paris: P.U.F., 1961) for a full discussion of the role of segmentation versus continuum and the role of cultural conditionings in the process of isolating and interpreting forms.

26. Reproduced from Francis Edeline, *Ian Hamilton Finlay: Gnomique et Gnomonique* (Liège: Atelier de l'Agneau/Yellow Now, 1977), p. 12.

27. In fact, as Stephen Bann shows in his article "Le talon de saint Thomas," *Revue d'esthétique* (Paris: Union générale d'éditions, 1977), five languages are involved.

28. Reproduced from Suzi Gablik, *Magritte* (London: Thames and Hudson Ltd., 1970), p.128–137, Fig.111.

29. *Chicago Review, Anthology of Concretism*, ed. Eugene Wildman (Chicago: The Swallow Press, Inc., 1968), p. 129. First published in *Chicago Review*, vol. 19, no. 4 (1967).

30. *Selected Shorter Poems:1950–1970* (New York: New Directions Publishing Co., 1975; 1st ed., 1958), p. 122. Reprinted by permission of New Directions.

31. "The poetic function projects the principle of equivalence from the axis of selection into the axis of combination." "Linguistics and Poetics," in *Style and Language*, ed. T. Sebeok (Cambridge: M.I.T. Press, 1960), p. 358.

32. *Selected Shorter Poems: 1950–1970*, p. 25. Reprinted by permission of New Directions.

33. See Francis Huxley, *The Raven and the Writing Desk* (London: Thames and Hudson, 1976) on Carroll's logical games. In chapter III he discusses "Doublets" and their rules. The two examples may be found on pp. 49 and 51.

34. *Jardin japonais* (Paris: André Silvaire, 1978). No pagination.

35. On the subject of sound icons and anamorphosis see Mireille Calle-Gruber, "Anamorphoses textuelles," *Poétique*, no. 42 (1980), 234–249.

III.

BAD REFERENCES

Gerald Prince

> They told me you had been to her,
> And mentioned me to him:
> She gave me a good character,
> But said I could not swim . . .
> —*Alice in Wonderland*

Of all the factors which make certain works of fiction difficult to process,[1] perhaps the most remarkable are the perturbations occurring in the referential system, in the set of references through which a (fictional) text constructs the model of a world and thanks to which we can know what the text is about.

I will not attempt in what follows to determine the ontological nature of fictional referents, of objects, entities, concepts, or states of affairs identified in a work of fiction through referring. Nor will I attempt to describe and explain their relation to referents in the real world.[2] I am more interested in the fact that a work of fiction makes use of reference and that the objects it refers to can be talked about (Roquentin lived in Bouville and Madame Bovary in Yonville; Sherlock Holmes solved the Case of the Speckled Band; Anna Karenina had a black velvet dress). In other words, I am interested in the fact that fictional discourse says certain things about certain entities rather than in the status of these entities.

I should point out, however, that students of reference have often insisted on two (possible) differences between fictional worlds and the real world. First, whereas the latter is said to be complete, the former are considered incomplete: for each entity a in a fiction and some relevantly applicable predicate F, it will normally be the case that neither "Fa" nor " $\sim Fa$" is true (what is Roquentin's weight? what is Meursault's date of birth? what are the exact dimensions of Jean-Baptiste Clamence's room?). Second, whereas the real world is taken to be consistent, fictional worlds are sometimes inconsistent: in Ray Bradbury's "A Sound of Thunder," for instance, Keith is elected president in 2055 and Keith is not elected president in 2055; and in Roger Martin du Gard's *Jean Barois*, the protagonist's daughter is eighteen years old in 1913 but also in 1910 and 1916. Of course, fictional worlds need not be inconsistent: there is no inconsistency in Perrault's *Little Red Riding*

Hood or in something like *John was unhappy, then he met Mary, then he became very happy*; moreover, it may well be that faith in the consistency of the real world is just a matter of faith. Of course too, fictional worlds need not be incomplete: "it might be possible to so write a story that every statement about its characters would be decided. For example one might write 'and everything not explicitly stated or implied here is false.' "[3] Besides, without invoking entities that no longer exist in our world (did Racine have an ingrown toenail? what was Shakespeare's weight?) and with respect to existing entities, it may well be impossible, given some predicate *F*, to determine whether or not *F* is true of an entity *a*. The differences between a fictional world and the real world may thus not be that easy to establish; but it is certainly less difficult to live with a lack of consistency and a lack of completeness in fiction, and writers—especially modern writers—have taken full advantage of this fact.

Instead of focusing on the referent in (a) fiction, I will discuss reference, that is, the relation holding between a given series of signs (the referring expression) and what the series stands for on particular occasions of its use.[4] Reference can be singular (when the signs refer to some specific entity) or general (when they refer to a class of entities). It can be anaphoric (backward-looking) or cataphoric (forward-looking). Most importantly, it can be correct (if what the referring expression says of the referent is true) or successful (if the referring expression allows for the identification of the referent) or both.

Consider *La Jalousie* [*Jealousy*],[5] which I take to be exemplary of modern fiction (at least in its handling of reference). It starts out pretty well; innocuously, at any rate, for what could be more innocuous than its title? The first word of the text proper is a deictic: *now*. It must be related to an "I." Patience is the only thing required and surely that "I" will appear. Many entities, perhaps too many, are introduced in the first two or three pages through definite descriptions: *the shadow, the column, the roof, the terrace, the flagstones, the sun, the walls, the gable*, and so on and so forth; but this is not unusual in fiction: after all, such definite descriptions help establish "what is (already) there" in the world represented. Very quickly, however, the start turns out to have been a false start (does a title come at the beginning or the end? isn't any *now* always tied to a past?) and the novel proves to be—among many other things, no doubt—a treatise on how not to refer successfully, a catalogue of bad references.

The first real difficulty occurs on page 11: "Mais le regard qui, venant du fond de la chambre, passe par-dessus la balustrade, ne touche terre que beaucoup plus loin" [page 40: But from the far side of the bedroom the [look] carries over the balustrade and touches ground only much further away]. What does the initial referring expression (if it is one!) refer to? Whose look is "the look"? That of anyone who would be in the back of the room (the familiar "observer" of nineteenth-century fiction)? that of the "I" announced by the liminary *now*? or that of A . . . who has entered the room on page 10? We will never know for sure. Several referents could satisfy this referring expression just as several can satisfy other referring expressions in the text. There are three different ships that something like *the ship* could refer to: the one anchored in the harbor, at the edge of the wharf; the one represented on the calendar; and the one mentioned in the African novel discussed by Franck and A . . . ; there are at least two lamps that *the second lamp* might designate; there are several windows evoked by *the corner window*, and several sheets of paper corresponding to *the sheet of paper*; and there are numerous stains in harmony with *the stain*: the stain left on the wall by the crushed centipede, the stain on the tablecloth, the stain on the blue letter paper, the oil stain in the courtyard, the red stain (is it blood?) under the window, the paint stain on the bannister, and more. In fact, there seems to be a stain everywhere:

> La tache est sur le mur de la maison, sur les dalles, sur le ciel vide. Elle est partout dans la vallée, depuis le jardin jusqu'à la rivière et sur l'autre versant. Elle est aussi dans le bureau, dans la chambre, dans la salle à manger, dans le salon, dans la cour, sur le chemin qui s'éloigne vers la grand-route. (p. 141)

> [The stain is on the wall of the house, on the flagstones, against the empty sky. It is everywhere in the valley, from the garden to the stream and up the opposite slope. It is in the office too, in the bedroom, in the dining room, in the living room, in the courtyard, on the road up to the highway. (p. 102)]

The innocuous title itself could designate a feeling (that of the mysterious "I," of course, but also that of Christiane who has every reason to be jealous, and even that of Franck or that of A . . .) just as well as it could refer to an object (but which of the many blinds would it be?). It is emblematic of the problems of reference in the novel.

Obviously, I do not mean to suggest that, for reference to be successful in *La Jalousie* (or any other text), the class of *potential* referents for every referring expression must be a class of one. I do not mean to imply that there should be one and only one ship, one and only one lamp, one and only one stain; nor do I mean to imply that, in case there are several ships or several stains, each should be named differently. Given any natural language and given any world but a singularly impoverished or heterogeneous one, it is impossible to have a different sign for every entity. Besides, it is not necessary. If, while eating a hamburger, I say to my dinner companion *The hamburger is delicious*, I can be pretty sure that the reference will be successful; and if I write to my wife who is away on vacation *The roof is leaking*, I think that she would understand which roof I am talking about. What is needed for reference to succeed is not so much referent uniqueness as referent uniqueness in context.

Sometimes, of course, a certain degree of linguistic precision, a few more specifications can help. Thus, instead of simply telling my friend something like *The guy asked me to check his car*, I would tell him *The guy you introduced me to yesterday asked me to check his car*. Now, *La Jalousie* is often very precise, not to say excessively or exhaustingly so:

> La main droite saisit le pain et le porte à la bouche, la main droite repose le pain sur

la nappe blanche et saisit le couteau, la main gauche saisit la fourchette, la fourchette
pique la viande, le couteau coupe un morceau de viande, la main droite pose le
couteau sur la nappe, la main gauche met la fourchette dans la main droite, qui pique
le morceau de viande, qui s'approche de la bouche, qui se met à mastiquer avec des
mouvements de contraction et d'extension. (pp. 111–112)[6]

[The right hand picks up the bread and raises it to the mouth, the right hand sets the
bread down on the white cloth and picks up the knife, the left hand picks up the fork,
the fork sinks into the meat, the knife cuts off a piece of meat, the right hand sets
down the knife on the cloth, the left hand puts the fork in the right hand, which sinks
the fork into the piece of meat, which approaches the mouth, which begins to chew
with movements of contraction and extension. (p. 88)]

In fact, from the very "beginning," the text multiplies the specifying elements in
its definite descriptions or resorts to metalinguistic explanations: "Maintenant
l'ombre du pilier—le pilier qui soutient l'angle sud-ouest du toit" (p. 9) [Now the
shadow of the column—the column which supports the southwest corner of the roof
(p. 39)]; "Le côté droit (c'est-à-dire aval) n'a plus que treize bananiers" (p. 34)
[The row on the right (that is to say the lower) side has no more than thirteen banana
trees (p. 51)]; "Par devant brillent aussi le parallélogramme que la lame dessine
et l'ellipse en métal au centre de la gomme" (pp. 137–138) [In front of it shines
the oblong of the razor blade and the metal ellipse in the center of the eraser (p.
100)]. Yet, regardless of the number of specifying elements or metalinguistic explanations, *La Jalousie* is often not precise enough and its (potential) decoder can
become as perplexed as someone listening to Franck and A . . . discuss an enigmatic
novel: "Il est à présent question d'une jeune femme blanche—est-ce la même que
tout à l'heure, ou bien sa rivale, ou quelque figure secondaire?—qui accorde ses
faveurs à un indigène, peut-être à plusieurs" (p. 194) [Now they are talking about
a young white woman—is it the same one as before, or her rival, or some secondary
character?—who gives herself to a native, perhaps to several (p. 126)]. Indeed, by
and large, no amount of precision turns out to be sufficient because the decoder
does not know the context in which the references apply. If, in the middle of a
race, I tell one of my competitors *The big, juicy, medium-rare hamburger is delicious*, he will probably feel that I am very tired; and he will feel the same way
if I describe the quality of the meat in even more detail. What makes for bad
references in *La Jalousie* is, above all, the impossibility of finding the appropriate
context for many of the referring expressions. Fiction, it has been said, provides
only a distant context. Robbe-Grillet's novel provides no context at all or, at best,
a most distant and uncertain one.

In the first place, such questions as Who speaks? or Who sees? only find ambiguous answers. It is not quite enough to claim that everything is presented in
terms of a protagonist, "I," one who is, if anything, radically incomplete, one
who never appears as such yet who, like Flaubert's invisible novelist, is everywhere.
We cannot be sure that what the text presents are the perceptions of this "I" rather
than his thoughts, his memories, or his hallucinations. Besides, many passages
could be attributed to an omniscient narrator, a kind of unsituated voice of truth:

"A . . . , sans y penser, regarde le bois dépeint de la balustrade" (p. 14) [A . . . absently stares at the paint-flaked wood of the balustrade (p. 41)]; "pour se rendre à l'office, le plus simple est de traverser la maison" (p. 48) [To get to the pantry, the easiest way is to cross the house (p. 58)]; "La nuit ensuite n'est pas longue à tomber, dans ces contrées sans crépuscules" (p. 137) [The night does not take long falling in these countries without twilight (p. 100)]; and many seem explicitly related to A . . .'s point of view: "A . . . écoute le chant indigène lointain mais net encore, qui parvient jusqu'à la terrasse" (p. 105) [A . . . listens to the native chant, distant but still distinct, which reaches the veranda (p. 85)]; "La voix grave du second chauffeur arrive jusqu'à elle" (p. 119) [The low voice of the second driver reaches her (p. 92)]. The ambiguity is further compounded by the extraordinary number of verbs used intransitively: "Le gris du bois y apparaît [à qui?], strié de petites fentes longitudinales" (p. 11) [The gray of the wood shows through *[for whom?]* streaked with tiny longitudinal cracks (p. 40)]; "Il serait difficile [pour qui?] de préciser où, exactement, il néglige quelque règle essentielle sur quel point particulier il manque de discrétion" (p. 23) [It would be difficult *[for whom?]* to specify exactly in what way he is neglecting some essential rule, at what particular point he is lacking in discretion (p. 46)]; "Vu de la porte de l'office le mur de la salle à manger paraît [à qui?] sans tache" (p. 51) [From the pantry door, the dining-room wall seems *[to whom?]* to have no spot on it (p. 59)]; and by the numerous definite descriptions— the eye, the gaze, the ear, and the fingers—which function just as well generically as specifically (pp. 11, 13, 28, 70, *et passim*, or pp. 40, 41, 48, 68 in the translation). The problem of origin in *La Jalousie*, like the problem of destination (how would the textual addressee be described?), must remain a problem.

The time of events is undeterminable. The many temporal deictics used throughout the novel cannot be related to a given "I" with any certainty and they cannot be ordered chronologically. A centipede is squashed perhaps before a trip taken by Franck and A . . . , perhaps during that trip, and perhaps after it.[7] *Maintenant* is *maintenant* is *maintenant*. The text itself makes clear that *now* does not constitute a good answer to *when?*: "A une question peu précise concernant le moment où il a reçu cet ordre, il répond: 'Maintenant', ce qui ne fournit aucune indication satisfaisante" (p. 50) [To a vague question as to when he received this order, he answers: 'Now', which furnishes no satisfactory indication (p. 59)]. The present tense, which is used almost exclusively, provides little help: in French, as in English, the use of the present does not necessarily imply that the event or situation described is contemporaneous with the act of description. As for the prepositions and conjunctions of time (*after, next, as soon as, after a few minutes or a few seconds*), they can apply either to several well-defined contexts or to none at all. As with many other features of *La Jalousie*, "plusieurs solutions conviennent, par endroit, et ailleurs aucune" (p. 52) [several solutions seem possible at some places, and in others, none (p. 60)].

If the time of events is baffling, so is the space in which they presumably occur. Granted, the text not only abounds in detailed descriptions of objects and of their spatial relations but also manifests a remarkable affinity for demonstratives. Thus, we get "Il se dirige . . . vers la petite table, s'empare de celle-ci et . . . dépose le tout un peu plus loin" (p. 110) [He walks . . . toward the little table, picks [*this*] up and . . . sets the whole thing down a little farther away (pp. 87–88)], instead of "s'en empare et dépose le tout un peu plus loin" [picks it up and sets the whole thing down a little farther away], and "Entre cette première fenêtre et la seconde" (p. 121) [Between this first window and the second (p. 93)] instead of "Entre la première fenêtre et la seconde" [Between the first window and the second]. Sometimes, the affinity for demonstratives leads to passages which would be most welcome in a book of French grammar for beginners: "Quand aux oiseaux eux-mêmes, ils ne se montrent pas . . . restant à couvert sous les panaches de larges feuilles vertes, tout autour de la maison. Dans la zone de terre nue qui sépare celle-ci de ceux-là . . ." (pp. 78–79) [As for the birds themselves, they [*do not show themselves*] . . . remaining in hiding under the clusters of wide green leaves on all sides of the house. In the zone of naked earth which separates [*it from the former*] (p. 73)]. Sometimes, it even leads to infelicities: "puis il se lève de sa chaise sans bruit, gardant sa serviette à la main. Il roule celle-ci (la main?) en bouchon et s'approche du mur" (p. 63) [Then he stands up, noiselessly, holding his napkin in his hand. He wads it (*the hand*?) into a ball and approaches the wall (p. 65)]. What the demonstratives point out or point to, however, what they designate, what they "demonstrate," often remains elusive because of numerous and sudden changes in scenery.[8] Anaphora and cataphora are confused (pp. 56, 99, 124, 126, *et passim*). *Here* is no different from *there*, *this x* is no different from *that x* and, like *now*, they constitute poor answers. For all its apparent precision, geography becomes chaotic and many events—not to say all events—are so difficult to situate spatially that they do not seem to take place.

"Où maintenant? Quand maintenant? Qui maintenant?" [Where now? When now? Who now?][9] If I do not know who, when, and where, I cannot know what. It is difficult to specify what happens in *La Jalousie* because Robbe-Grillet's novel contains little, if anything, that is firmly rooted.[10] Whereas the hallmark of most texts is certainty, *La Jalousie* lives in uncertainty. It is astonishingly hesitant about what happened, what is happening, what will happen, what might happen: "une tache noirâtre marque l'emplacement du mille-pattes écrasé la semaine dernière, au début du mois, le mois précédent peut-être, ou plus tard" (p. 27) [a blackish spot marks the place where a centipede was squashed last week, at the beginning of the month, perhaps the month before, or later (p. 47)]; "Combien de temps s'est-il écoulé depuis la dernière fois qu'il a fallu en rétablir le tablier?" (p. 103) [How much time has passed since the bridge underpinnings had to be repaired? (p.84)]; "Il rentre en scène aussitôt—ou un autre à sa place—et rétrécit bientôt son orbite" (p. 148) [It immediately returns to view—or another returns in its place—and soon [*narrows*] its orbit (p. 105)]. *La Jalousie* does not institute certain constants—save inconstancy!—which could be assimilated. It does not propose a body of knowledge which is to be acquired and shared. It consists, in large part, of ambiguous statements, and the possibly unambiguous ones are all contaminated. It is amnesic, forgetting what it has or has not yet established, resorting to indefinite articles when definite ones are expected and vice versa (pp. 115, 197, 216, *et passim*, or pp. 90,

128, 137 in the translation), assigning contradictory predicates to what may be the same entity and the same predicates to different entities (pp. 108 and 109; 27, 61 and 211; 216; *et passim*, or pp. 87, paragraphs 2 and 4; 47, 64 and 135; 137, in the translation). Untotalizable, unsummarizable, defeating memory and anticipation, defying spatio-temporal distinctions and hierarchies (in *La Jalousie*, we never know what to skip!), the novel disintegrates the scene of reading.

Consider, for instance, the passages describing or alluding to the partial squashing of a centipede on a wall (pp. 27, 63, 64, 97, *et passim*; or pp. 47, 65, 82, in the translation). If I take them to refer to one and the same referent, I have to deal with inconsistencies in the information I process: the insect is such that it can be squashed repeatedly, at different times, in different places, with different results. In other words, I cannot, until the very last page of the novel, take anything for granted and relax. I cannot assume that I know what there is to be known about the squashing. I cannot trust the conclusions I reach after any one set of descriptions. I cannot presume that what new information I gather will confirm or conform to the information already gathered. I cannot foresee, from what I learn, what may or may not happen. At any point in the novel, regardless of the context, the squashing of the centipede may occur in circumstances that I can neither predict nor expect. Suppose I try to eliminate inconsistencies by taking contradictory passages to refer to different places.[11] I would still be faced with the same problems. Once again, at any point, a new squashing of a centipede may occur. Once again, what I learn from the text does not allow me to expect or predict, even in part, what will or will not happen. Once again, it is a case of "le possible à chaque instant" [What is possible at each instant].

To try to account for the text by saying that it is basically about a husband jealous to the point of insanity (or that it illustrates the crumbling of colonial mastery) does not solve the problem either. It is merely another way of recognizing that the text is mad (schizophrenic: it is not modeled in terms of a receiver), that the language used is referentially inadequate, and that the novel cannot be processed and digested in conventional, sane, masterful ways.[12] There is no world I can abstract from *La Jalousie*, no material with which I can fill its gaps and plug its holes, no algorithm in terms of which I can distinguish what is said from what it is said about. *Here* must be *here, at this point in the text. Now* must be *now, at this moment in the text. It* must be *it, here and now in the text*, whatever *it* may be.

By subverting reference (and thus rejecting linguistic transparency as well as metaphoricity), *La Jalousie* places itself out of any communication circuit. It does not transmit. It is. The requisite distinctions for the construction of a world related to the "real world," the distinctions between likely and certain, same and different, old and new, before and after, here and there, are impossible to make. By multiplying bad references, *La Jalousie* multiplies potential meanings while destroying meaning and it aspires to pure fiction; that is, not merely what does not refer (directly) to events and existents in our world but what refers poorly to any world, what shows without showing, designates without designating, speaks without speaking; in a word, writes.

NOTES

1. On legibility and textual processing see Philippe Hamon, "Un Discours contraint," *Poétique* no. 16 (1973), 411–445; and Gerald Prince, "Questions, Answers, and Narrative Legibility" in *Retrospectives and Perspectives: A Symposium in Rhetoric*, ed. Turner S. Kobler, William E. Tanner, and J. Dean Bishop (Denton: Texas Woman's University Press, 1978), pp. 75–90.

2. On this problem, see John Woods, *The Logic of Fiction* (The Hague: Mouton, 1974) and "Formal Semantics and Literary Theory," ed. John Woods and Thomas G. Pavel, *Poetics* VIII, 1–2 (April 1979).

3. This was suggested by Dudley Shapere to John Heintz. See John Heintz, "Reference and Inference in Fiction," *Poetics* VIII, 1–2 (April 1979), 91.

4. John Lyons, *Semantics*, vol. I (Cambridge: Cambridge University Press, 1977), pp. 174–229, provides a helpful introduction to the problems of reference. M. A. K. Halliday and Ruquaiya Hasan, *Cohesion in English* (London: Longman, 1976) contains many interesting examples.

5. Alain Robbe-Grillet, *La Jalousie* (Paris: Les Éditions de Minuit, 1970). Translations are taken from *Jealousy* in *Two Novels by Robbe-Grillet: "Jealousy" and "In the Labyrinth,"* trans. Richard Howard (New York: Grove Press, 1965). All references will be to these editions. Any italicized words within square brackets in the translated version are my interjections or the editors' more literal translation.

6. I said *exhaustingly* because defamiliarization through detailing can be exhausting.

7. Cf. M. Mouillaud, "Le Nouveau Roman: Tentative de roman et roman de la tentative," *Revue d'Esthétique* XVII (août-décembre 1964), 228–263.

8. In *Les Romans de Robbe-Grillet* (Paris: Editions de Minuit, 1963), p. 131, Bruce Morrissette writes: "tous les changements de scène sont amorcés en début de paragraphe, à l'exception peut-être de ce 'fondu enchaîne' où le regard du mari passe d'une terrasse de café à la photo de A, puis à la terrasse réelle de la maison" (p. 126). This is not entirely correct. To give but one example among many, *la table* on page 110 (page 88 in the translation) may designate the little terrace table (first mention) and the dining-room table (second mention).

[Editors' note: The difference between this quotation and Morrissette's subsequent English translation, p. 134 in *The Novels of Robbe-Grillet* (Ithaca and London: Cornell University Press, 1975), is perhaps indicative of Morrissette's own doubts as to the accuracy of his original statement. The translation of the above runs thus: "almost all the transitions between scenes occur at the beginning of a paragraph. The rare exceptions pass almost unnoticed except on the most minute reading and represent only very brief alternates between tightly linked elements."]

9. Samuel Beckett *L'Innommable* (Paris: Editions de Minuit, 1953), p. 7 [*The Unnamable* (New York: Grove Press, 1970), p. 3.]

10. In this respect, at least, *La Jalousie* is very similar to the novel read by Franck and A . . . as it is described on page 216 (137 in the translation).

11. Such a solution is hinted at (then seemingly rejected) by the text on page 171: "Combien de fois s'est répété le choc léger contre les dalles? À peine cinq ou six, ou même encore moins. . . . La chute d'un gros lézard, depuis le dessous du toit, produit souvent un 'flac' étouffé de cette sorte; mais il aurait alors fallu que cinq ou six lézards se laissent tomber l'un après l'autre, coup sur coup, ce qui est peu probable" [How many times was the faint impact repeated against the flagstones? Barely five or six, or even less. . . . The fall of a big lizard from the eaves often produces a similar muffled "slap"; but then it would have taken five or six lizards falling one after another, which is unlikely p. 115].

12. I do not mean to suggest that Bruce Morrissette, *The Novels of Robbe-Grillet*, and Jacques Leenhardt, *Lecture politique du roman: "La Jalousie" d'Alain Robbe-Grillet* (Paris: Editions de Minuit, 1973), are hopelessly wrong. Indeed, I have found both works excellent

and I have profited enormously from them and from Barthes's superb preface to Morrissette, just as I have profited from Jean Alter, *La Vision du monde d'Alain Robbe-Grillet: Structures et significations* (Genève: Droz, 1966), Olga Bernal, *Alain Robbe-Grillet: le roman de l' absence* (Paris: Gallimard, 1964), and Stephen Heath, *The Nouveau Roman: A Study in the Practice of Writing* (London: Elek, 1972).

IV.

WAITING FOR THE REFERENT
WAITING FOR GODOT?
On Referring in Theatre

Jean Alter

To deal cogently with *referents* in *theatre*, it is essential to clarify the meaning of both terms as well as the manner in which I shall be using them. Both concepts have given rise to considerable confusion and misunderstanding. The fact that my approach will be semiotic (in contrast to that of most previous studies on this topic) may further explain why, in this preliminary discussion, I must question and largely discard some current definitions, and replace them with more workable ones.

I. Theatre

In theory, a semiotic definition of theatre does not present any special problem. Here (as elsewhere), I take theatre to mean the entire process which culminates in a theatrical performance, and involves both internal and external factors. Theatre may thus be defined as an iconic representation of events by means of a number of codes and corresponding systems of signs. The latter are either text or stage signs. The interaction between the two categories during the theatrical process, the resulting transformations, further subdivisions of signs, and so forth, are all matters that can be conceptualized and even formalized.[1]

However, moving from the safe ground of theory into praxis, one is caught in a triple bind resulting from the ephemeral nature of the theatrical performance. As no two performances are ever identical (even of the same play on two successive nights), nothing guarantees that the choice of a particular performance for study will yield more than contingent observations. Furthermore, since the performance lapses into non-existence at the very moment it comes into being, there is no opportunity either for a second look at a specific feature or for a reproduction of the entire experience for purposes of verification. Finally, in the absence of a reproducible performance, any statement made about its stage signs must first translate them into verbal signs, with resulting semiotic confusion and risk of subjective bias.[2] It is possible that in the future, as progress in video, laser, and computer recordings leads to the establishment of vast *theatre archives*, the elusive character of performance may be overcome. If so—some problems will still remain—it will affect future scholarship only. At present, a theory which postulates the unity of the entire theatrical process from text to performance (within a specific cultural framework) cannot justifiably draw its illustrations from all the significant steps in that process, simply because not all are available or acceptable as evidence. Of course, critics can and do recreate performances from memory, notes, or photographs, but, in so doing, they are making personal statements which must be taken on faith, at best as second-hand accounts of authentic impressions. For purposes of analysis, discussion, and scholarship, such accounts are largely inadequate, however persuasive and stimulating they may be. One is reluctant to reject them, especially when they express one's own experience; but ultimately one must come back to the written text which alone allows for meaningful communication. Such a strategy has its own risks, but most can be avoided if the text of the play is clearly conceived as only one step in the entire process, and the work on that text inscribed in this process. Hence, when testing my hypotheses about the theatrical referent on Samuel Beckett's *Waiting for Godot*, I shall rely primarily on the written text of the play. Beckett's text, however, will not be considered as an autonomous literary work, but as an initial set of verbal signs intended to generate additional sets of stage signs and, after some transformation, to become part of a performance.

II. The referent

Defining the referent is by no means easy. While the notion may seem clear, its applications to the semiotics of theatre are far from being so. Obviously, the referent is "that which is referred to" (Webster), but what is meant by referring? A great deal has been written on the problem—from Meinong to Russell, Frege, and Austin, and other speech-act theoreticians such as Strawson or Searle. The referent has been central to the concerns of philosophers, logicians, formal linguists, and semanticists, interested in and working with ordinary language (utterances, acts), rather than with fictional discourse or other semiotic systems.[3] Much controversial ink has been spilled over the conditions of true or false referring, with the temptation to restrict reference to objects *existing in the actual world*.[4] And when a new generation of philosophers of language finally undertook the analysis of reference in fiction, their efforts were channelled by constraints of tradition into contrived and contradictory explanations of the aberrant practice of referring to non-existent objects: fascinating but inconclusive theories of possible or fictional worlds, story operators, "say so" authority, guises, etc.[5] Some of their points can be adapted, *mutatis mutandis*, for the semiotics of theatre; in particular, I am indebted to their notion of the "incompleteness" of fictional referents[6] and to the image of "in the mind's eye" representation.[7] But not much of this scholarship is directly relevant to the study of *theatrical* (text or stage) signs.

More specifically semiotic studies are not very helpful either, since they do not provide *much* semiotic discussion of reference, referring, or referents. Semioticians who deal with these notions are often unclear and many are heavily influenced by linguistics. If Ducrot and Todorov, for example, accept the concept of the referent, as a complement to the Saussurean theory of the sign, they add (cautiously) that the former, "in the easiest to imagine case," is a "real object" with which the sign is "linked"; referring is equated with denoting; and the single illustration of the process links the word "apple" to "real apples."[8] There is little difference between their supposedly semiotic definition and the frankly linguistic one offered by Dubois *et al.*, where the referent is "that to which a linguistic sign refers in extra-linguistic reality,"[9]—a restrictive notion which excludes fictional referents. A similar emphasis on verbal *reference* is apparent in Michael Issacharoff's decision to restrict the referent to "its properly linguistic meaning," based on Strawson and Searle.[10] But he qualifies this by citing a more semiotic source, Ogden and Richards, for whom the referent is "whatever we may be thinking of or referring to," that is, much more than a "material substance," and where, by inference, the referring may be done by signs other than words.[11] Patrice Pavis, in his recent *Dictionnaire du Théâtre*, also alludes to Ogden and Richards, but is somehow sidetracked by Benveniste's distinction between semiotics and semantics, with the result that the referent is reduced either to a material object on stage, to an illusion thereof, or to what it could have been at the time the dramatic text was written: an unnecessarily confused entry.[12] A much broader definition of the referent in theatre appears to be given by Anne Ubersfeld, who holds it to be "an image of the world," possibly an idea or an ideal embodied in a specific reference; but further analysis shows that this embodiment always requires an initial reference to some material object, and that the entire process attributes to both signs and referents an impossibly dual presence on the stage and in the world.[13] In all these instances, recent scholarship on reference in theatre seems to err in its hasty acceptance of often incompatible concepts. The theoretical bases require rethinking and would benefit from systematic reformulation.

It is evident, in that perspective, that the study of theatre must retain Saussure's split of the sign into its material manifestation, the signifier, and its coded meaning, the signified. Peirce's sign/referent relationship, especially the distinction among the icon, the index, and the symbol, can also be of use (though most of his other material may be discarded in the name of methodological austerity). Ogden and Richards proposed an attractive tripartite system: Referent/Thought/Symbol, but at the price of discarding the signifier/signified duality, which is essential for stage signs.[14] The Prague School's contributions came close to a workable synthesis of their predecessors, but tension between aesthetic and social concerns, inherited from Russian Formalism, stood in the way of a simple theory.[15] Instead of attempting to develop (and betray) any of these approaches, I am proposing to use Occam's razor and borrow from all of them in such a way that the triad Signifier/Signified/Referent may simply, sufficiently, and efficiently account for referring in theatre. Hence my definitions:

1) *The Signifier*: The material manifestation of a sign (graphy, sound, color, facial expression, costume, light, etc.), coded in the appropriate semiotic system as signifying by conventional association with:

2) *The Signified*: The definitional concept provided in the code, such as a dic-

tionary, or an internalized cultural code, consisting generally of essential or class properties,[16] which, in an existential discourse, may receive:

3) *A Referent*: A particular manifestation of the signified, conceived of or perceived as having a unique individual existence, real or fictional.

The first two definitions are standard. The third requires further comment.

(i) *Ontology* of the referent: I am postulating that the referent can be anything at all: real or fictional persons, objects, events, feelings, ideas, and combinations thereof, provided that they are perceived as having a unique real or fictional existence;

(ii) *Identification* of the referent: It may be assumed on pragmatic evidence that any semiotic referential discourse supplies not only the concept of the referent, as coded by the signified for a given signifier, but also at least one more property and possibly many more, and that the identification of the referent by receivers is made possible at some *sufficient level of specificity* dependent on the number or type of these properties;

(iii) *Incompleteness* of the referent: However specific, a reference can never be assumed to be complete, that is, to comprise all possible additional properties that may be attributed to the referent "in the mind's eye" of the sender or the receiver of the semiotic discourse; namely, those which the referential sign may trigger, in the form of a "display of internal representations," from among the complex network of latent representations recorded in memory and adding up to the internalized Representation of Reality;[17]

(iv) *Identity* of the referent: Strictly speaking, the referent therefore cannot be identical in all points for the sender and the various receivers of the semiotic discourse even when there is easy agreement on its identification. In practice one may assume, however, that either because of a high degree of referential specificity in the discourse, or because of a high degree of correspondence between internalized representations in each memory, a properly identified referent, however different it may be in each "mind's eye," will be perceived with a sufficient number of overlapping properties to insure, under normal circumstances, a similar understanding of its function in the discourse by the sender and the various receivers, regardless of the real or fictional nature of that discourse.

III. Literary referents in *Waiting for Godot*: primary and secondary referents

In order to see clearly how these concepts work as well as to explore the basic problems of *Godot*, it will be useful to start with a "literary" reading of the play, the one accessible to most people who forget that it is theatre. In this sense, *Godot* yields an experience not entirely dissimilar from that of some genuine "new fiction": a minimal and rather tedious plot, a very individual style, sparse characterization, and considerable ambiguity. It also yields a network of referents situated in some outside world where the action takes place; characters with their words, gestures, emotions, ideas; a sequence of events; and ultimately a meaning of the story which, as shall be seen, has a special status. In order to survey the referential process in each of these categories, I need to posit three types of referents, as follows:

1. Verbal referents

Even read as literature, *Godot* obviously privileges the type of referent which, in verbal discourse, may be expected to achieve the highest identity concordance for sender and receivers: *the quoted text*. Under normal circumstances,[18] the quoted text, dialogue or monologue, emerges as the fundamental referential constant of the literary reading. One reader, for example, may identify Lucky as strong, cynical, and distant; another as emaciated, sincere, and pathetic. Lucky's lines may then receive a different referential meaning; but the fact that he speaks these lines will not change and, especially, the lines themselves will remain the same and always available. The quoted text, as such, is thus almost "complete": ideally, it needs a minimum of additional properties to become its own referent. It is the stablest of the signs—in literary readings.[19]

2. Narrative referents

This category includes all the referents which make up the "story," on the basis of either didascalia or discrete signs contained within the quoted text. The reader progressively decodes them, that is, moves from signifier to signified, and then, in "the mind's eye," links the signified to a particular referent which has properties provided in the text but also other properties generated by associations that the concept triggers in the reader's memory, that is, in the network of his internal, individual representations. Thus first the location: the (incomplete) referent supplied by the text is an area along a road; but the process of visualization[20] may add properties which will diversify the individual referent of the receiver along such variables as: A path? A street? A highway? A turnpike? Straight, turning, or sinuous? Level or steep? Paved, concrete, or dirt surface? Grass or rocks or earth or rubbish around? Perhaps a stream or bushes or ditches? and so on. Some of these properties are less likely than others to be added, and not all categories will be covered by each reader. Some overly hasty or unimaginative may even not add any significant property, and thus visualize a referent very close to the concepts given by the signified. But variations will occur, contaminating other referents as well. Vladimir on a flowery bank near a country road will not be the same, *ceteris paribus*, as Vladimir on a concrete slab near an industrial highway. Yet all these variations will not affect the general agreement among readers about the identification of the locale and its function in the story. Besides, as reading progresses (and comes to an end), the initial visualization may be revised, enriched, or impoverished until, gradually becoming hazier, it fades in the memory and is absorbed into the general network of individual representations.

Let us now turn to the characters, to Vladimir, Pozzo, and Godot in particular. The minimal referent yielded by the complex sign Vladimir[21] is that of a "bum," wearing a hat, and moving around; he performs actions and makes statements which stress that he and Estragon are waiting for Godot. Clothing, gestures, voice, face, figure, etc., but also emotions, personality, ideas, are left to individual visualization. The latter may vary considerably, and yet a general identification of Vladimir's function in the story will not be dramatically affected: he will remain a "bum," and the source of the stable verbal referents that his lines generate. In the case of Pozzo, no clear status properties are displayed in the minimal referent, though it provides for physical deterioration (blindness) and a change of relationship with Lucky; on the other hand, his speeches and actions will suggest to most readers a number of psychological properties: vanity, cruelty, etc. Again, there is no real problem about his function in the story.

And Godot? Very few signs refer to Godot in the text; they amount to a name, the power to give messages, and the state of being expected. There is very little to trigger individual visualization, since even a human shape is uncertain, so that the specificity of the minimal referent in fact appears *insufficient* both for the purpose of identification and for a clear perception of Godot's function in the story. During the reading process, this insufficiency may serve, like a vacuum, to entice the reader hoping to find new signs which would generate new properties and permit a satisfactory visualization. The average reader, no doubt, gives up halfway, declaring the story to be nonsense. The sophisticated reader, already intrigued by possible divine connotations of the name, may persist to the point where, frustrated by the insufficiency of the minimal referent, he will feel the need for "a daring hypothesis" (about Godot's role in the story) and postulate a referent for Godot which does not rely on signs provided in the text. In other words, this reader will visualize or conceptualize a number of properties which, attributed to Godot, would make sense for the other referents in the story, by integrating them into a coherent "meaning." For many, this hypothetical referent of Godot will indeed be God, endowed in their "mind's eyes" with various God-like properties, and so perceived by anyone who accepts the hypothesis. Of course, all the other referents, such as Vladimir, Pozzo, and the locale, may then have to be appropriately adjusted, through a change of or additions to their properties. This entire process, however, calls for a different type of semiotic operation than in the case of verbal or narrative referents. The latter can be called *primary* referents in that they are given directly by the textual signs, whereas the process just discussed involves *secondary* referents, based on primary referents when they are treated as signs.

3. Secondary referents: meaning

In the literary reading of *Godot*, the insufficient minimal referent of Godot entailed recourse to the notion of "meaning" lest the story be declared nonsensical. In reading fiction (which does not present such problems) the determination of meaning depends on the individual choice of the reader, and may not take place. Nevertheless, since it is always possible, and involves *referential* processes, it should be further explored. The Godot case enables us to make the following observations:

(i) Before an "in-the-mind's-eye" referent can assume the function of a sign, a process of *reverse encoding* of properties added by the individual reader must first occur. The signifiers of these properties are encoded with the same signifieds as in the general cultural code. If Vladimir is visualized with a bum's clothes, emaciated body, clasped hands, and an inspired face, these material features will be viewed as signifiers associated with signifieds corresponding to the concepts of "bumming," asceticism, religiosity, holiness. Together, they will add to a *definition* of Vladimir in the reader's ideal dictionary: An inspired bum who, for example, is eagerly and trustfully waiting for Godot at the top of a mountain. The reader's Vladimir is thus reconstituted as a sign.

(ii) Such a sign, however, may be more or less complex or complete. In an extreme case, it will contain all properties visualized for Vladimir, with the result that its only possible referent will be Vladimir. Critics who carry anti-reductionism to this extreme in fact claim that this entire operation is therefore circular, and that, in general, only the totality of primary referents defines the meaning of fiction. Readers (and critics) who look for more manageable meanings are prepared to accept a *reduction* in the complexity (completeness) of the sign, scanning its signified properties with a view to retaining only those which will serve the original purpose of the operation: to supply a reduced (and hence distorted) concept of Vladimir which could be easily integrated with the other similarly derived concepts so as to form a coherent meaning. Such a reduction, depending how far it is carried, will yield a hierarchy of Vladimir concepts, from the one quoted above to, say, "an inspired person who, on some high place, is waiting for Godot," or "an inspired man who is waiting for Godot," or "a man who is waiting for Godot." The "best" level, of course, is determined by the ease with which it can combine with the other concepts to form a coherent unit.

(iii) A coherent unit of this kind entails a retroactive impact on most concepts in question. If Godot, for example, is reduced to God, then the Vladimir concept may be modified, at a convenient level of reduction, to that of "a man who is waiting for God," or "a pilgrim who is waiting for God," etc. Any of these individual variations modify the ideal individual dictionary of fiction, providing a different definition, or signified, for Vladimir and all other "in-the-mind's-eye" referents treated as signs.

(iv) At this juncture, the referential process enters its final state where the new signified is again translated into a particular manifestation. A semiotically trained reader will now state that Vladimir's referent is a particular man (or pilgrim) named Vladimir, waiting for God. Extended to the entire story, the (highly simplified) referent—or meaning—of *Godot* could be stated as follows: "The story of two men, Vladimir and Estragon, who are waiting for God, who does not show Himself, and of two other men, Pozzo and Lucky, who are involved in earthly matters, and deteriorate," or "The story of men who wait for God and of those who do not."[22] Such a meaning can now serve to clarify and adjust any discrete referent in the text.

(v) By their very individualized nature, secondary referents of sender and receivers may be expected to vary much more than primary referents, to the point where identification could be undermined. Most controversies about fiction turn indeed on differences in "meanings" (secondary referents). However, such differences rarely entail a failure in communication, a lack of identification. Secondary referents operate at such reductive levels that, when disagreements occur, they do not involve misunderstanding but rather the choice of meanings. When, for one reader, Vladimir is seen as a pilgrim awaiting God, and for another as a nihilist awaiting Death, neither reader has trouble identifying the other's referent when rejecting it. In other words, literary referents encourage rather than discourage discussion, critics, and scholarship.

(vi) As secondary referents reach the highest levels of reduction, the corresponding formulation of the meaning of a story comes increasingly close to the formulation of a concept. Thus, the referent draws closer to its signified, at least in form. For the sake of clarity, I have reserved the term "meaning" for the highly simplified, integrated sum of all secondary referents of a fictional creation; and I propose to use "message" to designate the equivalent integrated sum of the signifieds of that fiction. Like all signifieds, the message will be likely to occur as a universal cognitive or imperative statement. The message of *Godot*, corresponding to the particular meaning obtained above, could be formulated thus: "There are men who wait for God, and others who do not," or "One should believe in an uncertain God rather than in earthly life which is sure to end in death." The process whereby meaning yields a message is not at issue here, but one may speculate again that it involves a kind of reverse encoding whereby the reader, looking for a concept behind the referent, scans his memory of representations until he encounters an acceptable cliché (that he could find in an ideal dictionary of messages) or, if none fits, makes one up on the model of the others. Of course, any message may then in turn be embodied in various particular meanings, including the first, with additional properties determining the differences. Any further development of this process moves from the area of reading to that of writing.

IV. Theatrical referents: The "virtual performance" of *Godot*

Now that the basic referential processes have been identified, as well as the main problems in *Godot*, it is easier to understand what happens when the play is not read as fiction but as a step in the theatrical process, a performance-to-be. Such a reading will yield, "in the mind's eye," what shall be called a "virtual performance," an anticipation of, and substitution for, the elusive real performance. Obviously, this virtual performance must be first related to the script of the play, especially in ways which affect referential processes; but, as will be shown, its assumed potential manifestation as a real performance must also be taken into consideration.

1. The virtual performance as referent

When read as theatre, *Godot* no longer refers to an outside world but to an outside stage, real or imaginary, and its characters no longer refer to people but to actors playing the role of these people. In the virtual performance, which takes place in the "mind's eye," all referents of *Godot* thus become parts of that performance which, in itself, becomes the referent of the text of the play. The question is: can these theatrical referents be identified, communicated, and discussed with the same success as the literary referents?

The first significant difference occurs in the process of visualization. Indeed, the mimetic associations of concepts with the representation of reality are now made to compete with associations derived from the experience of theatre, namely, representations of staging practice.[23] A road, for example, may be visualized on the stage with additional properties drawn from the memory of roads seen (or imagined) on some particular stage during some past (or imaginary) performance. It could be an empty space, scaffolding, a wooden plank, a roof-like surface, or swinging ropes, or even a "realistic" road. Similarly Vladimir and Pozzo may be visualized (and probably *will* be by adepts of theatre) not in the context of lived experience, and thus as unstable characters, but with features associated with specific and even codified acting styles and stock characters. In other words, while a literary reading basically moves from signs to referents which are intellectual realities, a theatrical reading can move from signs to other signs before reaching the referents. It has often been said that a cube on the stage may stand for a chair, a table, a car, a bed, and so on, alternately. We know too that the referent chair, table, or bed in turn functions as a sign referring to an outside (mental) reality; I shall return to this. What interests me here, however, is that the awareness of stage codes increases the variety of referents perceived by readers, since the use of coded signs as referents on stage expands the pool of additional properties in the reader's memory. Just as a road can be visualized as a wooden plank, so Vladimir or Pozzo can be visualized as stock Commedia dell'Arte characters, or Pierrots, or men with sandwich-boards appropriately inscribed, or masked figures in body-stockings, and so forth. For these examples, I am drawing on my experience of theatre; it supplies me with a much richer choice of referents than my experience of real roads or bums. Furthermore, my theatrical experience is likely to be quite different from that of other readers of *Godot*, and certainly quite distinct from our experience of reality. As a result, the referents I visualize during a virtual performance are far more likely to differ from other readers' referents, and more unpredictably than in the process of a literary reading. But does that mean that the principle of identification is subverted, and that no communication about the theatrical referents of *Godot* can occur? Not quite. For a virtual performance places upon its referents the ultimate constraint of coherence and stability. Once visualized as a stage element, in whatever form, the road will remain firmly anchored in the "mind's eye," directly and constantly linked to the visualized movements of the actors. The latter, with their fixed physical appearance and specific style of acting, will be constantly checked for the skill and consistency of their performance. If, say, I visualize Vladimir as a slender, saintly-looking man, with a face like Von Sydow, I shall not have him turn playful summersaults. And whereas I could visualize Pozzo as a truly protean character, moving through a whole gamut of expressions, nonetheless, even in his case, I shall be forced to eschew contradictions. In short, not only will my referents be relatively fixed (in my version of the virtual performance), but also their interaction will have to remain coherent, since they are viewed as elements of the dramatic space of a

specific stage. Thus, my theatrical reading of *Godot* will yield a much more controlled and better perceived network of referents than my literary reading. A much
clearer overall meaning will emerge from this network. We have seen that there is
no problem in identifying meanings, however they may vary; by the same token,
the organized network of referents in the virtual performance may also be readily
communicated.

But where and when does this unified meaning originate? During the literary
reading, it was posited to supplement the insufficient referential properties of Godot.
A theatrical reading, in theory, does not have to deal with Godot since Godot is
not visualized on stage. The need for the meaning, however, generally appears to
be more imperative for the virtual performance than for a literary reading. It does
not derive from the (optional) wish for a better understanding of the play, but from
the *necessity* of organizing the referents on stage. The problem then is how to locate
that meaning. The referents in the virtual performance cannot function the way the
primary referents in literary readings do, because rather than generating the meaning,
they depend on it. The formulation of the meaning must precede the visualization
of the performance. Where then does it originate? It would seem that only one
answer fits: the meaning must be drawn from the literary reading. The virtual
performance, when viewed as the referent of the text, thus always occurs after the
play is read as literature, though the two readings may conceivably be simultaneous.
All other things being equal, and despite a basic difference in referential processes,
the problems of literary and theatrical referents could then be related without any
risk of confusion. I shall stage Vladimir as a Von Sydow figure *because* I read him
first as a pilgrim waiting for God.

2. The virtual performance as sign

However, all other things are *not* equal. When the written text of a play is viewed
as a step in the theatrical process, its virtual performance must also be seen as
leading to (or substituting for) an actual performance—a conglomeration of (verbal
and stage) signs which in turn refer to some outside world. In other words, when
I visualize a plank on a stage slanting from right to left, and at the top of it an actor
looking like Von Sydow, hands clasped and eyes lifted in hope, I must not forget
that these referents of the text are intended to function as signs for the fictional
pilgrim Vladimir waiting for God at the top of an imaginary mountain; or that the
actor playing Pozzo is supposed to generate, in the "mind's eye" of the audience,
the image of a pathetic (or insufferable) ham. In many cases, this dual nature of
the virtual performance (referent of the text and sign of an outside referent) is in
no way problematic; the reader simply postulates that the ultimate outside referent
is the same as the initial literary referent, at least insofar as the principal meaning
is concerned. If his initial reading yielded God as referent of Godot, a pilgrim as
the referent of Vladimir, an earthly, emotional, ambitious, pathetic character as the
referent of Pozzo, a mountain road as their meeting place, and a story of believers
and disbelievers as the meaning of the play, then his virtual performance will
manipulate the verbal and stage signs so that the virtual audience will end up with

a similar set of referents. (Such a practice is generally justified by a pretended loyalty to the author, and provides arguments for critics who claim to be able to discuss a future [virtual] performance of a play on the basis of the written text.) Yet an actual performance is not the translation of a text. It is a social act, and though it uses the text as its pretext, its motivation and intention cannot help being primarily social or psychological (profit, self-expression, the need to make an ideological statement, professional success, and so forth). Motivation and intention often play a crucial role in shaping the final referents of the performance, imposing a meaning different from the literary meaning. A specific ideological commitment (political or sexual), for example, can use the text of Godot in order to advance a particular cause such as political freedom or homosexual rights. Godot, in such cases, would be identified pessimistically as the embodiment of the ideal, or optimistically as the embodiment of the competing ideal. The rest belongs to imagination, and only Theatre knows its limits. I can only suggest, for the first instance, a prison court-yard setting, guards on a ramp above, Pozzo as an army officer, Vladimir in army fatigues; and, behind the massive Gate, through which Pozzo enters, a pastoral landscape, etc. For the second instance, one would probably rely on nudity, projected images, suggestive decorations, scrims, screams, and so forth. *Godot* does not lend itself particularly to such a performance, but it could be done. And if such happens to be the intention of a particular reader, his virtual performance of *Godot* will be oriented by his committed meaning, since it will contain an abundance of stage signs which no other reader could have foreseen, or imagined, and which certainly cannot be deduced from the written text of the play. One may add that these signs, as always in theatre, inevitably contaminate and transform other signs, especially verbal (that is, text) signs, so that one cannot speak of two meanings but of one.

For such virtual performances, where signs are dictated by externally defined referents, identification becomes arbitrary. Each reader's visualization contains too many individual properties and signs to insure effective communication. There is no discussion possible. By the same token, all referents become elusive for all but a single reader, dreams waiting for a future performance. In other words, one cannot find a referent for such virtual performances; one should not discuss it, and critical discourse ought to avoid it. Of course, there are other virtual performances which rely on the literary referents, and present no problem in identification and communication. And no doubt many mixed categories lie between the two extremes. But why look for their referents? The identification we have seen is all the more successful when the virtual performance keeps closer to the literary reading; so why not be satisfied with the literary referent, as the only one which can be safely grasped?

V. Conclusion

The preceding observations were intended to help clarify the function of referents in theatre. They entailed redefinition of a number of basic notions and scrutiny of referential processes at work in a specific play. This analytical operation, based on the hypothesis that plays should be read as a part of the theatrical process and not as a literary genre, brings me to a startling conclusion. The only safe way to deal with referents in theatre under present circumstances is to keep to the literary referents. No doubt, an extensive verbal transcription of a performance may supply the possibility of discussing theatrical referents; but such a transcription becomes itself a literary text, and the supposedly theatrical referent becomes largely literary. This does not mean, however, that plays should be read as literature. A theatrical reading, especially a semiotic reading, may indeed lead to a clarification of one related problem so far unexplored: the likelihood that a particular play will generate performances with referents close to or remote from the literary referents. Because the referents of performances, virtual or real, seem to elude present critical discourse (at least as a topic for scholarly discussion), it is all the more important to assess the practical influence literary referents (which *can* be studied) may have on future productions. One way of approaching this problem is to rely on the experience of theatre critics by examining their reviews of actual performances of particular plays; on this impressionistic basis, some plays appear to generate a whole range of referents while others generate only a limited number which a literary reading would yield as well. Such an approach, however, does not offer any basis for comparison between plays, since the range of referents observed on stage may simply correspond to the potential derived from the written texts; plays obviously differ in their degree of complexity, ambiguity, looseness, and so on, to the same extent as novels or poems. Furthermore, the reasons for repeated performances of a play depend on many factors, and likewise, the possibility of a comprehensive range of referents. Thus, I have identified elsewhere some of the properties of a written text which stimulate (or impede) the transformation of its verbal signs by stage signs, thus increasing the likelihood of productions. But plays with a higher "theatricality quotient" do not necessarily invite a change in, or departure from, the literary referent, although they make it likelier. *Godot* is a very theatrical play which has had many original productions, yet, so far as I am aware, even the most innovative have been derived directly from a literary reading of the text, without the interference of extraneous issues such as I suggested for my two improbable virtual performances. Perhaps, then, some plays, *Godot* included, privilege literary referents, despite, or rather because of, their inherent theatricality? Maybe the least theatrical plays are in fact the most likely to generate referents totally alien to the text? Or, finally, perhaps the answer lies not in any property of a given play, but in the encounter between some properties of the text and social concerns at a particular moment of history? Whatever the case, any further exploration of this problem obviously cannot rely on the evidence of the critical reaction to actual performances, but must focus instead on a careful reading of plays as plays, that is, as part of the whole theatrical process, in which the verbal signs already exist in a state of potential transformation by the stage signs. A successful analysis of the stability of literary referents of a play may then perhaps help solve another basic problem recently raised by Steen Jansen: the permissible limits of stage transformations of a text.[24] When does a production of *Godot* no longer qualify as a production of *Godot*? Can one determine a "field" of a dramatic work, within which all possible productions define the total potential of that work, and beyond which another work emerges? Is it conceivable that the literary referent, today's *parent pauvre* of theatre semiotics, holds the key to that problem?

NOTES

1. See J. Alter, "From Text to Performance," *Poetics Today* 2:3 (1981), 113–139.
2. One of the most successful accounts of this type, M. Corvin's description and analysis of D. Benoin's avant-garde production of *George Dandin*, while quite impressive in its wealth of detail and persuasive in its argument, nevertheless remains one man's experience, not necessarily shared by others. See M. Corvin, "Sémiologie et spectacle," *Organon 80* (Lyon: CERT, 1980), 93–152.
3. Cf. J. L. Austin, *How to Do Things with Words* (Oxford: Oxford University Press, 1962), especially pp. 93, 96, 135–136, 141–143; John R. Searle, *Speech Acts: An Essay in the Philosophy of Language* (Cambridge and London: Cambridge University Press, 1969), especially pp. 23, 26, 77–78, 89, 158–162, and p. 172 on the referring function of proper names; Willard Van Orman Quine, *Word and Object* (Cambridge, Mass.: The M.I.T. Press, 1960), especially pp. 112 and 119–121; P. F. Strawson, *Logico-Linguistic Papers* (London: Methuen, 1971), especially pp. 1–27.
4. Thus Searle, *Speech Acts*, p. 77, accepts as an axiom of reference that whatever is referred to *must exist*. See also Quine, p. 112. Most of the controversy concerns the notoriously bald king of France, statements shown to be false, neither true nor false, infelicitous, unsatisfactory, etc.
5. The seminal work in this field was no doubt J. Woods, *The Logic of Fiction* (The Hague: Mouton, 1974), but a good survey of recent work on referring in fiction is provided by the April 1979 issue of *Poetics* (Vol. 8, Nos. 1–2), where Jens Ihwe and Hannes Rieser's "Normative and Descriptive Theory of Fiction: Some Contemporary Issues" (pp. 63–84) and Robert Howell's "Fictional Objects: How They Are and How They Aren't" (pp. 129–179) offer an excellent overview of latest controversies and issues.
6. See Richard Routley "The Semantic Structure of Fictional Discourse," *Poetics* Vol. 8, Nos. 1–2 (1979), 9, and Ihwe and Rieser, p. 68; R. Howell, pp. 134–136.
7. Cf. Howell, pp. 172–173, who refers to an activity of the imagination, but does not limit it to strict "visualizations" since it may also involve conceptualizations.
8. Oswald Ducrot and Tzvetan Todorov, *Dictionnaire encyclopédique des sciences du langage* (Paris: Seuil, 1972), p. 133 (*Signe*).
9. Jacques Dubois *et al.*, *Dictionnaire de linguistique* (Paris: Larousse, 1973), p. 415: "On appelle référent ce à quoi renvoie un signe linguistique dans la réalité extra-linguistique."
10. Cf. Michael Issacharoff, "Labiche, la farce et la sémiotique," *Saggi e Ricerche di Letteratura Francese* XIX (1980), 209–221: "Il est indispensable, en utilisant ce concept de référent, de s'en tenir au sens linguistique propre; . . . pour que l'on puisse parler de *référent*, il faut qu'une *référence verbale* soit faite explicitement" (p. 211).
11. C. K. Ogden and I. A. Richards, *The Meaning of Meaning*, 8th ed. (New York: Harcourt, Brace, 1956), p. 5: "The word 'thing' is unsuitable for the analysis here undertaken, because in popular usage it is restricted to material substances. . . . It has seemed desirable, therefore, to introduce a technical term to stand for whatever we may be thinking of or referring to. . . . The word 'referent,' therefore, has been adopted." Elsewhere, Issacharoff (who has written several articles on theatrical reference) underwrites Strawson's definition: "We very commonly use expressions of certain kinds to mention or refer to some individual

person or single object or particular event or place or process; in the course of doing what we should normally describe as making a statement about that person, object, place, event, or process. I shall call this way of using expressions the 'uniquely referring use.' " "Espaces mimétiques, espaces diégétiques," *Sartre et la mise en signe*, Issacharoff and Vilquin, eds. (Paris: Klincksieck, and Lexington: French Forum, 1982), p. 66.

12. Patrice Pavis, *Dictionnaire du Théâtre* (Paris: Éditions Sociales, 1980), pp. 368–370 (*Signe théâtral*).

13. Anne Ubersfeld, *Lire le théâtre* (Paris: Éditions Sociales, 1977), pp. 35–38.

14. In fact Ogden and Richards strongly opposed Saussure's scheme because, they claim, as a result "the process of interpretation is included by definition in the sign," and the scheme, "by neglecting entirely the things for which signs stand, was from the beginning cut off from any contact with scientific methods of verification" (pp. 5–6). As for Peirce, while acknowledging the interest of his extensive analysis of the sign, they criticize his cumbersome conceptual apparatus which discourages practical applications (pp. 279–290).

15. Thus Mukarovsky, studying an art object as a sign, distinguishes: 1. a signifier (to be perceived), 2. an *aesthetic* "signification" (coded in the collective consciousness), and 3. a relationship to a thing signified (in the total social, cultural, historical context). See Jan Mukarovsky, "Art as Semiotic Fact," *Semiotics of Art: Prague School Contributions*, L. Matejka and I. Titunik, eds. (Cambridge, Mass.: The M.I.T. Press, 1976), p. 9. His "signification" no doubt corresponds to the signified, but why must it be aesthetic? And why, again, reduce the referent (i.e., the "thing signified") to a historical reality, however mediated by cultural factors? Other Prague semioticians who specifically studied theatre, anticipating by several decades the current scholarship in that field, hardly used Mukarovsky's scheme, and in general focused their studies on relations between signs rather than on the referential problem. Cf. (in the same volume) the articles by Jindrich Honzl, Jiri Veltrusky, and Karel Brusak.

16. My use of the word "property" is borrowed from formal semantics, but does not imply commitment to that discipline. Terms such as "quality," "aspect," or "feature," for example, though synonymous, have confusing connotations.

17. Ogden and Richards speak in a similar vein of engrams, an unnecessary complication. It suffices to postulate that memory contains, in the form of representations, visualized or conceptualized experiences (personal or second-hand) which add up to a Representation of Reality, consisting of signs belonging to many systems. How a particular sign triggers the association with some of these representations is not pertinent here. It is more important to note that such associations, and the resulting additional attribution of properties to the referent, do not essentially vary with the real or fictional nature of the referent.

Thus, even a very concrete table perceived by sender and receiver at the same time is not necessarily identified by them with all the same properties. A table simultaneously referred to by the utterance "this table" and a pointing gesture may be seen differently by two persons and attributed different additional properties (rustic vs. elegant, small vs. big, etc.). *A fortiori*, real people, living or dead, though easily identifiable within a homogeneous social group, obviously cannot be expected to have similar properties attributed to them by the sender and various receivers, since everyone relies on a different network of representations. What was the color of Churchill's eyes? Was he flexible or rigid? Of course, one may object that most properties added in the "mind's eye" are somehow relevant to the topic of the discourse, and that such relevant properties can be expected to be generally shared. While this is largely correct, and, of course, insures easy identification of historical characters or personal acquaintances, the same observation can be made about fictional characters, say Anna Karenina who, for twentieth-century Americans who have read the novel, is probably perceived with additional properties similar to their representation of a Russian aristocrat of the nineteenth century. In both situations, however, there always remains the possibility of some variation, which in each case may cause a significant diversity of referents.

18. By 'normal circumstances,' I mean those in which there is no particular ambiguity as to the author of the quoted speech (as in some "new novels") or its mode of existence

(spoken, written, imaginary, etc.). Furthermore, and arbitrarily for the sake of a clear argument, I am assuming here as elsewhere that sender and receivers (author and all readers) not only share the same linguistic code, but have similar competence in that code—a totally implausible assumption which, however, underlies all critical discussion. Finally, I am also excluding from these considerations all problems related to the existential (social) circumstances under which the quoted speech may be sent and received. The entire notion of historical relativity and resulting variations is taken for granted, and as such, discounted.

19. In theatrical readings, of course, the quoted speech, placed on a stage and attributed to an actor, becomes totally unstable: one knows how voice, pitch, intonation, tempo, and accompanying gestures can alter any quoted speech! A literary reading generally eschews such speculations, and approaches the quoted speech as the most reliable element of a narrative, which may explain the prevalence of dialogues in so-called popular literature. That the quoted speech has its own referents, when it is referential, is not here at issue.

20. I shall be using the term "visualization" as an abbreviation for "in-the-mind's-eye representation," implying not only visual but also auditory, olfactory, tactile representation, where relevant, and even "conceptualization" when the representation deals with more abstract notions such as feelings, ideas, and so forth.

21. By a complex sign, I mean the totality of discrete signs, and their relations, which relate, or are related by a reader, to a single referent, in this case Vladimir. Whether the proper name *Vladimir* is itself a sign, or a "rigid indicator," is irrelevant in this respect. In practice, the proper name functions during the literary reading as a property, and in most cases as one of the essential properties composing the concept of Vladimir, coded in the ideal dictionary of fictional characters as a character in Beckett's *Waiting for Godot*. The referent of this sign (signifier and signified) is then the Vladimir that the sender or receiver perceives (with some additional properties) as having a particular existence in the world referred to by the play.

22. Three observations are essential here:

1. The meaning thus presented, at a very high level of reduction, must not be understood to be in any way privileged among many other meanings which could be suggested for *Godot*. In fact, it is probably one of the least original (though most popular) interpretations, which is why I have chosen it to illustrate the procedure. Among other meanings, similarly derived, one may even include the following "ambiguous" (though not meaningless) explanation, based on the "daring hypothesis" (suggested by the author) that Godot cannot be identified: "The story of men who are waiting for something which could be anything, and of those who are not waiting for anything." It should be observed that literary readings provide many meanings, and that a play read as literature remains largely an open work.

2. Obviously, the process of reduction, shown here in its end result, may follow various strategies, so long as it satisfies the requirement of integrating various referents into a coherent unit or story. The choice of strategies depends on the reader's (critic's) preferences, gifts, and internalized models of interpretative approaches (e.g., Souriau's system of functions, Greimas's actantial model). My own method, leading to a reductive account of Godot quite different from that which I am presenting here, is based on a theory of dramatic units whereby Godot is identified as "the meaning of life" (See J. Alter, "En codant Godot," *Sémiologie de la Représentation*, ed. André Helbo [Brussels: Éditions Complexe, 1975] pp. 42–62).

3. The "meaning" must not be confused with the notion of a "summary," though when very simplified, the two may appear similar. A detailed summary does not clarify the meaning, whereas a short summary, because it must select and simplify, often involves the elaboration of a meaning.

23. Similarly, cinematographic practices in styles of acting and types of characters such as a "bum" (Chaplin, for example), and so forth.

24. Cf. Steen Jansen's paper, "Texte dramatique et représentation scénique," read at the Congress of the British Comparative Literature Association in Canterbury, England, November 18, 1980.

V.

TOPOLOGICAL POETICS
ELUARD'S "LA VICTOIRE DE GUERNICA"

Jean-Jacques Thomas

> On April 26, 1937, the German air force, acting
> under the orders of General Franco, bombed
> and almost destroyed the defenseless city of
> Guernica on a crowded market day. This first
> example of modern mass bombing, during the
> Spanish Civil War, was a grim foretaste of what
> would happen on a larger scale in World War
> II.[1]

Of all the military atrocities perpetrated between the two world wars, the bombing
of Guernica probably had the greatest impact upon the writers and artists of that
era.[2] Fixed in time:

> *Le 26 avril 1937, jour de marché, dans les premières heures de l'après-midi, les
> avions allemands au service de Franco bombardèrent Guernica durant trois heures
> et demie par escadrilles se relevant tour à tour;*[3]

[In the early afternoon of April 26th (market day) Guernica was bombed for three
and a half hours by relays of German Air Squadrons under General Franco's orders;]

and in space:

> *Guernica. C'est une petite ville de Biscaye, capitale traditionnelle du Pays basque.
> C'est là que s'élevait le chêne, symbole sacré des traditions et des libertés basques.
> Guernica n'a qu'une importance historique et sentimentale.*[4]

[Guernica: a small town and the traditional capital of the Basque country. It was here
that grew the oak of Guernica, sacred symbol of Basque traditions and Basque freedom. Guernica's importance is purely historical and sentimental.]

the reality of this event was bound to attract the attention of the author of *Yeux fertiles* and *Donner à voir* who held that poetry should first and foremost reveal "le visage de la vérité"[5] [the face of truth]. The event obviously lent itself to journalistic writing and was reported in great detail.[6] Nonetheless it was to this same event (perhaps better suited to the epic form since it so magnified reality) that the poet turned for material he later exploited to symbolic effect. While depleting the events of their referential value, this symbolic effect progressively drains them of their reality, transposing them into a system founded on language universals and totally independent of the mimetic event which originally triggered production of the poem's verbal system.

The mere name *Guernica* binds the text to reality since, as Derrida points out, it acts on a "monumémoire"[7] or "monumemory" and constitutes a whole store of information related to this particular event.

Now, for there to be reference, the referent (the sign's third element and its only non-symbolic one—contingent on objective reality and thus "parasitic"), must figure explicitly in the text so that its textual presence can act as an extra-linguistic shifter, as something which speaks about reality while acting as a support for the other purely symbolic constituents of the verbal sign.

The name *Guernica* constitutes the poem's only historical emblem: it indicates the constraints and imperatives of time and space, imposed by history, and acts both as milestone and textual boundary. Against this background of reality the text constructs an autonomous sign system of its own. Thus from the title onwards, the exclusively referential value of the name *Guernica* is negated since, though primarily designating an atrocious massacre, the effect is counterbalanced by its link with "victoire"—"victory" being a term which contradicts what "we know" about events in Guernica as reported in the press.

This system of bipolar opposition provides a preliminary model for the entire text in that it is based on the principle of contradiction. Thus the referential presence underlined by *Guernica* exists for the sole purpose of allowing the opposite pole (signaled by *victoire*) to be developed. *Guernica*'s denotation and connotations have no value *per se*, since here Eluard is not concerned with pseudomimesis of the type found in the Annals of History.

Inevitably, though, one must recognize the proper name's particular function in this system. As Benveniste points out, the proper name's distinguishing linguistic feature is that, by its very nature, it incorporates its own actualization and self-determination, these being intrinsic components of any proper name. Whence the special referential status of a text engendered by a verbal component of this type. In an utterance such as *la victoire du génocide* [the victory of the genocide] one could recognize a contradiction similar to the one expressed in *la Victoire de Guernica*. There is, however, a fundamental difference between the two: "genocide" refers to an atopical and, alas, universal reality, while *Guernica* implies the reader's encyclopedic knowledge—knowledge which cannot possibly be anhistoric. The poem's contradiction, that is to say its *meaning*, is, of course, clear without referring to the event. But the event's importance (it justifies the text in relation to a particular system of meaning) in no way diminishes it as a referential anchor, one which functions as a *trigger* rather than a matrix. This is demonstrated by the fact that when Eluard wanted to commemorate the actual historic event, its site and meaning, he eliminated *victory* from the title (and consequently the principle of contradiction the word provided), keeping only "Guernica." This transformation in turn alters the way the text is treated: its meaning fades and what was elliptic, paratactic, and antithetical in the poem becomes direct, explanatory, and justificatory in the commemorative discourse:

> On a tout lu dans les journaux en buvant son café; quelque part en Europe, une légion d'assassins écrase la fourmilière humaine. On se représente mal un enfant éventré, une femme décapitée, un homme vomissant tout son sang d'un seul coup.[8]

> [People read all about it in the newspaper over coffee at breakfast: somewhere in Europe a legion of murderers had crushed a human anthill. It is hard to imagine a child disembowelled, a woman beheaded, or a man suddenly vomiting all his blood.]

Whereas the poem only exists by virtue of the tension created between deceptively vague reference on the one hand, and a system of symbols that refer to a highly specific context on the other, the commemorative discourse refers only to the specific event. If one compares the two versions, written fourteen years apart, the differences between the two modes of writing are quite obvious from the very first verse.

> Beau monde des masures
> De la mine et des champs

> [Beautiful world of hovels
> mines and fields]

becomes, in the second version,

> Les gens de Guernica sont de petites gens. Ils vivent dans leur ville depuis bien longtemps. Leur vie est composée d'une goutte de richesse; et d'un flot de misère.[9]

> [The people of Guernica are humble folk. They have been living in their town for a very long time. Their life is made up of a drop of wealth and a flood of poverty.]

Although in 1919 Eluard wrote in *Littérature* "Let us reduce, transform the displeasing language which satisfies mere talkers, language as dead as the crowns which sit upon our equally dead brows," and goes on to propose an aesthetics "aiming at an immediate rapport between the object and the person who sees it" *(Physique de la Poésie*[10] [Physics of Poetry]), when he speaks of the event itself, he cannot help developing an explanatory, metadiscursive level of discourse. Even when interpolating fragments of the original poem in the prose commentary, he feels it necessary to modify them so that the gap between the two not be too obvious.
Thus:

Ils vous ont fait payer le pain
Le ciel la terre l'eau le sommeil
Et la misère
De votre vie

[They made you pay for the bread
the sky the earth the water the sleep
and the misery
of your life with your life]

becomes

Ils vous ont fait payer le pain
De votre vie
Ils vous ont fait payer le ciel la terre l'eau le sommeil
Et même la misère noire
De votre vie.[11]

[They made you pay for the bread
of your life with your life
they made you pay for the sky the earth the water the sleep
and even the black misery
of your life with your life.]

The repetition of *De votre vie* and the interpolation of *même* introduce a hierarchical distinction, whereas originally the mere juxtaposition and accumulation of words suggested equivalent, similar components, all equally essential to the life of the *beau monde*. "Bread" becomes something one acquires, the result of work; "sky," "earth," "water," and "sleep" are something given. *Même* is the author's intervention and a comment since the adverb hails both a reiteration and an amplification, so that *misère* becomes a sort of superlative in relation to the other terms, as is further underlined by the addition of *noire*. Or, if one were to use the terminology of traditional rhetoric, one might say that whereas a metabole suffices in "La Victoire de Guernica," "Guernica" is more explicit and takes the reader from one step to the next. And in case the reader or listener did not notice these distinctions, the prose commentary points them out quite unequivocally:

Leur vie est composée de tout petits bonheurs et d'un très grand souci: celui du
lendemain. Demain il faut manger et demain il faut vivre. Aujourd'hui, l'on espère.
Aujourd'hui, l'on travaille.[12]

[Their life is composed of small joys and one great worry: that of tomorrow. Tomorrow
they must eat and tomorrow they must live. Today they hope. Today they work.]

This type of discourse is quite foreign to that of our poem, since, as Nicole Charbois notes, in the poem

"Eluard makes an utterance, then remains silent: no comment whatsoever. . . . Picasso conveyed the violence by the shrieking and convulsed colours and shapes he used, but Eluard chose silence to make us aware of this violence. He holds in his cry, masters his language—but he says all."[13]

There is no need for further demonstration since examples so far given abundantly prove the difference between the way the poem and the commemorative text treat the referential given. The didascalic inscription differs too: in the poem the symbolism generated by the referential trigger leads one to the meaning without there being any need for circumstantial reference. In the commemorative text, reference is the force which maintains the legitimate meaning, controlling and producing it by the discourse's underlying naturalism.

Thus a study of "La Victoire de Guernica" is also a study of a language system whose only postulate is to negate precise reference and endow it with a symbolic importance which transcends any *mimesis* of the specific, transposing it into a universal and anhistoric mode.

In our introduction, we pointed out the *antithetical* character of the title and, to that end, emphasized that the antithesis was not founded solely on the semantic qualities of *Guernica*, since this word, being a proper name, retains its essential designatory quality and implies, in the process of perception, the actualization of a set of extra-linguistic connotations that are indissociable from its denotative function. Indeed it is this aspect which creates the poem's special status, and leads me to place it in the category of *topological poetics*, since the fundamental trigger of the poem's system appears as a sign-signal. This process is distinct from the poetic practice of opposing two verbal signs in such a way that each is deprived of its complete sign status. For example, when Leiris writes *Étrusques aux frusques étriquées* [Etruscans in tight togs], *Étrusques* is only used so that it can appear as a reverse contraction (or porte-manteau word) of *frusques étriquées* and vice versa: *étr*(iquées fr)*usques*. Here language is only fighting itself: no extratextual reference is ever involved in this type of game which never goes beyond the simple sign's specific properties—that of the meeting of signifier and signified.

It would not be rash to claim that once the title's emblematic effect and its value as a referential trigger are established, the poem's significance and its role as a "universal and atemporal monument" are created in a language which brings into play an exclusively verbal system. Extratextual reference plays only a minor role in relation to the poem's main preoccupation, which is to show language pitted against itself. Thus in topological poetics, the status of reference is that of a pretext which legitimizes and justifies the creation of a complex sign whose referent is the excluded third component. Nonetheless its impact is felt marginally all along the symbolic chain, since, within the framework of the co-presence of an encyclopedic knowledge in each linguistic element's field, an allusion to the name *Guernica*—and, by the same token, to its referential context—can be attributed to each element.

This explains how, in the first stanza, *masures, mine,* and *champs* [hovels, mine, and fields] can be seen as offering a precise description of the lifestyle of Guernica's inhabitants; though one would have to be sufficiently well-informed to assess the accuracy of such a statement—a geographer's or sociologist's task rather than a literary commentator's. In fact, *masures, mine,* and *champs* all serve as general signs for a hard and laborious life; they are used in order to contrast with *beau monde,* a fixed expression which in French usually designates the idle, elegant world of the privileged. The sole purpose of this antithetical disjunction is to herald a theme which runs through the entire poem: namely, that the little these people possessed was a "treasure" compared to their plight after the disaster. This theme of life seen as a treasure as long as there is hope returns covertly in stanzas V, VIII, IX, XII and overtly in stanza XIII in a paradoxical formulation accentuated by the homophony of the two rhyming words:

> Hommes réels pour qui le désespoir
> Alimente le feu dévorant de l'espoir
>
> [Real men for whom despair
> feeds the devouring fire of hope.]

The importance given here to *espoir*—and it is of some intertextual comfort that Malraux was later to choose it as the title of his own account of the Spanish Civil War—brings to the text a set of variants such as: *feuilles vertes* [green leaves], green being associated with hope in French; *de printemps* [of spring], the season of germination; and *lait pur* [pure milk], *milk* is a metonym for motherhood, for promise, and *pure* contributes the image's meliorative value by connoting natural innocence and fragility.

The thematic pole opposing this *beau monde* is obviously *mort* [dead] and *vide* [empty], lines 6–7, which transform *feuilles vertes . . . dans les yeux* [green leaves in their eyes], line 20, into *roses rouges dans les yeux* [red roses in their eyes], lines 26–27. For here "red" is doubly overdetermined, first by *sang* [blood], line 28, which follows it, introducing violence into the field of utterance, and, second, by the fact that *rose rouge* is a metonym for extreme intensity and also the very end of a cycle.[14] A metaphoric extension of this opposition between foliage and flower is embodied in the formula which contains the poem's exhortation: *ouvrons ensemble le dernier bourgeon de l'avenir* [let us open the future's last leaf bud together]. *Bourgeon* [bud] refers directly to "leaf," to "green" and thus to "hope," whereas in the flower system the precise term for bud would be *bouton* rather than *bourgeon.*

The asyndetic construction of the third stanza and of its first line introduces a new cumulative series of notations which are presented as a figurative description not of a lifestyle, this time, but of the inhabitants themselves—though the description's "naturalist" flavor is again transformed into a negative value by an exclusively verbal semantic artifice. However, unlike the first stanza where the semantic opposition to the "beautiful world" was direct, disjunction now occurs within the syntactic framework implying the restitution of the fixed expression "bon à quelque chose" [good for something] and indicates a positive value, good for action or a particular state. Here *feu* [fire] and *froid* [cold] represent the entire paradigm of climatic conditions since they evoke its two extremes. *Bons au feu . . . bons au froid* [good for the fire good for the cold] is thus the interchangeable equivalent of "good for all weather" as far as meaning is concerned, but adds a certain concreteness to the utterance. The accumulation which follows it brings together a group of negative elements: *refus, injures, coups* [refusals, insults, blows] which, through analogical contamination, give *nuit* [night] (an *a priori* neutral element) a similar pejorative value that it retains from this first context when it recurs a second time in *la couleur monotone de notre nuit* [the monotonous color of our night]; "monotonous," usually laden with negative presuppositions, confirms this value. Thus the effect of semantic contrast relies upon the opposition between "good," considered as positive, and the negative value of the elements to which this term is structurally attached and which all indicate the natural or man-made atrocities these people suffered.

This type of syntactic dislocation of a fixed structure is used again in stanza V, since the syntagm *de votre vie* [of your life] can be linked equally well to both the preceding nouns (*le pain, le ciel . . . la misère de votre vie* [the bread, the sky . . . the misery of your life]), and to the verb if one allows for a stylistic inversion such as *Ils vous ont fait payer de votre vie le pain Le ciel . . .* [They made you pay with your life for the bread, the sky . . .]. In this case, the phrase would imply a simple *quid pro quo*, whereas the first structure would elaborate upon the idea of "treasure," by insinuating that "they" [*ils*] have so indulged in excess that they even put a price on the most complete destitution. This interpretation would concur with *ils exagèrent* [they exaggerate] in line 18. One should note, however, that any partial interpretation matters little here: for the dislocation of the syntactic structure creates ambiguity and, unlike what happens in the second stanza, where the ensuing disjunction concretizes the semantic opposition between the two poles (good/bad), in stanza five, dislocation reinforces meaning to the point of redundancy, since the co-presence of the two formulations serves to reinforce both of them and corroborate the notion of excess, being themselves a type of "overflow" of meaning.

In both cases, the use of syntactical possibilities forces language into a state of internal ambivalence and the resulting dichotomy removes any possibility of direct, unitary denoting: it produces a meaning which establishes either redundancy or opposition, as the case may be. It seems clear, then, that referential mimesis, always based on an utterance's direct meaning, is overshadowed by a symbolic process which introduces a certain number of exclusively verbal distinctions which then proceed to take over.

The asyntactic utterance in line 8, *La mort coeur renversé* [death heart overturned], derives its force from the encounter of verbal effects on different levels. The absence of an explicit grammatical or semantic link between the two parts is naturally perceived to be a case of symbolic disorder, the precise nature of their relation depending on how the reader construes it. Yet one cannot overlook the well-known expression *coeur renversé*, which adds to its physical meaning (upside down, upset, or even knocked over) a quite special psychological, figurative value making it the semantic equivalent of "emotionally upset" and "overwhelmed."

Such an interpretation would create a consecutive link between "death" and "upset heart": it is death that upsets. But *renversé* is also a synonym of "changed to the exact opposite," which is precisely what death has done in relation to the victims' former state. In this case *renversé* would simply appear as an expansion of "death," with a more limited meaning focusing on the result of the latter. Naturally one would still have to explain its association with "heart" since, given this meaning, "upset" and "heart" cannot constitute a fixed expression. But one can envisage that the sequence *coeur renversé* (taken in the sense of upside-down heart), instead of being a pseudo-mimetic representation of the victims' situation, plays an emblematic role in relation to "death" and that both terms could be joined to make a heraldic description. If a "beating heart" is a symbol of life, *coeur renversé* is its opposite: the blazon of death. The structure *La mort coeur renversé* would thus introduce the bearer (the enemy) and his sign, his "speaking arms." This brings us back, indirectly, to the original context, war; and also introduces the adversary, an undefined *Ils* [They] mentioned in the fifth stanza. Here again meaning results from symbolic densification (compression) and cannot, therefore, be reduced to singular, unequivocal reference.

Just as the hovels, mine, and fields could be seen as referring directly to the real world of Guernica's inhabitants, so the characterization in the sixth stanza could make us think that these are fragments of description referring metonymically to the chronicle's "nazi pilots." In fact the undefined "They" marks the moment at which the poem breaks loose from its specific frame of reference and introduces a generic dimension devoid of any specific actualization. What appear are thus generic qualities—hypocrisy, vanity, avarice. The opacity of *Ils saluaient les cadavres* [They saluted the corpses] hides a semantic short-cut which plays on the choice of a term indicative of finality instead of something in progress as expected.[15] "Corpses" can refer just as well to "dead heroes" as to victims of military atrocities—but that is beside the point. What the expression "They saluted the corpses" does indicate is a fetishistic and ritualized (salute) taste for death, the complete opposite of "life" (fifth stanza) and thus of the positive pole presented here as the only remaining goods of (future) victims. So it is that the overall effect of these connotations is to establish a semantic field based on the notion of excess. This is confirmed semantically in line 18 by *Ils persévèrent ils exagèrent ils ne sont pas de notre monde* [They persevere they exaggerate they are not of our world]. "They are not of our world" doubly defines the definition since, over and above the opposition life/death, the utterance also incorporates the opposition excess/destitution continued in the stanzas which follow. The "leaves," "spring," and "pure milk," in addition to their previously mentioned values, characterize women and children and so connote the victims' natural simplicity (these victims being "real men") in contrast, let us say, to *sou* in line 15; for a cent connotes a society which is organized, artificially based on monetary exchange (a society of conventions, just as the use of "salute" has already indicated).

The antithetical formulation of stanza XI

> La peur et le courage de vivre et de mourir
> La mort si difficile et si facile

[The fear of living and dying and the courage to do both
death so difficult and so easy]

could be put anywhere in the poem,[16] since it merely restates in an explicitly paradoxical and abstract formulation what the various concrete expressions have thus far sought to reveal: living out one's daily life is a continual and hard-won victory, so precarious that at any moment it may be interrupted. Similarly, death, always easy, within reach the moment one gives up, is nonetheless relentlessly deferred by effort and work. As it stands, this statement applies not just to the inhabitants of Guernica, but to many others, and this explains the way we interpret "pariahs" (line 36) in the final stanza: as a term used to generalize, it destroys once and for all the poem's specific meaning and gives it a collective dimension.

If it were still necessary to prove that stanzas VI, VII, XIII, and XIV lead us to read the poem as a generalization, it would suffice to note that they are the only ones which do not appear in "Guernica"; that is to say, the only ones excluded from the substance of the chronicle, since, necessarily, the latter was restricted to specific events in a particular place at a given time. But this demonstration provided by "Guernica" is not essential, merely a confirmation, since a careful reading will undoubtedly reveal that, through this *generalizing process*, the text frees itself of referential implications. And indeed in each of the poem's sections one notices a type of formulation which makes retroactive generalization a model of language function, thereby allowing the text to expel the real and the specific and attain the general and the universal. Thus each element of a paradigmatic series is picked up by a term which both resumes and contains the whole series. This term, then, can be regarded as a condensed version of the series and also appears, retrospectively, as a particularizing and redundant anticipatory expansion of the series' closing generic term. Thus *bons à tout* [good for everything], line 5, picks up *bon au feu, au froid, au refus, à la misère, aux injures, aux coups* [good for the fire, the cold, refusal, misery, swearing, blows]. *Ils vous ont fait payer . . . la misère* [They made you pay for your misery] in line 11 picks up *ils vous ont fait payer le pain, le ciel, la terre, l'eau, le sommeil* [they made you pay for the bread, sky, earth, water, sleep] of lines 9 and 10; *les femmes les enfants ont le même trésor . . . de durée* [women and children have the same treasure of lasting], lines 19 and 21, picks up *de feuilles vertes de printemps de lait pur* [of green leaves of spring of pure milk] of line 20; finally *la couleur monotone de notre nuit* [the monotonous color of our night], line 38, picks up *la mort, la terre, la hideur de nos ennemis* [death, earth, the hideousness of our enemies] of lines 36 and 37.

The repetition of the process, coupled with the practice of adding juxtaposed terms, compounds, on a formal level, the semantic value of "monotonous" and gives the poem a canonic structure typical of the plaintive ballad traditionally used for the tragic poem. Here, however, instead of being based on a repeated refrain, the repetition is maintained by the reappearance of the same asyndetic syntactic structures and by the use of a general term to sum up the paradigmatic series. The ensuing monotony is only broken by the final line *Nous en aurons raison* [We will overcome them]: a collective appeal with which the poet associates himself—something already anticipated by *notre monde* [our world], line 18, *ouvrons ensemble* [let us work together], line 35, and *nos ennemis* [our enemies], line 37, and which is another way of subverting Guernica's topical specificity "your life," "your death" (in lines 12 and 7) to give it a general and symbolic dimension. Moreover, one can hardly fail to notice that the exceptional quality of the last line conforms to the pattern of the *envoi* or *coda* which constitutes the traditional climactic ending of this type of poem.

Eluard concludes "Guernica" by extending the lesson of this particular agony to other grimly remembered landmarks: *"Guernica comme Oradour et comme Hiroshima sont les capitales de la paix vivante"* [Guernica like Oradour and like Hiroshima is the capital of living peace].[17]

The subject then broadens, and Guernica returns as one of several examples of a pattern of conflict which transcends all particular circumstances: *"Guernica! l'innocence aura raison du crime"* (Guernica! innocence will overcome crime).[18] From this standpoint the lessons of "La Victoire de Guernica" and "Guernica" are similar. But in "Guernica" Eluard is forced to abandon the chronicle form so that he can proclaim the event's universal and perennial quality. The referential model is brutally stripped of its specific value and becomes confused with other Guernicas, thus losing its particularity and all the spatio-temporal characteristics which make it a unique place and subject. In "La Victoire de Guernica" the process is more closely linked to intrinsically symbolic procedures and it is language which, by exclusively verbal operations (opposition, expansion, condensing, etc.), strips specific extra-linguistic reference of its naturalistic identity, thus transforming what is said into a victorious song of hope which is both plural and universal.

La Victoire de Guernica

I.	Beau monde des masures	
	De la mine et des champs	
II.	Visages bons au feu visages bons au froid	
	Aux refus à la nuit aux injures aux coups	
III.	Visages bons à tout	5
	Voici le vide qui vous fixe	
	Votre mort va servir d'exemple	
IV.	La mort coeur renversé	
V.	Ils vous ont fait payer le pain	
	Le ciel la terre l'eau le sommeil	10
	Et la misère	
	De votre vie	
VI.	Ils disaient désirer la bonne intelligence	
	Ils rationnaient les forts jugeaient les fous	
	Faisaient l'aumône partageaient un sou en deux	15
	Ils saluaient les cadavres	
	Ils s'accablaient de politesses	
VII.	Ils persévèrent ils exagèrent ils ne sont pas de notre monde	
VIII.	Les femmes les enfants ont le même trésor	
	De feuilles vertes de printemps et de lait pur	20
	Et de durée	
	Dans leurs yeux purs	

IX.   Les femmes les enfants ont le même trésor
Dans les yeux
Les hommes le défendent comme ils peuvent   25

X.   Les femmes les enfants ont les mêmes roses rouges
Dans les yeux
Chacun montre son sang

XI.   La peur et le courage de vivre et de mourir
La mort si difficile et si facile   30

XII.   Hommes pour qui ce trésor fut chanté
Hommes pour qui ce trésor fut gâché

XIII.   Hommes réels pour qui le désespoir
Alimente le feu dévorant de l'espoir
Ouvrons ensemble le dernier bourgeon de l'avenir   35

XIV.   Parias la mort la terre et la hideur
De nos ennemis ont la couleur
Monotone de notre nuit
Nous en aurons raison.

Cours Naturel
Paul Eluard

The Victory of Guernica

I.   High life in hovels
In mines and in fields

II.   Faces staunch in the fire staunch in the cold
Against denials the night insults blows

III.   Faces always staunch   5
Here is the void staring at you
Your death shall be an example

IV.   Death heart overturned

V.   They made you pay for bread
Sky earth water sleep   10
And the poverty
Of your life

VI.   They said they wanted agreement
They checked the strong sentenced the mad
Gave alms divided a farthing   15
They greeted every corpse
They overwhelmed each other with politeness

VII.   They insist they exaggerate they are not of our world

VIII.   The women the children have the same treasure
Of green leaves of spring and of pure milk   20
And of endurance
In their pure eyes

IX.   The women the children have the same treasure
In their eyes
The men defend it as best they can   25

X.	The women the children have the same red roses	
	In their eyes	
	All show their blood	
XI.	The fear and the courage of living and of dying	
	Death so hard and so easy	30
XII.	Men for whom this treasure was extolled	
	Men for whom this treasure was spoiled	
XIII.	Real men for whom despair	
	Feeds the devouring fire of hope	
	Let us open together the last bud of the future	35
XIV.	Pariahs	
	Death earth and the vileness of our enemies	
	Have the monotonous colour of our night	
	The day will be ours.	

(Translated by Roland Penrose
and George Reavey)

NOTES

1. Anthony Blunt, *Picasso's Guernica* (New York and Toronto: Oxford University Press, 1969).

2. Cf. *Les écrivains et la guerre d'Espagne*, ed. Marc Hanrez (Paris: Panthéon Press, Les Dossiers H, 1975).

3. Paul Eluard wrote two texts on the subject of Guernica. "La Victoire de Guernica," the subject of our analysis, was composed in 1937, at the same time that Picasso was working on his famous painting *Guernica*, which was exhibited in the Spanish pavilion at the International Exhibition in Paris in 1937. The poem accompanied the painting. It was first published in *Cahiers d'art*, nos. 1–3, 36, in 1937. The English translation by Roland Penrose and George Reavey appeared in 1938, in the *London Bulletin*, no. 6, 7–8.

The full text of this poem and the translation appear at the end of this chapter. Any subsequent more literal translations are by Terese Lyons.

In 1949, Eluard wrote "Guernica," a text meant to accompany Alain Resnais's film on Picasso's painting. The text was published in *Europe*, nos. 47–48, Oct. 1948, 47–50. All italicized quotations in this chapter have been taken from this second text. The editions of these two poems on which the present study has been based can be found in Paul Eluard, *Oeuvres complètes*, ed. L. Sheler and M. Dumas (Paris: Gallimard, "Pléiade" 1968, 2 vols.). "La Victoire de Guernica" can be found in *Cours naturel*, vol. I, pp. 812–814, and "Guernica" in *Poèmes retrouvés*, vol. II. pp. 913–917.

4. "Guernica," p. 913.

5. "Baudelaire," in *Poèmes retrouvés*, p. 912.

6. Cf. this account of the event in *The Times* (April 1937):

Guernica, the most ancient town of the Basques and the centre of their cultural tradition, was completely destroyed yesterday afternoon by insurgent air raiders. The bombardment of the open town far behind the lines occupied precisely three hours and a quarter, during which a powerful fleet of aeroplanes consisting of three German types, Junkers and Heinkel bombers and Heinkel fighters, did not cease unloading on the town bombs and incendiary projectiles. The fighters, meanwhile, plunged low from above the centre of the town to machinegun those of the civil population who had taken refuge in the fields. The whole of Guernica was soon in flames, except the historic Casa de Juntas, with its rich archives of the Basque race, where the ancient Basque Parliament used to sit. The famous oak of Guernica, the dried old stump of 600 years and the new shoots of this century, was also untouched. Here the kings of Spain used to take the oath to respect the democratic rights [*fueros*] of Vizcaya and in return received a promise of allegiance as suzerains with the democratic title of *Senor*, not *Rey Vizcaya*.

7. A porte-manteau word, coined by Jacques Derrida in *Glas* to designate a *monument à la mémoire*, i.e., a monument in memory (of someone or something).

8. "Guernica," p. 914.

9. Ibid.

10. "Le langage déplaisant qui suffit aux bavards, langage aussi mort que les couronnes à nos fronts semblables, réduisons-le, transformons-le . . . il y aura recherche d'un rapport immédiat entre celui qui voit et ce qui est vu." Paul Eluard, "Les animaux et les hommes," *Littérature* 5, July 1919.

11. "Guernica," p. 913.

12. Ibid., p. 914.

13. Nicole Charbois, "Eluard et Picasso," in *Europe* 525, "Rencontres avec Paul Eluard," January 1973, 188–207.

14. Consider, for example, these famous lines of Malherbe in "Ode à Duperrier sur la mort de sa fille":

> *Et rose, elle a vécu ce que vivent les roses,*
> *L'espace d'un matin.*

15. Cf. in French, "cuire le pain," or in English,"to bake bread," said instead of "cuire la pâte," "to bake dough," the process whose result is the production of bread. Cf. also "percer un trou," "to drill a hole," *vs.* "percer un mur," "to drill (a hole in) a wall."

16. And indeed, in "Guernica," these lines come at the beginning of the poem.

17. "Guernica," p. 917.

18. Ibid.

VI.

RENAMING IN LITERATURE
FACES OF THE MOON

Françoise Meltzer

Frege's distinction between the *sense* (*Sinn*: connotation, meaning) of a sign and its *nominatum* (the object to which it refers) provides an indispensable complement to Saussure's concept of the signified. The *associated image* which Frege attaches to the configurations of reference is crucial in this respect:

> Both the nominatum and the sense of a sign must be distinguished from the associated image. If the nominatum of a sign is an object of sense perception, my image of the latter is an inner picture arisen from memories of sense impressions and activities of mine, internal or external.[1]

Literature poses an immediate problem, because the "nominata" evoked in the text are apparently designated objects, on the one hand, and on the other, are left for the reader to visualize, since they are not objects of sense perception. Moreover, the "associated images" which the literary object evokes in the reader must not interfere with its *customary sense*. The latter is problematic because one may say that an associated image gains strength when the object is described or named, but not physically or directly presented. This is the essence of literature. Indeed, Frege notes that in indirect discourse, what is referred to is not a designated object at all, but rather the customary sense of the sign.[2]

It would follow, then, that literature is an extended form of indirect discourse (narration), because what is referred to within the text is the sense of the sign and *not*, strictly speaking, a designated object. Since, as Frege says, "a sign expresses its sense and designates its nominatum," literature can be said to have no nominata at all, and to deal exclusively in sense and, it will be argued, in associated images.

Frege's position is quite explicit:

> A sentence as a whole has perhaps only sense and no nominatum? It may in any case be expected that there are such sentences, just as there are constituents of sentences which do have sense but no nominatum. Certainly, sentences containing proper names without nominata must be of this type. The sentence "Odysseus deeply asleep was disembarked at Ithaca" obviously has a sense. But since it is doubtful as to whether the name "Odysseus" occurring in this sentence has a nominatum, so it is also doubtful

that the whole sentence has one. However, it is certain that whoever seriously regards the sentence either as true or false also attributes to the name "Odysseus" a nominatum, not only a sense; for it is obviously the nominatum of this name to which the predicate is either ascribed or denied. . . . But why do we wish that every proper name have not only a sense but also a nominatum? Why is the proposition alone not sufficient? We answer: because what matters to us is the truth-value. . . . In turning to the question of truth we disregard the artistic appreciation and pursue scientific considerations. (p. 90)

His view that fiction can have no assertoric force or reference is therefore logo-centric, in that it assumes that language *outside* of fiction (sentences having both sense and nominata) has truth-value and signifies truth by referring "directly" to a nominatum. The person who regards the sentence about Odysseus as either true or false is attributing a nominatum to the name "Odysseus," but cannot, in Frege's view, ascertain truth-value. In other words, because fiction has no nominata, it is incapable of signifying truth. But the person reading the sentence about Odysseus clearly understands to whom the name "Odysseus" refers, creating what we may call a "cognitive nominatum." If we suspend the logocentric view that language may signify truth, then we may see in literature the mimesis of language's most cherished *fiction*: the notion that there is a logical, fixed connection between signifier and signified. If the language of fiction insists upon creating in the reader what I shall call "cognitive nominata," it does so because it mimics the fiction of language, which insists upon guaranteeing the connection between the signifier and the signified. It is precisely because literature has no "real" nominata that it becomes a fertile field for examining systems of naming. If for Frege literature can only be non-referential, then it becomes all the more intriguing that the reader provides the name "Odysseus" with a nominatum. Thus this essay will disregard "scientific considerations" with their assumptions of "truth value" and pursue "artistic" ones, with their assumptions of suspended belief.

Frege suggests, though does not develop, the implications of his position that literature is without nominata: "It would be desirable to have an expression for signs which have *sense only*. If we call them "icons," then the words of an actor on the stage would be icons; even the actor himself would be an icon" (p. 91). "Icon" is a strange choice of words (the original is *Bilder*), since it suggests an *object* of representation. But Frege seems rather to be emphasizing icon as representation in a more abstract mode: that which signals a sense.

It is to be noted that Frege omits the associated image in these kinds of signs, and yet the term *Bild* means, precisely, image or picture. And Frege is quick to link image to literature: "Surely, art would be impossible without some kinship among human imageries; but just how far the intentions of the poet are realized can never be exactly ascertained" (p. 89). One might say that it is this indefinable kinship among human imageries which allows for language in the first place and, in the second, for writing. The associated image can never be entirely personal and subjective because it is so largely derived from, and inextricably bound with, the sense. In discussing the sense and nominatum, and the subjectivity/kinship dialectic of associated images, Frege uses a simile: a person viewing the moon through a telescope. The moon is the nominatum. The "real image" projected by the lens is the customary sense, and the retinal image in the eye of the observer is the associated image. He comments:

> The real image inside the telescope, however, is relative; it depends upon the standpoint; yet, it is objective in that it can serve several observers. . . . One could elaborate the simile by assuming that the retinal image of A could be made visible to B; or A could see his own retinal image in a mirror. In this manner one could possibly show how a *presentation itself can be made into an object*; but even so, it would never be to the (outside) observer what it is to the one who possesses the image. However, these lines of thought lead too far afield. (p. 88; my emphasis)

What is to be noted from this passage is the following: the "real" image (customary sense) in the lens is what permits the retinal image (associated image) in the viewer. Thus the latter is made possible by the former, and we may add "associated image" to Frege's "icon." Secondly, *icon* (or *Bild*) in rhetoric traditionally means simile, or likeness, and it is precisely a simile which Frege uses to make his point.[3] In so doing, Frege repeats the gesture of fiction vis à vis the assertory. The simile itself necessitates a "cognitive nominatum" in order for the argument to be grasped. In this way, then, *Bild* becomes redundant, repeating as both simile and signs-with-sense-only the *likeness* of sentences with nominata.

But what happens in literature when there is a presentation of a "real" icon—a portrait? Is this comparable to A seeing his own retinal image in a mirror? Of a presentation itself being made into an object? If the portrait of a literary character is presented, then (to continue Frege's simile) the "real image" of the telescope lens reflects another image of the moon, but not a real moon. In other words, is the evocation of a portrait in a literary text—a portrait with only textual "presence"—yet another addition to the system within the signifieds? Since the portrait cannot have a nominatum, is its existence in the text any different from the other "icons"?

Frege's article on sense and referring concerns itself with proper names only: "From what has been said it is clear that I here understand by 'sign' or 'name' any expression which functions as a proper name, whose nominatum accordingly is a definite object (in the widest sense of this word)" (p. 86). It is at this point, then, that we depart from Frege, for whom the discussion that follows would be futile, centered as it is on fiction. Fregean terminology, however, will be retained as a useful scaffolding, as will the assumptions it betrays.

The actual portrait of a character in a literary work is an icon (simile) for the individual named in the text. In Madame de Lafayette's novel, *La Princesse de Clèves*, the title itself is a proper name which refers to the character in the text so named by the narrator. Here we already have what Frege calls an icon, one for which the customary sense is not yet established, as yet conjuring up in the reader only a limited sense and associated image. When the text refers to the portrait of the princess, however (our sense and image of her have by this point been established by our reading of the text), we have a double image, neither half of which has a "real" nominatum. The absence of nominata ("real," designated objects) which characterizes literature is thus further problematized by the presentation of a *textually* concretized object: the portrait. For the portrait is the iconization of the textual proper name.

In order to examine the function of the portrait in fiction, or at least part of its function, I have chosen portrait scenes from two French novels, *La Princesse de Clèves* and *Le Rouge et le noir*. While my choice of these two passages is somewhat arbitrary, my purpose is to explore Frege's sign system in the context of textual naming. More precisely, we will be applying Frege's system of references to the very area he discounts as non-referential: fiction.

Strawson noted that the sentence "the so and so is such and such" is neither true nor false if the "so and so" does not exist.[4] In this sense, the proper name in literature (the "so and so") is, as in Frege, a non-existent, since its presentation is limited to the world of the text and cannot be concretely identified. But we have said that what is at issue here is precisely not the true and false, but the relation between the proper name *per se* and its expression in the text. Within the bounds of the text, moreover, rhetorical systems are at play which have their own "proper names," and which mirror Frege's delineations. What I will attempt to show in my readings of the two texts is that within the given passages, the portrait functions as a predicate for the passage, and that the predicate concerns not the true or false, but a system of description which is at the heart of textual "naming."

Before examining the two (French) portrait scenes, however, let us consider a traditional portrait in Sir Walter Scott's *Waverly*. (The passage, describing a portrait of Waverly as Hero of the Highlands, comes from the end of the novel):

> There was one addition to this fine old apartment, however, which drew tears into the Baron's eyes. It was a large and spirited painting representing Fergus Mac-Ivor and Waverly in their Highland dress, the scene a wild, rocky, and mountainous pass, down which the clan were descending in the background. It was taken from a spirited sketch, drawn while they were in Edinburgh by a young man of high genius, and had been painted on a full-length scale by an eminent London artist. Raeburn himself, (whose Highland chiefs do all but walk out of the canvas) could not have done more justice to the subject; and the ardent, fiery, and impetuous character of the unfortunate Chief of Glennaquoich was finely contrasted with the contemplative, fanciful, and enthusiastic expression of his happier friend.[5]

This description, unlike the two we are going to consider, gives the reader a relatively vivid account of the canvas. We know, for example, what the surroundings are, what the background contains, how Waverly and Mac-Ivor are dressed, and the impression these two characters convey. We also know when and under what circumstances the portrait was painted, the size of the painting, and that it was done by an "eminent London artist" after having been sketched by a young man at the time the scene depicted took place. The irony of the portrait is that it shows Waverly as the "ardent, fiery, and impetuous" leader of the Highlanders—whereas the novel itself shows Waverly to be what his name implies: a waffling, confused, and gullible follower. Thus Scott's portrait shows us a Waverly who, rather than being a likeness of his ''real'' self, is rather an ironic opposite thereof. The portrait itself, however, is a clear rendering which the reader has no difficulty visualizing.

Such is not the case in the passage to be considered next. But like the *Waverly* passage, the following scene, taken from Mme. de Lafayette's *La Princesse de Clèves*, is iconic in two ways: it represents the princess, the figure whom the title names; and it is Frege's sign which has only sense and no nominatum.

Il y avait longtemps que M. de Nemours souhaitait d'avoir le portrait de Mme. de Clèves. Lorsqu'il vit celui qui était à M. de Clèves, il ne put résister à l'envie de le dérober à un mari qu'il croyait tendrement aimé; et il pensa que, parmi tant de personnes qui étaient dans ce même lieu, il ne serait pas soupçonné plutôt qu'un autre.

Mme. la Dauphine était assise sur le lit et parlait bas à Mme. de Clèves, qui était debout devant elle. Mme. de Clèves aperçut par un des rideaux qui n'était qu'à demi fermé, M. de Nemours, le dos contre la table, qui était au pied du lit, et elle vit que, sans tourner la tête, il prenait adroitement quelque chose sur cette table. Elle n'eut pas de peine à deviner que c'était son portrait, et elle en fut si troublée que Mme. la Dauphine remarqua qu'elle ne l'écoutait pas et lui demanda tout haut ce qu'elle regardait. M. de Nemours se tourna à ces paroles; il rencontra les yeux de Mme. de Clèves, qui étaient encore attachés sur lui, et il pensa qu'il n'était pas impossible qu'elle eût vu ce qu'il venait de faire.

Mme. de Clèves n'était pas peu embarrassée. La raison voulait qu'elle demandât son portrait; mais, en le demandant publiquement, c'était apprendre à tout le monde les sentiments que ce prince avait pour elle, et, en le lui demandant en particulier, c'était quasi l'engager à lui parler de sa passion. Enfin elle jugea qu'il valait mieux le lui laisser, et elle fut bien aise de lui accorder une faveur qu'elle lui pouvait faire sans qu'il sût même qu'elle la lui faisait. M. de Nemours, qui remarqua son embarras, et qui en devinait quasi la cause, s'approcha d'elle et lui dit tout bas:

—Si vous avez vu ce que j'ai osé faire, ayez la bonté, Madame, de me laisser croire que vous l'ignorez; je n'ose vous en demander davantage.[6]

(La Princesse de Clèves)

[For a long time M. de Nemours had wanted to have the portrait of Mme. de Clèves. When he saw the one belonging to M. de Clèves, he could not resist the desire to steal it from a husband he believed to be tenderly loved. And he thought that, among so many people who were in the same place, he would not be suspected more than another.

Mme. la Dauphine was sitting on the bed and speaking softly to Mme. de Clèves who was standing in front of her. Through one of the curtains which was but half-closed, Mme. de Clèves caught sight of M. de Nemours, his back against the table which was at the foot of the bed, and she saw that, without turning his head, he was adroitly taking something on that table. She had no difficulty in guessing that it was her portrait, and she was so upset by this that Mme. la Dauphine noticed that she was not listening to her and asked her out loud at what she was looking. M. de Nemours turned at these words; he met the eyes of Mme. de Clèves which were still fixed on him, and he thought that it was not impossible that she had seen what he had just done.

Mme. de Clèves was not a little embarrassed. Reason wanted that she ask for her portrait. But to ask for it publicly was to inform everyone of the sentiments this prince had for her; and to ask for it privately was quasi to engage him to speak of his passion. Finally, she deemed it better to leave it to him, and she was quite pleased to grant him a favor which she could do without even his knowledge that she was doing it for him. M. de Nemours, who noticed her perplexity, and who quasi-guessed its cause, approached her and said in a very low voice,

—If you have seen what I have dared do, have the goodness, Madame, to let me believe that you are in ignorance of it. I dare not ask more of you.]

The first thing to be noted in this passage is that there is no description of the portrait. And yet description is unnecessary because the *effect* of the portrait centers on its presence and its theft, not on its specific artistic qualities. Moreover, the princess herself is never really described in the novel: we only know that she is the most beautiful, the most noble, the most virtuous personage at court—a series of superlatives which emphasize the absence of detail concerning her appearance. Thus the undescribed portrait remains as vague as its subject.

The question to be raised here, however, is how such a passage can be descriptive when there is no straightforward depiction of the art object. Part of the answer must be that, while the passage does not give us any overt description of the portrait, its presence in the text is effective because it evokes a chain of senses. The portrait represents the princess; the princess is represented by her name. The symbiotic relationship between naming and description thus begins to emerge: a name has no meaning without description. For Frege, such is certainly the case. Indeed, as one Frege scholar has put it, "the logical behavior of descriptions is, for Frege, indistinguishable from that of (denoting) proper names."[7] It follows then that the portrait in the passage works according to Frege's moon simile: the "lens image" is true to the "real object" it reflects, for since the princess is never physically described, the reader must remain equally ignorant of the physical characteristics of her portrait. Further, the proper names in this passage are as prominent as they are in the rest of the text, signaling the importance of rank and title (with all that these imply). This abstract but rigid social hierarchy is foregrounded by the very scarcity of individualized facial traits. The proper names here become to a large extent their own signifieds—the "phantom of duty" which the princess obeys is dictated by her rank, that is by her proper name. The situation is further complicated by the fact that the proper name in a text, as we have said, refers to sense and image only, and not to an existing person. We may then formulate the textual situation in this way: the customary sense of "la Princesse de Clèves" becomes a collection of abstract, moral convictions—the necessity of virtue in the dangerous world of a flighty and precious court; a commitment to speaking the truth despite the flowery and hyperbolic (therefore false) language of the society; the rigid ideals of conduct which must not be jeopardized in spite of emotions which are in conflict with those ideals (the princess's love for the duke), and the fact that the ideals are in direct contradiction with the superficial code of courtly love which her society has espoused. The appearance of the portrait in this passage, then, comes to *mean* the iconic rendering of the princess who, in turn, means a specific conflict of morals. The portrait, then, serves as an example of the power of description, for oblique as it has been, the name of the princess, and her portrait, ultimately designate a cognitive nominatum. Were this not the case, of course, the text would be nonsensical. The etymology of the word "description" reinforces this point: from the Latin *describere*, "to write down," description is in some measure any form of writing; conversely, any writing is a form of description. The mental proximity of name and description is then particularly evident in a text where a name is granted meaning without direct description, and where a portrait can be imagined by the reader as designating the figure it signifies.

The theft of the portrait in *La Princesse* is crucial: it is a purloining, the symbolic power of the duke over that moral code which is precisely emblematized by the princess's *good name*. When we say that in this novel the proper name begins to generate its own referent, we may say this of the portrait as well, for it is the simile (icon) of the princess's good, proper name. Wittgenstein's reminder is worth mentioning here: "don't confuse the meaning of a name with the bearer of a name."[8] The proper name of "La Princesse de Clèves," her title and that of the novel, provides us with a name which comes to mean itself, not the "bearer." Sense and image take on so much importance that the character designated by her name gradually loses vitality in its presence. It is her name, and not her emotions, which dictates her behavior, so that her name attains a life of its own, at her expense.[9] In this passage, she herself is silent, her interior monologue serving only to underscore her powerlessness. The portrait is referential in that it demonstrates the power of the name; but it is also referential in that its presence functions as a silent description designating that power.

Just as "real" nominata are absent from literature, allowing sense and image all the more emphasis, and creating a "cognitive nominatum" in the reader, so too the naming in this passage seems stripped of its normal function, becoming instead "description" at its most abstract, a figure of thought in its most literal sense. It is to be noted that the passage is filled with verbs of *sight*—surely a component of direct description. And yet what we are led to visualize is neither the portrait's qualities, since we are not given them, nor a vivid ocular image of the figures in the passage, since they are left essentially undepicted. Rather, it is the situation and the conflict of ideals (= names) and emotions which are vividly portrayed. Indeed, the function of the portrait is *reversed* in the same way as is the movement of the sign when the name in a text comes to designate itself: the figure of the princess in this text comes to represent her name, as does her portrait. Like the retinal image cast by the "real" lens image and generated by the real moon, the portrait of the princess represents her name, the sense of which is generated by the name itself. The portrait is the simile of the princess, though no two readers will "see" the portrait in exactly the same way.

For Russell, proper names are abbreviations for description.[10] But in this passage, the portrait is obliquely ecphrastic in the same way that the referential context (nominatum) is oblique ("cognitive"). The portrait, we have said, functions as clearly *as if* described, in the same way that we understand what the princess "means" as clearly as if she were designated. For Mill, a proper name's sole function is to denote the referent.[11] But in a text, there is no concrete referent, no "other," to be designated. It is only for Frege that, as Leonard Linsky puts it, "names contribute to the senses of the declarative sentences containing them by themselves expressing their senses."[12] It is ironic that while for Frege, literature must be non-assertoric, no formulation can better explain than does the one just cited the semantic weight the name assumes in literature, or explain its cognitive power. The Lafayette passage we have examined demonstrates this point: the names contribute to the senses of the text containing them by themselves expressing their senses. It is this process which makes what I am calling the "cognitive nominata" possible.

We have seen that for Frege, artistic appreciation (for example, a literary text) is at odds with scientific considerations and with "the truth-value." Scientific considerations have truth-value for Frege because they concern sentences which have both a nominatum and a sense. Indeed, it is Frege's constant wish that there be a Utopia of language which would *always* have an unchanging reference:

> A logically perfect language [*Begriffsschrift*] should satisfy the conditions, that every expression grammatically well constructed as a proper name out of signs already introduced shall in fact designate an object, and that no new sign shall be introduced without being secured a reference.[13]

Such a utopian language would, presumably, allow for a constant truth value, by virtue of fixed signs with fixed referents. Thus Frege's utopia of language not only grants power to a proper name, but also vests it with the truth. This view is the opposite of Socrates' position in the "Cratylus":

> Whether there is this eternal nature in things, or whether the truth is what Heraclitus and his followers and many others say, is a question hard to determine, and no man of sense will like to put himself or the education of his mind in the power of names. Neither will he so far trust names or the givers of names as to be confident in any knowledge which condemns himself and other existences to an unhealthy state of unreality.[14]

For Socrates, then, truth has little to do with the arbitrary process of naming. Indeed, language can only veil the truth by naming it. It is significant that Frege's search for truth-value is posited on an ideal ("logically perfect") language with unambiguous references. But these two views, apparently diametrically opposed to one another, are in fact essentially identical, in that they assume the presence of truth to begin with, and the ability of language to convey that truth (even if it is only to state the "truth" that language cannot name truth). It is further significant that this same view, expressed differently, necessitates the rejection of fiction as bearing truth-value. "But why do we wish that every proper name have not only a sense but also a nominatum?" Frege had asked, and answered: "because what matters to us is the truth-value." Literature, like the sentence about Odysseus, is thus discarded. So too, Socrates, after briefly considering returning Homer's poetry to the Republic, again rejects it as lacking in truth, "for we have come to see that we must not take such poetry seriously as a serious thing that lays hold on truth."[15]

In both views, the referent is a transcendental concept, designating Truth; in both views, literature (poetry) has no such referential potential and thus remains non-assertoric. But once again, if we suspend this insistence upon the Truth, we can see the systems of naming within literature as precisely indicative of, rather than in contrast to, the myth of pure reference. For the act of reading is mimetic of the power to reveal Truth which logocentrism vests in language: in literature, too, *nomen est omen*. The literary text is rejected by philosophers who insist upon purity of meaning and, therefore, on an inside/outside. Utopian language or "Republic": literature stands exiled. To grant identity (reference) to the literary would be to taint the purity which philosophy seeks to maintain, and undermine the concept of transcendental meaning, which is the fiction of language. Thus philosophy, by rejecting literature for not being "a serious thing," creates its own fiction of truth. Frege's *Begriffsschrift* is the "Republic" of Plato in print.

The problem is compounded when literature alludes to a historical figure—a figure known to us, precisely, by *description*. The next portrait scene to be examined, taken from Stendhal's *Le Rouge et le noir*, provides us with just such a figure. The protagonist, Julien Sorel, has become a priest because Napoleon has fallen; thus the military life no longer offers the possibility for an ambitious young man of modest circumstances to rise above his birth. A tutor in a rich man's house, M. de Rênal, Julien is also courting the virtuous Mme. de Rênal, and simultaneously playing the role of the pious clergyman. When Julien learns that the mattresses in the Rênal household are being restuffed, he realizes that his secret will be discovered: for Julien keeps a portrait of his hero, Napoleon, under his mattress. Julien asks Mme. de Rênal to steal the portrait back for him, and he begs her to do so without looking at it. She carries out both orders, convinced that the box containing the portrait encloses the likeness of another woman, a rival:

> Assise sur une chaise dans l'antichambre de cet appartement, madame de Rênal était en proie à toutes les horreurs de la jalousie. Son extrême ignorance lui fut encore utile en ce moment, l'étonnement tempérait la douleur. Julien parut, saisit la boîte, sans remercier, sans rien dire, et courut dans sa chambre où il fit du feu, et la brûla à l'instant. Il était pâle, anéanti, il s'exagérait le danger qu'il venait de courir.
>
> Le portrait de Napoléon, se disait-il en hochant la tête, trouvé caché chez un homme qui fait profession d'une telle haine pour l'usurpateur! trouvé par M. de Rênal, tellement ultra et tellement irrité! et pour comble d'imprudence, sur le carton blanc derrière le portrait, des lignes écrites de ma main! et qui ne peuvent laisser aucun doute sur l'excès de mon admiration! et chacun de ces transports d'amour est daté! il y en a d'avant hier.
>
> Toute ma réputation tombée, anéantie en un moment! se disait Julien, en voyant

brûler la boîte, et ma réputation est tout mon bien, je ne vis que par elle . . . et encore, quelle vie, Mon Dieu![16]

[Seated on a chair in the antechamber of the upstairs apartment, Mme. de Rênal fell prey to all the horrors of jealousy. Her remarkable ignorance was particularly useful to her at this point, since astonishment tempered her grief. Julien appeared, snatched the box without a word of thanks or a word of any sort, and ran to his room where he lit a fire and burned it on the spot. He was pale and haggard; he exaggerated the extent of the danger he had just run.

"The portrait of Napoleon," he said to himself, shaking his head; "and found on a man who professes such hatred for the usurper! Found by M. de Rênal, a black reactionary and in a bad humor! And as the height of all imprudence, on the cardboard mounting of the portrait, lines written in my own hand which leave no doubt of the depth of my admiration! Each one of these raptures of love is dated, too, and the last one just the day before yesterday!"

"My entire reputation fallen, destroyed in one moment!" said Julien as he watched the box burn, "And my reputation is my fortune, it's all I have to live for—and good God, what a life!"]

At first glance, this passage seems quite the opposite of the first: the language is different (over- rather than understated) and the lover, Mme. de Rênal, is actually *ordered* to steal the portrait. And yet what is at the heart of the Stendhal excerpt is also central to Mme. de Lafayette: the fear of shattering a reputation; a good name which is both a personal ideal and a willed identity. As in the Lafayette text, the portrait is never described. But because it is of a historical figure, it is easier to observe how it achieves its effect. The portrait (that is, its mere presence) owes its power to the scene in the novel: as in *La Princesse de Clèves*, possession is what counts. Like the princess, Julien lives for his reputation. Indeed, the words he chooses could just as well be uttered by the princess: "my reputation is my fortune, it's all I have to live for." For the reader, two things make the portrait "live": the historical description of Napoleon, which the text assumes is familiar to most readers; and the sense that that figure is given for Julien by the text and by the historical period of the novel's setting. For Julien, Napoleon "means" everything that he wishes to be: powerful, rich, and glorious, despite his humble origins. For nineteenth-century France, the name of Napoleon erases the determinist quality of the family name in the social hierarchy, for Napoleon's rise to power showed that title no longer need depend upon birthright. Thus the text plays upon several senses of the name "Napoleon": the nominatum of the historical figure, the specific sense that figure has for the protagonist, and the ironic fact that, in worrying about his own "good name," Julien hides the very figure whose name "means" the end of the tyranny of names within the class structure of nineteenth-century France.

The protagonist himself, however, is non-existent: that is, the name "Julien Sorel" has no nominatum, only sense. Here again, we have the same literary situation of an "icon" which depends upon sense and associated image alone. But within that iconic context is the portrait of a historical figure who even according to Frege does have a designated nominatum: Napoleon. In writing of Odysseus, Frege pointed out that a sentence can have sense and no nominatum. We have shown that in literature, however, the context of sense-only can ultimately designate a "cognitive" nominatum. In referring to historical figures, literature "deconcretizes" a direct referent by putting it in an "iconic" context. On this level, the name "Napoleon," when it is used in fiction, comes to be as void of "truth-value" as that of "Julien." Conversely, however, the nominatum of Napoleon, the historical figure, adds weight to Julien's "presence" in the mind of the reader. The very proximity of Julien to the figure of Napoleon in the text (his possession of the latter's portrait, his handwriting upon it, his identification with Bonaparte's life, etc.)—at once fictionalizes the "real" Napoleon, since we know the entire scene to be the invention of Stendhal; and simultaneously concretizes Julien, since he is placed in the same cognitive sphere as a figure whom we know by "real" description. If fiction neutralizes the reality quotient of a historical figure by placing it in a fictional context, it can also make us realize the extent to which the names "Julien" and "Napoleon" do, finally, have a nominatum of cognitive value, granted them by the text.

Unlike the vague princess, Julien is physically described in some detail by Stendhal. Nevertheless, both the names "Princesse de Clèves" and "Julien Sorel" mean something quite specific to the reader: they are particular figures who can, in fact, be mentally designated. Even if no "truth-value" may be attached to a predicate modifying literary proper names, the reader's comprehension relies upon the same cognitive mechanism: knowledge by description, rendering a cognitive nominatum for the name. It is not because we know that Julien is fictional that we cannot conceptualize him, any more than it is not because we have not met Napoleon that we cannot designate him. Our ability to identify Julien Sorel rests upon the same mental procedure as our capacity to do so with historical figures or even personal acquaintances on description. It is this mental knowledge which Plato sees as essential to understanding a designated object:

> For everything that exists there are three classes of objects through which knowledge about it must come; the knowledge itself is a fourth, and we must put as a fifth entity the actual object of knowledge which is the true reality. We have, then, first, a name, second, a description, third, an image, and fourth, a knowledge of the object. . . . In the fourth place there are knowledge and understanding and correct opinion concerning them, all of which we must set down as one thing more that is found not in sounds nor in shapes of bodies, but in minds, whereby it evidently differs in its nature . . . from the aforementioned three.[17]

It is this "true reality," however, which is, of course, the problem. In Plato's *Phaedrus*, writing and painting are compared, because the images of both are considered to be *less real* than those of existing beings. Here again is the problem of Frege's "icon"—and indeed, as Paul Ricoeur notes, the icon itself is the issue at stake in much of our thinking on mental optics:

The question here is whether the theory of the *eikon*, which is held to be a mere shadow of reality, is not the presupposition of every critique addressed to any mediation through exterior marks. . . .

Far from yielding less than the original, pictorial activity may be characterized in terms of an "iconic augmentation," where the strategy of painting, for example, is to reconstruct reality on the basis of a limited optic alphabet. This strategy of contraction and miniaturization yields more by handling less. In this way, the main effect of painting is to resist the entropic tendency of ordinary vision—the shadowy image of Plato—and to increase the meaning of the universe by capturing it in the network of its abbreviated signs.[18]

The present essay would seek to make the words "painting" and "pictorial activity" in the above citation interchangeable with "writing." Ricoeur notes, in fact, "If it could be shown that painting is not this shadowy reduplication of reality, then it would be possible to return to the problem of writing as a chapter in a general theory of iconicity."[19] Naming in texts is, in Frege's own terms, a form of "iconic augmentation." But Frege stops where Ricoeur would begin in the development of the problem of writing as a chapter in a general theory of iconicity. The irony is that the same philosophy of a transcendental Truth (Frege, Plato) rejects written fiction because of its "unhealthy state of unreality"—that is, because such referents are "shadowy images" without "real" nominata. The difference which philosophy insists upon maintaining between fictional and historical names is self-serving, because it gives "seriousness" to the latter by dint of trivializing the former. But since the systems of referring within the literary text necessarily resemble "real" reference, then the distinction between what is a "designated nominatum" versus an "iconicized" name becomes, at best, a privileging of speech, or of writing which conveys direct speech. If I speak the Truth, I am relating history, and may then write it down. If I tell stories, and then write them down, I am referring to nothing save, perhaps, my own text—this is the conclusion implied in the *Begriffsschrift* and the *Phaedrus*.

Rhetorical systems in general function to "clarify" the textual system of signs in much the same way that Frege's terms "explain" direct reference in naming: to designate a metaphor in a text, for example, by delineating its parts (vehicle and tenor) is the same act as disentangling the sense, image, and nominatum of a sign. Whether the two portrait scenes we have considered are labelled ecphrastic or iconically referential, the system in both cases is the same: naming. And in both cases, aspects of naming are renamed, like two telescopes projecting different faces of the same moon.

My point is not, of course, to argue that literature be viewed as the Truth; it is rather to insist that all writing be seen as referring to our mythologies on the Truth, to the names we choose to give to it, and to the assumptions we have concerning the power of the name. In this sense, literature indeed captures, through its abbreviated signs, the meaning we choose to agree upon. And the portrait in a literary text becomes the iconization of an *eikon*, yielding more by handling less. Fiction is then the best of "places" in which to look for the fictions of language.

NOTES

1. "On Sense and Nominatum," tr. Herbert Feigl, in *Readings in Philosophical Analysis*, H. Feigl and W. Sellars, eds. (New York: Appleton-Century-Croft, 1949), pp. 85–102. The citation is from page 87. The article was originally published as "Uber Sinn und Bedeutung" in *Zeitschrift für Philosophie und philosophische Kritik*, 100 (1892), pp. 25–50. The more standard translation is "On Sense and Reference" in *Translations from the Philosophical Writings of G. Frege*, P. Geach and M. Black, eds. (Oxford: Blackwell, 1952). I have chosen to use the Feigl translation because his terminology (based on that of R. Carnap in *Meaning and Necessity* [Chicago: University of Chicago Press, 1947]) is easier for my purposes. Feigl's use of "nominatum" rather than "reference," for example, allows a more subtle differentiation between all types of reference and the individual designated by a proper name. All future citations are from the Feigl translation and will hereafter be situated by page number only.

2. Feigl tr., p. 87: "In order to formulate this succinctly we shall say: words in indirect discourse are used *indirectly*, or have *indirect* nominata. Thus we distinguish the *customary* from the *indirect* nominatum of a word; and similarly, its *customary* sense from its *indirect* sense. The indirect nominatum of a word is therefore its customary sense."

3. The *OED* lists "simile" as one of the definitions of icon. And Lanham says, for example, "From Aristotle onward, *simile* is often the vehicle for *icon* or *image*." Richard A. Lanham, *A Handlist of Rhetorical Terms* (Berkeley: University of California Press, 1968), p. 93.

4. Strawson, P. F., *Introduction to Logical Theory* (London: Methuen, 1952). All of chapter six concerns itself with this idea.

5. (New York: Dutton, 1976), p. 473.

6. (Paris: Gallimard, 1958), pp. 106–107. Translation mine.

7. Leonard Linsky, *Names and Descriptions* (Chicago: University of Chicago Press, 1977), p. 7.

8. Cited by Linsky, p. 22. Wittgenstein, Linsky summarizes, was taking issue with Russell's idea that the meaning of a proper name is its denotation. In his notebooks of 1914–16, Wittgenstein also says, "In our language, names are *not things*; we don't know what they are: all we know is that they are of a different type from relations." *Notebooks 1914–16*, 2nd edition, tr. G. E. M. Anscombe, ed. Wright and Anscombe, (Chicago: University of Chicago Press, 1979), p. 111. And in another passage, Wittgenstein takes Russell and Frege to task, in a manner which (consciously or not) parodies Frege's telescope simile:

> The comparison of language and reality is like that of retinal image and visual image: to the blind spot nothing in the visual image seems to correspond, and thereby the boundaries of the blind spot determine the visual image—as true negations of atomic propositions determine reality. Logical inferences can, it is true, be made in accordance with Frege's or Russell's laws of deduction, but this cannot justify the inference; and therefore they are not primitive propositions of logic. (p. 100)

In the same notebooks, Wittgenstein adds another comment on naming and description: "One cannot achieve any more by using names in describing the world than by means of the general description of the world" (p. 53).

9. An extended, if differently focused, example of the loss of vitality in the face of an increasingly powerful "iconicizing" is to be found in Edgar Allen Poe's short story, "The Oval Portrait." In the story, a painter gradually saps his wife of life by putting, it would seem, all of her essence into the portrait he is painting of her. When the portrait is completed, she dies; the portrait, on the other hand, is life-like to the point of being terrifying. The

portrait scenes discussed in this article are shortened versions of readings of the same scenes, to a different end, in my *Salome and the Dance of Writing: Portraits of Mimesis in Literature* (Chicago: University of Chicago Press, 1987).

10. *The Principles of Mathematics*, 2nd edition (New York: W. W. Norton, 1938). Russell, however, creates a special group, the logically proper name, as distinct in logical function from description. See Linsky, p. 7, on this distinction.

11. John Stuart Mill, *A System of Logic* (London: Longmans, Green, 1900). See John R. Searle's attack on this view in *Speech Acts: An Essay in the Philosophy of Language* (Cambridge: Cambridge University Press, 1980), p. 93 ff.

12. Linsky, p. 9.

13. *Translations from the Philosophical Writings of G. Frege*, p. 56.

14. *Plato: the Collected Dialogues and Letters*, E. Hamilton and H. Cairns, eds. (Princeton: Princeton University Press, 1973), p. 474.

15. Ibid.

16. (Paris: Garnier, 1973), p. 56. My translation.

17. *Collected Dialogues*, Letter VII, pp. 1589–90.

18. Paul Ricoeur, *Interpretation Theory: Discourse and the Surplus of Meaning* (Fort Worth: Texas Christian University Press, 1976), pp. 40–41.

19. Ibid., p. 40.

I am grateful to my colleague at the University of Chicago, Professor Leonard Linsky, for his very helpful reading of this essay. I should add that for him this essay is not grounded consistently enough in Fregean logic. While this is a tactic which I have consciously chosen, Professor Linsky is in no way accountable for any ensuing complications.

VII.

HOW PLAYSCRIPTS REFER
SOME PRELIMINARY
CONSIDERATIONS

Michael Issacharoff

It is tempting to oversimplify the nature of fictional discourse by claiming that since it does not, supposedly, refer in precisely the same way as definite referring expressions in ordinary language do, it is a 'parasitic' form of discourse. Or so the argument usually runs in works on speech-act theory. Stanley Fish has convincingly argued that the simplistic 'serious' (or referential) language vs. fictional (or non-referential) language dichotomy is far from being as valid as some philosophers of language would have us believe.[1] It in fact may do a disservice both to speech-act theory and to literary theory.

The problem I propose to examine in what follows is the nature of referring in dramatic discourse. My inquiry will entail a preliminary consideration of the (referential) specificity of the dramatic *script*, that is, the features which distinguish it from other literary texts. It is my contention that the playscript *is* distinct and that its peculiar referential status enables us to establish its difference.

It is probably true to say that any literary text may be an amalgam of utterances referential and non-referential. Utterances closest to what philosophers of language such as Strawson, Linsky, and Donnellan call 'definite reference' (or 'definite descriptions')[2] in 'serious' discourse can be found in the form of references made by fictional characters or made by real authors to historical persons or places (that is, existents), for example. Thus, in *Travesties*, Tom Stoppard refers in the didascalia (and likewise his characters in the dialogue) to real people: James Joyce, Tristan Tzara, Lenin, among others. Stanley Fish is right in pointing out that the fictional vs. serious language debate has tended to oversimplify and thus cloud the issue. *Fictional discourse is not pure fiction, and 'serious' discourse utilizes techniques and games—pretending, lying, joking—more commonly associated with literature.* J. L. Austin's position on this problem, expressed rather (too) succinctly, has been distorted and did not, perhaps, help to clarify matters:

> A performative utterance will, for example, be *in a peculiar way* hollow or void if said by an actor on the stage, or if introduced in a poem, or spoken in soliloquy.

This applies in a similar manner to any and every utterance—a sea-change in special circumstances. Language in such circumstances is in special ways—intelligibly— used not seriously, but in ways *parasitic* upon its normal use—ways which fall under the doctrine of *etiolations* of language. All this we are *excluding* from consideration. Our performative utterances, felicitous or not, are to be understood as issued in ordinary circumstances.[3]

Austin himself may be criticized for his confusing, if not question-begging, category, "ordinary circumstances." Serious discourse is not necessarily coextensive with "ordinary circumstances," and likewise, fictional discourse is not always merely 'parasitic' or simply an "etiolation of language." Searle has shown, by quoting a passage from a novel by Iris Murdoch, that "not all of the references in a work of fiction will be pretended acts of referring; some will be real references as in the passage from Miss Murdoch where she refers to Dublin."[4]

Whereas Searle recognizes that fictional discourse is not perhaps as simple as Austin would have us believe, neither he nor Fish (who quotes him) resolves another fundamental problem central to the referential process: *who* (in a literary text) is doing the referring? Searle, it will be remembered, insists that it is not *expressions* which refer, but *people* using them. This problem is particularly relevant to the *dramatic* text, given that contrary to other kinds of literary texts, the author *writes a script for performance by other speakers*. When we seek to identify the person referring in a play, all will hinge on whether we are considering the script *read* or the script *performed*. In the case of the read script, as we shall see, there is at least one level of discourse—the didascalia—which contains many of the attributes of serious discourse used in "normal circumstances," and is intended (by the author) to be taken seriously. The performed script, on the other hand, is, of course, the text minus the didascalia, but the actors can be considered as persons making references (in the technical sense), even though one can perhaps accept Austin's view that their utterances may be void of perlocutionary effect. The illocutionary force, however, may be perfectly valid.

While Austin excludes from consideration performatives in fictional discourse, Searle provides criteria for definite reference which, upon examination, are in fact at least partly relevant to the literary and, for our purposes here, the dramatic script. According to Searle, the criterion for definite reference is twofold:

1. There must exist one and only one object to which the speaker's utterance of the expression applies (a reformulation of the axiom of existence) *and*

2. The hearer must be given sufficient means to identify the object from the speaker's utterance of the expression (a reformulation of the axiom of identification.)[5]

Now dramatic discourse, despite Searle's comments about fictional discourse being "parasitic,"[6] *may* contain utterances true to the first criterion which requires the existence of a specific (that is, constant or fixed) object to which an utterance applies. The obvious instance is the mention of an existing place or person, existing, that is, either at the time of writing or prior to it. In such cases, mention may occur either in the didascalia or in the dialogue. Consequently, in drama just as in fiction, there is an obvious distinction to be drawn between, say, Balzac's Paris or Dickens's London and Butler's Erewhon. The former two places exist, the latter does not. Similarly, literary mention of Napoleon, De Gaulle, Churchill, Kennedy, and so on, should be regarded as referentially distinct from mention (in the dialogue or didascalia) of imaginary characters.

As Searle himself explains, the axiom of existence can be extended so that when *we* speak of a fictional character—Searle uses the example of Sherlock Holmes— we are able to make a valid reference, given that we are speaking of a character (or other entity) that exists in a particular fictional world. One could, though, go beyond the case Searle envisages and argue that *a character onstage can make valid references* (to other characters, places, or objects in the same play) since they, too, are referential acts which focus on *someone or something that exists in that particular fictional universe*. In the case of a script in performance, instances such as these in fact fulfill *both* Searle's criteria for definite reference: the axioms of existence and identification. In drama, then, it can be said that a character X refers to characters Y and Z who either appear in the same play or, failing that, hold some crucial part in the logic of the plot. The axiom of *identification* stipulates that "the *hearer* [my emphasis] must be given sufficient means to identify the object from the speaker's utterance."[7] Again, one can go further in applying this criterion than Searle undoubtedly intended, and maintain that the hearer in this case could be either another character onstage or, of course, the audience.

My remarks so far have been confined essentially to a commentary on Searle's and Austin's observations on fictional discourse and the various ways one can adapt Searle's axioms so as to find (unexpectedly, from Searle's point of view) cases of definite reference in fictional discourse. The preceding comments, however, are no more than a preliminary discussion pertinent to dramatic discourse, whose referential status is more complex than either of the two philosophers of language would lead us to believe. The axiom of existence may, as I have attempted to show, be fulfilled in at least two possible ways: through a mention in the dialogue (or in the didascalia) of a person, place, or thing that exists either in the real world or in a particular (coherent) fictional universe. References to imaginary persons, etc. may be termed, to borrow Strawson's phrase, "story-relative reference."[8]

Let us now attempt to examine the referential status peculiar to the dramatic script. While it is true to say that the author of a play (or a novel) provides a (contractual) label describing his mode of discourse—"A play in five acts," "Comédie," "Farce tragique," "A novel"—authorial intention in this respect is by no means a foolproof criterion for reference versus non-reference. Sartre, for example, on writing his *Les Séquestrés d'Altona [The Condemned of Altona]* had no intention of making a real (that is, definite) reference to Von Gerlach (a real person) whose name he used for a character in his play, imagining it to be fictional. Sartre realized his gaffe too late and added the following prefatory note in the printed edition of the play:

NOTE BY THE AUTHOR

I thought that I had invented the name Gerlach. I was mistaken. It was hidden in my memory. I regret my mistake even more because the name is that of one of the bravest and best-known opponents of National Socialism.

Hellmuth von Gerlach devoted his life to the struggle for *rapprochement* between France and Germany, and for peace. In 1933 his name was high up in the list of those proscribed by the Nazis. His property was seized, together with that of his family. He died in exile two years later, having devoted his last efforts to providing help for his refugee compatriots.

It is too late to change the names of my characters, but I beg his friends and relatives to accept this as an earnest expression of my apology and my regret.[9]

This means, of course, that someone who knew the real Gerlach in Germany during World War II would have some difficulty, despite Sartre's published apology, in reading the play non-fictively.

Furthermore, that referential intention is not a watertight guideline is clearly demonstrated, as Richard Gale points out, by the fact that authors of fictional texts have sometimes been found guilty of libel. "This is so," writes Gale,

even when the resemblance of his story to real life is purely coincidental. E.g. if in a fictional work there is a character named Frank Jones who lives at 547 Industrial Drive in Pittsburgh, is president of the United Steel Workers Union and embezzles union funds, and by coincidence there is a real-life Frank Jones who fits these descriptions with the exception of not being an embezzler, he could sue the author of this work and collect damages. This shows not only that a fictive use of a sentence can say something true (false) but also that a purely locutionary act of referring which is what a fictive reference is, can succeed in referring to some existent.[10]

In short, then, successful reference is by no means contingent on a speaker's or writer's intention; it may occur by accident or even by coincidence. In addition to instances such as these, of course, one need hardly mention the more felicitous cases where a play (or novel) acquires a new referential focus, unimagined by the writer, due to the impact of historical events. Thus in a work of satire, or in a play with political overtones, reference (to people) may be transformed, due to circumstances external to the text, from the indefinite or open-ended to the definite. A producer may decide, say, to make a Shakespeare play such as *Julius Caesar* or *Macbeth* 'refer' anachronistically to World War II. This may be achieved, without changing a word of the script, through the use of appropriate costumes and set. Reference in drama can therefore be *conveyed obliquely* through the visual channel.

The discrepancy between reference intended and reference inferred (a problem too often overlooked by speech-act theorists) is not confined to drama. It is common to all forms of literary (as well as to non-literary) discourse. What *is* peculiar to the (modern) drama script and distinguishes it *referentially* from other types of literary discourse is its two-layered structure consisting of dialogue plus didascalia.[11]

I say *modern* drama, since in many pre-nineteenth-century playscripts by such authors as Racine, Corneille, Shakespeare, and Molière, didascalia—especially information about the set and properties—tended to be inscribed in the dialogue, and not set apart in italics in accordance with modern convention. The upshot of this is a category of dramatic discourse distinct from fictive discourse. It need hardly be pointed out that the didascalia in a playscript are the equivalent of an authorial voice, normally intended to be taken seriously, that is, non-fictively. Every playscript contains at least a minimal form of didascalic discourse, be it simply the dramatis personae on the first page and the names of the characters at the beginning of every speech. Stage directions are equivalent to a real speech act insofar as they amount to a set of instructions to the director and cast on how to (1) stage the dialogue, and (2) deliver the lines. It is this part of the text that frames the playscript. Didascalia are addressed by a *real person* (the author) to other *real people* (director and actors), and, save in cases where the dramatist is satirizing convention—the examples of Ring Lardner and Ionesco[12] immediately come to mind—are intended to be taken non-fictively. It should be remembered, though, that didascalia refer *not* to a speech event (that is, to what was said and how), but to a *future speech event*, namely to how something *should be said* and in what circumstances. Thus they are *not* merely a set of instructions akin to the directions for baking a cake, as Searle suggests,[13] but, usually, indications not only of *contents* (personages and objects present) but also information on the manner in which they *interact*. Didascalia, then, are the element of the playscript providing cohesion for the purposes of the reader, director, and cast.

The fact that the didascalic portion of the script refers to a future speech event has important referential consequences. It means that didascalia fulfill one of Searle's criteria for definite reference. In a word, whereas the *axiom of existence* is not strictly adhered to (since didascalic utterances apply to objects and persons which change from one stage production of a given play to the next), the *axiom of identification* is certainly complied with (since the hearer can identify the object mentioned in the speaker's utterance). Finally, in this matter of didascalic discourse, it should be observed that the fact that didascalia may be in referential contradiction with the dialogue (as in Ionesco's *Les Chaises*) proves that (1) there must be a distinction between author's and characters' speech acts; and that (2) there is a hierarchy. Stage directions are normally cut-and-dried rather than tongue-in-cheek. Thus, even if the dialogue portion of a playscript is experimental or absurdist, as in Beckett's *Endgame*, Stoppard's *Dogg's Hamlet*, or Tardieu's *Un Mot pour un autre*, the didascalia tend to be quite conventional and 'serious.' If this were not the case, the production of such plays would be even more difficult than it is already. In technical terms, if the axiom of identification were not strictly adhered to in the didascalia, the reader as well as the producer would be totally confused.

The preceding comments on didascalia should enable us to achieve at least two objectives: (1) to note the referential specificity of the playscript in contrast to other kinds of literary texts, and (2) to make preliminary observations on the mechanics of reference in playscripts. It follows from all of this that the process of reference in the playscript as read is fundamentally distinct from the case of the playscript as performed. Clearly, when the playscript is staged, the explicitly authorial channel disappears from view.

We now need to turn to reference in dramatic dialogue. When considering the playscript *in toto*, it was apparent that we were dealing with what is usually a referential amalgam of (almost) genuine definite reference (the didascalia) and possibly non-referring discourse (the dialogue). But, in fact, what kind of beast *is* dramatic dialogue? Could it not also be considered an amalgam of referring and non-referring discourse? Obviously the answer must be sometimes in the affirmative. However, before reaching such a conclusion, it will be necessary to examine the identity of the utterers, since, if we follow Searle's criteria, it is not expressions that refer, but people using them. When an utterance is heard onstage, *who* is speaking? Clearly, it is not the author. There are exceptions, though. The obvious example is Molière, who chose to forego conventional authorial detachment by playing the lead or important parts in most of his plays—Arnolphe in *L'École des Femmes*, Orgon in *Tartuffe*, Sganarelle in *Dom Juan*, Alceste in *Le Misanthrope*, Argan in *Le Malade Imaginaire*, Jourdain in *Le Bourgeois Gentilhomme*, the title role in *Georges Dandin*, and so on.[14] One could argue, though, in cases such as these, that the playwright fictionalizes himself by becoming a player. For the contemporaries of the playwright, however, who saw the original productions, the referential ambiguity surely remained. Utterances would have had a different ring to them. Instances in which the ambiguity is greater, as the line between nonfictional speech event and theatrical speech act becomes more tenuous, are those in which an author gives his "fictional" character his own name as Molière does in *L'Impromptu de Versailles*, and likewise Ionesco in *L'Impromptu de l'Alma*. Molière even played the part of the character to whom he lent his name, and given that the character is Molière the theatre director, the degree of fictionalization becomes minimal.

These instances do not of course reflect standard practice in which the author *lends his voice* to his characters (and indirectly to his producer). If, then, the speaker in a dramatic dialogue is not normally the playwright-player or the fictionalized playwright, it is not the actor either. He is using borrowed utterances he has been instructed (or, rather, paid) to use. He does not have to believe what he is saying, although nothing precludes his so believing. (As for the characters—Macbeth, Lady Macbeth, Ophelia, Hamlet—they do not even exist!) It need hardly be emphasized that the lines spoken onstage are framed by the context of theatrical performance. To use Austin's terms, the locutionary force is normal, whereas the illocutionary and perlocutionary forces are weakened, if not eliminated entirely. Yet it would surely be wrong to consider that utterances spoken onstage are entirely cut loose from their regular illocutionary and perlocutionary anchors and are heard as so many innocent sounds floating freely in the air. An audience (just like a reader) is always at liberty to hear them non-fictively and transform them into fully engaged discourse. That this is so is clearly demonstrated by the fact that plays are sometimes censored or banned in totalitarian societies as well as in democracies, under certain circumstances when freedom of expression is temporarily curtailed. As we have noted already, a dramatist may also be charged and found guilty of libel. Presumably, in a court of law, a playwright could not disclaim responsibility for words spoken onstage on the pretext that he had not uttered them in person. Furthermore, the playscript does of course remain the writer's *literary property*, even if the apparent utterer of the text in performance is not the author. Thus, needless to say, an author can bring an action for plagiarism against anyone who tries to misappropriate his literary property.

Acts of definite reference, however, are not necessarily contingent on the hearer's knowing the identity of the utterer. Provided that an utterance in no way focuses on the speaker or on the hearer, its referential force is not in the least impaired. This means that all statements in a dramatic dialogue concerning real persons (living or dead) or places and so forth have virtually the same referential status as the same statements in a non-literary context. I say *virtually* since the only difference is the context of usage. Stoppard's *Travesties* provides us with an interesting illustration of this. His principal characters, James Joyce, Lenin, and Tristan Tzara, were all living people. In addition, nearly all of Lenin's lines (as Stoppard himself tells us) come from his own *Complete Works*. Many speeches, in fact, are taken verbatim from Lenin's published correspondence. Thus, for example, when we hear lines such as the following:

> LENIN: September 15, 1919, to A. M. Gorki, Dear Alexei Maximych . . . Even before receiving your letter we had decided in the Central Committee to appoint Kamenev and Bukharin to check on the arrests of bourgeois intellectuals of the near-Cadet type, and to release whoever possible. For it is clear to us too that there have been mistakes here.[15]

we are dealing with an unusual instance of discourse spoken by an actor playing the part of Lenin, using the Russian's exact words. Referentially, then, the only difference in the status of the lines as they were originally used in a letter written by Lenin and in the play is *the new context of usage*. In short, all the definite references occurring in the passage in its reincarnation still retain their illocutionary force. What is modified, however, is their perlocutionary force, since what has changed in the new context is Lenin's addressees. Lenin, of course, never met Tristan Tzara and James Joyce. Thus many of his lines, though still addressed directly to their original (though absent) addressees, are overheard by additional (indirect) addressees, not present at the time of the original speech event. In short, what has occurred is that an original speech event (a letter) has acquired a modified complementary referential status by virtue of its new discursive context. In fact this phenomenon is about the same as the referential status of a *quotation*, rejuvenated through reincarnation.

The Stoppard play eloquently exemplifies the problem of the referential status of dramatic dialogue. We are dealing with a multi-stranded mode of discourse which, at one extreme, can be the quotation of words actually spoken or written by a real person (living or dead). The definite referential force may still be valid, if at least some of the circumstances of the original speech event are retained. The minimum condition would be that speaker and hearer are unchanged. The Stoppard example, then, is about the closest that dramatic dialogue can come to definite reference in nonfictional speech events, although another technical possibility would be the use of a radio recording of an interview with a real person. (A device such as this would be comparable to the use of extracts from a newsreel in a feature film.)[16] Next to this are two other forms of definite reference, allusions to or mentions of real persons or places or things, and play-relative references. In Stoppard's *The Real Inspector Hound*, Moon's speech is an obvious example of definite reference: "Faced as we are with such ubiquitous obliquity, it is hard, it is hard indeed, and therefore I will not attempt, to refrain from evoking the names of Kafka, Sartre, Shakespeare, St Paul, Beckett, Birkett, Pinero, Pirandello, Dante and Dorothy L. Sayers."[17] An intentionally playful list of names, all of real people. Given, however, the purposely tenuous connexion between these names, their playfully alliterative linkage, together with the context of their mention in the play, they probably acquire some degree of unreality, if not fictionality. The same process occurs, of course, when a dramatist mixes definite reference to existents and story-relative referents.

Story-relative reference (or, to coin a term, play-relative reference) is the other mode of singular definite reference that is the norm in traditional dramatic dialogue. By this we mean that a character (or place or event, etc.) referred to by other characters in the same play remains constant and can thus be reliably identified. Strawson's definition: "The identification is within a certain story told by a certain speaker. It is identification within his story; but not identification within history."[18]—makes it clear that this form of definite reference does not imply or entail the axiom of existence. Almost any non-experimental play will furnish examples of this referential mode, ranging from, say, references to Molière's protagonist in *Tartuffe* (prior to his appearance onstage in act III, for instance) to comments about Macbeth made by other characters in Shakespeare's play. In all such cases we are dealing with an identifiable constant referent, a character whose existence is confined to a fictional universe. The reverse process is to be found in experimental drama where a title (such as *En attendant Godot*) names a character who *never* appears onstage and thus does not really 'exist' even in Beckett's fictional world. The other type of anti-reference is exemplified by the Bobby Watson anecdote in Ionesco's *La Cantatrice chauve* (The Bald Soprano). The name Bobby Watson, contrary to normal exclusive naming and identifying practice, 'refers' to several members of the same family (living and dead!) in the same sentence.

Two types of reference, both characteristic of dramatic dialogue, remain to be examined (though only in summary form here): referential mixing and referential subversion. By referential mixing, I mean that dramatic dialogue is normally an *amalgam* of referential modes and comprises concurrently at least two of the following: (1) definite singular extratextual reference (that is, reference to real persons, living or dead; places, events, etc.); (2) story-relative reference (that is, reference to entities existing solely within a given fictional universe); and (3) intertextual reference (that is, reference to other texts by the same writer or other writers or to literary conventions). A brief example from Stoppard's *Night and Day* will illustrate what I mean by mixed reference. Wagner, a reporter, comments: "I go to fires. Brighton or Kambawe—they're both out-of-town stories and I cover them the same way. I don't file prose. I file facts."[19] Brighton is a real place—a city on the southeast coast of England; Kambawe is a fictitious African country which provides a setting for Stoppard's play. This utterance, then, exemplifies mixed reference consisting of definite singular extratextual reference (Brighton) and story- or play-relative reference (Kambawe). A referential cocktail such as this is, of course, peculiar to literary discourse. The aesthetic result is double-edged and one of two things may occur. Either the reality (a sort of Barthesian *effet de réel*) of the definite reference may rub off onto the story-relative referent(s), or the fictionality of the latter may affect (and possibly undermine) the former.

Finally, referential subversion is a referring mode commonly present in dramatic dialogue and may occur on various channels, visual and auditory. It need hardly be pointed out that drama is the one literary medium in which the verbal may be enhanced, transformed, or even subverted through visual means, including costume, decor, and lighting. It would not be difficult to transform a play such as *Hamlet* or *Othello* into a farce by undermining it referentially with the aid of appropriate costumes and prosodic tampering. Hamlet's famous soliloquy could easily be dislodged from a tragic to a comic mode through a change in intonation and rhythm and, perhaps, with the addition of a few derisive sound-effects.

In the preceding discussion, my focus has been primarily on modes of extratextual reference that are peculiar either to the playscript or to the playscript-in-performance. Needless to say, there are probably other referential mechanisms at work, but I would contend that they are not characteristic of dramatic discourse *per se*. One such area that I have purposely left unexplored in this paper (and that I have examined elsewhere)[20] is the complex problem of *intertextual reference*. This phenomenon includes not only the obvious category of allusion to and parody of other literary (and non-literary) texts, but also reference to dramatic stereotypes and conventions. In research on this topic, I have discovered a general tendency (especially in the genre of dramatic parody) for the intertextual to expel and even obliterate the extratextual.

In this paper I have attempted to show that the position according to which fictional discourse is referentially quite distinct from non-literary discourse is untenable. The dramatic script contains various modes of definite reference ranging from the didascalia to story- (or play)-relative reference, and including virtually regular definite reference. In fact I have argued that, surprisingly perhaps, dramatic discourse often fulfills the criteria for definite reference as defined by Austin and later reformulated by Searle. To say, then, that dramatic discourse is somehow "parasitic" or an "etiolation of language" seems very far from the truth.

NOTES

1. Stanley Fish, *Is There a Text in This Class?* (Cambridge, Mass.: Harvard University Press, 1980); see especially pp. 97–111, "How Ordinary Is Ordinary Language?" and pp. 268–292, "Normal Circumstances . . ."

2. See P. F. Strawson, "On Referring," *Mind* LIX (1950), 320–344, reprinted in Strawson, *Logico-Linguistic Papers* (London: Methuen, 1971), pp. 1–27; Leonard Linsky, *Referring* (London: Routledge & K. Paul, 1967); Keith S. Donnellan, "Reference and Definite Descriptions," *The Philosophical Review* LXXV (July 1966), 281–304. See also J. Searle, *Speech Acts: An Essay in the Philosophy of Language* (London & New York: Cambridge University Press, 1969).

3. J. L. Austin, *How to Do Things with Words* (Cambridge, Mass.: Harvard University Press, 1962), p. 22.

4. J. Searle, "The Logical Status of Fictional Discourse," *New Literary History* VI (1975), p. 330; quoted by S. Fish, *Is There a Text in This Class?*, p. 235.

5. J. Searle, *Speech Acts*, p. 82.

6. Ibid., p. 78.

7. Ibid., p. 82.

8. P. F. Strawson, *Individuals: An Essay in Descriptive Metaphysics* (London: Methuen, 1959), p. 18.

9. J. P. Sartre, *Les Séquestrés d'Altona* (The Condemned of Altona), trans. S. & G. Leeson (New York: Alfred A. Knopf, 1961), p. 2.

10. Richard Gale, "The Fictive Use of Language," *Philosophy* XLVI (1971), 329–330.

11. I have attempted to examine the status of didascalia as a form of discourse central to the reading of drama in *Le Spectacle du discours*, (Paris: José Corti, 1985), pp. 25–40.

12. See especially Ring Lardner, *Taxidea Americana*, in *The Ring Lardner Reader*, ed. Maxwell Geismar (New York: Scribner's, 1963), pp. 621–623; *The Tridget of Greva*, in *Theatre Experiment: An Anthology of American Plays*, ed. Michael Benedikt (New York: Anchor Books, 1968), pp. 48–56; *Quadroon*, in *The Ring Lardner Reader*, pp. 603–608. See also Ionesco's parodic use of didascalia in *La Cantatrice chauve*, in *Théâtre* I (Paris: Gallimard, 1954); for example, pp. 19, 22, 29.

13. J. Searle, "The Logical Status of Fictional Discourse," *New Literary History* VI (1975), 319–332, reprinted in Searle, *Expression and Meaning* (Cambridge: Cambridge University Press, 1979), pp. 58–75.

14. See Georges Couton's notes to the individual plays in his edition of Molière, *Oeuvres Complètes* (Paris: Gallimard, 2t., 1971).

15. Tom Stoppard, *Travesties* (London: Faber & Faber, 1975), p. 88. In a note of acknowledgment at the beginning of the playscript, Stoppard tells us: "Nearly everything spoken by Lenin . . . herein comes from his Collected Writings" (p. 15). Verification in Lenin's *Collected Works* confirmed this. Passages used are indeed quoted verbatim, though in a slightly abridged form in some cases. The letter cited here appears in the *Collected Works*, Vol. 44 (Moscow: Foreign Publishing House, and London: Lawrence & Wishart, 1970), pp. 283–285. In the same way, letters used elsewhere in *Travesties* for Lenin's lines, for example on pp. 81 and 87, are taken from the *Collected Works*, Vol. 36 (p. 420) and Vol. 34 (pp. 385–386), respectively. Similarly, Lenin's famous lines on p. 85 of the play ("Today, literature must become party literature. Down with non-partisan literature!" etc.) come from a speech made in 1905 which appears in Vol. 10 (1962), pp. 44–49.

16. An interesting example was provided recently in Woody Allen's *Zelig*, in which three real people, Saul Bellow, Irving Howe, and Susan Sontag (played by Saul Bellow, Irving Howe, and Susan Sontag) are interviewed about the fictional protagonist Zelig! By their appearance in the movie, the three real persons are fictionalized. This example is, of course, distinct from that of a real interview that actually occurred and is later re-used in a fictional context.

17. Tom Stoppard, *The Real Inspector Hound* (London: Faber & Faber, 1968), p. 36.

18. P. F. Strawson, *Individuals*, p. 18.

19. Tom Stoppard, *Night and Day* (London: Faber & Faber, 1978), p. 38.

20. See, for example, "Labiche et l'intertextualité comique," *Cahiers de L'Association Internationale des Etudes Françaises* 35 (mai 1983), 169–182.

VIII.

ARE BAUDELAIRE'S "TABLEAUX PARISIENS" ABOUT PARIS?

Ross Chambers

"Poetic discourse is the equivalence established between a word and a text, or a text and another text."[1] This definition lies at the heart of the only currently prominent theory of poetic reference, that of Michael Riffaterre, who perceives poetic discourse as having "meaning" by virtue of its mimetic function but "significance" by virtue of purely textual and intertextual relationships, to which the reader's attention is directed by mimetic "ungrammaticality," that is "mimetic anomalies, interference with apparent referentiality."[2] Text, in this view, is "shaped like a doughnut,"[3] the hole being the absent and unexpressed verbal referent, or "hypogram."

Although it is true that mimetic representation "is founded upon the referentiality of language,"[4] the modes of linguistic referentiality are not exhausted by mimesis. All language (literary or otherwise) derives its meaningfulness from its use in context, and its reference is consequently best described as a relationship between the discourse and the total context in which it "makes sense." Such a context includes understandings about the nature of the "real world" in which the discourse is produced and received, and to which it is thought to refer (what is sometimes called the "encyclopedia of the text"); but it includes also understandings between speaker and receiver about the illocutionary relationship pertaining between them (that is, about such matters as the social purposes fulfilled by the communication and the constraints upon it, the rights and responsibilities which are distributed between the participants in the communicational act, the code employed, and so forth). In short, the illocutionary situation is as much a part of the reference—the situation in which discourse makes sense—as is the "referential" situation proper (in the "mimetic" sense); and indeed the latter is actually included in the former, if one understands the illocutionary situation to embrace *all* the relevant speaker-hearer understandings on which the communicational act depends.

In light of this, it seems very probable that such categories as the "literariness" of literature or the "poeticity" of poetry are most suitably described, not in terms of specific features of literary/poetic discourse, but in terms of the illocutionary understandings which prevail in given cultures and at specific historical moments as to which texts are literary or poetic, and what it *means* for a text to be so classified. In this respect, Riffaterre's most important contribution to literary theory lies perhaps in his long-term insistence on the fact that the literary phenomenon "resides in the relationship between text and reader, not between text and author, or text and reality."[5] However, the text-reader relationship is, unfortunately, not so much a simple given as a theoretical problem in its own right, and one of great magnitude. One reason for this is the inadequacy of the simple speaker-discourse-receiver model of communication to the literary situation, which in our modern Western culture defines literature in terms of its ongoing ability to produce meaning in situations of reception remote from the initial situation of production. Literature thus becomes one example among many of "deferred" communication, in which the notion of context is radically complicated not only by the fact that the context of reception is by definition distant from the context of production, but also by the fact that "meaning" is subject to continual drift, as it evolves from one changing context of reception to another. It is for this reason that literary referentiality appears so much more problematic than the referentiality of discourse situations in which production and reception co-occur (although many would argue that the more complex model is apposite, as well, to the apparently simpler situations of "everyday life").

But if interpretative indeterminacy is an actual criterion of literarity in the modern age, this fact perhaps accounts for a notable characteristic of texts which pretend to literary status. The paradox is that, in order to lay claim to a future history of indeterminacy, such texts must initially *determine* themselves as literature; their own literariness being subject to interpretative "drift" along with everything else, it becomes necessary for them to safeguard their own esthetic status from the outset. They do it by self-reference. I am not referring here to the well-known phenomenon of literary self-referentiality (poems about poetry, theatre in the theatre) as an autotelic device. Rather I am suggesting that this supposed autotelic device has a communicational function in establishing, or attempting to establish, for a future readership, the illocutionary situation which makes sense of the text, that is, those understandings about the purposes and means of the discourse which are necessary for an appropriate act of reading to take place. For this purpose, it is not enough, of course, for such texts to define themselves simply and generally as "literature," or as "poetry," "novel," etc., since such categories are subject to future drift; they must define themselves *specifically*, as a certain kind of poetry, or poetry in a certain sense, so as to determine future reading situations in such a way that they will be decoded in ways which speech-act theory might call "felicitous;"[6] and that is why a claim to a future of indeterminacy (as literature) must start by determining in a quite specific way the reading conditions of the text.

In my view, then (to summarize), so-called "self-referentiality" functions, in fact, as reference to an illocutionary situation, the contextual understandings posited by a text as necessary for it to make sense (to make sense as literature, that is, to *go on* making sense). Thus conceived, the illocutionary situation amounts to a set of instructions for decoding the text; and indeed, the distinction between "code" and "situation" is at best a heuristic one, since a felicitous illocutionary situation is a function of an agreed code, just as the existence of an agreed code implies a whole illocutionary situation. In texts, such illocutionary reference may be entirely implicit; or it may be directly expressed (by means of explicit textual self-comment); or—the most frequent case—it may be obliquely presented by means of figures of the text contained within the text. Such figures, like narrative "mise en abyme" as analyzed by Lucien Dällenbach (and "mise en abyme" is an example of the techniques in question), may reproduce the text as utterance (énoncé), as speech-act (énonciation), or as code;[7] but from the point of view of the illocutionary self-contextualizing of the text, it is the latter two types of figuration which are directly relevant. They "produce" within the text the text's own illocutionary situation, as it is conceivable or formulable in the circumstances of the text's production, and thus guarantee the survival of this illocutionary context as an essential component of all future contexts of reception. (Needless to say, if texts can produce their own contexts in this way, it becomes urgent, as a philosophical issue, to ask to what extent *all* the contexts, which in the ordinary way we regard as being distinct from discourse, are in fact products of discourse; but that is a line of thought I do not need to follow up here.)

"Tableaux Parisiens" [Parisian Pictures] is the title Baudelaire gave, in the 1861 edition of the *Fleurs du Mal* [Flowers of Evil], to a group of eighteen poems— some previously published in the 1857 edition, others not—which he placed between "Spleen et Idéal" and "Le Vin." Such a title appears to imply mimetic intent and to refer to descriptive poetry concerning visual aspects of the city of Paris. A superficial glance at the poems, however, quickly gives the lie to this inference and reveals an "ungrammaticality": relatively few of the poems are specifically set in Paris,[8] a number of the others might be more broadly described as "big city poems,"[9] but certain texts are not clearly or specifically related to city life at all.[10] One poem, "Rêve parisien" [Parisian Dream], although it incorporates Paris in its title, is mimetic not of the city of Paris but of an entirely imaginary spectacle.

This last title is instructive, however, because it offers an obvious coupling with the title of the section as a whole, "Tableaux Parisiens." For "Rêve parisien" does not necessarily mean a dream having Paris as its object; the sense could equally be a dream dreamt in Paris or a dream inspired by Paris, and this sense is supported by the narrative content of the poem, with its conclusion set in the "horreur de mon taudis" [horror of my hovel]. Similarly "Tableaux Parisiens" might be taken to imply "pictures inspired by Paris," "pictures done in Paris," or even (at a stretch) "pictures done by a Parisian." In these cases, the word "tableaux" would begin to suggest less the idea of mimetic *representation* and rather more that of artistic *production*, since a picture is, after all, as appropriately defined as a created product of art as it is in terms of the reproduction of its object. Thus, although the lines from "Les Petites Vieilles" ["Little Old Women"]:

> j'entrevois un fantôme débile
> Traversant de Paris le fourmillant tableau,

[I catch a glimpse of a flimsy ghost
Passing through the swarming Parisian landscape,][11]

might support the mimetic sense of the word; those from "Rêve parisien" ["Parisian Dream"]:

peintre fier de mon génie
Je savourais dans mon tableau
L'enivrante monotonie
Du métal, du marbre et de l'eau,

[just like a painter
I enjoyed in my picture
The entrancing monotony
Of metal, marble, and water,]

quite clearly imply esthetic production—while in addition, the text as a whole authorizes the equation "tableau" = mental representation, dream. The meaning of "imaginary production" would apply without strain to *all* the non-city poems in the section.

It seems, then, that the word "tableau" in the "Tableaux Parisiens" section may mean either mimetic reproduction or mental representation, depending on the individual poem,[12] but that its primary or nuclear meaning lies in its suggesting the creative involvement of a seeing subject, *producing* spectacles mimetically as "fourmillant tableau" [swarming picture] or imaginatively as "L'enivrante monotonie/ Du métal, du marbre et de l'eau"[The entrancing monotony of metal, marble, and water]. A subject, then, whose function is to make sense of the visual object, be it actually seen or a dream: "tout *pour moi* devient allégorie" [for me everything becomes an allegory], comments the *ego* of "Le Cygne" [The Swan], while the *ego* of "Rêve parisien" refers to:

ces prodiges
Qui brillaient d'un feu *personnel*!

[these marvels,
which shone with an intrinsic fire!]

(where "personnel" of course means "proper to the dream objects"; but also inevitably suggests subjective involvement in the vision).[13]

This subject (as some of the above quotations illustrate) figures as an actor in the poems, which dramatize his effort to produce meaningful representations. Thus, on seeing a swan:

Andromaque, je pense à vous!

[Andromache, my thoughts are turned to you!]
("Le Cygne")

or, a propos of the blind:

> Je dis: Que cherchent-ils au Ciel, tous ces
> aveugles?
>
> [I ask myself—What are they looking for
> in the sky, all those blind men?]
> ("Les Aveugles")

or again:

> Voilà le noir tableau qu'en un rêve nocturne
> Je vis se dérouler sous mon oeil clairvoyant
>
> [such is the sombre picture that in a dream,
> one night, I saw unfold before my seer's gaze]
> ("Le Jeu" [Gambling])

But also, this seeing subject *in* the poems becomes a speaking subject *through* the poems which produce him, and relate in verse the visual encounters and mental representations of which he is the subject. The *ego* who is the subject of the poetic utterance is the truly universal factor present in *all* of the poems of the "Tableaux Parisiens," all but one of which are couched in specifically first-person discourse, while the only third-person poem in the section, "Le crépuscule du matin" [Morning Twilight], dramatizes the speaking situation and the presence of "je" through a curious use of the imperfect tense as a deictic.[14] Consequently, one may conclude that the best sense attributable to the title is "Tableaux d'un Parisien" [A Parisian's Pictures], since it is the speaking *ego* who takes responsibility for the discourse through which the experiences of the seeing subject are conveyed. In this final interpretation of the title, the word "tableaux," in addition to its visual connotations, can be read as metaphoric of the poems themselves.

But in what sense is it accurate to say of the speaking *ego* that he is a Parisian? (I am taking it for granted that he is a "he.") I want to suggest that he is a Parisian in the sense that Paris is less the place he writes about than *the place out of which he speaks*, and hence the place *in which* the poems are supposed to be understood— the place, in short, which gives point to the poetic text as an utterance, and hence does so not as mimetic object but as illocutionary situation. But since the poems are presumably intended to be read wherever the French language and the conventions of its verse are known, and not just in the city of Paris, the "Paris" out of which the *ego* speaks and in which his voice must be heard cannot be too closely identified with the "real" Paris in which Charles Baudelaire produced his poems (to be fussy, some of the work was done at Honfleur). In other words, it is not so much the historical city which was the capital of France in the Second Empire as an imaginary Paris which figures as a cultural item in the encyclopedia of speakers of French, the "Paris" invented by Baudelaire and his contemporaries as a symbol of modern life, and which *we* continue to recognize, in Walter Benjamin's useful phrase, as capital of the nineteenth century. It is for *this* reason that the illocutionary situation in which "je" [I] produces his discourse functions to indicate the specifically modern status of that speech and to invite the reader to receive it in the same spirit. The "décor," in short, functions as code.

Within the poems themselves, the speech of "je" as a communicational act is frequently dramatized, and it is striking that the overall effect of these dramatizations is to convey a sense of his speech activity as lonely, and most often futile, verbal gesturing.[15] The interlocutors he takes and whom he addresses or questions are usually unable to hear him, let alone to reply: "Andromaque, je pense à vous!" [Andromaque, my thoughts are turned to you!]; "Telles vous cheminez" [Thus you pass on]; "O cité! . . ./ Vois! je me traîne aussi!" [O city . . . behold I also drag myself along!]; "Fugitive beauté . . . / Ne te verrai-je plus que dans l'éternité?" [O fleeting beauty . . . shall I never see you again except in eternity?]; "Dites, quelles moissons étranges/ Tirez-vous . . . ?" [Tell me, what strange harvests are you bringing in?]; "Quand je te vois passer" [When I see you pass by]; "*Je* n'ai pas oublié . . . / *Notre* blanche maison" [I have not forgotten . . . our white house]; "Endormeuses saisons! je vous aime et vous loue" [O drowsy seasons! I love you and praise you]. Consequently, the rhetorical question is one of the most characteristic speech patterns of "je": "Avez-vous observé que maints cercueils de vieilles . . .?" [Have you ever noticed that many old women's coffins . . .?]; "Viens-tu troubler, avec ta puissante grimace,/ la fête de la Vie?" [Do you come with your fearful grimace to disturb Life's festivities?]; "Es-tu le fruit d'automne . . . / Es-tu vase funèbre . . .?" [Are you Autumn's fruit? Are you a funeral urn?]; "Que pourrais-je répondre à cette âme pieuse . . .?" [What reply could I give this pious soul?]. So too is self-address: "Contemple-les, mon âme . . . / Je dis: Que cherchent-ils au Ciel . . .?" [Observe them, O my soul . . . I ask myself—What are they looking for in the sky?]; "Recueille-toi, mon âme, en ce grave moment" [O my soul, withdraw into yourself at this grave hour]. And finally, simple deixis: "Voici le soir charmant" [Here's the delightful evening]; "Voilà le noir tableau" [Such is the sombre picture]; "De ce terrible paysage/ . . . Ce matin encore l'image/ . . . me ravit" [The image of this terrible landscape entrances me again this morning]; "C'était l'heure où . . ." [It was the hour when . . .] functions to betray the presence of a speaker addressing—who knows whom?

The lack of contact thus dramatized is heightened by the hostility or indifference of the city environment in which "je" speaks. In one poem,[16] the city is too noisy for the poet's speech to be heard:

                                                    O cité!
Pendant qu'autour de nous tu chantes, ris et beugles,

. . . .

Je dis: Que cherchent-ils au Ciel, tous ces aveugles?

[O city, while you sing, laugh and bellow

> around us
> I ask myself—What are they looking for in
> the sky, all those blind men?]

In another, the street environment, "La rue assourdissante autour de moi hurlait" [The deafening street was howling round me], prevents communication between "je" and the woman passing by, the "passante." Finally, urban noise accounts for the movement of withdrawal by which the poet's speech comes to be completely inner-directed:

> Recueille-toi, mon âme, en ce grave moment,
> Et ferme ton oreille à ce rugissement
>
> [O my soul, withdraw into yourself at this
> grave hour, and stop your ears against this
> roaring din]

—and it is not accidental that this poem, "Le crépuscule du soir" [Evening Twilight], introduces the whole series of poems of mental representation (desire, nostalgia, the dream) which compose the nocturnal panel of the section. Urban noise, as the adversary of poetic speech, thus defines the illocutionary circumstances not only of the diurnal poems (the series of street-poems beginning with "Le Soleil" [The Sun], but also of the nocturnal poems (from which explicit indications of din are absent.)

Yet this speech, which is either drowned by the city's hubbub or else confined to a self-directed monologue, is one which we (the readers of Baudelaire) are permitted to hear, or to *overhear*, as it were. The speech which is dramatized in the poems as futile becomes available *through* poems which presuppose effective channels of communication. Thus, the lonely words in "Les Aveugles" [The Blind]:

> Je dis: Que cherchent-ils au Ciel, tous ces aveugles?
>
> [I ask myself—What are they looking for in the sky,
> all those blind men?]

are reported in a sonnet of deliberately jumpy prosody, perhaps, but one which is readable (and in which the jumpiness is *expressive*) to anyone familiar with the conventions of French verse. And the miscommunication in "A une Passante" [To a Woman Passing By], Car j'ignore où tu fuis, tu ne sais où je vais, / O toi que j'eusse aimée, ô toi qui le savais!" [For whither you flee I know not; nor do you know whither I am bound—O you whom I could have loved, O you who knew it!], is similarly related in a sonnet of essentially conventional structure. The reader, such poems assume, is one with whom acts of communication are possible because, on the one hand, he or she is culturally equipped and trained in the traditions of French poetry, and on the other, he or she is assumed to be familiar with the dilemmas of modernity, notably the experience of lack of contact which is the subject of the texts; and hence to be responsive to the poet's plight as it is dramatized in the poems.

What this means is that the dramatization of problematical circumstances of communication within the poems serves as a specific cultural *code* for readers who, in fact, have no technical difficulty in "reading" the texts: by such means, we are asked to read this relatively classical verse as the speech-act of a "modern" poetic subject. The poems' reference to Paris is, consequently, not so much representational and mimetic as it is metaphoric of an illocutionary situation outside of which the poems themselves would be meaningless (that is, could not be appropriately read). In this way, Baudelaire solves the difficult artistic problem of communicating a sense of the powerlessness to communicate, of writing meaningfully about the difficulty of being meaningful. The apparent contrast between the illocutionary situation presented in the poems and the illocutionary situation presupposed by them need not disturb us, then: the poems simply depend on a prior, conventional read-ability in order to indicate those non-conventional circumstances which can only be produced *in* the texts but which give them their "true" point. Of course, it happens also that this combination of the traditional and the modern meshes well with Baudelaire's doctrine of Beauty, as being formed of an absolute and continuing component, and a relative and changing one. It corresponds too to the actual sen-sation of Parisian experience developed in a poem like "Le Cygne" where continuity ("Andromaque, je pense à vous!" [Andromache, I am thinking of you!]) and change ("Paris change!" [Paris is changing]) are dramatized as the joint components of a specific tension:

> la forme d'une ville
> Change plus vite, hélas! que le coeur d'un mortel.

> [a city's pattern changes,
> alas, more swiftly than a human heart.]

But one final point emerges from the above considerations: if "Paris" as illo-cutionary context, or code, is metaphoric of the modern, the street, then the "deaf-ening" street is itself metonymic of Paris. As such, it comes to be a figure, within certain poems, of those poems themselves as modern discourse. It is not simply that in the diurnal series the events of the poems actually take place in the street, but that the street itself is projected as a model of modern poetic language (in short, here too the décor is the code). As I have shown elsewhere,[17] "Le Soleil" is strategically placed at the head of the diurnal series so as to establish the street not just as their locus but as the model of creative experience for the poetic *ego*:

> Le long du vieux faubourg, . . .
> Je vais m'exerçant à ma fantasque escrime,
> Flairant dans tous les coins les hasards de la rime,
> Trébuchant sur les mots comme sur les pavés,
> Heurtant parfois des vers depuis longtemps rêvés.

[Through the old suburb . . .
I go practising my fantastic fencing all alone,
Scenting a chance rhyme in every corner, stumbling
against words as against cobblestones, sometimes
striking on verses I had long dreamt of.]

But here, poetry of the street is conceived in terms of a poetics of encounter (experiential encounters and linguistic serendipity). The poem on which I shall now focus at greater length also proposes the street as simultaneously locus and code, but it does so more specifically in terms of a poetics of modernity, conceived precisely as a fusion of the traditional and the urban. This is "Les sept vieillards" [The Seven Old Men], a poem which has been frequently read as allegorical, but which can most fruitfully be interpreted—like Mallarmé's "sonnet en -yx"—as a poem allegorical of itself.[18]

"Vous créez un frisson nouveau" [You create a new shiver, a new thrill]: Victor Hugo's comment on receipt of "Les sept vieillards" echoes the observation made by Baudelaire himself to Jean Morel: "it is the first number in a new series I am attempting and I fear that I've merely succeeded in going beyond the limits assigned to Poetry."[19] What defines this novelty, by which the limits of poetry are transcended? Much discussion has surrounded the question; I will content myself with citing Baudelaire's essay on Gautier, written the previous year:

Besides, the nature of true poetry is to flow evenly like mighty rivers approaching the sea, which is their death and infinity; and to avoid sudden haste and jerkiness. Lyric poetry rushes, but its movement is always elastic and undulating. Poetry rejects anything abrupt or broken up, relegating it to drama or the social novel.[20]

This is the conception of poetry *against* which "Les sept vieillards" is written, the conception which is both assumed and transcended in the "new series" to which the poem belongs—assumed, that is, in order to be transcended. The new poetry has in common with the theatre and the social novel—those realist genres—a certain angularity and discontinuity in its movement, even while the image of the poem as a river approaching its infinite and its death in the sea is retained; for in the urban context it is streets, with their harsh angles and sudden encounters, which, as the "canaux étroits du colosse puissant" [the narrow veins of this mighty giant], replace streams.

The frequency of enjambment and irregular breaks in the versification of this poem (and other street poems such as "Les Aveugles" or "A une Passante") indicates, as Graham Chesters has pointed out,[21] an attempt to achieve in verse the condition of prose, with a view to matching the characteristics of the urban environment. But if one recalls the elastic and undulating movement which was said in the Gautier essay to be essential to the lyric, it is clear that the manner of a poem such as "Les sept vieillards" is more than a merely mimetic device; it is a means of rendering poetic discourse itself problematic, and of creating a new lyric code

suitable to modern life, at the risk of "going beyond the limits." This latter circumstance is in fact thematized in the poem itself, with its reference to an encounter
with absurdity and madness—that which lies beyond the limits of meaning, and
constitutes "its infinity and death." But I shall suggest that it is precisely this
transcending of the limits which constitutes the new poetic code, and that consequently the encounter related in the poem is synonymous with the adventure of
encountering the poem itself.

The narrative structure of the poem is that of a voyage to the sea. The river of
the outset:

> Les maisons . . .
> Simulaient les deux quais d'une rivière accrue,
>
> [The houses
> looked like the two banks of some swollen river,]

becomes the infinite sea of the final lines:

> Et mon âme dansait, dansait, vieille gabarre
> Sans mâts, sur une mer monstrueuse et sans bords!
>
> [And my spirit danced, danced, old barge
> With no masts, on a monstrous endless sea!]

But the river was a metaphoric river only, simulated by a street ("Le faubourg
secoué par les lourds tombereaux" [the suburb shaken by the heavy tumbrils]) in
which the vehicles of death (cf. the connotations of "tombereaux" [tumbrils] go
rumbling to their destination; *ego* is walking down that same street). The common
element of street and stream is a threatening liquidity: it is the fog which produces
the illusion of a river ("Les maisons, dont la brume allongeait la hauteur" [the
houses which the fog made taller]), and this same yellow mist invades the soul of
the poet just as it inundates space:

> décor semblable à l'âme de l'acteur,
> Un brouillard sale et jaune inondait tout l'espace.
>
> [decor resembling the actor's soul,
> A dirty yellow fog was inundating all space.]

But liquidity is the mark also of "mystery," of that which defies understanding
and challenges meaning:

> Les mystères partout coulent comme des sèves
> Dans les canaux étroits du colosse puissant,
>
> [Everywhere mysteries flow like sap

In the mighty giant's narrow canals,]

the poem announces at the outset; whereas at the end the protagonist has been "Blessé par le mystère et par l'absurdité!" [Wounded by the mystery and the absurdity]. It follows, then, that not only is the "âme de l'acteur" invaded by the liquidity of mystery, but that that mystery is directly identified with the encounter which "wounds" him, that is, with the proliferating series of old men, even though these old men are characterized by their sharpness and angularity, and described with words like "roide," "cassé," "faisant . . . un parfait angle droit" [stiff, broken, making . . . a perfect right angle]. This sharpness explains their ability to wound; but it is not incompatible in the poem with the liquidity of mystery, since initially the first old man of the series is seen as a kind of emanation of the fog:

> un vieillard dont les guenilles jaunes
> Imitaient la couleur de ce ciel pluvieux.

> [an old man whose yellow rags
> Imitated the colour of that rain-filled sky]

Several observations are called for at this stage. First, all the components of the poem's action—the "actor," the "décor," the old men—bathe in a common element which is that of mystery. The soul is invaded, like a swamped boat (soon to become the "vieille gabarre/ Sans mâts" [the old wreck/ without masts]) by the yellow fog of which the old men are themselves an equivalent. The poem is thus subverting traditional distinctions such as those of self and other, the soul and the world, by making them all subject to the category of absurdity, meaninglessness. Secondly, the liquidity of mystery and the angularity of the street are here identified, both by the metaphor which makes rivers of streets and by the double quality of the old men. But, sharing its mysterious liquidity and its dangerous harshness, the old men are consequently equivalents of the street in its double aspect, a kind of emanation of it. Both street and old men thus recall Baudelaire's definition of the lyric as smooth flowing and of what opposes it as "anything abrupt or broken up," except that in this poem the two are uncannily combined in such a way that flow comes to represent "mystery" as the suggestion of elusive meaning—a last residue of traditional meaningfulness, perhaps—while the harsh and the angular represent the hostility of such "mystery" to traditional concepts such as the self, "mon âme déjà lasse" [my already weary soul]. Correspondingly, the poetic persona of *ego* reveals itself to be double also, and composed of an element already succumbing to the flow ("my soul") and a combative and heroic element more attuned to the realities of the world of the street:

> Je suivais, roidissant mes nerfs comme un héros
> Et discutant avec mon âme déjà lasse,
> Le faubourg secoué par les lourds tombereaux.

[I was making my way, steeling my nerves heroically
and nagging my already weary soul, through the
suburb shaken by heavy tumbrils.]

My final observation is this, that this world of equivalences (where soul, décor, and old men bathe in the common element of mystery and where liquidity and angularity, the stream and the street, are themselves identified) is a fictional or poetic world, a world of figuration and falsity. The street is a theatre, a "décor" in which the narrative *ego* is an "acteur"; similes underline the falsity of this world: "roidissant mes nerfs *comme* un héros" [steeling my nerves *like* a hero], and undermine the equivalences they produce: "décor *semblable* à l'âme de l'acteur" [a background comparable to the actor's soul], while two key verbs explicitly point to the false, and let us say hallucinatory, quality of this universe:

> Les maisons, dont la brume allongeait la hauteur,
> *Simulaient* les deux quais d'une rivière accrue,

> [the houses seemed to be stretched upwards by
> the mist and simulated the two banks of some
> swollen river,]

> Tout à coup, un vieillard dont les guenilles jaunes
> *Imitaient* la couleur de ce ciel pluvieux, . . .
> M'apparut

> [Suddenly an old man whose yellow rags imitated
> the colour of the rainy sky, . . . hove in sight]

What is real here is the street (the houses, the suburb) and the fog; the rest (the mystery, the river, the invaded soul, the old man) is a product of vision, of the vision which produces equivalences through the operation of metaphor. Thus, although the poem begins by presenting the city as a place "Où le spectre en plein jour accroche le passant!" [where the ghost accosts the passer-by in broad daylight], it hastens in the following stanzas to reverse this relationship by suggesting that the spectral quality of the city is a product of the metaphorizing vision of the "passant"—and on reflection that is the ultimate force of the run-on "M'apparut" [hove in sight] which concludes these introductory stanzas. Thus, the world of equivalences and mystery which is so threatening to the soul of the poet may itself be the product of that poet's vision: it is poetry as a factor of equivalence and indifferentiation, the poetry of the city as ant-bed—"fourmillante cité" [swarming city], *fourmi* means *ant*—which appears as the real source of the uncanny.

Certainly, if poetic equivalence is the key to the opening stanzas of the poem, a different aspect of poetic repetition is figured by the proliferating old men whose encounter forms the mediating event in the narrative structure of "Les sept vieillards." Poetry, as the type of discourse which constructs metaphoric equivalences, is also the type of discourse which, repeating itself stanza by stanza (just as the old men proliferate), approaches an infinity of resemblance and calls into question the distinctions from which meaning is derived. It is significant that the stanzas in which the appearance of the eight old men is related (seven effective appearances, plus one hypothesized) themselves number eight (from stanza 4, "Tout à coup" through stanza 11 "Mais je tournai le dos . . ."); the first apparition begins in the first stanza (although it spills over, by enjambment, into the second), and the eighth apparition is evoked in the eighth stanza. The poem does not, of course, proceed with a stanza-by-stanza identification of the verse structure and the old men; but it does suggest the resemblance between stanzaic repetition and that of the "vieillards" in a number of ways.

Thus, the early stanzas are concerned with the angular appearance and limping gait of the first of the men—a break and a syncopation which recur in the heavily run-on verse itself. The lines concerning

> la tournure et le pas maladroit
> D'un quadrupède infirme ou d'un juif à trois pattes
>
> [the ungainly shape and gait of some ailing
> quadruped or a three-legged Jew],

run on as they are from the *third* to the *fourth* stanzas of the description, clearly metaphorize the verse itself in its metric structure. The remaining four stanzas are concerned with the proliferation of old men; that is, their sameness and their repetitiveness. Here the verses themselves exploit various forms of repetitiveness, summarizing the previous four stanzas by an enumeration: "barbe, oeil, dos, bâton, loques" [beard, eye, back, stick, rags]; repeating lexical items and syntactic structures: "du même enfer venu,/ . . . Marchait d un même pas" [from the same hell . . . plodded at the same speed]; "A quel complot infâme . . . / Ou quel méchant hasard . . . ?" [What infamous conspiracy . . . or what evil chance?]; "de minute en minute" [minute by minute]; introducing phonetic patterns and parallels: "je comptai *sept fois* . . ./ Ce *s*inistre *v*ieillard"; "*s*aisi d'un *f*risson *f*raternel"; "*s*aisi . . . *S*osie" [I counted that sinister old man seven times; seized with a brotherly chill; seized . . . an identical double]; metaphorizing in various ways the notion of similarity and repetition: "jumeau centenaire"; "vieillard qui se multipliait"; "Sosie"; "Phénix"; "fils et père de lui-même" [centenarian twin; multiple old man; a double; phoenix; his own son and his own father].

In this way, then, the "cortège infernal" [hellish procession] figures the language of the poem itself, a language in which the *poetic function*—exactly Jakobson's projection of the principle of resemblance onto the syntagmatic axis—no longer reproduces the majestic flow, the smooth flow of the poem as stream, but embodies the absurdity and lapse into meaninglessness inherent in modern discourse, in the poem as street. The flow has not disappeared: it is still present in the slippage of one old man into the next, a slippage reproduced by the stanzaic enjambment in the text; but discontinuity and repetition now predominate (as the jerkiness of the enjambments also records) and now constitute a sense of meaninglessness, the meaninglessness of signs which have undergone a loss of differentiation, so that they flow dangerously into each other and frighteningly repeat each other in endless absurdity: "Ces sept monstres hideux avaient l'air éternel" [These seven hideous freaks had a look of eternity about them]. The problem of meaning in a world of signs which has lost its transcendental guarantee, the consequent "drift" of signifiers which cannot be anchored to a single, stable signified, thus constitute the major problematics of the diurnal poems of the "Tableaux Parisiens" (that of the nocturnal poems being the closely related problematics of desire); but it is only in "Les sept vieillards" that this sense of meaninglessness is carried to its extreme in the intuition that ultimately all signs, despite their apparent diversity, are one sign and simply repeat each other indefinitely.

This is not the place to enlarge on the philosophical import of indifferentiation in "Les sept vieillards"—a topic which would require, in any case, a joint reading with the other poems of the diurnal series. What is interesting, in terms of my present inquiry, is the fact that, in the abstract, it is obviously not *necessary* to read lines of French verse structured like those of the central stanzas of "Les sept vieillards" (by enjambment and repetition) as expressive of a poetics of the modern—of angularity and indifferentiation, an (urban) poetics of the street as opposed to, or superimposed upon, a (natural) poetics of the stream. The difference, at the technical level of versification, between such lines and (say) Baudelaire's own earlier practice is perhaps not so striking as to justify *in itself* such a reading of them. If I do read into the poem in this way, it is because the poem *asks me to*—and it does so by projecting its *apparent* mimetic referent (Paris as "décor") as an *actual* indicator of poetic code, an illocutionary context: Paris as the site of a modern experience of threatening indifferentiation, that is, Paris as a "décor semblable à l'âme de l'acteur" [decor resembling the actor's soul]. "Décor sembla-ble": a manifestation of the problematics of indifferentiation; but "décor semblable à l'âme de l'acteur," a *constructed* site ("décor"), emblematic of the "place" ("l'âme") out of which the poet speaks—and, perhaps, constitutive of that place.

Michael Riffaterre would point out, justly, that my reading of the poem was triggered by a "mimetic" anomaly (the *invraisemblance* inherent in the poem's fantastic mode); and that I have read the poem like a doughnut surrounding an absent textual matrix—the word "indifferentiation," perhaps, or the text from the essay on Gautier cited at the outset. My point is not to dispute his theory but to add to it the observation that the referential apparatus characteristic of poetry is that which makes us read it as poetry (or as a specific kind of poetry), that is, the illocutionary context assumed by the text and communicated, by various means, to the reader as a guide to his/her reading. The literary phenomenon is indeed best described in terms of the text-reader relationship; but that relationship is inscribed (implicitly, obliquely, or directly) within the text.

This is perhaps clearest in the opening lines of "Les sept vieillards," which summarize the narrative and thematic content of the poem, but simultaneously dramatize its illocutionary status:

> Fourmillante cité, cité pleine de rêves,
> Où le spectre en plein jour accroche le passant!

> [O swarming city, city full of dreams,
> where the ghost accosts the passer-by
> in broad daylight!]

Who is this passer-by? In narrative terms, he is the protagonist of the poem, the *ego* who is to encounter the spectral old men; in thematic terms, he personifies mortality and points to the narrative encounter as a meeting with death in the guise of the city's proliferation, its undifferentiated *fourmillement*. But in illocutionary terms, he figures the reader of the poem, whose function is to be accosted by the spectre *as a figure of the poem*; and to be involved in his or her dangerous encounter with the text in just the way that the *ego* of the poem is caught up in, and wounded by, *his* encounter with the phantoms. Here, then, is a final identification which completes the set of equivalences installed by the opening stanzas: the reader, like "je," is invited to experience the adventure of a soul encountering that—the street-river, the text-spectre—which puts its existence in jeopardy. The whole poem, as narrative, thus figures the process of reading it; it serves as its own illocutionary code.

What more striking way could be imagined of illustrating the function of poetic reference as a self-reference which figures its own illocutionary context? By establishing the code common to the text and to its readership, it seeks to make of the reader the *only* subject such a text—as literary discourse, set adrift from its original context—can hope to have.

NOTES

1. M. Riffaterre, *Semiotics of Poetry* (Bloomington and London: Indiana University Press, 1978), p. 19.
2. "Les anomalies de la mimésis, les troubles de la référentialité apparente." M. Riffaterre, *La production du texte* (Paris: Ed. du Seuil, 1979), p. 77.
3. *Semiotics of Poetry*, p. 13.
4. Ibid., p. 2.
5. ". . . se situe dans les rapports du texte et du lecteur, non du texte et de l'auteur, ou du texte et de la réalité." *La production du texte*, p. 27.
6. I am using "felicitous" to describe a speech-act in which the illocutionary understandings of speaker and receiver coincide. But the "felicitousness" of an interpretation depends not only on the relationship between interpreter and text, but also on that between interpreter and audience. See R. Chambers, *Meaning and Meaningfulness* (Lexington, Ky: French Forum, 1979), pp. 172–180.
7. *Le récit spéculaire* (Paris: Ed. du Seuil, 1977).
8. Cf. "À une mendiante rousse" ("Au seuil de quelque Véfour/ De carrefour''); "Le Cygne" ("Comme je traversais le nouveau Carrousel/ . . . Paris change!''); "Les Petites Vieilles" ("Traversant de Paris le fourmillant tableau''); "Le squelette laboureur" (" . . .

sur ces quais poudreux/ Où maint livre cadavéreux/ Dort . . .''); "Le crépuscule du matin"
("Et le sombre Paris, en se frottant les yeux,/ Empoignait ses outils . . ."). Cf. in translation:
"To a Red-Haired Beggar-Girl" (At the door of some shabby cornerhouse); "The Swan"
(As I was crossing the new Carrousel bridge . . . Paris is changing!); "The Little Old
Women" (Passing through the swarming Parisian landscape); "The Digging Skeleton" (In
the book-boxes on the dusty quays where many a corpse-like book sleeps); "Morning Twi-
light" (And gloomy Paris, rubbing his eyes, laid hold of his tools).

   9. "Paysage"; "Le Soleil"; "Les sept vieillards"; "Les Aveugles"; "A une passante";
"Le crépuscule du soir"; "Le Jeu." In translation: "Landscape"; "The Sun"; "The Seven
Old Men"; "To a Woman Passing By"; "Evening Twilight"; "Gambling."

   10. "Danse macabre"; "L'amour du mensonge"; "Je n'ai pas oublié . . ."; "La servante
au grand coeur . . ."; "Brumes et Pluies."

   11. Where possible the translation is taken from F. Scarfe, *Baudelaire* (Harmondsworth,
Baltimore, and Victoria: Penguin Books Ltd., 1961).

   12. In fact the "mimetic" poems and the poems of mental representation form two sets
of serially arranged poems, which structure the section as a whole in terms of "diurnal" vs.
"nocturnal" experience. Cf. R. Chambers, " 'Je' dans les 'Tableaux Parisiens,' "*Nineteenth
Century French Studies*, XI, 1–2 (Fall-Winter, 1980–81), 59–68.

   13. My italics in the quotations. From a different perspective, Karlheinz Stierle has also
concluded that the focal point of the "Tableaux Parisiens" lies in the figure of the observer
and his lyrical transformation of the scene. See K. Stierle, "Baudelaires *Tableaux Parisiens*
und die Tradition des *Tableaux de Paris*," *Poetica* (Juli 1974), 285–322; and cf. my " 'Je'
dans les 'Tableaux Parisiens.' "

   14. The poem is built on a series of verbs in the imperfect tense ("La diane chantait,"
etc.). These appear to be setting the scene for the eventual introduction of a narrative event,
which however never occurs. The only possible point can therefore be to dramatize the
speaking situation itself, as a present opposed to the past being described.

   15. See Klaus Dirscherl, *Zur Typologie der poetischen Sprechweisen bei Baudelaire*
(München: Fink, 1975).

   16. See R. Chambers, "Saying and Seeing in Baudelaire's 'Les Aveugles,' " in R. Mitchell,
ed., *Pre-Text/Text/Context* (Columbus: Ohio State University Press, 1980), pp. 147–156.

   17. "Baudelaire et l'espace poétique; à propos du 'Soleil,' " in *Le lieu et la formule:
Hommage à Marc Eigeldinger* (Neuchâtel: La Baconnière, 1978), pp. 111–120.

   18. On allegory in Baudelaire, see especially Nathaniel Wing, "The Danaïdes' Vessel:
On Reading Baudelaire's Allegories," in *Pre-Text/Text/Context*, pp. 135–144. N. Wing
shows that in "Les sept vieillards" the poem deconstructs its own allegorical structure by
"figuring the reiteration of an allegorical figure as a repetition cut from any link to its
signified." By reading the poem as an allegory of itself (of its own failure to produce
meaning), one incorporates this deconstruction as a component of the poem's own code (of
its illocutionary axioms).

   19. C. Baudelaire, *Correspondence I: 1832–1860* (Paris: Bibl. de la Pléiade, 1973), p.
583. Translation by Anna Whiteside.

   20. C. Baudelaire, "Théophile Gautier," in *Oeuvres complètes II* (Paris: Bibl. de la
Pléiade, 1976) p. 126. Translation by Anna Whiteside.

   21. "Baudelaire and the Limits of Poetry," *French Studies* XXXII, 4 (October 1978),
420–434.

IX.

REFERENTIAL INTERTEXTUALITY
PRE-CODE, CODE, AND POST-CODE

Bruce Morrissette

Referential polyterminology proliferates in current literary criticism to such an extent that the term "reference" becomes an element in that other quasi-universal terminological mix of our times, generative structure. No doubt reaction will set in, so that eventually the dozens of words and phrases, many of them neologisms and figurative usages, that have revolutionized critical vocabularies will diminish or disappear; but for the moment their heady brew intoxicates us, and we feel we are making critical discoveries of real importance as we add to the Saussurian innovations of *sign, signified, langue,* and *parole* such spin-offs as (poly)semantics, (poly)semiotics, destructuration, metaphoric displacement, metonymic condensation, syntagmatic and paradigmatic, metalanguage, diegesis, narrativity, and generative chains based on the concept of the code. It was while reading certain remarks by Roland Barthes on code and pre-code that it struck me that the coding process in literature also involved an essential further step, the post-code, in order to avoid creative stagnancy and to allow an endless creative spiral: this article is an effort to justify such an assumption.

The term code is, of course, so widely applied that it transcends literature and cinema. It originated outside these artistic domains, making literary and cinematic codes in a strict sense metaphoric or metonymic transfers. Indeed, there seems to be no form—written, auditory, visual, sociological, political, intellectual, or instinctive—that does not correspond in one way or another to some *code.* Man's mental content appears to be as codified as the very structure of his brain. And as cerebral codes demonstrably evolve, vary, and change forms in the course of mental activities, one is easily persuaded to see analogies between this procedure and the evolution of codes within the creative structures of literature and the arts.

In the life or progress of a code, we may search out its origin (often as a development of other pre-existent codes), its use in one or another art form (narrative literature, for example), its "infraction" (in a moment of rupture engendered by an intrusion of one or more contradictory codes), and finally its state of "pre-code," in which the code of an art work of advanced structure seems to disappear, before becoming in its turn—either in the same work, or in a later intertextual work—a "post-code," appearing in the chain of forms as a new coded point of departure.

The works of Alain Robbe-Grillet offer, both theoretically and at the level of *écriture*, perhaps the most highly developed and successful example of generated and generative chains of codes. The procedure can be seen in retrospect as already present in his first novels and films, with their radical manipulations of the traditional narrative modes of chronology, point of view, and scene linkages. Moreover, in his early works, extensive use is made of thematic sub-codes, such as the Oedipus myth-complex, parodied semi-seriously in *Les Gommes* [*The Erasers*], Steckelian sado-eroticism in *Le Voyeur* [The Voyeur], textbook schizophrenic paranoia in *La Jalousie* [*Jealousy*], and even, in the same work, conventional socio-political codes observed first by Jean-Paul Sartre and then treated in book length by Jacques Leenhardt.[1] Without here attempting a complete re-examination of code structures in these early works (something that remains to be done), we will use as a take-off point the theoretical and practical code processes described and illustrated by the preface, the text, and the film *Glissements progressifs du plaisir* [Progressive Slippages of Pleasure],[2] moving on then to the even more complicated stages of intercodes found in Robbe-Grillet's most recent works, *Topologie d'une cité fantôme* [*Topology of a Phantom City*][3] and *Souvenirs du triangle d'or* [*Recollections of the Golden Triangle*].[4]

The system expressed and developed in *Glissements progressifs du plaisir* and subsequent works is based on the passage from pre-code, code, and infraction of code to a re-coding through what Robbe-Grillet terms "un mouvement de rétrogradation du sens à mesure que l'oeuvre s'accomplit" [retrogradation of meaning as the work develops; *Glissements*, p. 13]. The "degraded" elements are thematic and structural materials drawn from literary and cultural conventions: folklore, detective stories, horror films, horror legends (for example, Bluebeard), pornographic paperbacks—what Robbe-Grillet calls a "panoply" of popular sources, reminiscent of Rimbaud's taste for "low class" literature and art as he describes them in the "alchimie du verbe" section of *Une Saison en enfer* [*A Season in Hell*] and of the Fantômas predilections of Breton and the surrealists. These codes create in the reader of the novel or the viewer of the film certain established expectations of situational development, of character, or of plot, based on familiar assumptions of interpretable themes. These assumptions Robbe-Grillet calls *sens*, or meaning, and it is the goal of his new code structure to destroy them, downgrade them, contradict them, make them impossible of logical understanding (as done almost unobtrusively with the time patterns of *La Jalousie*). As the new code progresses, the retrogradation of meaning creates what Robbe-Grillet terms "the irreplaceable Saussurian opposition between *langue* and *parole*." This structuralist analogy implies for the idea of the Saussurian *parole* a division between language or *préparole* and *parole* itself not unlike the distinction proposed here between pre-code and code. The borrowed, popular elements of Robbe-Grillet's system make up the *parole* of our culture, created by man and his groups out of the elements of *langage* found in the "dictionary" of our cultural life, the source of our popular Saussurian artistic-cultural *langue*. But, the author points out in his preface to *Glissements*, the cultural *parole* becomes merely the source or *langue* from which the writer-cinéaste takes the elements of his own *parole*: or, in our terms, the code (the source materials, already structured) becomes pre-code for the artist's new codes and forms. Thus, "les scènes de comédie, le goût du sang, les belles esclaves, la morsure des vampires, etc., ne représentent pas la parole de ce film, mais seulement sa langue" [the comedy scenes, taste for blood, enslaved beauties, vampire bites, etc., only represent this film's *langue* and not its *parole*): popular *parole* becomes *langue*, the source of a new *parole*. Robbe-Grillet adds, "C'est la parole d'une société qui a été découpée en morceaux afin de la faire rétrograder à l'état de langue." [It's the *parole* of a society which has been cut up into little pieces to make it regress to a state of *langue*.] This new *parole* formed by the structure of the created work, is "une structure non réconciliée . . . ma propre parole" [an unreconciled structure . . . my own *parole*]. The base elements (*langue* or pre-code used by popular writers and artists) are first structured in a cultural *parole* (code), which in turn becomes *langue* or pre-code for a passage into creative *parole* or post-code.

Adopting the three terms of pre-code, code, and post-code avoids a certain ambiguity in Robbe-Grillet's use of the same word, *parole*, to identify first his material sources (popular speech), and then my own speech or his own restructured encoding, or post-code. It should be noted that Robbe-Grillet's re-use of objects, themes, narrative situations, and the like from pre-existing coded materials creates a new *parole* or post-code in a sense different from that of Raymond Queneau, for example, in his famous *Exercices de style* [*Exercises in style*], in which the re-coding introduced by the author imitates so wittily stylistic elements from various domains of popular rhetorical codes. Robbe-Grillet's "infractions" and "degradations" function quite otherwise, passing by a sort of entropic process to a topological reconstruction leading to a degradation (rather than to a heightening, as with Queneau) of pre-existing codes and new structures at a level of heightened contradictions, in which the creative energy does not enhance (even satirically) the source code (as in *Exercices de style*), but surpasses and replaces it.

To name an object, said Mallarmé in an often quoted text, is to eliminate most of the enjoyment of a poem, which consists in gradual discovery; to suggest is the ideal.[5] Similarly, to point out or emphasize the transition from pre-code to code, or from code to post-code, runs the risk of making too obvious a reconstruction of the original and subsequent coding processes. Robbe-Grillet recognizes this danger: the various explanatory passages in the printed text of *Glissements*, which are numerous, alter or partially nullify the code infraction or the degradation of meaning intended by the writer: "rupture ceases to be abrupt, subversive, scandalous," he writes, "at the moment that I call it a rupture, and thereby integrate it into the structural continuity that it was supposed to destroy" (p. 12). This threat to the system's code inversions makes necessary a new movement towards deconstruction, described by Robbe-Grillet as a suite "de fragments, de ponctuations, de plans isolés (comme situés entre parenthèses), de répétitions ou de dédoublements" [of fragments, interruptions, isolated (and seemingly bracketed) shots, repetitions, or doublings] which appear to block the formation of a new code, meaning, or coherent discourse.

At the same time, another danger arises: if the fragmenting or deconstructive procedure applied to a given code involves the length or duration of narrative elements, if this time span is insufficient to allow, in the reader-spectator, the recognition or esthetic sensation of the presence of the original, point-of-departure code, the resulting incoherence leads not to a new *parole* or post-code but to a total absence of code, and a failure to establish a *parole*. The attack against coded meaning cannot therefore be absolute, since there must exist, at every moment of text or image, "un sens précaire, glissant, toujours prêt à s'effondrer" (p. 13), [a precarious, slippery meaning, constantly on the brink of collapse]. The "glissements progressifs" of Robbe-Grillet's title are metaphoric then not only of the slipping movements of erotic pleasure, but also of the slippages between elements of successive manipulated codes.

At this point, critical scrutiny reveals an apparent contradiction in the system described thus far: namely, the presence and identification of a new *sens* or coded meaning in the author's "proper parole" that in principle proposes only a progressive degradation of meaning. *Glissements progressifs du plaisir* illustrates this problem, and its preface and inner commentaries show Robbe-Grillet's awareness of it. In principle, as stated, the massive decoding of basic thematic elements (violence, falsehood, tortures, blood, death, and the like) aims at the annihilation of all meanings, and yet the metaphoric and metonymic interplay of images and dialogues in the film, the constant interaction of digital/linear and analogous/non-linear structures creates an immense figurative code of meanings surrounding the central code of sexuality that engulfs the smallest elements (for example, the shoe fetish), as well as scenes and décors of widely varied magnitude (dismembered mannequins, girls tied to wheels, secret torture caves, and many others), all leading to more complicated sequences that become the subject (in the printed text) of authorial commentaries that constitute baroque extravaganzas of analytic terminology: "rapport réaliste direct . . . rapport métaphorique . . . liaison métonymique . . . (où) chaque type de liaison peut subir des glissements vers les autres catégories . . ." (p.126), [a direct, realistic connection . . . a metaphorical connection . . . a metonymic link . . . (in which) every type of linkage can merge with the other categories . . .], commentaries which establish the idea of the title phrase, *glissements progressifs du plaisir*, as the central metaphoric meaning of the work, the multiform image junction between artistic creation and prolonged coitus. In a sense, the post-code of image slippages or *glissements* among the structural elements reverts to the pre-code of point of departure: for, as in traditional Freudian doctrine, the eroticism of the basic elements (popular sado-masochistic materials) all arise from the Freudian pleasure principle.

Thus, parodied, retrograded, inverted popular erotic images, supposedly annihilated in their transformation into the personal *parole* of the author, emerge reconstructed at a higher creative level in which Freudian desire reappears (as in the paintings of Magritte, who constantly uses the term *desire*) and assumes supremacy in the esthetic constructs of man, if not domination over his basic libido. If this interpretation is valid, it must be admitted that Robbe-Grillet does not totally destroy meaning: his deconstruction or de-coding is followed by a subtly coherent new and personal reconstruction or post-code, with its own identifiable meaning.

The creative artist, such as Robbe-Grillet, has recourse to yet another coding/re-coding technique analogous to the procedure thus far discussed. Again, the basic elements have already passed through one or more textual codings, in the form either of a published text by another writer (or a visual image by another artist), or of a pre-existing text, already printed or not, by the author himself. For this procedure I have used the term intertextual assemblage, a technique or procedure which at the present time forms the principal generator or encoding process in the newest fiction of Robbe-Grillet.

The intertextual technique of generative assemblage recalls procedures dating far back not only among writers who re-use portions of their previous works, with or without textual changes, but also among painters and, especially, composers; Bach's *B-minor Mass* is an assemblage of seven cantatas composed by Bach over two preceding decades. The music critic Andrew Porter, in an important article on Pierre Boulez,[6] describes Handel's *riscritura* of his own works, the self-quotations of Prokofiev, and other examples. Boulez's work uses as a structural base the fact that Mallarmé towards the end of his career wished to incorporate all of his texts into a single Work. Boulez, similarly, makes a final assemblage of his own Mallarméan compositions, some of which date back to 1958. The Italian critic Renato Barilli has studied the *riscritura* of such devotees of assemblage as Calvino, and everyone knows that the central idea of Balzac's *Comédie humaine* involved a total re-framing of his life work.

Such re-coded assemblages from the distant and recent past are, however, exceeded by what Robbe-Grillet has proposed and accomplished in his latest works in a number of ways. Most of the re-integrated texts have their origins in composite compositions already involving more or less intercalated elements of a visual nature (pictures, photographs, lithographs, etchings) by artists whose works played or still play a self-reflexive role in the author's structural processes. The novel *Topologie d'une cité fantôme* (1976) contains texts taken from two early illustrated books with photos by David Hamilton (1971–72), a work with eleven etchings by Paul Delvaux (1975), a text accompanied by some twenty-one lithographs by Robert Rauschenberg (ca. 1976), the text of a Japanese advertisement for Suntory liquors (ca. 1974), and one large portion of a composite work using seventy-six reproductions of drawings and lithography by René Magritte. *Topologie* has been followed by *Souvenirs du triangle d'or* (1978), an assemblage containing the rest of the text related to Magritte pictures, the verbal text of a composite work using eighty-three black-and-white or sepia photographs by Irina Ionesco (1977), and the written portion of the catalogue prepared by Robbe-Grillet for the Jasper Johns exhibit held in June 1978 at the Georges Pompidou Centre National d'Art et de Culture. Titles, cuttings, transpositions, and other details of these sometimes complicated splicings are given in my book *Intertextual Assemblage in Robbe-Grillet from Topology to the Golden Triangle*.[7] In the case of the living artists involved (Hamilton, Rauschenberg, Delvaux, for example) a kind of pseudo-collaboration has occurred; in the case of an already dead artist, Magritte, it is Robbe-Grillet who creates the illusion of collaboration, as he does with a living artist when he merely appropriates and uses existing works by Jasper Johns or integrates the photographs of Irina Ionesco into the developing text of a novel in progress.

Since the only creative hand involved in the Robbe-Grillet/Magritte work *La Belle Captive*[8] is Robbe-Grillet himself, it is instructive to examine the coding, recoding, and other structuring processes used to produce the work, and to which the production of the "collaborative" books (for example, with Rauschenberg and Delvaux), may be compared and contrasted. On the back of *La Belle Captive*, Robbe-Grillet pays homage to Magritte as "un peintre qu'il aime entre tous" [one of his favorite painters]; elsewhere he has identified his susceptibility to the force of Magritte's neo-surrealist objects, such as the bowler hat, crescent moon, the famous *quille* (bilboquet, ninepin, chessman, baluster, spindle), drinking glasses, eggs, pipes, birds, *grelots* or harness bells, keys, candles, musical objects, doors, stones, and so on: a list which imperceptibly melds with "Robbe-Grilletian" objects already established in the author's *chosiste* dictionary, as they are joined by bicycles, shoes, eyes, valises, masks, phonographs, bottles, pistols. . . . All these become generators of diegesis for Robbe-Grillet, but they generate more than diegetic story line or narrative plot, for the Magrittian objects, along with the titles of the pictures in which they figure, undergo a chronological rearrangement and a titular evolution which impose on Magritte's works a narrative organization which at once engenders and reinforces a wholly new fictional form. This derived yet invented diegesis is sometimes quite close to the subject matter or title of an accompanying illustration, sometimes so far from the picture that the visual element seems denied, contradicted, decomposed. An example of close *rapport* between picture and plot is Magritte's painting "L'Assassin menacé" [The Threatened Assassin] and its development as the criminal on his own traces which underlines the story of *La Belle Captive* [The Beautiful Captive] as well as that of the other intercalated plots in both *Topologie* and *Souvenirs du triangle d'or*. Astonishingly coincidental, in the manner of the surrealist *hasard objectif*, Magritte's picture (admittedly discovered fairly late in Robbe-Grillet's career) seems already to "illustrate" pre-existing scenes from the author's early novels, films, or short texts. The killer pursued, watched, threatened: Mathias in *Le Voyeur*, Johnson in *La Maison de rendez-vous* [*The House of Assignation*], the interchangeable murderers in *Projet pour une révolution à New York* [*Project for a Revolution in New York*], Elias in the film *Trans-Europ-Express*, Alice in *Glissements progressifs du plaisir*, the Magrittian hooded killer of *La Chambre secrète* [The Secret Room], which was dedicated to another painter of similar scenes, Gustave Moreau. The fact that Magritte's picture derives from a scene in Feuillade's 1912 movie *Fantômas* further extends the chain of intertextual assemblage. Such is Robbe-Grillet's insistence on deconstruction that even where he accepts a wide general similarity in decor and plot, as in "L'Assassin menacé," he introduces alterations both large and small. In Magritte's picture, it is the two massive figures armed with cudgels and nets, watching from the sides of the door, who wear bowler hats; in the text, it is the murderer standing beside his victim. The phonograph in the painting is the old-fashioned mechanical type of the "His

Master's Voice'' era; and in the text, an even older one using a wax cylinder. The murdered girl on the divan in Magritte's painting becomes a mere "mannequin assassiné" in the text, diluting the diegetic realism. This constant interaction between text and image becomes a game for the reader-spectator: parallelism and deviation accompany the interplay of visual and verbal codes.

Of equal interest is the presence or absence in Robbe-Grillet's text of actual titles of Magritte pictures. A very few are used in quotation marks, referring directly to an illustration; most, if they are found at all, are worked into sentences and diegetic phrases. Not all of these, in turn, appear in the text proper of *La Belle Captive*: for example, the page of *Topologie* which precedes the beginning quoted passage from the Magritte/Robbe-Grillet work contains a "message" on a crumpled piece of paper reading: "Après les vendanges, l'assassin menacé prendra garde aux oeufs de l'oiseau qui brûle," an amalgam of (forthcoming) titles (after the grape harvest, the threatened assassin) and visual images (eggs, bird on fire) from Magritte. A number of persistent themes used by Magritte prefigure and reappear with an air of inevitability in Robbe-Grillet's narrative: such is the theme of the double. I have discussed elsewhere the many doubles in his early novels and films, relating them to the doubles of such literary predecessors as Poe and Dostoevsky. Magritte himself intercalates and quotes Poe extensively, and in the Poesque painting of the man looking into a mirror at the back of his own head ("La Reproduction interdite"[The Forbidden View]), the allusions to Poe there and elsewhere are reinforced by the presence of a book lying on the mantlepiece before the mirror, "Adventures d'Arthur Gordon Pym." It is especially the double of Poe's *William Wilson* that links paintings of Magritte to many passages in Robbe-Grillet's *Topologie* and *Souvenirs* in which the central narrator pursues one or another double of himself, "le criminel déjà sur mes [sic] propres traces" [the criminal already following me [sic]]. Intertextual assemblage becomes itself a series of mirror images and doublings; again, creative method, textual coding, becomes metaphoric of itself, of its own diegesis.

A final example of the complexities of coding or re-coding to be found in *La Belle Captive*, along with that of the enigmatic valise of the title page (the valise of the criminal-narrator, which does not appear in the picture of that title, but in other paintings of Magritte reproduced in the book), is the initial visual image, "Le Château des Pyrénées," minutely described in the novel's first pages. Research reveals that this picture of an aerolithic falling rock, with a château on its top, contains interrelated references to an early essay by Robbe-Grillet on Raymond Roussel, Breton's edition of Mathurin's *Melmoth* and his preface to that Gothic novel, Gautier's *Les Jeunes-France*, and an 1803 novel erroneously attributed (by Magritte as well as others) to Ann Radcliffe, author of the much admired *Mysteries of Udolpho*. Just as Magritte himself, in later paintings, removed the château and joined the large rock (now fallen) to the image of a woman with a rose, so Robbe-Grillet omits any reference to the château which he had formerly used in his Roussel analysis, and makes an important diegetic linkage with his rose/woman construct. We find in all this a kind of code-within-code operation which could be termed a spiraling *mise en abyme*.

Turning to Robbe-Grillet's fiction involving visual materials from living collaborators, such as Delvaux and Rauschenberg, we move towards a new dynamics of coding, decoding, and re-coding. Robbe-Grillet has described, in interviews and lectures, how the Delvaux section of *Topologie* (which appears with the Delvaux etchings in *Construction d'un temple en ruines à la Déesse Vanadé* [Construction of a Ruined Temple for the Goddess Vanadé], 1975) was produced: each of the 10 "chapters" was first written by the novelist, then sent to the artist, who made his etching and returned it to the writer, who then "transformed" the pseudo-illustration, creating in principle the same kind of interplay of similarities and differences, of reinforcements and contradictions, that the author had established alone in his work with the Magritte paintings. A picture-by-picture, text-by-text, study of *Construction* reveals that Delvaux's etchings do not constitute the kind of "transformation" of Robbe-Grillet's "chapters" that the author had in mind; it is possible to find almost everything that appears in Delvaux's pictures in the texts that precede them, so that the deconstructive generation sought by Robbe-Grillet becomes entirely a matter of his own re-codings, alterations, and departures. Instead of leading Robbe-Grillet towards new elements, Delvaux's etchings cause him rather to abandon specific visual correspondences. Nevertheless, a certain Delvaux atmosphere, doubtless due to the author's familiarity with Delvaux's style and the fact that, after all, the work was to be a kind of collaboration, persists in *Construction* and may be felt in reading the unillustrated corresponding pages of *Topologie*: neo-Roman architecture, reclining nudes, tramway lines, columns, wharfs, beaches, and the like. Just as Magritte's paintings seem like already existing illustrations of Robbe-Grillet, so does a certain neo-baroque, neo-romantic stylistic imagery already present in Robbe-Grillet seem to correspond almost naturally to Delvaux's subject matter and style.

Although stylistic similarities between the works of Rauschenberg and Robbe-Grillet are less evident, they too may be discerned as early non-"intentional" relationships in the case of Robbe-Grillet's use of objects already employed by Rauschenberg. As early as 1963, Marceline Pleynet in *Tel Quel*[9] pointed out possible relations between the Pop Art *chosisme* of the everyday objects of Rauschenberg's "combine" paintings (Coke bottles, chairs, neckties, ladders, and the like) and the minute object-descriptions of Robbe-Grillet's early novels. At the same time, the anti-war collages of bomb-blasted cities, urban blight, and other strongly socially-oriented pictures of Rauschenberg bore, at the time, little if any resemblance to the concerns of Robbe-Grillet. It was, and is, the formal materials used by Rauschenberg that attracted Robbe-Grillet, and a study of the over two dozen lithographs made by Rauschenberg for the joint work *Traces suspectes en surface* [Traces Suspect on their Surfaces] (1972–78), whose written text has been inserted into *Topologie*, reveals borrowings and transformations by the novelist and a lesser number of images created by the artist from materials of a purely verbal nature. A key work used by Rauschenberg in one lithograph, "Construction," is developed by Robbe-Grillet into a central metaphor for the fictionalization of his phantom city; Rauschenberg's familiar objects (wrecked cars, corridors, ruined buildings) are worked into Robbe-Grillet's diegesis. An enormous black bull, with dilated nostrils and bloodstained eyes, emerges from a lithograph and enters the text. Even the three eggs already excerpted from a Magritte picture for *La Belle Captive* occur coincidentally, and not suggested by any text sent to Rauschenberg, in one of his lithographs. Now and then, a written text furnishes material for a lithograph: thus the smoking volcano on page 20. But in general, the interchange between the writer and the artist involves constant transformations and re-codings, corresponding more closely to the compositional method used with less "success" in the case of Delvaux.

Much remains to be done to study *Traces suspectes en surface*, a task made difficult by the non-availability of the expensive book of lithographs and zinc plate written texts. The critic Tony Towle has described the physical and some of the structural aspects of the joint work in a valuable article which reveals how, even at the level of printing and coloration, various codings are involved:

> Rauschenberg's images were created for the book as he has created lithographs before, by transferring materials torn or cut from magazines to lithographic stones. He may alter images, or combine them before transferral. . . . There is an occasional image that exactly coincides with the text—for example, that of an egg, or a bull—but that is not usual.
>
> The crayon and brushwork with which Rauschenberg often enhances his images are themselves master strokes of abstraction. . . . There are three main color themes: red, in the variations of cardinal, lake, and fire; gray, in the form of silver gray, graphite, and blue graphite; of off-white and ocher. . . . There is also some orange, an occasional accent of green, an occasional light blue. A touch of color on one page often foreshadows its more extensive appearance on the next; there are rhythms of contrast and similarity from page to page.[10]

By far the most complicated fictionalization of visual inserts into narrative text thus attempted by Robbe-Grillet is found in a twenty-page section of *Souvenirs du triangle d'or* (pp. 130–150): a tour-de-force in which a dazzling array of image objects taken from the works of Jasper Johns is not only worked into diegetic situations and actions, but is reformed into interlocking relationships between hitherto discrete pictures. Robbe-Grillet supplied his text, as indicated earlier, to serve as a "Catalogue" for a large Jasper Johns exhibit in Paris, and published the text accompanied by reproductions of Johns's works from Michael Crichton's *Jasper Johns*, (Abrams, 1977); readers of *Souvenirs* can use Crichton's book as a readily available visual adjunct to the text. Robbe-Grillet's catalogue bore the title "La Cible" [the target], one of the central sources of images used repeatedly by Johns, and a natural diegetic source for the related fictional episode by Robbe-Grillet. The basic re-coding procedure used by Robbe-Grillet issues from the fact that whereas Johns subjects his image materials to almost unlimited formal variations (numbers overlapping or in separate units, in black, gray, and almost all other colors and arrangements; targets with and without faces and other objects, in many colors), he never interlocks different elements to create structural or metaphoric relationships. Between the twisted coat hanger of one picture and the bent spoon of another, Johns makes no specific connections. Robbe-Grillet, conversely, in diegetizing such elements, animates them in a narrative that brings together, in astonishing connections, almost all of Johns's materials; as the narrator in the *Souvenirs* text says, "tous les éléments . . . sont forcément reliés entre eux" (all elements are necessarily linked with each other). Johns's various number sequences generate narrative circles in which each number takes on coded meanings involving items from other Johns pictures: ale cans, broken mirrors, hand prints, light bulbs, strings ("bout de corde avachi, dit 'du voyeur' dans le rapport" [a length of old string, supposedly belonging to 'the voyeur' in the report]), shoe with mirror on the toe, flashlight, ruler, and other objects become the essential features of the diegesis, as the narrator pursues his complicated description of and escape from the "generative cell" in which he is imprisoned. So persuasive are the intercalations and reinterpretations of Johns's forms that one has the feeling that the painter himself *should have* foreseen all these possibilities. It would be difficult to find a clearer example of the intertextual progress from pre-code (the "real" pop objects, such as light bulbs and coat hangers), code (Johns's paintings and lithographs of Ballantine ale cans and the like), and post-code (Robbe-Grillet's narrative structures incorporating and extending these objects: a sort of "tels qu'en eux-mêmes Robbe-Grillet les change").

Auto-citation, *contaminatio*, *riscritura*, allusions and references to other authors, fictionalization of visual objects, rearrangements and redefinitions, in short all the techniques of generative intertextuality produce in *Topologie* and *Souvenirs du triangle d'or* a veritable *stretto* of coded forms in which appear such "combine materials" as the eggs of Rauchenberg and Magritte, the umbrella of Magritte and Lautréamont's *Maldoror*, the phonograph of *Projet pour une révolution à New York* and of Magritte's "L'Assassin menacé," the circles of Johns's numbers and the time-cell architectures of the narrator's prison in *Souvenirs*, and a vast panoply of old and new Robbe-Grilletian codes involving, in other "generative cells," chains, broken glass, keys, iron beds, bound girls, painter's easels with *mise en abyme* repetitions of narrative sequences, nudes descending iron stairs, fractured doubles, and so on and on. The post-code thereby becomes the state often referred to as post-modernism, with its doctrines and techniques of the anti-referential, the deconstructive: rupture of previous codes, annihilation of meaning, destruction of existing forms. But these negative creative operations lead, as we have seen, to a massive new coding in which meanings reappear and proliferate, since they are transformed into the new constructions themselves. The analytic process thus carries the critic into a new quasi-symbolic forest of intermixed images and texts, among new correspondences of metaphoric and metonymic condensations and displacements, in a domain of new codes of contemporary fiction which look out at the reader/spectator "avec des regards familiers."

NOTES

1. Leenhardt, J. *Lecture politique du roman: "La Jalousie" d'Alain Robbe-Grillet* (Paris: Minuit, 1973).

2. *Glissements progressifs du plaisir* (Paris: Minuit, 1974) has not yet been translated into English. My translations of passages cited.

3. *Topologie d'une cité fantôme* (Paris: Minuit, 1975); tr. J. A. Underwood, *Topology of a Phantom City* (New York: Grove, 1977).

4. *Souvenirs du triangle d'or* (Paris: Minuit, 1978), *Recollections of The Golden Triangle*, tr. J. A. Underwood, (London: Calder, 1984).

5. "Nommer un objet, c'est supprimer les trois-quarts de la jouissance du poème qui est faite du bonheur de deviner peu à peu: Le suggérer, voilà le rêve." Mallarmé, "Réponse à une Enquête" (1891).

6. "Alphabet of the Stars, à propos of Boulez' *Pli contre pli: Portrait de Mallarmé,*" *New Yorker*, March 20, 1978, 130–138.

7. (Fredericton, N. B.: York Press, 1979); cf. "Constructional Appendix," pp. 79–80.

8. *La Belle Captive* (Lausanne and Paris: La Bibliothèque des Arts, 1975).

9. No. 13 (Printemps 1963), 68–69.

10. Tony Towle, "Rauschenberg: Two Collaborations—Robbe-Grillet and Voznesensky," *The Print Collector's News Letter*, Vol. X, No. 2 (May-June 1979), 37–41.

X.

PRODUCTION, RECEPTION, AND THE SOCIAL CONTEXT

Patrice Pavis

Sign production: some theoretical problems

That theatre begins with a script which culminates in stage presentation is self-evident. Yet some scholarship in the semiotics of drama has taken as its premise the unity of the sign and the final product (performance) as a collection of signs. This approach does not reflect the development of signs and sign series, which starts with the writing of the text and ends with its vocal and visual emission by the actor. To forget that production stems from diverse sources and rhythms (including, for example, isolated signs such as lighting or costume, or complex signs with several levels such as plot or character), is to oversimplify signifying systems, and to fail to account for performance as a hierarchically structured entity. Moreover, the attention given to particular signs taken out of context fragments the performance and often leads to the naïve realist illusion that these signs are given in the theatre with their referent actualized on the stage and that it suffices, therefore, to examine them in isolation without relating them once more to the whole signifying structure from which they have been extracted. This "referential illusion" (that we see the *referent* of the sign, when, in fact, what we have before us is only its *signifier*) is the basis for the spectator's pleasure (seeing the real world represented before him). But this same referential illusion is the root cause of the theoretician's dissatisfaction (seeing the sign confused with reality). This misunderstanding results from a confusion of several levels of reality. Ingarden,[1] for example, suggests the following three categories:

1) Objects discursively referred to. Those not shown on stage, except "negatively," by their absence, and by the emotive impact they may have on what is made visible (actors, decor, etc.). Such "objects," then, are never made tangible; their function is to convey signifieds and their significance is the link between them and the visible action of the play.

2) Objects shown directly (actors, props)—not discursively referred to. To a large extent it is they that trigger the referential illusion, for the playgoer, like the theoretician, is convinced that such objects are the referents of the theatrical sign, or are both referents and signs.[2]

Now, from a semiological point of view, this kind of object is not the referent of a sign, but the signifier (tangible element) enabling one to reconstruct signified object X or character Y. We shall see, on examining the relationship between the sign and the world, that the *referent* is very closely linked to the signifier through the signified. But it is not the referent that we actually have before us on stage.

3) Objects discursively referred to and shown on stage. Here again, we get the impression of *being in the presence of* a stage referent which actualizes the referent of the linguistic sign. A common error is to assume that stage production, or *mise-en-scène* (literally, 'putting-on-stage,' namely, putting-on-view) consists solely in showing the referent of the text. This is where illusion reaches its peak, for it may seem that the stage is the exact referential translation of the referent spoken about in the text. In fact, in both categories of objects (shown and evoked), we have a sign whose signifier is present. The object/table that is seen and spoken about interests the spectator only insofar as he "semiotizes" it, by transforming it into a sign. What is perceived on stage, be it a "real" object or discourse about such an object, is not a referent but a signifier, the illusion of a referent. In the theatre *everything* is real *except* reality. Everything, including stage machinery, colours, forms, actors; *except reality*, since reality is transformed into signs as soon as it appears on stage.[3]

The spectator is thus the victim of a *referential illusion* when he thinks he sees Hamlet, his crown, his madness, whereas he perceives merely an actor, a stage prop, and the simulation of madness. In this kind of communication by ostension, therefore, it is not the referent of an object which is shown, but simply "an element of the class of objects to which it belongs."[4] As Evelyne Ertel rightly points out: "whether the stage object (a term which includes everything—human beings, stage sets, movements—produced on stage) is frankly a sign or pretends to be real, its fundamental status as a sign is not modified, only its ideological and aesthetic function varies."[5] Thus the referent is not actualized; it is fiction that we take to be real. Theatre (in the Western mimetic tradition) could be defined as a reality that the audience continually transforms into signs. One could invert Anne Ubersfeld's happy turn of phrase used to define theatre semiologically: "un référent (un *réel*) qui fait signe"[6] [a referent (a *reality*) which makes a sign], and say that theatre is also *un signe qui fait réel* [a sign which seems real].

Does this mean that everything becomes a sign on stage? This is Evelyne Ertel's position in the wake of Saussure, whose thinking had a profound impact on the Prague Circle (especially Mukařovský, Honzl, and Veltruský). For Anne Ubersfeld, however, the stage should not be regarded as a total "mise-en-signe" [putting-into-signs]. Referential elements are still left (stage objects, and so forth) which are signs of nothing more than themselves, with the result, as Ubersfeld puts it, that "the concrete theatrical sign is both sign and referent."[7]

As I have tried to show, what is seen on stage, then, is not an actualized referent, but the *illusion of a referent*. Furthermore, the stage is perceived in two distinct modes which constantly overlap:

1) *Fiction*: character, plot, illusion, and consequently a semiotic system formed by coherent groups of signs.

2) *The real world*: the awareness of an actress's body, real stage, stage lighting, a space we share with the actors, and so on. Here the spectator refuses to cooperate by exchanging his real world for the fictional world that the actors offer him. He sees only real objects which have not been semiotized and translated into signs. This naïve mode of reception is obviously not "prohibited"—it is the prerogative of children and distracted persons, and it is conceivably one of the pleasurable sensations experienced by the spectator.

The fiction/real world dichotomy has nothing to do with the sign/referent distinction. What we are dealing with is the contrast between 1) the *possible fictional world* of an illusion created by systems of signs, *versus* 2) the *real world* in which we, the members of the audience, with our particular desires and powers of perception, exist.

The complexity of the semiotics of drama (just like the pleasure of the spectator) stems from the interplay between these two worlds. In fiction we always find, strung together, bits and pieces of our own reality and of our psychological and social universe. Identification with a character or with an ideological situation is thus possible only on the basis of lived experience. Curiously enough, it is ideology— through the phenomena of recognition and eroticism (the combined effects of familiar reality and the actor's body)—which attracts us and draws us into the spectacle. Hence ideology and the social context superimpose, on the fabric of a work of art, a living trace of the *spectator's* reality. In the ideology given form by the artistic sign, just as in the body lent by the actor to his character, there is always a "physical residue" which cannot be semiotized and which Anne Ubersfeld calls "L'être-là de l'acteur" [the actor's physical presence]. It is first and foremost this body and the living and unpredictable person that we have before us. The "physical residue" could, for example, be the pretty legs of the actress which have an erotic effect on me; it will also be, on an ideological plane, what I recognize in the fiction that corresponds to my own ideological situation. Thus it becomes necessary, in order to understand the fiction offered, to compare the *possible world* of the dramatic universe with the *real world* of an audience, at any given moment of reception. It would thus seem that in considering the production of the sign and determining its meaning, attention needs to be refocused on the problem of reception and on a comparison between the sign and the ideological universe of the receiver. The sign cannot therefore be taken as a self-contained entity; it is necessarily to be interpreted as a unit forming part of a discursive and ideological whole.

It follows that the theatrical sign does not refer to a visible and isolated referent. Its meaning is contingent on a discursive construct. Discourse has become a major preoccupation of linguistics, for it was soon realized that Saussure's distinction between language and speech did not hold when the meaning and usage of words in the linguistic system had to be defined, and that the meaning of a word depended on a concrete speech (discourse) situation: "It is in discourse," remarks Émile

Benveniste, "that language is formed and takes shape. That is where all language begins. As the classical saying has it: *nihil est in linguo quod non prius fuerit in oratione.*"[8]

This semiological principle of an exchange between a system (language) and speech (discourse) is fundamental for the semiology of art, in which every element of the message derives its meaning from its context in the whole in which it appears. This is true of every sign produced in a text or in a performance. The sign is subordinate to the social and historical situation of its use. Benveniste called this relation between the sign and the exterior world *semantics* (as opposed to *semiotics*, the interrelationship of signs): "With semantics we enter into a specific world of meaning which is engendered by discourse. . . . The semantic order is identified with the world of enunciation and the universe of discourse."[9] This entails decoding *theatrical* signs not only structurally, in their internal relationships with other systems of the text and performance, but also *semantically*, that is, from the perspective of their discursive and ideological context. Mukarovsky's semiological model will help illustrate how meaning (the *signified*) is produced, beginning with the *signifier* and passing through the "total context of social phenomena" (the discursive referent). His model (fig. 1) will enable us to synthesize modes of production and reception in the light of some major existing theories.

I shall be concentrating here on two aspects of production and reception: concretization, and ideology and text theory. Is the exclusion of the element that connects text and stage, the production of textual and stage signs and their reception by the audience? (Needless to say, this is a vast problem in itself, which would require an appropriate theory of fiction to account for the ambiguities and multiple possible readings of the same text, as well as the staging of spatial, temporal, and actantial aspects of a playscript.)

The diagram, which divides artistic communication into production and reception, should first be read vertically, starting with the four main columns which include the main theories of production and reception: (1) formalism, (2) sociology of contents, (3) aesthetics of reception, (4) the theory of speech acts. The distinction between (1), (2) and (3), (4) is determined by the function of the sign. *Production* will entail examining the sign with special emphasis on its signifier, by establishing syntactic oppositions (formalism), or by focusing on its signified and its reference to reality as expressed through the work of art. For *reception*, the determining factor is the relation between the sign and its user; in other words, the pragmatic dimension. The aesthetics of reception is concerned with the way the reader (or spectator) receives signs. The theory of speech acts (which will not be discussed here) examines the ways an utterer produces meaning by analyzing utterances in the context of their use.

1A) Emphasis on the signifier and the syntactic dimension led to a *formalist method* concerned exclusively with the functioning of signs within a closed system. A distinction should be made between two kinds of formalism: the first, stemming from the Russian Formalists, with a focus on literary forms and their evolution, and the attempt to determine the specific properties of the literary text (literariness)

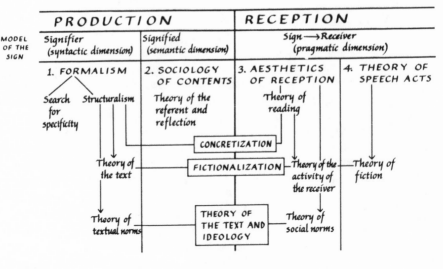

Figure 1

or the dramatic text (theatricality), by comparison with so-called ordinary language. Its failure was to be foreseen, given that no account was taken of the pragmatic criteria of the circumstances of usage of a text.

1B) The second mode of formalism, *structuralism*, has been far more fertile, for it has (sometimes) succeeded in opening the text to history. The semiological variant of structuralism (the Prague Circle, for instance), has even managed to produce a model integrating, with a certain degree of flexibility, the reader or the spectator.

2) These two modes of formalism developed as a reaction against a sociology of contents centred on *the signified*. This sociological approach, informed by the social and psychological circumstances of literary production, nevertheless always lacked a theory of the text (which stems from structuralism), leading thus to a dead end, all the more regrettable for having blocked a Marxist theory of literature, which might have been more exacting than a simple doctrine about the way reality is reflected in a work, or about ideology as an inextricable jumble or false consciousness.

3) With regard to *reception* and the pragmatic dimension of the sign, methodologies which normally reject production theories have evolved recently, privileging phenomenology (Ingarden), hermeneutics (Gadamer) and especially "Rezeptionsästhetik" (the Konstanz School—Jauss and Iser in particular).[10] This reversal, although necessary in view of the stagnation of traditional aesthetics, has tended sometimes to adopt too unilateral an approach by confining itself, for example, to the effect produced on the audience to the exclusion of the techniques that triggered a particular reception. Nevertheless, reception studies have provided useful theories regarding the different levels of reading and the history of effects produced (*Wirkungsgeschichte*), reader response, as well as social and literary accounts of literary history.

In what follows, my purpose will be to build bridges among the four production and reception theories briefly outlined by utilizing in each case elements common to all four. Three links will be emphasized (see fig. 1): 1) *Concretization*—structuralism, in its very opposition to the theory of the work as reflection, can be taken as a theory of reading and therefore as a structuring of dramatic and stage material by the spectator. 2) *Fictionalization*—the theory of fiction, stemming from studies on convention, possible worlds, and rules of fictional discourse, can be confronted with the structuring activity of the reader, who himself organizes narrative material according to a theory of the text, structuralist in origin. (This problem will not be dealt with here.) 3) *The Theory of the Text and Ideology*—brings together a theory of the text (as devised by various semiologists) and a theory (which has not yet been fully articulated) of the relationship between the text and discursive and ideological structures.

Reception and Concretization

We have so far observed the inadequacies of two theories. In the one, the sign is inward-looking and autonomous; in the other, on the contrary, the sign surreptitiously becomes the referent. Ideally, both pitfalls should be avoided. To achieve this, a semiological model is needed which transcends Saussure's binary system and offers a mediation between the sign and the social reality in which it is produced and received. Mukarovsky's concept of ''art as a semiological fact'' provides an excellent starting point. Mukarovsky distinguishes between the artifact (the signifier), the aesthetic object (the signified), and the ''relation to the thing signified'' in these terms:

> ''Every work of art is an autonomous sign composed of: 1. an '*oeuvre-chose*' (a work of art as a thing) which functions as a tangible symbol; 2. an 'aesthetic object,' lodged in the collective consciousness and which functions as meaning or 'signification'; 3. a relation to the thing signified; this relation aims not at a separate existence—since it concerns an autonomous sign—but at the total context of social phenomena (science, philosophy, religion, politics, economy, etc.) of a given milieu.''[11]

Mukarovsky's semiology, going beyond Saussureanism, is concerned with the production and reception of a work of art (literary, or if theatrical, a dramatic text, a performance or specialized aspects of theatrical form such as the stage, dialogue, stage signs, and so forth). Production and reception occur as follows: a) perception of the artifact, namely the signifying substance and structure of the work: whether it be the text heard, a lighting effect, or a gesture, the ''*oeuvre-chose*'' is first perceived as a tangible symbol; b) in order to be assimilated (endowed with a signification ''lodged in the collective consciousness'') in its capacity as signified, the signifier must first be located by the receiver (reader or spectator) in the ''total context of social phenomena'' (hereafter designated as the *Social Context*). The sign therefore acquires its signified (its meaning) only after contact with the social context of the work and its receiver (interpreter). The aesthetic object (the meaning of the work of art) thus comes into being only after the sign (whose signified is so far only approximately determined) is linked to Social Context. At the end of this process, as we shall see, the *"oeuvre-signe"* (the work of art as a sign) becomes a specific aesthetic object or concretization.[12] The latter is a particular reading of the work more or less clearly objectified (in a commentary or series of reactions). To be explicit, the concretization itself must be reconstituted. In the theatre, the director concretizes his reading of a play through his production (a "concretization of a concretization"), while the spectator engages in a "concretization of a concretization of a concretization." In order to *read* the text produced, the spectator experiences a dramaturgical reading, then the director's stage reading (or, if the latter does not yet explicitly exist, the production). In practice it is not possible for the spectator to differentiate between the reading of the text by the director (its first concretization) and the latter's work of stage transposition (its second concretization). This is not important, though. What counts is the result—the work as produced on stage. Reading a production, reading theatre [*Lire le théâtre*], to borrow Anne Ubersfeld's expression, means reading a visual performance as well as reading a theatre director's reading of a playscript.

The most complex phase of signification and concretization is the linkage with the Social Context. Suffice it to say here that this includes: 1) the content of the work (as well as elements referred to therein in various ways), and 2) the social and ideological link with the receiver performing the concretization. This link determines and elucidates the content of the work. Linkage with the Social Context enables the receiver to construct the imaginary referent of a work and its fictional world; this, in other words, is the process of fictionalization.

It follows that a work is neither a single 'correct,' signifying structure, nor an infinite number of amorphous possibilities; rather, it assumes meanings which are historically differentiated according to changes in the Social Context. Consequently, the structuring of a work results not from formalist games, but from the awareness of a change in the Social Context of reception.

Thus for the first time, perhaps, it is possible to assert with Mukarovsky the structural and therefore the formal significance of social and ideological awareness. Structuralism and ideological content are therefore not incompatible, but may be linked dialectically, thereby shedding light on the whole of the production/reception dimension of a work. This is close to the position of Adorno, who placed even greater emphasis on the dialectical tension between a work and society: "The immanence of society in the work is the essential social relationship of art, not the immanence of art in society. Because the social content of art is not established externally in its *principium individuationis*, but is inherent in individuation, itself a social element, the social essence in art is hidden, and can only be grasped by interpretation."[13]

Let us return briefly to the fundamental difference between the artistic sign and the linguistic sign as devised by Saussure (fig. 2). In the Saussurean model, the linguistic sign is defined only as the unbreakable bond between a signifier (the sound) and signified (the concept); the referent is not taken into account at all,

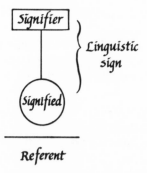

Figure 2

except insofar as it is seen as identical to the signified. The referent is detached, and so created and named, by the linguistic division, and follows in "the wake of the signified." Saussure claims that the relationship between signifier and signified is arbitrary. Benveniste corrects this assertion by showing that "what is arbitrary is that one particular sign rather than another is applied to a given entity rather than to another."[14] The break which takes place is therefore between the sign and the referent; there is no relationship of motivation (necessity or iconicity) between the world and the sign. Benveniste posits two types of sign relationship. The connection between signs within a system he calls *semiotic*, and that between the sign and its referent, *semantic*. Saussure's theory does not require a third term for the sign, the referent, since the latter is constructed by the division of the sign. Whether it is "real" or discursive, the referent is never more than an extension of the signified. Furthermore, the referent is constructed and stabilized by the practice of language. Its existential dimension can be verified by the concrete relationship between us and the world.

The artistic sign, and consequently the semiology of art, cannot be based simply on the linguistic model. In fact, the artistic sign (be it literary, theatrical, cinematic, architectural, etc.) is not initially given as a recurrent unit already detached from the continuum of the work and clearly divided up into signifier and signified. For a work to become meaningful, the artistic sign can only be defined by a receiver external to the work and thus belonging to (Mukařovský's) Social Context, in fact, to the referent. The latter is created by fiction; it has no existential value. Hamlet's court or a scene represented in a painting do not exist as such, as an autonomous external world. They are no more than a referential illusion. Nonetheless, it does have close links with the reality of the Social Context (our real world). This is why the artistic sign always has a motivated rather than a "mimetic" link with the referent of the Social Context (even in the case of abstract art, music, or concrete poetry). The motivated link, however tenuous, is never broken. A cow, whether it is represented by a photograph, a drawing by Picasso, or even the gestures of mime, always has something to do with the cows we come across daily—quite simply because we can identify the cow in the photo, picture, or gesture on the basis of our experience or knowledge. From his vantage point in the Social Context, the receiver perceives in the signifier forms, colours, sounds, material elements to which he can give meaning.

Unlike the linguistic sign (which is already isolated and determined by a code and an accepted convention, grammar), the artistic sign must be identified and extracted from a work of art by the receiver. Obviously this cannot be achieved without reference to the work of art itself, which contains signifiers linked to the Social Context, and specifically, to ideology. The latter is thus not the content "above" or outside the work, but a semiotization or codification of the referent in the form of discursive practices. Ideology is therefore "textualized," absorbed into the work in the form of a discursive referent. A reciprocal process then occurs from the Social Context (the referent) to the signified. Thus defined, the sign becomes the concretization of the work, with the result that a specific signified (or concretization) corresponding to a given response on the part of the reader/spectator can now be associated with the signifier.

Figure 3 illustrates the process.

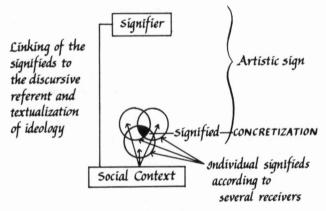

Figure 3

Textualization of Ideology

I now come to the central problem to be examined here: the infiltration of ideology into a literary work and its textualization. The fictionalization that occurs in reading any text provides the links between the text and Social Context. In order to construct the possible world of a text, we must refer to our own real universe. Any theory of ideology or of the ideological must necessarily examine the make-up of the Social Context. By "ideological" I do not mean a closed system of (distorted) ideas about the world, but rather a characteristic of the text on a par with the autotextual and the intertextual. The ideological is not limited and locatable like a theme at a specific point in a literary text, but present at all levels, especially in a text's structure, form, and materiality. The ideological is a mediating force between production and reception, between the text and social context, as well as between literary *form* and social *content*.

It is, of course, very difficult indeed to determine the precise nature of the relationship between ideology and the artistic text. Rather than oversimplify a complex problem, my remarks will be confined to a textual and semiotic analysis of ideology, the latter thus being firmly anchored in dramaturgical and stage materiality. Any reflection on ideology must begin with Marxism and the *camera obscura* in which ideology is glimpsed as false consciousness and a mystification of social relationships: "Consciousness can never be anything but the conscious Being and the Being of men is their process of real life. And if, in the whole of ideology, men and their relationships appear in an upside-down position as in a *camera obscura*, this phenomenon results from historical being, in exactly the same way as the reversal of objects on the retina results from physical being."[15] This inverted image, linked, according to Marx, to the ideological domination of the middle class, has become the unique and universal characteristic of ideology seen as "false consciousness" (Lukacs) or even, significantly, as the hallmark of all literature, since the literary text is defined (by Étienne Balibar, for example) without any concern for nuance, as "the *operator* of a reproduction of ideology in its entirety."[16] A typical Marxist standpoint. Thus it seems that Marxist aesthetics often limits the role of ideology to that of gamekeeper in the economic domain of the middle class. Even France Vernier, whose work represents a notable advance in Marxist literary theory, restricts dominant ideology to the role "of helping to maintain the power of the dominant class as part of the complex and contradictory processes whereby capitalism strives to reproduce the production relationships necessary to it."[17] The purpose of ideology, the enslavement of others for the benefit of one class, has been taken for granted for a long time; it still remains to be seen whether this is its sole function and above all why it is so effective and so difficult to eradicate from man's consciousness and from the literary text. The conceptual figures of the traditional theory of ideology (the distorted reflection, the inverted image, darkness and obscurantism, and so forth) do not use visual metaphors innocently. This is the confusion that a modern theory of ideology can avoid with the help of a semiological system whose focus could be the signifying structure of text or stage. It is thus possible to eschew the nebulous vision of the text as a slavish reflection of the social element or of a specific ideological allegiance. Ideology is, on the contrary, absorbed into the very fabric and structure of the literary text.

The coupling of text to referent is not done directly. It is contingent on a theory of the referent and referentialization that links the text to an ideological frame; it is, of course, the task of the reader or spectator. The theory of reception is therefore particularly well suited to studying the manner in which a literary work acquires meaning by being linked to an ideological discourse extraneous to it. To conclude from this, as does Bernard Valette, that "if there is an ideology, it can scarcely be anyone's but the reader's,"[18] is a step we must be careful not to take, for this would privilege the reception mode to an excessive degree, entrusting it with full responsibility for the construction of meaning. Clearly, though, as we have seen, the work foregrounds the signifier in ways that linkage with the Social Context cannot entirely eliminate.

The coupling of text to discursive referent brings us back to the link between discourse and the world (words and things), and implicitly to the distinction between signifier, signified, and referent. The referent, in my view, not to be conceived of as a real object, is the mediator between words and things.[19] Things do not exist autonomously, but are constructed by discourse. Of course, this does not mean that the external world does not exist and that there is only a maze of words, but that the world is contingent on discourse, needs to be named. Thus, for example, we can identify the object to which the expression *the little blue table near the radiator* refers in the real world; but *a coffee table* only refers if the situation in which this kind of table is used is reconstructed. The referent "coffee table" only means in a specific context of usage; the same applies *a fortiori* to literature. If I read that Orgon hides under the table, I must, in order to understand this utterance, construct in my imagination a fictional world (a story told by Molière) in which Orgon and his table assume meaning. This is true even in the theatre. Orgon's table may be in front of me on stage, yet it is no more real for all that; the table on stage is not the actualized referent, but a re-presentation of what it could be in Molière's fictional universe. (My position is thus diametrically opposed to the frequent argument that theatre, unlike the other arts, represents its referent).

The linking of the text to an ideology extraneous to it is not merely a process of recognition (of the signified); it is, rather, a semiotic mechanism, connecting text to a field of discourse (that is, a discursive referent). As Baudrillard rightly points out, Marxism nearly always has a "mythical" conception of ideology, for it defines it as an extraneous thought content: "The [Marxist] 'criticism' of ideology rests on a magical notion of it. It does not decipher ideology as form, but as content, as a given transcendent value, a sort of *mana* which might attach itself to a few great representations, magically imbuing floating and mystified subjectivities called 'consciousnesses.' "[20]

To understand a text, then, is not to visualize or imagine the realities of which it speaks (a virtually impossible task in many cases), but to link it to the discursive practices in which it is rooted. This is particularly essential when a text mentions things (a palace, a prince, a counsellor) that I cannot comprehend from my solitary standpoint and knowledge of relevant history alone, without referring them to discursive and political practices peculiar, say, to the eighteenth century. But is it enough to refer the reader/spectator to a discursive structure that can be reconstructed from contrastive forms of discourse? Can one, like Foucault, hover between words and things, by confining oneself to a discursive structure to which words refer, without determining their referent?

> From an analysis like the present one, *words* are as deliberately absent as *things* themselves; there are no more descriptions of vocabulary than there is recourse to the living plenitude of experience. One cannot return to the nether side of discourse— where nothing has yet been said and where things can barely be discerned in the grey

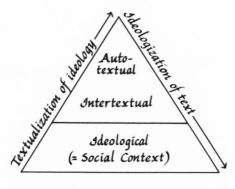

Figure 4

light; one cannot transcend discourse to rediscover forms it has deposited and left behind; one remains, one endeavours to remain, on the level of discourse itself.[21]

"To endeavour to remain on the level of discourse": is this not tantamount to admitting a very precarious balance between two extremes: a closed syntax of discursive mechanics described "from the inside" (constraining the critic and the historian by forcing them to describe the rules of a game whose implications escape them), and a materialist theory of discursive structures (be they economic, political, or infrastructural)? Thus, after taking the one step forward that Foucault hesitates to take (despite the encouragement of his Marxist critics) there is this new pitfall: a materialist and historical theory of ideological relationships.[22]

In the light of the preceding discussion of concretization, fictionalization, and discursive and ideological structure, I propose to delineate some guidelines for the study of ideology in a literary text and beyond it. Between a text and its discursive anchor, several constraints govern the manner in which ideology is textualized and the reader/spectator locates ideology in textual, dramaturgical, and stage forms. Both two-way processes occur simultaneously. 1) *Textualization of the Ideological*: A discursive referent and a given ideology culminate in a specific text, concretized in a signifying structure. This process occurs on two levels, autotextual and intertextual. 2) *Ideologization of the Text*: The linking of text to ideology occurs first on the autotextual, then on the intertextual level, and thus entails a filtering process, culminating in the text in its final concretized form. In figure 4,[23] three levels (ideological, intertextual, autotextual) are apparent; each represents a modalization of the previous one, and thus a semiotic structuring of a given discourse or ideological perception of reality.

1) *The ideological* was examined in detail earlier in the discussion on the discursive referent. This is the first phase of the structuring process. The main object is to link snatches of discourse on the basis of common social practice. The constructed text continues to refer to this as a "they say" level which guarantees textual content.

2) *The intertextual* comprises the various subtexts (verbal as well as visual and

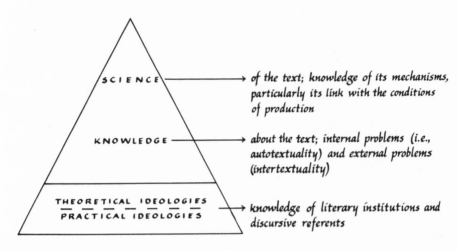

Figure 5

artistic) with which a literary work is (or can be) associated thematically, structurally, or stylistically. The intertextual is both what the text is made up of and
what it is written against. Though invisible at first glance, the intertextual is an
integral part of a literary text.

3) *The autotextual* is the self-contained, self-referential level whereby a text claims
autonomy and adopts the perfectly rounded form of a monad, thus fending off
outside influence, intertextual or ideological. This type of self-referentiality, though
common especially in modern literature, is to be found in any text which calls
attention to the processes it employs. In the theatre, where it takes the form of
theatricality, it is the crux of the illusion/disillusion dichotomy, hovering between
the "real" and the "theatrical."

There is a dialectical tension between the autotextual and the intertextual (and
hence between unity and multiplicity); the artistic text aims either at originality or
at the imitation of earlier models. A second, deep-seated tension is to be observed
between the autotextual, purportedly autonomous, and the ideological, supposedly
universal and pervasive.[24] Thus, surface text itself is no more than the tip of the
iceberg: it is made up of the same "ice" as its self-referential parts and its subtexts,
the whole being linked to ideological roots. It is up to the reader, though, to
"concretize" it. We could superimpose on figure 4 a new diagram (see figure 5),
drawing on theories of Althusser, Foucault, and Lecourt, linking ideology, science,
and knowledge. Some reservations are in order, by way of caution and clarification:
1) The concretized text is comparable to a science for the reader who masters the
mechanisms that control it. 2) Knowledge about the text concerns the autotextual
and intertextual dimensions, which are contingent on the relationship between signifiers and intertext. The "science of the text" stems from this knowledge, which
denotes the activity of the reader in the semiotic process of textualization. 3) Ide-

ology is divided into practice and theory, practical ideologies determining the form and limits of theoretical ideologies.[25] For literature and theatre, institutions (type of theatre, control and circulation of books, etc.) constitute practical ideology and form part of the Social Context and social status of the writer and text.

Figures 4 and 5 illustrate in broad terms the impact of ideology on concretized text; detailed analyses would help ascertain the permeability of the various levels. Ideology infuses a text gradually, but the process only rarely (and usually unreliably) permits identification of an ideological theme. It is located more subtly in the formal properties—in the signifying structure and in passages where autotextuality invites reflection on the means it employs to conceal its ideological origin. In the theatre, the process is exemplified by phenomena such as the Brechtian alienation effect, characters' conflicting points of view, the so-called objectivity of theatrical communication, or theatrical foregrounding (or sign effects).

Ideology thus encourages focus on the *form* of a work of art. This has the immediate effect of enabling the receiver to escape from the autonomous work and to link the text to the discursive referent outside it. Ideology is not located on the "direct" level of content, nor on the level of pure forms, which are meaningless until linked to the Social Context.

Ideology plays the role assigned by Barthes to connotation, which expels from the text secondary signifieds, only meaningful in the context of the referent and ideology: "These signifieds are closely linked to culture, knowledge, history; one could say that through them the world penetrates the system; in short, *ideology* is the *form* (in the Hjelmslevian sense of the term) of the connotation signifieds, while *rhetoric* is the form of the connotators."[26] Thus literary form alerts the reader to what ideology instills into him subconsciously. But ideology is neutralized by literary form as soon as it enters the work of art. For Adorno, this is art's only merit, for it allows ideology to speak through it: "Works of art are great only insofar as they reveal what ideology hides."[27]

Thus the debate between form and content, temporarily rejected, though not eliminated, by structuralism, is reopened. It raises many complex issues, difficult to pursue methodically. If ideology is indeed *the other* in the text (which the text seems to deny) and if as Baudrillard had it, "it is a ruse of form to be continually veiled in the conspicuousness of content,"[28] it is a waste of time to look for forms which conceal other forms. It is, however, the task of unveiling forms behind forms (or, to use Brecht's words, "processes *behind* processes") that we must now pursue in two directions: the textualization of ideology and the ideologization of the text.

NOTES

1. R. Ingarden, "Les fonctions du langage au théâtre," *Poétique* 8 (1971).
2. A. Ubersfeld, "Sur le signe théâtral et son référent," *Travail théâtral* 31 (1978), p. 123.
3. To illustrate the ideological linking of the sign, a simple example will suffice: the

sign /prince/ in a play by Marivaux. For the linguistic sign, like the visual sign (the actor who portrays the prince), there is no direct referent; to understand this term one has to look for its meaning not in the thing, but in the word, or rather, in discursive practice in the eighteenth century and today. It is the discursive referent and the possible context of usage which enable us to determine its meaning. See C. Buzan, "Dictionnaire, langue, discours, idéologie," *Langue Française* 43 (1979), p. 41.

4. U. Eco, *A Theory of Semiotics* (Bloomington: Indiana University Press, 1976).

5. E. Ertel, "Eléments pour une sémiologie du théâtre," *Travail théâtral* 28–29 (1977), p. 147.

6. "Sur le signe théâtral et son référent."t p. 121.

7. Ibid., p. 123.

8. *Problèmes de linguistique générale I* (Paris: Gallimard, 1966), p. 131.

9. E. Benveniste, *Problèmes de linguistique générale II* (Paris: Gallimard, 1974), p. 64.

10. R. Ingarden, *Das literarische Kunstwerk* (Tübingen: Niemeyer, 1931); *Von Erkennen des literarischen* (Tübingen: Niemeyer, 1968). H. G. Gadamer, *Wahrheit und Methode-Grundzüge einer philosophischen Hermeneutik* (Tübingen, 1972, 3rd ed.).

On the "Konstanz School" see R. Varning, *Rezeptions-ästhetik* (München: Fink, 1975); *Poétique* 39 (September 1979), "Théorie de la réception en Allemagne." For an approach to reception in the theatre, see A. Ubersfeld, "Notes sur la dénégation théâtrale," *La relation théâtrale*, R. Durand, ed. (Lille: Presses Universitaires, 1980); P. Pavis, "Pour une esthétique de la réception théâtrale," ibid.

11. Jan Mukarovsky, "L'art comme fait sémiologique," *Poétique* 3 (1970); originally published in *Actes du huitième congrès international de philosophie* (Prague, 2–7 septembre 1934), Prague, 1936, pp. 1065–1072.

12. This theory on concretization, borrowed from Mukarovsky (*The Word and Verbal Art*, tr. John Burbank and Peter Steiner; New Haven & London: Yale University Press, 1977), is developed by F. Vodička who uses Ingarden's term, concretization. The latter is a convenient label for several theatrical concepts including individual readings, dramaturgical analysis, and stage presentation.

13. Th. W. Adorno, *Asthetische Theorie* (Frankfurt: Suhrkamp, 1970), p. 345 (my translation).

14. E. Benveniste, *Problèmes de linguistique générale I*, p. 52.

15. K. Marx, F. Engels, *L'idéologie allemande* (Paris: Editions Sociales, 1968), p. 50.

16. E. Balibar, P. Macherey, "Sur la littérature comme forme idéologique: Quelques hypothèses marxistes," *Littérature* 13 (février 1974), p. 46.

17. France Vernier, *L'Écriture et les textes: Essai sur le phénomène littéraire* (Paris: Editions Sociales, 1974), p. 53.

18. B. Valette, "*Cendrillon* et autres contes: lecture et idéologie," in C. Duchet, ed., *Socio-critique* (Paris: Nathan, 1979).

19. M. Pêcheux, on rereading Althusser, makes this point very clearly: "everything said here about 'words' concerns in fact the entire area of discursive processes, and is *ipso facto* applicable to the most general of expressions, formulations, etc., which happen to represent, in circumstances of varying historical importance, politico-ideological *stakes* . . . (by expressions like 'the oil crisis', 'the dictatorship of the proletariate', 'the purpose of history' . . . or utterances such as 'man makes history', 'class struggle is the mainspring of history')." *Les Vérites de la Palice* (Paris: Maspero, 1975), p. 195.

20. J. Baudrillard, *Pour une critique de l'économie politique du signe* (Paris: Gallimard, 1972), p. 174 (my translation).

21. Michel Foucault, *L'Archéologie du savoir* (Paris: Gallimard, 1972).

22. Althusser seems to warn him of this danger in a long comment in *Positions* (Paris: Editions Sociales, 1976), pp. 124–125. Similarly, D. Lecourt, in his review of *L'Archéologie du savoir*, advises Foucault to quit his intermediary stance "between words and things" and to draw the materialistic conclusions from his descriptions of discursive regularities. See also Lecourt's *Pour une critique de l'epistémologie* (Paris: Maspero, 1974).

23. Figure 4 owes much to Wladimir Krysinski's excellent diagram and analysis of modalization in fiction in his *Carrefours du signe* (Paris & The Hague: Mouton, 1981), pp. 1–75.

24. Cf. Adorno, *Théorie Esthétique* (Paris: Klincksieck, 1974), p. 14.

25. Dominique Delcourt, *Pour une critique de l'epistémologie: Bachelard, Canguilhem, Foucault* (Paris: Maspero, 1974), p. 130.

26. R. Barthes, *Eléments de sémiologie: Le degré zéro de l'écriture* (Paris: Gonthier, 1971), p. 165.

27. Th. W. Adorno, *Noten zur Literatur I* (Frankfurt: Suhrkamp, 1958), p. 77. Adorno arrives at a negative dialectic which opposes art (form) to the social element (content).

28. J. Baudrillard, *Pour une critique de l'économie politique du signe* (Paris: Gallimard, 1972), p. 175.

XI.

POLAND OF NOWHERE, THE BREASTS OF TIRESIAS, AND OTHER INCONGRUITIES, OR REFERENTIAL MANIPULATION IN MODERN DRAMA

Wladimir Krysinski

I.

In the *Poetics*, Aristotle interprets the relationship between the dramatic text and reality as one of dependency. Occurring on several levels, this dependency primarily affects the realization of the dramatic fable (the plot) which in various ways imitates "human actions." One can contend that *logos* (the dialogue) or *lexis* (the expression) supports the dramatic fable (*muthos*) solely to the extent that what is said by a character confirms the logical and referential presuppositions of the dramatic fable (*muthos*). These refer to a given "reality" composed of actions, human agents, and events. Imitation (*mimesis*) is a verbal, structural, and specular linkage between reality and the tragic text. When Aristotle says: "Thus tragedy is the imitation of an action, and of the agents mainly with a view to the action,"[1] or "Tragedy is an imitation of an action that is complete, and whole, and of a certain magnitude," or "Tragedy is an imitation not only of a complete action, but of events inspiring fear or pity,"[2] he emphasizes the need for textual restraint in relation to a world wherein there are actors, completed actions, and past events. Their relation is referential insofar as the action (*praxis*, which supports the *muthos*) occurs as the necessary or probable outcome of what has already taken place.[3]

We may describe the referent in tragedy as a reality represented by the *muthos* and transcribed textually in diction, song, and spectacle. Such transcription is possible, however, solely because there are objects to represent: that is, the dramatic fable (plot), characters, and thought, all related to what has already taken place. In Greek tragedy, the dramatic fable reflects the logical and referential presuppositions of a mythic or real world. Their verification by the spectator is possible insofar as the logical and referential presuppositions are given him by the tragedy in its role as transcriber of representable objects. These objects exist in a mythical and ideological world which the spectator recognizes as transformed; yet, at the same time, as sufficiently referential for the structure of tragedy to be recognizably imitative. Every sign and referent in tragedy partakes of this referentiality. Tragedy necessarily reflects a reality whose referents are already given to the spectator as the relations between the gods and men, and as action and thought.

This referentiality implies a referential solidarity between the characters' thoughts and actions. Antigone cannot say "God does not exist; it is a myth." Likewise, no character in Greek tragedy can say, like a character in Mrozek's *Tango*: "Give me God and I'll make an experimental theater."

II.

In the light of these preliminary (Aristotelian) considerations, the following characteristics of the referent in drama can be delineated:

1. The dramatic fable is doubly constrained. As *muthos*, it must already exist in reality; as *praxis*, it must be textually and structurally transcribed in order to be represented.

2. A referential solidarity exists among the *logos*, *lexis*, and plot, as well as between the actions and systems of referents (mythological, ideological, real).

3. The concept of the referent (as proposed by Frege and applied by Russell, Strawson, Quine, and, in semiotics, by Greimas, for example) allows, within the limits of the drama, a logical and semantical formulation of verbal communication, plot-structure, and function of the characters.

4. The referent has thus a primarily heuristic function, situating the text and its interpretation according to presuppositions implied by referents common to the dramatist and the spectator.

III.

The transition from Aristotelian to non-Aristotelian drama is one of the semiotic programs of the modern theater. Where can the process first be observed? In Victor Hugo or, even earlier, in Shakespeare? Certainly "referential restriction" and "referential solidarity" in modern theater assume specific forms and manifest a range of referential manipulations similar to those of tragedy or Aristotelian drama. In modern drama from Strindberg to Beckett, references to logical and referential presuppositions will be of a different order. They will be subverted by a specifically modern manipulation of the text. The Aristotelian *vs.* non-Aristotelian drama dichotomy is generally equivalent to mimetic and referential drama as opposed to autonomous drama. However, even in the case of a clearly formulated program as in Brecht, dramatic autonomy cannot dispense entirely with reference to reality. In fact, this is especially so in Brecht's case. We refer to him, however, since he introduced the distinction between his own non-Aristotelian drama and traditional Aristotelian drama.[4] Brecht's semiotic activity is autonomous, that is, further removed from the real, as the distancing seems to imply. The epic plot is distanced by the stage manipulation of the message and even of the act of communication, dialectically reflected in the prism of the Distancing-effect (*Verfremdungseffekt*). Between the fictitious plot and the audience, an interpretive space is created which is at once open and restricted. This space is implicitly posed above and beyond catharsis. Here, "verifiable reality" corresponds to a system of values established by the stage's play on distance. In Brecht's theatrical system (semi-realistic compared to that of Ionesco or Marinetti), the referent retains its heuristic function. The spectator must recreate distance, but always in terms of the systems of logical and referential presuppositions of a second-degree reality, rendered dialectical by its ideological and historical prerogatives.

In recent avant-garde (non-Aristotelian) playscripts, the referential mechanism is multiple. Though the real is not altogether dismissed, it is treated allusively and manipulated to serve as one of the subversive components of a theatrical process which will claim its own autonomy.

IV.

In modern drama, the disruption of mimesis occurs through a series of referential strategies that transform the referent into a tool, object and sign of theatrical autonomy.

However, the stage manipulation of the referent is not our main consideration here. Rather, given the complexity and polyvalence of theatrical signs, we will consider a certain number of examples of early avant-garde theater. Plays by Jarry, Apollinaire, Pirandello, the Italian Futurists, and Witkiewicz constitute a sort of semiotic laboratory where theatrical autonomy is developed. Various procedures are used, some more coherent and systematic than others, but each relating the text to the referent.

The concept of referent and of referentialization[5] thus acquires a specific meaning in the theater, in that each text or theatrical system is subject to specific constraints. Thus, our purpose will be to examine the modalities of referential manipulation in the modern theatrical text even before the advent of the so-called "Theater of the Absurd," where referential manipulation becomes a systematic procedure. The latter is probably best exemplified by *The Bald Soprano* in which the relation between sign and referent constantly changes. Ionesco thereby establishes a deceptive model of communication in which signs are deprived of possible referents. Ionesco's purpose is to show how the audience can be semiotically manipulated. The title "The Bald Soprano" has no denotation; the number of times that the text requires the chiming of the clock bears no relation to the time announced by the characters. The dialogue between the Mr. and Mrs. Smith, the citations from the newspaper,

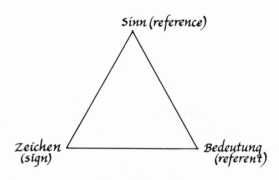

Figure 1

as well as the gratuitous statements of the characters contribute to this deceptive form of communication.

Lexis and *logos* are not linked to what is happening on stage, because the stage action no longer has any meaning. Without wishing to repeat the commentaries on the elements of the absurd in this play, let us sketch briefly what is "produced" in *The Bald Soprano*. Our interpretation will be based on Frege's triangle, the first attempt in modern philosophy to formulate the problem of communication by means of verbal signs.[6] Frege's triangle shows the mental and semiotic mechanisms which render human communication possible and meaningful. Each sign refers back to what it represents (its denotatum), not a particular object but rather, as Umberto Eco has remarked, a class of objects[7] (table, star). However, the *Sinn*, the meaning, is the mode of mental representation of the object, or rather the way in which the object referred to is understood. Frege's often cited example, "morning star" and "evening star," are two *Sinnen* of the same object, the planet Venus.

Frege's system (fig. 1) can help account for referential manipulation of verbal signs. This triangle and its variants in Ogden and Richards, Morris, or Carnap[8] allow us to observe the complexity of the mechanisms of encoding and decoding theatrical messages. Our focus here is confined to messages considered as *lexis* and *logos*, be they dialogical or monological, and related to a system of references which, in each case, requires definition.

V.

To return to *The Bald Soprano*, we observe that the characters speak. What they say does not contain referents common to the characters, readers, or spectators. The tripartite relation between sign, referent, and reference is constantly disrupted by statements which preclude reconstruction, or semantic linkage. Thus, the "dialogue" (in fact non-existent) is based on a series of monological, abrupt, and even laconic statements: a gratuitous verbal performance.

How can one formulate the problem of reference in this series of verbal, non-referential performances? The use of the semantic triangle for understanding what "occurs" in *The Bald Soprano* would have to be based not only on the unities of minimal dialogue, on phrases such as "the bald soprano," but also on the necessity of evaluating the "meaning" of Ionesco's use of the theater since, as we have already noted, the process of referential manipulation culminates in *The Bald Soprano*. It stems as much from a critique of language as from the limited autonomy of the dramatic text. It is comparable to other plays in which the referent and reference are specifically manipulated.

We shall examine the mechanism of this referential manipulation in the relation between title and text before looking at further examples in the play. The title implies a twofold relation: the referential constraint it imposes upon the text, and the title as a function of the text. In the first case, the conventions of production, as well as the habits of reader and spectator of drama, require the title to refer to the text and *vice versa*. This requirement may be due to an implied relation which can be thematic, pronominal, or nominal as in the case of *Antigone*, *Hamlet*, and *King Lear*, or generally thematic, as in the case of *The Tempest*, *Death of a Salesman*, and *Galileo*. The referential relation between title and text is broken in *The Bald Soprano*,[9] as there is no "bald soprano" referent. Reference is made to the title, though, when the Fire Chief asks Mr. and Mrs. Smith: "By the way, what about the Bald Prima Donna?" and Mrs. Smith's reply eliminates the referent through a disruption of the logical relation between "The *Bald* Prima Donna" and "She always wears her *hair* the same way." These contrastive expressions are mutually exclusive. One could contend that the soprano in question is wearing a wig and conclude that sopranos whose hair is not particularly attractive usually wear wigs. This hypothesis is shown to be wrong, as the title, the Fire Chief's question, and Mrs. Smith's reply suggest. An evaluation of the title by the spectator or reader is presupposed, however. Here, we may refer to Jakobson's metalinguistic function. What is the code implicit in the title? Does it supply the spectator or reader with a system of referents and reference which would permit its acceptance? The title is evaluated according to Ionesco's constant referential disruption of the relation between language and reality. The series of empty yet constantly manipulated referents in *The Bald Soprano* entail the creation of a certain referential "fullness." The empty referents such as the title, the statements about the Watson family, or even the running-on of dialogue where the characters haphazardly cite pseudo-proverbs, aphorisms, and sayings such as:

"Social progress is much better coated with sugar." (p. 116)
"I am looking for a monogynist priest to marry our maidservant." (p.116)
"I'd rather slaughter a rabbit than whistle in the garden." (p. 117)
"Sullivan Alfred" (p. 118)
"Tennyson Arthur" (p. 118)

stem from the disruption of a referential relation, neutralization of the referents, a textual positioning of the empty referents, as well as to what we have termed a referential "fullness" of the empty referents. The latter refers to the fact that the

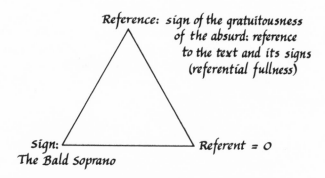

Figure 2

absurdity of the text (and its distorted referential systems) constitutes a new paradigm of the text, in which referential emptiness is functional. It will become re-referential by virtue of the metalinguistic code which the spectator reconstitutes from the theater of the absurd, a certain social function of language and, finally, from theatrical practice in the play itself. The title functions metalinguistically. It refers to a code which refers back to it via the text. The metalinguistic code is thus determined by the constraints of the text.

The Bald Soprano exemplifies a dramatic process, characteristic of the avant-garde text, which systematically disrupts referential and mimetic systems by "referential manipulation." The relation between the signs, referents, and references does not have a logical and referential stability which would permit the receiver to decode messages in terms of the triple elements of the triangles of Frege or of Ogden and Richards: sign, reference to the object of discourse (reality, the class of objects); meaning, as the limitative relation between the object and its differential, verbal representation ("morning star" = planet of Venus; "evening star" = planet of Venus). In Ionesco, this process of decoding can be represented as in figure 2. *The Bald Soprano* may thus be considered an autonomous and self-referential dramatic text. This is so because it uses the artifice of the referential fullness of a language, autonomous insofar as it systematically permits the improbable and the absurd.

Analyzing *The Bald Soprano* as a series of "semiotic experiments," Olga Karpinska and Izaak Revzin show how Ionesco subverts the basic principles of human communication. There are six such principles:

1. The sender and receiver refer to the same reality.
2. The sender and receiver refer to the same world-model.
3. The sender and receiver have a certain "common memory," that is, a certain fund of common information about the past.
4. The sender and receiver make more or less similar predictions about the future.
5. The sender must describe the world in a concise and elliptical manner.
6. The sender must communicate something new to the receiver.[10]

They govern what Karpinska and Revzin call "correct" human communication. They are applicable to the theatre if we assume that the disruption of human communication in *The Bald Soprano*, while eliminating the code, contact, and context according to Jakobson's categories, leaves the metalinguistic code intact. Thus, paradoxically, while human communication is rendered impossible and ironic in *The Bald Soprano*, its disruption focuses theatrical communication through the metalinguistic code.

VI.

Let us now consider some other principles of theatrical communication in the light of the specificity of the dramatic text and its evolution. The modern, dramatic text tends to be autonomous due to its metalinguistic code, which is contingent on referential manipulation and incongruity, a technique common to several of the textual strategies involved. The principle of incongruity, which subverts "correct communication," entails the use of shock, surprise, the improbable, the fantastic, and the absurd. It results in the destruction of mimetic referentiality and the autonomy of the dramatic text.

In examining plays by such authors as Jarry, Apollinaire, Pirandello, Witkiewicz, and Ionesco, we will offer a definition of the dramatic text based on Jakobson's concept of the poetic function. The latter projects a principle of equivalence from the axis of selection onto the axis of combination. The *autonomous* function of the dramatic text disrupts the axis of the mimetic and projects the principle of incongruity onto the axis of the autotelic. The mimetic axis presupposes a referential restriction of the dramatic plot and of the *logos*, *lexis*, actions, and systems of referents shared by dramatist and spectator. The autotelic axis entails disruption of the principles of "correct communication." It is coextensive with the performance, whose referents are manipulated by the text because of their emptiness.

These categories become clearer when applied to avant-garde authors cited earlier.

VII.

Thus, Jarry's *Ubu roi* (King Turd) exemplifies the principles of incongruity and referential manipulation. In *Ubu roi* we find:
1. The use of the empty referent: Poland.
2. The discursive manipulation of the elements specific to the empty referent.
3. Ubu-speak ("Le parler Ubu") as a referential manipulation.

Our concept of the empty referent can be compared to the position taken by Michel Arrivé, which maintains that the literary text has no referent, or rather that it has a "simulacrum of a referent":

> A text such as *Ubu roi* is sandwiched between the comment that 'the scene takes place in Poland, that is, Nowhere' and the final sentence 'If there were no Poland,

there would be no Poles,' where the word 'Poles' functions as a sign of the text whose subtitle it is (*Ubu roi ou les Polonais*).[11]

While "Poles" is indeed a sign, it entails textual and referential manipulation. That is to say, Jarry manipulates the referent "Poland" in order to disrupt its denotative (as opposed to connotative) reference. For *Ubu roi* to exist as a system of autonomous signs, the referent "Poland" must exist prior to the text. The empty referent is contingent on the full referent "Poland." For, when Jarry states: "As to the action which is about to begin, it takes place in Poland—that is to say, nowhere,"[12] he presupposes a system of reference which must account for 'Poland' as well as 'Poland = nowhere.' In the first case, he must manipulate the "Polish" elements both discursively and referentially. In the second, he must neutralize them. Thus he says:

> The curtain rises on a set which is supposed to represent Nowhere, with trees at the foot of beds and white snow in a summer sky; the action also takes place in Poland, a country so legendary, so dismembered that it is well qualified to be this particular Nowhere, or in terms of a putative Franco-German etymology, a distantly interrogative somewhere.[13]

And also

> Nowhere is everywhere, but most of all it is the country we happen to be in at the moment. And that is why Ubu speaks French. But his assorted vices are reinforced by Captain Bordure who speaks English, Queen Rosamund who gabbles away in double Dutch, and the Polish masses talking through their noses and all dressed in gray. Certain satirical elements may be evident, but the play's setting relieves its exponents from any responsibility.[14]

Hence the associative and connotative chain Poland → Nowhere → Distantly Interrogative Somewhere → Everywhere → the country one happens to be in at the moment. This connotative chain implies complete topological indeterminacy, yet it underscores the incongruity which has become the organizing principle of the text. Poland-as-Nowhere thus displaces geographical and historical "Poland."

We agree with Michel Arrivé that the literary and theatrical text has no referent, because Poland, which is the same as Nowhere, Somewhere, etc., does not exist. Yet, at the same time, Poland as referent makes referential manipulation possible. In *Ubu roi*, the principle of incongruity depends on referential manipulation. The continuity of drama and narrative in *Ubu roi* is provided by the exploits, deeds, and gestures of Ubu. Incongruity is a form of textual extravaganza that discards referents such as Poland or denotative language (whence "*merde et finance*" becomes "*merdre et phynance*").

The geographical and historical referent "Poland" is emptied of its own reference in *Ubu roi* by the confusion of names and facts. In the first case, we have a series of Polish or so-called Slavic names: King Wenceslaus, Queen Rosamunde, and their sons Boleslaus, Ladislaus, and Bougrelas. Neither Rosamunde nor Bougrelas are Polish names. Functionally they render everything absurd, unreal, and incongruous. Judith Cooper has aptly pointed out:

> The sound of the names seems to be of primary importance rather than any specific historical reference. Their foreign sound would automatically seem comic to French ears. And once more we notice the repetition of sounds in all four names which increase the comic effect. The most important character of the four is Bougrelas and his is the most unusual of the four names. It is nothing more than a derogatory epithet with the Slavic-sounding ending -*las*. A hero with such a name could not possibly be taken seriously, just as no audience could sympathize with a character named Bordure.[15]

The first name Bougrelas (Buggerlaus) is a sign without a referent, or rather a sign-index which feigns the existence of a referent. It thereby becomes an autonomous textual sign which evolves thus: empty referent → textual sign → referential fullness.

Besides these Polish or pseudo-Polish names, there are some historical Polish names in the play: Jan Sobieski, Stanislas Leczinski, Nicholas Rensky, General Lascy. The latter have human referents, but they contribute nonetheless to incongruity, given their historical and geographical context but unreal and absurd situation. Jan Sobieski, King of Poland (1673–1696), is one of King Ubu's soldiers, killed in the battle with the Russians. Stanislas Leczinski, King of Poland in the first half of the eighteenth century, is none other than the peasant from whom Ubu wants to extort taxes. We shall examine more closely the case of this peasant who bears the name of a king of Poland. At the time of his reign, Leczinski was well known in France, where he was governor of the duchies of Barrois and Lorraine. Leczinski lived in Nancy; Place Stanislas was named after him. Marie Leczinska, his daughter, was the wife of Louis XV. All these facts, familiar to the educated Frenchman, are references which Jarry manipulates and renders inoperative.

In act II scene iv, the following conversation takes place:

> Papa Turd: Which one of you is the oldest? (A PEASANT steps forward.) What's your name?
> The Peasant: Stanislas Leczinski.
> Papa Turd: Well then, hornstrumpet, listen carefully or these gentlemen will cut off your years. So are you going to listen to me?
> Stanislas: But Your Excellency hasn't said anything yet.[16]

Given the status of the referent "Leczinski," what is said can be analyzed in the two models shown (figs. 3 and 4).

The autonomy of the text is the result of referential manipulation emptying the normal referent of its verifiable, existential, and historical content, thereby displacing even the historical truth.

When in act III scene ii, Ubu requests that someone state his heritage, the following list is given:

> The Herald: Principality of Podolia, Grand Duchy of Posen, Duchy of Cortland,

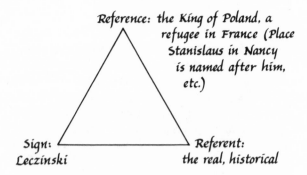

Figure 3: Semiosis I (historical, real)

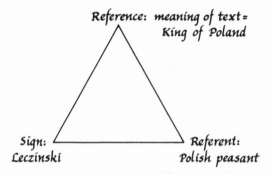

Figure 4: Semiosis II (textual autonomy)

Earldom of Sandomir, Earldom of Vitebsk, Palatinate of Polackia, Margraviate of Thorn.[17]

Given that the action of *Ubu roi* takes place in Poland as well as nowhere, this list must be construed as a referential manipulation of geographical and historical data, despite some correct references. No Poland, in fact, can serve as referent for this list, or match the geographical and administrative names or the historical Polish, Russian, and German references.

Because of the incongruous mixture, this list seems exotic to the French reader. Ubu-speak (*"Le Parler Ubu"*) creates incongruity insofar as it is repetitive, energetic, excessive, and vulgar, yet also fundamentally non-referential. It is composed of recurrent lexical items: *merdre, phynances, croc à merdre, cornebleu, cornegidouille*, etc. If they are connotative and nonreferential it is because they are composed of phonemes, syllables, and keywords whose referents are emptied of reality.[18] This mechanism produces textual autonomy. The action of *Ubu roi* does not take place in Poland or "Nowhere," but upon the stage where the drama is enacted.

VIII.

In *Les Mamelles de Tirésias*, Apollinaire also claims to create theatrical autonomy. His play bears a resemblance to Jarry's, though the text is more varied,
being a surrealistic theatrical scenario and a vaudeville. *Les Mamelles de Tirésias*
mingles the improbable with the comic, the surrealistic with music and farce. The
internal and external referentiality accentuates the essential theatricality of the characters, as well as the pomp of the stage-setting. The continuity of the text does not
seem to stem from the narrative but seems accidental and based on the mixture of
dialogue and song. *Les Mamelles de Tirésias* shows a twofold metamorphosis:
Thérèse becomes a man (Tirésias) and the husband becomes the wife. The result
is a series of *quid pro quo* that makes the stage performance self-referential due to
the displacement of the tripartite relation of sign, referent, and reference. The double
metamorphosis is linked to, or rather generated by, the metalinguistic code, which
can be defined in the exact terms of the Director of the Troupe in the Prologue:

> The great unfolding of our modern art can join, without any apparent connection as
> in life, sounds and gestures colours, cries, and clamour music, dance, acrobatics,
> poetry and painting, Chorus, action and varying decors
>
>> You will find here the actions which accompany the main drama and
>>   embellish it
>> The changes of tone from the pathetic to the burlesque
>> The prudent use of improbabilities
>> As well as the actors, collective or not,
>> Who are not necessarily part of Humanity
>> Nor of the whole universe
>> For the theater must not be an art of illusion
>>
>> It is fitting that the dramatist use
>> All the tricks at his disposal
>> . . . .
>> Right that he should make the hoard of inanimate
>> objects speak
>> If it pleases him and that
>> he should take no more account of time
>> Than space.[19]

In his preface, Apollinaire insists upon the autonomy of the theater whose goal is
"to amuse and interest." Yet he says of his play that "its aim is the highlighting
of a vital question for those who hear the language in which it is written: the problem
of repopulation."

There are thus two referential levels: 1) verifiable reality: France is becoming
depopulated, the number of births has diminished; and 2) stage "reality," which

is non-verifiable and surrealistic according to Apollinaire's definition. The text mixes the two levels in accordance with the principle of incongruity.

The double metamorphosis operates thus: Thérèse → Tirésias; husband → wife. In both cases there is a transition from a probable referent to an autonomous stage sign, which also serves as the pretext for the creation of a specific referent, namely the woman changed into a man and *vice versa*. In fact, this double metamorphosis also creates comic stage sequences, songs, and wordplay. The metamorphosis is thus a semiotic operation with syntactical and semantic consequences. Syntactically, it creates a series of actions and stage gestures; semantically, it transforms the real referent of the first level—a woman (Thérèse) and a husband, etc.—into stage signs. This transformation, then, is the outcome of referential manipulation. The transformation of real characters into stage signs is better illustrated by the breasts of Tirésias which need further examination.

Referentially, the breasts stand for the feminine attributes of Thérèse. They are represented somewhat negatively because Thérèse loses them and gradually changes into a man:

> Oh, now it seems a beard begins to appear?
> And now my bosom's disappearing.
>
> (She partially opens her blouse from which her breasts fly out, one red and the other blue, and as she loosens them they fly away. They are children's balloons which are held back by strings.)
>
> Fly fly away Oh birds of woman's weakness
> Aren't they lovely things such lovely lovely things?
> Sweet delicate charms
> Full delicate charms
> Aren't they lovely things
> Aren't they lovely things[20]

The sign-referent-reference triad is thus disrupted. The breasts represent femininity solely on condition that they form part of the woman's body, thereby serving as the referent for the sign "breasts."[21] The reference of the sign "breasts" is sexuality, attractiveness, and maternity. In *Les Mamelles de Tirésias*, the sign "breasts" is severed from its reference and referent. The text operates a stage materialization of the breasts, which change into children's balloons, a materialization which is, in fact, meta-textual. Thus, the breasts in the text are no longer those of a woman, or even of a man (Tirésias); they become autonomous stage sign-objects created through incongruity, and the paradoxical title. In fact, *Les Mamelles de Tirésias* is a sign which no longer corresponds to any real referent. Tirésias, a masculine name, cannot be given feminine attributes. Tirésias, in the play, is Thérèse changed into a man, but he is also a stage character. As such, Tirésias is a stage-sign, an empty referent (metamorphosed woman, deprived of her attributes, a man-woman) transformed and reequipped with referential fullness as the "*mamelles de Tirésias*," that is, as neither man nor woman, but text. Apollinaire's strategy is to detach the sign from its referent and reference and to allow the text its autonomy. This consists of a play upon words, leading to verbal breakdown, of song and gratuitously referential stage operations. Apollinaire thus creates an autotelic text through the use of incongruity.

An excerpt from scene vii of the first act illustrates the principle of incongruity as well as textual autonomy:

The People of Zanzibar, the Policeman, the Husband

(dressed as a woman)

The Policeman: The duellists of the landscape will not prevent me from saying that
 I find you
As pleasant to touch as a rubber ball.

The Husband: Ah choo. (A dish breaks.)

The Policeman: A cold is exquisite.

The Husband: Atchi. (Drums. The husband lifts up his skirt which is bothering him.)

The Policeman: Shameless woman. (He winks.)
 What matter, she's a beautiful girl.

The Husband: My he's right
 Since my wife's a man
 I must be a woman (bashfully to the Policeman)
 I am an honest woman-man
 My wife is a man-woman
 She has taken the piano, the violin, the butter-dish.

The Policeman: she is "*mère des cygnes*"
 Ah! how they sing, those who are going to perish
 Listen. (Bagpipes, sad air.)[22]

The device used is phonic echo which creates autotelic effect. The connecting elements are: caoutchouc → atchou → exquis → atchi → femme-monsieur → homme-madame → merdecin → mère des seins → merdecine → mère des cygnes. The stage signs have no real referent or simulacra. The breakdown of the mimetic coincides with the enhancement of the autotelic.

From Jarry to Apollinaire and Ionesco, the autonomy of the theatrical text is contingent on an intensified use of incongruity and the emptying of referents and references of their real content, a process culminating in *The Bald Soprano*. Two other theatrical processes should also be mentioned, and are exemplified by Pirandello and Witkiewicz. Both strive for theatrical autonomy, Pirandello through the subversion of the mimetic text, Witkiewicz through his theory of "Pure Form in the Theater."

IX.

Six Characters in Search of an Author is structured on various levels of reality,[23] which we shall call referential as in the case of *Les Mamelles de Tirésias*:

Level A: that of the characters. Here we must further distinguish sublevels, since each character represents an "idiosyncratic code."[24]

Level B: that of the author.

Level C: that of the actors.

Pirandello's play is generally taken to be "a play about the impossibility of drama."[25] It presupposes three referential levels and is based on a specific referential manipulation which consists of pushing "referential conflict" to its limit. This presupposition is a trap set by the dramatist, part of his semiotic strategy which allows him to dramatize and dedramatize the melodramatic situation of the characters. Pirandello's strategy is thus an attack upon the mimetic signs of Aristotelian theater of representation. These signs are: the characters representing personages or human beings, the actors signifying consonance between the roles they play and their referents, and, finally, the author (whose stage equivalent is the director). The latter functions in the text as a mimetic sign insofar as it is a textualization of the real; here the dramatic fable functions both as *muthos* and as *praxis*. Each of the referential levels thus corresponds to its mimetic sign, which Pirandello highlights, but also renders ineffectual.

The first referential conflict occurs between level A and level B. For the author, the characters seeking to be represented by the stage script are signs without fixed references. Moreover, they are psychologically unfathomable and, in the narrative, their accounts are confused and contradictory. The six characters are signs of a melodrama; their only referents are their bodily presence. If their confused and contradictory lines reflect the wish to identify the drama, the characters evidently cannot agree about its meaning. The discussion between the Father and the Beautiful Girl is a play on various references: who is the Father in relation to the whole family? Why has he come to Madam Pace's house? what relation exists between the Father and the Beautiful Girl? These questions are present, explicitly or implicitly. Their constant recurrence creates a tense conflict between the characters and levels B and C, precluding a mimetic representation of the conflict or of the story of the six characters. Nor can the actors perform something confused, exaggerated, and indeterminate. There is thus a referential struggle between the ideas which the characters have of themselves and the implicit postulates of mimetic theater as defined earlier.

The Father's soliloquy on consciousness ends with the conclusion of the impossibility of self-knowledge and even of communication among levels A, B, and C.

> *The Father*: For the drama lies all in this—in the conscience that I have, that each one of us has. We believe this conscience to be a single thing, but it is many-sided. There is one for this person, and another for that. Diverse consciences. So we have this illusion of being one person for all, of having a personality that is unique in all

our acts. But it is not true. We perceive this when tragically perhaps, in something we do, we are, as it were, suspended, caught up in the air on a kind of hook.[26]

This soliloquy allows us to define one of Pirandello's principal thematic structures; the multiplication of "I"'s and the dissolution of the stable personality. This can be linked to the sign-referent-reference triad as in the model shown (fig. 5).

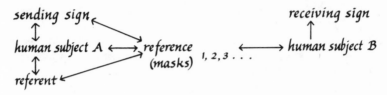

Figure 5

The same human subject A as the sending sign of his "I," in confrontation with human subject C as the receiving sign, will use other references (masks). Thus, the schema of failed communication is shown in figure 6.

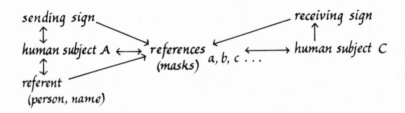

Figure 6

This model of failed communication can be applied to real human interaction and referential conflicts. Such as Pirandello's conclusion, despite the constant attempts of his drama to demythify human communication and the meaning of being for others.

The following dialogue excerpt exemplifies referential conflict (common in Pirandello) between level A and level C.

The Manager: Now, look here! On the stage, you as yourself, cannot exist. The actor here acts you, and that's an end to it!

The Father: I understand. And now I think I see why our author who conceived us as we are, all alive, did not want to put us on the stage after all. I have not the least desire to offend your actors. Far from it! But when I think that I am to be acted by . . . I don't know by whom . . .

Leading Man: (on his dignity). By me, if you have no objection!

The Father: (humbly, mellifluously). Honored, I assure you, sir. (Bows.) Still, I must say that try as this gentleman may, with all his good will and wonderful art, to absorb me into himself . . .

Leading Man: Oh chuck it! "Wonderful art!" Withdraw that, please!

The Father: The performance he will give, even doing his best with make-up to look like me. . . .

Leading Man: It will certainly be a bit difficult! (The actors laugh.)

The Father: Exactly! It will be difficult to act me as I really am. The effect will be rather—apart from the make-up according as to how he supposes I am, as he senses me—if he does sense me—and not as I inside of myself feel myself to be. It seems to me then that account should be taken of this by everyone whose duty it may become to criticize us.[27]

Two signs are at odds here: "to play" and "to represent." For the Father, "to play" and "to represent" refer to being unique, personal, unrepeatable. For the Leading Man, "to play" and "to represent" signify imitating, feigning.

In *Six Characters in Search of an Author* sending and receiving signs do not share common references. The play ironically reduces the problem of mimetic, Aristotelian drama to the sole function of signs (the soliloquies of the characters, the dialogue of the actors and director) involved in referential conflict. Mimetic theater's signs fail as vehicles of communication. It is not so much theatrical communication, as we saw in Jarry, Apollinaire, and Ionesco, that is at stake in the semiotic practice of Pirandello, as metatheatrical communication. Pirandello questions the stability of references in mimetic theater, whose premises are the permanency of character and personality, the linear development of plot, and the exchange and functional harmony of the textual roles, imitated reality, and the actor-agents of mimetic stage representation.

Six Characters in Search of an Author is thus a spectacle composed of signs which have been detached from the ordinary reference presupposed by the dialogue. The referents of the signs are there; they are the characters and actors in person. Yet this in no way insures referential solidarity between *logos* and *muthos*. What Pirandello calls *commedia da fare* therefore fails to occur. Pirandello's critical and ironic discourse is akin to a scalpel which dissects the living body of mimetic theater, revealing the artifice of mimetic communicaton, the basis of the narrativity and dramatic representation.

X.

The theoretical propositions of Witkiewicz center on his theory of "Pure Form in the Theater." This "Pure Form" must, by analogy with abstract painting, be an abstraction. That is to say, it must liberate itself from a dependency on reality or what Witkiewicz calls "vital meaning." However, Witkiewicz admits that this "vital meaning" can never totally disappear. He thus envisages a whole series of possibilities and combinations in which the actions and dialogue can exclude each other without depriving each action or statement of its "vital meaning." Witkiewicz proposes the following schema:

    a) actions in accordance with the dialogue and having a vital meaning;

    b) actions not in accordance with the dialogue;

    c) actions in accordance with a dialogue which does not have a vital meaning;

    d) a complete division between actions and dialogue without meaning, and dialogue without meaning.[28]

In this system, the semiotic triad reflects both the manipulation of the referent, the real (vital meaning), and the construction of a new formal referent, namely, the materiality of the stage signs as well as the development of the spectacle. The formal referent combines with the stage signs. In this combination, though, there is no reference other than that of "Pure Form." The problem of theatrical autonomy is therefore represented by Witkiewicz both as incongruity (referential "distortion," to use Witkiewicz's term) of empirical reality, and as the self-referent of the self-reflexive spectacle. It can be represented as in figure 7.

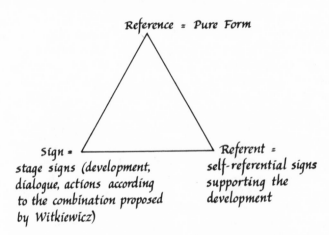

Figure 7

Crucial metalinguistic elements are in this way incorporated into the theory of "Pure Form." In modern theater, this theory, along with that of Artaud, is perhaps the most consistent and complete. It is not, however, devoid of ambiguity, and Witkiewicz himself implicitly acknowledges this. Theater, as he puts it, cannot divest itself of human presence or human speech. The development of the drama requires both gesture and narrative even though these may be presented as absurd.

The self-referentiality of the spectacle is contingent on signs which are, so to speak, semi-referential. The dialogue and actions may embody a "vital meaning," but not because of the development of the spectacle. "Pure Form" in Witkiewicz's theater is an obsessive caricature of the real on which it depends. There is a discrepancy between Witkiewicz's theory and practice insofar as he holds that the abstraction of painting can be realized upon the stage through the development of spectacle and through the combination of actions with referential and non-referential dialogue. Yet his theater, as caricature of the real, is particularly dependent upon verbal fullness. It is only in theory that the text of the spectacle attains a certain purity of stage signs which focus the spectacle through the incongruity of gesture, dialogue, and narrative. Witkiewicz's concept of ''Pure Form in the theater'' is exemplified by the following description:

> Three characters dressed in red enter the stage and greet one knows not whom. One of the characters recites a poem (which must appear at this moment as indispensable). An old man with a gentle appearance enters leading a cat on a leash. All this takes place in front of a black curtain. This opens and reveals an Italian landscape. Organ music is heard. The old man addresses one of the characters already on stage, saying something in line with what has already preceded. A glass falls from a table. Everyone drops on their knees and weeps. The old man changes then into a wild deer and assassinates a little girl who has just entered on stage from the side of the garden. At this, a handsome young man interrupts, thanking the old man for the crime he has just committed and the characters dressed in red begin to sing and dance. After this, the young man weeps near the corpse of the little girl, saying very funny and cheerful things. The old man assumes his original appearance of a mild and good man and laughs in a corner, saying things simple and sublime.[29]

Continuity is contingent on constant interchange of gesture and word, a series of discrete entities detached from all reference to a reality in which logically justifiable actions occur and in which words adhere to these actions.

XI.

In the modern dramatic text, therefore, reference to the real is manipulated, with the aim of subverting the latter or subordinating it to the principle of incongruity. The process stems in part from the use of empty referents as well as from their transformation on the stage, where they become self-referential signs.

The autonomous signs of drama, as defined above, are relational signs. They are the product of a distancing from reality, and of a conflict or series of conflicts among the signs, referents, and reference.

The modern drama script thus achieves autonomy through a modification of the semiotic triangle in which the tripartite solidarity and continuity are no longer determined by a reality understood according to logical and mimetic parameters.

NOTES

1. Cf. Aristotle's *Theory of Poetry and of Fine Art*, translated and with critical notes by S. H. Butcher and a New Introduction by John Gassner (New York: Dover Publications Inc., 1951), p. 29.

2. Op. cit., pp. 31 and 39.

3. Cf. op. cit., pp. 39–40: "A Complex action is one in which the change is accompanied by such Reversal, or by both. These last should arise from the internal structure of the plot, so that what follows should be the necessary or probable result of the preceding action. It makes all the difference whether any given event is a case of *propter hoc* or *post hoc*."

4. See, for example, the series of studies collected in "Sur une dramaturgie non-aristotélicienne 1933–1941." References are to the French edition of Berthold Brecht's *Écrits sur le théâtre*, I (Paris: L'Arche, 1963), 1972.

5. The concept comes from A. J. Greimas and J. Courtès in their *Sémiotique, dictionnaire raisonné de la théorie du langage* (Paris: Hachette, Université, 1979). They define referentialization as follows: "The problem which arises when one considers the discourse from a generative point of view is not that of the referent given *a priori*, but of the referentialization of the statement which implies the examination of the procedures by which 'referential illusion'—the 'reality' or 'truth' meaning-effect proposed by R. Barthes, is established." Pp. 312–313; my translation.

6. See "Sinn und Bedeutung" written in 1892. We translate *Zeichen* by "sign," *Sinn* by "reference," and *Bedeutung* by "referent"; we are using this terminology in conformity with the practice of certain French semioticians, such as Michel Arrivé, to whom we refer in our analysis of *Ubu roi*.

7. Cf. Umberto Eco, *Segno* [Sign] (Milano: Enciclopedia filosofica ISEDI, 1973), p. 25.

8. In analysing the sign as an element in the process of communication, Umberto Eco (op. cit.) includes in the triangle the different terms which correspond to Peirce's use of Frege's sign, referent, and reference ('object' for referent, 'interpretant' for reference), in Ogden and Richards ('symbol' for sign and 'reference' for reference, that is, the *Sinn* of Frege), in Charles Morris ('signifying vehicle' for sign, 'denotatum' for referent, and 'designatum' or 'significatum' for reference). In Carnap's terminology 'extension' corresponds to referent and 'intension' to reference.

9. We cite *La Cantatrice chauve* [*The Bald Soprano*] in the translation of Donald Watson; Eugène Ionesco, *Plays*, volume I (London: John Calder, first published in 1958); the numbers in parentheses refer to this edition.

10. Cf. Olga Karpinska and Izaak Revzin, "Expérimentation sémiotique chez E. Ionesco (*La Cantatrice chauve* et *La Leçon*)," *Semiotica IV*, 3 (1971), 240–262.

11. Cf. Michel Arrivé, "Postulats pour la description linguistique des textes littéraires," *Langue française* 3, (septembre 1969), p. 6 (my translation).

12. Cf. Alfred Jarry, *King Turd* [*Ubu roi*], translated by Beverley Keith and G. Legman (New York: Boar's Head Books, 1953), p. 13.

13. Cf. *Ubu roi*, the article written by Jarry for the program issue of *La Critique* for the Théâtre de l'Oeuvre, and distributed to the audience on the first night. In *Selected Works of Alfred Jarry*, edited by Roger Shattuck and Simon Watson Taylor (New York: Grove Press Inc., 1965), p. 79.

14. Cf. ibid., p. 79.

15. Cf. Judith Cooper, *Ubu roi: An Analytical Study*, Tulane Studies in Romance Languages and Literatures, no. 6 (New Orleans: Tulane University Press, 1974), p. 47.

16. Cf. Jarry, *King Turd*, p. 47.

17. Op. cit., p. 42.

18. Cf. the very detailed analysis of "le parler Ubu" by Michel Arrivé in his *Les langages de Jarry: Essai de sémiotique littéraire* (Paris: Klincksieck, 1972); cf. especially "Essai de description du métalangage jarryque" and "Dictionnaire d'*Ubu roi*," pp. 43–113; 165–307.

19. Cf. Apollinaire, *L'Enchanteur pourrissant suivi de "Les mamelles de Tirésias" et de "Couleur du temps"* (Paris: Gallimard, 1972), p.114.

20. We cite, only for this passage, the English translation of Robert Goss in *Les Mamelles de Tirésias*, opéra-bouffe en deux actes et un prologue, Poème de Guillaume Apollinaire, Musique de Francis Poulenc (Paris: Au Ménestrel, Heugel et Cie., 1970), pp. 17–18.

21. We exclude, for the moment, the fact that in phantasmic structures of the libido and of fetishism the breasts can be regarded as what Freud calls a "partial object."

22. Cf. Apollinaire, *Les Mamelles de Tirésias*, Gallimard, pp. 130–132.

23. Cf. Gérard Genot's comments in his *Pirandello* (Paris: Seghers, 1970), pp. 59–60.

24. See W. Krysinski, "La dislocation des codes, l'accroissement des récits et la brisure de la représentation dans *Six personnages en quête d'auteur*," *Études littéraires*, No.3, 1980, p. 501 (my translation), in which the point was made that "The discourse of the Father and of the Beautiful Girl refer to the personal, subjective codes which one can call idiosyncratic codes which disrupt the stability of the 'sub-codes' such as those of *ethos*, *dianoia*, and *hamartia*."

25. Cf. the chapter "Speil von der Unmöglichkeit des Dramas" in *Theorie des modernen Dramas* by Peter Szondi (Frankfurt am Main: Suhrkamp Verlag, 1963).

26. Cf. Luigi Pirandello, *Six Characters in Search of an Author*, English Version by Edward Storer, in *Naked Masks; Five Plays by Luigi Pirandello*, edited by Eric Bentley (New York: Dutton, 1952), p. 231.

27. Cf. op. cit., pp. 244–245.

28. Cf. S. I. Witkiewicz, "Précisions sur la question de la Forme Pure au théâtre," in *S. I. Witkiewicz* (Paris, *Cahiers de la Compagnie Madeleine Renaud-Jean-Louis Barrault*, Gallimard, no. 73, 1970) tr. Koukou Chanska and Jacques Lacarrière; p. 56.

29. Cf. S. I. Witkiewicz, "Théorie de la Forme Pure au Théâtre", op. cit., pp. 27–28 (my translation).

XII.

THE REFERENTIAL ACT

Thomas E. Lewis

No one shall ever develop a theory of literary referentiality. The present renewal of concern with "referring in literature" promises less the possibility of explaining such a process than the creation of new reading practices that break with dominant twentieth-century assumptions in the West about the nature of literary textuality. Diversity of approach to this problem signals an eagerness on the part of critics professing various methodologies to enter a domain of inquiry that, until recently, they happily left to the occasional philosopher and a handful of Marxists. Indeed, the once welcome notion that "literary" texts identify themselves by being "self-referential" now appears overly to constrain critics in their accomplishment of scholarly and pedagogical goals. A legitimation of referential studies within the academy, therefore, may first be understood as a symptom of general dissatisfaction with a particular ideology of the aesthetic.

Attention to literary referentiality, however, should fully permit a break with aesthetics as such. In its present stage of elaboration, this attention will never succeed in doing so. Even as the aesthetic of self-referentiality is laid to rest, discussions of "referring in literature" widely reproduce the enabling premise of the older notion: namely, that processes of "literary" signification differ from other processes of signification. Despite the collapse, even within Russian Formalism, of distinctions between standard and poetic language, the idea that literature constitutes a mode of signification *sui generis* dies hard. Thus, at the same time as an understanding of literature as solipsistic is repudiated, inquiry into literary referentiality often preserves an assumption of literary essence. This assumption in fact hinders analysis of "referring in literature" because it imposes upon such effort the traditional concerns of epistemology.

I shall not rehearse here the arguments that have convinced me of both the impossibility of an intrinsic definition of literature and the unworkability of the epistemological categories upon which such definitions depend.[1] I can, however, illustrate how underlying epistemological interests muddle thinking about referentiality. When reading *The Odyssey*, for example, readers encounter the epic, a genre which, for Roman Jakobson, "strongly involves the referential function of language," even as it displays the dominance of the poetic function.[2] Significantly,

Jakobson does not attempt to collapse the poetic and referential functions of epic into one special function: that of "poetic referentiality." By implication, he considers that analysis of the referential function in texts dominated by the poetic function would follow the same semiotic procedures as analysis of referentiality in texts dominated by any of the functions, including the referential function itself. Despite his famous contribution to defining aesthetic function through its "self-referential" impulse—insofar as an essentially "self-focussing" message is constituted—Jakobson never suggests that, in poetic texts, the properly referential function of language undergoes metamorphoses so strange that it thereby acquires new methodological status.

But most of us today would tend to discuss the referential function of *The Odyssey* under the auspices of that mulish term, "literary referentiality," which Jakobson so carefully avoids. Here it happens that epistemology can begin to mislead analysis of referentiality in two ways: first, with respect to the object of representation, and second, with respect to the determinacy of representation. Assumptions about literary referentiality often extend so far as to posit a specifically "literary" referent, that is, a referent that differs from other possible kinds of referents as a result of the special use of language through which it is constructed. Implicitly or explicitly, a claim is made that there exists a unique *object*, to which only aesthetic perception affords adequate access; thus, aesthetics becomes a mode of cognition in its own right. When critics endorse the notion of a "literary" referent, therefore, they admit something important and deny it in the same instant. In the admission, literary signification is seen as an effect of reference to the world. In the denial, properly "literary" signification is seen as the effect of aesthetic cognition alone. Whereas cultural meaning constitutes the object of representation in the admission, intrinsically aesthetic meaning constitutes the object of representation in the denial. So it is that, from a referential point of view, an epistemological approach to the object of "literary" representation paradoxically recuperates textual meaning for aesthetics and throttles attempts to ascribe textual meaning to the world. Here arises a second understanding of the present interest in referentiality: while embodying the potential to inspire a vigorous cultural criticism, study of referentiality is often too readily accommodated to the institutional discourse of literary specialization.

Not everyone concerned with literary referentiality, however, upholds the existence of a specifically "literary" referent. Some critics acknowledge that referents signified by "literary" discourse may be signified by "nonliterary" discourses as well. Although all referents now enjoy the same methodological status, literary signification is still considered as a special semiotic; hence, the task of criticism is to distinguish a specific mode of referring in literature from other possible modes of referring. Pursuit of this task usually assumes a broadly tripartite division of signifying modes into denotative semiotic (standard language), connotative semiotic (literary language), and metasemiotic (scientific language).[3] Even this more moderate essentialism, however, can prompt an injudicious approach through epistemology to study of the determinacy of representation in literature. By "determinacy of representation," I do not mean consideration of specific techniques of sign production through which texts that are conventionally regarded as "aesthetic" manage to generate meanings. Classification of certain techniques as "aesthetic" varies historically and in relation to developments in several cultural spheres; "aesthetic" sign production can be, and often is, studied historically and not epistemologically. Rather, by "determinacy of representation," I mean consideration of the modality of a literary text taken as the sign of an object that it determines. For the moment, as in the preceding paragraph, I am equating the notion of the "referent" with that of an "object" that is determined by representation.

Epistemological concerns trouble this consideration when an *origin* is sought for the connotative meanings engendered by literature. Traditionally, critics have conceived of the literary text either as a connotative sign that is undercoded with respect to the object that it determines, or as a connotative sign that is overcoded with respect to the object that it determines.[4] In the first instance, the referent of literary representation surfaces as a social text that constitutes the conditions of literary *production*; in the second, the referent of literary representation surfaces as a social text that constitutes the conditions of literary *reception*, or interpretation. The referential text of *The Odyssey*, for example, may be considered either as a set of contemporary perceptions or representations in function of which Greeks lived the experience of an immense social revolution (ca. 750 B.C.) that powered the transition of their civilization from its Dark Age (1200–800 B.C.) to its Archaic period (800–500 B.C.), or it may be considered as a set of culturally coded representations of problems or values that persist into our own era and which comprise the basis, though not necessarily the identity, of modern apprehensions of the text. To the first manner of conceiving of the referent apply such terms of literary criticism as "conditions of possibility" (Macherey), "ground" (Peirce), "invention" (Eco), and "referential subtext" (Jameson). To the second manner of conceiving of the referent apply such terms as "resymbolization" (Bleich), "gap" (Iser), "interpretant" (Peirce), and "symbolic order" (Lacan).

No doubt this seeming exclusivity of referential perspectives is unwarranted. Conditions of both production and reception play a part in constituting the "object" that is determined by literary representation, and several of the critics whose vocabulary I have just cited take due notice of this phenomenon. Any epistemological approach to the determinacy of representation in literature, however, demands such exclusivity. To submit literary referentiality to a determinacy *of origin* requires predication of a denotative semiotic—a social text of either productive *or* interpretive conditions—in relation to which literature stands as a connotative semiotic. Now there is, of course, no such thing as a denotative semiotic, but this objection alone remains insufficient to restore deserved complexity to the question of the determinacy of literary representation. Indeed, only abandonment of the notion of origin can accomplish this end. Once origin has been abandoned, however, the notion of determinacy itself shifts perceptibly in the direction of that more fruitful notion of the *overdeterminacy* (or overdetermination) of representation in literature. Here a determinacy based on articulation of systematic relationships eventually replaces a determinacy based on predication of direct (whether mediate or immediate) causality. The referential text of *The Odyssey* may now be constructed as the site of a complex, even contradictory, conjuncture of multiple conditions of writing and reading.

To structure a theoretical terrain without recourse to origins does allow critics to account more adequately for the variety of objects determined by literary representation and their relations. It also suggests what an epistemological approach finally conceals about literary referentiality itself: "the function of the concept of origin, as in original sin, is to summarize in one word what has not to be thought in order to be able to think what one wants to think."[5] Most of us concerned with literary referentiality want to think that we can specify determinate referents for the literary texts we read. In order to do this, we often isolate one or another origin of literary signification that serves as ground and anchor of textual meaning. A third insight, therefore, into the present concern with referentiality is that, with the successive demises of authorial intention, decidable language, and competent readers as guarantors of literary intelligibility, we seek to discover still another inviolable sanctuary of literary meaning. Yet our search remains possible for only so long as we continue to think of literary referentiality as something that occurs, rather than as something that *is made* to occur. To abandon myths of origin makes analysis of referring in literature no longer an epistemological but an ideological and political enterprise.

Fulfillment of what I do not hesitate to call the political vocation of referential studies depends precisely on judgments made as to the nature of both the determinacy and the object of representation in literature. A notion that "literary" signs, like all signs, are governed by inference can foster an understanding of the determinacy of literary representation such that referentiality is perceived as an *activity* of intertextual inscription. A notion that "literary" meanings, like all meanings, are comprised by cultural units can suggest a definition of the object of literary representation such that referentiality is perceived to involve the social commerce of *ideologemes*.

The "literary" text, taken as a sign of an object that it determines, cannot be thought of as obeying its own rules of sign. The notion of an intrinsically "literary" sign rests on the spurious claim of being able to isolate specifically literary connotators in texts.

> The analysis of connotators may help describe a text, any text, but it could never ascertain that text's literariness, for we would search in vain for the specific connotators of literature. A text can be attributed to the category of literary objects only if one resorts to purport, to extralinguistic reality, which means to explanations of a sociological, psychological, and ethnological kind. In practice, I must again repeat, only a sociocultural investigation can tell us whether or not a text is to be considered literary in a given age and by a given audience. Naturally, this is so of all kinds of connotators because every connotator must be referred to a content-purport once the analysis has shifted to the metasemiotic of connotative semiotics. (Di Girolamo, p. 63)

In fact, the "literary" does not constitute a connotator at all. The appearance of those connotators that critics often consider as distinctive of literary discourse is by no means limited to texts that are said to belong to literature; rather, "the literary 'overtones' we might observe in some signs or sets of signs are the result of a combination of connotators which, when taken individually, do not qualify as 'literary,' but, for example, as 'archaic,' 'learned,' 'dialectal,' 'figural,' etc., which are connotators common to everyday speech, scientific language, and the like" (Di Girolamo, p. 63). Even consideration of styles and genres fails to provide sufficient reasons to establish the "literary" as a connotator. Various studies reveal that so-called "literary" structures inform as well the conventions of composition, and often of interpretation, of texts classified as historiographical, religious, philosophical, scientific, and political. No semiotic reasons exist, therefore, that warrant a view of the governance of "literary" signs as inherently different from the governance of signs in general.

Nevertheless, if the literary text, taken as a sign of an object that it determines, must obey the general rules of sign, it is erroneous to invoke a linguistic, or Saussurean, model of sign in order to explain the determinacy of representation in literature. The notions of the arbitrariness and biconditionality (signifier/signified) of sign finally construct signs as "bastions of identity, equivalence, and forced unifications."[6] Indeed, if the relation of signs to the world seems duly problematic for Saussure, the relation of signifiers to signifieds seems unduly secured:

> From this perspective, the sign, ruled by the law of definition and synonymy, represents the ideological construct of a metaphysics of identity in which signifier and signified are biconditionally linked. By opposition, textual practice would consist in a challenge, a denial, a dissolution of such a rigid and misleading identity. Texts are the necessary liturgical ceremony where signs are sacrificed at the altar of significance, of *la pratique signifiante*. (Eco, "Theory of Signs," p. 38)

Yet, in Eco's view, the polarity created here remains false; signs can be analyzed as texts, and texts can be analyzed as signs. The wedding of a theory of language to a theory of sign, which produces the polarity between signs and texts, is a historical, not an ontological, fact. The history of this rocky marriage has exercised a debilitating influence precisely on study of the determinacy of representation in literature. For the view promoted by the linguistic model (that signs and texts differ) is really only applied to alleged differences between linguistic signifiers and textual signifiers. The linguistic model still assumes that attribution of textual meanings to textual signifiers proceeds on the basis of relations of equivalence between textual signifiers and textual signifieds. Thus the effect of extratextual determinations of meaning is denied.

Far from entertaining relations with their objects that can be specified by a problematic of identity/nonidentity, however, texts maintain relations to their objects that are specified by an inferential model of sign based on abduction. Abductive signs do not depend on relations of equivalence with their own meanings ($p \equiv q$), but, from the point of view of a theory of communication, on inferences ($p \supset q$) anticipated as probable by sign producers, and, from the point of view of a theory of signification, on inferences actually made by sign interpreters. Like deduction and induction, abduction represents an activity of synthetic inference; it distinguishes itself from other inferential modes insofar as it involves reasoning from a specific result, to formulation of a law, and, finally, to formulation of a case.[7] With respect to literary texts taken as signs of referential objects, abduction suggests that readers infer from a given text the existence of a world whose laws and processes enable the text to be interpreted (or naturalized) as a statement about that world. Thus, any textual sign, or sememe, "must be analyzed and represented as a *set of instructions* for the correct co-textual insertion of a given term" (Eco, "Theory of Signs," p. 43). So it is that referentiality in literature, like referentiality in all types of discourse, surfaces as an activity of *intertextual inscription*.

Only through recognition that literary texts are governed by inferential rules of sign can discussion of the determinacy of representation in literature begin to take place without recourse to essentialist assumptions involving one or more metaphysics of identity. To pose the question of the determinacy of literary representation is also to ask, "How do texts constrain meaning?" Eco, of course, devotes much space in his writings to discussion of how texts attempt to program certain readings within themselves as part of their own process of production. That this concern betrays a residual essentialism becomes quickly evident in such phrases as "*the correct* co-textual insertion of a given term" (my emphasis). Yet the logic of an inferential model of sign, especially when elaborated through notions such as that of an "inferential walk," pushes beyond this position. According to Eco's own scheme, readerly inferences always involve ideological determinations that are spatially located outside or beyond the text.[8] Once such determinations have been admitted, however, it is no longer possible to maintain either that what readers confront is "the text" or that what constrains readerly inferences is "the text."

For the crucial concept here is not "constraint," but the very notion of "the text itself." As Tony Bennett argues, texts can be said to participate in the constraint of meaning only if what is meant is that

> the text that the reader or critic has in front of him or her is encountered as a resisting force, constraining the interpretive and analytical options that may be adopted in relation to it. . . . What most needs to be stressed, however, is that, whatever the material form or social context in which the text reaches the reader, it does so only as already covered by a pre-existing horizon of interpretive options, options which are encountered as limits, as a force which has to be reckoned with. . . . It is not some shadowy ideal text, a text hidden within the materiality of the text, but the text in its specific material form as inscribed within a definite set of social relations and as already covered by an accumulated history of readings that, in the present, exerts a determinacy over the modes of its consumption. It is the readings already produced in relation to a text, and not some . . . 'text itself,' which bear upon and limit present and future possible readings. It is for these historical and not at all essentialist reasons that texts are encountered as a resistance.[9]

A notion of "the text itself" remains an illusion because texts are only available as entities that are always already imbued with meanings through various practices of interpretation, appropriation, distribution, and classification of texts.[10] The theoretical perspective implicit in Eco's logic, and explicit in Bennett's formulations, thus becomes one of displacing "the text" from the center of focus in analysis of the determinacy of literary representation. An inferential model of sign must finally locate the site of such determinacy as a "reading formation, a set of intersecting discourses which *productively activate* a given body of texts and the relation between them in a specific way."[11]

On this view, already constructed, or culturally activated, readers confront already constructed, or culturally activated, texts. Not only, therefore, is referentiality to be conceived of as an activity of intertextual inscription, but also the determinacy of such activity is to be conceived of as provided by operations of historically variable ideological conjunctures. While these assertions in no way imply that "new" readings may not issue from the encounters between readers and texts, they do deny that "referring in literature" consists of a direct cue by "the text" of an "hors-texte" of history, transcendental subjectivity, personal experience, or the like. Here the problem of origins that plagues epistemological approaches to the determinacy of literary representation disappears. For, instead of positing the literary text as a sign that is to be played off against an "object" that it is said to determine, the view afforded by an inferential model of sign suggests that a text is inseparable from the determinations in which it is inscribed.

Any concept of the object of representation in literature, or what I shall begin to call the "referent," must fulfill the conditions imposed by this understanding of the determinacy of representation in literature. The referent of literary representation should thus surface as an entity susceptible to construction such that it appears as already inscribed within its determinations. Now the "referential fallacy," as premised by semiotics, eliminates "things" from the field of "objects" to be considered here. Because "*every attempt to establish what the referent of a sign is forces us to define the referent in terms of an abstract entity which is only a cultural convention*," the meaning of a term can exist only in the form of a *cultural unit*; the abstract entity through which a referent is defined, moreover, is itself "another representation referred to the same 'object,' " or an interpretant.[12] Interpretants guarantee the cultural validity of signs (for some group of interpreters) by displacing signification into a series of further sign functions. The referents of literary texts, therefore, are initially to be conceived of as determinate constellations of "cultural units."[13]

In his discussion of aesthetic value, Jan Mukařovský offers an exemplary formulation of the object of representation in literature such that it appears as a cultural unit already inscribed within its determinations.[14] While Mukařovský seeks ultimately to answer the question, "Is objective aesthetic value a reality or a false illusion?" (Mukařovský, p. 70), his argument involves less a transitive use of the notion of value, in the sense of "evaluation," than a substantive use of the notion of value, in the sense of "values." Mukařovský first maintains that, because of its nature as a sign, the work of art is a social fact. Yet the artistic sign differs socially from the more frequent communicative sign in that the information it conveys is no longer inflected toward empirical objects or events about which receivers may inquire as to their actual existence or occurrence. Rather,

> the change which the material relationship of the work—the sign—has undergone is thus simultaneously its weakening and its strengthening. It is weakened in the sense that the work does not refer to the reality which it directly depicts, and strengthened in that the work of art as a sign acquires an indirect (figurative) tie with realities that are vitally important to the perceiver, and through them to the entire universe of the perceiver, as a collection of values. Thus the work of art acquires the ability to refer to a reality which is totally different from the one which it depicts, and to systems of values other than the one from which it arose and on which it is founded. (Mukařovský, p. 75)

In Mukařovský's view, communicative signs situate sender and receiver in a signifying process for which a depicted reality, known to the one and about which the other is informed, serves as the source of the material connection between sender and receiver. In art, however, depicted reality does not constitute the source of the material connection in the signifying process, but rather, only its intermediary.

> The real tie in this situation is a variable one, and points to realities known to the viewer. They are not and can in no way be expressed or even indicated in the work itself, because it forms a component of the viewer's intimate experience. This cluster of realities may be very important and the material tie of the art work with each of them is indirect, figurative. The realities with which the art work can be confronted in the consciousness and subconsciousness of the viewer are squeezed into the general, intellectual, emotional and willful attitude which the viewer assumes toward reality in general. . . . Also, the attitude which the individual takes toward reality is not the exclusive property even of the strongest personalities, for it is to a considerable extent, and in weaker persons almost totally, determined by the social relationships in which the individual is involved. (Mukařovský, pp. 82–83)

Hence, artworks refer to that which Mukařovský calls "extra-aesthetic values." This assertion, moreover, derives its authority from analysis of the expression plane, as well as the content plane, of aesthetic sign functions. In a lengthy discussion, Mukařovský shows that, even for the most abstract styles of art, formal features acquire semantic value in the interpretive encounter. Indeed, he suggests that interpretation of nonrepresentational art becomes possible only after the perceiver has begun to ascribe certain extra-aesthetic values to such features as line and color, in painting, which themselves embody semantic potential. These notions—that aesthetic texts take extra-aesthetic values as their objects, and that interpretation proceeds from extra-aesthetic values toward perception of the internal organization of the artwork—eventually lead Mukařovský to a compelling conclusion about the nature of the aesthetic process.

> We said earlier that all elements of a work of art, in form and content, possess extra-

aesthetic values which, within the work, enter into mutual relationships. The work of art appears, in the final analysis, as an actual collection of extra-aesthetic values and nothing else. The material components of the artistic artifact, and the manner in which they are used as artistic means, assume the role of mere conductors of energies introduced by extra-aesthetic values. If we ask ourselves at this point what has happened to aesthetic value, it appears that it has dissolved into individual extra-aesthetic values, and is really nothing but a general term for the dynamic totality of their mutual interrelationships. . . . The influence of aesthetic value is not that it swallows up and represses all remaining values, but that it releases every one of them from direct contact with a corresponding life-value. It brings an entire assembly of values contained in the work as a dynamic whole into contact with a total system of those values which form the motive power of the life practice of the perceiving collective. (Mukařovský, pp. 88–89)

The referents of literature, or "extra-aesthetic values," therefore, are here already inscribed within their determinations. Mukařovský posits no distinct object that would qualify as an intrinsically "aesthetic" referent. As I have shown, to posit the existence of a properly "aesthetic" referent makes the object of representation in literature subject to an essentialist determination, even when so-called "extrinsic" factors are acknowledged to exercise determinations on this object as well. Yet the argument set forth by Mukařovský fully breaks with epistemological problematics structured by spatial metaphors of "inside" and "outside."[15] Precisely because his referents are already "extra-aesthetic," Mukařovský can consistently assert that textual meaning is an effect of reference to the world.

Mukařovský's formulations furnish the protocol by means of which the referent of literary representation may be analyzed as already inscribed within its determinations. Nevertheless, his definition of the referent as an "extra-aesthetic value" requires further precision. Indeed, Mukařovský's affirmation—that extra-aesthetic values involve "the general, intellectual, emotional, and willful attitude which the viewer assumes toward reality"—strongly anticipates a twentieth-century Marxist definition of ideology:

> Ideology, then, is the expression of the relation between men and their 'world,' that is, the (overdetermined) unity of the real relation and the imaginary relation between them and their real conditions of existence. In ideology the real relation is inevitably invested in the imaginary relation, a relation that *expresses* a *will* (conservative, conformist, reformist or revolutionary), a hope or nostalgia, rather than describing a reality.[16]

Furthermore, Mukařovský's notion that aesthetic processes release extra-aesthetic values "from direct contact with a corresponding life-value" itself anticipates a concept of the "pseudo-real" and implies recognition of the "contextual mobility" of fictive significations.

Terry Eagleton defines the "pseudo-real" as "the imaginary situations which the text is about."[17] Paralleling Mukařovský's distinction between the communicative sign and the artistic sign, he argues that signifieds within fiction refer not to concrete situations but to certain ideological formations that concrete situations have produced. The meaning of the imaginary events presented in a text, therefore, "lies not in their material reality but in how they contribute to fashioning and perpetuating a particular process of signification" (Eagleton, *Criticism and Ideology*, p. 74). As does Mukařovský, with respect to the distinction between "aesthetic" and "extra-aesthetic" value, Eagleton arrives at a bold elision of boundaries between the fictional and the ideological:

> It is useful in this respect to think of the text not merely as the *product* of ideology, but as a *necessity* of ideology—not in an empirical sense, since ideologies without literature have certainly existed, but theoretically, in that fiction is the term we would give to the fullest self-rendering of ideology, the only logical form that such a complete rendering could assume. And this is not, of course, because fiction is 'untrue,' and so a fit vehicle for 'false consciousness,' but rather that in order to reconstruct a society's self-representations we would finally encounter the need to cut them loose from particular 'reals' and mobilise them in the form of situations which, because imaginary, would allow for the range, permutation, economy and flexibility denied to a mere reproduction of the routinely lived. (Eagleton, *CI*, pp. 77–78)

Thus, for Eagleton, literature stands out as a vast enterprise of ideological representation in which multiple fictive strategies encode varying attitudes, or relations, of individuals to their experiential world. On this basis, moreover, Mukařovský's concern with depragmatized "extra-aesthetic values," as well as his concern with their articulation into social "systems of values," can be assimilated to Marxist theory:

> It could be claimed, indeed, that what constitutes a product as 'literary' is exactly [its] contextual mobility. . . . The 'literary' . . . is whatever is detached by a certain hermeneutic practice from its pragmatic context and subjected to a generalizing rein-scription. Since such reinscription is always a particular gesture within determinate ideologies, 'literature' itself is always an ideological construct.[18]

Hence, in place of Mukařovský's notion of the referent as an "extra-aesthetic value," Marxist criticism substitutes the more enabling concept of the "ideologeme" to define the object of literary representation. According to Fredric Jameson,

> the ideologeme is an amphibious formation, whose essential structural characteristic may be described as its possibility to manifest itself either as a pseudoidea—a conceptual or belief system, an abstract value, an opinion or prejudice—or as a proto-narrative, a kind of ultimate class fantasy about the 'collective characters' which are the classes in opposition. This duality means that the basic requirement for the full description of the ideologeme is already given in advance: as a construct it must be susceptible to both a conceptual description and a narrative manifestation all at once.[19]

Thus the texts of literature may be said to consist of various unfoldings of the narrative potential embodied in the very ideologemes to which such texts refer.

Jameson understands what Eagleton calls the "pseudo-real" of individual texts as providing an imaginary solution to unresolvable social contradications; thus, from the outset, the aesthetic is here inscribed within the ideological by conceiving of the social as immanent to form (Jameson, p. 77). When the individual text is later "refocussed as a *parole*, or individual utterance, of that vaster system, or *langue*, of class discourse," then "this larger class discourse can be said to be organized around 'minimal units,' " or ideologemes (Jameson, pp. 85, 87). Finally, in a formulation that refines and resonates with Mukařovský's views, the individual text, now restructured through the ideologeme, emerges as "a field of force in which the dynamics of sign systems of several distinct modes of production can be registered and apprehended" (Jameson, p. 98). At every moment, therefore, this view of the object of representation in literature avoids the essentialist fallacy, for the referent defined as ideologeme remains wholly inscribed within its determinations.

What conclusions follow for the study of referentiality from a definition of the object of literary representation as an ideologeme and from a notion that the determinacy of literary representation is provided by activities of intertextual inscription? Analysis of referentiality in literature may be said to encourage repudiation of a narrow concern with aesthetics and augur the development of a vigorous cultural criticism. In conjunction with the referential fallacy, the essentialist fallacy deprives the referent of the fixity that is accorded to essences and things. Now subject to ongoing processes of the social determination of meaning, the referent can no longer stabilize the reading of texts. Referentiality, therefore, does not just happen. It *is made* to happen when a reading formation activates a particular inscription of texts into an ideological practice. Analysis of referentiality has little to do with the epistemological attempt to discover an absolute ground of textual meaning. It has everything to do with the political struggle over the forms of use and effectivity that texts enjoy within the broader social process.[20]

For Hispanists, the social destiny of Benito Pérez Galdós's *Fortunata y Jacinta* may perhaps prove illustrative of the foregoing arguments. What is the referent of this text? If I bracket consideration of popular readings of the novel, I feel confident in asserting that no critic today would progress very far toward an answer to this question before having to take account of the relevant debate carried on by Stephen Gilman and Carlo Blanco Aguinaga in three articles published in *Anales Galdosianos* between 1966 and 1970.[21] *Fortunata y Jacinta* comes before critics today as already carrying a political charge; no academic interpretation of this text currently can be circulated without its being evaluated and classified in light of the interpretive options that have accrued as a result of the polemical exchange between Gilman and Blanco. Yet, for my purposes, the exemplariness of *Fortunata y Jacinta* resides not only in that studies of the novel now enjoy explicitly political resonance, but also in that ideological decisions made in regard to the referents of the novel can be shown to inform how its structure is perceived by the critical discourses in question.

In 1981, quite independently of one another, there appeared two of the more recent attempts at describing a referent for *Fortunata y Jacinta*. One of these attempts was made again by Gilman in his *Galdós and the Art of the European Novel 1867–*

1887.[22] The other was made by me in an essay entitled "*Fortunata y Jacinta*: Galdós and the Production of the Literary Referent."[23] While I still endorse the major arguments of my article, the presence of the term "literary referent" in its title should indicate that I would today formulate somewhat differently the theoretical framework within which my analysis takes place. I do not want, however, to use this space as the occasion upon which to defend my reading of *Fortunata y Jacinta* as one that is "more something or other" than Gilman's reading. Rather, I want to examine aspects of both readings in order to suggest that the particular predication of referents enacted by each of us depends on the reading formations into which the text of *Fortunata y Jacinta*, and we ourselves, are inscribed.

In my essay, I consider that *Fortunata y Jacinta* produces as referents a set of progressive middle-class values that are addressed to the "vacío ideológico" created in Spain during the process of ideological assimilation of the landed and financial middle classes by the traditional nobility, 1875–1900. I argue that Galdós's *costumbrista* representation of lower-middle-class experience in *Fortunata y Jacinta* unfolds a narrative logic that remains at odds with the dominant tendency of the overall structure of the novel. For example, the social implications of the representations offered in "Costumbres turcas"(III, 1) resist the synthetic and reconciliatory movements of the plot and formal argument that govern the text generally. Based on descriptions that establish the *café* as a representational space informed by special psychological strategies of identification and aggression (Lacan's "Imaginary"), "Costumbres turcas" constructs an image of a possible form of subjective relation to Restoration society that counters the more conservative image of subjectivity represented through the Santa Cruz *tertulia*. Thus, Juan Pablo Rubín's eventual assimilation into the political machinery of the Restoration is portrayed as a disheartening, though unavoidable, repudiation of progressive values that seem embedded in the very texture of lower-middle-class life. Even in this chapter, therefore, I perceive that the narrative surface of *Fortunata y Jacinta* is traversed by various historical perspectives: the fictional return to the apparent possibility in 1875 of elaborating an effective ideological practice of the middle class, coupled with narrative awareness in 1887 of the impending integration of the landed and financial middle classes within the Restoration "bloque de poder." I claim, then, that it is the project of this novel to organize and to transform cultural representations available in the 1880s in a way that seeks to restore a specific kind of ideological presence to the middle class. In the form of a contradiction between its guiding structural premises and the representational logic of its textualization of the lower middle class, however, the work may be said to acknowledge its own failure to accomplish this task. It is through recognition of this structural dissonance that the full significance of the production of the referent in *Fortunata y Jacinta* may be grasped. For, by undertaking in the mode of the Imaginary to articulate elements of a progressive middle-class ideology, the novel constructs the referent in a manner that replenishes in consciousness the absence of such a practice from the ideological problematic of the Restoration.

Now, my perspective on the referents of *Fortunata y Jacinta* depends on a specific understanding of how the novel is structured; and my understanding of textual structure here depends on a series of more general assumptions that may be said to comprise my reading formation. Thus, my perception that the temporality represented in the novel surfaces as a peculiarly conflictive and uneven one, involves my own view that historical moments are best conceptualized through the categories of contradiction and overdetermination. My willingness to base so much of my reading on a "secondary" character such as Juan Pablo Rubín is owing to my view that characters can never be understood as adequate embodiments of qualities or attributes; therefore, marginal agents or *actants* in a text deserve special consideration, not as inadequate representations of a universal consciousness, but precisely as indexical components of an overall system of relations that represents determinate positions for subjectivity. My assertion that the novel reveals an internal dissonance depends on my convictions that literature does not present "reality" or express the author's intention, that it does not provide knowledge or truth (in an epistemological sense), and that certain of its significations always escape its dominant explanatory strategies. My location of this text in relation to the ideological problematic of Restoration Spain is motivated, of course, by my understanding of the place and function of literature within social formations generally. In other words, I construct the form of this text through a poststructuralist optics in which an Althusserian Marxism serves as the dominant factor. When I read this text, therefore, I productively activate it by inscribing it within a particular set of intersecting discourses that themselves constitute a specific ideological practice.

In *Galdós and the Art of the European Novel: 1867–1887*, Gilman seems to recognize that at least some acts of predication of referents for texts consist of the inscription of texts into an ideological practice by means of a reading formation.

> Once having aided us in posing the problem, . . . Marxist critics, at least in the case of *Fortunata y Jacinta*, offer an incorrect solution. Here is a story, in their view, of an innocent, proletarian victim caught in the "engrenage" of an immense and complex bourgeois society, which literally cries for a revolution. All of Galdós's social and historical "materias reunidas" are justifiable artistically because they are "socially realistic" and show us vividly the mechanisms of corruption and exploitation.
>
> Why is this, at first glance, apparently reasonable interpretation of our novel, . . . "incorrect"? (Gilman, p. 229)

It seems, then, that not all acts of predication of referents for texts are considered by Gilman to consist of an ideological inscription, for, as this passage illustrates, Gilman inscribes his own reading of *Fortunata y Jacinta* into the position of truth. I shall suggest, however, that Gilman's reading accomplishes the inscription of "our" text precisely into a determinate ideological practice.

Gilman's discussion of *Fortunata y Jacinta* is a lengthy and challenging one, so I must limit myself here to presentation of his argument largely as it appears in the opening chapter of Part III, the section devoted exclusively to *Fortunata y Jacinta*. Gilman argues that, as does Cervantes, Galdós exploits "the temporal paradox of fiction (or the fictional paradox of time) in order, not just to make us laugh or to attract our attention, but to make us aware of who we are and who we could be or should be, to lead us to become, as it were, working members of the 'Wortkunst-werk,' whose consciousness of society and self is heightened and changed by that membership'' (Gilman, p. 233). According to Gilman, the temporal paradox of fiction is that the past tense of the author's discourse becomes the present tense of the reader's experience: in fictional narrative, "then" becomes "now." Neverthe-less, "in the greatest nineteenth-century novels (and *Fortunata y Jacinta* is surely one of them), after the scrupulous documentation of social illness and the poetic expression of intensely lived experience have been completed, 'then' and 'now' become 'forever' " (Gilman, p. 245). I take this to mean that Gilman believes that great novels afford access to universal and transcendent truths about human nature that are immune to those conditional, transitory, and perhaps all too fragile phe-nomena that give concrete shape to the present and past of human beings. In *For-tunata y Jacinta*, then, it is "the sheer health of Fortunata's consciousness" (Gilman, p. 240) that becomes the vehicle through which readers accede to such truths. Unlike *all* the other characters, who "fill the pages of the novel, but whose ample assortment of eccentric reactions to their metropolitan milieu amounts at best to 'costumbrismo' on a grand scale" (Gilman, p. 239), Fortunata "is or becomes a *presence*" (p. 240): "she may also be in her own novelistic way a savior" (p. 240). According to Gilman, therefore, "although it is not an argument that Marxist critics who do not live in Marxist societies are likely to agree with" (p. 244), it is through the consciousness of Fortunata that "Galdós intended to show us that salvation is possible" (p. 244).

Hence, Gilman posits the referent of *Fortunata y Jacinta* as a transcendent con-sciousness that embodies awareness of a path to salvation. I now want to inquire further into the contours and motivations of this consciousness: who is to be saved? From what are they to be saved? What path do the elect follow? Except on rare occasions, answers to these questions are not directly forthcoming from Gilman; yet such answers would surely make explicit some aspects of Gilman's own reading formation. Since he praises in Galdós, and prescribes for Galdós's readers, the exercise of what he calls "the art of listening," perhaps you and I should "listen" carefully to Gilman in the hope of discovering some indication of the ideological practice into which I shall allege that he inscribes this text.

> Discussion of what Galdós intended and what he in fact achieved in the creation of his masterpiece must wait until a step-by-step exploration, from style, through poetic imagery, into Fortunata's consciousness, is completed in the chapters to follow. Naturally, Marxist readers will not be convinced, insofar as they are committed to a definition of what novels are (and should be) antithetical to that of Galdós. (Gilman, p. 230)

Authorial intention; unity of intention, style, imagery, and subject matter: the as-sumptions about the nature of textuality that Gilman brings to his reading of *For-tunata y Jacinta* are here apparent. Masterpiece: also apparent are his evaluative interest in transcendent art and his institutional concern to demonstrate that *For-tunata y Jacinta* deserves recognition by non-Hispanists as one of "the greatest nineteenth-century novels." Consciousness: consistent with an emphasis on authorial intention, he makes the assumption that the possibility of discursive meaning depends on identifying a source of self-aware expression ("the presence of Fortunata as a perfect conductor of experience" [Gilman, p. 243]). Even more telling, there is here revealed Gilman's tendency to displace responsibility for his own assumptions and to give them author-ity by projecting them onto Galdós. Let us listen again to the closing sentence of that quotation: "Naturally, Marxist readers will not be convinced, insofar as they are committed to a definition of what novels are (and should be) antithetical to": . . . "mine"? No, "antithetical to that of Galdós."

This last tactic should be recognized for what it is: "a political strategy for reading in which the critic's own construction of authorial intention is mobilized in order to bully other interpretations off the field."[24] Gilman repeatedly indulges in disguises and displacements of this sort that attempt to secure the truth of his position by inscribing both the text, and Gilman's own readers, within the discourses of quite specific ideologies. Let us listen again:

> For passionate readers and rereaders of *Fortunata y Jacinta*, Fortunata is the woman who, among all women, is the most profoundly known. We know her from within, and we know her at length, from spiritual birth to physical death and believed-in resurrection. We know her in a way we can never know women of flesh and blood— our mothers, our sisters, our wives. (Gilman, p. 320)

Who is included in the "we" here? Certainly not women, unless women are to be judged incapable of coming to know themselves as intimately as they may come to know a fictional character. Rather, it is "we men" who are supposed to know Fortunata in this way. And, in Gilman's analysis, to know Fortunata is to know and to possess the meaning of the text—the text as woman—just as Galdós knew and possessed the meaning of the text. For, after all, the text *is* the masterful expression and perfect representation of Fortunata's consciousness.

Who, then, is saved by Fortunata, and from what? I want to listen to Gilman one last time as he writes the image of his own subjectivity, and perhaps ours, into his discussion of the referent of this novel.

> Galdós is not trying to excuse nor does he still aspire (as does Zola) to cure the diseased society portrayed in the novel. Like Mark Twain's Mississippi shores, Stendhal's Parma, or Cervantes' "la Mancha," it is both unjustifiable and in its own terms chronically ill, but Galdós does see, with the clear, distant vision with which great novelists are blessed, the ironical interdependence and interaction of society (sick almost by definition) with those rare incited souls who inhabit it but are immune to its debasement and who at the end find their individual paths to a reevaluation of the human condition. (Gilman, pp. 245–246)

Like great novelists, are perhaps literary critics blessed with "clear, distant vision"? Do literary critics stand in need these days of abandoning a society that is "sick almost by definition"? Are literary critics some of those "rare incited souls"—the elect—who find their individual and transcendent paths to salvation? It is Gilman's own consciousness, and the image of subjectivity made possible by a complex ideological practice, that are saved by Gilman's Fortunata. And, in the end, by elevating themselves above those common unincited souls who also inhabit society, and yet who are not immune to its mechanisms of debasement, what these rare incited souls are saved from is any responsibility to or for a chronically ill society.

So it is that, when Gilman reads *Fortunata y Jacinta*, he productively activates the text by inscribing it within a reading formation that Catherine Belsey has called "expressive realism": "This is the theory that literature reflects the *reality* of experience as it is perceived by one (especially gifted) individual, who *expresses* it in a discourse which enables others to recognize it as true."[25] As a reading formation, expressive realism is constituted by the intersecting ideological discourses of humanism, empiricism, and idealism. Expressive realism holds "that 'man' is the origin and source of meaning, of action, and of history (*humanism*). Our concepts and our knowledge are held to be the product of experience (*empiricism*), and that this experience is preceded and interpreted by the mind, reason or thought, the property of a transcendent human nature whose essence is the attribute of each individual (*idealism*)" (Belsey, p. 7). Gilman's referents, therefore, arise from the intertextual inscription of *Fortunata y Jacinta* into these ideological practices by means of the reading formation of expressive realism.

The referents of *Fortunata y Jacinta* that I posit in my essay on the novel also arise from a process of inscribing the text into an ideological practice by means of a reading formation. Throughout his discussion, Gilman's constant assertions regarding what Marxist critics can or cannot do, and what they will or will not believe, suggest that, at least to some degree, he understands that his formulation of the referent of the novel is in struggle with alternative formulations, or, as I have tried to show, with rival referential acts. And so it is! This is what I meant when I wrote that analysis of referentiality has little to do with epistemological attempts to discover an absolute ground of textual meaning. Rather, it has everything to do with political struggles over the use and effectivity that texts enjoy within the broader social process.

NOTES

1. See especially Tony Bennett, *Formalism and Marxism* (New York and London: Methuen, 1979); Mary Louise Pratt, *Toward a Speech Act Theory of Literary Discourse* (Bloomington and London: Indiana University Press, 1977); Costanzo Di Girolamo, *A Critical Theory of Literature* (Madison and London: University of Wisconsin Press, 1981).
2. "Linguistics and Poetics," in *The Structuralists: From Marx to Lévi-Strauss*, ed. Richard and Fernande DeGeorge (Garden City, N.Y.: Doubleday, 1972), p. 94.
3. Di Girolamo, p. 6.
4. Overcoding occurs when, "on the basis of a pre-established rule, a new rule [is] proposed which govern[s] a rarer application of the previous rule"; undercoding represents "an operation by means of which in the absence of reliable pre-established rules, certain macroscopic portions of certain texts are provisionally assumed to be pertinent units of a

code in formation, even though the combinatorial rules governing the more basic compositional items of the expressions, along with the corresponding content-units, remain unknown." Umberto Eco, *A Theory of Semiotics* (Bloomington and London: Indiana University Press, 1976), pp. 133, 135–136.

5. Louis Althusser and Etienne Balibar, *Reading Capital*, trans. Ben Brewster (London: New Left Books, 1970), p. 63.

6. Umberto Eco, "The Theory of Signs and the Role of the Reader," *Bulletin of the Midwest Modern Language Association* 14, 1 (Spring 1981), p. 38.

7. Deduction entails reasoning from a law, to a case, to a result; induction entails reasoning from many results and many cases to formulation of a law. See Eco, "Theory of Signs," pp. 44–45.

8. *The Role of the Reader* (Bloomington and London: Indiana University Press, 1979), pp. 22–23.

9. "Text and Social Processes: The Case of James Bond," *Screen Education* 41 (Winter/ Spring 1982).

10. "Texts come before us as the always-already-read; we apprehend them through sedimented layers of previous interpretations, or—if the text is brand-new—through the sedimented reading habits and categories developed by those inherited interpretive traditions." Fredric Jameson, *The Political Unconscious: Narrative as a Socially Symbolic Act* (Ithaca and London: Cornell University Press, 1981), p. 9.

11. Tony Bennett, "Texts, Readers, Reading Formations," *Bulletin of the Midwest Modern Language Association* 16, 1 (Spring 1983), p. 5.

12. Eco, *A Theory of Semiotics*, pp. 66, 68.

13. For more detailed discussion of the referent as cultural unit, see my "Notes toward a Theory of the Referent," *PMLA* 94, 3 (May 1979), pp. 459–475.

14. *Aesthetic Function, Norm and Value as Social Facts* (Ann Arbor: University of Michigan Press, 1970).

15. A problematic structured by spatial metaphors of "the inside" and "the outside" is common to both empiricist and idealist epistemologies. See Althusser and Balibar, *Reading Capital*, pp. 35–40.

16. Louis Althusser, *For Marx*, trans. Ben Brewster (New York: Random House, 1970), pp. 233–234.

17. *Criticism and Ideology* (London: New Left Books, 1976), p. 80.

18. Terry Eagleton, *Walter Benjamin, or Towards a Revolutionary Criticism* (London: Verso Editions and New Left Books, 1981), p. 123.

19. *The Political Unconscious: Narrative as a Socially Symbolic Act* (Ithaca and London: Cornell University Press, 1981), p. 87.

20. See Tony Bennett, *Formalism and Marxism* (New York and London: Methuen, 1979), pp. 167–168.

21. See Stephen Gilman, "The Birth of Fortunata," *Anales Galdosianos* I (1966), pp. 71–83; Carlos Blanco Aguinaga, "On 'The Birth of Fortunata,' " *Anales Galdosianos* III (1968), pp. 13–24; and Gilman, "The Consciousness of Fortunata," *Anales Galdosianos* V (1970), pp. 55–66.

22. (Princeton: Princeton University Press, 1981).

23. *MLN* 96, 2 (March 1981), pp. 316–339.

24. Bennett, "Texts, Readers, Reading Formations," p. 15.

25. *Critical Practice* (New York and London: Methuen, 1980), p. 7.

CONCLUSION

THEORIES OF REFERENCE

Anna Whiteside

I: The Frame of Reference

I, 1: Preamble

First, a word about what this essay is not about. Since the subject of this volume is *literary reference*, we shall not be dealing with the problems of truth or existence *per se*, for the simple reason, as Leonard Linsky and John Searle, amongst others, have pointed out, that successful reference is contingent on neither. On the whole the literary reader (as opposed to the historian, sociologist, anthropologist, philosopher, and all those who use literary texts as source material) and *a fortiori* the literary critic, are not particularly interested in the truth value of a literary text, or in the ontological status of the literary referent. These are rather the problems of logicians and a certain school of semanticists, and have been dealt with by such authors as Woods, in *The Logic of Fiction*, and Heintz (1979).[1] Nor shall I be dealing with the linguistic aspects of reference, except initially in as far as they contribute to literary pragmatics.

What this essay does hope to do, however, is to outline some of the specific ways reference functions in literary discourse as opposed to ordinary discourse. In so doing I will inevitably draw on the findings of both philosophers and linguists, since it is they who have so far formulated and described the concepts and processes of referring, thus providing the tools for this inquiry. In fact, now that the ontological issue—raised by Bertrand Russell, Ryle, Strawson (in his earlier works), and Quine, and largely evinced by Linsky, Searle, and Keith Donnellan—is no longer considered an essential part of referring, we find that philosophers and linguists present an increasingly complementary picture of what referring is. Broadly speaking, the philosopher is interested in the *relationship* obtaining between an expression and its referent, while the linguist's concern is with the act and process of referring— the *ways* we use language to draw attention to what we are talking about. In effect, then, both approaches necessarily consider 1) pragmatics, since the context of utterance determines the referent and thus reference, and 2) semantics, since meaning is contingent on the precise nature of the referent as established pragmatically. By the same token, this essay will examine both the relationships obtaining between literary discourse and its context-determined referent, and the ways in which the associated semantic evolution of literary referents work. This will entail some discussion of speech-act theory as propounded by philosophers such as Austin, Strawson, and Searle, and by linguists such as Emile Benveniste, and, obviously, Jakobson. For it is Jakobson's communication model which links the referential function to context and underscores the importance of a more complex referential function in literature, given the importance of speaker-receiver related context or contexts and the poetic function. Coincidentally, this discussion may induce a modest measure of Anglo-French semiotic *entente*, the aim being to show how it is possible to envisage fusion of Saussure's binary sign and the mainly Anglo-Saxon ternary one by combining their complementary functions—the former being strictly linguistic, the latter more philosophical.

But why this interest in referring in literature? Ever since Plato, and, somewhat more recently, since the discussion sparked by Frege's inquiry into the relation between sense and reference, followed by Russell's response in "On Denoting," philosophers and linguists have been debating the problems of reference. Relatively few, however, have turned their attention from ordinary discourse to *literary* discourse. Those who have (mainly logicians) are more interested in accounting for the fact that literary texts can indeed refer (to real or imagined things, states of affairs, etc.) than in discussing the specifics of literary referring: its pragmatic and socio-cultural dimensions, its modes, contexts, codes, types, levels, and, above all, the ways in which it functions and how these affect interpretation. Literary exegetes are no less to blame since few have tackled the problem. Yet surely, to claim to discuss the meaning or meanings of this or that text, as most of us do at some time or other, is necessarily to imply the whole question of reference. For though the signs of literary discourse constitute a text's linguistic dimension, its particular ideological significance lies beyond, and is determined by, the referent and all that this presupposes. Contrary to the belief of some latter-day structuralists and semioticians, literature does not and cannot live by signs alone—at least not in the Saussurean sense.

I, 2: Referring and Literary Theory

True, some aspects of literary reference have been dealt with separately; but though critics such as Woods (1974), Ihwe and Reiser ("Normative and Descriptive Theory of Fiction"), and Lewis ("Notes Towards a Literary Referent") have integrated many of them, no one, to our knowledge, has attempted to provide an overall theory of referring in literature. This volume is intended as a first step in that direction.

Let us briefly consider the individual referential issues already raised by literary critics and theorists, linguists, and philosophers. Glosses discreetly tell us what obscure archaic, or specialized terms, expressions, and names refer to—sometimes so discreetly that the referent lacks its socio-cultural frame of reference as well as its semantic and phonic connections and evolution. Unless the textual context is particularly enlightening, a gloss is not designed to provide complete reference, with the result that the text's full potential meaning may not be realized. But critical editions and the traditional *explication de texte* type of commentary spring into the breach explaining much of the rest, adding pre-textual (that is, from earlier drafts), intratextual, and intertexual references (in both the notional and structural sense of the latter).

Semiotics reinforces intratextual, and to some extent intertextual, reference by interpreting literary discourse as a series of interrelated signs: discover the scotomized code and the appropriate signs will reveal their meaning through their relationship to one another. Little codes breed bigger codes, and as sign-systems are decoded, so they form a macro-sign-system, a master-code to which, hindsight tells us, they had been pointing all along, and which, in this unscrambled text, spells out *meaning*. But if, for semioticians, signs refer syntagmatically to one another and hence to their code, if their decoded referent in turn becomes a sign and so, through the chain of semiosis, eventually refers to a particular literary form, and if form is meaning (as Patrice Pavis's chapter suggests), then there exists a strange paradox: the majority of literary semioticians in fact use the notion of referring while pretending to ignore the referent. Having adopted a linguistic model (Saussure's signifier-signified), they are caught referring without a referent—ever mindful that for Saussure the referent, being strictly extra-linguistic, was irrelevant. But Saussure, like many a philosopher, strangely enough, confused the referent with existence, and referring with affirmation of existence. Critics and literary theorists, however, be they semioticians or no, must deal with referents, contexts of reference, and thus reference itself if they are to refer, say, to *Anna Karenina*, to its heroine or to any other of the text's entities. Even Barthes or Foucault, who claim that form is the ultimate meaning, have, by so doing, acknowledged reference: reference to a particular form or consciousness of form.

Socio-criticism, from Dilthey to Goldmann, Althusser, Adorno, or Foucault (and to some extent structuralism and semiotics, as Patrice Pavis's chapter shows), pushes back referential horizons by examining texts in their sociological, cultural, historical, and thus, in their complete ideological context. They thereby transform the context of production into the referent itself—a referent variously coloured, as will be shown (see section II, 2) by the context of reception.

A narrower and more linguistic view of pragmatics has also contributed significantly to discussions of literary reference as an integral part of the speech-act, and thus of explicit and implicit speaker-addressee contexts of discourse. Reference-determining factors such as modalisors, spatio-temporal deixis, anaphora, and other related components certainly have their uses, but the pitfall of literary vivisection is to insist on treating the text as ordinary discourse, thereby disregarding its literary difference. (Michael Issacharoff's chapter examines the difference and shows how serious vs. non-serious discourse—see II, 3 "Modes"—can be a useful consideration when examining playscripts.) Jakobson's literary sensitivity has helped us avoid such dangers. His communication model provides an indispensable framework for our present discussion. Not only does he integrate sender, receiver, speech-acts, and context by defining the message in terms of its referential function to all four, he also examines the literary text's specifically aesthetic ("poetic") function in terms of textual self-reference.

In philosophy the debate has waxed wider and longer, but, being primarily concerned with logic (and modal logic), it has shed little light on the specifics of literary reference. Indeed many philosophers deny the possibility of a literary referent at all. Exceptions exist, however, as the issue of *Poetics* on reference and literature shows (Vol. 8, Nos. 1–2, 1979) and as the work of some speech-act theorists has demonstrated. John Searle's "The Logical Status of Fictional Discourse" is one such example. It is significant that his main argument deals more with the nature of the literary speech-act than with the different ways texts, or rather the "speakers" in and behind them, refer. Nevertheless, this discussion of the special status of the literary speech-act is useful and corroborates Linsky's and Strawson's views.

The logical status of the referent is one of the focal points of discussion on referring, and, latterly, on referring in literature. Frege dismissed the referent's logical status as having nothing to do with truth; Russell would not even countenance a non-existent referent, let alone a literary one. Meinong, however, opened the door to two types of existence: being and so-being (*Sein* and *So-sein*). It soon became clear that the heart of the matter lay not in things referred to, but in the act of referring itself—which brings us back to pragmatics. After all, the Golden Mountain, Cerberus, Mr. Pickwick, and Wells's time-machine may not exist, but we can still refer to them.

Indeed, as Linsky points out (1967) when discussing the question "Does Santa Claus live at the North Pole?" there are two possible answers: "Yes, he does," and "No, he does not really live at the North Pole. It is just make-believe." Now what is at issue here and in literary discourse is not so much the intrinsic status of the referent as the mode of the speech-act: the first reply respects the make-believe mode; the second rejects it for the existential mode. In literature the speaker (writer or character) pretends to perform illocutionary acts which are in turn perceived by the reader as what Searle calls "non-deceptive pseudo-performance." The difference between ordinary and literary speech-acts, then, is not so much that in one world things exist while in the other they do not, or that in one they are true, in the other not, or that meaning changes (after all "words still have their normal meanings" in fiction); but that the mode of performance and interpretation varies. As Blanchot remarks, the reader reading fiction reads with an altered attitude (Linda Hutcheon's chapter explores this problem).

In fact reference, far from having to be true, as Russell would have us believe, does not even have to be accurate. A speaker can use a definite or seemingly definite description to refer, according to Donnellan (1966) and Linsky (1967), even if 1) it does not fit the referent, that is, is false, or 2) if the presupposition of existence is not satisfied. In the first place, to use Linsky's example, a speaker who says of an unmarried lady enjoying the amiable company of some gentleman at a party, that her husband is nice to her, may successfully refer—as even a reply like "But that's not her husband" will confirm. Similarly, in literature, a writer or character may incorrectly describe New York, Napoleon, or the Holocaust, yet still refer . . .

initially to the entity in question, or rather to our image of it, but above all to the author's (re-)creation of it, that is, to his, and consequently the reader's, "secondary" referent; a hyphenated, doubly connoted writer-reader artifact. For example, Robbe-Grillet refers to New York in *Topologie d'une cité fantôme* precisely by disclaiming any intention of referring to the "real" New York—a disclaimer which, while implying, albeit tenuously, the very relationship it refutes, nevertheless attests to the supremacy of secondary reference in literary discourse. Similarly, when Stendhal refers to Napoleon, Baudelaire to Paris, Chekhov to Moscow, and Dickens, Mark Twain, Balzac, and Steinbeck to particular social conditions, however realist or naturalist their art (and there is a distinction as Gombrich [1960] shows), they refer not so much to the extratextual primary referent mentioned as to their own highly connoted intertextual and intratextual literary artifact (something Thomas, Chambers, Meltzer, Krysinski, and Issacharoff all explore in different ways). Barthes, talking of *"l'effet de réel"* (the reality effect), and Ricoeur corroborate the view that literary reference is existentially false reference, a referential illusion whose very force is the illusion it manages to create. Literary critics interested in the role of the reader have further undermined primary reference in literature by showing that from a single description readers construct fairly different imagined or secondary referents.

It would seem then that the distinction between primary and secondary reference in literature is a question of degree rather than of absolutes. For it is arguable that in literature their roles are perhaps reversed, that is, that the primary or "real" referent may actually be subordinated to the secondary referent which recreates and thus replaces it, that is to say, becomes primary by virtue of its literary foregrounding and immediacy. What then of the reader whose knowledge of the "real thing" is primarily second-hand? Where does one distinguish between primary and secondary reference? Although there are two criteria involved here, one existential (which is real, which not?), the other perceptual (which seems most immediate?), both are in fact inextricably intertwined, since from a materialist's (and probably many a reader's) point of view, existence is just as much an image in the mind's eye as in the beholder's. All this prompts one to wonder whether, in literary discourse, the distinction between referent and signified, or indeed between signifier and referent, where a text's form is its signifier, is as unambiguous as is commonly held.

Three self-evident conclusions stem from the discussion of literary reference by critics, theorists, and others: first, that literary critics and theorists, philosophers and linguists are all aware that referring in literature is possible; second, that they feel the need to account for it; third, that it is considerably more complex than referring in ordinary discourse. From these conclusions we derive an obvious fourth. An overall theory is needed which will both account for the specificity of literary reference and combine its apparently divergent facets and functions.

I, 3: Reference defined

Before going any further, it might be well to state what we mean by reference. Let us start with Lyons's definition, since it is one of the broadest. It is "the relationship which holds between an expression and what that expression stands for on particular occasions of its utterance" (1977, Vol. I, p. 174). Here, then, are the three basic considerations concerning reference: an *expression*, *what it stands for*, and the *context* of utterance. In a more Saussurean vein one might translate this trio as 1) signifier within the sign-system of a given *langue*, 2) referent, and 3) *parole*. But, as we hope to show, the highly connoted literary referent in fact tends to become an integral part of the literary sign.

The danger of this definition is that it presupposes an element which has too often been overlooked: the speaker. For an expression alone does not refer—or at least may not be deemed to do so in a very reliable way, despite the arguments (summarized by Linsky, 1967 and 1971, and Quine, 1966), of philosophers who, in any case, are primarily interested in non-literary discourse. Rather, it is the person using the expression who refers, as Lyons shows, and Strawson, Linsky, Donnellan, and Searle all emphasize. So we should perhaps read Lyons's definition bearing in mind Linsky's discussion of uniqueness of reference and the referring expression: "to secure uniqueness of reference through increased determination of the 'referring expression' is otiose, for what secures uniqueness is the user of the expression and the context in which it is used *together* with the expression" (Linsky, 1967, p. 117). If it seems obvious that "expression" and "context of utterance" imply both speaker (author or literary character) and addressee, it was not always so, and indeed much ink has been devoted from Russell to Ryle to the cause of uniquely referring expressions.

Life, let alone literature, would be somewhat problematic if we did not take these aspects of referring for granted: that is to say referring as an *act* (an aspect which Lewis's chapter develops), and its implied contextual (and thus illocutionary and perlocutionary) correlates. For example, if someone tells you he has just bought "a rabbit," reference (albeit indefinite), and thus the referent, are contingent on contextual definition. If the context is a) a visit to a toyshop, the rabbit in question could well be a pink polyester monstrosity; but if he has just returned from b) a Volkswagen dealership, we immediately visualise a car; if, however, the context is c) a pet-shop, presumably the rabbit would be alive; if d) a game and poultry shop, then it should be dead. Here context suggests both state (or mode): a) artificial, b) figurative, c) alive, d) recently dead; and type: c) one of the varieties sold in petshops, for example, a white angora, or d) one of the edible sort. Similarly, if you say to someone "I would like the rabbit," this referent (definite or indefinite) will vary considerably according to 1) the context, 2) the identity of the speaker and receiver, and 3) to the perlocutionary function. Should the addressee be a waiter, the perlocutionary function would be that of a hungry client ordering rabbit; here again the context allows you to assume that "the rabbit" will arrive not live, or frozen solid, but cooked—and in the style specified on the menu of the restaurant where the speaker has chosen to eat.

So in literature, context, speaker and addressee, mode, types of illocutionary acts, and their perlocutionary function all help determine reference and referents, as will be shown in more detail in the sections which follow. In a sense one might even say that literary discourse is more referentially biased than ordinary discourse, in that readers tend to assume the writer's intention to refer, however indirectly.

Contrary to ordinary discourse, literature thrives on the ambiguities of contextual mobility and disguised singular reference. Satires, parodies, and all forms of intertextuality depend upon them. Titles, too, exploit them. *The Old Man and the Sea* initially appears contradictory; its definite descriptions seem to refer, but to what old man, to which sea? *Une saison en enfer* (*A Season in Hell*), though apparently indefinite, refers, since one could say that it actually refers to a specific period in Rimbaud's life as interpreted by him, to a particular imagined construct as it appears in this literary creation—or both, the latter evoking the former. In fact titles always refer—to the texts they identify as well as to their own descriptive deictic function.

Before examining *contexts* (see II, 2), a word about the other two terms in Lyons's definition: the referring expression and its referent. Given literature's enormous contextual elasticity, duplicity, and multiplicity, the literary referent has an unusually protean and dynamic propensity. Describing the phenomenon thus leads to certain pitfalls. In the first place, a referent itself may act as a referring expression: the name Moby Dick refers to a whale which in turn is used to refer to, and thus comes to represent, certain concepts. Similarly characters such as Ahab or Scrooge refer to literary characters whose mere names, by evoking their literary context, come to refer symbolically to particular human qualities. Whether the referent is used as a symbolic or metaphoric referring expression, and regardless of how many stages it may evolve through (in poetry these can be particularly numerous), it is clear that some referents are more equal than others. Although the terms *primary* and *secondary* referent are useful in that they indicate derivation, their suggestion of hierarchy causes problems, given the constantly shifting nature of this hierarchy in literature. Some philosophers use the terms existentially; others, including linguists, anaphorically. To borrow Charles Chastain's example in "Reference and Context" (1975), the philosopher's primary referent when he speaks of "the house" is some "real" world house. From this evolves another referent: the memory image someone has of this house set in the context of his memory, that is, store of memories. In effect this is already a hypothetical intermediary referent, since it is unlikely to be the original memory image, but rather a remembered and thus modified memory image, set inevitably in an altered memory context. Still more removed is the related or so-called secondary referent, set this time, for example, in a literary context. So when I read of Marcel's family home in Combray in *À la recherche du temps perdu* (*In Search of Time Past*), my mental image refers back to a selection of associated memory images or to a conglomerate image of a suitable house or houses I have seen. This does not preclude the possibility of the house being Proust's house at Illiers-Combray, which I may have visited, since this cannot be identical to the one Marcel remembers, despite strong architectural similarities, for different eyes in a different age make a different world. How this memory selection takes place is in turn determined by context association and connotation; thus, here again, contexts not only determine reference, but become referents themselves, as Thomas

Lewis shows. As for connotation, it plays a far greater role in literary reference than has hitherto been admitted. The reader can continue this chain indefinitely; either intertextually, by using his Combray-connoted house to form the basis of another fictional house whose context reminds him of Proust's evoked one, or intratextually, by constantly referring back to the preceding image of Marcel's ever-modified home.

Linguists link referents too, but for them, secondary reference is anaphoric and therefore intratextual. Thus, apparently indefinite expressions may, in fact, refer when considered anaphorically—and in literary discourse, except for the opening sentences (and sometimes even then in the case of the *roman fleuve*, satire, parody, transposed myth, or history, for example), these indefinite expressions usually pre-suppose anaphoric links. Going beyond obvious pronominal anaphora, a literary character may speak of "a room with a view"; from the context it is clear that, in fact, this apparently indefinite and non-referring expression definitely refers . . . in a most specific way. Or again, in *A la recherche*, we may read that "a visitor" used to ring at the garden gate on summer evenings before dropping in for a talk, when clearly "a visitor," considered anaphorically, is a singular definite referring expression, the referent being Swann.

Literary texts play considerably on tension created between apparently referring and non-referring expressions. Jane Austen may speak of a house near or in the town of M., but subsequent description and narrative anaphorically subvert initially non-referring appearances. Legends or tales beginning "Once upon a time there lived a damsel, king, etc.," though they may not establish spatio-temporal reference, do create character or role reference. Such a damsel is never a mere damsel, but the one who is about to become the heroine, etc. Conversely, Balzac's lengthy definite descriptions may fail to refer, despite his and our intentions, if the reader's memory is defective, or he or she misses certain cues.

Although we should be aware of these two distinct uses of primary and secondary referent, they are not quite as different as they may appear. First, an anaphoric chain, and *a fortiori* its referent, relies on the perceived mental image which refers back to a given thing or event. Second, both anaphoric referents and perceptual or imagined referents, symbolic or otherwise, are at least similarly if not equally distorted by changing contexts and permeable memory images, which both lose and gain something each time. In a sense, symbolically invested referents display the same ambiguity as anaphoric ones, in that the concurrent referents of a given referring expression—be it a name, a pronoun, or, say, an indefinite noun—rely on readers' differing abilities to reconstruct and perceive changing reference. But here we anticipate reader-writer collaboration.

The distinction between referring in ordinary and in literary discourse, then, is rather one of degree; it presupposes greater elasticity in addressee (that is, reader) expectations and responses. It involves most of what is involved in ordinary discourse reference; namely, pragmatic considerations including both addresser and addressee within and outside the text, types of speech-acts, multiple contexts, levels, and modes of reference, and ambiguous or changing perception of what constitutes the sign and thus its referent. But, here again, these concepts become considerably more elastic in literary discourse and the interplay between them more complex. So that the overall effect is what might be called the dynamics of "shifting" reference and referential identification (referents, like Mukarovsky's sign, being contingent on cultural—apperception—as Jean Alter and Thomas Lewis show).

In what follows I shall endeavor to present these interwoven aspects separately and then reassemble them in a two-tone semio-semantic view of the literary text.

I, 4: The Referent

Since referring inevitably presupposes discussion of what a referent is, let us consider, briefly, some of the ways in which this concept has been construed. (See fig. 1.) Although the conventional triangle is used throughout, this by no means implies that the different triads are synonymous—though in some cases it may enhance certain similarities.

The discrepancies among these triads require explanation. First the strictly linguistic points of view which separate sign and referent: Saussure divorces the sign (signifier and signified) from the extra-linguistic hypostatized referent (1916, p. 100). The second triad, Benveniste's correction or revised interpretation of Saussure (*Problèmes de linguistique générale*, II, p. 82), reinforces this split, as he remarks that it is not so much the relation between the signifier and the referent which is arbitrary, as that between the sign and the referent.[2]

Ogden and Richards's triad (in *The Meaning of Meaning*) contains the most concrete, behavioristic referent of all those formulated by the philosophers. For them it is an object or state of affairs in the external world, identified by means of a word or expression; reference is the mediating concept. This seems close to the way in which Umberto Eco interprets the referent within his "Theory of Codes" (in *A Theory of Semiotics*), where he appears to dismiss the referent as a "referential fallacy." "The referential fallacy," he says (p. 62), "consists in assuming that the meaning of a sign-vehicle has something to do with its corresponding object." He equates this referential fallacy with what he calls "the extensional fallacy" by relegating reference and extension to a theory of mentions and of sign production involving a truth-value which posits actual existence. Hence, when talking about *mentioning*, he says "The act of *referring* places a sentence (or corresponding proposition) in contact with an *actual circumstance* by means of an indexical device" (p. 163). Thus, in one fell swoop, his own, Ogden and Richards's, Saussure's, and Benveniste's referent, Carnap's extension, and Morris's denotatum appear to be relegated to the wastepaper basket as mere fallacy. But, in a sense, Eco is making much ado about ontological nothings, since here he is concerned with meaning and lies, or statements which do not refer to an actual thing or state of affairs. (Incidentally it should be noted that Morris's "denotatum," being the object which actually exists, corresponds to what is now usually called designatum; conversely his "designatum," evoking the "kind of thing or class of objects or the 'significatum' " [Morris, 1938], is now more commonly known as a denotatum.)

Although these positivist and rather narrow interpretations of the referent may at a first glance appear unsuitable for our purpose, they constitute the very spring-

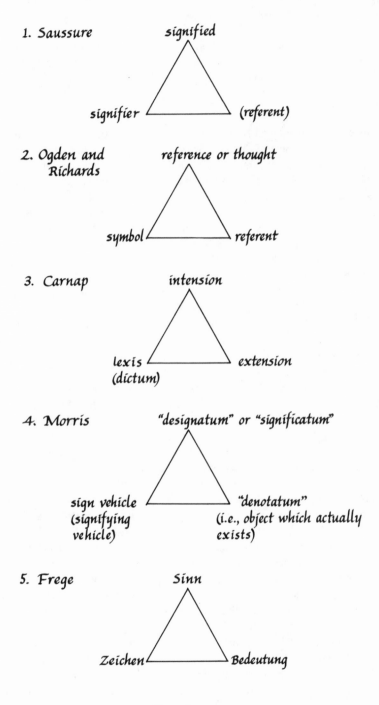

Figure 1

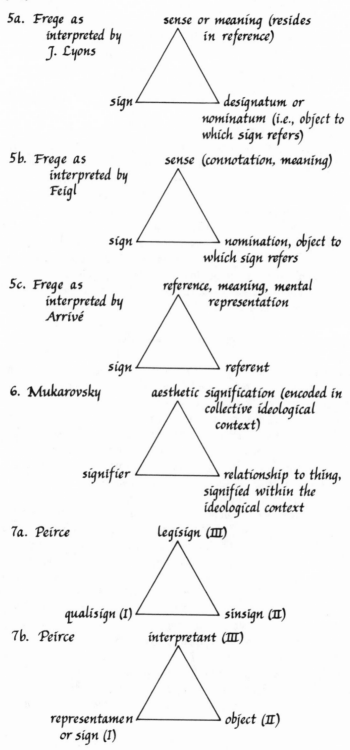

5a. Frege as interpreted by J. Lyons

sense or meaning (resides in reference)

sign — designatum or nominatum (i.e., object to which sign refers)

5b. Frege as interpreted by Feigl

sense (connotation, meaning)

sign — nomination, object to which sign refers

5c. Frege as interpreted by Arrivé

reference, meaning, mental representation

sign — referent

6. Mukarovsky

aesthetic signification (encoded in collective ideological context)

signifier — relationship to thing, signified within the ideological context

7a. Peirce

legisign (III)

qualisign (I) — sinsign (II)

7b. Peirce

interpretant (III)

representamen or sign (I) — object (II)

board for literature's less concrete referents, and are essential in that they express
reference (relationship and act) in its simplest, most immediately recognizable form,
which is reference to a thing. Incidentally, a materialist would claim that a mental
image provoked by an expression, description, etc., is a thing, does exist as a
particular brain activity, just as television images exist and are produced by an
analogous electronic activity. This then makes the expression a referring expression
and the image the referent.

But what of Frege, Mukařovský, and Peirce? Their views will take us up the
primrose path to secondary reference—to the worlds within worlds, ideologies
within ideologies, forms within forms, entities within entities, that are the stuff of
referring in literature. Frege's theory has unfortunately fallen prey to misleading
terminology—partly through translation into modern nomenclature, partly through
translation from German into other languages. In his *Sinn und Bedeutung* (*Sense
and Reference*, Geach and Black's 1960 translation) his use of *Bedeutung*, as Lyons
points out in his discussion (in *Semantics*, Vol. I, p. 199), is in fact closer to
Beseichnung (designation). So Lyons proposes translating Frege's *Zeichen-Sinn-
Bedeutung* triad as sign, meaning, (that is, meaning which resides in reference),
and designation. Feigl's earlier 1949 translation of Frege further clarifies the issue;
here *Sinn* is "sense" (connotation, meaning) and *Bedeutung* is "nominatum" (the
object to which the sign refers). This is roughly the same as the version used by
such French transcribers as Michel Arrivé: sign, reference (that is, meaning, mental
representation), and referent, as shown in Wladimir Krysinski's chapter. In a sense
these cumulative interpretations of *Sinn* and *Bedeutung* help show, contrary to
Saussure's claim and Eco's referential fallacy, that meaning and reference are indeed
related. Frege raises a further problem, which takes us closer to the question of the
literary referent, when dealing with the term "icons." As Françoise Meltzer's
chapter points out, these are closer to the Greek meaning of "likeness," "image,"
"picture," than to their other object meaning. Thus we move from the referent as
object to the referent as the literary image or imagined form of the object, so that
the object referent is seen as the basis of the reader's individualized, imagined
referent. So, in this more literary sense, the original "real" referent becomes a
class or type, and the "iconic" referent, portrayed by description, narration, scenic
representation, or shapes on a page (in concrete poetry) becomes a token. Frege
puts it as follows: "It would be desirable to have an expression for signs which
have *sense* only. If we call them 'icons,' then the words of an actor on the stage
would be icons, even the actor himself would be an icon" ("On Sense and Nominatum," *Readings in Philosophical Analysis*). What is interesting in Frege's argument is that these icons, these mimetic images (to use Wladimir Krysinski's
Aristotelian parallel) are directly concerned with the aesthetic, and, as Françoise
Meltzer points out in her chapter, Frege opposes them to truth and existence. "In
turning to the question of truth," says Frege, "we disregard the artistic appreciation
and pursue scientific considerations." But even though Frege opts for the latter,
his contribution is significant for a theory of the literary referent, since he reduces
the gap between signified and referent and paves the way to their symbiotic relationship.

Mukařovský, dealing with the art object as a sign, further develops both the aesthetic dimension, briefly mentioned by Frege, and, in so doing, the signified-referent symbiosis. For him the signifier is the object to be perceived; the meaning or signified is the aesthetic signification (coded in collective consciousness), and the referent is interpreted as the relationship to a thing signified in the total cultural and historical (that is, ideological) context—an aspect which Patrice Pavis's, Jean Alter's, and Thomas Lewis's chapters elaborate.

Thus referring is shifting ever further from the concrete referent of the linguists and Ogden and Richards. Reference is now relative, encompassing both referent and signified, since it goes beyond specific meaning for a particular readership, to show that meaning is but one meaning in relation to many others.

I too have slipped from referent to reference, for at this level of symbiosis and ever-broadening horizons of context, it becomes increasingly difficult to limit discussion to the referent: the relationship between sign and referent becomes the dominating factor. Similarly, as we shall see in the next section, literary reference, viewed in its widening contexts, shifts from relatively concrete referents, having little obvious meaning or sense, to an increasingly Platonic ideal form, defined by relationships between forms which generate a dialectical synthesis of meaning and referent.

I have left Peirce's triads till last because his theory, integrated in his immense, all-encompassing semiotic scheme, is by far the most sophisticated—far more so than any diagram could ever suggest. Since, as David Savan's excellent monograph (1976) shows, Peirce's triad presupposes an understanding of his categories of Firstness, Secondness, and Thirdness, which govern his entire theory of semiotics, let us briefly consider these categories. Firstness is the possibility of some abstractable quality in what we perceive. Secondness is the state of what he calls "haecceity": being-there-ness, existence, or occurrence. Thirdness is the Hegelian or Kantian "synthesis"—a third entity connecting two others, a transforming or mediating law, a becoming, a process. The terms of the first and most familiar triad (qualisign, sinsign, and legisign) reflect these three categories. "A *Sinsign*," Peirce begins, "is an actual existent thing or event" (Buchler, p. 101). This then is our referent, and the legisign corresponds to reference. But the sinsign, as its name indicates, is also a sign, and the complete quotation runs as follows: "A *Sinsign* is an actual existent thing or event which is a sign." Thus we move beyond the signified-referent relationship, suggested by Mukařovský and Frege, to semiosis, the dynamics of the literary referent. For in literary discourse, as structuralists and semioticians have observed, literary elements (expressions, objects, roles, actions, units, structures) may themselves become signs, referring to and thus transforming other referents into more signs which in turn refer . . . and so on *ad infinitum*.

So this qualisign-legisign-sinsign triad is in turn contained in, and thus becomes, a single element of a more encompassing triad, made up of the sign (or Representamen, as Peirce often calls it), the Interpretant, and the Object. Peirce presents them according to his categories, so that once again, as its name indicates, the Interpretant (a Third; that is, in the category of thirdness) plays a mediating synthesising role, roughly the equivalent of reference, being between the Sign (a First) and the Object (a Second), comparable to the referent. Now what is interesting for us is that the Object, as Peirce sees it, is "much more than that to which a sign refers or purports to refer." Peirce is aiming at a conception of an object which will be adequate to the whole range of signs, from the "Jacquard loom . . . to the most advanced cosmological theories" (Savan, p. 18). Pursuing Peirce's thinking on the relation between object and context (for he did not resolve the problem), Savan has suggested that "the object might be defined as that part of the context which is common to the sign and all its interpretants" (p. 19). If this is the case, then the literary Object or Referent, as well as being *dynamic* in the way that Peirce's first triad suggests, also entails the possibility of *unlimited semiosis*: hyphenated sign-referents which refer to an ever-widening multitude of contexts. If this is so in the world of literature, and we hope to show that it is, then referring in literature is indeed a cumulatively semio-semantic process: a dynamic transcontextual linking of referents, as they evolve from referent to referent, from context to context. The logical extension of this, shown by Michael Riffaterre's work, is intertextuality, as Genette's *Palimpsestes* would seem to corroborate.

But here we are anticipating our conclusion. So let us first turn to more specifically literary considerations, to literary referents in particular, or rather the merging of these referents into reference and, ultimately, into the contexts that both identify and endow them with meaning.

II. LITERARY REFERENCE

II, 1: Construing the Literary Referent

The foregoing tentative conclusion that referring in literature is a dynamic, transcontextual, and ultimately semio-semantic process, leads me back to Lyons's definition of reference as a relationship. Indeed, this relationship between sign, referent, and context is so close-knit that it is hard to consider any single element separately. Thus, although this section will be dealing mainly with various *forms* of the literary referent (ranging from the most concrete to the most abstract), it will necessarily be considered in terms of a) the signs it evolves both from and into, and b) its defining context.

At the concrete end of the scale, what could seem more obvious than concrete poetry or futurist texts? The very tools of writing—letters, words, and sounds— are arranged in such a way that they draw attention to themselves. But, readers being what they are, even such apparently concrete self-referential referents tend to a double role and act as signifiers too. Thus, relatively concrete referents also refer to an identified form, sound, or process of signification—despite the manifestoes decrying this activity. Ideograms in fact use shape(s) to refer to the elements that create them and *vice versa* (Anna Whiteside's chapter develops this). Even pure sounds are strung together in an order, or orders, by the writer (however unconsciously) and the reader (however stochastic the composition), and so compose a form, forms, or possible sets. In all cases, form still leads beyond itself and, as in music, refers the interpreter to a structuring process which will enable him, ultimately, to make sense of the perceived form(s). (So, too, even nonsense rhymes refer—not to nothing, not to sense either, or at least not directly; but to nonsense as the denial of sense and to our need, albeit frustrated, as readers reading a text, to make sense. They refer, then, to themselves as contradiction and, indirectly, to reading as a structuring activity.)

Other putative tangible referents that come to mind include do-it-yourself poem or novel kits such as Queneau's *Mille et Un Poèmes* or Marc Saporta's *Composition No. 1*, each comprising a collection of discrete units (pages of individually cut lines in the first case, loose pages in the second) to be combined by the reader in any order or orders, and thus pointing, yet again, to compositional and reading processes.

The dramatic text can also be considered from this point of view. It "exists" both in its dramatized form and as a printed text whose typographical arrangement refers to the dramatic genre. Similarly, typographical page arrangements usually afford immediate recognition of verse or prose; and subsequently determine, or at least help determine, the reader's generic expectations by providing instant cues to a frame of reference. Genre, though, is not a particularly concrete referent (despite typography, which *is*), so let us return to literature's relatively concrete ones.

When a writer says to his Dear Reader (and he too can exist as a token, rather than always being the virtual reader, the represented type) that "this book" recounts the events which befell, let's say, Tristram Shandy, what book is it? the one the writer is writing or the one you, dear reader, hold in your hand as you read? Already contexts of reference lead us not just to other referents, but to different worlds: the writer's world, the reader's world, and the fictional worlds each and both create. (Of possible worlds, more later, since here we are already anticipating the question of modes to be dealt with in section II, 3.)

Obviously, stage objects and characters are also relatively concrete referents, though they have a double status. As Keir Elam (1980, p. 8) notes, they are referents *and* signs representing a thing. One might call them iconic or mimetic referents; they comprise props, scenery, costumes, and make-up, as perceived through various lighting effects; though, clearly, all do not have the same status. Some may be referred to in the dialogue, some by gestures, some only by the didascalia (Michael Issacharoff examines these different ways of referring in detail). Others may be perceived, but not mentioned in the text: costumes, lighting, make-up, accents, and prosody may be ancillary and used to direct attention to a particular referent at a given moment, enhancing a quality or qualities which help define it. Finery or rags refer to a character's assumed role or status within a given society—a dramatic cliché which has led to many a double dramatic referent (*dramatic* in the sense that it relies on audience participation and awareness, as opposed to *theatrical*—that which happens on stage, to use Keir Elam's nice distinction; *Semiotics of Theatre*, p. 2). A kilt, a period costume, or even an accent may do more for spatio-temporal reference than any decor—however elaborate. Malvolio's yellow stockings, though the rest of his body be hidden, refer to him and also to a particular culture's chromatic code, and so, metonymically, to his personality, with mirth and mockery. Moon-beams may help define the love-lorn hero or romantic heroine, just as garish make-up or talcum powder differentiate between the vamp and, say, the tuberculosis victim's impending exit.

Then there is the implied referent (discussed by Michael Issacharoff). A strange paradox, but nevertheless referred to (diegetically if not mimetically) in the dialogue or in the didascalia: Macbeth's dagger, which he sees and tries to clutch; Caliban's music so eloquently described, Ionesco's unseen Primadonna, or Beckett's Godot.

Nor should we forget the actors themselves who, however strong our powers of suspension of disbelief, are, nevertheless, there on stage in a very real way. For although mimesis refers back to what it imitates, it is simultaneously an event, as exemplified by Pirandello's *Sei personaggi in cerca d'autore* (*Six Characters in Search of an Author*; see Wladimir Krysinski's chapter). In our search for meaning, we see that these actors and their producer refer to the problems of dramatic creation. Of course, for the naïve spectator or reader (mentioned in Patrice Pavis's and Linda Hutcheon's chapters) there is no double or ambiguous referent, no referential chain, no dynamic reference. Jill playing Hedda Gabler is always Jill for Jack—so much so that reference is forever blocked within the immediate frame of reference.

Paradoxically the text an actor quotes is also a referent—a verbal referent (see Jean Alter's chapter). Indeed, a logical extension of this would be to say that any *actualized* text, be it a stage-production or individual reading of any type of text, both is referent and refers back to the written text. Thus the written text is both referent and referring expression (or sign) in that it is the virtual text lending itself to different "concretizations," to use Ingarden's term, and interpretations.

If each production is an actual event in its own right, coincidentally it is an ideological statement (see the chapters by Jean Alter, Patrice Pavis, and Michael Issacharoff) referring, mimetically, to dramatically appropriate socio-cultural phenomena in order to enhance meaning. The Vitez production of *Britannicus* in punk make-up and hair dyes, and Ariane Mnouchkine's *Richard II* in Japanese Kabuki style, are just two such ideological statements, suggesting that *Richard II* can be meaningful in the context of Japanese feudal power struggles and that *Britannicus* can be perceived as a play of our times. Incidentally, this flexible ideological referent revives an old controversy often linked to the use of proper names in literature (Thomas, Meltzer, Issacharoff, Alter, Krysinski, and Chambers all deal with this problem in their chapters). Which *Britannicus* or "Britannicus" are we referring to? Racine's seventeenth-century creation, depicting seventeenth-century ideals? Racine's hybrid classical ideology as seen through neo-classical eyes? A neo-classical interpretation of a decadent interpretation of a classic of Roman history or fable? Or a twentieth-century interpretation of one or all of these? Mukarovsky evokes "the total context of social phenomena" (science, philosophy, religion, politics, economics, etc.) "of a given milieu," as chapters by Lewis, Pavis, and Alter point out. So the dramatic referent becomes ever more elusive, ever less fixed.

But what of poetry and fiction? As well as obvious textual referents (characters, things, events, places, and so on) referred to in the text, many others are similar to those of plays. Visible signs, such as *Tristram Shandy's* marbled page and two blanks, are mimetic referents. In their diegetic context they also refer, rather like

Macbeth's unclutched dagger, to three implied abstract referents: the author's work (of which the marbled page is a "motley emblem"), a missing chapter, and paper for the reader to paint, in his own mind, Toby's lady love. Subsequently these same referents become the reader's concretizations, as is corroborated by the author's comment immediately after the second blank: "—Was ever anything in nature so sweet!—so exquisite!" Because these iconic signs are also self-referring, they are analogous to drama's sign-referents. Other visual signs (formal symmetry or anomalies) and phonetic ones (assonance, onomatopoeia, rhyme, rhythm) may also be discrete and, to some extent, self-referring, whilst also contributing to the text as a global concretized referent.

Form constitutes a more abstract referent. Baudelaire's *Tableaux parisiens* (see the chapter by Ross Chambers) refer beyond topology to the conventional form of the *tableau*, and so back to his particular use of it. Eluard's "La Victoire de Guernica" (Jean-Jacques Thomas's chapter) also reaches beyond topological reference by referring to implied opposition between the extratextual Guernica and this textual recreation, to the conflict between horror and callous acceptance, *and* to the very form chosen to describe it—one which plays on a system of internal opposition. So the poetic function refers to ideology as form, and the referent, whether fictional, poetic, or dramatic, becomes ever more elusive. As Barthes said, "The work of art is a form which history spends its time filling in."

We can perhaps go one stage further before toppling into nothingness and say with Foucault (discussing Barthes in *Pour une archéologie du savoir*, 1978) that this very form is the only reality, the only sure referent. Althusser's refinement of Marxist ideology corroborates this. He advocates stepping outside history to show that Marxist interpretation of realism was, in its own different way, as biased as the bias it was busy demonstrating. Even if a text is construed as an ideological Product, this product remains "symptomatically deformative of its historical reality" (Lewis, 1979, p. 459). It refers in the last instance to an ideological space, its own blind spot, defined as a dialectical absence deriving from an unrepresented relation to other non-identical cultural referents.

II, 2: Contexts

a) Intersecting Contexts

The referent is determined by contexts of production and reception. But literary context, like the referent it defines, is complex, protean, and elusive, given its several and often coexistent levels, which we will now examine. Before even discussing meaning, and *a fortiori* socially symbolic meaning, we need to show how reference is contingent on context. Jakobson's theory of communication raises this issue. It needs some expansion for our present purpose.

The three fundamental contexts which underlie all reference, both in the sense of reference as an act (see Thomas Lewis's chapter for a full development of this aspect), and as a relationship which establishes meaning are: the utterer's, the receiver's, and the so-called encyclopaedic context (see fig. 2).

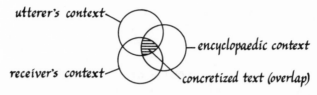

Figure 2

That these three overlapping contexts and their interaction are fundamental to reference is inevitable for, as Benveniste remarks, reference is an integral part of the speech-act and, thus, of the speaker's and receiver's literal, cultural, and ideological situation. This in turn implies the encyclopaedic context of available knowledge constituting their known world. Otherwise, how do we know what "I" or "you" or "his words" refer to, let alone "He" or "God" or "Rome" (to use a more obviously encyclopaedic-oriented context)? So this triad of contexts stands as the foundation for the second set of contexts—however wide or narrow these may be and regardless of their degree of coexistence.

This second set's three main contexts are 1) intratextual, 2) intertextual, and 3) extratextual, with metatextuality sitting on the fence between intra- and intertextuality. They lead to the interpretation of referents within 1) the "work-as-a-symbolic-act," 2) the work as *parole* or "*ideologeme*," 3) perceived "reality" as ideology of form (see Fredric Jameson, 1981). The boundaries between these three contexts are not fast, nor does one context preclude another. It is rather a question of interpretation and degree.

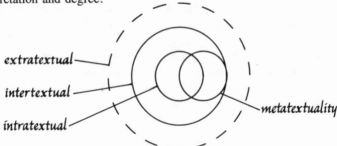

Figure 3: Expanding concentric circles of reference of a concretized text: i.e., secondary set of contexts. This figure represents in detail the shaded area of the fundamental contexts shown in fig. 2.

Since Althusser carries literary reference to its ultimate form by setting it in the widest context imaginable, I shall start from this Ultima Thule and work inwards, proceeding from extratextual to intertextual and, via metatextuality, to intratextual contexts (or "levels" of reference, as Linda Hutcheon calls them). All such contexts involve the interaction of utterer and receiver/reader contexts as well as a common encyclopaedic one. The reader has an image of the text as a "cracking tower of ideologies" (Holquist and Reed). According to these authors, texts provide, not photographs of societies, but "X-rays of the systems out of which they are constituted." Patrice Pavis likens the phenomenon to an iceberg whose vast and invisible base sustains the recent visible layers that rise above the water level. All three metaphors point to the coexistence of multiple layers and to the fact that they are, for the most part, hidden. The cracking tower affords a glimpse, the iceberg shows here and there a few of its numerous layers, the rest changes colour as seen dimly through the water. So too, X-rays are selective, making certain aspects visible, but obscuring or distorting others.

The reader's context, likewise, tends to obscure the writer's, even though it is the latter which originally created reference. When Verlaine says "Dans le vieux parc," whose "old park" is it? his, or one that we remember? Even if our park were the same as his, our impression of it would be different. Yet again, we stumble on another problem which has occupied philosophers and linguists: who or what is doing the referring? The answer, after much debate, is that though words alone may denote (in the linguistic sense), they do not refer. It follows that texts alone do not refer, although this seems nonsensical—and is . . . in a sense. Even an anonymous text is obviously *by* someone, so that directly or indirectly it refers to its context of creation (the literary equivalent of a context of utterance). If we did not know who wrote *La Jalousie* or when it was written, the text's very form would refer us indirectly to a particular extratextual context of creation—that of the *nouveau roman*, and thereby (intertextually speaking), to a literary reaction against so-called realist novels. At all levels reference is an integral part of the speech-act, so that what an author or character says refers directly or indirectly to the author's context of utterance. Dickens's writings refer explicitly to English nineteenth-century society, and so do his characters, their language, and their behaviour. Nabokov's *Lolita* and the lollipop heroine it depicts refer to his un-American view of an aspect of a particular American society; Dante's *Divine Comedy* to fourteenth-century Florentine socio-political conditions, beliefs, and prevailing ideology, and thus to himself as a writer defined by and against his times. John Barth's *The Sot-Weed Factor* refers anachronistically to eighteenth-century mores and literary conventions whose parodic effect relies on a twentieth-century perspective.

Barthes's autobiography, *Roland Barthes par Roland Barthes*, exemplifies a speech-act which fuses and confuses extratextual and intratextual speaker reference. By the title he chooses, Barthes admits extratextual reference; yet he tells his reader that the text "should be read as though it were a novel." He is "I" and "he," subject and object of his speech-act, "I" and "you," speaker and addressee, dialoguing intertextually with himself as author of previous texts of which this autobiography is but a rewriting, a metatext. Thus Barthes exploits reference among all contextual levels whilst enshrining the (polyvalent) speech-act as the necessary means to his referential end: self depicted as a kaleidoscope of *personae*.

Intratextual and extratextual contexts are, in fact, related in all texts, since a literary *microcosm*, or *heterocosm*, is defined as just that: a partial reflexion (and ideological deflexion) of the extratextual *macrocosm*. So, for the reader, the intratextual context is contained in the outer extratextual one, as indeed are metatextuality and intertextuality. The dotted line of the extratextual context represents the expanding and contracting horizons of the latter in the reader's ideological eye. From Althusser and Barthes's standpoint, all the second set's contexts (extra-, inter-, meta-, and intratextual) share this centrifugally biased protean quality (as chapters by Alter and Lewis show). Conversely, chapters by Prince, Thomas, Chambers, Krysinski, Hutcheon and Whiteside all emphasize a centripetal focus, thereby implying a heightened metatextual awareness of text *qua* text in current writing and reader reception.

b) Shifting Contexts

Thus, neither fundamental nor secondary sets of contexts are fixed in a rigid pattern. Just as the secondary set of reader-construed reference moves outwards *and* inwards between contexts, so the focussing of the fundamental overlapping reader, writer, and encyclopaedic contextual lenses enhances first one, then another aspect. Like the lenses of a telescope (or microscope) they focus differentially, enhancing any one of the three ways of seeing, in any combination. For example, when reading a historical play, we can privilege the encyclopaedic contextual lens so as to emphasize historical "facts." Alternatively, we may prefer to construe it as a writer's or society's biased version, and so bring to the fore the utterer's context. By identifying with this utterer's context or dissociating himself from it, a reader may also focus on his own context. A stage-production can emphasize a particular receiver's (reader's, producer's, or culture's) context, in which case, the interaction between utterer, receiver, and encyclopaedic contexts again shifts. In fact, as we shall see later, the relationship between this fundamental contextual triad and the superimposed frames of intra-, inter-, and extratextual reference is one of inevitable interdependence, since, in any text, both sets are automatically implied in their different permutations.

For example, the Babiyar massacre in D. M. White's *The White Hotel* refers, at the level of fundamental contexts, to a particular utterer's transposition of encyclopaedic reality. The problem is to define the utterer. Do we mean the author, the psychoanalytic narrator, his tortured and hysterical female protagonist, or some other narrator? The answer is probably the whole gamut, its shifting hierarchy depending on their roles, and on the receiver's (that is, character's and reader's) conscious or unconscious perspective—and this too is protean and complex. Moving into the second set of contexts, we construe this episode extratextually by relating it to the documented 1941 massacre outside Kiev, and intratextually by linking it to other events and elements in the novel. The hotel fire could thus be construed as a premonition of the holocaust, or as a re-enacting of the original or derived meanings of "holocaust" (whose etymology goes back to the Hebraic sacrificial burning and thence to the Greek *holos kaustos*, "burnt whole"), or perhaps all of these. Thus the episode may also be seen as referring to the text's attempt at Freudian analysis and portrayal of a particular (Jewish) collective unconscious. This same death camp episode also provides a text (and context) for the other chapters by metatextually relating their versions of the protagonist's hysteria to her experience of this catastrophe. Indeed metatextual commentary seems to condition interpretation from the outset of *The White Hotel*: the opening letters' comment on the poem in chapter 1, chapter 2 is a parallel prose version of the poem, then poem and journal form the basis of the Freudian analysis "Frau Anna G." in chapter 3.

This Freudian account also refers intertextually to Freud's famous case history of Anna O., and the chapter on Babiyar to Yevtushenko's *Babi-Yar*. The maze of interwoven contexts compound the *illusion* of confusion between extratextual and all other reference, for ultimately intratextuality subsumes all other contexts.

For the literary reader then, as chapters by Hutcheon, Prince, and Chambers show, there is no "real" referent—since the referent is first and foremost a textually created, that is, an imagined construct. Thus all levels of this secondary set's contexts imply the interaction of various contrasting ideologies, making the reader a reader of ideologies *qua* ideologies.

One of the distinctive features of the literary text is the play on multiple and equivocal contexts, leading inevitably to simultaneous levels of reference and to what is in fact a *polyreferent*. As we have seen, Barthes's autobiography, like other examples cited, exploits polyreference by presenting the subject's different facets and *personae*. In poetry, the tradition of multiple contexts is so taken for granted that it defines the very way the genre is read. Thus the coexistence of literal (extratextual) and symbolic (that is, intratextual, and sometimes intertextual) levels, in a text other than poetry, is often deemed to lend it a "poetic" quality. In theatre, as Wladimir Krysinski shows, reference shifts from "historical" or "real" extratextuality to intratextuality. Apollinaire's *Les Mamelles de Tirésias* (*The Breasts of Tiresias*) is meant to refer, as the author's prologue tells us, to France's need for repopulation. The play also refers to the scriptural and theatrical creation of a dramatic text whilst being played. Even the floating balloons, once theatrical breasts, ultimately corroborate the predominance of intratextuality by referring to dramatic creation *within* the play.

Modern literature, particularly, plays on plurality and equivocation of contexts (termed "opacity" by Quine, 1976; "obliqueness" by Frege) because of an apparent perfusion and concerted confusion or lack of context. As Gerald Prince points out (see chapter 3), bad (confused or contradictory) references make it impossible for the reader to interpret the numerous examples of intratextual spatio-temporal deixis. However seemingly precise, "now," "next," "here," etc. do not refer, or rather they refer to themselves: "here" is here in the novel; "now," at this moment in the novel. In other words, they refer to fiction, namely the reading and writing processes. So context is deferred until finally it is seen to surround the invisible central speaker. This referential hide-and-seek in turn refers intertextually to the *nouveau roman's* refusal of the realist novel's referential practice, and, hence, to reader expectations relating to ideology, period, school, genre, form, and conventions.

Thus, when Robbe-Grillet, in *Glissements progressifs du plaisir*, refers intertextually to the thematic and structural materials of pop culture (folklore, detective stories, pornography, horror films and stories), he intentionally misleads the reader. For having established this context of codes, he destroys them by slipping into another set of codes. These eventually refer, metatextually, to the process of the creation (and destruction) of reference *and* meaning in terms of reference to particular contexts (see Bruce Morrissette's chapter). This self-referential device again signals the official bankruptcy and illusion of absolute or "real" extratextual fictional reference. In so doing it stresses the integral role of the reader in the creative and recreative process of imagined, or rather reconstructed, reference.

So, whether texts, and thus writers and readers, in fact refer (or should one say writers and thus texts and readers?) extratextually, intertextually, intratextually, or metatextually ultimately depends on the reader's recognition of reference. Now the potential variety of contexts and ensuing divergent referents are considerable. My mental images of Emma Bovary, of Henry James's Paris, or the events in *War and Peace* will not necessarily match someone else's, because, in spite of the same descriptions, we bring different contexts to our construction of them. Furthermore, the way we construe and construct the text's created context is a dynamic semiotic process. Referents become hyphenated referent-signifiers as contexts shift and meaning blurs. If signs fail to refer in one context, they are reinterpreted in another. In fact, one of the pleasures of reading (and rereading) is that reference, and thus meaning, is never complete. The referent can always be reoriented, refocussed, and redefined, as Robbe-Grillet's *Glissements* illustrate, and Krysinski's and Pavis's chapters explain: the former tracing the metamorphosis of the historical referent into the autotelic one, the latter its ideological translations.

The reader constructs a mutually defining referent-signified dipole within a given context (his own, alias the text's) and so arrives at a tentative meaning. This meaning then modifies, enhances, or deflects some other aspect (or aspects) of the referent, and so on in a never-ceasing hermeneutic spiral, similar to those postulated by Iser and Ingarden.

So too, intratextually, a text's characters, places, events, conversations, descriptions, narrators, narratees, speakers, pronouns, symbols, significant narrative and structural entities, are all defined in terms of their reference to one another. The links between them constitute units which in turn refer to and fit into larger and larger units. And so the intratextual, multilayered construct is, rather like the extratextual context, constantly referring to ever-widening contextual spheres.

Thus we have gone full circle, and the ideology or ideological space which was the text's ultimate referent for Althusser has become the context which defines reference. This is hardly surprising—after all, ordinary discourse too, though to a lesser degree, links the sign, not directly with real things, but with a world perceived within the ideological framework of a given culture. Biographers and autobiographers, chroniclers, realists, and naturalists, however scrupulously honest their intentions, are, and ever shall be, interpreters. Inevitably the line separating referent and context appears increasingly fuzzy, and the distinction becomes one of degree rather than of absolutes.

In fact one can say, without being unduly Platonic, that even the most apparently absolute (that is, "primary") referents are only relatively so. "The page" may well be the page a writer writes, or writes upon, in his authorial context; but it cannot be unequivocally so, as it is also your page as you read in your context and, in a secondary way, your image of the writer's page as he wrote those words at his writing desk. The question of which is real is superfluous; all are, in a sense, and we accept the convention of this referential multiplicity, knowing that literary reference obtains by virtue of the contexts we, the readers, bring to it (an aspect dealt with in Bruce Morrissette's chapter). Inevitably, then, literary reference assumes its own phenomenological implications, and increasingly "reality" or extratextual reference is replaced by the concept of validity. Nevertheless, because the notion of the referent as extratextual reality has enjoyed wide credence (despite Althusser's, Foucault's, and Barthes's insistence that it too is relatively artificial, being an ideological construct), and because this notion has somehow infiltrated literary exegesis, it is worth considering the implications of the two modes which the notion of contexts of reference apparently suggests, namely: the *"real"* mode (derived from the extratextual context) and the *fictitious* or *imaginary mode* (derived primarily from the intratextual context).

II, 3: Modes of Reference

How do we reconcile a statement such as Michel Arrivé's that "there is no literary referent," with the assumption which underwrites literary creation (and, *a fortiori*, the reader's recreation): namely, that we can indeed refer—as can literary characters (Heintz, 1979)—to Mr. Pickwick, Anna Karenina, Pegasus, Banquo's ghost, Macbeth's perturbed state of mind, Lilliput, Picrochole's war, Achilles' shield, Ulysses, and so on? Clearly, Arrivé would side with Russell (1905) and Strawson (1950), in claiming that because literature does not deal with "real" entities, it fails to refer. And yet, as Linsky points out in *Referring* ("Reference and Referents"), fiction has a reality of its own. It exists, after all! It constitutes an important part of our extratextual context.

All agree with Searle who says, in "The Logical Status of Fictional Discourse," that in fiction words have their normal meanings (p. 319), since there are no special dictionaries for fictional discourse (Gale, 1971). The difference between ordinary and fictional discourse (and I extend Searle's "fictional" to include all literary discourse) lies rather in the way readers interpret and writers perform (or have fictional characters perform) their fictional speech-acts. This is a difference not of meaning but of discursive mode. In normal discourse it is assumed that we mean, more or less, what we say—any deviation from this norm is marked by prefatory or postfatory riders such as "let's imagine that . . . ," hypothetical riders such as "perhaps . . . ," and disclaimers, "she says that . . . ," "that's his version," "but that's not what really happened," "but no one believes it," "Have you heard the joke, story, etc. about . . . ," "I was inventing," "I didn't really mean that," and so on. Deviations not marked by a spoken or situational disclaimer (storytelling, acting, postulating, etc.) are considered violations of the assumption that we mean what we say (Grice, 1957), and are interpreted as lies (Grice, 1968), that is, intentionally deceptive discourse.

In fictional discourse, writers indulge in "nondeceptive pseudo-performance," to use Searle's expression. In other words, there exists between writer and reader an unwritten pact that the writer is referring, not to the real world, but to his own interpretation of the real world, or to his own created world, or both. This does not mean that the reader will not recognize many aspects of it—character types, objects, general truths, place descriptions and events or proper names, etc. He certainly will, and this recognition, or as Patrice Pavis calls it, this "referential illusion," is one of the sources of the reader's pleasure. Carried further, this referential illusion may cause referential confusion. Such an extreme case would be Ricardou's naïve reader, mentioned by Linda Hutcheon, who talks of a fictitious character as though he were real, saying "If I were so-and-so I would have done such-and-such"—or better still, "X should have done this, not that."

So, although we can say that literature refers, we should be careful to distinguish the two modes of reference. On the one hand the "real" or indicative ordinary discourse mode (that is, meaning what we say or meaning to deceive) ranges from concrete to ideological to abstract referents in a world that exists, or is assumed to have existed; on the other, a fictional or subjunctive mode posits possible worlds and their story-related referents (see Thomas Pavel, 1975, and Kripke, Quine, and Linsky in Linsky, 1971). Since the second mode presupposes the first, it is hard to know where to draw the line. Yet there is a difference, and it constitutes one of the important idiosyncracies of literary reference. The literary referent is a construct which both relies on an affirmative, recognizably plausible or "real" entity (or a negative one as in science fiction, fantasy, utopic, or dystopic writings), and modifies our awareness of it, making it "more real" by removing the patina of use and habit (Schklovskii, 1965; Barthes, 1968) and by iconic augmentation (Ricoeur, 1976). As such, it reinvests the text with its particular enhanced meaning, so that, in fact, the relationship between "real" and "make-believe" is symbiotic, each lending meaning and referential potential to the other.

A brief comparison of "real" and literary referents will show this, as well as help define the literary referent's role and the way it functions within the text. A chair in a play such as Ionesco's *Les Chaises* (*The Chairs*) is, as Anne Ubersfeld remarks when discussing stage props, both a real and a make-believe chair: a referent, in the most concrete sense, and a representation of a chair, that is, a sign (1977, p. 37). Eco, for whom performance is a sophisticated form of ostension (1977, p. 110), corroborates this by remarking that one uses the concrete object as "the expression of the class of which it is a member" (1976, p. 225), while Keir Elam (p. 21–27) stresses the iconic quality of a dramatic referent of this sort, thereby treating it as a sign too (p. 21–27). Ionesco's chair is also a literary symbol, evoking the absence of people, of God, and of material presence (Ionesco, 1962), and, as such, far exceeds its initial reference. In so doing, it underlines the use of words, naming, and the relationship of a referring expression to its referent, or indeed of a sign to what it represents—to its denotata, and to its contextually determined designatum.

Instead of comparing a real chair and a fictional one, let us compare Ionesco's ,double signifier-referent chairs with, say, a unicorn, (Snark, or other fantastic creation).[3] The fact that unicorns have only secondary denotation (Goodman, 1952) is irrelevant to considering them as literary referents. It is not so much a question of what their existential status is as of how they are used and how this use is effective in endowing them with referential status, that is, by providing solid contextual backing and an identifying definite description. Indeed the more "memorable" the entity, the more readily subsequent reference may be established; and memorability is usually determined by events or context-related factors. Curiously enough, and precisely because unicorns are odd, our mental image of a unicorn is probably more memorable than that evoked by the word "chair."

For those concerned with referring in literature, all this talk of unicorns, states of disembodiment, Utopias, and other fictional entities is a referential red herring started by Russell and continued by Lavis (in "Le Texte littéraire, le référent, le réel, le vrai," 1971). It is now deemed to have little to do with referring, in the sense that once a definite description has been provided, once the mental image exists, then, even if none of us has actually seen or experienced the real thing, we can refer to it. For referring, as Thomas Lewis's chapter insists, is something we do, an act, and a link we establish between an expression (verbal or gestural) and what we thereby refer to, whatever its ontological status. After all, a writer or character (and thus a reader) may refer to Cleopatra, as did Shaw and Shakespeare, without having seen her. This does not mean that they have not really referred to her, or to someone's description of her. It merely means that, as in most literature, they refer to their interpretation, and ensuing mental representation, of someone else's description. Now this version may also be second- or third-hand—as in Shakespeare's use of North's second-hand translation (from Amyot's French version) of Plutarch's *Bioi paralleloi* (*Parallel Lives*). It is a question of degree, but not, and especially not in literature, one of existence or reality.[4]

In fictional discourse, a writer or heterodiegetic story-teller can also set the action in a period or place that he has never known, in the same way that you or I can refer to a time or place that neither we (nor, perhaps, the reader) have ever actually experienced. In fact, sometimes we simply do not know what is meant to be real or imagined. But again, the question of reality is irrelevant, for reference is nevertheless established, first and foremost, within the literary construct and fictional mode. Victor Hugo, when writing about Villequier in "A Villequier," deals with this problem. He juxtaposes his mental image of a bygone Villequier and a more recent one which, for him, in no way resembles the first, completely shattering not only many of its remembered denotations, but also its concomitant connotations. So which Villequier is Hugo's referent? Is it one of these, or both, or the geographical entity of that village in Seine-Maritime? (Ross Chambers's chapter on Baudelaire's *Tableaux Parisiens* and Jean-Jacques Thomas's chapter raise similar questions about Paris and Guernica respectively, as do the chapters by Krysinski, Meltzer, and Issacharoff about Poland and historical figures used and quoted in fiction.) One might also ask which Hugo do we mean? The father whose daughter was drowned near Villequier, or the older Hugo returning there years later to visit his daughter's tomb? If we were interested in the ontological status of either Villequier or Hugo in this poem, we might say, contrary to Frege, that though the referent (and the name) Villequier is the same, the sense of Villequier past and Villequier present is different (even if this sameness is perhaps more disputable than the sameness of Venus alias The Morning Star and The Evening Star, to Frege's stargazers). But this sameness is of little use in a literary discussion. Rather, we would draw the conclusion that reference in the two cases is different, since the context of reception (taking Hugo to be the observer, the person who experienced the situation) is different. Both mental images—even if the denotata had been identical—are surprisingly different because of the vital role connotation plays in literary reference.

In other words, mere designatum is not enough here; for literary reference relies on and is created, primarily, by intratextual linkings and connotation, so that the similarity between a literary referent such as Robbe-Grillet's New York in *Projet pour une révolution à New York* and our New York is merely a realistic illusion. In fact he has tricked us into interpreting a proper name in the real mode and trying to construe fiction as reality. This trick merely serves to remind us that, in fiction, all constructs are fictional within the fictional mode (however "real" or fantastic they may seem), and that the reader's readiness to draw parallels with his known world, to "identify" or to "recognize" fictional elements, by situating them in his own mental context, is unremitting.

Jarry, as Wladimir Krysinski's chapter shows, goes one stage further than Hugo, Baudelaire, or Robbe-Grillet, in that, having established a pseudo-"real" mode (Poland), he makes it entirely fictional. He then proceeds to transform this nowhere into a somewhere—the somewhere of his literary creation. But by calling it Poland when it is not Poland, he insists on the illusion of literary "real" reference and on the autonomy of the literary sign which can, in fact, refer to whatever the writer will, be it a substitute referent or the very process of creating reference.

If we move on from things, periods, and places to a comparison between "real" and make-believe *qualities*—avarice and ubiquity (to use Lavis's example) or disembodiment, the difference between the modes of ordinary and literary discourse becomes more apparent. Avarice, taken out of context, is something we can experience; ubiquity or disembodiment is not (not in our normal state anyway). Yet Scrooge's or Harpagon's avarice is no easier to refer to than Ariel's or Satan's ubiquity, or Banquo's ghost: the question is irrelevant. All can be referred to, providing we have the necessary context, in the make-believe mode (just as all qualities can be referred to in a non-fictional mode by our speaking about them). In fact it would seem, yet again, that the fictional referent, because so tightly bound to its context, is more memorable than the non-fictional one, for Scrooge has passed into "real" mode discourse as a metonymical expression of extreme avarice. So rather than saying that there are two types of referents, it is generally more useful to say that there are two modes of discourse: the serious and the make-believe.

Obviously this pretence of mode-mixing is a common literary device and relies on the assumption that proper names are the purest and most readily recognized referring expressions.[5] This mixing of modes not only enhances fiction's putative realism, it also works the other way around and imbues transposed home truths of real events with a fictional aura. Satire relies on it, and so too do moralistic or socially relevant *tranche de vie* writings such as those Diderot advocated for the theatre.

Michael Issacharoff and Françoise Meltzer deal at length with mode mixing in playscripts and novels, as does Wladimir Krysinski, using (amongst others) what is probably one of literature's most sophisticated crossing of modes: Pirandello's *Six Characters in Search of an Author*. Within the fictional mode, it shows the play as a *single* text created by author, characters, producer, and spectators, and also as *several* simultaneous interpretations. Thus combined, they debunk any claims that in theatre (or other literary forms), real and fictional modes are separable, by fusing the two into a single fictional entity. Probably the only case in which modes are consistently distinct is the playscript: here the traditional type of didascalia is in the serious mode and the dialogue in the non-serious mode (see Michael Issacharoff's chapter).

Fiction thus points ultimately beyond modes to the processes of literary creation and interpretation—that is, interpretation as recreation. Distinguishing between the different contextual horizons of the secondary set (fig. 3) depends on interpretation in the fictional mode, which may pretend to mix serious and non-serious modes. The "reality" of fiction's extratextual referents is a question of *degree of illusion*, of this or that literary referent *seeming* more real than another. In other words, it seems real because we are the better able to fill in the skeleton the text's construct provides—the form which is literature's only constant. So, we have come full circle back to Plato, Foucault, and Barthes, for whom form is the only literary reality. Perhaps, then, metatextuality (see Linda Hutcheon's chapter) is the closest thing to a real mode in literature, since its object, being a text, must, like some overt poetic function, inevitably refer to the text's form.

II, 4: Dynamics of Referring in Literature

If form is the ultimate referent, our apperception of it necessarily depends on the process of filling and emptying it. For it is this very process which delineates form. Reference as a deictic process is thus essential to our recognition of form, so that the linguist's focus (reference as process) and the philosopher's (reference as a relationship) are contingent on each other and mutually defining. It would seem that one of the differences between ordinary discourse and literary discourse is precisely the latter's propensity to sustain the dynamics of this process. By way of conclusion, we will briefly summarize these dynamics.

Literary reference is forever protean. It evolves with the reader's (and, to some extent, the writer's) constantly changing perception, whilst developing within a given textual context, itself being shaped by the symbiosis of all contextual spheres. Furthermore, a constantly fluctuating contextual hierarchy forever keeps us reassessing and refining our perception of the referent and the evolving act of reference. For reference, seen as a relationship, is not suddenly established and immutably maintained. Being, rather, a question of perception, it depends on the reader's interpretational strategies, and on his constant testing and reappraisal of reference. At the same time, he is also measuring the validity of his interpretation by elaborating parallel complex coreferential systems, which constitute both a tentative interpretation and a means to interpretation.

As Mary Louise Pratt shows, in *Towards a Speech Act Theory of Literary Discourse* (p. 3–37), the literary text is not to be viewed so much as an object possessing special properties, as "an *act* performed in a context." It is performed, ultimately, by the reader who brings out unending subjects and countersubjects as they evolve in this polyphonic fugue, first in one voice then in another, variously colouring, reshaping or inverting, enhancing or subduing them, as all play together in evolving contrapuntal combinations. Nor are any two performances identical, so that, while the text provides referring expressions or signs, it is the reader who ultimately makes them refer, makes them refer within the text and without, and thus creates meaning. "Never ask for the meaning of a word in isolation, but only in the context of a sentence," warns Frege (see Quine, 1953, pp. 20–46). "Reference," adds Benveniste, "is an integral part of the speech act," and only when this sentence or text is seen as a speech act, and thus in a particular framework (that is, textual and related to both speaker and reader), that reference obtains and meaning is possible. Otherwise the signs remain empty; no sign-systems or contingent meaning(s) coalesce.

Fortunately for the posterity of the literary text, as already suggested, the reader looks for meaning, and thus reference, behind every bush—literal and metaphoric. (In fact, of course, the order is the reverse, since he must first establish some sort of reference for there to be meaning). It matters little to him that what he reads is in the fictional mode, or indeed in mixed modes, since neither precludes the possibility of reference, even though referential status is altered. In fact mode-mixing is a trigger which propels reference towards a dialectically enhanced dynamics. If all other reference fails, the fictional mode will merely refer to itself as fiction, as Gerald Prince shows. Or, caught between the two modes, like the balloon-breasts in Wladimir Krysinski's chapter, referents may refer to their own transformation: to the very creation, destruction, and recreation of reference before our very eyes. Even such startlingly non-referring texts as Surrealist writings, which systematically (but in asystematic fashion) cut coreferential bonds, refer . . . to themselves as innovation, to new para-syntactic strategies. In a similar way, as Riffaterre remarks (1979, pp. 199–234), many metaphorically overloaded and referentially contradictory texts point, like a boomerang, to themselves as semiotic structure.

It is interesting to note that often the triggers which propel signifiers to refer, and thereby to signify specifically, are either the overfull or the empty sign. Grojnowski, analysing literary decadence and its discourse (1978),[6] shows how the aesthetically overcrowded sign, ceasing to refer coherently and thus to mean, turns in upon itself till it reaches an altered state of reference by referring to the very nature of the decadent sign, which, like the work of art, refers ultimately to itself. Moving from the high-piled paradigms of decadent, poetic, and highly metaphoric discourse to empty paradigms, such as "Poland of Nowhere," this very emptiness seems to display an irresistible referential attraction for the reader, who, in his "performance," seeks to fill it. Often referential or semantic opacity will simultaneously empty and trigger a text's signifiers to polyvalent referential contexts. For instance, in Apollinaire's poem "Fête" ["Celebration"], the poet-soldier describes fireworks and roses. Looking down he suddenly mentions his cocked revolver. Though a soldier, this barely provides sufficient context for meaningful reference. So what "revolver" is he speaking of, and why? Reference, now blocked, floats in a vacuum, forcing us to cast around for a new context, and, in this case, to switch to a latent erotic context. Thus we discover a speech act far more subjectively and symbolically oriented than the bucolic third-person description initially implied. The deictic function of the typographical arrangement (capitalized key words such as "TO LOVE," ambiguous indented lines, and the artifice they explicitly mention), reveals new reference within a new code, and, thereby, converts diegesis into referential mimesis. Here, then, as in many such cases, referential blocking points to hidden reference, breeds polyreference, and unleashes semiosis, allowing different interpretations to enhance one another. For subsequently these exotic flowers, like the pointing revolver, are not as innocent as first they seemed, now that a hidden trigger has reforged and interwoven the text's anaphoric and cataphoric referential chains.

Indeed, referential subversion and diversion, and the semiosis they engender, are instrumental in creating and weaving the many strands of the textual cloth. Our awareness, and thus performance of the text's perlocutionary function, triggered by our awareness of its predominantly fictional illocutionary force, is probably one of the most important factors in literature's referential dynamics. Thus we see, through the surface, other inferred levels of reference, as we perceive, for example, the perlocutionary referential function of symbolism, irony, or "historical" recreations. Irony, parody, *mise en abyme*, covert intertextuality (as when Nabokov's opening lines in *Ada* refer to Dostoievsky's world), metaphor, symbolism, and allegory are just some examples of the text's deictic role in the reader's boundless perlocutionary referential and semiotic enthusiasm. By the same token, we also see inferred concretizations, both diachronic and synchronic, mutually reinforcing one another, as emphasis shifts with the text's unfolding and the reader's constant adjustments to his recreation.

In literature, unlike most ordinary discourse, no one level ever precludes another: they all coexist, and in a constantly shifting hierarchy. It is perhaps this very coexistence of contexts, of modes, and of diverse illocutionary and perlocutionary acts which makes literary reference essentially an *act*, a dynamic self-referential process; one which never ceases and never shall. For in literary discourse the referential function encompasses far more than mere context (though this, too, is complex): it implies the metalinguistic, conative, emotive, and, above all, the poetic functions.

In literature, reference creates the tension that propels the dialectic movement of interpretation between reader and text. For this dialectic is contingent upon that of the text's double referential function. Form (as perceived by virtue of its metamorphic content) *and* process are the two poles, the two dynamic generators of this referential dialectic in literature. As such, they are its ultimate and necessarily symbiotic referents, the very foundation of literary creation and reader recreation. For referring, in literature, is the *sine qua non* of the literary act; and literature, in the last analysis, must be literary *praxis*.

NOTES

1. All references are to be found in the bibliography at the end of this volume.

2. We have already commented on the non-referential semantic and semiosical fallacy this leads to. Since it will also be dealt with in the next section, and since the purpose of the present section is to present the referent, and thereby reference, in relation to the sign and meaning, our remarks will be limited to 1) the separation of the sign (and apparently of meaning) from the referent, and 2) the latter's perceived degree of concreteness.

3. Unicorns have come under fire from Russell who, refusing anything but the real mode, would not admit that unicorns can exist in any form or shape—not even in heraldry. But what is the precise nature of their ''existence''? They are fictional entities, just as Ionesco's chairs are fictional entities for the reader. We can represent both by drawing them or including them in fictional discourse, and both representations will refer to some previous image of them. Whether the source of this image is secondhand (seeing a painting of a unicorn) or real (sitting on a chair) matters little—literature is rarely concerned with referring to the real thing—and we are able to refer equally well to the mental image of both: looking at paintings and sitting on chairs are both events, and mental images of both exist in our minds.

4. The same problem also applies to ordinary discourse. Am I to say that before we knew Troy was where Hissarlik now stands, or before the mound called Cadbury Castle was identified as one of King Arthur's castles, no one could refer to these places? For the untravelled or ignorant reader, the possibility of referring to these places is no less than for the initiated. For centuries people have been referring to Troy; does it make a qualitative difference to the validity of their referring act that they can now add, to their erstwhile historico-literary referent, layer upon layer of archeological rubble? The answer must be no, for the act itself is not changed, even if the widening context, which now includes both the fictional and real mode, has enhanced our mental image by the archeological proof of what one suspected all along.

5. Some have argued the only ones—see Plato's *Theaetetus*, Russell's ''Philosophy of Logical Atomism,'' and Wittgenstein's earlier writings in the *Tractatus*; Frege, and Wittgenstein in *Philosophical Investigations*, para. 40, represent the opposite point of view, i.e., that names necessarily have meaning, but only contingently reference, and are like disguised definite descriptions; more recently both views have been debated by Strawson (1950 and 1959), Kripke (1972), Donnellan (1970 and 1974), and Pavel (1979), to mention but a few.

6. *Littérature* 29 (1978): 75–89.

BIBLIOGRAPHY

Only basic and seminal works on reference and closely related problems are listed. Writings on specific literary texts and genres are not included.

Adorno, T.
  1970 *Aesthetic Theory* (tr. C. Lenhardt). London & Boston: Routledge & Kegan Paul.
Althusser, L., & Balibar, E.
  1970 *Reading Capital* (tr. B. Brewster). London: New Left Books.
Arrivé, M.
  1969 Postulats pour la description linguistique des textes littéraires. *Langue Française* 3:3–13.
Balibar, E., & Macherey, P.
  1974 Sur la littérature comme forme idéologique: Quelques hypothèses marxistes. *Littérature* 13:29–48.
Barthes, R.
  1964 Eléments de sémiologie. *Communications* 4:91–135. (Tr. A. Lavers & C. Smith, *Elements of Semiology*. London: Cape, 1967 & New York: Hill & Wang, 1968).
  1968 L' Effet de réel, *Communications* 11:84–89.
Benveniste, E.
  1966 *Problèmes de linguistique générale* I. Paris: Gallimard. (Tr. M. E. Meek, *Problems in General Linguistics*. Coral Gables: University of Miami Press, 1971).
  1974 *Problèmes de linguistique générale* II. Paris: Gallimard.
Buchler, J. (ed.)
  1955 *Philosophical Writings of Peirce*. New York: Dover.
Carnap, R.
  1942 *Introduction to Semantics*. Cambridge, Mass.: M.I.T. Press.
  1947 *Meaning and Necessity*. Chicago: University of Chicago Press.
Chastain, C.
  1975 Reference and Context, in K. Gunderson (ed.), *Language, Mind and Knowledge*. Minneapolis: University of Minnesota Press, pp.194–269.
Donnellan, K.
  1966 Reference and Definite Descriptions. *The Philosophical Review* LXXV:282–304.
  1970 Proper Names and Identifying Descriptions. *Synthèse* 21:335–358.
  1974 Speaking of Nothing. *The Philosophical Review* LXXXIII:3–32.
  1978 Speaker Reference, Descriptions and Anaphora, in *Pragmatics,* vol. 9 of P. Cole (ed.), *Syntax and Semantics*. New York: Academic Press, pp.47–68.
Eco, U.
  1973 Langage artistique, segmentation du contenu et référents. *Degrés* 3:b–b15.
  1976 *A Theory of Semiotics*. Bloomington & London: Indiana University Press.
Elam, K.
  1980 *The Semiotics of Theatre and Drama*. London & New York: Methuen.
Feigl, H. & Sellars, W. (eds.)
  1949 *Readings in Philosophical Analysis*. New York: Appleton-Century-Crofts.
Foucault, M.
  1969 *L'Archéologie du savoir*. Paris: Gallimard. (*The Archeology of Knowledge*, Tr. A. M. S. Smith. New York: Pantheon and London: Tavistock Publications, 1972).

Frege, G.
   1892 Über Sinn und Bedeutung. *Zeitschrift für Philosophie und philosophische Kritik* 100:25–50.
   (Tr.: 1) On Sense and Reference, in Geach & Black, 1960, pp. 56–78; 2) Feigl & Sellars, 1949, pp. 82–102.)
Gale, R. M.
   1971 The Fictive Use of Language. *Philosophy* 46:324–40.
Geach, P. T.
   1962 *Reference and Generality*. Ithaca: Cornell University Press.
Geach, P. T., & Black, M. (eds.)
   1960 *Translations from the Philosophical Writings of Gottlob Frege*. Oxford: Blackwell.
Gombrich, E. H.
   1960 *Art and Illusion*. Princeton: Princeton University Press.
Goodman, N.
   1952 On Likeness of Meaning, in Linsky, 1952.
Grice, H. P.
   1957 Meaning. *The Philosophical Review* LXVI:377–88.
   1968 Utterer's Meaning, Sentence Meaning and Word Meaning. *Foundations of Language* 4:225–42.
Halliday, M. A. K., & Hasan, R.
   1976 *Cohesion in English*. London: Longman.
Heintz, J.
   1979 Reference and Inference in Fiction. *Poetics* Vol. 8, Nos 1–2:85–99.
Holquist, M., & Reed, W.
   1980 Six Theses on the Novel—and Some Metaphors. *New Literary History*, Vol. XI, No. 3:413–23.
Ihwe, J. F., & Rieser, H.
   1979 Normative and Descriptive Theory of Fiction: Some Contemporary Issues. *Poetics* Vol. 8, Nos. 1–2:63–84.
Ingarden, R.
   1973 *The Literary Work of Art: An Investigation on the Borderlines of Ontology, Logic and Theory of Literature* (1965). Evanston: Northwestern University Press.
Iser, W.
   1978 *The Act of Reading: A Theory of Aesthetic Response*. Baltimore: Johns Hopkins University Press.
Jakobson, R.
   1960 Closing Statement: Linguistics and Poetics, in T. Sebeok (ed.), *Style in Language*. Cambridge, Mass.: M.I.T. Press.
Jameson, F.
   1981 *The Political Unconscious: Narrative as a Socially Symbolic Act*. Ithaca: Cornell University Press.
Kripke, S.
   1963 Semantical Considerations on Modal Logic. *Acta Philosophica Fennica* 16:83–94. [Reprinted in Linsky, 1971, pp.63–72].
   1972 Naming and Necessity, in D. Davidson & G. Harman (eds.), *Semantics of Natural Languages*. Dordrecht: Reidel, pp. 253–355.
Lavis, G.
   1971 Le Texte littéraire, le référent, le réel. *Cahiers d'Analyse Textuelle* 13:8–22.
Lemon, L. T., & Reis, M. J. (eds.)
   1965 *Russian Formalist Criticism: Four Essays*. Lincoln: University of Nebraska Press.
Lewis, T. E.
   1979 Notes Toward a Theory of the Referent. *PMLA* Vol. 94, No. 3:459–75.

Linsky, L.
    1967 *Referring*. London: Routledge & Kegan Paul.
    1977 *Names and Descriptions*. Chicago: University of Chicago Press.
Linsky, L. (ed.)
    1952 *Semantics and the Philosophy of Language*. Urbana: University of Illinois Press.
    1971 *Reference and Modality*. London: Oxford University Press.
Lyons, J.
    1977 *Semantics* (Vol. 1). Cambridge: Cambridge University Press.
Morris, C.
    1938 Foundation of the Theory of Signs. *International Encyclopedia of Unified Science*, Vol. 1, No. 1. Chicago: University of Chicago Press.
    1946 *Signs, Language and Behavior*. New York: Prentice Hall. (Reprinted in Morris, 1971).
    1971 *Writings on the General Theory of Signs*. The Hague: Mouton.
Mukarovsky, J.
    1977a Art as a Semiotic Fact, in J. Burbank & P. Steiner (eds.), *Structure, Sign and Function: Selected Essays by Jan Mukarovsky*. New Haven & London: Yale University Press, pp. 82–88. (Originally published as "L'Art comme fait sémiologique," in Actes du huitième Congrès international de philosophie à Prague, 2–7 septembre 1934, Prague, 1936, pp. 1065–72; and reprinted in *Poétique* 3: 1970).
    1977b *The Word and Verbal Art* (tr. and ed. J. Burbank & P. Steiner). New Haven & London: Yale University Press.
Ogden, C. K., & Richards, I. A.
    1923 *The Meaning of Meaning*. London: Routledge & Kegan Paul.
Pavel, T.
    1975 'Possible Worlds' in Literary Semantics. *Journal of Aesthetics and Art Criticism* Vol. 34, No.2.
    1979 Fiction and the Causal Theory of Names. *Poetics* Vol. 8, Nos. 1–2:179–191.
Peirce, C. S.
    1932 *The Collected Papers of Charles Sanders Peirce* (eds. C. Hartshorne & P. Weiss). Cambridge, Mass.: Harvard University Press.
    1982 (*Writings of Charles S. Peirce: A Chronological Edition* is currently being prepared by the Peirce Edition Project at Indiana University–Purdue University at Indianapolis. Volumes 1 (1857–1866), 2 (1867–1871), and 3 (1872–1878) have appeared as of 1987. [Bloomington: Indiana University Press, 1982–.])
Piaget, J.
    1961 *Les Mécanismes perceptifs*. Paris: Presses Universitaires de France.
Plato
    (1973) *Theaetetus* (tr. J. McDowell), Oxford: Clarendon Press.
Poetics Vol. 8, Nos. 1–2 (Special issue on reference in fiction).
Pratt, M. L.
    1977 *Toward a Speech Act Theory of Literary Discourse*. Bloomington & London: Indiana University Press.
Quine, W. V. O.
    1953 *From a Logical Point of View*. Cambridge, Mass.: Harvard University Press.
    1960 *Word and Object*. Cambridge, Mass.: M.I.T. Press.
    1971 Reference and Modality (reprint of Quine, 1953, pp. 139–157), in Linsky, 1971.
    1976 *The Ways of Parodox and Other Essays*. Cambridge, Mass.: Harvard University Press.
Ricoeur, P.
    1976 *Interpretation Theory: Discourse and the Surplus of Meaning*. Fort Worth: Texas Christian University Press.
Riffaterre, M.
    1978 *Semiotics of Poetry*. Bloomington & London: Indiana University Press.

1979 *La Production du texte*. Paris: Seuil. (*Text Production*, tr. T. Lyons; Columbia University Press, 1983).

Russell, B.
1905 On Denoting. *Mind* XIV:479–93. (Reprinted in Russell, *Logic and Knowledge*; London: Allen & Unwin, 1956, pp. 41–56).
1940 *An Inquiry into Meaning and Truth*. London: Allen & Unwin.

Ryle, G.
1957 The Theory of Meaning, in C. A. Mace (ed.), *British Philosophy in the Mid-Century* London: Allen & Unwin. (Reprinted in F. Zabeeh, E. D. Klemke, & A. Jacobson [eds.], *Readings in Semantics*; Urbana: University of Illinois Press, 1974).

Saussure, F. de
1916 *Cours de linguistique générale*. Paris: Payot. (*Course in General Linguistics*, tr. and annotated by R. Harris; London: Duckworth, 1983).

Savan, D.
1976 *An Introduction to Peirce's Semiotics: Part One*. Toronto Semiotic Circle Monographs, Working Papers & Prepublications, Toronto: Victoria University.

Searle, J.
1969 *Speech Acts: An Essay in the Philosophy of Language*. Cambridge: Cambridge University Press.
1975 The Logical Status of Fictional Discourse. *New Literary History*, Vol. 6:319–32. (Reprinted in Searle, *Expression and Meaning*; Cambridge: Cambridge University Press, 1979, pp.58–75).

Shklovsky, V.
1917 Art as Technique, in L. T. Lemon & M. J. Reis, eds., 1965, pp. 3–24.

Strawson, P. F.
1950 On Referring. *Mind* LIX:320–44. (Reprinted in Strawson, *Logico-Linguistic Papers*; London: Methuen, 1971, pp. 1–27).
1959 *Individuals: An Essay in Descriptive Metaphysics*. London: Methuen.
1964 Intention and Convention in Speech Acts. *The Philosophical Review* LXXIII:439–60. (Reprinted in Strawson, 1971).

Wittgenstein, L.
[1921] *Tractatus Logico-Philosophicus* (tr. D. F. Pears & B. F. McGuiness). London: Routledge & Kegan Paul, 1961 & 1974.
1968 *Philosophical Investigations* (tr. G. E. M. Anscombe). Oxford: Blackwell.

Woods, J. H.
1974 *The Logic of Fiction*. The Hague & Paris: Mouton.
1979 *Soundings of Deviant Logic*. The Hague & Paris: Mouton.

NOTES ON CONTRIBUTORS

JEAN ALTER, Professor of Romance Languages, University of Pennsylvania, is author of *La Vision du monde d'Alain Robbe-Grillet, Les Origines de la satire anti-bourgeoise*, and *L'Esprit anti-bourgeois sous l'ancien régime*. He is founding editor of *Forum*, an international newsletter for the semiotics of theatre.

ROSS CHAMBERS, who is Marvin Felheim Distinguished University Professor of French and Comparative Literature at the University of Michigan, recently published *Story and Situation: Narrative Seduction and the Power of Fiction* and is working on two new books, *Narrative in Opposition* and *Mélancolie historique, textualité moderne* (on the 1850s in France).

LINDA HUTCHEON is Professor of English at McMaster University (Canada) and a member of the Associate Faculty of the Center for Comparative Literature, University of Toronto. She is author of *Narcissistic Narrative, Formalism and the Freudian Aesthetic, A Theory of Parody* and articles in *Diacritics, Contemporary Literature, Poétique*, and others.

MICHAEL ISSACHAROFF is Professor of French at the University of Western Ontario. His most recent books include *L'Espace et la nouvelle, Le Spectacle du discours*, and *Discourse as Performance*. He is editor of *Langages de Flaubert* and co-editor of *Sartre et la mise en signe* and *Performing Texts*.

WLADIMIR KRYSINSKI is Professor of Comparative Literature and Slavic Literature at the University of Montreal. He is author of *Carrefours de signes* and numerous articles on comparative literature and literary theory.

THOMAS E. LEWIS, Associate Professor of Spanish and Comparative Literature, is Chairman of the Department of Spanish and Portuguese at the University of Iowa. He is author of *Fiction and Reference* and has published several essays on reference and literature in such journals as *Diacritics, PMLA*, and *MLN*.

FRANÇOISE MELTZER, Associate Professor of French and Comparative Literature, University of Chicago, is author of *Salomé and the Dance of Writing: Portraits of Mimesis in Literature* (forthcoming).

BRUCE MORRISSETTE is Sunny Distinguished Service Professor Emeritus of Romance Languages at the University of Chicago. His recent books include *The Novels of Robbe-Grillet, Intertextual Assemblage in Robbe-Grillet: From Topology to the Golden Triangle*, and *Novel and Film*.

PATRICE PAVIS teaches drama at the Institut d'Etudes Théâtrales, Université de Paris III. He is author of *Problèmes de sémiologie théâtrale, Voix et images de la scène, Dictionnaire du théâtre*, and *Marivaux à l'épreuve de la scène*.

GERALD PRINCE is Professor of Romance Languages and Chair of the Program of Comparative Literature and Literary Theory at the University of Pennsylvania. His *Dictionary of Narratology* is forthcoming from the University of Nebraska Press.

JEAN-JACQUES THOMAS is Associate Professor of Romance Languages and

Linguistics at Duke University. He has written widely on literary theory and linguistics, edited special issues of *Langages* and *Sub-stance*, and translated Michael Riffaterre's *Semiotics of Poetry*. His *La Langue la poésie*, just completed, is soon to appear.

ANNA WHITESIDE is Associate Professor of French and Comparative Literature at McMaster University (Canada). She is the author of works on autobiography, semiotics, speech act theory, and reference in *Semiotica, Neophilologus, Romanic Review, French Forum, Revue des Lettres Modernes*, and others. She is currently writing a book on Apollinaire's *Calligrammes* and visual poetics.

INDEX

STARTING OUT

Ephrata Washington is where I call home.
I live on a farm, but I don't live alone.
I live with my wife of fifty-two years.
We once fed some heifers and also some steers.

I farmed and ranched most all of my days.
Now I'm turned out to pasture and left there to graze.
So instead of working like I've done all my life,
I just make life miserable for my dear little wife.

I've done part of the jobs on her "honey-do" list.
Now I'm doing fun things that I formerly missed.
I'm doing some traveling and also some writing.
I'm going to gatherings and doing reciting.

When I finish this book I'll have it for sale.
I write poetry to friends by using e-mail.
My poems are short and I try to be funny.
I do it for fun and not for the money.

I attended a gathering in nineteen ninety-one.
I thought it a blast so I joined in the fun.
I write of experiences on the ranch I once had
And also of stories told to me by my dad

Who once was a cowboy way back in the teens
When they lived on sourdough, sow belly and beans.
If I remember a joke someone told me one time
I set it all down in both meter and rhyme.

Since that fateful day in ninety-one
I've recited in Idaho and in Washington.
In Nevada and Utah I've recited my rhymes
And also in Canada several times.

I only do poetry, I don't sing worth a hoot
Nor play a guitar or even a flute.
Now I'm retired and have sold all my stock
Now poetry is my role and my wife is my rock.

SNAKE BIT

We were two young kids
Just starting out in life,
A man with big dreams
And his pretty young wife.

When we started life together,
We had a tar-paper shack.
Two small rooms to call our home
With a path to an outhouse in back.

We had hopes, dreams and ambitions.
Lots we wanted to do.
With a place of our own and a herd of cows
We'd raise a family too.

In the sagebrush land of the Basin
Our fortune would be made.
We started by planting a garden,
And trees to have for shade.

One day while hoeing the garden
I heard some sort of a buzz.
Being new to this environment
I didn't know just what it was.

I turned in time to see a snake.
He was coiled and ready to strike
So I just turned and ran from there
For snakes I do not like.

I surely avoided that snake,
Instead of me he bit the hoe.
How many times he struck at that hoe,
I just don't really know.

He struck at it several times
And it swelled up big as a log.
When I returned the snake was dead,
Killed by my old yeller dog.

I made plans for that big log.
Which I knew would please my spouse.
So I sawed it all up into boards
And I built a chicken house.

My wife was oh! so proud of me.
She said I was a saint.
She said she'd even be prouder yet
If I'd give it a coat of paint.

I went and got some turpentine
And primed that chicken coop.
But the thing that happened next
Sure threw me for a loop.

The turpentine was so strong
It drew the swelling out of the wood.
Now a little bird house stands
Where that chicken house once stood.

1957

OUR KIDS

Every other year beginning in 1958 our five kids Lyndon, Wendy, Amy, Maxine and Tim were born two years apart as regularly as clockwork. Now we had a haying crew, harvest crew, round-up crew... whatever crew we needed, we had. And believe me we had a crew that was better than any we could hire. I know because in time the kids had to be replaced after they grew up and deserted us for greener pastures.

Of course there were all the legendary spills and scrapes and even a few broken bones that all farm kids have to endure growing up. There was the time Jake, our Border Collie, ran in front of the motorcycle and caused Lyn and Wendy to take a bad spill, as well as the time Lyn fell off his horse and broke his collar bone. And the time someone lost a post, which was used to prop up wheel lines, out in the hay field and dear old dad hit it with his motorcycle and took a nasty spill.

First day of school 1971

4

PANIC

As Jack and I were finishing changing the hand lines one evening, I became more and more apprehensive about having left Lyndon by himself in the pickup. After all he was only three years old. I had convinced myself that I would only be gone a few minutes and that I really wouldn't be that far away. But as I looked over my shoulder to see if he was all right, the setting sun shone in my eyes and there was no way I could see the pickup. I frantically finished hooking up the last pipe and ran for the pickup which was parked next to the sump from which the irrigation water was pumped. Out of breath, I staggered to the pickup and looked inside. He was gone. "Lyndy!" I called, sure that he was lying in three feet of water at the bottom of the sump. No answer. The irrigation pump was making too much noise so I turned it off and called again. This time I heard a noise behind me, but the setting sun blocked my view until I shaded my eyes and saw him about a hundred yards away stuck in the mud up to his knees. Never in my life have I been so happy to see anyone. This is only one example of the many stupid things I have done in my 51 years of being a dad.

Having heard that story, you'll understand my fear that Tim would not heed my order to stay in the truck in the following account.

When Tim was about six years old, he and Lyn, who was then about 14, and I went up in to the hills on the Valley Grazing Association ranch to look for cows. It was late in the fall and it was getting cold. We unloaded the horses and I sent Lyn up along the fence to the north where he was to turn back when he came to the corner of the fence about two miles away and push any cows he might find back down the hill.

Tim rode with me on old Paint. When we returned from riding our circle, it was getting cold and nearly dark, but Lyn had not returned. Once again, panic! "I'll ride up the hill and try to find him. You stay in the truck and don't leave it for any reason," I told Tim. I hunted for about half an hour with no luck and headed back to the truck praying that Lyn would be there when I got back. To my great relief, he was loading his horse into the truck as I rode up. Experiences like these are the reason for my white hair. (What little I have left.)

L=

I grew up on a farm, not a ranch, so I didn't learn to rope and do all the things that cowboys do. Even to this day I don't ever rope and drag 'em, I just push them up the chute and let somebody snag 'em. But we had cows to milk and fences to fix and haying to do just the same as on a ranch. I even had a horse from the time I was nine or ten years old, but he didn't buck so I didn't learn to ride a bucking horse until I grew up and bought a place of my own.

Since then I've been bucked off several horses. In 1969 my wife and I bought into a grazing association, so for the last forty years or so I've been acquiring the education that I didn't get when I was a kid. I wrote this poem to tell about it.

I'M REALLY NOT A COWBOY

I'm really not a cowboy, though I have owned a lot of cattle,
And many's the time I've spent a long day in the saddle.
I've ridden the hills for days upon days
Gathering cows and looking for strays.

I've worked lots of cattle, and I do mean 'lots'
I've branded and dehorned and given them shots.
I've been bucked off and kicked and broke a few bones,
I've rode blacks, bays and pintos and also some roans.

I've worked in the hot sun putting up hay,
I've worked building fences day after day,
I've rode on mowing machines and walked behind plows,
I've tried grafting calves on some ornery old cows,

I've castrated and branded and marked the calves' ears,
It's a job that I've done for quite a few years.
I've baled lots of hay. I've fed and done chores.
I've spent the biggest part of my life out-of-doors

But I've never had time to rodeo or team rope,
It's only a dream that I couldn't even hope.
For cow penning or cutting, I've never had time,
Kept my nose to the grindstone to earn every dime.

I've had some good cutting horses. They got the job done.
But we didn't go out and compete with someone.

6

So I'm just not a cowboy, I don't fit the mold.
And I guess I won't start now. I'm getting too old.

Besides, I don't have a pickup with a fancy gun rack.
And I don't have a Dingo dog to ride in the back.
I don't have no Copenhagen 'twixt my cheek and my gum.
I tried it one time, but it made my gum numb.

And I don't have a mustache like real cowboys do
And I don't drink and also I don't chew.
So I can't pass for a cowboy, you won't dispute that.
And I'm really not a cowboy, I just found this hat.

Lyndon on Lucky, Amy on Paint

ROCKY MOUNTAIN OYSTERS

Let me tell you of a time I had this
Fall-out with my wife.
Of course it happened other times
In our blissful married life.

We were just a couple greenhorn kids,
Married a real short time ago.
Lots of things we hadn't learned,
Things we didn't know.

We needed someone to help us out,
To lead us by the hand,
Show us how to care for cows
And how to work the land.

We had a little bunch of cows,
Maybe twenty head or so.
Her dad had come to help us out,
Teach things we didn't know.

It was time to work the calves,
To dehorn and castrate.
That's the part that caused the trouble
Between me and my mate.

Now Loyd was a cowman
Who'd been 'there' once or twice
I reckoned that he knowed the ropes
So I heeded his advice.

He knew most every cattle trick,
His advice to me was free,
So when he came to help me out
I greeted him with glee.

I didn't have a roping horse
So to rope I wasn't able
We stretched 'em out and burned their hides
On a Powder River table.

When we started in to castrate
He ordered a pail of water.
Which was brought out by my wife,
Who was his darling daughter.

We worked real hard 'til almost noon,
Branded and marked their ears,
Gave them all a bunch of shots
And changed bull calves to steers.

He said, "We'll save the testicles.
They're real good to eat."
I thought he'd be our chef that night,
Provide us with a treat.

Rocky Mountain oysters
Have a taste beyond compare,
A delicacy that can't be found
In restaurants anywhere.

We finished up that job real quick.
It didn't take us long
But he didn't stay to cook for us
I guess I'd figured wrong.

When we finished up the job,
He must have changed his mind.
For he got into his pickup truck
And he left those treats behind.

He couldn't take them home with him.
His wife would have a fit.
And to do the job of cooking them?
She wouldn't hear of it!

I could have fried those jewels myself,
But what was I to do?
How to marinate or season them
I didn't have a clue.

If he don't want to cook them up
And enjoy their subtle taste
My faithful wife will do the job
They'll not go to waste.

I was pretty sure my little bride
Liked exotic things to eat,
So I knew that she would cook for me
Those little balls of meat.

But she wasn't very happy
When I brought that bucket in.
She didn't seem to understand
The ways of cattlemen.

And when she saw them sitting
In that bucket by the sink
Repulsed was her reaction
To those hors d'oeuvres bright and pink.

She asked me why he'd left them there,
She acted kinda mad.
Now who had got her dander up?
Was it me or was it dad?

She knew just how her mother felt.
Some things wives won't do.
She said, "You can tell your dad-in-law,
That I won't cook them too."

She threw them out into the yard,
To protest I'd waste my breath.
Don't she know that kids in China
Are starving half to death?

Now it's true those dainty morsels,
Our table didn't grace,
But our cow dog made a meal of them.
They didn't go to waste.

DAD! DAD!

Dad! Dad! There's a cow in the neighbor's hay field! This is a refrain that strikes fear in the heart of any cowman. What if a car hits a cow and someone is injured? What if a neighbor's crop is ruined? What if they get so far away that they are never found? Any one or all of these scenarios could happen. At the very least it is a nuisance and takes time to get them back in and repair the fence.

FENCES

I awoke one morning to the sound of cows bawling under my bedroom window. I jumped out of bed and ran to the window. Sure enough, the cows had broken down the fence and come back to their calves. We had weaned the calves the day before and trailed the cows to a neighbor's where they would feed on alfalfa stubble and corn stalks during the winter. By the time I got outside, opened the gates and got the cows back in to the corral, they had made a mess out of the haystacks. After breakfast we fixed the broken-down fences and took the cows back to the

pasture. This time they stayed put.

One other time, I weaned the calves, moved the cows about two or three miles from home and put them in to a field of corn stalks which was enclosed with only an electric fence, turned them over to 16-year-old Kenny Youngers to watch for me and took off for the weekend for Thanksgiving. I don't know what I could have been thinking about to do such a dumb stunt as that, but everything worked out alright. Fortunately, they respected that hot wire fence.

SCAB ROCK PASTURE

It didn't look like anything but sagebrush and cheat grass but the chance to lease 1,800 acres for spring pasture only three miles from home was really quite appealing, so in the spring of 1971, I made the deal with the Bureau of Reclamation, checked out and repaired the fences and turned the cows out. In the Columbia Basin of Central Washington, grass only lasts about two months but it turned out to be better grass than I thought. It wasn't cheat grass at all, but instead it was what is known as June Grass, a highly palatable and very nutritious grass.

As things turned out, the quality and quantity of the grass is not what I should have been most concerned about. The wind had been blowing tumble weeds against the fence all winter and the fences looked like great long walls. The ground was very rocky and the posts had only been set into the ground about eight or ten inches deep. When the strong spring winds blew against the tumble weeds it was like the wind blowing on a sail and something had to give. The fence posts were what gave. A few days after I turned out the cows, we had a great strong wind that lasted for about three days. It blew all the fence posts out of the ground and rolled the wire and weeds up like a long rope. I should have taken the cows back to the corrals, but I had fed up all the hay so I had no choice but to leave them in the pasture while I untangled the wire, redug the post holes and restrung the wire. My wife and kids lived with the cows while I rebuilt the fence. Have you ever tried to keep cows in a pasture with no

fence? Very time consuming! Have you ever tried to unroll, untangle and rebuild three miles of fence and keep the cows in at the same time? Very time consuming! After about three weeks we finally got the job done. By the way, I set the posts deeper this time.

Before the next year rolled around, I built about five more miles of fence and then I had 3,500 acres of pasture. Needless to say that wasn't the end of our problems, the cows still got out sometimes. As a matter of fact, a calf got out of my new three wire fence one morning the next spring and a neighbor girl driving to school swerved to miss it and rolled her car on the opposite side of the road.

The trooper who investigated the accident, suggested that a citation would probably be issued because he didn't think it was a good enough fence. After he left, I hurriedly put up another wire on that stretch of fence before anyone could verify his complaint and I dodged the bullet. No ticket... at least not that time.

Fx

I was warned of a potential ticket another time. Our irrigation sprinklers sometimes watered the highway in front of our farm and I had been cautioned about it several times by the county sheriff. One day when the kids were home alone, the sheriff stopped in and probably would have ticketed me if I had been home. He told the kids to tell me that was my last warning; the next time there would be a fine to pay.

Everyone at the sheriff's office knew my name and telephone number. It got to the point that any time there were any cows out within ten miles of our place, we were the first to be notified. Actually ours were the only beef cows within ten miles, so our neighbors also knew who to notify when they saw cattle out.

⩅

If you have cattle, they'll get out at times. If you have cattle on pasture, you'll have fence problems. Then you have your work cut out for you. I've built and repaired many miles of fence in the last 50 years.

Horses are not nearly as hard to keep inside the fences as cattle. However we had horses get out a time or two also but they are easy to

catch. Just shake a bucket of grain near enough to them so they can hear it and they will come running.

JUVENILE DELINQUENTS

Our kids drank homemade root beer by the gallon. It was cheap and easy to make. We had a bottle capper and bottles were easy to find along the road. We weren't too particular whether they were pop or beer bottles, but we were embarrassed one Fourth of July at the gymkhana at George. We packed a lunch, four horses and five kids and intended to make a day of it.

Along about thirsty time the kids each grabbed a bottle of root beer and carried it around with them as they drank it and played with the other kids. All of a sudden we noticed folks looking askance at our kids like they thought they were poison or maybe had the plague. We didn't realize what the problem was until one little guy expressed astonishment that our kids were allowed to drink beer. After that we made sure to take root beer that was bottled in pop bottles anytime we were to be in the public eye.

BIRD HUNTING

One fall when hunting season opened, I took all five kids with me to teach them the sport of bird hunting. One man with a shotgun over his shoulder and five little tykes following behind with their dog is not very conducive to sneaking up on a rooster, but we had a nice outing anyway. Along in the afternoon when everyone was getting tired enough to call it a day, we came upon another man who was also teaching his kids the fine art of Pheasant hunting. The only difference being that he had seven kids following him, plus they had a real bird dog, not a Border Collie.

This was the beginning of a longtime friendship with Doctor Gehrig and his family from Mercer Island, Washington. We hunted together on our farm and on some of my neighbor's farms for several years. One summer they invited us to come visit them at their home on the island. We cleaned out our cattle truck, threw in some straw and sleeping bags, stretched a tarp over the racks and headed for the big city. We must have

been quite a sight in that up-scale neighborhood with our foul smelling rig and five noisy kids but it sure didn't bother us or our hosts.

Our little 130 acre farm was not big enough to support a family. Consequently, I had to work off the farm for the first four or five years. I spent two winters working at the sugar factory, one winter on road construction, and in my spare time I drove truck or whatever job I could find. One fall I had a corral full of steers but the price was so low that I wanted to keep them until spring and fatten them. I went to see Alan Sircin, the owner of A and W feedlot and asked him if he would custom feed them for me. He told me that if I would work for him during the winter, I could drive a load of feed home every night and feed them in my own corral thereby saving the yardage fee. That sounded good to me because I needed a job and he was paying $300 a month.

We trailed the steers to my father-in-law's scales, weighed them and determined a value per pound and the deal was struck. When we sold the fat cattle the next spring, I had to pay him one-half of the profit over and above the original value of the cattle plus the feed cost. Fat cattle at that time were bringing about 26¢ a pound, so I came out about even and worked all winter for nothing. But I had a job!

9

Every year in January, the Western Folklife Center puts on a week-long fun filled western bash in Elko Nevada. It consists of cowboy poetry, music and western art displays, as well as workshops on many subjects such as saddle making, western cooking, training horses, etc.

ELKO OR BUST

Two old cowpokes named Jake and Joe
Headed for the gathering way down at Elko.
The place where they lived was far from there,
Since horses are slow so they traveled by air.

They boarded the plane early one night.
It's their first time flying so they held on tight.
Their knuckles were white as they flew along
Though the stewardess assured them, "Nothing will go wrong,

"This old plane has four 'power plants'
and the pilot don't fly by the seat of his pants."
Suddenly an engine conked out and the pilot came on
He said, "We're a little short of power but we'll carry on.

"Four engines are needed for maximum speed
But three is all we really need.
We'll still get to Elko but we'll be a little late.
We're scheduled for six. Should get there by eight."

Soon another engine quit. Now the captain was miffed.
He explained how three engines give extra lift.
"Two engines," he said, "will still get us there
But we sure won't have any time to spare.

"That eight o'clock arrival I'll have to extend
We probably won't get there til way after ten.
Each engine we lose makes the plane go slower."
Said Jake, "I sure hope we don't lose any more."

They flew along for quite a spell,
And everything seemed to be going quite well
When engine number three started to sputter and spit.
"Oh oh," said the stewardess. "Another one just quit."

"But don't you worry," she said to Joe.
"We'll still get to Elko but it's gonna be slow.
Each engine that quits slows us more, that's true
One engine will be much slower than two.

"So we'll be pretty late. You got that one right.
We may not get there 'til after midnight."
Now Jake said to Joe in a voice filled with fright,
"If that fourth engine quits, we'll be up here all night"

25¢

FOUR WHEEL DRIVE

I never had a four wheel drive pickup when I really needed one. When feeding cows in the deep snow or mud, I would load up as many bales as I could get on the rig, put on the chains and go feed about half of the hay.

15

I always left enough on so that I had the needed traction to make it back for another load. It took longer to feed that way but it was better than getting stuck. Several years later, I bought a new four wheel drive rig and figured my problems were solved. I can go through mud, snow or sand. I've never been so badly stuck as I was one time the next winter when I tried to negotiate a snowdrift while on my way to load hay. Four wheel drive is great, but use a little common sense, Larry!

EXOTICS

In the early 1970s exotic cattle became all the rage. We wanted to be in on the cutting edge of technology so we purchased a liquid nitrogen tank and several vials of Simmental semen which was imported from Switzerland. I went to an artificial insemination school and soon we were in the exotic cattle business. It was very expensive to import live cattle at that time and they had to be quarantined for a lengthy period at a government facility which increased the cost even more. I artificially inseminated about 70 cows each year for four or five years and we soon had a herd of one-half blood and three-quarters blood Simmental cows. At that time the Simmental breed was getting very popular and we sold some half blood cows with three-quarter Simmental heifer calves at side for as much as $3,700 at auction sales in Spokane and Portland. If I had just had foresight enough to realize that the bubble would soon burst, I could have sold all of the Simmental cows we had and paid off the mortgage. They were bringing that much money at that time. But I have never been known for my intelligence, so I hung on to most of them until they went down in value.

Artificially breeding cows is a time consuming job. When I started doing it I used a "gomer" bull, but found that to be rather ineffective. Even though the kids considered it boring, they took turns spotting for cows in heat. The best time to breed a cow is twelve hours after she exhibits heat symptoms. Therefore, rather than trying to find her again twelve hours later, she and her calf were locked in the corral for future reference. Cutting her from the rest of the herd and keeping her calf with her was always a challenge but one that Peanuts and I relished. The kids all tried to do it but could not ever get to the corral with both cow and calf. It was usually fairly easy to find which calf went with the cow

16

because with her "bulling" and riding other cows, she was neglecting her calf and wouldn't be standing still long enough for it to suck. Therefore it was hungry and would usually tag along. As soon as I would get the cow and the right calf together and Peanuts knew which ones we were after, all I had to do was hang on and he would keep them together and get them to the corral pretty much by himself.

Maxine and Cricket

A.I.

When I was a young man so many years ago,
Exotic cattle were all the rage, A.I. the way to go.
Plastic sleeves, heat detection, gomer bulls and all
And a cutting horse to bring the cows in to the A.I. stall.

The bulls I used were Simmental and also Maine Anjou,
Charolais and Limousin were in that bull pen too.
Like crooked politicians, the best that could be bought.
And real good bulls like politicians cost an awful a lot

There has to be a catch. I don't have that much dough.
I was just a broke young cowman some thirty years ago.
But I didn't have those bulls and I didn't have to feed 'em,
I took straws from the semen tank whenever I would need 'em.

17

In about 1971, I was getting overly anxious to get into the Simmental business and couldn't wait to build up my own herd so I bought a load of Hereford cows in Havre, Montana which were A.I. bred to Simmental bulls. I hadn't yet bought a cattle truck of my own, so I hired Harvey Ottmar to haul them for me. We left his place at Moses Lake early one morning and drove to Havre, loaded the cows (after waiting for hours for a brand inspector) and headed back home late in the afternoon. We drove all day and all night and finally arrived back at our place about eight a.m. the next day.

This adventure reminds me of the time Dick Heath had purchased a load of Hereford cows which were bred to Simmental bulls and he asked Lois and me to drive his truck to Billings and haul them home for him. We left Billings in the middle of a snow storm about noon. The locals warned us about snow storms in Montana but we were anxious to get home as we had left Lyn in charge of the cattle and he was only a lad of about thirteen. Besides I figured if the weather worsened we could unload in Bozeman and wait out the storm there. When we got to Bozeman, the roads were still passable so we decided to try for Butte. When we got to Butte, we were brave enough to think we could make Missoula. About the time we hit Missoula the snow had turned to rain so we decided to take advantage of the better driving conditions and just kept going.

North Meadow VGA

By this time I was getting pretty sleepy, so I turned the driving over to Lois. That woke me up real quick! She had a hard time seeing because of the dark pavement and all the rain so I again took over the wheel. The passes were not really all that bad so when we got down the west side of Fourth of July Pass, we figured we were home free and we hightailed it for Ephrata. We sang songs, told stories, opened the windows, did driver calisthenics, and every trick in the book to stay awake. We got home in time to get the kids off to school, check the cows and then we hit the sack for a few hours.

As I write this book, nearly 40 years later, Simmental cattle are not really very popular. They are large animals, and they produce large calves which gain well and have high weaning weights but they have a lot of waste because they are big in the shoulders and have a big brisket and extra "leather". When the calves are born, they are so big they cause problems. Ninety to one hundred pound calves were not uncommon. Simmental calves have big heads and shoulders which makes passage through the birth canal difficult. As you can well imagine, this was very hard on the cows. Most of my cows were Angus and in those days Angus cows were not as big as they have been bred up to be nowadays. I had to assist in the delivery of a very large percentage of the cows which were bred to Simmental bulls. Sometimes the calves had to be taken by Cesarean operations. Some of the cows were paralyzed or crippled to some extent because of the injury to the pelvis. I figured that when I got the herd bred up to three-fourths or seven-eighths Simmental, the cows would be big enough to handle those big calves. Due to the high value put on the Simmental at that time, I thought the extra work and expense to produce them was warranted although I don't really know for sure. Due to the fact that Brucellosis decimated my herd, I was unable to continue my Simmental program and so I still don't know.

(11)

Instead of riding a horse one morning to check on the cows, I drove my new pickup. That's what new pickups are for, right? Wrong!! I found a cow that was having a problem calving so I drove up close to her, got

out and threw a rope over her head. I quickly jammed a stick into a stake pocket and dallied. The cow jumped up, took off and hit the end of the rope then she turned around and came back toward me and around the other side of the pickup, pinning me to the side of the pickup with the rope and slamming into the far side of the pickup with such force that she caved in the left door. That just wasn't my day.

–N

I thought it might be helpful to relate a few experiences I've had throughout the years with cattle, horses, kids and dogs to tell the story behind some of the poems I've written. All the mishaps in the following poem did not happen on the same day…but they all did happen to me.

MY NEW RIG

It sure was nice to have some help
Feeding cows that day.
My dad had come to visit us
He could help me load the hay.

He was downright glad to tag along,
And ride in my old truck
And it wouldn't take us long to feed
With any kind of luck.

Well, luck just wasn't with us.
The battery, it was dead.
I dug up some jumper cables
Hitched up to black and red.

I hit the switch but all I heard
Was just a little click
Then I saw a puff of smoke
Which darned near made me sick

"Not to worry," I says to him.
"I know what we can do.
We'll take my new rig out to feed,
Fix this when we're through."

I had bought a brand new pickup
A few short days ago.
It was equipped with four wheel drive
To make it go in snow.

And even though we had no snow
It filled me up with pride
To show off my new pickup truck
And take him for a ride.

First we had to load the hay,
An everyday event.
A bale fell down from off the stack
And made a great big dent.

We finished loading up the hay,
Drove to where the cows were kept
I did a stupid thing that day,
Which proves I am inept.

A cow was lying on the ground,
Her calf was coming breech.
I tried to throw a rope on her
But the rope just wouldn't reach.

I knew I'd have to catch that cow
And I'd have to pull her calf.
If I tell what happened next,
Please promise you won't laugh.

I cautiously walked up behind,
Threw a loop around her neck,
I didn't realize it then but
We were about to have a wreck.

I didn't have a saddle horn
To dally up the rope.
The cow jumped up onto her feet
And took off on a lope.

I dallied on a 2x2 that
I kept to use this way
I figured that for roping cows
It would some time save the day.

21

I jammed it in the stake pocket
On the rail of the bed.
I gave that cow a lot of rope
And let her have her head.

She hit the end and headed back
So mad that she was blind.
I didn't have a single thing
That I could hide behind.

She came so fast I couldn't move.
I was frozen where I stood
I made a desperate feeble try
To climb up on the hood.

She pinned me up against the truck.
The rope, it squeezed me tight,
And then she turned and headed back,
She was really on the fight.

But it loosened up the rope a bit
'Cause then it had some slack.
There wasn't any place to hide
So I jumped into the back.

She jumped, pulled and bellered
And ran around that rig once more.
She slammed into the other side
And caved in the left-hand door.

She scraped a horn along one side,
Peeled off a bunch of paint
When a cow gets riled up that way
She don't show much restraint

I guess I could have turned her loose
But that's the coward's way
Besides, I need to pull that calf
It's his birthday today

I got another rope on her
And gently laid her down.
I figured I could pull the calf
While she was on the ground.

We pulled the calf but it was dead.
We laid it on the grass.
The cow jumped up and hit the truck
And broke a window glass.

I guess by now you've figured out
That this was not my day.
Sometimes no matter what you do
It just don't seem to pay.

Amy on Tammy

ORPHAN CALF

Who says you need a horse and a rope to catch a calf? When you are out checking cows in your pickup, you don't have all the necessary tools of the trade. If you need to do a job, you do it the best you can with the resources at hand. I once chanced upon a dead cow and upon further investigation found a poor hungry calf running around bawling for its mom. There was no way I could catch it without a horse. As I pondered my dilemma and watched, the calf made its way to where the dead cow was lying. It discovered the cow and began sucking so I just sneaked up behind, grabbed it by the hind leg and dragged it to the pickup. I took it home where it was adopted by the kids and raised on a bottle.

Tim with Frisky

The secret to success is to buy low and sell high, Right? In the late seventies the bottom dropped out of the cattle market so I decided that it was time to increase the size of my herd. (Buy low.) I bought about 50 cows that had come out of Nevada. Good, big, young cows and the price was "right"... at least it was less than it had been previously.

Well, to my sorrow I found that those cows were infected with brucellosis. A year and a half later after they had also infected my original herd, I sold every cow I had for about 20¢ a pound. The price was really "right" then. I had gambled and lost. I knew better than to gamble. My mother taught me better than that.

GAMBLING MAN

Mama taught me not to gamble.
Said it would bring me grief.
"Work at something safe," she said,
That's the reason I raise beef.

I'm glad I took my mom's advice,
No horses, dice or poker.
Otherwise I know by now
I'd be a whole lot broker.

Once I had four hundred cows
And a big debt at the bank.
But safe and secure as I could be,
And I had my mom to thank.

Well, brucellosis struck my herd,
I wound up in the red,
So I decided to buy some steers
And feed them out instead.

But the price went down, I lost my shirt,
My life was sure in shambles.
But at least I took my mom's advice
When she told me not to gamble.

My wife and I, we bought a farm,
Thought hay would raise some cash,
But Mount St. Helens blew her top
And covered it with ash.

I plowed up the hay, planted winter wheat,
A brilliant move I know,
But all the wheat froze out that year.
It had no cover of snow.

I plowed and planted spring wheat then.
That crop, it was a whopper.
Then we were hit by another plague —
Great hordes of big grasshoppers.

I thought I'd try some corn next time,
It's always in demand.

One cold spring night we had a frost
Which left a real poor stand.

Then there's the year we had no rain.
The grass, it didn't grow.
How we weathered that disaster,
I just don't really know.

The advice my mother gave to me
Sure didn't do no harm,
But it should have included a warning
That I'd not try to farm.

I don't know what the next thing is
To come along and plague us
But I think that I'd be better off
Gambling in Las Vegas.

I'm sure anyone who has ever tried to help a little kid put on his
shoes can identify with this experience that I once had with one of my
grandsons. And he was serious, too.

COWBOY LOGIC

My grandson Neil is quite a kid
And bright as he can be.
He sure is one in a million
And he means the world to me.

So just like grandpas everywhere
Who dote on their grandkids,
I like to tell of the things he said
And the cute things that he did.

Gram and I had the good fortune
To baby-sit one day,
And Neil was putting on his boots
To go outside and play.

Just like most little three-year-old buckaroos
He can get confused when putting on his shoes.
"Neil," I says, "You're doing great,
But you're putting them on the wrong feet."

He gave me one of those looks
That makes grandkids so sweet.
And with respect his answer was
"But Gramps, I don't have any other feet."

THE PERFECT SQUELCH

This Texas cowman liked to brag, he really was a boor.
If anyone told of things they had, he claimed to have much more.
One day he got into a discussion with a cowman from Idaho,
The more he bragged about his ranch, the bigger it did grow.

"When I ride around the fence line in my old pickup truck
I don't get home 'til midnight even with the best of luck."
The Idaho cowman smiled, reached up and took off his hat.
(He held it over his heart)
"I know how you feel old partner. I once had a pickup like that."

RUNAWAY CALF

Speaking of grandkids, I bought Cody a Holstein calf when he was about five years old. He raised it on a bottle and by the time it was a couple years old it was worth quite a lot of money. Of course that was all profit for Cody because I bought the calf and his dad furnished the feed. Consequently when he was about seven years old he had a couple hundred dollars or so to spend on some more cattle. He wanted to buy some heifers and start a herd of his own so I took him to sale to see what we could find. They ran three little red heifers, as alike as peas in a pod, in to the ring so I bought all of them and told Cody that I would keep one for myself since he didn't have enough money to pay for all three.

We hauled them home and unloaded them in my corral. They were kinda spooked after all the excitement at the sale yard and the ride home. They hit the ground running and one of them jumped the fence and took off across the field. It headed for the dairy up on the hill where I figured it would stop. I told him we would give it a chance to calm down and go after it later. We went to the house where he had to relate his adventure to Grandma. "We bought three calves, two for me and one for Grandpa." He told her. "But when we unloaded them Grandpa's calf got out and ran away."

Cody and his calf

28

Pabst the Blue Ribbon Steer

PABST

Amy is the middle kid of five kids and the animal lover in our family. She had rabbits, cats, dogs, sheep, goats, horses and steers during her growing-up years. She didn't show the cats and dogs at the fair, but everything else was "fair" game. She loved them all so much that she couldn't bear to part with any of them and she surely couldn't stand the thought of one of them being slaughtered. Consequently, they all they lived to a ripe old age. She once had a steer which she was convinced would be a blue ribbon winner. She named him "Pabst" the blue ribbon steer. (I think she'd been watching too much television.)

Along toward fair time she got to worrying about the fact that he would have to go to slaughter so she devised a scheme which she hoped would save his life. She wrote a letter to the Pabst brewing company and asked if they would buy her steer since it was named after their beer. She explained to them how they could keep it and use it for an advertising mascot. She was convinced it would become even more famous than the Budweiser horses.

The folks at Pabst evidently got a kick out of her proposal. They wrote her back a nice letter but declined her offer. They did, however, send her a gift of a radio encased in a beer can which we recently found in a box of her junk still stored at our house 30 years later.

Amy grew up, married and now has three boys, one of which is blind. He began losing his sight when he was about six years old. He is now completely blind. I wrote this poem about him.

MY GRANDSON

When you were little, I'd read to you
But I could hardly see the book.
When I'd ask you to move your head,
You'd say, "But gramps, I want to look."

We didn't realize what was going on then,
But later we were to find
That you could barely see the page.
You were slowly going blind.

The doctor said it was genetic,
That you'd slowly lose most of your sight.
But that you may retain a little,
And we pray every day that you might.

You'll never again see the face of your brothers
Nor the likeness of your mom or your dad.
They're only a vision in your memory
And it makes your grandpa real sad.

To think of all the sights that you're missing
Like the flowers that bloom in the spring
And the different scenes of nature
That the changing seasons bring

Like the pure white snow in the winter sun.
It's blinding, it's sometimes so bright.
But with your limited vision
You can barely tell day from night.

And you'll never see the wonders of nature
Like a cow when giving birth
And watching her calf growing big and fat
And knowing his ultimate worth.

And you can't take part in the branding,
You'd never catch a calf with a rope.

Colin, Amy, Cameron, Mark — 2008

But you can ride a horse though my heart skips a beat
When I see him break in to a lope.

And I really get anxious when you ride out of sight.
I get nervous and then start to sweat.
But old Peanuts has been on this ranch all his life.
He'll bring you back home, you can bet.

So ride out and have fun with the wind in your face,
But to make sure you're not caught in a bind,
Old Gramps will be there riding too,
And you can bet that he's right close behind.

    We recently learned that his youngest brother, who is now six years
old, also has Cone-Rod Dystrophy and he's going blind too. (Five years
Later: Cone-Rod Dystrophy was the wrong diagnosis; both these boys
have since been diagnosed with Batten's syndrome, a fatal disease.)

31

Amy wrote this poem for me several years ago.

FATHER'S DAY

My Daddy is a Cowboy
He taught me to be one too
Except I am his daughter
Guess I'll have to think that through

He raised five kids and ran a ranch
He is a true 'cowdad'
He showed us love and patience
He's the best I could have had

He taught me how to ride a horse
To sort the cows for brandin'
And when I got bucked off — again
To find a spot for landin'

And every time it happens
To get back on that horse again
Sometimes you're bruised and dirty
But if you don't, you just can't win

So every time I bite the dust
I figure…next time I'll stay on
He taught me how to think that way
It is the cowboy song

You see, a cowboy keeps a goin'
Doing what needs done
Sometimes it's hard and lonesome
Sometimes it's not much fun

But there are, oh so many blessings
When we count them as we should
He taught me what's important
Life is hard, but God is good

I am my father's daughter
I see it when we dream
We talk and plan and figure
How we'll make skimmed milk into whipped cream

I will always be his cowgirl,
Though I now have children of my own
He still teaches me the cowboy way
Now that I am grown

Why, I will even take a crack right now
At writing cowboy rhyme
To take a chance, try something new
Heck, he does it all the time

And now he is a 'cowgramps'
To my sons one, two and three
He teaches them the cowboy way
Just like he taught me

FIRE!

Along with drought and other things,
Farmers worry about fire.
Out of control it can burn and grow
With consequences dire.

I can think of several times
That glow gave us a scare.
Through the years that's one true cross
We have had to bear.

The first time that comes to mind
Was one day long ago,
Joe McMains came down the road,
His truck was all aglow.

I saw him at a distance
And ran out to the road
And motioned to him frantically
To pull in with his load.

When I saw his signal flashing
I knew that he would turn
So I ran and grabbed the garden hose
Before his truck could burn.

As he pulled into my yard
I took a careful aim
And turned that garden hose on him
To try to douse the flame.

Joe didn't have the slightest hint
His truck was belching fire,
So when I turned that hose on him
It surely raised his ire.

He jumped right out and I could see
That blood was in his eye,
But I knew I had to douse that flame
Or else his truck would fry.

He'd been heading for the landfill
With his burning barrel and junk.
That barrel was the igniter,
Just like a stick of punk

The kind for lighting firecrackers
On Independence Day
When we celebrate our freedom
Which is the American way.

DP

I once had a fire in my own truck
That I won't soon forget.
And before I got that fire out
I worked up quite a sweat.

I'd headed for the ranch one day
With a pickup load of hay.
I'd settled down to make that trip
On a cold but sunny day.

As I was driving down the road
I looked into the mirror,
A puff of smoke came from the load,
My heart was filled with fear.

I pulled the pickup off the road
And jumped out real quick.
The sight that I was greeted with
Darned near made me sick.

It was just barely started
Coming from the bottom of the load,
But I knew I'd have to fight that fire
Right there by the road.

I unloaded every bale of hay
That was on that pickup truck.
No one came by to help that day,
I didn't have that kind of luck.

The fire was caused by a hot exhaust pipe
Underneath the bed.
I don't quite think it prudent
To repeat the words I said.

I covered the hole in the bed
With a board that I had found
Right there beside the road
Lying on the ground.

A fire of greater consequence
Happened late one summer night.
It took us hours to get it out,
It put up quite a fight.

An electric fence in the corral
Must have had a short in it.
It sent a spark onto the straw
Until a fire was lit.

Sparks from that electric fence
And the wind partnered up just right
To set the corral on fire
And light up the summer night.

Haystacks ringed the corral,
The wind blew a terrible gale.
We and the firemen worked so hard
We didn't lose one bale.

We quenched those flames with hand lines,
Buckets and hose
And though we didn't have much loss,
I will tell you it was close.

Then when that night was over
It was such a great relief
Instead of what it might have been:
A time of pain and grief

OT

One summer day long ago
I was baling up some straw
When I looked up from my work
And a sickening sight I saw.

From the top of the Harobed load
Came a little puff of smoke
And I knew in a flash
That I would soon be dead broke.

Paul was driving my new Harobed
Stacking straw that day.
On a hot, windy day,
Nothing burns faster than straw or hay.

Straw had gathered on the manifold
Which was very hot.
If that happens when fully loaded
Then trouble you have got.

The neighbor came with tractor,
He disced the field all 'round,
But the Harobed was a total loss,
It burned down to the ground.

An incident like that
Can really set a feller back,
And don't expect your banker
To cut you any slack

A loader that I used for hay
I was driving down the road.
I was driving to the neighbor's
For I had some hay to load.

Oil sprayed on the manifold
And the manifold was hot.
The fire that I had that day
Cost me quite a lot.

The power steering hose
From whence the oil came,
Blew out and caused this accident,
It was the thing to blame.

When you lose your power steering
And you have a fire to boot,
You might as well just bail out
'Cause your life ain't worth a hoot.

I quit that rig right then and there
And into the road I lit.
The loader kept right on agoin'
Into the borrow pit.

When I bailed out that day,
I was at least ten miles from town,
So then I just stood idly by
And watched that rig burn down.

DH

One morning long ago
We got an awful scare,
We looked out the window
And saw lots of smoke out there.

It was early in the morning
And as we looked around,
It looked like someone tried
To burn the whole world down.

It was haystacks that were burning,
The smoke was thick and black.
I jumped into my pickup
And went to check my stack.

I found it still was standing,
There was no fire there.
So I bowed my head in silence,
Sent aloft a thankful prayer.

We turned on the radio
And we heard the newsman say
That there was fire all around us,
Many haystacks burned that day.

A poor disgruntled farmer
Is the guy who did this crime
And this poor disgruntled farmer
Later did some jail time.

UNPREDICTABLE

Kids , dogs and horses sometimes make you a liar. Case in point: One
time at the Grant County Fair, the kids were ready to ride in the grand
entrance to the rodeo, but little Nancy Owens didn't have a horse to ride.
Since none of our kids intended to ride him, I volunteered to let her ride
Paint. She was concerned that he would balk at the bright lights and the
crowd. I assured her that he was "bomb proof" and she had no need to
fear.

So with great confidence in Paint and in me, she took off at a lope for the entrance only to have Paint come to a screeching halt when he broke in to the arena.

When Bonnie Ray came out to borrow a couple horses one day, I told her where to find them in a pasture about a mile from the house. Our horses were easy to catch and load and I assured her that they would not give her any trouble at all. About an hour later she came back all hot and sweaty and asked me to help.

·R

When you are a farmer or a rancher, things don't always work out according to plan. Sometimes money is kinda scarce and you may have to break a promise that you made to your kids like in the following poem.

YOU BET YOUR LIFE WE WILL

I promised you a new saddle, son,
But I've a sad story to tell.
We've got the money for the calves
But they didn't do too well.

The crops were not too good this year,
Calf prices mighty low.
Having to replace that worn out tractor
Was sure an awful blow.

We won't do that again next year
And repeat that great big bill.
We'll buy that saddle next year for sure,
You bet your life we will.

Calving was kinda all strung out,
I think the bull's to blame.
He got in a fight with the neighbor's bull
And came up kinda lame.

The one we bought to replace him
Is working out just great.
The calves, next year will be bigger,
The cows won't calve so late.

39

And spring came real late this year.
The rains came later still.
Next year we'll do a whole lot better.
You bet your life we will.

I think El Niño's run its course
So when spring comes round again
We'll probably have much warmer days
And get a lot more rain.

And then the grass will grow knee high
Up there in the hills.
With grass like that, we can buy that kack,
You bet your life we will.

Repairs, I'm sure, will cost us less
And calves won't get so sick.
We'll get a better stand of hay
And weeds won't grow as thick.

The doctor bill was outta sight
When you broke your leg last May
It's good we had some cash
Laid up for a rainy day.

It's sure too bad that your old horse
Took that nasty spill.
With no doctor bills we'll have more dough,
You bet your life we will.

So hang in there another year
And things will turn out great
With a better yield and higher prices
Things will be first rate.

With calf weights up and prices too,
We'll be able to pay the bills
With dough like that we'll buy that kack.
You bet your life we will.

Fair Time

I went to see a friend in the hospital who had just had heart surgery. He told me that his heart valve had been replaced with a heart valve from a cow.

HEART SURGERY

Up in the hospital in room one ten
Lies old Art Brossoit, a longtime friend.
I went to the hospital to visit with Art.
He's had an operation. They fixed up his heart.

I learned how they'd fixed him. He's doing just fine.
They added some cow parts now he's partly bovine.
He had calves in his legs and cowlicks in his hair
Now his heart's bovine too, they put a cow's valve there.

I know that a pig valve is the usual spare part
That's used when overhauling a worn out heart,
But who'd want the valve of an ornery old sow
When he could choose the valve of a contented cow?

With those cow innards used in Art's bypass
He'll probably have to live on hay and grass.
Art was once known as a bronc riding stud
Now he just lies around chewing his cud.

41

One day my brother-in-law told me a couple of jokes, so I wrote them out in the form of poems.

TEXAS RAIN

You don't really know what a real rain is
'Til you've lived on the Texas plain.
Sometimes you wait six months in the heat
While you just keep praying for rain .

When it does finally rain, it rains real hard,
It's usually a big downpour,
And before that storm has blowed itself out
You might get six inches or more.

Well that's what happened at Cliff and Ed's place
And it sure caught them off guard.
It musta rained for two or three days
And it flooded their house and yard.

As they sat on their roof contemplating their plight
They noticed a hat float by.
It went around the corner and then it came back,
And they sure couldn't figure out why.

They sat and watched as that hat made its rounds
Back and forth across the yard.
Cliff said, "I sure don't know what's going on,
Have you figured it out, old Pard?"

"Oh sure," said Ed, "I talked to gramps last night
So you know that I sure oughta."
He said he was going to mow the lawn
And he'd do it come hell or high water."

RURAL ELECTRIFICATION

Across the length of Oscar's ranch
The R.E.A. was building lines.
Ted, the boss, soon found out
That help was hard to find.

He made a call and with some luck
He hired a Mexican crew.
That still wasn't quite enough help,
They had so much to do.

So he made another call next day
And hired some Norwegian guys.
They'd never built power lines before
But they were willing to try.

Ted told the crews where to go
To set the poles that day.
He told them where the shovels were
And how much he would pay.

The Mexicans he sent across the river
Where they could do their thing.
They had holes to dig and poles to set
And a bunch of wire to string.

The Norskies he sent up on the hill,
They were a greenhorn bunch.
Both crews worked all morning long,
Then they came in for lunch.

"Well," Ted asked the Mexican boys,
"How did it go today?"
Juan said, "We worked hard, set ten poles.
We sure earned our pay."

"Set ten poles in half a day,
Why you've worked at a furious pace!
A couple days working like that
And we'll be done on Oscar's place."

He turned his attention to Ole then
To see what his crew had done
"Vell," said Ole, "Ve vorked hard too,
But ve only yust set vun."

Ted was kinda vexed at that
He threatened to can that crew.
"If the Mexican boys set ten poles
Can't you Norskies do it too?

"They dig the holes and set the poles.
They're the best I've ever hired.
But your crew set just one pole
And you act like you're plumb tired."

Ole really felt kinda bad
That he hadn't pleased old Ted,
But he thought they'd done a pretty good job
And this is what he said:

"Yew tink dose udder guys did a better yob
Vhen day set so many poles,
And maybe day are faster dan us
Vhen it comes to digging holes

"But dere is vun ting to keep in mind
Though your reasoning, it is sound
Did you notice how much your Mexican friends
Left sticking up out of the ground?"

BULL FIGHTER

I once had a couple Charolais bulls that I had used several summers
and had now outlived their usefulness so I decided to take them to the
livestock auction yard at Ellensburg. I went out and brought them in to
the corral so I could load them. These two bulls had grown up together

44

and had been together all summer but when they entered the corral they began fighting so ferociously that they were about to tear the corral apart. I hurriedly opened the tailgate, ran them up the loading chute into the truck and quickly slammed the tailgate down on them. They were fighting so violently that I feared they would wreck the truck. I quickly jumped in, started the engine and slammed the rig into gear and lurched ahead about ten feet, then slammed on the brakes, slamming the bulls in to the front of the truck.

By this time they were trying so hard to maintain their footing that they momentarily forgot to fight. However, it didn't take them long to regain their mutual animosity and again begin fighting. When they did, I again slammed them in to the front of the truck by alternately applying the brakes and the throttle. They behaved themselves most of the way, but resumed their feud when I slowed to turn in to the sales yard. I quickly backed up to the loading chute and got rid of my load. As soon as they were on solid ground again they went at their fight with renewed vigor but they were now consigned to the auction yard and I figured it was no longer my problem.

POLLED

It was not an Angus nor a polled Hereford steer,
But this city dude thought it looked kinda queer.
"How come that cow don't have horns he inquired?"
The cowboy who answered him truly was inspired.

He explained how some cattle are naturally polled,
Some others are hornless for reasons untold.
Some are dehorned at the time they are branded,
Sometimes with a saw though some are just banded.

There's an acid-like paste that'll kill off the horn
If applied to the nubbin when the calf is first born
Most cattle are dehorned to prevent injury to others
Such as cowboys, other calves or maybe their mothers.

"There's a whole lot of reasons cows don't have horns
If naturally polled they were that way when born.
There are many sound reasons, and most I endorse.
But that particular critter ain't a cow. It's a horse!"

LONG-WINDED PREACHER

Dan was a good old cowboy,
And patient as could be,
And about as good a horseman
As ever you'd hope to see.

He had a lot of patience
When he took a colt to break,
And he didn't even fret about
How long that it might take.

He was so even-tempered
That he never lost his cool,
Whether he was breaking horses
Or was working with a mule.

Dan was known both far and wide
For his firm but gentle touch.
About his expertise and patience,
I can never brag too much.

He was also patient with his kids,
He was never rude nor loud.
Patience was a virtue
With which Dan was well endowed.

That's the way he was with horses
And with kids and simple critters.
He never acted mean and
He was never, ever bitter.

But when it came to grown-ups
Of the human variety,
His patience had a limit
Somewhat short of infinity.

He'd put up with their nonsense
'Til his fuse burned plumb out.
When Dan lost his patience,
You knew there'd be a rout.

Which is just about what happened
When in church last Sunday morn,

He sat in rapt attention
As the preacher preached up a storm.

And he kept right on apreachin'
'Til the clock showed half past one.
Dan believed that preacher
Never, ever would get done.

He got up and walked right out
With the preacher standing there.
He was going into town
To have the barber cut his hair.

"Whoa there," said the preacher,
"I'm not ready yet to stop."
Dan said, "I need to take a trip
Down to the local barber shop."

The preacher then informed him
That he needs to plan ahead.
"Why don't you do that kind of thing
Before you come?" he said.

Dan was very, very patient
And this is what he had to say:
"I didn't need a haircut
When I came to church today."

BEN

There were vaudeville shows and minstrel shows
To entertain back then,
But this was a traveling one-man show,
A man with his dog named Ben.

Folks came on horses from miles around,
Though a few I'm sure had to walk
To see this dog known far and wide,
A dog that was trained to talk.

They all settled down in their seats that night
And the lights were turned down low.
They waited with great anticipation
To see this one-dog show.

Ben and his owner came onto the stage,
The applause was raucous and loud.
Ben and his owner were very well pleased,
For they'd drawn a monstrous crowd.

The owner of Ben was a man named Jack,
He had trained old Ben real well.
He asked Ben questions and Ben answered back
In a voice as clear as a bell.

"Ben," Said Jack, "I'm sure you know Noah,
The man who built that big ark.
What was the cover he peeled off the logs?"
To which Ben replied, "Bark, bark."

The folks in the audience were not much impressed,
They booed the dog and they hissed.
One fellow threw a rotten tomato,
But his aim was poor and he missed.

Then Jack asked Ben, "What is sandpaper like?"
To which Ben replied, "Rough, rough."
The crowd was getting unruly by now
For they'd just about had enough.

"Wait," said Jack. "He really can talk.
I'm telling the gospel truth.
Ben, name that famous baseball player."
To which Ben replied, "Ruth, Ruth."

With that the crowd came all undone,
They ran Jack and Ben out of town.
As they trudged along in the middle of the night,
Jack was really feeling down.

Ben could sense his master's mood,
He's a real smart dog, don't you know?
He looked up at Jack with soulful eyes,
"Joe DiMaggio?

48

HYBRID VIGOR

Before we gelded Cherokee (Paint) we bred him to Smoky. Smoky, who was a Shetland, produced a colt which the kids called Lucky. There has never been a better example of hybrid vigor than that demonstrated by Lucky. He wasn't very big. He probably stood about thirteen hands and may have weighed eight hundred pounds but he was all horse! One day up at the ranch, Jerry Hanson who is about six foot two and weighed about 250 pounds, was making fun of my little horse.

"Jerry," I told him, "I'll bet this pony can carry you all day and do it better than that nag of yours." Jerry pointed out a hill near the corral and scoffed. "He couldn't even take me up that first hill." I told him, "Not only can he carry you up that hill. He can go all the way at a dead run and he won't slow down until he brings you back." Jerry looked kind of comical on such a small horse, but Lucky made him a believer.

F2

We always had half a dozen horses around so it seemed only prudent that I should shoe them instead of always hiring it done. I bought all the necessary tools, several pairs of shoes and some nails and I was in business. I was young and ambitious and thought there wasn't anything I couldn't do if I set my mind to it.

Well, I probably could have done it if I had more time but the learning curve for a new chore sometimes makes it impractical when there is so much other work that needs done.

GREENHORN HORSESHOER

The price for shoeing horses has gone plumb out of sight.
It's up to nearly twenty bucks, it surely is a fright.
Well I don't need that horse shoe man, he's dispensable.
I'll learn to do the job myself, that seems to be more sensible.

Of course I'll need to buy some tools. A pincer, rasp, and such.
I might even need an anvil but that won't cost too much.
I've never done that job before but it can't be hard to do.
I'll trim the hoof, shape the shoe and put in a nail or two.

I've watched Gene do it several times, he does the job with ease.
He just bends over, picks up the foot, clamps it twixt his knees.
With his pincers, cuts off some hoof then smooths it with a file.
I'll just watch and learn from him. I'll save myself a pile.

I went to town to buy some tools. I needed quite a few.
I felt like I'd been robbed when that hardware clerk got through.
When Jesse James robbed someone he always wore a mask,
But this hardware man just wore a grin as he carried out his task.

I finally paid the price he asked. Though he really was a jerk.
I went back home and caught my horse and then I went to work.
I didn't know a hoof that small could be so hard to lift,
And when I clamped it twixt my knees, the horse, he had to shift.

I tied my horse up in the shade underneath a great big tree.
I picks up a foot and starts to work, the horse just leans on me.
By the time I got the first hoof trimmed I was working up a sweat.
Before I got the second done I had come to know regret.

There just might be an easier way that I could save some dough.
The horse slammed down his foot just then, nearly broke my toe.
I think I'll take a break from trimming and nail on some steel.
That way I can rest a while, give my toe a chance to heal.

Before I get the shoe nailed on my back is getting sore.
This nag is getting awful heavy, can't hold him up no more.
Before I get the nails clinched, he jerks his foot away.
It cut my hand and tore my pants much to my dismay.

I haven't added up the cost of pants and shoes and tools.
But I've come to one conclusion — bull riders aren't the only fools.
Tightwad ranchers better leave it to those who know the trade,
Horse shoers, after all, aren't really overpaid.

BEEF, IT'S WHAT'S FOR DINNER

Since the days of cattle drives
On the prairies of the West,
The taste and safety of our beef
Has always passed the test.

But there's been a lot of problems
Since that cattle driving time.
Sometimes we work a year or more,
And hardly make a dime.

There's heel flies and horn flies
And ticks that chew their ears,
And also storms and prairie fires
That drive a man to tears.

There's Bangs and Mange and Lepto
And other things as bad,
Sometimes I sit and wonder
How we keep from going mad.

Now we've got mad cow disease
And E. coli to boot
And nutritionists who advocate
Vegetables and fruit

And if by chance supplies are low
And the price should rise a bit
Consumers think that they're abused
And then they throw a fit.

But I am here to tell you friend,
That beef ain't high at all
And to gripe about a thing like that
Sure takes a lot of gall.

Folks pay the price for beer and smokes
And not think twice, you know?
They'll even pay a buck or more
For plain old H-two-O.

They wouldn't give a second thought
To expensive French champagne.
But let the price of beef go up
They howl and complain.

But if the price of beef should rise
And the rancher is a winner,
I say "Hallelujah folks!
Beef, its what's for dinner!"

PHRED

Noel Reid, a neighboring dairyman, came to see me one day with an offer to sell me an Angus cow that he had in his milking string. "She's a nice gentle cow but she doesn't give enough milk to be profitable for a dairy cow," he explained. "But she would make a good family cow and she would raise the kind of calves that you could sell right along with your others." I bought her and Lyn promptly named her Phred.

We kept her in the barn and fed her the choicest hay we had which was some very green fourth cutting alfalfa that was nearly all leaves. Lyn took over the job of milking her because her teats were too small for my hands. One morning when he went out to milk, he found her lying in the barn bloated up and dead. I guess she wasn't accustomed to such royal cuisine.

CATTLE BUYER

He was talking on the phone
In a booth in Ma's café,
The place was almost empty
I could hear him plain as day.

He was a shyster cattle buyer
Which was not too hard to tell,
It seems a local rancher
Has some calves he needs to sell.

And while he was dealing
As he sat there in that booth
I noticed he was having
Real problems with the truth.

He was telling this here rancher
How the price was going down
And of all his rancher neighbors
Who have calves to take to town.

And how they all will hit the market
On the same day of the week...
I could tell where this was going
And I detested his technique.

53

As I sat and ate my breakfast
On that cold and windy day,
I wasn't really being nosy
But this is what I heard him say:

"Your neighbors all have calves to sell,
There's lots of calves around
And I can buy them all day long
For sixty cents a pound.

"Demand is what will set the price.
Right now demand is nil."
The way that buyer laid it on,
It darn near made me ill.

"But I'll do my best to get 'em sold
Though competition's mighty tense.
Oh! I know a feedlot has some room.
I'll see if I can get you sixty cents."

He hung up the phone then picked it up,
Dialed and asked for Mick
He must have dialed the feedlot then
And he laid it on real thick.

He explained the implications
Of the cattle-on-feed report
And how the price was going up
Because supplies were short.

He told this man how scarce calves were,
How very few he'd found.
How anything worth hauling home
"Brings eighty cents a pound."

That's a mighty different story
Than the one I just had heard,
And both men probably trusted him
And took him at his word.

He said he'd beat the bushes
And try to find some steers,
But cattle were more scarce right now
Than they had been for years.

"I'll do my best to get some bought.
But competition's mighty tense.
OH! I know a rancher has a few
That I'll try to buy for eighty cents.

"If you'll agree to that high price,
I'll see what can be done.
If he won't sell for eighty cents,
I'll offer eighty-one."

He hung up the phone, then picked it up
And dialed it once again
"Hello," he said with nervous voice,
"I'd like to talk to Ben."

I think he'd called the rancher back,
He was generous as could be...
"I convinced the buyer to raise his bid
And I got you sixty-three."

FLOOD

One winter we moved the herd to Wayne Shimke's corn field. He had just built a new basement and moved a house which he bought from Jesse Siebert and put it on the basement. The construction job wasn't completed yet and there was no one around, so I found a water faucet on the side of the basement wall, screwed on the hose, turned on the water and went home to eat lunch. I came back to find the cows had gotten their fill and the tank was about to run over so I went to the house and turned off the water. It was then that I heard water running and saw that there was about six inches of water in the basement. Wayne had his tools in the basement as well as a pile of sheetrock and other building materials. My wife and kids were with me so we went to work and bailed water for a couple of hours but didn't get the mess cleaned up before Wayne came and caught me.

/ꙅ/

I couldn't afford Powder River corral panels so I bought a truckload of used pipe at the local scrap metal dealer and built my own. I also built my own portable loading chute and used this setup when loading at our spring pasture and hauling to our summer range which was about 150 miles away. We would go out with our horses in the evening and pair up a load of cows and calves and run them into our pipe corral so that they would be ready to load early next morning. The only way we had to hold the panels together was with haywire. (Why not? … that holds together everything else on the ranch.)

One morning when we came to load up, the panels were lying on the ground and the cows were all scattered and we had to get the horses and gather them all over again. I guess I'll have to invest in a better grade of haywire.

CACKLEBERRIES

When we moved to Ephrata we inherited a herd (flock?) of Bantam chickens. The former owners had just let the chickens run loose all over the farmstead and multiply with abandon. Of course there were

eggs under every tumbleweed, loose board, haystack, and anyplace a hen could find to hide them. One Saturday all my kids, plus a couple neighbor kids were out playing when they came upon a nest of rotten eggs. They threw the eggs and broke them. This was all kinds of fun so they went looking for more nests which weren't hard to find. Soon they were throwing eggs at each other.

It wasn't long until someone hit me with one that was rotten and then the war was on! This was just like a snowball fight except that it was a little more aromatic. We had a lot of fun but we had eggs splattered on everything on the place, some of which were still apparent several years later.

$$ \mathrm{L_K} $$

Mrs. Bergstrom came over one day and found three-year-old Tim digging a hole. When she asked him the purpose of his excavation project, he informed her that he was making a trap to catch some chickens. He must have had the hole at least five or six inches deep and he told her he was ready to put some weeds and grass over it for camouflage and when a chicken fell in he would be nearby to catch it.

$$ \mathrm{wZ} $$

COLD WATER

Russell was an orphan lad
And life for him was tough.
Most days he had a meal or two
But most days not enough

He was well in to his teenage years
When he met his old Grandad
Who became the only father figure
Russell ever had.

Now Grandad was a lot of things
But he was not fastidious
The way he washed the dishes
Didn't set too well with Russ.

Russ complained to Gramps one day
The dishes weren't quite clean
Gramps said, "Cold water does as good a job
As anything I've seen.

"Now you go out and feed the stock
And check the heifer pen,
I'll have some grub for us to eat
Whenever you come in."

At half past dark Russ came back,
He'd had a busy day.
He hoped to have a good hot meal
And then he'd hit the hay.

He pulled a chair up to the table
And looked down at his plate.
The durn thing looked as dirty
As if he just had ate.

"Your cookin's good," he said to Gramps,
"But these dishes just ain't clean."
Gramps said," Cold water does as good a job
As anything I've seen."

"I've got a job for you to do,
So get a good night's sleep."
At break of day Russ hit the floor
To work and earn his keep.

"Sit down and eat your breakfast first
Then saddle up old Pete
And take your rifle to the woods
And bring us home some meat."

Russ sat down to have his meal
But lost his appetite.
The dishes were as dirty as when
He finished up last night.

"I don't like to complain," he said to gramps,
"But these dishes just aint clean."
Gramps said, "Cold water does as good a job
As anything I've seen."

Russ sat down and ate his eggs
And then he saddled up.
He climbed aboard and then he called
For Grandpa's faithful pup.

But Grandpa called his cow dog back.
Here's what he had to say,
"You stay here with me, Cold Water,
You'll scare the deer way."

⅂

IKE

A redheaded freckle-faced kid,
He was known to all as Ike.
Not a mean bone in his body
But a real mischievous tyke.

With practical jokes his stock-in-trade,
He was a holy terror.
His teacher bore the brunt of his pranks,
To Ike that seemed to be fair.

Whenever he got the best of her
It gave him quite a lift.
To make amends, Ike thought one day,
He'd bring Miss Brown a gift.

He walked into the classroom,
His hand behind his back,
He had a nice surprise for her
And he carried it in a sack.

"Guess what this is I have for you?"
He asked her with a grin,
Then he extended his hand
With the sack that it was in.

The proverbial apple was the thing
His teacher guessed at first,
Little Ike was so doggone proud
His shirt just dang near burst.

But he allowed her guess was wrong
So she'd have to guess once more,
Suddenly the sack sprang a leak
And was dripping on the floor.

It wasn't heavy and so he held it out
And from his hand it swung,
With her finger she caught a drip
And touched it to her tongue.

She smacked her lips and with a smile
Said, "It tastes just like pickle."
Little Ike was all aglow
And his eyes began to twinkle.

He said to her with impish grin
All the while her eyes agog,
"You'll never guess and so I'll tell.
It's a little puppy dog!"

Molly's Puppies

Panhandle Phillips was a character in a book by Richmond P. Hobson. According to Hobson, this is a true story which he told in a book titled "Nothing Too Good for a Cowboy."

PANHANDLE PHILLIPS
AND THE GRIZZLY BEAR

I have a story to tell that's hard to believe
And I'm not real sure that it's true
But it's a story that's been around for years
Up north in the Caribou.

Before the Nechaco had been explored
And the Algacs not yet mapped
The wolves and the moose had never seen man,
No beaver had yet been trapped.

It happened up north of Anahim lake
On the Blackwater River, I'm told
The story of a man who encountered a bear,
So scared that his blood ran cold.

Panhandle Phillips was this cowhand's name
A man of courage and pluck,
A transplanted puncher from down in the states
But now for sure a Canuck.

He'd got off his horse to give him a rest
And was rolling himself a smoke
When up on the bank not twenty yards back,
A big Grizzly Bear awoke.

Old Grizzly gave them the once over slow,
No man had he ever seen
For up until now there'd been no man
In this land so wild and pristine.

Old Piledriver, the black he rode,
Quit him right there on the spot.
The terrified horse stumbled and fell,
Gained his feet and was off like a shot.

Pan couldn't afford to excite the bear
So he slowly rose up to his feet,
He carefully unholstered his old forty-four
Though he knew that he was dead meat.

It would be futile to try to scare him away,
To yell or to fire in the air.
It would be a short race if he started to run,
He could holler but bears don't scare.

He could smell the acrid stench of the beast
As a breeze drifted in from the south.
He spoke in a slow and soothing tone
As he aimed at the bear's open mouth.

"I'll put two in you mouth and two in your chest
But I know that you won't stop.
Even at close range, this ain't enough gun
To ever make you drop.

"Though I don't have a chance
I'll get off four shots and I know that you will die,
But as close as you are, you'll get to me first.
You'll die but so will I."

Well it's just as though the bear understood
And he slowly dropped down on all four.
He turned and ambled on down the trail.
Said Pan, "Good riddance old boar."

Now Pan was a man who knew the ways
Of critters wild and free
And the one most feared in the whole northwest,
The Grizzly Bear was he.

The nature of Pan's makeup didn't allow
Emotions to get in the way
That's reason for his cool actions
That saved his life that day.

Pan didn't have time to make a plan
Nor time to think things through,
But if you would ask him for his advice
Here's what he'd say to you:

Bell your horses, make some noise,
Let bears know you're there,
Above all else stay away from her cubs
Try to never surprise a bear.

A Grizzly, of course, will kill for food
And he'll eat most anything
He's master of all that he surveys,
In his world he's the king.

But if perceives that there's no threat,
He won't kill just for fun,
So he may let you live to ride again
If you just don't cut and run.

BRANDING DAY

Working the calves each spring was one job our kids always looked forward to. It was a long day of hard work, but we usually scheduled it for a weekday and allowed them to stay out of school, which made it all worthwhile for them. As I mentioned in one of the poems in this book, I'm not really a cowboy, so I didn't do things the old-fashioned way. I did them the modern way. We didn't rope the calves and drag them to

the fire. In fact, we didn't even have a fire. We used a Powder River calf table and an electric branding iron.

With one man and five kids doing the work, it was an all-day job to work our herd of about two hundred head. First thing in the morning, we'd bring the herd into the corral, separate the calves from the cows, run the calves into the crowding alley and then up the chute. It was the kid's job to push the calves, one at a time, up to the calf cradle where I would catch them, pull the handle which laid them over on their side readying them for branding and all the other operations which needed done.

While Lois kept the syringes filled, the kids and I spent our time branding, castrating, implanting, vaccinating, and earmarking the calves. On one branding day, Wendy, then a high school junior, had a date to go to the prom with Bill Sieverkropp. I didn't realize how late it was getting and worked her so late she nearly didn't get ready in time. As it was, the sunburn she got that day didn't quite match her gown. In another branding which comes to mind, Maxine who was then about nine years old, took on the job of being the cook for the day, and did she ever do a great job. She did everything from boiling and mashing the potatoes and making gravy, to cooking some veggies and baking a pie.

CR

MIKE'S THERMOS

Old Mike had been out on the ranch
For thirty years or more
He hardly ever went to town
To go into a store

But way last spring he went to town
And to a hardware store
Where shelves were lined with lots of things
That he'd not seen before

His eyes fell on a quart sized jug
He thought it looked unique.
When he asked the clerk what it was for
She thought he was a geek.

"What," he asked, "is that thing there
If I may be so bold?"
"Why that's a thermos jug," she said,
"It keeps things hot or cold."

Now Mike, he knew how handy
A thing like that could be
"Hey! That looks good. Wrap it up.
I'll take it home," says he.

For he knew how cold he often got
When riding on the range,
Now he'd use this thermos jug
It would be a welcome change.

He took it to the bunkhouse
Where he put it on display,
He'd fill it with hot coffee
And he'd be warm today.

A warm Chinook came up that day
A blowin' from the west
He'd just fill up that thermos jug
And give that jug a test.

Old Mike, he kinda vacillated,
Did he need it hot or cool?
But then he figured what to do,
He sure was no one's fool

That afternoon he stopped to rest,
He was getting kinda sore,
Then Joe saw that jug and asked old Mike
What that jug was for

"Well," said Mike, "it keeps things hot,
It also keeps things cold.
It's real high tech and works real good,
At least that's what I've been told."

"When we left today, it was cold
So I'd need a good hot drink.
But with that warm Chinook a blowin'
I didn't know what to think,

"So I put in two cups of good hot coffee
In case the day is cool
But with a wind as warm as that
I knew I might get fooled.

"So just in case the day is warm
Instead of cold, you see.
I topped it off with two more cups
Of frigid cold iced tea."

A BEAR STORY

Behold, the mighty hunter
With his rifle in his hand
He goes into the mountains,
There he takes his hunting stand.

The object of this hunting trip
Is to get a warm fur coat,
Be it from a Grizzly Bear
Or from a mountain goat.

Behold the mighty Grizzly Bear,
He's in the mountains too
He's a whole lot more intimidating
Than the one that's in the zoo.

He's looking for a meal today,
He's "hungry as a bear"
He doesn't need a nice fur coat.
He has a coat to wear.

Both hunters have specific wants
Though their needs are not the same,
And though they both have serious goals,
This hunt is just a game.

If the bear sees it as a game
It's one of hide and seek,
And if he doesn't win the game
His dinner outlook's bleak.

To the hunter it's a game also
But of lesser consequence,
And if he should be the one to win
It's at the bear's expense.

It's the hunter and the hunted
Those names apply to both,
And so they hunt and stalk each other
Through the undergrowth.

Finally later in the day
When the sun is going down
The man's about to pack it in
And head back in to town.

He rounds a bend and in the trail
They meet there face to face,
He turns around and starts to run
But he'll surely lose this race.

He yelled a lot and acted brave,
He waved and hollered SCAT!
But the bear was not intimidated,
He didn't savvy that.

And so they sat upon a log
To negotiate then and there,
It's life and death for the hunter
And likewise for the bear.

Although it's hard to negotiate
When your life is on the line
Anything else at this point
Would just be asinine.

Both had their wants and needs
Which to them were very real.
The man wanted a warm fur coat,
The Grizzly Bear a meal.

So this is how the hunt turned out,
It was fair as it could be
For each of them must give a little
And compromise, you see?

As the bear went merrily on his way,
Each hunter was a winner.
The man got his warm fur coat,
And the bear? He got his dinner.

BRRR...COLD

The spring pasture which we leased from the USBR contained a small lake where the cows could get water so we left them there and hauled hay to them during the winter of 1977. Sometime in January the weather got cold enough that I was having a hard time keeping the ice chopped off the lake. One morning when I went to feed I discovered two cows that had walked out on the ice and broke through. They were standing in about three and a half feet of water and were shivering violently. I walked out on the ice and threw a rope on one of them but couldn't drag her out.

In those days we didn't have a four wheel drive pickup so I went home and got a tractor. After both cows were safely on dry land I returned the tractor and came back to check on them. I guess they decided it was

warmer in the water. They were both in the lake again so I had to go back and get the tractor. This time when I got them out, I tried to chase them around and warm them up, but they were so cold they didn't want to move. After a while I gave up in frustration and left. When I returned the cows were still on dry land but both were dead.

In those days we pastured our cows on corn stalks in the winter time. We'd buy the aftermath corn stalks of harvested fields from neighboring farmers and throw up a temporary electric fence. One morning when I went to check the cows I noticed tracks and cow sign on the road, and I could see where the cows had knocked down the fence, but when I counted, I could see that there were no cows missing, and the fence was repaired. Later I learned that Bud Wizer was moving his cows down the road past where mine were and they broke the fence down and they all got mixed up. He and his men tried to separate the cows and take theirs home. They finally gave up, took all his cows and mine up to the Short ranch about five miles away, put them in a corral sorted them and then trailed mine back to where he found them and repaired the fence.

2L

During the winter time, when moving cows from field to field, we also moved the water tanks and would usually fill them with a hose from the house of the farmer whose aftermath crops we were using. Oftentimes the cows would cause the hose to fall out of the tank and/or we didn't get the water turned off soon enough and ice would build up around the tanks.

One winter a cow fell with her legs spraddled out so far that it broke something and we had to butcher her. Of course I knew that she would be tough eating so I made her all in to hamburger. I didn't know hamburger could be so tough. Even though it was finely ground, it was so tough that we could hardly get our forks into the gravy.

The next time we had to butcher an old cow, we had her made into pepperoni. It was tough too, but that's the way pepperoni is supposed to be. My kids always wondered why we had to eat those old tough cows.

They thought that since we had so many, why not butcher a nice fat steer and have some good meat? I understood their argument but it seemed like we often had an old cow got injured and couldn't be sold. If we didn't eat her, who would? Besides, those fat steers are worth more to sell than old cows are.

A BLONDE JOKE

Jerry lived out on a ranch,
His wife was a blonde named Jean.
She wasn't quite the smartest chick
That I have ever seen.

Cattle prices hit the skids
And they couldn't make ends meet
So they sold the ranch and moved to town
And lived on Basin Street.

'Twas in the year of sixty-nine
A winter to remember,
The mercury fell plumb out of sight
The last day of November.

And then it started snowing
And the snow got real deep,
The only way to get around
Was by horseback or a Jeep.

The snow all needed to be plowed
But cars were in the way
So the mayor and the street crew
Devised a plan that day.

They needed the help of the citizenry
To execute their plan,
They enlisted the help of the radio station
And also the weatherman.

The radio announcer was loud and clear
His message short and sweet.
He asked the folks to move their cars
To the odd numbered side of the street.

So Jean went out to do her part
To help that snowplow crew,
She was a real good citizen
And that's the least that she could do.

All went well, the streets were clear
But next week it snowed some more,
The radio announcer came on again
For order he must restore.

Once again Jean went out
And did her job with pride,
She did exactly as she was told
And parked on the even numbered side.

A few days later another storm
Brought traffic to a stop,
There was no way that anyone
Could go downtown and shop.

But this time when the word came out
The blonde was left in the dark,
All were asked to move their cars
But they weren't told where to park.

Now Jean was left in a tizzy,
She was confused and in a stew,
She wanted so much to be helpful
But she needed to know what to do.

And she sure didn't want the snowplow
To cover up her new Dodge.
Then cool-headed Jerry suggested,
"Why not just leave it in the garage."

This poem came from a poster on the wall in Kenny Ardell's feedlot scale house/office. I thought it would make a good poem so here it is. It was my first attempt at poetry.

LOST DOG

There's a little old auction yard in my hometown.
And the folks come in from miles around.
They bring horses and cows and Billy goats too.
And ducks and chickens and pigs and ewes.

It's not limited to horses and cows,
They even sell tractors and mowers and plows.
They have a bulletin board to advertise things
That don't sell too well through the auction ring.

It was there that I read about a dog that had strayed
And a big old reward just awaitin' to get paid.
According to that note pinned up on the wall,
He was a good little dog. Though not really that small.

He's black and white and walks with a limp.
He was hit by a car and broke one hip.
His tail was docked when he was a pup
So all he has there is a short little stump.

Three toes are gone from his left front paw.
He was kicked by a horse and has a crooked jaw.
He lost one eye in a fight last year
And in that fight he lost one ear.

He has a big old scar on the top of his head,
The result of a wreck with a kid on a sled.
Four teeth are missing from the side of his mouth.
Don't blame this dude for headin' down south.

The note also said in an offhand way,
"There's one more thing about this stray —
We neutered him last week and it left him sorta lame.
If you see him, just call to him. 'Lucky' is his name."

72

MULE RAFFLE

"White mule for sale: five hundred dollars"
Read the ad in the paper that night,
Now in case you don't know, I'll tell you now
A white mule is an unusual sight.

Ben decided to answer that ad
For he needed a mule real bad,
He'd have a team if he hitched it up
With the mule he already had.

So he wrote a check for the mule that night
Five hundred dollars it read,
He returned next day to haul it home
But the doggone mule was dead.

Now Sam who sold it really felt bad
That the mule had died that way,
He'd spent the money and now was broke
So really what could he say?

Ben hauled it home and devised a plan
At which you'll probably scoff,
The county fair was coming soon
He'd just raffle that dead mule off.

Six hundred tickets at a dollar each,
He had his money back and more,
Sam asked, "When the winner found out
That the mule was dead, wasn't he kinda sore?"

Well yes," said Ben, "he really was,
He was mad as old wet hen,
But I don't see how he can be mad now,
I refunded his dollar to him."

The following poem was inspired by Robert (or Raymond... at that time I'd known them for ten or fifteen years and still couldn't tell them apart) Sieverkropp. One day at a farm auction he informed me that he didn't have to go to college to get his Ph.D. This poem will explain why.

THE COWBOY WITH THE PH.D.

I have this rancher neighbor
Who's just as smart as he can be.
Well, at least I think he's smart,
He has a Ph.D.

I asked what field of knowledge
Was this Ph.D. he'd earned.
Did it help his ranching skills,
All the things he'd learned?

He didn't tell me right away
What was his specialty
So I could only speculate
On this great advanced degree.

A Ph.D. in range management
Would sure be good to have.
He could improve his range that way,
Raise some real good calves.

Or a Ph.D. in horses
Would surely be worthwhile,
He could raise some real good stock
And then cowboy in style.

A Ph.D. in agronomy
Would really save the day,
Then maybe he could grow
Some good nutritious hay.

A Ph.D. in nutrition?
Yeah, I like the sound of that.
He could improve the ration
And get his calves real fat.

With a Ph.D. in genetics
He could develop a superior breed.
They'd grow a whole lot faster
And consume a lot less feed.

Now a Ph.D. in mechanics
Is a real important one.
He could fix that broke down tractor
And maybe make it run.

The Ph.D. my neighbor has
Ain't none of these I've mentioned.
So when he told me what it was
It sure got my attention.

'Cause a Ph.D. is something
That's a real useful tool,
And anyone who has one
Is surely no one's fool.

The Ph.D. he brags about
Does help his cowboy skill
And when it comes to ranching
It really fills the bill.

I know The Ph.D. my neighbor has
Don't make his calves grow bigger.
'Cause I finally found out what it is.
It's just a <u>P</u>ost <u>H</u>ole <u>D</u>igger

TIM'S WRECK

"Mom, my head hurts," Tim complained from his hospital bed.

"After a nasty spill like that, you have a right to have a headache," countered the doctor. This was when Tim was about seven or eight years old and Lois had found him unconscious in the bath tub. He had wrecked his motorbike and fell in the dirt so he had gone home, filled the bath tub, climbed in and passed out. She rushed him to the emergency room and found that he had a concussion. We later discovered that he had his wreck a couple miles from home and we're not sure how he made it home by himself.

WHAT'S IN A NAME?

I'm sure everyone is aware that kids often come up with some rather weird names for pets. Our kids were no different. Maxine and Tim had cats which were named Blarts, Jockey-box, Mouse and Milkery, and of course what else but --- Kitty.

When Wendy was real young, she tacked the name "Book" on to a colt. A horse she had in high school, she named Shandy.

We had too many cows to put names to them but the kids did raise some bucket calves which they named. I recall such names as Hannigan, Hoolihan, Eyelash, Frisky, Sagebrush Charlie, Candy, Nellie and a Holstein calf they called Holster.

Our paint horse was originally named Cherokee but most times we referred to him as Old Paint. Other horses carried such monikers as Peanuts, Cloudy, Tampico (later shortened to Tammy), Sinew, Cody, Smoky, Hap, Lonesome, Yeller, Lucky, Toby, Flag, Misty-Dawn, Calija and Cricket.

Lyn once named a milk cow Phred.

Of course, their 4-H steers that they took to the fair all had names: Pabst the blue ribbon steer, Tyrone, Doc, Bo, Snuffy, Pizzazz.

The few dogs' names I remember are Jake, Mollie, Pete, Blondie, Ralph, Gilligan, Sloan and Babe.

Then the sheep: Bongo, Sadie, Ojo, Jiffy, Barney, Pete and Fred.

And goats: Clementine, Cappie.

Rabbits: Grandma and Grandpa. Yes, you read that right, Grandma and Grandpa.

Maxine even named her motorcycle Ol' Number 7.

The kids even named some bulls we had. One was called Hector. Another was El Capitan. Then another one, because several times we caught him sitting like a dog, they called "Sitting Bull."

Mollie had many puppies and the kids decided they would name one litter for characters in a book about McBroom's farm in which the soil was so fertile that every crop he planted grew overnight. Some of these names were: Will, Jill, Hester, Chester, Peter, Polly, Tim, Tom, Mary, Larry, and little Clarinda. These names didn't stick because we gave away all the pups.

I called on my kids to refresh my memory and it took a lot of concentration on the part of all five of them to come up with all these names most of which I had forgotten.

SWIMMING HOLE

Lyn was twelve years old when we moved to Ephrata. He was a very resourceful lad. He decided we needed a swimming pool so he hitched the Kilifer scraper to the tractor and dug one. He had better equipment for digging than what Tim had when he tried capturing chickens. When he finished the job he had a pool about four feet deep.

The ground around our house is very rocky and the pool wouldn't hold water so he lined it with a huge piece of plastic. After it was filled with water the kids had a lot of fun on those hot summer days playing in the water. After a while the water became dirty and needed to be changed.

He'd made no provisions for draining, so Lyn dove to the bottom with a knife and cut a hole to let out the water. Bad mistake! He could never get the hole repaired and the swimming pool was abandoned.

This is a true story about a little neighbor kid who was confused about a horse's name.

RIDING DOUBLE

We had to move some cows one day,
It was cold and the wind was strong.
Gary and Dale were bundled up warm
And they wanted to go along.

Two little kids, just four and five,
So you see they were quite small.
Their dad was riding a half-broke mare
And she couldn't be trusted at all.

So Grandpa Don took Gary,
He rode behind the saddle on Mike.
Dale wanted to ride with us too,
Just four years old, but a game little tyke

So his mama said to me, "Larry,
If it's not too much trouble
That horse of yours is pretty gentle,
Can you and Dale ride double?"

"Why sure," says I, "I think we can.
We sure can give it a try."
So she lifts Dale up. He's kinda scared,
But cowboys, you know, don't cry.

Now I was riding Peanuts,
A flashy little quarter horse bay,
Dale was holding on real tight.
He was up there and he aimed to stay.

The ride was uneventful,
We brought the cows all in.
When Dale saw his mother waiting,
He broke into a grin.

When he got back on the ground,
He was proud as punch of course.
He said, "I sure do like to ride 'Double'
He's really a nice old horse."

Maxine, Amy and Tim

Dale wanted to ride with me on "Double" when we were moving cows another time that same winter. We were about a hundred yards from where his mother stood watching when Peanuts started to buck.

Of course my reaction was to protect Dale and keep him from falling off. He was riding behind me, so I reached around behind my back to hold him on while trying to control the horse and stop him from bucking. Dale hung on and all was well, but mama came running and rescued her boy. I'm not sure how Dale felt but I don't think Linda considered "Double" such a nice old horse anymore.

–N

FORMAL DINING

I took my wife out on the town
One night in Moses Lake,
I had an urge for seafood.
She wanted T-bone steak.

We went into a fancy joint
Where folks were dressed to kill.
I hoped that I was rich enough
To pay the entire bill.

The Maitre d' looked at me
And gave the evil eye.
"You're not allowed in here," she said
"Unless you wear a tie."

"I would oblige, If I could,
So I can taste your fare
But a necktie is a garment
That I hardly ever wear.

"And since I didn't bring one,
I just can't quite see how
I can do what you require
And wear a necktie now."

"If that's the case," she countered then,
"Get out, don't come back."
For making friends and acting nice
She didn't have the knack.

I went out to my car
Which was parked out on the street,
I found a pair of jumper cables
Underneath the seat.

To my surprise they looked real good
When hung around my neck.
I went back to the restaurant then.
I figured what the heck!

If I can get away with this,
I'll have nice fillet,
Fill my belly, have a drink
And soon be on my way.

Well, "Grouchy" had some other plans,
She met me at the door.
When she saw the jumper cables
She let out an awful roar.

But after the initial shock
She broke into a grin.
She said if I'd behave myself
That she would let me in.

"You may as well come in,"
She said. "You're such a dingaling.
But you will have to promise me
You won't start anything."

HARD TIMES

During the Depression when I was a kid
Times were really tough.
Oh, we always had something to eat,
But sometimes not nearly enough.

But with a vegetable garden,
A few old hens and a bony old Jersey cow
And by skimping and scraping and saving our pennies,
We always got by somehow.

That big apple tree out in the yard
Provided us with apples to eat.
We'd pick them and store them down in the cellar.
In the winter we'd have them to eat.

"One bad apple can spoil the bunch."
Wise words in more ways than one
So we took great care as we put them away
Spoiled apples in lunches ain't fun.

Those spoiled apples weren't a total loss.
They still had parts good to eat.
We could use them to make pies or sauce,
Even eating them raw was a treat.

All winter on weekends we'd sort out the bad ones,
The good ones we'd leave in the bin,
Every Saturday morning we'd go back to the cellar
And sort them over again.

We'd cut out the bad parts that had started to rot
And eat as much as we could,
But we ate spoiled apples all winter long
And never ate one that was good.

81

Though I may complain about eating rotten apples, I'm really very thankful for all that God has blessed me with. I wrote the following prayer for Thanksgiving dinner.

A THANKSGIVING PRAYER

Lord of wonder, love and grace.
God of earth and sky and space,
We do exalt Thee Almighty God.
By Your greatness we are awed.

We're so thankful You're mindful of us,
And though we're sinners You still love us.
You sent your son, He bled and died,
And now He reigns at Your side.

We're very thankful for this land,
For the way You've touched it with Your hand.
Warm summer days You've sent our way.
It ripened grain and dried the hay.

We thank You Lord for all You've done.
You've sent the rain, also the sun.
You've blessed us with a big calf crop.
Our blessings just don't ever stop.

We thank you Lord for what we have.
Those mama cows with big fat calves.
The pasture grass is belly deep,
A heavenly feast for calves and sheep.

Round-up time will soon arrive,
We'll sell our calves and pay our tithes
To honor You which is our aim
And give you thanks in Jesus name.

Amen

◊=

When calving season rolls around it always seems to be cold, stormy and damp. Cows always seem to have their calves on the coldest, wettest (not day but) night of the year. And they always find a good hiding place to calve if they are going to have problems.

Consequently, we tried to determine when each cow was close up and get her in to the corral ahead of time so we could keep an eye on her. The one looking two weeks off would be left out on the hill. Of course she calved that night and the ones that were brought in to the corral waited two weeks to have their calves.

CALVING TIME

There's one big job that comes around
On a cattle ranch each year,
It's usually cold and stormy and wet
When calving time draws near.

Cows always calve in the dark of night
Or in the middle of a storm.
They never do it in broad daylight
Or when it's nice and warm.

Every day we'd ride through the herd
We'd check the cows real good.
Bring in those we thought would calve,
But of course they never would.

They'd lay around for a week or two
Before they'd ever do it.
But the ones we left outside the corral
Were mamas before we knew it.

In the spring of 1969, we traded our farm near Moses Lake for three hundred acres south of Ephrata. At that time the preferred method of irrigation was hand lines and wheel lines. In order to get around fast enough to get the water all changed before school in the mornings, we each had a Honda motorcycle to ride out to the fields (and out through the fields).

We lacked knowledge and experience, but we did have lots of determination and ambition. It is Lois' contention that we did things backward because the first thing I did was to fence the place, after which I built a shop and corral, and finally a house.

OUR DREAM RANCH

My wife and I, we bought a ranch
In the foothills way out west.
The trees and grass were lush and green,
Our friends were all impressed.

A stream meandered through the place
From the mountains to the south
And culminated at a lake
With the ranch house near its mouth.

The lake was stocked with lots of fish,
The woods had deer and bear.
If there's another ranch this fine,
I'm sure I don't know where.

The cattle in the meadow
Grazed on knee high Orchard Grass.
We thought we were in heaven
And we sure did live first class.

After several years of living high,
Things sorta hit the skids
Which accounted for some problems
For me, my wife and kids.

A downturn in the weather cycle
Brought a drought into our life,
Which was a lesson in humility
For this cowman and his wife.

The lake dried up and got real low,
The creek was just a trickle.
The pasture was a dry dust bowl,
We sure were in a pickle.

We lived and breathed the dust and dirt
For a year or maybe more.
We'd had a taste of living high
But now we sure were poor.

In the second summer of the drought
On a hot and windy day
The sky was getting dark with clouds.
A storm was on the way.

The wind was whipping dust around,
And then the lightning flashed.
And on its heels the deafening sound
Of thunder as it crashed.

We ran down to the storm cellar
We were so filled with fright.
We could hear that awful storm a blowin'
As it raged throughout the night.

It wasn't 'til next morning
When the thunder boomed no more,
That I ventured from my hiding place
And stood there in the door.

Then as I stood and checked things out
The rain began to fall.
The thing that happened to me next
It seems I can't recall.

The sudden change from dry to wet
Hit me like a rock.
The rain that hit my dusty face
Caused me to go in shock.

My wife came from the shelter then
And saw me lying there.
She knew she must revive me quick,
She had no time to spare.

She grabbed a bucket in her hand
And ran down to the creek
To throw some water in my face
Would be the right technique.

Because we'd had a two-year drought
The creek was now plumb dry.
There was no water she could use,
She thought of something else try

The drought had lasted for so long
And the dust was so familiar
Anything else she might have done
Could not have been much sillier.

She knew she had to act real quick
Or suffer the consequences,
So she threw a bucket of dust on me
And brought me to my senses.

A SURPLUS OF CATTLE GUARDS

Our President, they say, is seeking a way
To cut the budget in half.
He has found a way, but I'm here to say,
It's sure to give you a laugh.

A way to save dough, he wants you know:
"Lay off cattle guards out in the West"
And so he will cut right down to the gut
And he'll save only the best.

The rest will get canned and wherever they land
I'm sure is beyond their control,
But he really does care so he'll be there
To sign them with the border patrol.

If they don't qualify, there's no need to cry
Even though they no longer work,
He'll find a way to retain their pay
And keep their bennies and perks.

'Cause he does have a plan, that compassionate man
To prevent a terrible wreck,
A retraining program, courtesy of Sam
And a great big severance check.

87

GOOD DOG

Let me tell you about a dog we had. He was a Border Collie and his name was Jake. He was a very good watch dog and also a good cow dog. We also had an Australian Shepherd named Mollie. These two dogs presented us with a couple litters of pups every year for several years. These pups were in big demand and we never had any trouble getting rid of them.

One day I was driving down the road about fifty miles per hour with Jake in the back of the truck when he saw my reflection in the rear view mirror and reached up to lick my face. It wasn't my face he was trying to lick, it was the mirror, and he fell off the truck. I looked back and saw him bouncing and tumbling over and over again. I got stopped about the same time he stopped rolling. He jumped back up on the truck and we proceeded on home. Poor old Jake was one sore pooch for a few days but he never showed any permanent scars or disability.

Like I say, Jake was a good watch dog. One day we heard a commotion out in the yard, but there was nothing there. Upon further investigation, we realized the noise was coming from the front yard. We went around the house and found Jake standing beside a car growling and a young woman was sitting on top of the car calling for help.

Jake was very protective of the kids, too. Jerry Hansen was teasing Tim one time and started being a little too playful to suit Jake. Jake let him know in no uncertain terms that he'd better leave that kid alone if he wanted to retain all his body parts.

Jake always wanted go along wherever I went, But I sure didn't want him with me when checking cows at night during calving. My herd consisted of mostly Angus and they are very protective mothers and they go haywire if a dog is around their babies. One time when he got loose and followed me, an irate cow thought she had him in her sights and charged. She had become disoriented and it wasn't the dog she had in her sights at all but a calf standing out there in the dark by itself. She hit that calf going about twenty miles per hour and threw it ten feet in the air. (Do you detect a little exaggeration there?) After that little episode, I decided I'd had enough of his company so I locked him in the truck cab. I knew he couldn't get out of there! But he fixed me. When I let him out next morning, he had torn and chewed up all the upholstery — headliner,

seats and all.

When we moved from Moses Lake to Ephrata, it took several loads over the course of several days. Every time we took off with a load Jake would stand by and watch. He could see that we were taking everything except him. Finally when we were hauling the last load, he couldn't take it any longer and decided he was going along so he climbed up on top of the load. We hadn't intended to haul him on the truck because the load was too high, but there was no way we could get him down. He didn't want to be left behind.

Like all Border Collies, he was so full of energy that he had to be on the go all the time. If he didn't have anything else to do he would chase birds, but he sure was not a bird dog. With the first crack of a gun during hunting season, Jake disappeared under the house, and didn't come out until all was quiet. But Jake was a lot of help around the cattle and he saved us a lot of time and steps in the corral and a lot wear and tear on the horses when we were up in the hills looking for cattle.

JAKE

He'd find the cows that hid their calves
Where cowboys couldn't ride,
He'd always flush those crafty cows
That tried their best to hide.

He'd catch a cow and bring her back
Even in headlong flight,
He could mother up a cow and calf
And he always paired 'em right.

Another thing about this dog
And I don't aim to lie,
He'd stand in the alley beside the gate
And sort cattle "in" or "by,"

He'd run up hills and get through brush
Where horses couldn't go,
He could cover an awful lot of ground
And was anything but slow.

89

If you have a friend who works that hard
You gotta treat him right,
So I let him ride behind my saddle
When we headed home at night.

On a gunny sack behind my kack
He'd scramble up and stay,
When we headed back to bunkhouse
At end of a long, hard day.

Black and white with a bushy tail,
We called that old dog Jake,
He worked so hard and did so much
We fed him eggs and steak.

He slept on the floor in the bunkhouse,
He was spoiled as could be,
We couldn't make him sleep outside
He was family, don't you see?

Sad to say, the time did come
When Jake just up and died.
He'd been a friend tried and true
And when he died we cried.

Just like "Old Shep," Jake has gone
Where all good doggies go.
Now he's in heaven herdin' cows
And havin' fun I know.

FORTY-DOLLAR DOG

I was in the feed store one day and there was a cute little Kelpy/Border Collie cross pup for sale for only $20. We were between dogs at that time and darned if he didn't somehow follow me home. That was the most stupid dog I've ever seen. He had a mind of his own. (If, in fact he had a mind at all.) He wouldn't come to me when I called him even if I was offering him something to eat. I could never teach him anything, no matter how I tried. He loved to chase cattle, but I could never call him back. No, he wasn't deaf, he just ignored me.

The next thing I knew he was chasing cars. I had to keep him tied up to keep him out of trouble. I was so mad at that pooch that one day when Melvin Simmons came by, I told him I would give $20 if he would take that stupid dog and shoot it. Melvin was the kind of guy who never had a dime to his name and $20 sounded like a real windfall to him. He agreed to my terms but he would have to come back later and get the dog.

A few days later he came back but said he would just take the dog home and keep it. I gave him the dog, a $20 bill, and a sack of dog food and my dog problems were solved.

TD

HIGH PRICED VETERINARIAN

Sam's sheep dog was looking poor. He really was quite sick
Sam took him to the vet who checked him out real quick.
The method that he used that day was quite unorthodox,
He put that little dog into a great big cardboard box.

He took him to the X-ray room and laid him on the table
To see if all his vital signs were erratic or were stable.
He reached up in the cupboard and took down a kitty-cat
When shown that sickly dog, the cat he hissed and spat.

He passed the cat above the dog and then to Sam he said,
"According to my diagnosis, I can tell your dog is dead."
"Well," said Sam, "I thought he was. But I didn't really know.
Tell me what I owe you doc, 'cause now I gotta go."

91

"Well," said doc, "I think three hundred would be fair."
When Sam heard the vet say that, his cursing filled the air.
"Dang it doc, don't you think three hundred's kinda steep?
I aint a wealthy vet you know. All I do is raise some sheep.

"Why do you have to charge so much?
Surely you must jest."
"Well," said doc, "fifty dollars for the office call,
The cat scan cost the rest."

CR

OOPS!

I bought a little bunch of steers at the auction yard one day and took them home and unloaded them in the corral but one got out into the pasture right away. Well, I figured I could just go out there on foot and run him back in. Surely it would be a cinch because all the rest of his peers were in the corral and he would be anxious to get back with them. He had evidently never seen a man on foot before and he really went haywire. He ran back toward the corral but instead of going through the gate, he tried to jump the fence. He almost cleared it but one front foot caught a wire as he went over and he landed on his head and broke his neck.

Another time I bought some steers and took them to the corral and branded them. When I turned them out into the pasture, unbeknownst to me one of them ran up into the crowding alley, tried to jump or climb over the alley fence. When he came back down, he hung himself up in the space between the squeeze chute and the alley fence and choked himself to death. I didn't find him until I went back to the corral next morning.

$\hat{C}$

HORSE ACQUISITIONS

When Lyn was just a little guy about five years old, he and I went over to Chuck McInroy's one day and saw a yearling paint colt in his pasture. Lyn thought that it was just the horse for him so we bought it for $35. When he got old enough to break, I started riding him. After I thought I had him pretty well broke, I was riding along one hot summer day about half asleep, when all of a sudden I found myself sitting on the ground with the dog licking my face. I guess Paint was about half asleep too, and when the dog came up behind him and startled him, he bucked and off I went. He ran home by himself and I had to walk. Another lesson learned: Be Alert! The world needs more lerts.

Paint wasn't really that great a horse but he was good with the kids so we kept him until we no longer needed a kids' horse.

I really got ripped off one time when I bought a horse for my oldest daughter, Wendy. We looked at a horse in Dryden and she liked the horse, so we decided to take it. The lady wouldn't take a check but said that if I would have the cash ready when she came next day, that she would deliver the horse to us. He was a young horse and was well broke and seemed to be sound. About a week later he went lame and we then

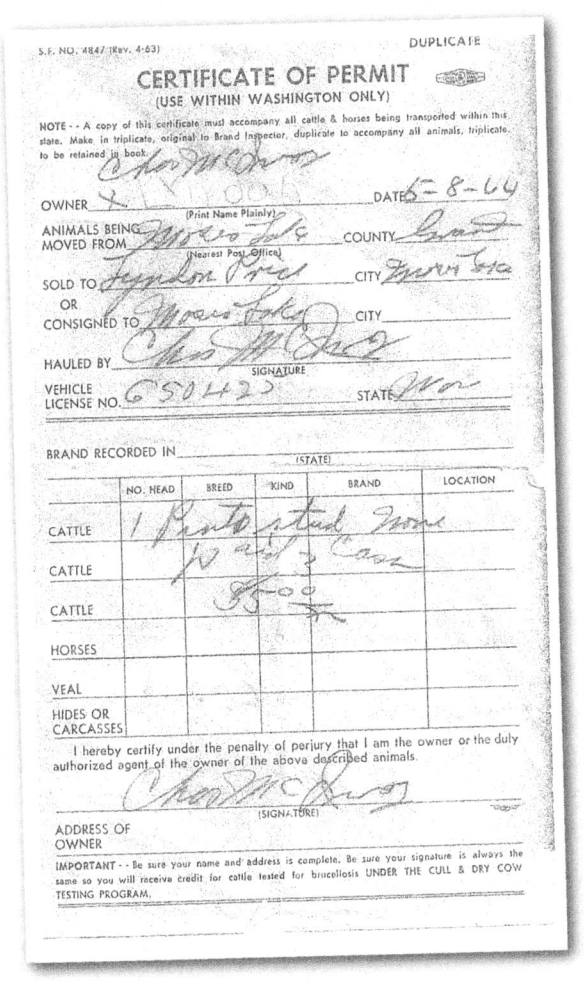

Bill of sale for Old Paint. The price was right, $35.

realized that she had him doped up so that his lameness wouldn't show. Then we figured out the real reason she didn't want a check. I couldn't stop payment on a cash sale.

In the early sixties, a high school girl from Moses Lake asked me to board two horses for her. One of them was a pretty good cow horse, the other may have been a good horse at one time but he was well past his prime. The younger horse, she called "Sinew." I don't remember the

name of the other one but Methuselah would have been an apt moniker. After dutifully paying the board bill for several months, she suddenly stopped coming out to ride or to pay the rent. One day she showed up and informed me that she was going to give me the horses. I told her that if she did, I would send Methuselah to the glue factory. She agreed that it would be alright but that she didn't have the stomach to do such a thing herself, because she had owned him since she was a little girl and that she was too attached to him to do it.

We kept Sinew for several years and put him to good use. He had a lot of "cow" and was a good rope horse. One day I was riding him on roundup when he suddenly stopped and turned to look at a thicket of trees over to our left about a hundred yards away. I nudged him on but he stopped and looked again after taking only four or five more steps. I said, "Horse, if there is something over there that interests you that much, let's go see what it is." When we approached to within a few yards, out jumped four or five big fat calves and three cows and headed down the mountain. If Sinew hadn't been any more alert than I was, we would have missed them.

Tim and Maxine with Paint

95

There was another time when he let me know that I wasn't living up to his expectations. Just by his body language, I could tell what he thought of me and my cowboy-ing abilities. I can't really explain his body language, but it was sufficient to let me know what he thought of me. In the spring when the cows are calving we always keep a close watch on them in case they need assistance. We also watch out for any calves which might get sick and need doctoring. As I was riding through the herd one morning, I spotted a calf that looked a little peaked. I shook out a loop and maneuvered around to the side where I could catch him.

About the time the horse figured out which calf we were after, the calf figured it out too and he started to run. He was no match for Sinew who had had a lot of experience catching calves. He soon had me in the perfect position to catch the calf so I threw the rope. He set up ready for the calf to hit the end of the rope. It didn't happen. I missed the calf and the rope fell on the ground. Sinew threw a look back over his shoulder that seemed to say, "Do you call yourself a cowboy?" Man, was I ever embarrassed!

I went to a farm auction sale in the spring of 1972 and bought a yearling colt for $50. He was out of an Arabian mare and a high powered Quarter horse stud. He'd been babied and was pretty badly spoiled but was real quiet and easy to catch. I broke him and he turned out to be a very good horse. We called him Peanuts.

We had him for more than 22 years. It wasn't all roses with him however. He put me in the hospital one time. Following is a poem which tells that story.

THE LUMP-JAWED CALF

Ross and I were down by the corral
And I didn't like what I saw.
One of the steers didn't look too good,
He had a swollen-up jaw.

Ross suggested we get him in
So we could give him a shot.
"His jaw don't look too good," he said,
"And I think he's got foot rot."

96

He turned him around and headed him back
But he ran past both of us.
I said, "Stop right there, I'll get my horse.
We'll catch that ornery cuss.

"I have a colt I'm starting to break
And he has a lot of 'cow'
I try to ride him most every day,
So I might as well use him now."

I cut that steer from the herd
And I headed him toward the gate.
That little horse knew just what to do,
He was really working great.

But the calf went by that open gate
Like he was shot from a gun.
Then my pony started to buck
'Cause he was having so much fun.

It caught me off guard, I dropped my reins,
I was in trouble then I knew.
I reached down then to gather the reins
Not knowing what else to do.

As I straightened up, he bucked again,
I landed astraddle the horn.
As I pushed back to regain my balance
I cursed the day he was born.

Before I got my balance back
I came down on that horn once more.
My pride was hurt, but not only that,
I sure was getting sore.

I says to myself, "I think I'll get off,
Though I'd much rather stay.
'Cause no matter what I do,
The horn gets right in my way."

But try as I might, I couldn't fall off,
I bounced on that horn again.
If ever I've been in such pain before
I'm sure I don't know when.

I finally fell off and hit the ground
And I just laid there in the dirt.
Then Ross came and checked on me
To see how bad I was hurt.

He picked me up, I stood on my feet
But I tell you it hurt like sin.
He said, "I think maybe your back is broke,"
So he laid me down again.

The ambulance came, took me to town,
I was laid up a week or two.
My back wasn't broke, but my pelvis was,
And my body was black and blue.

My family came to see me
In the hospital where I laid.
It was Tim's birthday
Amy brought a cake she had made.

I sure enjoyed that birthday party
'Til somebody told me a joke.
Cause when I laughed it really hurt
The side where my ribs was broke.

When the kids saw how it hurt my ribs,
They told me a joke again.
They sure were having a lot of fun
Seeing old dad in pain.

The more they joked, the more it hurt.
Though I tried real hard not to laugh.
Just my luck to end up hurt
When I was only trying to help a poor calf.

R\

WINTER PASTURE

It was early spring and the cornstalks were pretty well used up so it was time to take the cows home. We got an early start that day because we know how hard it is to move cows when they have baby calves. Some of the calves that day were as young as two or three days. It was nearly noon when we finally got them out the gate and started down the road. The calves were bawling and trying to find their mothers and the cows were bawling and trying to find their babies. We were not making a lot of progress, but we traveled the four miles by late afternoon.

We corralled the herd and soon most of the cows and calves were paired up and it began to quiet down. However two or three cows continued bawling until after dark so we know that we had inadvertently left their calves behind. We didn't want to let them go back to find their calves because we didn't want them on the roads after dark. But Lois went back to the pasture where the cows had been and rode around but couldn't find any calves, so we turned the cows loose next morning.

They high-tailed it back and found their babies right where they had left them. It wasn't hard moving them that day because there were only a few and they trailed easily.

TBO

ELECTRIC FENCES

In those Basin farmers' cornfields
Ringed by an electric fence,
Wintering a herd of hungry cows
Doesn't make a lot of sense.

It's a good thing all those cows
Are real thick skinned
'Cause the fences don't provide
Much protection from the wind.

Just what kind of nourishment
Is in that dry old feed?
It's not the kind of nutrients
That a pregnant cow would need.

So to supplement the fodder
And to satisfy the herd
You bought a lot of cotton cake
And a big debt was incurred

When a cow would have a calf
In the stubble and the snow
The day was always cold and
The wind was sure to blow.

So you rode out there amongst 'em
Every hour or maybe two,
If a cow was having trouble
There was work you had to do.

If the calf was freezing
You would call upon your spouse,
And you'd warm him in the bathtub
If she'd let you in the house.

Then you'd get the critter warm
And keep him 'til he's dry
You sure hoped the cow'd accept him
So the bugger wouldn't die.

And if you were successful
And you pulled the feller through

It was only the beginning
Of the work cut out for you.

'Cause there's a couple hundred more
And the calvin's just begun.
You'll play nursemaid night and day
Until calving season's done.

Then finally when it's over
And you think you can relax
And you've gone to your accountant
And you've paid your income tax,

Then it's time to do the branding
And to change bull calves to steers
Then you move them to the mountains
Just the way you've done for years.

Now that winter's work is over
And it's time for summer chores
It's a lot more gizzard pleasing
'Cause it's warmer out-of-doors.

So you spend your time a riding,
Scattering salt and moving cattle.
This is much more to your liking,
Spending time out in the saddle.

But too soon the summer's over
And it's roundup time once more,
So you go up to the mountains
To the job you can't ignore.

Then you gather all the cattle
And you wean and sell the steers,
Then you take the money to the bank
To pay your financiers.

Then you cull out all the old cows
And you preg test all the rest
Then you take a tally of your herd
Just to see if you've progressed.

Then around about the corn fields
You will build more hot wire fences
If you prefer this to the mountain scene,
Then you must have lost your senses.

CHECKING THE COWS

One day while riding and checking on cattle I came upon a cow that was lying in a slight depression of the ground with her feet higher than her body and by the looks of the ground around her, I could tell that she had been threshing around for a long time trying to get up. I got off my horse and put my shoulder to hers and pushed as hard as I could but even with my assistance she was unable to get onto her brisket and get her feet under her and get up. By this time she was too weak to help herself very much so I just grabbed her by the feet and rolled her over onto her back and then to her other side so that her feet were now lower than her body. I figured she would be able to get up then but she just laid her head back to the ground, shuddered and gasped for breath and died right there on the spot.

¬∏

It was early spring and as I sat on my horse surveying the landscape, checking on the cows, I turned my attention back to a couple cows that I had noticed earlier. They were both in labor so I just sat and watched them in case they might need some help. After about a half hour, one of them finally had her calf, but before she could get up and start cleaning it up, the other cow was attracted by the struggling calf, so she came over and claimed it for her own. She was very bossy and wouldn't let the real (very frustrated) mother come close. About the time she got it cleaned up and on its feet, she laid down and gave birth to her own calf, got right up and went back to the original baby. Meanwhile the cow which had calved first was frantically trying to find her baby. When she noticed the new one lying there by itself, she glommed on to it, licked it clean and everyone was happy, including me.

GRAZING ASSOCIATION

In 1968 several other fellows and I put together a cattle ranch which we dubbed Valley Grazing Association. With the help of FHA we purchased 5,200 acres of grazing and timber land near Republic in Ferry County, Washington. Along with our purchase we acquired about 10,000 more acres of grazing on BLM, DNR, National Forest and private land where we ran about 1,400 head of cow calf pairs. Seventeen years later we received an offer that we "couldn't refuse" and sold it for enough that we each came out with more than $100,000 profit to show for our investment.

We really thought we'd "cut a fat hog," but now we have neither the ranch nor the money. But those years of having that ranch and all the experiences it afforded could fill a book.

(11)

THE STUMP

My kids and I were out one day
Just riding here and there,
When on the hill ahead of us
I thought I saw a bear.

"No," I thinks, "It's not a bear,
It's a snag of a dead old tree,
But I can fool these kids of mine
And have some fun, by gee."

And so I said "Just look right there,
A bear is on that hill.
He's standing there eyeing us
And standing very still."

I knew that it was not a bear
But thought I'd have some fun
I told the kids that it's too bad
We didn't bring a gun.

"Oh dad," they said, "you can't fool us.
That's not a bear at all.
The bears are all asleep in caves
To hibernate this fall."

"Don't kid yourselves," I said,
"It's nice and warm today
All the bears wake at times
And they come out and play."

So the banter went that day
As we kept that stump in sight.
When suddenly I realized
After all that I was right.

The kids and I, we sat and watched
And got a real thrill.
That stump jumped up ahead of us
And scampered up the hill.

CAMOUFLAGED

There was a time when out riding by myself that I wished I'd had a movie camera. I stopped to give my horse a breather. And after sitting still for several minutes, something caught my eye. I sat and watched, as a deer which had been lying in the shade slowly got up and carefully slipped away hoping that he had not been seen. I marveled that I had not noticed him before even though he had been close and I had scanned the area where he lay in hiding.

As I sat there, wondering how he had escaped my vision, another deer rose up from the same patch of shade and also slowly slunk away. Now I was really amazed. How could I have missed this one when I now knew that the patch of shade was a deer hiding place? As I sat there berating myself for my lack of acuity, a third deer arose and sneaked off.

Now I was truly amazed, so I then looked intently at the shady area from where the deer had emerged and watched as four more deer slowly stood up one by one and sneaked away.

In 1969, when we first started our grazing association, traffic was light in northern Ferry County and we often drove cattle down the road when we moved them from pasture to corrals or vice versa. One evening after riding all day, we decided it was too dark to drive them down the road, so

we loaded several head into a truck and hauled them to the corral.

It took several loads to get them all moved and because it was nearly dark, Gene, who was driving the truck, was hurrying too much and rolled the truck and spilled cows all over the road. Most of them weren't hurt and they ran off in to the woods. A couple were badly hurt with broken legs and other injuries so we had to butcher them right there on the spot.

By the time we got them killed and bled and had gone after butcher knives, it was getting pretty late and pretty dark. We built a big bonfire for light and butchered cows until far into the night

A LOOK BACK AT VGA

Remember the day Gene was hauling cows
And he tipped over the cattle truck?
He got a little careless, he was driving too fast.
You could say he was pushin' his luck.

He didn't get hurt when the truck went over
But the cows sure did get scattered
All over the road where he had that wreck
Their blood and guts were splattered

We had gathered the cows and penned them up
In a little old pole corral.
We'd gathered quite a bunch, it was almost dark,
We thought we'd done real well.

We knew it was safer to truck them
Than to drive down them down the road
It worked real well, we were almost done,
He was hauling his very last load.

But as it turned out we weren't done yet,
Much work still had to be done.
Doug reached in the back of the pickup
And pulled out his trusty old gun.

We finally got those cows all butchered,
We finished in the middle of the night.
It sure is hard to butcher cows
When you have only a campfire for light.

106

Our range was spread out over several miles of mountainous terrain so we quite often hauled our horses out in the morning when gathering cattle in the fall. One day Don Liggett, Gene Robbins and I loaded our horses into my one-ton and drove up several miles north, unloaded and rode up in the hills from there. Shortly after starting out, Don was stung by a bee. He told me that he was allergic to bee stings and that he often swelled up. I suggested that we go to town and get him a shot of Epinephrine. He didn't want to do that. After all, we had already driven ten miles or so. He went his way and I went mine looking for cattle.

About an hour later, while driving some cows ahead of me, I came upon him with a few head that he had found. I took one look at him and realized that I needed to get him to a doctor Pronto! We abandoned the cattle that we had found and ran the horses as fast as was safe, tied them to trees, jumped in the truck and headed for the hospital. By the time we got there, he was in bad enough shape that the nurse hustled him in and gave him a shot. They kept him in the hospital overnight.

Remember the day we were riding up north
When Don Liggett was stung by a bee?
His eyes swelled up nearly all the way shut,
He could hardly even see.

We got off the mountain and jumped in the truck.
I drove as fast as it'd go.
But even at that it seemed to me
We were going much too slow.

Don said, "Slow this thing down.
What are you doing, trying to have a wreck?
I'd just as soon die of a poison bee sting
As to die of a broken neck."

$$\overline{CC}$$

It usually took us about a month to round up all the cattle. We rejuvenated an old log house and used it as a bunkhouse. Nobody had yet heard of insulation when that house was built, and it had cracks between the logs so it was a pretty cold place to live in the late fall. We put a corrugated steel roof on it and found an old pot-bellied stove and a wood

burning kitchen stove. When we came in at night, we'd build a fire in both stoves and hang up our wet clothes, cook some supper and feed the fires all night to stay warm.

Remember those nights when it got so cold
During roundup late in the fall?
The wind and cold came in through the cracks
That were there in that drafty wall

Of that big log house that stood up there
In the pasture that we called the "Hill"
It was colder inside than out
Because outside there was no wind chill.

We built a fire in that pot-bellied stove
That stood in the middle of the floor,
And I don't know for sure, but I think it was warmer
When we opened up the front door.

One day after gathering cattle on the Baker range and getting them all settled for the night in the corral, Ron Tebow said he knew a shortcut to get back to where we had left the trucks. We headed south up a long hill, to the corner of the fence and went through a gate. He rode between and around several big trees and headed back north again on the other side of the fence.

I told him that he was going the wrong way but he insisted that he was right so the rest of us decided to go along with him and see how long it took him to realize he was wrong. It wasn't until Baker's house came in to view that he admitted he was lost.

Remember when Ron Tebow knew a shortcut
He said he'd show us the way
To get off of the mountain and back to the meadow
Real quick at the end of the day?

We knew right away where he'd made his mistake
And now he was on the wrong trail
But he was so confident, we gave him his head
And we stayed right there on his tail.

We kept on going 'til late in the day
When the shadows began to grow long,
We came to the fire where we'd eaten lunch
Then he had to admit he was wrong.

/ƨ/

Bulls are sometimes hard to find when they are in such a mountainous range as we had in Ferry County. After breeding season, they will often times go off by themselves and hole up in the trees or brush. After the main roundup, most of the grazing association members needed to get back to their farms in the Columbia Basin to care for their cattle. Doug and Lucy Pearce, our hired help, were then left to ride daily until they found the few cattle which we had missed during the main roundup. It was usually late in the fall when all were finally found. One year, it wasn't until late December that they came up with all the missing bulls. Gene Robbins and I went to Republic on December 30th, stayed overnight in the bunkhouse and got an early start the next morning.

The first problem we had was the diesel jelling up in the tanks which prevented the trucks from starting. We built a fire under the tanks and in a couple hours we had them running. Gene loaded his truck first and when he pulled away from the loading chute, the truck slid sideways and got stuck in the snow. After some shoveling and installing the chains, he got away. We put chains on my truck, loaded it and took off for home.

It was well past noon by this time. The road over Cache Creek Pass was covered with packed snow. The front compartment of Gene's trailer was empty, which meant there wasn't enough weight over his drive axel. We figured if he kept his momentum and didn't miss any gears when shifting, he could make over the top. We chained up again and he took off. I gave him about five minutes head start and I headed up the mountain. As I rounded a corner about halfway up I saw him spun out and sort of crossways in the road. I squeezed by on the left side of the road hoping there was no one coming from the other way. I knew if I stopped, we'd both be stuck.

I got to the top of the hill after passing a car which was also stuck. As I waited at the top, along came a wrecker to rescue the car that I had seen. I told the driver about Gene's truck and rode back down with

him to try to help even though I knew there was nothing I could do. His wrecker was much too small to do Gene any good. I rode back up with him and drove on in to Nespelum and sent a big wrecker after Gene. That night about midnight as we were celebrating New Year's Eve, Gene came barreling by my house and gave me a blast on his air horn as he sailed by.

What a day!

Remember Gene on Cache Creek Pass
With his truck crossways in the road?
We called a wrecker to come up from Nespelum
So that he could get it towed.

He and I were hauling cows
And it was late on New Year's Eve.
The troubles we had all day that day
Are downright hard to believe.

The cold weather caused the diesel to jell
And our trucks did not want to run.
We slid in the ditch and we got stuck in the snow
It sure as heck was no fun.

Remember the time that airplane flew over
With a supersonic force?
The horses jumped, out of fear I guess,
And little Timmy fell off his horse.

We all got down to see if he was hurt
But he was hardly hurt at all.
He'd fallen on a great big rock and he said,
"I'm lucky. That rock musta broken my fall."

Remember how Morrie used to get sleepy
On those sunny warm fall days?
He'd ride off by himself and hobble his horse
And then he'd just let it graze

Then he'd find a soft spot and lie right down
In the shade of one of the trees,

And while the rest of us worked rounding up cows
He'd catch himself a few z-z-z-z's

Remember how Carl, when he was riding drag,
Would crack his big long whip?
It would make those calves that were lagging behind
Move along at a pretty fast clip.

Remember those hippies back in the seventies
Who lived up there in the hills?
We'd chase a few cows right through their camp
And we did it just for the thrills.

Doug on his horse rode right through their garden
He really tore up their yard.
He sure made them mad, which of course was his plan,
And you know it wasn't very hard.

Remember the time when we had our cows pregged
It was done by a young lady vet?
We slipped in a steer, she declared him "open,"
I'll bet she's mad at us yet.

G

Remember how Chet would go out and wrangle
And bring in the whole darn cavvy?
Now that was a job that Chet liked to do
And it was something he sure did savvy.

Then we'd each catch a horse, saddle up and ride out
To see what we could find.
We could ride all day and come up empty,
It sure does boggle the mind.

In the springtime, before the sun brought the grass
Up on the hillsides awake
We'd start the cows out on the meadow,
Down south of curlew lake.

Then as the hills came alive with the grass
That grew in abundance there,
We moved the cattle up to the mountains
To graze with the deer and the bear.

Later, we kept them out of the meadow,
Gave the grass a chance to grow tall.
Then we'd use it when we brought the cows down
From up in the hills in the fall.

Then we'd haul them all home and sell the calves
And hope that they'd made a good gain.
Next year we'd come back with the cows and new calves
And we'd do it all over again.

And just like Doug was heard to say
 One day while talking to Morrie,
"We don't do this for the money we make,
We just do it all for the glory."

Remember back in about '77
When brucellosis was the current crisis
But the only cattle that caught that bug
Were the ones that belonged to the Prices?

We tested the cows most every month,
Doctor Horseman drew the blood.
We tested them in the dust and the heat,
We tested in the mud.

We tested in the dead of winter
When the snow was on the ground,
But brucellosis in the Price herd
Was the only thing we found.

So everyone except the Prices
Drew a sigh of great relief,
But to Larry and his family
It was a time of stress and grief.

DP

112

Remember the time we canned our help
And moved the herd on our own?
We started them up toward Copper Butte
But they turned and headed back home,

So we had to regroup, it was late in the day,
We camped out in the woods that night.
We woke up early and started moving cows
Next morning before it got light.

It was getting late in the day
When we arrived at our destination.
A real hot day when we made the summit
All covered with perspiration.

The horses were dry and the riders were too,
So we headed for the water tank.
We all were so thirsty we just didn't care,
Right along with the horses we drank.

One hot summer day Gene and his brother, Mitt and some others who
I don't remember, were riding up on Copper Butte. Gene got separated
from the others and was lost. He evidently rode around for a while until
he found his bearings but by then his horse was so exhausted that when
Gene came to a stream and let him drink, he stumbled and fell in the
water. Gene did all he could to get the horse back on his feet but finally
gave up, took off the saddle and walked all the way back down to the
trailhead, a distance of about seven miles, dutifully closing all the gates
he went through on his way.

Meanwhile Mitt and the others after searching for hours to find Gene,
finally rode back down the mountain and were contemplating their next
move. When they rode up, there was Gene sitting on the tailgate waiting
for them. Mitt told him that if he hadn't closed the gates, they would
have known he had gone through them and they wouldn't have searched
for him as long as they did. Mitt told him, "If I weren't so glad to see
you, I'd give you a whipping for scaring us like that."

Gene's horse showed up at the ranch house the next day. We still don't
know how he got through those closed gates.

Remember the time Gene was riding Copper
When he lost his horse in the creek?
That was the most excitement we'd had
Around here in many and many a week.

He unsaddled his horse but couldn't get him up
So he left him there for dead.
He was all by himself with no horse to ride
So he had to walk instead.

Seven long miles back to the trailhead,
Though it's downhill most all of the way,
But the best part of this story is
The horse came back next day.

Remember that fireplace in the Niedefer house?
We'd build a big fire in a storm.
Then we'd all crowd around that fireplace
And try our best to keep warm.

Remember one day up on the Niedefer
We found an old cow on the fight?
She had a wire wrapped around her foot.
It had cut off the blood 'cause it was tight.

We had a lot of trouble helping her out
Because of her bad attitude,
We removed the wire and turned her loose
But she didn't show a lot of gratitude.

ⵀ

Most of us flatlanders were pretty impressed with all the deer that
were on the ranch and could hardly wait until hunting season. I think
we each got a deer that first year but after that we were always so busy
rounding up cattle during hunting season that we had little chance to
hunt. After soft hearted Morrie Wilson shot his deer, he got to thinking
about it and he felt so bad for killing it that he said he couldn't feel any
worse if he'd shot his horse.

114

·3·

Remember when we remodeled the house
And fixed it for Lucy and Doug?
Then we appointed a committee to decorate,
Remodel and pick out a new rug.

The committee worked on that for many a day
But never got it done
We found out then that the best committee
Is a committee of only just one.

TRUCKING CATTLE

In the early seventies I decided it was too expensive to hire someone
to haul my cattle up to the ranch and back every year, so the only "smart"
thing to do was to buy a tractor-trailer of my own and haul them myself.
Yea right! I found a 1963 KW cab-over with a 318 Detroit engine and a
forty foot steel cattle trailer that weighed more than I like to admit and
I was in the cattle hauling business. I could haul 30 pairs and one bull.
Was I ever loaded! Or maybe I should say overloaded. With that little
318 engine it was more than a five-hour trip from Ephrata to Republic, a
distance of about 150 miles.

I left home one morning at 4 a.m. to haul home my first load. About
thirty miles from home it started snowing hard and I considered turning
around but I sure didn't want anyone calling me a quitter, so I gritted
my teeth and forged ahead. By the time I got to Cash Creek Pass it was
snowing so hard I could barely see the road. The road down the other
side was compact snow and ice with a tree in the road at the bottom of
the hill. If you don't stop for the stop sign you go over the bank, so I
decided I should stop now and chain up. That was the hard part but after
several tries and finding a relatively level spot I finally brought the truck
to a sliding stop and got out.

As I was getting the chains out of the storage compartment, the truck
started sliding down the hill with nobody in it. I made a run for it and
grabbed the door handle, twisted it open and climbed aboard. Before I

finally got it stopped and installed the chains I was wishing I had just stood back and let it go.

After all this, I still had to go another forty or fifty miles, load up a load of cattle and then drive all the way back. The trip home with a load was even more stressful. Driving all day with chains on the truck and going as slow as five miles per hour down some of the long hills was more than stressful. All the way back I was trying to figure out where I could find a sucker stupid enough to buy my cattle truck from me.

When I finally got home I heard the news and found that there were lots of wrecks and many trucks and cars all over this part of the state that didn't make it home that night because of the slippery roads, so I felt pretty lucky for a rookie.

That was the beginning of a trucking adventure which lasted about three years. That was an adventure that I could have done without. Joe Kelsey came by one day with an offer to buy the trailer to haul his rodeo stock. I sold it to him before he could change his mind. Bud King heard that I had sold the trailer, and he offered to sell me his trailer to replace it,

but about that time Alan Chlarson decided he needed another tractor so I made him a deal he couldn't refuse and I was out of the cattle hauling business. I don't know if Bud is still hauling cattle or not, but Chlarson has many trucks and is in it in a big way. Lyndon drove for him for a few years.

THE HONEYMOONERS

Sam and Sue got married
In that big white church in town.
It was a warm spring day in June
When he changed her name to Brown.

When the ceremony was over
And everyone had kissed the bride,
They headed for home in the buggy
Seated side by side.

Now the buggy horse was old
She didn't see too well,
She tripped upon a big ole rock
And right there down she fell.

Sam got down from where he sat,
Up on the buggy seat,
He unharnessed that poor old mare
And he helped her to her feet.

He put the harness back
They soon were on their way.
As he climbed back in the buggy,
"That's once," was all he had to say.

They continued on their journey.
They were so much in love
They didn't see the storm clouds
As they gathered up above.

The thunder crashed! The mare got scared
And she fell again, right there,
Once again Sam got down
And helped that old gray mare.

The shower passed, the sun came out
The flowers smelled so nice,
As Sam gathered the lines in his hands
He muttered, "Well, that's twice."

They drove along for quite a spell,
Just holding hands and such,
They both were kinda quiet kids
And they didn't talk too much.

As they topped the ridge above the river
There sprang up quite a breeze,
The old mare shied at a tumble weed
And fell down to her knees.

Sam sprang from the buggy in a single bound,
He was agile for his size.
"That's three," he said kinda quiet like
And put a bullet between her eyes.

Now Sue had been pretty quiet
Up until this point
But when she saw what Sam had done
She came plumb out of joint.

"How could you do a thing like that?"
She screamed as her face turned red,
They were having their first big fight
Right after they were wed.

She really read him the riot act
As he stood there like a dunce,
When she finished her big long mad tirade,
Sam simply said, "THAT'S ONCE!"

"C" SECTION

I had a young Angus X Simmental cow coming with her second calf. By the looks of her, she was several days overdue. She had made a big bag and one day I noticed she was switching her tail and acted real uncomfortable, so I put her in the corral where I could keep an eye on her and give any assistance she might need. I watched her pretty closely and she never did really go into labor but just stood around for a couple more days and then stopped eating. I called the vet out and he looked her over and concluded that she had a big calf in her but that it was dead and had probably ruptured the uterus and was lying in the peritoneal cavity.

He said he could do a cesarean operation but that she would probably die anyway. I didn't see any reason to spend my good hard-earned money on an operation that would kill a perfectly good cow so I told him to nevermind. He said, "I'd like to do it anyway and just make sure my diagnosis is right. I won't charge you for the operation."

I told him to be my guest, so we put her in the barn where we had some light and captured her in a stanchion that we used for the milk cow. He gave her a spinal, clipped the hair off her right side, washed her off with a germicide solution and started to work with his scalpel.

As soon as he cut though the hide, the calf was right there. There was no need to go into the uterus because it was ruptured just as he thought it would be. He got the huge calf out, pumped in a lot of penicillin and sewed her up. Next morning, just as he had predicted, she was dead.

COWS GET ARTHRITIS TOO

One fall when we hauled the cattle down from the ranch, one old
Angus cow was so skinny and arthritic that I felt sorry for her. I don't
know for sure why I kept her but I did. I threw up a special small pen just
for her and fed her by herself and gave her the best of feed but she didn't
gain a pound all winter. I guess she probably didn't have any teeth left.
She was so gaunt that it didn't look like she had enough capacity in her
gut to hold more than two or three pounds of hay at a time. I would have
taken her to the sale and got rid of her but it seemed like I was too busy
to take the time to do it.

One morning when I went out to feed, there she was nursing a great
big bull calf. I was dumfounded. How could a cow like that ever have
had that big a calf in her? I could have sworn that she wasn't even
pregnant.

THREE HOURS WASTED

It took more than a month in the fall to round up the cattle on the
Valley Grazing Association. We fenced off a separate pasture for each
owner and we made it a practice to sort the cattle by owner each time we
brought a bunch down from the hills. We had saved grass on the meadow
for this purpose, but these individual pastures didn't have enough feed
to hold cattle for very long. Therefore whenever there was a load of any
one owner's cattle, they were trucked home to that owner's farm in the
Columbia Basin. If a particular unit didn't include a part of the creek or
lake, we used a pump with a gasoline engine to pump water from the
creek to a tank in the pasture.

The pasture which was designated for Dave Adam's cattle was too far
from the creek to pump the water. Because of the fact that it was on low
ground, we decided we could dig a hole which we hoped would fill with
water seeping in from the nearby lake sufficient to satisfy the need. We
built a fence to keep the cattle from falling in the hole and pumped water
from it to a tank.

This arrangement worked well until we let the water get low in the

tank and the cows started crowding the fence. We arrived at the scene one morning to find Dave's biggest cow in the hole. It was late in the fall and she was wet and cold. Dave had some huge Simmental cows and this one was the biggest one he had. She weighed all of eighteen hundred pounds and a saddle horse on the business end of a rope couldn't begin to budge her out of that hole.

We tried a four wheel drive pickup all to no avail. We borrowed a loader tractor and drove it up to the fence which scared the cow sufficiently that she scrambled and clawed and dug her way out by herself.

ROLLING ROCK

In the days of Little Beaver and of Pocahontas too
A hunter was judged by the meat he brought back for the stew
An Indian hunter was judged by the trophy he brought back,
So he always hunted for a monstrous head or an even bigger rack.

To win the love of a sweet young maid, he'd go into the woods
If his aim was straight and true, he'd come back in with the goods
So if he bagged a Grizzly or a buck with a great big rack
He was considered worthy when he dragged that big one back.

Now Chief Cochise had a daughter with beauty beyond compare
A young and shapely maiden with long and silky hair.
He announced a hunting contest, the prize his daughter so fair
A brave, in order to win her, would kill a deer, a moose or a bear.

The brave with the greatest trophy when the hunt was done
Would win another trophy. "Little Flower" was the one.
The hunter who was to win her would risk his limb and life,
The reward in the end was worth it, a beautiful, loving wife.

Many hunters set out that day, each with great ambition.
To win the woman of their dreams was their collective mission.
The hunt had lasted into week four
When "Rain In The Face" returned with a boar.

"Sly Fox" came back a couple days later,
He had a trophy he considered much greater.

Then "Two Feathers" came back and later "Running Bear"
Then "Spotted Owl and "Crazy Wolf" and also "Wild Hare."
Now "Rolling Rock" was last of all. He hasn't come back yet.
The whole darned tribe has looked for him 'til they are in a sweat.

Two hundred years have since gone past,
And still they hunt for hope does last.
In the hearts of his tribesmen, his memory lives on,
They just can't believe that he really is gone.

So they've enlisted the help of everyone in the land
To return their hero to their dwindling band.
They've posted big signs for all to see,
To be a big help for you and for me.

So as you drive out in the West today,
Or even if you choose to walk
You'll see this sign by the side of the road:
"WATCH FOR ROLLING ROCK"

CALVING

During calving season I made it a practice to check the cows every two hours around the clock so that I'd know if they needed assistance. After four or five years of that I realized I was wasting time and losing sleep all for nothing. There were a few times, however, when it paid off. One night on my midnight rounds, I discovered a cow that had just calved and was prolapsed. It was about zero degrees Fahrenheit that night and she hadn't cleaned her calf so I took it to the house, woke Lois to help and we went out to repair the prolapse.

As anyone who has ever tried to shove a prolapsed uterus back into a cow knows, it is a very tough job. She was lying down of course, so I got down on the ground, braced my feet against a frozen cow pie and pushed. I don't know what the cow had her feet braced against, but she pushed back harder than I was pushing. The more I pushed, the more she pushed. I finally won the battle, poured her full of warm water and went in and got the calf on its feet, fed it some colostrum milk and went back to bed.

I didn't have to get up and check the cows at 2 a.m. because we were still up working on the cow until then. At 4 a.m. when I checked again

122

the darned old heifer was prolapsed again so it was the same battle all over. When I got it back next time I sewed her up. Then she tore out the stitches and the job had to be done again. By the third time she had stopped laboring so it finally held together.

What a night! That experience inspired this next poem. I embellished it a little near the end to make a more interesting poem out of it.

CALVING PROBLEMS

I rode out one night on my midnight rounds
In the middle of calving time.
Calving came round in January,
When sleeping's most sublime.

The wind was blowing, it was ten below
And the ground was covered with snow.
I spied this cow that just had calved
But was prolapsed, don't you know?

She hadn't got up to clean up her calf
So I guessed it was up to me.
I had to get that cow on her feet
There was no one else I could see.

It was too cold to wait for the vet to come out
It had to be done right now,
So I woke up my wife, she stumbled awake
And we headed back out to that cow.

I pushed and pushed, and she pushed back,
Truly a Herculean feat.
I finally got that tough job done
And got her back on her feet

I poured hot water down inside
It accomplished a double objective,
It held the uterus down in its place
And warmed up that heifer's perspective.

Two hours of hard work, but don't you know,
It was all pretty much in vain,

For when I checked her next time round
She was prolapsed once again.

Again I tackled that distasteful job
With the help of my devoted spouse,
We got her all done and sewed her up
And headed back to the house.

I looked for that cow when I made my rounds
Next morning at half past six.
She was lying there by the water trough
And her prolapse I still had to fix.

Again I called my lovely bride to
Come and give a hand.
Three times that night she's willing to help,
My but ain't love grand?

Now the third time's the charm or so they say,
But this ought to make you all grin.
That cow wasn't really prolapsed at all.
If I'd left her alone, she'd have had twins.

DEAD CALVES

The winters in our part of the state are usually not all that severe so we calved early in order to have most of the cows bred back before we took them to the ranch in mid May. By doing it this way, we could be assured that they would be bred to our own bulls. Consequently, calving season started about the last of January. Sometimes the weather was bad enough that we regretted starting so early.

One winter, when the cows started calving, we had about four or five inches of snow and the weather was warm enough that it was very wet and slushy. Calves born under conditions like that have three strikes against them for they can melt down into the slush and soon die of hypothermia. Even if they survive the first few days, they often get the scours which can run through the whole herd in a short time. I spent a lot of time that winter doctoring calves but before the winter was over, there was a pile of dead calves to be disposed of.

124

What do you do with a cow that has no calf? Well, you go to a local dairy and try to buy a Holstein calf to graft on her. Sometimes you can make it work and sometimes you can't. Holstein calves look rather out of place in a herd of beef cattle, but you can't afford to keep a cow for a year without raising a calf so it's either that or send her to slaughter.

Anyone who has ever had a cow lose its calf and tried to graft on another calf knows how hard it is to get a cow to take another cow's baby. I've tried everything from rubbing the new calf with afterbirth from the original calf, to skinning the dead calf and tying the skin on the new calf, to a dog in the pen, tranquilizers, hobbles, squeeze chute and even a club. Every rancher I know has his favorite method which he swears will work. And they all do (once or twice). But none were foolproof.

Here's one that is foolproof: take a cup of maple syrup, molasses, or honey, cut it fifty-fifty with water and spray it on the calf and watch that old cow lick it off. By the time she finishes licking off the sweet stuff and gets down to licking the calf, she has accepted the calf. Guaranteed to work without fail (once or twice).

That's not my baby!

·R

In the days when my parents were growing up, a lot of kids had to stay home and help with the farm work. Consequently they didn't spend a lot of time in school. Some kids quit school when they became big enough to work full time and because they had spent such a little time in school while they were younger they may not have attained a very high grade before they had to end their education. This poem tells about the end of my dad's education.

THE SCHOOL MA'ARM

He was just a country boy
And always behind in school.
Mostly, he worked at home on the ranch,
In his day that was the rule.

After roundup in the fall
He'd start to school late,
In the Spring he'd have to quit again
Ahead of calving date.

With this kind of schedule
He was always in a bind
And every year he'd fall
A little farther behind.

With calvin' and brandin' in the spring
And roundup every fall
And fixin' fence and makin' hay
Didn't leave much time at all.

But he went to school as much
As time from work allowed.
He learned to cipher and to read,
His parents were so proud!

He knew most all he had to know
When he finished up grade six.
He was just as smart as any
Of those other country hicks.

The reason why he quit school
Wasn't 'cause he knew it all.
He had another reason why
He stayed away that fall.

He'd learned love his sixth grade teacher,
She was a lovely lass.
But he couldn't marry someone
Who had him so outclassed.

Besides, there was too much difference
In their ages, don't you see?
Why, she was all of eighteen years.
BUT HE WAS TWENTY THREE!!!

After my dad quit school, he went to work on a ranch in Wyoming. The following poem tells the story of a kid who came to work on the ranch where he worked.

THE SNIPE HUNT

A city boy born and bred
But it was time to leave the nest,
He grew strong and tough on the city streets
But always dreamed of the West.

He longed to be where there's lots of room
Out in the open spaces.
Reared in the east, but rarin' for the west.
It was time for trading places.

He hopped a freight to get out of town,
He carried his clothes in a poke.
He hoped he could find a job real soon,
'Cause of course the poor kid was broke.

Well he ended up at the Rocking "A" ranch
He didn't even own a saddle,
But that didn't really matter to him
'Cause he had another battle.

For the boys who worked at the Rocking "A"
Were an ornery bunch of blokes,
Whenever the boss hired a new hand
They'd pester him with practical jokes

So when he hired this greenhorn kid
Who was a city boy to boot
They figured they'd take him on a big snipe hunt.
Now that would be a hoot!

They explained to him the habits of snipes,
Their way of flocking together
And the way they'd run to an open sack,
Especially in cold weather.

They always run and hunt for cover
Whenever they're spooked at night
And hide in a cave or a gunny sack
To get plumb out of sight.

They rode way out in the hills that night
With their sacks to catch the game,
They tied their horses to some trees out there
To fool this dude was their aim.

They got off their horses and walked awhile
'Til they came to a little hill,
They told him to hold his "snipe sack" there,
He'd have to be quiet and still.

They said they'd go and round up the snipes,
He should stay and hold the sack.
When he caught the snipes they'd bring the horses
And they would come right back.

Now this here kid's from the city,
We know that this is true,
But he had a good idea
What these jokers were going to do.

So he went along with their little game.
He'd have some fun of his own.
He watched as they walked away in the dark
And left him there alone.

When they were gone he took right off
As fast as he could run,
He beat them back to the horses.
That sly little son-of-a-gun.

He took the horses and headed home
As fast as he could go,
He left them afoot ten miles from home
And it was starting to snow.

When the crew couldn't find their horses
They knew that they'd been had
They came limping back next morning
Tired, sore footed, and mad.

They'd been beat at their own game
They felt kinda sheepish and small,
But they had to admire that city dude.
Now he's one of their gang afterall.

A few years later, my dad bought a team of horses.

IDENTICAL TWINS

The team of two looked so alike
He couldn't tell them apart.
The name of one, I think was Ben,
The other one was Bart.

In order to tell just which was which
He cut off the tail of Ben,
But the identity crisis struck once more
When the tail grew out again.

He tried and tried to figure out exactly what to do
To find some kind of easy way to tell just who was who.
He looked for differences in the color of their eyes
Or which one's ears were longer.

Which walked faster or which pulled harder
To know which one was stronger.
Maybe one was harder to catch
Or ornerier, or maybe just plain lazy.

He fretted about how to tell them apart
'Til it nearly drove him crazy.
But he couldn't believe he'd been so blind
The answer came out of the blue one day.

So he measured them up and to his surprise —
The black was three inches taller than the gray.

HEART ATTACK

Cows out of feed, gotta get them some hay
Grandson Cody came and helped me that day.
We jump in the truck and head for the scales
Then back to the stack, load up a few bales.

As we go down the road, I feel a pain in my chest
When we get to the scalehouse, I'll take a short rest.
Now the pain's getting worse, that is for certain,
Won't let Cody know how badly I'm hurtin'.

"Cody, you weigh the truck I think I'll sit down
We'll get back to the haystack, Lyn can take me to town."
Cody could drive me but he's only a lad
Fourteen years old, I'll leave it to his dad.

In that slow gutless truck we go back to the stack
Then it's back to the house and get the Cadillac,
For a fast trip to town to the emergency room
Where the doctor will fix me and I'll feel better soon.

I get out of the truck, tell Lyn of my pain,
Then back in the truck and on the road once again.
Not to the house for the car I'd hoped for
But still in the truck with his foot to the floor.

To make a story short, before we got there
The pain was more than I thought I could bear.
The folks at the hospital poked holes in my skin,
They needed a place to put the medicine in.

Before they got through I looked like a sieve,
About an hour later they assured me I'd live.
"Well, said the doctor, "I've done all I can.
Now it's a helicopter ride to Spokane

"Where they'll do an operation in a couple of days
And preach you a sermon about changing your ways
No more steaks and gravy and greasy french fries
No sweet rich desserts and apple pies."

After an angioplasty and a stent or two
They'd done all the damage that they could do,
So they sent me home to a new lifestyle,
Every day I'd have to walk at least a mile

And eat the kind of feed my cows like so well
Like grains and roughage and chlorophyll.
They say this diet will make my heart grow strong
I won't live any longer but it sure will seem long.

25¢

OH! OH!

I've been in the hospital for a couple of days,
It's not a place where I'd want to stay.
I'm ready for discharge, but what do you s'pose?
They've taken my shoes, confiscated my clothes.

When I boarded the 'copter I was halfway undressed,
At Sacred Heart Hospital they took off the rest.
I needed moral support and a ride back home,
I was in strange surroundings and all alone.

My wife came later with some very good news,
She'd brought me clean clothes and also some shoes.
I'm anxious to go so I put on my clothes,
But I ask you again, "What do you 'spose?"

When the doctor released me I put on my suit
Then reached in the bag to pull out my boots.
What I was greeted with left me in despair,
My boots were not even a matching pair.

So I walked from the hospital
A hilarious sight.
Two boots for the left foot
But none for the right.

END OF THE LINE

When the state veterinarian, Dr. Horseman, told me I would have to liquidate my herd because they had brucellosis, I made a deal with a packing house in Portland where I was offered 22¢ a pound which was more, even after paying the freight (I had my own truck to haul them) than I could get anywhere else. It was in the spring of the year and many of the cows had already calved. I asked the buyer if they would take the calves too. He assured me that they would but that he couldn't quote me a price for them, but he also assured me that it would be worthwhile to send them along. When I received payment, I was shocked to see how generous the packing company was. They paid $1 each for the calves.

$\widehat{c}$

HITCH GLITCH

I loaded up a load early one morning and was about to leave when I found that I had a broken spring on my Semi-tractor. I called Carl Burck and asked if he could haul them since they were already loaded. While I waited for him, I cranked down the landing gear and unhitched my rig. As soon as I pulled out from under the trailer, the landing gear sunk down into the soft ground.

Fortunately, Myron Bergstom had a big forklift at his hay cubing plant a couple miles down the road, so I went down and borrowed it. With the forklift and a jack and some blocking, I was able to lift the trailer enough to get some boards under the landing gear and get it high enough for Carl to get his truck under and hitch up. I knew Myron would soon need the forklift so I returned it before Carl arrived.

When I got back Carl was all hitched up and ready to go. When he pulled out of the yard he turned to the left to head toward the freeway and was about half way across the highway when the trailer came unhitched and fell onto the frame and rear wheels of the tractor. There he was with a fully loaded trailer blocking a busy highway and ready to fall onto the ground. It's hard to think rationally at times like that. There was a side door on the trailer which I could open and let the cows out of one compartment, but with all the motion of the cows moving and the trailer being so unstable while resting on the frame of the truck, I was afraid it would tip over. Maybe I could get several boards and railroad ties and block it up. That would take time and by now a sheriff was adding to my frustrations by telling me to get it off the road. Couldn't he tell that I was trying?

I finally calmed down enough to remember the forklift. Because of the fact that the trailer was crossways in the road it was hard to get the forklift close enough to lift the trailer but we finally got it done somehow. Before Carl pulled away this time I made sure the fifth-wheel was securely locked. By this time it was getting late in the day and it was next morning before Carl finally returned from Portland.

133

2009

THE GOOD LIFE

The wife and I have owned this ranch
For forty-some odd years.
Mostly it's been good to us,
Though you know we've shed some tears.

We worked our fingers near to the bone
To keep the wolf from the door.
And though we've never had much money,
You can't say we've been poor

We've got each other and we've got a home
And we're proud of the things we've done
We know we've worked some long hard days
But we've also had some fun.

After workin' and doin' the chores
There was time to play and laugh.
The kids would ride and run the barrels
And maybe rope some calves.

We'd work the calves in the middle of the week
About the end of May.
The kids would always look forward to that,
They could all skip school that day.

We'd ride in the hills and move the cows
And camp out under the trees,
We'd listen to sound of the coyote's howl
Come drifting in on the breeze.

When hunting time came in the fall
We'd load up the truck with our gear
And go to the mountains and camp for a while
And come back home with a deer.

And we'd fish in the lakes and pan in the streams
And maybe find some gold,
Whatever we did, we did it together
It never got boring or old.

Well, the kids grew up and they all left home
Deserting us one by one,
But they come back home with our grandkids now
And we still have our share of fun.

FROM THE KIDS' PERSPECTIVE

~ Lyndon ~

Sometime in the mid '70s, Dad decided he needed more cows. To get more cows he needed more pasture. That was about the time a fellow by the name of Archie had a ranch for sale north of Winthrop. So Dad and

Mr. Jorgenson
    My father rented some land from you for spring range. Well, me & some other guys built us a nice Rodeo arena on it & we want to know if it would be all right if we disced the middle of it up so we will have a soft landing.... We were thinkng maybe we could pay some extra rent for that land. We will have insurance on the arena before ever let anyone ride. It is going to be our practice arena so we can get in shape for the rodeos. Please send your Reply as soon as possible. THANK YOU!! Lyndon Price

Mr Jorgenson's Reply:

October 28-1972
Lyndon,
    I received your nice letter and since this is urgent with you I am answering promptly. You sound like a responsible boy to me. If your dad writes me a little note vouching for you, nothing says you can't get busy on your practice arena.
                                  Yours truly, Mr. Jorgenson

136

I loaded up a couple of horses and headed from the ranch at Winthrop to take a look at this place.

As I recall, the ranch consisted of a couple hundred acres of ground and forest permits for about 250 pairs. The forest permits rotated between two pastures. One year you run on one pasture, the next year you would move over to the other. Some kind of government summer fallow program I guess. As I recall each pasture was around 250,000 acres. I had a little trouble trying to figure out why you needed 500,000 acres to run 250 pairs for a few months in the summer. But I am sure that the guys working for the government know a whole lot more about cattle and grass that anybody else.

The first day we spent looking over the homestead and the deeded ground. We were able to see most of that from the cab of a four wheel drive pickup. But the next week we were to ride into the Pasayten Wilderness to look over his forest service permits, and while we were at it we would move some cattle to higher grass and put out some salt. I don't remember for sure, but I think that there were about five humans, five saddle horses, five pack horses, and two dogs. The second day we loaded the horses and headed north to the end of the pavement, unloaded the horses, loaded the packs with food, supplies and salt, and headed up the trail. Archie kept a camp about fourteen miles up the trail, all set up with a tent, stove and some supplies.

As I recall it was late afternoon before we got to camp. Everybody got busy making camp, giving the horses some grain and hobbling them so they could graze around the camp. After supper we all sat around and listened to each other tell lies. Archie told stories of bears that had come into camp in the past and showed us the rips on the tent where a bear had gotten in and decided to claw his way out instead of using the door. When it was time to turn in, my dad and I had to sleep out on the ground under a tarp stretched over a pole fastened to two trees. I remember it took me awhile to fall asleep after listening to those bear stories.

Around 2 a.m. I woke up screaming, "BEAR, BEAR!!" It seems one of the hobbled horses had come up to me in my sleep and started nibbling on my hair. I guess I really scared that horse as much as he scared me. I don't remember if I was able to go back to sleep that night or not.

During that trip we had another interesting experience while we were fishing in a high mountain stream. We rode to a little meadow

a stream running through it. The stream was in the middle of the adow and the trees where we tied the horses were 300 or 400 feet m the stream. We had been fishing for an hour or two and had caught fair amount of those delicious little trout, when all of a sudden on the pposite side of the meadow a bull came crashing out of the brush just a bellering and carrying on like he was loco. He spotted us fishing and started at us like we were going to be his lunch. Archie started yelling for us to run for the horses, and we obeyed our leader without hesitation. By the time we got to the horses the bull was not far behind, but I guess he decided we weren't worth messing with and he turned and headed off into the brush on his pursuit of the cows he had lost. It really got my adrenaline flowing though. That night back at camp we had a great feast of delicious high mountain brook trout.

The rest of the trip was mostly uneventful. We rode, moved cows, and put out salt. Although we enjoyed the country and the experience we decided that having to ride over 250,000 acres to gather and move cattle would be way too much work for 250 pairs.

Lyn, Lucky and Larry

~ Wendy ~

I remember one time in the middle of the night, on[...]
trying to have her calf, but she was having problems. Da[...]
vet to come out to perform a Cesarean section on her. They[...]
the barn light, just outside the door. My sister and I climbed [...]
barn roof, and watched the whole thing from that bird's eye vie[...]

I remember when I was very little, Dad would have the butcher c[...]
out to butcher one of our animals, and we kids watched the whole thing.
From the shooting, to the skinning, to the gutting. We never thought
anything about it. It was just a normal part of life on the farm.

As kids we spent a lot of time in the fields. We had to change the
irrigation morning and night, and we spent many hours on tractors,
harobeds, and swathers. We were happy kids, and it just seemed like
songs always wanted to burst forth from us at any opportunity. Anytime
we were outside and by ourselves we were constantly belting out some
song or another. Singing was how we kept ourselves occupied for
hours and hours on the tractor or swather. (We didn't have radios in our
equipment in those days.) It wasn't until years later that I discovered
that our nearest neighbor, who was a mile away, often heard us out in the
fields singing at the top of our lungs.

One of the best parts of raising cattle in my opinion was the calves.
Sometimes the calves would be born on cold winter days, and Dad would
find them almost frozen to death. He sometimes had to bring the calf in
from the fields. Sometimes he would put them on the floor in his pickup
with the heater blasting away. He would leave them in there while he
finished feeding and checking the cows. If the calf seemed to warm up
enough, he would send the calf back to its mother.

Sometimes though, if the calf wouldn't warm up enough, or if the
calf was too near death and too cold, he had to bring it into the house. I
always liked taking care of them. We put them in the bathtub with some
warm water to try to get their body temperature up. Then we laid them
on the floor in the bathroom, and dried them off with towels, and blow
dryers. We would try anything to try to keep them alive. This method

to work pretty well most of the time.

re is one problem with trying to warm up a calf though. When
.o that, they lose their individual scent, and then many times their
.ners won't know them and won't take them back. We had to put the
ther in the squeeze chute, and try to make her hold still while the calf
rsed. Sometimes the mother would accept the calf, and sometimes
he wouldn't. Sometimes we had cows die while giving birth. Because
of these situations, we had calves that needed to be bottle fed. This was
my very favorite part. I loved taking care of these motherless calves, and
feeding them with the bottle. They often became beloved pets.

I remember one time we had to move a herd of cattle from one winter
pasture to another. I was riding Peanuts, who was a very smart "cow
horse." He was very good at figuring out what I was trying to do. I just
had to point his head at a cow, and he instinctively knew which cow I
wanted to cut. At that point all I had to do was hang on tight, because he
got down to business and got the cow sorted out despite anything I did
sitting up on top of the saddle.

This particular day, we were moving a bunch of cows with very young
calves. There were some small calves lagging behind, and Peanuts (being
as impatient and bossy as always) kept biting them on the rear end, trying
to tell them to get moving. I remember it was a very cold day with snow
on the ground. Our fingers and toes were freezing. At about noon Mom
came driving up in the old blue pickup. In the back she had a big pot of
split pea and ham soup. We all climbed off our horses, and warmed up
with a bowl of that steaming soup. I never have a bowl of split pea soup
even to this day, without remembering that cold day moving cattle, and
how mom came to the rescue.

I also had a lot of misadventures in rodeos and gymkhanas. One time
I was riding Cherokee in the Grand Entry in the Moses Lake Rodeo. As
my 4-H group went running into the arena, Cherokee decided this would
be a wonderful time to stop and lay a big pile of manure right there in
front of everyone. I could not get that horse to move, no matter how hard
I kicked him. I had to wait while he took his sweet time, and when he
decided he was done, he slowly got moving again and we finished the
Grand Entry. Needless to say, my group was all the way around, and out

140

of the arena by then, and I was so embarrassed I never wanted to ride in another Grand Entry as long as I lived.

Somehow, though, I did get the courage to ride in another Grand Entry. This time I was riding Peanuts at a gymkhana in George, Washington. During the Grand Entry he started bucking and wouldn't stop. According to my dad, I just hung on and hung on while he kept on bucking. Finally I got tired of the whole thing, and decided to jump ship. I landed on a rock, and got the wind knocked out of me. I still have a numb spot on my shin from that episode. It is amazing though, how many times we all got thrown off horses and the only broken bone was when my older brother broke his collar bone when he was about five years old. On second thought, there is the time when my dad broke his pelvis. But that is another story.

One hot summer day, a man came walking up to our farm. He told my dad that his truck had run out of gas. Since we had a farm we had a large underground gas tank, dad hand pumped five gallons of gas into an old gas can and they hopped in Dad's pickup to gas up his truck, so that the man could be on his way. When Dad came back he had some cases of pop in his pickup bed. The man had been driving a delivery truck to Safeway in Ephrata. In payment for the gas, he gave my dad a bunch of pop.

Well, let me tell you, that was better than Christmas to us five kids. We rarely got to have pop in those days, and so it was a real treat. Mom

said we could have one can a day. We wanted each of those cans to last as long as possible, so instead of punching a hole with a can opener, we took a small nail and hammer, and punched a tiny hole in the top. That made our can of pop last much longer. There never was anything more fun than sipping on a cold pop, swinging in the swing on a hot summer day.

Here is my poem written in 1976. I guess I would have been 16.

My Home

I hear the wind madly blowing
Through the dreary desert land
A lonely kind emptiness
In sagebrush, rocks and sand.

The land all seems so hollow,
So meaningless to exist
Yet a serene kind of happiness
In this land the sun has kissed

The deserted land will always be there
Empty, dreary and unchanging
Yet the sunny days and still, dark nights
Seem to say the whole world's singing.

The wind keeps blowing on and on
'Til you notice it no more
But still it's where my heart belongs
We simple ones God made it for.

~ Amy ~

Following is a story we recently found in Amy's stuff which she wrote for a class in high school:

Her stomach swollen and her bag stretched tight with milk, this cow follows the others down the narrow trail they have trampled in the snow to reach the icy water trough. A few cows have already given birth and young calves frisk around in the snow, play tag and run back to the safety of their mothers. This cow is a Simmental-cross like many others in the herd. The cross-breeding gives her stripes and a white face and belly on a red body. As we watch them walk by, dad points her out, saying, "That one is due any time."

In the evening it begins to snow. We load hay on the pickup to take to the cows and some straw for bedding so the calves can get out of the muck. Our dog, Babe, a Border Collie, perches in her usual spot on top of the hay. She rides on top of the pickup looking around and getting snow caked in her black coat as we head down the highway.

The pickup is spotted by the hungry cattle as we come through the gate. Some come running as others plod their way slowly but surely to the pickup crowding and bellering. I drive slowly across the bumpy frozen field of corn stalks. By now the cattle have eaten most of the grain that was missed in harvesting. Dad cuts the twine on the bales of hay and throws them off the pickup feeding the cattle the leafy-green nourishment saved from the summer. Looking the herd over to see if any are ready to calve, we realize the one we had noticed in the morning isn't with the others crowding around the hay. We drive around looking for her, knowing she must have gone off to calve.

We find her in the far corner of the field below a hill that protects her from the wind but not from the muck that runs to the low spots from the melting snow. She stands looking at us glassy-eyed but not yet exhausted from labor. Two tiny soft hooves are showing with the promise of new life. Knowing that it will be a while, we leave her alone.

When we return in a couple hours we find that she has gone down in her effort to produce a calf. Her eyes are now glazed over from the strain. The weather has warmed, turning the snow to rain and the cow is lying in collected water. If the calf is born here it could drown. It must be a big calf and we decide that she probably can't do it by herself. She doesn't

143

appreciate the attention, but grunts as she rises on unsteady legs to move to higher ground. Each step seems like a major effort. She soon decides she has gone far enough and just stands in the night rain looking at us.

She is not a tame cow, but doesn't move as dad throws a rope over her head and quickly snubs it to a fence post. I slip a small chain around the forelegs of the calf. With only the headlights of the pickup and with rain drizzling down our necks, dad sets the strap of the calf puller across her heaving back and hooks the pulley to the chain around the calf's hooves, Cranking the pulley, the slack lessens.

This is a young cow and this is her first calf, we can see it is going to be a big one. Clicking, the cable becomes tighter and we see the small pink nose covered with film. The cow goes down again and is breathing hard, concerned only with the job she must do. We aid her efforts with another crank of the puller.

Eyes opening to the world for the first time appear. Once past the shoulders, the hardest part is done and we can see it is indeed a large calf. She would have struggled all night with this one. The calf slides the rest of the way out and lies flat on the ground all wet and slimy, but so beautiful. We slip the rope off the cow and she struggles to get up. It is a little bull calf and we clean the junk from his nose and give him a slap to start him breathing.

The cow is now up and nature takes over as she begins licking it off and starts it breathing. Red and white like his mother, he too shows the Simmental line. His big brown eyes blink as the harsh air enters his lungs. He snorts to clear a passage and his mother's rough tongue cleans his curly hair as she proudly gives him his first bath. We watch the scene for a couple of minutes then get in the pickup and turn the heater on our soggy bodies and drive away over the bumpy, frozen corn field.

We know that in an hour or two the calf will try out his wobbly legs and find the nourishment of his mother's warm milk. Soon the calf will be running and frisking with the others, testing his legs to see how they can buck and run, each time daring to get a little farther from the security of his mother's side.

~ Maxine ~

Growing up on a farm, we had a different perspective than most kids on animals and their deaths. While many tears were shed for the animals we had actually named, we were exposed to the deaths of many of the cattle we raised, as well as other farm animals. We didn't think much of the dead calf that the dogs proudly dragged up to the yard (until friends were over, and were totally disgusted). We also enjoyed front row seats when the butcher came to shoot and cut up one of our cows. So I was somewhat surprised at the odd reactions I got when I first told this story (in real society). And now, years later, it seems even stranger that I plan to relay it to an even bigger audience (I think — depending on if anyone reads this book).

At one point, we had a very old cow that would have been too tough even to make hamburger out of. I guess we finally decided to put her out of her misery — she was shot where she stood in the "North Forty." Soon afterward, I was out changing the wheel line on that section of land, and noticed her dead body. As I went for a closer look, I could see the bullet hole in her head. Since I had some time to kill waiting for the wheel line to drain, I picked up a nearby stick and poked it into the bullet hole. When I did, the cow's legs jerked — over and over. I remember it being very entertaining, the stuff of childhood memories.

~ Tim ~

Of course I have many memories of good times and "interesting" outcomes. I remember having a strawberry patch and eating strawberry shortcake nightly all summer. I remember shooting at birds in the cherry tree with my bb gun.

Moving wheel lines was a daily ritual from early spring to late fall and we had seven of them plus one hand line. The problem was, with about three or four of us getting up early every morning to change water, there was confusion as to who would move which one. Finally Wendy and Amy (in their infinite wisdom) decided that a proper nomenclature would

145

help ease the daily chaos. The names they came up with depicted the geographical location in relation to our house. There was Far Far, Close Far, Close Close, Far Close, Middle Far, Middle Close and of course the North 40.

Having the names down helped with the second part: Negotiating. We all had our own lines that we generally did day after day but there were times when one of us had an activity to do in the evening or a sleepover at a friend's house, so we had to get a sibling to take care of it for us. I don't know for sure, but I think the work usually got done.

Having opportunities to go to the "Ranch" at Republic and help with fall roundup was always a treat, especially the part about getting out of school with an excused absence. I remember one time when I was about ten years old, I had one such opportunity. We left from the headquarters, and rode out up past the big hill that we sledded down in winter (but that's another story).

The usual gang was there: Doug, and Lucy and their annoying dogs, Carl Jones on one of his big beautiful horses he was known for, Ross was there too. Of course Dad was riding Peanuts and I was riding Cody, a big gelding that was gentle and friendly. I am sure there were others along but those were the main people I remember.

It was a nice fall morning, a little brisk but just right. We headed up through several different pastures and crossed many gated fences. This was a big place! Thousands of acres and I only spent a couple of weeks a year there at the most, so I was lost from the get-go, but that was okay as long as I hung with the crowd I had nothing to worry about. We rode on for a while until we got to the furthest pasture where we would start gathering cows and bringing them back.

At that point we all spread out individually. The great big meadow on a south facing hillside was so incredible, it felt as though I was on top of the world as I loped Cody along, the sound of the hooves gave a deep hollow sound I still remember. The whole experience just kind of mesmerized me. There looked to be a couple of pair off in the distance. It didn't really seem too far but I realize now it was just an optical illusion, you know, kinda like the great big buildings in a city like Las Vegas seem to be close… until you try to walk there.

So finally I got to the animals I was looking for and turned them

around to head back and all the sudden there was no one around. I was all alone in the middle of nowhere. It was okay for an hour or two but then I started getting scared. Thinking of all the possible ways of my demise so far away from my mother's tender touch, the thing that scared me the most would be to starve to death.

Keeping the cows moving became more difficult as the day grew warmer and they wanted to hide in the shady brush. This distracted me from thinking if I would ever see the rest of the gang again. But then it is kind of hard to chase cows somewhere if you don't know where to go.

Finally after what seemed like hours of fret and worry and bargaining with God to get me safely back I looked at the sun and figured it must be getting close to dinner time and here I was no closer to finding the group. For all I knew they were back at the trailer eating Emma Jones' blue ribbon spaghetti. So I thought "the heck with those cows, they can freeze for all I care." So... angry, tired, frustrated, and weak with hunger Cody and I headed back to camp hoping to get there before winter set in too hard.

For the first part of the journey home, it was me against him. He tried to go one way while I wanted to go the other, so after a while I just gave up, I figured I was gonna die anyway I might as well not have the horse

147

mad at me too. After a bit, things started looking vaguely familiar, then we got to a gate and Cody just stood there waiting for me to open it. So I got down, opened it. He walked through and waited for me. Being a little guy, I couldn't get the gate closed so I let it drop and continued on, hoping I wouldn't get in too much trouble for leaving it open. This happened several times as things continued to get more and more familiar.

Finally a wave of relief filled my body as the house, corrals and bunkhouse came into view. It was a funny thing though; suddenly it didn't seem so late. None of the crew was around. Maybe they were on a search party for me, so I tied up at the trailer and went inside to see what was going on. Nobody there but Emma and when I walked in she seemed surprised to see me since it was only 1:30 in the afternoon. After that I was never really afraid of getting lost up there since the horses always seem know how to get home.

He rises with the sun
To another work-filled day
His eyes growing dim with age
The years, they slip away

She is always there beside him
Working at a steady pace
And tries to hide the solemnness
That tugs upon her face

Life was once experiences
Wild winds he tried to tame
But now it seems for ages
His life has been the same

Hours in the burning sunshine
Sweat dripping down his face
Somewhere the excitement died
Along life's busy race

**By Wendy Price
1976, age 16**

He pushes always onward
Fighting with the sun
The days are long, but oh so short
To do all that must be done

She slaves to get the cooking done
Wash the clothes and sweep
But there's a will that burns inside
That will not let her weep

And as her calloused fingers
Rub her wrinkled brow
Her old and tired body knows
That life's been good somehow

The blazing sun will rise again
And troubles never cease
But life goes on, they don't mind
For in their hearts, there's peace

Yes, life has been a struggle
But somehow they're content
They know they've done their part in life
For the reasons they were sent.

BRANDS

These are some of the brands we had a brush with through business and friendships. To illustrate how powerful a brand is, while these brands are (sorry) branded into my memory, I forgot who some of them belong to now! If you see yours with no name, give me a holler! I'd like to set that straight.

Reverse P Arrow — Lyndon Price

Lightning over LP Connected — Larry Price

L Hanging K — Loyd Goehri

Arrow Hanging L — Lester Rataezyk

Sundown 7 — Jack Goehri

C Arrow — Ralph Hagy

Rocking GH — Glen Hagy

DH — Don Hagy

Dot R — Ross Rathbun

2-Bit Rock Ranch — Fred Cook

Bear Claw — Glen Bair

Diamond Double Bar — Delbert Tebow

Slash Z Slash — Doug Pearce (Asotin)

✳C Spur — Chuck Yarbro

Circle Eleven — Bud Stewart ⑪

ĉ Hat Over C — Mike Cobb

Backward F Lazy L — Don Liggett ⅃」

ꟼ̶ Lazy LR — Louis Raap

McClure Ranches (Nespelum) ⑦

V̎ Virgil LaPlant

F2 — Ken Ardell **F2**

ꓤ 7R — Gene Robbins

F Hanging X — Jim Frost Fx

ᑕN CN Connected — Chuck McInroy

Don Floren ⊔⊔

OT OT — Will Latham

TBO — Ron Tebow **TBO**

ꟼ̲ Rocking Lazy P — Don Liggett

A Hanging R — Aaron Raap A𝖱

· 3 ·

Dot E Dot — Roger Edwards

Rafter M — Richard Miller

Made in the USA
Monee, IL,
23 December 2020

CONTENTS

at the sugar factory a couple winters, drove cattle truck, worked on construction and did custom wheat and pea harvesting, baling and hay stacking in the rest of my spare time for the next several years.

About the second year we were there, we decided we needed a house of our own so I wrote to the folks from whom we had bought the farm and asked them to loan us $5,000 to build a house. They were old folks in their nineties and had no family of their own so they were willing to help us get a start in life. We could never thank them enough.

Times were kinda tough the first few years (it must have been those $1,000 payments) but we slowly acquired equipment and cattle and more kids until our 130 acres were not enough to support our growing family. That's when we moved to the Ephrata area.

Few people have any idea of all the things that happen in a rancher's life. Mostly it is hard work and certainly not boring. When we look back through years we can find many noteworthy happenings to talk and write about. Most, but not all, of these memories are pleasant ones. Many of these things may be of interest only to the family of the person telling the story. I find it very interesting, however, when I have a chance to listen to some of the tales of others' experiences, and that is the reason I wrote this book for my family and close friends.

I have been asked by folks in my audiences for a book of my poetry, so I hope it will find its way to others. Please don't think I consider my experiences out of the ordinary. I am just telling it the way I remember it. Most everything in this book is factual to the best of my recollections... with the exception of the obvious embellishment of some poems.

~ Larry Price

AUTHOR'S FORWARD

"That's the last place on earth that I would ever live!" That was the answer that I gave to my dad when he asked me what I thought of Ephrata. I had been sent to Ephrata on an errand one spring day back in 1950 when he and I were working on a road construction job at Wilson Creek. Ten years later, my wife and I bought a farm east of Moses Lake. At that time, I still had a low opinion of Grant County and we agreed that this farm was only a temporary detour to something better.

Fast forward another ten years when we sold that farm in block 41 and purchased a three hundred acre farm in block 89. This had been our chance to leave Grant County, but by this time it was home. We might be induced to leave for a short winter sojourn to warmer climates now that we are retired but to actually move away? Forget it!

We started our life together on May 20, 1957. Lois was graduating from WSC (it became WSU two years later) with a degree in nursing and I was working for James Crick Construction Co. rebuilding the runways to accommodate the larger airplanes that now fly in and out of Gieger field in Spokane. After her graduation, we moved to Seattle, where I went to work at Boeing Airplane Company and she found a job at Maynard Hospital. After enduring the traffic and rain and fog of the great metropolis of Seattle for a year, we moved to Pullman where I enrolled at WSU on the GI Bill.

In 1961, we moved to our newly acquired farm near Moses Lake where I put my BS in agriculture to work and started making our fortune. We bought our farm from an old couple who lived in Rockford, WA. We paid $10,000 for 130 acres. We paid $1,000 for the down payment and our payments were $1,000 per year plus 4% interest on the unpaid balance.

We had first acquired the farm the previous summer and had planted winter wheat that fall. We had two small kids (18 months and three years), no farm machinery and only one last check from the GI Bill (I think it was $125) to last us until our first harvest. Lois' folks had a house that was used for hired labor so we made a deal to rent said house and to use their farm equipment in exchange for the use of fifty acres of our farmland and for my labor. At least I was fully employed because I had to work for her dad and do my own farming in my spare time. I worked

DEDICATION

This book is dedicated to my wife Lois, who has been there beside me every step of the way. Without her help I could not have accomplished all that we've done over the years and without her help this book would not have been done either. She put up with me and my foolish notion that I could be a poet. With her encouragement and help, here it is; for better or for worse.

ACKNOWLEDGEMENTS

My daughter, Amy, was the one I counted on to do all the computer work that was required to ready this manuscript for the printer. Without her able assistance it would have never been finished.

Thanks to all the rest of my offspring for their stories which add so much to this work.

Thanks to Lois for reading and rereading these pages and correcting all my mistakes and for reminding me of many of the things which I have written about.

Copyright © 2010 by Larry Price
Cover photos: (main photo) Tim and Buddy with Cherokee in 1971; (clockwise from top) Tim with Frisky; Wendy, Tim, Kenny Youngers, Lyndon and Maxine on branding day; Tim with Cherokee and Molly; (back cover) Tim, Amy and Maxine in 1968.

This revised printing contains new original poems and recollections shared by the author's family, combined with poems and stories from an earlier publication *Horses, Cows, Kids and Dogs*, printed in Nov 2004.

For sales or reprint information, please contact the author.

Edited in the USA by The Purple Coyote, Inc. July 2009

ISBN 978-0-7414-6344-9

Printed in the United States of America

Published November 2010

INFINITY PUBLISHING
1094 New DeHaven Street, Suite 100
West Conshohocken, PA 19428-2713
Toll-free (877) BUY BOOK
Local Phone (610) 941-9999
Fax (610) 941-9959
Info@buybooksontheweb.com
www.buybooksontheweb.com

"I'M REALLY NOT A COWBOY..."

cowboy poetry and recollections of
a Grant County ranch family

by Larry Price

Contents

Preface

BIOCATALYSIS AND BIOMIMETICS presents a cross section of recent advances in catalytic science and biotechnology. The chapters that follow will serve to illustrate how many of the key challenges in biotechnology can only be addressed by bringing together traditionally "separate" disciplines within chemistry and biology.

A subtitle for this volume might read, "A View of Biotechnology Through the Eyes of a Catalysis Scientist". As such it is not intended as an all-encompassing view of chemical opportunities for biotechnology, nor will it cover the recombinant-DNA or monoclonal antibody methods normally associated with modern biotechnology. Many such reviews are already available. Rather, it is meant to focus on emerging enabling technologies at the interfaces of catalysis and biology that will provide new opportunities for the chemicals industries. Key aspects to be presented within this major theme of catalysis and biotechnology are biomimetics and hybrid catalysts, biocatalytic applications of computers and expert systems, enzyme solid-state structure and immobilization, enzyme structure–activity relationships, and the use of enzymes under novel conditions.

The editors have been fortunate to have assembled contributions from world-class authorities in this field. We sincerely thank all who participated to make this not only a successful symposium, but an important contribution to the literature as well. We also thank the Biotechnology Secretariat for coordination of the symposium cluster on Biocatalysis and Biomimetics and the sponsoring Divisions of Petroleum Chemistry, Inc., and of Industrial and Engineering Chemistry, Inc. We greatly appreciate the contributions from E. I. du Pont de Nemours and Company, Monsanto Company, Eastman Kodak Company and B.P. America. The gracious support and understanding of our wives, Cindy Burrington and Molly Clark, and that of our families is most warmly acknowledged.

JAMES D. BURRINGTON
B.P. America Research
   and Development
Cleveland, OH 44128

November 11, 1988

DOUGLAS S. CLARK
Department of Chemical
   Engineering
University of California
Berkeley, CA 94720

Introduction

Biotechnology: Chemistry Is at the Heart of It

by Mary L. Good

Biotechnology is the study and application of genetic engineering techniques to improve the value of such things as crops, livestock, and pharmaceuticals. It is the adaptation of living systems to produce higher value-added products and processes. Planned are applications in medicine and agriculture that were considered impossible only 15 years ago. They include:

1. genetically altered bacteria for producing medicinals

2. alfalfa engineered to produce valuable proteins

3. livestock as factories for a human blood-clotting protein

4. cleanup of industrial wastes by bacteria

5. bacteria engineered as diagnostic tools

Chemistry is at the core of this fantastic new science of biotechnology. Jacqueline K. Barton of Columbia University has said, "You may notice that neither the words 'chemical' nor 'molecular' is incorporated into 'biotechnology', but the heart of what I think is exciting about this area is indeed chemical." Biotechnology depends on our ability to manipulate chemical structure in biological systems on the molecular level. We are learning how the structures of large biological molecules determine their functions. By altering chemical structure, we are learning how to design molecular properties with increasing precision and predictability.

We have also begun to understand that how well we manipulate these chemical structures may ultimately determine our nation's status in the global economy.

Several pharmaceutical and diagnostic products produced using recombinant DNA techniques are already on the market and more are on the way. It has been estimated that by the year 2000, the biotechnology market could reach $100 billion. The predictions are that high value-added specialty products are likely to appear first, followed by production of chemicals and feedstocks, and later, biomass conversion.

The U.S. chemical industry has been quick to recognize the potential of this new technology and invest in it. Howard E. Simmons of DuPont tells us that his company spends one-third of its billion-dollar research budget for biotechnology-related research. In the company's Central Research & Development Department, for instance, half of the scientists working on biotechnology programs are chemists. Dow, Monsanto, American Cyanamid, and Eastman Kodak are a few of the other companies following suit.

The U.S. lead in most areas of biotechnology research has been challenged by West Germany, Great Britain, Switzerland, Sweden, and France, but most aggressively by Japan. In the United States, although large companies are forming or acquiring their own biotechnology divisions, the biotechnology development effort is led by small start-up firms that derive early technology from government-sponsored research at the universities. In Japan, large firms such as brewing companies with extensive bioprocess experience lead in biotechnology R&D. Their time scale for strategic planning is 10–15 years, a long-term view compared with the usual 3–5-year planning period in the United States. The National Science Foundation has concluded that the quality of biotechnology research performed in Japan matches that done in the West.

A study commissioned by the U.S. Department of Commerce predicts that Japan will offer the United States stiff competition in biosensors for the medical market. According to the study, Japan already is competitive in cell culture technology; is now fourth in the world and gaining in protein engineering; and is scaling up its lagging effort in recombinant DNA technology.

What is the role of the American Chemical Society? We have the capabilities and resources, and in terms of our charter an *obligation*, to make a positive contribution toward solving our nation's economic problems and to lead the chemical profession into new areas. Biotechnology will be one of the significant areas for the employment of chemists in the future and will greatly affect our standard of living. The establishment of this Biotechnology Secretariat, which presented its first technical program two years ago, is one proof of ACS' commitment. We have also:

1. presented a Select Conference on Advances in Biotechnology and Materials Science to many of those who make and interpret national science policy.

2. considered launching a new journal in biotechnology.

3. developed *CA Selects* in several areas of biotechnology.

4. considered a definition for a new certified B.S. degree with an emphasis on biochemistry.

These initiatives, because they have broken new ground, presented a challenge to the Society, one that we have met. Quite frankly, a driving force for change has been the recognition that many trained as chemists are already working in biotechnology fields. As a result, new program initiatives in biotechnology will go through more easily. All we have to do is dream them up.

Allied-Signal, Inc.
Morristown, NJ 07960–1021

October 19, 1988

Chapter 1

Biocatalysis and Biomimetics

New Options for Chemistry

James D. Burrington

B.P. America Research and Development, Cleveland, OH 44128

As a dominant technology in the chemicals industries,
catalysis provides an important long-term commercial
target for biotechnology. While enzymes represent the
most efficient catalytic systems known, their impact on
the chemicals industry relative to traditional catalysts
is still small. Developments at the interface of biology
and chemistry will be key to overcoming the major
barriers to broad industrial application of enzyme
catalysis.

The Impact of Catalysis

The overwhelmingly dominant technology in chemicals-related
industries is catalysis. Commercial catalytic processes account for
over half of all fuels production and for 60% of the 135 MM metric
tons of organic chemicals produced annually in the U.S. In fact 20%
of the nation's GNP can be attributed to catalytic processes (1).
Thus, from a technical standpoint, advances in the chemicals industry
are strongly linked to advances in catalysis.
   A key property of catalytic processes is selectivity. Catalysis
has revolutionized process chemistry by replacement of wasteful,
unselective (i.e. multiple-product-forming) reactions with efficient,
selective (i.e. one-product-dominating) ones. For example, selective
catalytic methanol carbonylation (practiced by BP, BASF Monsanto,
Eastman) has to a large extent substituted unselective non-catalytic
n-butane oxidation (Celanese, and Union Carbide processes).
   Control of reactivity by catalysis provides the capability to
shift to lower cost feedstocks. In the twentieth century, advances
in catalysis have allowed the substitution of acetylene with olefins
and subsequently with synthesis gas as primary feedstocks. For
example, production of acrylic acid, traditionally produced by the
Reppe process from acetylene and CO, has now been replaced by
catalytic oxidation of propylene. The emergence of paraffins, the
hydrocarbon feedstock of the future, will depend on development of
catalysts for selective alkane C-H activation (2).

0097–6156/89/0392–0001$06.00/0
© 1989 American Chemical Society

Catalysis has also had a major impact on the functional and
specialty chemicals businesses, providing lower cost routes and
higher performance materials than would have otherwise been possible.
Major examples are from polymer syntheses including Ziegler-Natta,
anionic, cationic polymerization processes, for formation of
polyolefins, ABS resins, polyesters and other synthetic materials.
Future materials areas include high temperature composites,
electronic materials and conducting organics.

The role of catalysis in the petroleum industry has been equally
revolutionary. Metal-supported systems (e.g. of Topsoe and Shell)
for catalytic reforming, hydrodesulfurization and
hydrodenitrification, alkylation catalysts and shape selective
systems (e.g. zeolites and pillared clays) for catalytic cracking
(FCC) and production of gasoline from methanol (Mobil MTG) all
represent significant technical and commercial achievements.

Thus, the impact of new technologies on the chemicals industries
can be assessed to a large extent by its impact on the commercial
practice of catalysis.

Nature's Catalysts

At the molecular level, nature's catalysts, the enzymes (isolated or
as microbial systems) provide tremendous rate increases over the
corresponding uncatalyzed reactions and virtually quantitative
selectivity. The capability to both improve selectivity to a single
product and utilize alternate feedstocks is well documented (3-4).

A major selectivity advantage of biological catalysts over
traditional systems includes the ability to form single products
(chemical selectivity) as well as single optical isomers
(stereoselectivity). Specific examples where biological routes are
preferred commercially include fermentative processes for the amino
acids monosodium glutamate (MSG), lysine, aspartic acid, citric acid
and phenylalanine (5). Many other chemicals have also been produced
by fermentative processes (6).

Enzymes also provide a potential means to utilize alternate
feedstocks which cannot be selectively activated by conventional
catalysts, or to improve selectivity over traditional systems. For
example, the hydroxylase enzymes convert paraffins to alcohols with
virtually 100% selectivity, a reaction which has no analogue in
traditional catalysis (7). The Nitto acrylonitrile to acrylamide
process is an example of how biocatalysis can improve selectivity
over traditional catalysis (8-10).

Coaxing Nature to Work Harder

The exciting technical opportunities in biocatalysis are tempered by
the major barriers to commercialization which still exist. Most
notably, these include low stability of an expensive catalyst, and
the high separation and capital costs associated with low concentrations of reactants and products.

These significant barriers are largely responsible for the lack of
substantial commercial impact of enzyme and microbial catalysts on
the chemicals-related industries. High fructose corn syrup and amino

acids by fermentation remain the only significant chemicals produced by biotechnology and represent only a tiny fraction of industrial chemicals output.

Prospects

Advances in the life sciences over the past 30 years have produced the new enabling technologies normally associated with modern biotechnology, namely genetic engineering and monoclonal antibody methods. While these will surely be key to many new products, particularly in health care and agricultural markets, these methods alone are not likely to permit a major impact on the chemicals industries.

Along with the development of these enabling biological methods, catalysis and other technologies (such as computer modeling and expert systems), which already have a major influence on the chemicals industries, have also made major technical advances. The integration of biotechnology with these more traditional areas represents a means to capture the technical advances across a number of chemicals-related disciplines.

For example, the importance of the complimentary roles of surface, bulk and interfacial structure in heterogeneous catalysis (11-13), also indicates the need to address these issues in explaining and predicting catalytic behavior of enzyme systems as well.

From this cross-disciplinary approach a number of new enabling technologies are now emerging. The combination of biological and chemical catalysts to produce hybrid catalysis or "biomimetic" systems has shown some promise in capturing the high selectivity of enzymes with the favorable processing characteristics of traditional catalysts (see D. Clark, R. H. Fish, R. DiCosimo contributions, this publication). The growing body of information on structure/function relationships of enzymes is being accelerated by advanced crystallographic methods and the use of computer modeling and expert systems (see G. A. Petsko, G. Klopman, W.A. Goddard contributions, this publication). New methods of enzymology, including novel immobilization and reaction conditions (see T. A. Hatton, N. Herron, R. Sipehia contributions, this publication) have demonstrated the potential to improve catalytic performance.

These advances can collectively be viewed as the growing field of biocatalysis and biomimetics. Along with the biotechnical developments, these provide another option for exploiting the potential of enzyme catalysis in the chemicals industry. The following chapters present representative examples of current advances in this emerging field.

Literature Cited

1. Witcoff, H. Chem. Systems Report, Third Annual Review Meeting; New York, Jan. 17-18, 1985.
2. Weissermel, K.; Arpe, H. J., eds., Industrial Organic Chemistry, Verlag Chemie: New York, 1978, p 254.
3. Stiefel, E. I. Chemical Engineering Process, Oct 21, 1987.
4. Whitesides, G. M.; Wong, C-H. Angew. Chem. Int. Ed. Eng., 1985, 24, 617.

5. Sedovinikova M. S.; Belikov, V. M. Russian Chemical Reviews,
    1978, 47, 357.
6. Ouellette, R. P.; Cheremisinoff, P. N. Applications of
    Biotechnology, Technomic Publishing Co.: Lancaster, 1985, p 72.
7. Leak, D. J.; Dalton, H. Biocatalysis, 1987, 1, 23.
8. Nitto Chemical Industry. U.S. Patent 4 414 331, 1983.
9. Nitto Chemical Industry. U.S. Patent 4 421 855, 1983.
10. Nitto Chemical Industry. U.S. Patent 4 343 900, 1982.
11. Gates, B. C.; Katzer, J. R.; Schuit, G. C. A. The Chemistry of
    Catalytic Processes, McGraw-Hill: New York, 1979.
12. Grasselli, R. K.; Brazdil, J. F. Solid State Chemistry in
    Catalysis, ACS Symposium, Series 279, American Chemical Society:
    Washington, D. C., 1985.
13. Vedrine, J. C.; Coudurier, G.; Forissier, M.; Volta, J. C.
    Catalysis Today, 1987, 261.

RECEIVED October 17, 1988

BIOSCIENCE AND BIOTECHNOLOGY

Chapter 2

Biomedical Science and Technology

The Interdisciplinary Challenge

Paul B. Weisz

Departments of Chemical Engineering and Bioengineering, University
of Pennsylvania, Philadelphia, PA 19104-8393

Interdisciplinary bridges across chemistry,
chemical engineering science and medicine are
compelling challenges to progress basic
insights and solutions for major problems in
the life sciences and technologies. An
analysis of the molecular spectrum identifies
some trends, basic phenomena and skills
involved, and examples of basic focal points
for the joining of existing but largely
segregated skills.

Interdisciplinary Research - Vogue or Reality?

"Interdisciplinary" is a word used frequently these days.
Perhaps some of us think -or even hope- that it is a vogue
that will pass. It is a fact, however, that our
institutions, communications and activities in the sciences
have become increasingly subdivided into "specialties". As
researchers, we generally keep drilling deep in our own
specialty parcels, with but occasional excursions to
adjacent fields. Our institutions (organizational units,
departments, course structures, journals, funding
organizations, "peer" groups, etc.) are neatly subdivided,
categorized, organized. All these factors, by
interdependence and mutual perpetuation, mold the character
of education, attitudes, professional language, and the
opportunities as well as constraints in the choice, type
and execution of research, career, the structure of
knowledge, etc.
    Perhaps the word "interdisciplinary" will go away.
But the concept will not, because society needs it. There
is a growing awareness that real problems in our society

NOTE: This chapter was presented as the plenary address of the symposium, Impact of Surface
and Interfacial Structure on Enzyme Activity.

are not optimally served by the convenience (and comforts) of orderly compartmentation. We recall (1) a 1979 meeting in Princeton,attended by leading scientists from diverse fields,including Nobel Laureates, in which the keynote speaker, Ashly Montagu, observed that

"The present degree of specialization has resulted in a condition of intellectual isolationism. This manifests itself in .... inability to see ... relevance of content, methods and models of other ... disciplines, existence of an inbred ... philosophy ... largely irrelevant to ... problems of modern life."

Ten years before that, an observation, outspoken but humorously true, was that of E. Haskell (2) (Connecticut Review, p. 84, April, 1969):

"The multiversity has now become the modern tower of Babel, each of whose departmental languages grows ever less understandable to members of all other departments."

The evolving field of biomedical science and technology appears to be one that recognizes from the outset that it must deal with "real" and "relevant" problems of health, life, and, literally, with survival; that there is little time or value to engage in moral debate over what is "pure", basic, or applied research. Louis Pasteur, whom we could well call the father of biomedical science and technology, stated nearly a century ago "There is only one science: A basic science and its application."

As we address biomedical problems, as Pasteur did, we surely deal with "real" problems, "relevant" to society, and we are forced thereby to look to the skills of all the disciplines. It is significant that many of these most important pieces of knowledge to be embraced and used exist already at a quite basic level of the sciences, not buried in great depths of specialized sophistication.

In that spirit, let us examine some very basic science concerning the nature and behavior of the molecules that are the actors in all of life. From whatever we touch to the mechanisms of life itself, we deal with molecules and molecular processes. Figure 1 displays molecules, molecular complexes, and molecular systems of our world, in the order of their molecular weights (M.W.). From left to right we have molecular entities of ever increasing sizes and complexities.

Molecular Entities, Phenomena, Skills

Moving from simple gases, through inorganic and organic compounds, somewhere we get to peptides, oligomers and to polymers, macromolecules like proteins or polysaccharides; we move on to complexes or interacting systems of molecules, like neurons or cell organelles; to systems of systems, like cells, organisms, organs, people, and societies, each an associative, dynamic molecular system of ever increasing order. Mathematically and actually,

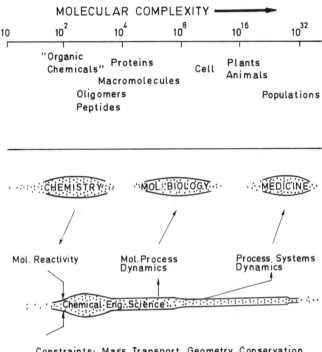

Figure 1. Molecules and Molecular Systems. Their size (molecular weights); increasing complexity; the relevant, major 'location' of activity of traditional disciplines.

diversity increases even more rapidly than molecular weight. One of us, as a molecular system, would correspond to a M.W. of about 10^{28}, and obviously, no two of us will have the same "molecular weight". Of course, we have yet ignored the immense diversity of possible variants in chemical composition and (e,g, isomeric) structure, within any given molecular weight.

Under this spectrum, I have indicated where the center of gravity, or focus of interest has been of a few of our named disciplines.

Starting on the left (Figure 1), chemistry has first dealt with the realm of chemical (atomic) composition and structure of molecules, and focused on reactivity of molecules (or its parts), progressing from simple toward more complex structures. At the other end of the spectrum, medicine has always dealt with the vast biological complexity of people.

Early in this century, a few chemical and medical scholars of a few universities in Austria-Hungary and southern Germany crossed the constraints of disciplinary boundaries. It led to the beginnings of biochemistry (3), to at least four Nobel Prizes (4), and to vitamins. It was a decisive step toward bridging the vacuum between the right and the left of our spectrum, by applying the chemical skills of composition and structure to various biological entities of relatively small to fair molecular complexity, with a growing and, finally, a major emphasis on the complexity of proteins.

Molecular biology is certainly a prominent outgrowth of that trend and discipline, with it's center of gravity heavily in the realm of structural detail of proteins, and the significance and relationship of that sophistication to informational phenomena (recognition, immune response, replication, genetics, etc).

We face the challenge of increasingly bridging the large remaining gaps. We might say that we know many pieces, but we know too little of how they effect the whole. What are some of the phenomena that are fundamental to a successful march across this bridge?

As we progress from left to right, we move from problems of composition, structure and reactivity of *compounds* to those of the dynamics of interacting *processes* and *process systems* ; generally we move from individual entities to systems, and these become directed to very specific *missions* to be achieved, with mandatory *efficiency*, and within the constraints of many physical and chemical parameters acting upon the process system as a whole.

During the last few decades, the study of processing systems, their constraints, behavior and performance for specific missions has centered largely in the compartments of chemical engineering science. It is important to discard any image of 100 foot towers that may arise at the word "engineering". Fortunately, the fundamentals of chemical engineering science are equally applicable to chemical process systems of any dimension.

Chemical Engineering and Bio-Medicine

For example, chemical engineering science has evolved much basic knowledge, qualitative and quantitative guidelines for the understanding and design of porous, heterogeneous catalysts for chemical processes. They deal with criteria that define how large the catalytic materials or regions may be to support a desired conversion rate; how that relationship depends on the concentration of the molecules undergoing conversion; how the size and geometry of catalytic regions can effectively accomplish a sequence of reactions, inhibit it, or side-track it (5,6).

All these considerations are basic and equally applicable to the broad variety of biochemical reaction systems. We can use them to determine the optimal size of catalyst particles in a giant petroleum cracking process; but they have interdisciplinary, i.e. universal applicability to any molecular process systems (7) including the biochemical transformation processes at the dimensions of organs, cells, organelles, and smaller molecular units.

By way of an example illustrated in Figure 2, "chemical engineering" criteria can provide relationships between the maximum allowable dimensions of the intra-cellular enzymatic reaction systems, or the minimum concentrations of metabolic intermediates they are to process, required to achieve certain desired magnitudes of turnover numbers (6b). At the time of this publication, applying chemical engineering science useful in the chemical process industry to cellular processes was an excursion with a very small audience, in spite of the universal applicability of its criteria. Only occasionally, the biochemist has applied the concepts, often after independent efforts; for example, Nevo and Rikmenspoel showed that such an "engineering" criterion links the optimal (and actual) physical length of the tail of spermatozoa firmly to the concentration of the ATP generated at its base (6c).

Today, chemical engineering science is logically able to apply its skills to phenomena of the molecular processing *systems* characteristic of bio-medicine and to their "modelling" to develop rigorous and quantitative foundations. The basic need for the bridges in our spectrum of knowledge (Figure 1) to span the territory of chemical systems, promises fruitful results from an increasing partnership between the sciences of medicine, chemical engineering and chemistry.

Quite in line with the above quoted comment by Haskell, such partnership will mainly require courage, effort and patience to overcome a divisive language barrier. It is, I believe, the only barrier that stands in the way to a meeting of minds, and to an explosive acceleration towards major insights and revelations.

The detailed interaction and dynamics of several molecular entities and parameters in an entire process *system*., is of crucial importance throughout biology and medicine. It is well illustrated by the battle of an army of macrophage, seeking, meeting and annihilating invading pathogens. A recent study of my chemical engineering and medical colleagues (8) is another example of the

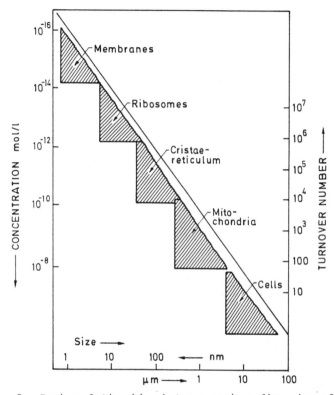

Figure 2.   Basic relationships between maximum dimension of
biochemical apparatus (e.g. cell component), achievable turnover
number, and concentration of metabolic intermediate to be
processed (see ref. 7).

combination of "chemical engineering" modelling with medical inquiry (9). The success of the vital process involves invasion rates, pathogen and macrophage concentrations, mobility behavior etc.. The results of their analysis, sketched in Figure 3, demonstrates the dramatic importance of the macrophage having a slight but critical chemotactic directivity superimposed on its general mobility. Below that critical value, the required time of battle goes to infinity , i.e. the war is lost.

By way of such insights, we can see how, like diffusion coefficients in chemical technology, cell motility and chemotactic coefficients are becoming fundamental parameters with rigorous significance. Aided by a symbiosis between the skills of chemical process science and medicine, they are bound to become routinely accessible by experiment, as rigorous descriptive parameters for bio-medical research, and potentially for medical, diagnostic purposes .

Trends

There are currently at least three notable and important trends observable that work in the direction of narrowing the gaps between the simple and the complex molecular world we described in Figure 1.

One is the increasing number of demonstrations that some less complicated chemical things on the left can do some things best known in the complex medical sector on the right. The best representatives of that trend are the researches devoted to chemical mimics for molecular recognition or enzymatic action. An example is the demonstration by Myron Bender and co-workers (10) of b-benzyme, a relatively simple molecule pictured in Figure 4A, as an efficient mimic of the enzyme chymotrypsin, a protein containing 245 amino acid residues. The reaction rate equals or exceeds that of the natural enzyme. In addition, its stability to denaturation is superior over a vast range of pH conditions, as shown in Figure 4B.

There is now a complementary trend quietly reaching from the complex right to the far left of our working spectrum (Figure 1). The bulk of biochemical science has focused on the nucleic acids and complex macromolecules, proteins, DNA and RNA. The skills of sequencing and determination of ever increasing structural detail have grown rapidly. We have become accustomed to expect, as a matter of routine, that all or most of such detail is essential for the functioning of any prominent bioactive entity, such as growth factor or any other "factor".

Now, the word *fragment* is beginning to make a dominant appearance. In diverse instances, smaller molecular entities derived from an important and complex macromolecule are found to have similar biochemical functions as the prominent parent, sometimes displaying one of the parent's several (desirable and undesirable) functions.

Bacterial Clearance Half-Time (Hours)

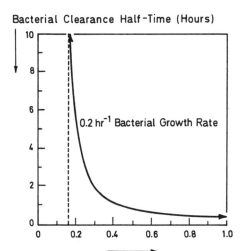

Macrophage Chemotactic Index

Figure 3.   Clearance of Bacterial Attack by Macrophage on the
Lung Surface. Success (represented by the time required for
clearance, the ordinate) depends critically on the coefficient
of chemotactic motility (abscissa). Initial macrophage and
bacterial densisities = 10^3 cm^{-2}; random motility coeff. =
$10^{-8} cm^2$/sec; speed = 3µm/min.

(A)

CHYMOTRYPSIN:

245 amino acid
sequence

β - BENZYME:

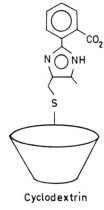

Cyclodextrin

Figure 4. Enzyme mimic for chymotrypsin. (A) Structure and molecular
weights. *(Continued on next page.)*

(B)

Reaction Rate

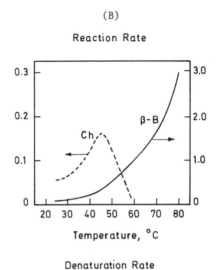

Denaturation Rate

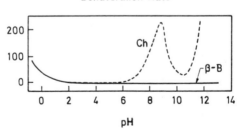

Figure 4. *Continued.* (B) Comparative reaction rates and stability to denaturation.

Soon after the discoveries by J. Folkman and his associates, of the powerful role heparin could play in promoting tumor induced angiogenesis (11, 13), and its dramatic capability, when combined with certain steroids, to inhibit such angiogenesis and thereby arrest tumor growth (12, 13), the modulating effects of the complex, 10,000 to 40,000 M.W. glycosaminoglycan, were shown to be obtainable from a *fragment* of but five to seven sugar units (12,13). Similarly, the antithrombic activity traditionally associated uniquely with heparin was shown to be obtainable from a small (five to seven glucose oligomeric) *fragment* of heparin (14,15,16).

We have some fascinating analogies in animal and plant biology. We are familiar with the release of biochemical factors (growth factors, glycosaminoglycans, etc.) that results from tissue injury and their vital role in the subsequent repair mechanisms. We now note that the destruction of plant cell walls also leads to important products. They are relatively small oligo-saccharide *fragments*. They have important functions in plant growth regulation and antibiotic defense (17).

Fragments of hyaluronic acid, in contrast to the whole parent compound, have been reported to be promoting neo-vascularization (18). *Sub-fragments* of myosin have been shown to be sufficient to cause movement of actin filament (19). Nicotinamide and nicotinamide group containing fractions of a tumor derived ethanol extract were reported to have angiogenic activity and would represent the first non-proteinic low molecular weight molecules tumor derived growth factor (20).

A third trend, now following the mushrooming discoveries of growth factors, is a phase of discovery of growth inhibitors. This, in turn, leads logically to a heightened awareness (21) that the condition for the normal, i.e. the non-pathological state, is the achievement of balance in a dynamic network of kinetics involving a number of stimulating and inhibiting molecular participants (factors) seeking to act upon one, perhaps more receptors. It is analogous, if not equivalent to the systems of heterogeneous catalytic chemistry, where receptors become sites, stimulating and inhibiting factors become promoters and poisons, and the role of more than one receptor in the accomplishment of a task becomes known as polyfunctional catalysis (6a).

Challenges

In the first two trends, we recognize indications of ripeness and fertility that awaits us in exploring the gap between "simple" chemistry and "complex" medicine. The third observation re-emphasizes the important role of evolving rigorous kinetic models which become essential, first for "keeping track" of, and subsequently for "making sense" out of the many interactive events in a multicomponent system, of promoters, inhibitors, protagonists and antagonists, in the real kinetic systems of biomedical chemistry. It underlines the future utility of the linking of skills between the biomedical and the chemical "engineering" sectors.

Linkages progress in many ways and instances. Many are catalyzed by ever widening capabilities of instrumental skills, exemplified by the study and use of nuclear magnetic resonance techniques. The joining of intellectual approaches and skills between disciplines will create major and *basic* advances such as to have multiple impacts on many branches of biomedical science.

Angiogenesis is an example of a *basic* process in biomedicine: It impacts on many aspects and branches of health and disease: Wound healing, ovulation and menstrual activity, inflammatory diseases including arthritis, tumor growth and management, neovascular ophtamological diseases, psoriasis, to name a few. It is a basic process *system*, where the biomedical and the chemical 'engineering' researcher can apply their respective *skills* for 'modelling' to advance the understanding of behavior, balance, and control of complex kinetic networks (and three interacting components already suffice to produce a "complex" network!). Dr. J. Folkman and I will report some results from such a cooperation in the following paper.

I will close with an example of where the pooling of knowledge from segregated disciplines could be of great potential importance:

Silicon and aluminum oxides and hydroxides are the most abundant compounds on our earth. They exist in rock, soil, the dust we breathe, and as components or trace components in just about all we touch or consume. Over decades, they have made their appearance in a number of segments of medicine such as fibrotic diseases, tumor induction, Alzheimer's disease, and aluminum related bone diseases. Of these Alzheimer's disease is perhaps one of the most serious diseases in our society. Here a still mysterious role of "aluminum" is observed and acknowledged by many researchers.

In traditional teaching of chemistry these oxides are considered among the stablest materials. On the other hand, in another discipline, namely in modern catalytic chemistry and technology, we know of and utilize the catalytic capabilities of trace amount of aluminum associated with silica (22). A major portion of petro-chemical technology depends on these sites (receptors). Yet the potential relevance of that extensive experience in catalytic chemistry of the rugged hydrocarbons, remains largely unrecognized and segregated from the world of delicate and diverse biochemical entities and processes.

Acknowledgment

Support by the Mobil Foundation for the initiation of interdisciplinary studies is hereby gratefully acknowledged.

Literature Cited

(1) Ashly Montagu, Keynote Address, "Crisis in Scientific Research", Princeton, N.J., October,1979;

(2) E. Haskell, Connecticut Review, p.84, April,1969;

(3) "The Origins of Modern Biochemistry", P.R. Srinivasan, J.S. Fruton, J.T. Edsall, Ed.'s, Ann. N.Y. Acad. of Sciences, Vol. 325, 358, 1979;

(4) H. Fischer (Vienna); O. Loewi (Graz); F. Pregl (Graz);A. Szent Györgyi (Szeged)

(5) P. B. Weisz and C.D. Prater,"Interpretation of Measurements in Experimental Catalysis", Adv.in Catalysis, Vol.6, Academic Press, New York, 1956; C.N.Satterfield, "Mass Transfer in Heterogeneous Catalysis", MIT Press, Cambridge, 1970; R. Aris,"The Mathematical Theory of Diffusion and Reaction in Permeable Catalysts", Clarendon Press, Oxford,1975;

(6) (a) P.B. Weisz, "Polyfunctional Heterogeneous Catalysis", Adv. in Catalysis, Vol. 13, 1962; (b) P.B. Weisz, "Enzymatic Reaction Sequences and Cytological Dimensions, Nature, 195, 772, 1962; (c) A.C. Nevo and R. Rikmenspoel, J. Theor. Biol. 26, 11, 1970.

(7) P. B. Weisz, "Diffusion and Chemical Transformation: An Interdisciplinary Excursion", Science, 179, 433, 1973;

(8) E.S. Fisher, D.A. Lauffenburger and R.P. Daniele, "The Effect of Alveolar Macrophage Chemotaxis on Bacterial Clearance from the Lung Surface", Amer.Rev. of Respiratory Diseases, in publ., 1988;

(9) D.A. Lauffenburger, "Mathematical Analysis of the Macrophage Response to Bacterial Challenge in the Lung", in "Mononuclea Phagocytes: Characteristics, Physiology and Function", R. van Furth, Z. Cohn and S.Goron, Ed.'s, Martinus Nijhoff, 1985;

(10) V.T. D'Souza, X.L. Lu, R.D. Ginger and Myron L. Bender, Proc. Natl.Acad. Sci. USA, 84, 673, 1987;

(11) S. Taylor and J. Folkman, "Protamine is an inhibitor of angiogenesis", Nature, 297, 307, 1982;

(12) J. Folkman, R. Langer, R. Linhardt, C. Haudenschild, and S. Taylor,"Angiogenesis Inhibition and Tumor Regression caused by Heparin or a Heparin Fragment in the Presence of Cortisone", Science 221,719,1983;

(13) J. Folkman, "Regulation of Angiogenesis: A new Function of Heparin", Biochem. Pharmacology, 34, 905,1985;

(14) R.J. Linhardt, A. Grant, C.L. Cooney, and R. Langer, "Differential Anti-Coagulant Activity of Heparin Fragments Prepared Using Microbial Heparinase", J. Biol. Chem., 257, 7310, 1982;

(15) J. Choay, J.C. Lormeau, M. Petitou, P. Sinaÿ and J. Fareed,"Structural Studies on a Biologically Active Hexasaccharide Obtained from Heparin", Ann. N.Y. Acad.Sci.370, 644, 1981;

(16) L. Thunberg, G. Bächström and U. Lindahl, "Further
      Characterization of the Antithrombin Binding Sequence
      in Heparin", Carboh. Res., 100, 393,1982;
(17) K.T.T. Van, P. Toubart, A. Cousson, A.G. Darvill,B.J.
      Gollin, P. Shelf, and T. Albersheim, "Manipulation of
      the Morphogenetic Pathways of Tobacco Explants by
      Oligosaccharins", Nature 314, 615, 1985; see the
      overview: P.Albersheim and A.G. Darvill,
      "Oligosaccharins", Scient. American 253, 58, 1985;
(18) D.C. West, I.N. Hampson, F. Arnold and S. Kumar,
      "Angiogenesis induced by Degradation Products of
      Hyaluronic Acid", Science 228, 1324, 1985;
(19) Y.Y. Toyoshima, S.J. Kron, E.M. McNally, K.R.
      Neibling, C.Toyoshima and J.A. Spudich,"Myosin
      Subfragment-1 is Sufficient to Move Actin Filaments in
      vitro, Nature 328, 536, 1987;
(20) F.C. Kull, D.A. Brent, I. Parikh and P. Cuatrecasa,
      Science 236, 843,1987;
(21) Jean L. Marx, "Cell Growth Control Takes Balance",
      Science 239, 975, 1988;
(22) J. Folkman, P.B. Weisz, M.M. Joullié and W.R. Ewing,
      in publication,Science;
(23) W.O.Haag, R.M.Lago, P.B.Weisz, "The Active Site of
      Acidic Aluminosilicate Catalysts", Nature 309, 589,
      1984.

RECEIVED January 25, 1989

Chapter 3

Interdisciplinary Challenges

Control of Angiogenesis

Judah Folkman[1] and Paul B. Weisz[2]

[1]Departments of Surgery, Anatomy, and Cell Biology, Harvard Medical
School and Children's Hospital, Boston, MA 02115
[2]Departments of Chemical Engineering and Bioengineering, University
of Pennsylvania, Philadelphia, PA 19104-8393

Angiogenesis is the normal process of growth
of capillary blood vessels, but unabated
angiogenesis is the basis to many diseases.
Heparin administered together with certain
steroids can inhibit angiogenesis. In
investigations guided by a "simplest possible"
chemical kinetic model for the interaction in
the heparin/steroid/cell system, we
demonstrate that low molecular weight
molecules of minimal chemical complexity can
take the function of heparin. A polysulfated
seven membered cyclopyranose is shown to be
nearly a hundred times more effective than
heparin.

We will briefly discuss the meaning, role and importance of
angiogenesis, and report recent progress concerning
angiogenesis inhibition, identifying chemical structures of
minimal complexity in the role of heparin, but equally or
more effective in antiangiogenic activity.

Angiogenesis

In the adult, new capillary blood vessels are normally not
formed except in females, during ovulation, menstruation
and pregnancy. Otherwise blood vessels remain quiescent.
Endothelial cells which constitute the lining of the vessels
divide slowly, if at all. Their turnover time **may** be as
much as ten years. By contrast, other cell systems
proliferate rapidly. For example, there are some 10^{10} cell
divisions per hour in bone marrow, and the whole bone
marrow mass is replaced in some five days.
During angiogenesis (1), however, endothelial cells
can change their resting condition into rapid cell
proliferation with similarly fast turnover times of a few

0097–6156/89/0392–0019$06.00/0
© 1989 American Chemical Society

days. Angiogenesis is the phenomenon of inducing sprouting
and proliferation of endothelial cells from an existing
vascular component, resulting in the generation and growth
of new capillaries and vessels; see Figure 1.

Angiogenesis is an active, desirable and necessary
phenomenon during healing processes after injury or after
myocardial infarction, i.e. after heart attack. On the
other hand, there are more than fifty diseases in which
angiogenesis turns on abnormally, continues out of control,
and causes devastating tissue damage. Therefore,
angiogenesis is a basic physiological process, with wide
ranging consequences in life and biomedicine.

For example, in ophthamology, angiogenesis is the most
common, basic physiological phenomenon that causes
blindness. The capability of adequate control of that
condition would have enormously beneficial consequences. In
another realm of medicine, tumors induce the most intense
angiogenesis by release of its own growth factors (2). It
is becoming increasingly evident that progressive tumor
growth and metastasis is dependent on angiogenesis for its
maintenance and growth, due to its dependence on the
endothelial network for nutrient transport (3,4). In view
of this linkage of tumor cell and endothelial cell
proliferation, successful agents for angiogenesis
inhibition would impact importantly on oncology. Targeting
the control of the endothelial process, as compared to
tumor cell biochemistry, offers an attractive and general
strategy (5), especially since tumor species release
different and often several angiogenic molecules. At least
four angiogenic polypeptides have been analyzed for their
complete amino acid sequence (4), but many more factors
exist.

Inhibition of Angiogenesis

Inhibition of angiogenesis has been demonstrated to be
possible by the unique, simultaneous action of *two*
compositions, a steroid of specific structure and heparin
(6,7,8,9). The steroid by itself has little or no effect;
heparin also has no inhibiting effect, and at some
concentrations may promote angiogenesis. Only the
simultaneous application of both agents can result in
successful inhibition.

Hydrocortisone has been used most frequently in
studies of antiangiogenesis. In view of the well known
clinical side effects of hydrocortisone it is of interest
that the angiostatic function can be separated from these
other steroidal activities by moving the 11-OH group from
its beta-position to the alpha-position (i.e. below the
plane of the molecule), to produce 11-alpha epicortisol.
Such variants of that steroid structure are now potentially
available to serve as "angiostatic steroids" (7,8,9).

Angiogenesis inhibition is most conveniently
demonstrated and measured in the chick embryo bioassay (CAM
assay, see further below). It sets in upon introduction of

about 10 μg of heparin (in 10 μl solution, containing 50 μg of hydrocortisone), for a "good" heparin or heparin fraction. Increasing heparin concentration leads rapidly to an optimal effect, followed by a decline.

On the other hand, the attainable effectiveness and usefulness of the heparin varies greatly with its source (6,10). It is usually manufactured from pig intestine. The product is a heterogeneous, polydisperse composition, its molecular weight in a range from some 10,000 to 40,000, varying among manufacturers, and from batch to batch. Furthermore, studies with heparin administered subcutaneously to mice have shown that heparin's anticoagulant activity is sufficiently close to its antiangiogenic dose requirement to risk bleeding as a serious side effect.

In view of these problems, the fact that heparins have been the only source of an effective co-factor for the anti-angiogenic pair effect, and the general importance of achieving reliable inhibition, we have examined potential mechanisms and structures for an effective alternative molecule.

The "Simplest Model" Approach
Heparin is a material of the family of glycosaminoglycans. Heparins contain some 20 to 60 sugar units bearing many and various substituents (O-sulfate, N-sulfate, glucuronic, N-acetyl, epimers of uronic acid residues) (11a,b,c). The polyionic substituents render the molecule hydrophilic and water soluble.

A customary approach to research concerning the biological activity of a macromolecule focuses on its very detailed chemical structure. If smaller portions of such a molecule exhibit the desired activity, one can more easily duplicate its detailed structure or vary and examine the significance of one or the other structural detail. Heparin fragments of 5 to 7 sugar units have indeed been shown to be active (6). However, the structural/chemical complexity is still so large that the creation of structural variants or duplicates by chemical synthesis requires an extraordinarily large number of synthetic steps (12,13).

We have undertaken an approach different but familiar in scientific system's analysis: Initial construction of a "simplest model" generally consistent with observed behavior and current knowledge, in terms of the smallest number of parameters and most basic (elementary) properties; in our case, the chemical system involves three participants, two molecular species and the cell. Adequacy of such "simplest" working model is tested experimentally, for either confirmation or added information for modification; but complexity is added only as required.

The necessity of simultaneous action of the two molecular components suggests involvement of a bimolecular complex. While the saccharide is highly hydrophilic in

nature, the anti-angiogenic steroids, hydrocortisone or structural variants, are hydrophobic structures. (This still applies to the bulk of the steroids' molecular structure, even when water solubility is attained for pharmaceutical practice by introduction of acetate, phosphate or other single polar group in 21-position). Superficially, this difference may discourage the thought of mutual interaction. However, an oligomeric chain of glucose rings, can and will attain a spiral (helical) configuration, especially with polar substituents directed outward to interact with the aqueous medium. Such helical configuration is observed for heparin (18,19). It offers an apolar, hydrocarbon-like region for hydrophobic interaction (14) within the configurational loops. This is, in fact, the basis for the strong inclusion of non-polar molecules by the cycloamyloses (cyclodextrins) where such a conformation is permanently offered (15,16,17).
          A simple working model is based on the following assumptions:
          1. Complex formation takes place between the steroid (the "angiostat') and portions of the saccharide. The saccharide thus facilitates fluid (aqueous) solubility and functions as the carrier;
          2. The carrier saccharide adsorbs strongly at the cell surface by hydrophilic (ionic) bonding, and thereby presents a high surface concentration of the active steroid (either to surface receptors directly or for facilitated channel diffusion).

Experimental Approach

The cyclodextrins (CD's) have a proven capability for the formation of complexes with many hydrophobic structures (14,15,16). The α, β, and γ cyclodextrins are cyclic oligomers of 6, 7, and 8 glucose (anylose) rings, respectively. The center cavity of the β form can easily include a large portion of a steriod molecule. The α cyclodextrin cavity can capture at best a small portion. Each cyclodextrin sugar unit has three hydroxyl groups, and no other substituents. These materials are not known, by themselves, to have any particular biological functions.
          Stability constants (equilibrium constants for complex formation, K_c) for many steroids in α-, β- and γ-cyclodextrin have been reported (17); for hydrocortisone and simple substitutions, they typically have magnitudes of K_c = 2000 to 4000 M^{-1} for β- and γ- CD's, and K_c = 50 to 200 for α- CD. They are hydrophilic and water soluble. We tested them for angiogenic activity in combination with hydrocortisone, with negative success.
          Although, they should satisfy the first criterion, of complexing with the cyclodextrin of our "simplest model", bonding to the cell surface would have to rely entirely on

hydrogen bonding with hyroxyls of the cyclodextrin. On the other hand, it has been shown that in sulfated glycosaminoglycans, like heparin, sulfate plays a major role in strong cell adhesion (20); their importance is particularly well demonstrated by the observation that adsorbed sulfated species such as heparan sulfate is displaced by a similar species of still higher sulfate density, namely heparin (20).

We therefore proceeded to examine two polysulfated ß-cyclodextrins, one with ca. 7 sulfate substitutions per molecule (ß-CD-7S), and another with about 14, i.e with two thirds of the available hydroxyl groups sulfated; this product is referred to as β-CD-14S, for β-cyclodextrin tetradecasulfate.

All of the angiogenesis inhibitors discovered have been found by using the chick embryo bioassay, also called the chorioallantoic membrane (CAM) assay: Using fertilized chicken eggs, the initial development and growth of blood vessels can be visibly observed and measured. On day 6, the angiogenesis inhibitor, contained in 10 ml of methylcellulose, is placed on the vascular membrane (the chorioallantoic membrane). Normally, its diameter doubles each day and new vessels grow with it. However, an angiogenesis inhibitor causes regression of growing capillaries over a period of 48 hours. The new capillaries disappear and leave an avascular zone of about 2 to 4 mm). The avascular zones are like those in a penicillin assay and can be used to generate dose-dilution curves.

Effective Replacement of Heparin for Angiogenic Control

The results (J. Folkman, P.B. Weisz, M.M. Joullié and W.R. Ewing, Science, in publication;) of antiangiogenic effectiveness measured by the CAM- assay (see below), using 25 mg saccharide with 60 mg hydrocortisone-21-phosphate (in 10 ml solution) are shown in the following table, together with the range of results with heparins (20 to 57 eggs per assay):

Saccharide	%Avascular Zones (Antiangiogenic Activity)
heparins	0 to 65
ß - CD	5
ß - CD-7S	7
ß - CD -14S	62
α - CD	0
α - CD -12S	4

The ß-CD-14S material is not only the first non-heparin material we have seen to have activity to promote

antiangiogenic activity with the steroid; it also produced
the widest avascular zones in the chick embryo assay.
       It is significant also that the alpha cyclodextrin,
having a smaller hydrophobic cavity for complexing, and
slightly smaller sulfate substitution showed very little
activity.
       A dose response study, keeping the hydrocortisone
constant, but changing the concentration of ß-CD-14S, gave
the results shown in Figure 2. The % avascular zones are
shown (bars represent results from 30 to 50 assays in each
case. Five replicate experiments were carried out over 10
months. The shaded area represents the area of past
experience with various heparins. The data obtained under
this area include those from many heparins and CHOAY
heparin pentasaccharide.
       The ß-CD-14S material is found to still maintain 40%
percent of the activities achievable with the best of
heparins, at two orders of magnitude concentrations.

An Example Application: Inhibiting Corneal Neovascularization

We have since confirmed the exceptional activity also using
the rabbit corneal test (19), in which endotoxin from a
corneal implant of a sustained release polymer induces
neo-vascularization, and a second implant contains the test
substances.
       Moreover, with the cyclodextrin polysulfate, in
contrast to heparin, we can obtain adequate transmembrane
transport into the cornea using topical application (eye
drops) to administer the anti-angiogenic pair of
substances. The photographs of Figure 3, taken during the
study, demonstrate: (a) the unabated corneal neo-
vascularization (induced by an endotoxin pellet) as, in
fact, it would be seen in a patient rejecting a corneal
transplant; (b) hydrocortisone alone (0.5 mgm/ml drops)
produces a slight suppression; (c) both components applied together completely stop all angiogenesis; (d)ß-CD-14S
alone (1.0 mgm/ml) causes some stimulation.

Model and Mechanism

The "simplest model" appears satisfactorily applicable to
the results. The two steps assumed to be operative are
familiar to chemical and biochemical interactions, subject
to elementary formalisms:
The first step is the bimolecular equilibrium between the
active component A (steroid) and the carrier C
(saccharide), capable of forming the complex CA,

$$A + C \overset{K_c}{\Leftrightarrow} CA$$

$$K_c = \frac{CA}{A \times C} = \frac{CA}{(A_0 - CA)(C_0 - CA)} ,$$

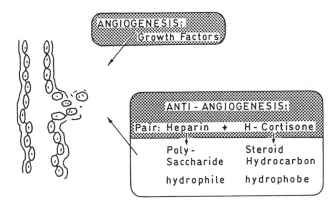

Figure 1. Angiogenesis and its Inhibition. Growth factors induce blood capillaries (left) to sprout; endothelial cells proliferate. Inhibition (anti-angiogenesis) is effected by the pair H-cortisone + heparin.

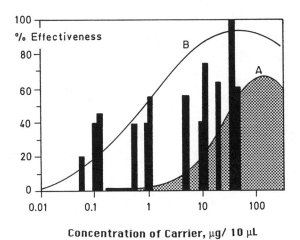

Concentration of Carrier, µg/ 10 µL

Figure 2. Anti-angiogenesis in the Chick Embryo Bioassay. Dose response for saccharide concentration (in µg in 10 µl sol.) with H-cortisone (60 µg in 10 µl sol.). For heparins the shaded area represents past experience; bars represent results with β-cyclodextrin tetradecasulfate. Curve A and B, see text.

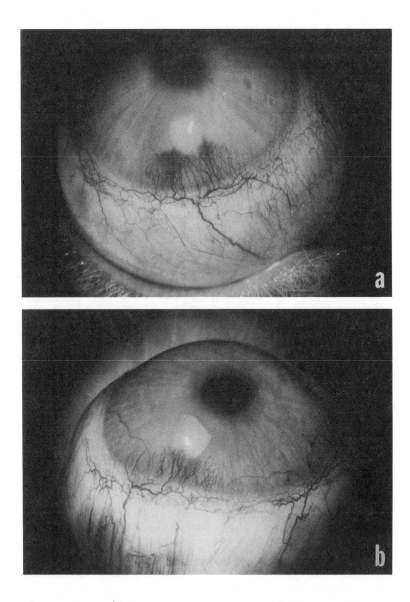

Figure 3. Inhibition of corneal vascularization by administration of H-cortisone (HC) with polysulfated β-cyclodextrin (CDS), by eye drops. (a) No intervention, (b) HC alone. *(Continued on next page.)*

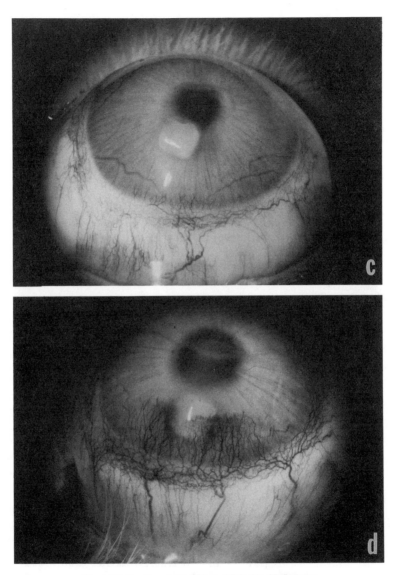

Figure 3. *Continued*. (c) HC + CDS, (d) CDS alone.

where each symbol represents molar concentration, and the
last relationship applies to initial concentrations A_0 and
C_0. From this follows that the fraction ε of carrier which
will be complexed as CA (will "carry" an A), $\varepsilon = CA/C_0$,
will be given by the relation

$$\varepsilon^2 - \varepsilon(1 + r + 1/C_0 K_c) + r = 0 , \qquad (1)$$

where r is the initially available molar ratio $r = A_0/C_0$.

The second step involves the surface (adsorption)
equilibrium between the carrier concentration in solution,
$C_t = C + CA$, and the concentration of sorbed carrier
species $C_t S$, on cellular surface sites (receptors) S:

$$C_t + S \overset{Ka}{\longleftrightarrow} C_t S ;$$

We assume that K_a, dependent mainly on polar bonding
substituents, will be similar in magnitude for the carrier,
whether or not it is associated with the hydrophobe. For
the case of excess carrier in solution, $c_t \approx c_0$, and
elementary sorption dynamics (Langmuir, or Michaelis-Menten
- depending on one's discipline) gives the fraction of
total available adsorption sites η as

$$\eta = C_0/(1/K_a + C_0) . \qquad (2)$$

The total effectiveness will be proportional to the
fraction of cellular adsorption sites occupied by complexed
(i.e. angiostat bearing) carriers,

$$\text{Effectiveness} \approx \varepsilon \times \eta.$$

In the CAM assay, the concentrations are in a dynamic
state, i.e. they are not in a steady state. They
ultimately dilute into an infinite volume. But the simple
model can be expected to give at least semi-quantitative
guidance for the early events, where the active volume is
limited by the diffusion distance.

Figure 4 shows the character of the relationships (1)
in A, and (2) in B, when plotted in terms of the variables
as they appear in the CAM assay; the abscissa is measured
in weight concentration of the saccharide.

To use the proper translation to molar quantities and
ratios, we accept that complexing of the steroid molecule
will involve a chain of about seven sugar units (as shown
by molecular model or the performance of the 'preformed'
cyclodextrins). Thus the effective molar saccharide unit
has a molecular weight of about 2500 (a seven-membered,
sulfated saccharide unit) even though the material used may
have anominal molecular weight many times greater
(heparin). This, in fact, is consistent with the

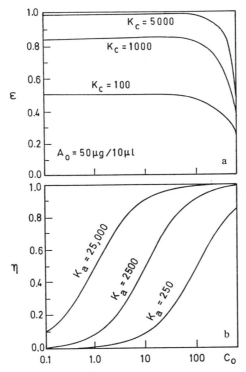

Figure 4. Basic Model Relationships for Interaction of the
Steroid/Saccharide/Cell System. The abscissa is the saccharide
concentration in μg/10μl as used in the Chick Embryo Assay (CAM).
a) ε is the fraction of saccharide complexed with (i.e. "carrying")
steroid; b) η is the fraction of available cell surface sites
occupied by saccharide (complexed or uncomplexed). Total
effectiveness is proportional to the product of ε and η.

observation that the optimal effects of all active heparin
materials, whether whole heparins or fragments (6), and now
with cyclodextrins, appear at similar *weight* concentrations
of the saccharide!

Figure 4A shows the course of the complexing phenomenon. Application of too large a saccharide concentration
can diminish its effectiveness. B shows the commanding
importance of the cell-saccharide binding equilibrium
constant K_a for obtaining effectiveness at very low
concentration. It is consistent with the need for sulfate
anions and their observed role in cellular adsorption (20).

In the experimental CAM plots pictured in Figure 2,
curve A, the envelop of past experience with the heparins,
fits well the curve obtained from (3), with $K_c \approx 1500$ M^{-1},
and a cell adsorption constant of $K_a \approx 800$ M^{-1}. The
performance of the ß-CD-14S material (curve B) represents
an increased adsorption equilibrium constant of $K_a \approx 50,000$
M^{-1}, i.e. nearly a hundred times greater. (The shift in K_a
is inversely proportional to the shift in concentration for
the half-way point in effectiveness, due to formula (2)).

We can estimate an additional binding energy which is
effective in the case of the cyclodextrin tetradecasulfate
(consisting of seven sugar units) as compared to a seven-
sugar fraction of the heparins from

$$\Delta E = RT \ln (K_{a,CD}/K_{a,heparin}) = RT \ln 100 = 2.9 \text{ kcal/mol}$$

This applies to a mole of seven-sugar-units and is a
reasonable, added contribution shared between some 14
sulfate bonds sterically and rigidly positioned on our
cyclic seven-unit oligomer.

Conclusions

The effective inhibition of angiogenesis by the co-action
of heparin and a steroid action depends sensitively on the
detailed structure of the angiostatic steroid (7,8,9). On
the other hand, there is no need for much of the chemical
complexity of heparin. The role of the saccharide appears
to be that of a carrier of the active steroid to the
endothelial cell surface. This action depends primarily on
two overall physical/chemical properties: 1. the capacity
to complex, in parts of its structure, a hydrophobic
portion of the steroid molecule, and 2. the ability to form
strongly interactive bonding with the cell surface protein.
An oligosaccharide structure of seven (generally about
five to eight) sugar units is sufficient to embrace a
steroid for complexing; a minimum number of anionic sulfate
groups alone suffice to provide sufficiently strong
saccharide-cell bonding.No other saccharide substituents
appear to be necessary.

A highly sulfated ß-cyclodextrin (the
tetradecasulfate) is a very effective, reliably

synthesizable heparin 'mimic' for angiogensis control, and is, in fact, effective at nearly one hundredth of the dose required of heparin. Its use in at least one application, the inhibition of corneal neovascularization, is demonstrated, while its wider therapeutic usefulness seems promising.

The advances in mechanistic understanding and in the discovery of the heparin-alternatives (J. Folkman, P.B. Weisz, M.M. Joullié and W.R. Ewing, Science, in publication;) were intimately coupled in this interdisciplinary effort. Further reports, on corneal angiogenesis (J. Folkman, W.W. Li, in preparation) and other studies related to this work are in preparation.

Acknowledgments

The authors acknowledge the contributions of M.M. Joullié and W.R. Ewing (University of Pennsylvania) in synthesizing the sulfated cyclodextrins, and William Li (Harvard Medical School) in developing the early data on corneal antiangiogenesis. We thank Racheal Levinson and Geraldine Jackson (Harvard) for help with the chick embryo assays, and Dr. Yasuhiko Kiwano (Takeda Chemical Industries,Ltd.) for synthesizing additional β-syclodextrin tetradecasulfate. We acknowledge the gifts of various cyclodextrin raw materials by American Maize Products Company and Chinoin Pharmaceutical Co. (Budapest). We thank the Mobil Foundation for the encouragement and financial seed support for interdisciplinary research.

Literature Cited

(1)   D. Ausprunk and J. Folkman, J. Microvasc. Res. 14, 53, 1977;

(2)   J. Folkman, "Tumor Angiogenesis", in "Cancer", F.F. Baker, Ed., Plenum Publ. Co., New York, Vol.3, 1976;

(3)   J. Folkman, in "Advances in Cancer Research,", G.Klein and S. Weinhouse, Eds. , 175 - 203, Academic Press, New York, 1985

(4)   J. Folkman and K. Klagsbrun, Science 235, 442, 1987;

(5)   J. Folkman, in "Important Advances in Oncology", 197-211, V.T. DevitaJr., S.Hellman and S..A. Rosenberg, Eds., J.B. Lippincott, Philadelphia,1985;

(6)   J. Folkman, R. LAnger, R. Linhardt, C. Haudenschild and S. Taylor, Science 221, 719-725, 1983;

(7)   R. Crum, S. Szabo and J. Folkman, Science 230, 1375-1378, 1985;

(8)   D.E. Ingber, J.A. Madri and J. Folkman, Endocrinol. 119, 1768-1775, 1986;

(9)   J. Folkman and D.E. Ingber, Ann. Surg. 206, 374-384, 1987;

(10)   J. Folkman, Cancer Res. 46, 467-473, 1986;

(11)   U. Lindahl, M. Hook, GH.Backstrom, I. Jacobsson, J.
        Riesenfeld, A. Malstrum, L. Roden and D.S. Feingole,
        Fed. Proc. 36, 19-23, 1977; b) T.C.Laurent, A.
        Tengblad, L. Thunberg, M.Hook and U. Lindahl,
        Biochem. J. 175, 691-701, 1978; c) R.J. Linhardt, A.
        Grant, C.L. Cooney and R. Langer, J. Biol. Chem. 257,
        7310-7313, 1982;
(12)   J. Choay, M. Petitou, J. Lormeau, P. Sinay, B. Casu
        and G. Gatt, Biochem. Biophys. Res. Comm. 116, 492-
        493, 1983;
(13)   C.A.A. van Boeckel, T. Beetz and S.F. van Aelst,
        Tetrahedron Letters 29, 803-806, 1988;
(14)   J. Sejtli, "Cyclodextrins and their Inclusion
        Complexes", Akademiai Kiado, Budapest, 1982;
(15)   M.L. Bender and M. Komiyama, "Cyclodextrin
        Chemistry", Springer-Verlag, Berlin, 1978;
(16)   W. Saenger "Structural Aspects of Cyclodextrins and
        their Inclusion Complextes", in "Inclusion
        Compounds", Vol.2, J.L. Atwood, J.E.D. Davies and
        D.D. McNicol, Eds. Academic Press, New York, 1984;
(17)   K. Uekama, T. Fujinaga, F. Hirayama, M. Otagiri, and
        Y. Yamasaki, Int. J. Pharmaceutics 10, 1, 1982;
(18)   E.D.T. Atkins, I.A. Nieduszynski and A.A. Horner,
        Biochem. J. 143, 251, 1974;
(19)   S.P. Perlin, Fed. Proc. 36, 101, 1977;
(20)   T. Barzu, P. Mohlo, J.L.M.L. Petitou, J.P. Caen,
        Biochem. Biophys. Acta 845, 196, 1985;
(21)   G. Grayson, W.W. Li, P.A.D'Amore and J. Folkman,
        Invest. Ophthamol.Vis. Sci. 29, 49a, 1988;

RECEIVED January 25, 1989

STRUCTURE–FUNCTION RELATIONSHIPS

Chapter 4

Crystallography and Site-Directed Mutagenesis of Two Isomerases

Thomas C. Alber[1], Robert C. Davenport, Jr.[2], Gregory K. Farber,
D. Ann Giammona[3], Arthur M. Glasfeld, William D. Horrocks[4],
Masaharu Kanaoka, Elias Lolis, Gregory A. Petsko[5],
Dagmar Ringe, and Gerard Tiraby[6]

Department of Chemistry, Massachusetts Institute of Technology,
Cambridge, MA 02139

The Ferrari of Enzymes vs. the Fiat of Enzymes
in a Drag Race for Protein Engineering

Suppose you want to travel from Stuttgart to Munich on the
Autobahn. The distance is about 200 km, the road is excellent and
there are no speed limits. The journey could be made in one hour
if one were driving a Ferrari Testarossa, the fastest production
automobile in the world. Its top speed of over 180 mph allows one
to cruise comfortably at 125 mph, which is over 200 km/hr. In
addition, the Ferrari is beautiful: it has a chassis designed by
the great Italian carrozeria Sergio Pinninfarina, and its 12
cylinder engine is the product of decades of development from the
original superb designs of Enzo Ferrari himself.

Of course, if you can't afford a Ferrari (one costs about as
much as some medium-field NMR spectrometers), you could drive a
Fiat. Some of the better Fiats were also designed by the
Pinninfarina organization, and since Fiat owns Ferrari now anyway,
one might hope that some of the Ferrari engineering would rub off.
But you get what you pay for. A Fiat Spyder costs 1/10th of what a
Ferrari costs, it has a four-cylinder engine, and its top speed is
under 100 mph. The trip from Stuttgart to Munich would take twice
as long.

Now suppose you want to get from an aldehyde to a ketone.
That is a race-course called isomerization (Figure 1), and it is
the simplest reaction in all of chemistry. One proton moves from

[1]Current address: Departments of Biochemistry and Chemistry, University of Utah, Salt Lake
City, UT 84112
[2]Current address: Department of Biology, Massachusetts Institute of Technology, Cambridge,
MA 02139
[3]Current address: Bolt, Beranek, and Newman, Cambridge, MA 02138
[4]Current address: Department of Chemistry, Pennsylvania State University, University Park,
PA 16802
[5]Corresponding author
[6]Current address: Laboratoire de Microbiologie et Génétique Appliquées, Université Paul-
Sabatier, Toulouse 31062, France

0097–6156/89/0392–0034$06.00/0
© 1989 American Chemical Society

one carbon atom to the adjacent one, a distance of 1.5 Å. You can
travel that distance via the enzyme triose phosphate isomerase
(Figure 2), and you will cover it in about $1/10,000^{th}$ of a second.
Or you can travel it via the enzyme glucose isomerase (Figure 3),
and it will take you more than a second.

Triose phosphate isomerase is a Ferrari, glucose isomerase is
not. Just as one can understand the difference between a Ferrari
and a Fiat in terms of their designs, it should be possible to
understand the difference between triose phosphate isomerase (TIM)
and glucose isomerase (GI) in terms of their structures and
chemical mechanisms. We have set out to do exactly that, using the
techniques of protein engineering. We have applied X-ray
crystallography and site-directed mutagenesis to both enzymes and
have discovered some of the reasons why their catalytic rates are
so different. This has in turn led us to ask the question whether
we might be able to alter GI so that it approaches the speed of
TIM.

Glucose isomerase is one of the most important industrial
enzymes. All of the high-fructose corn syrup used to sweeten soft-
drinks, candy-bars, and most other foods is made using glucose
isomerase. A reengineered GI that had the catalytic rate of TIM
would not only be interesting, it might be very profitable. In any
case, the fact that there are two enzymes that run the same course
with vastly different speeds provides the enzymologist with a
splendid opportunity to understand the origins of the catalytic
potency of enzymes.

The First Lap: The Kinetic Parameters

Triose phosphate isomerase enzyme catalyses interconversion of the
3-carbon triose phosphate dihydroxyacetone phosphate (DHAP) and
D-glyceraldehyde-3-phosphate (D-GAP). The reaction is just the
transfer of the pro-R hydrogen from carbon 1 of DHAP
stereospecifically to carbon 2 to form the D-isomer of GAP (Figure
2). Although the equilibrium constant on the enzyme is not known,
Keq for the overall reaction is 300 to 1 in favour of DHAP. The
large magnitude of this number arises from the combination of an
apparent Keq of 22 with a hydration equilibrium of 29 for the
hydrated and unhydrated forms of D-GAP (Trentham *et al.*, 1969); only
the unhydrated forms of the triose phosphates are substrates for or
even bind to the isomerase (Webb *et al.*, 1977).

The simplicity of the TIM reaction allowed Albery and Knowles
and their coworkers to determine the complete free energy profile
of the catalytic process (summarized in Albery and Knowles, 1976a).
These data showed that the highest free energy transition state was
that for the diffusion-limited bimolecular association of GAP with
the enzyme.

The free energy profile showed that TIM has reached
evolutionary perfection as a catalyst (for details see Albery and
Knowles, 1976b). In addition, the availability of the complete
free energy profile for the TIM-catalysed reaction meant that the
mechanism could be understood in great detail. In particular, if a
mutant made by site-directed mutagenesis caused a major change in

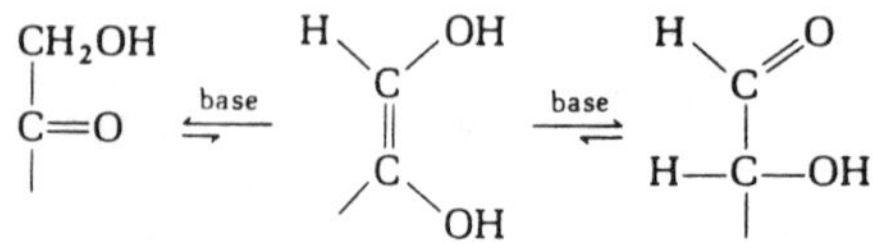

Figure 1.   The isomerization of a ketone to an aldehyde.
The reaction in aqueous solution is base-catalysed and is
thought to proceed through a cis-enediol intermediate.

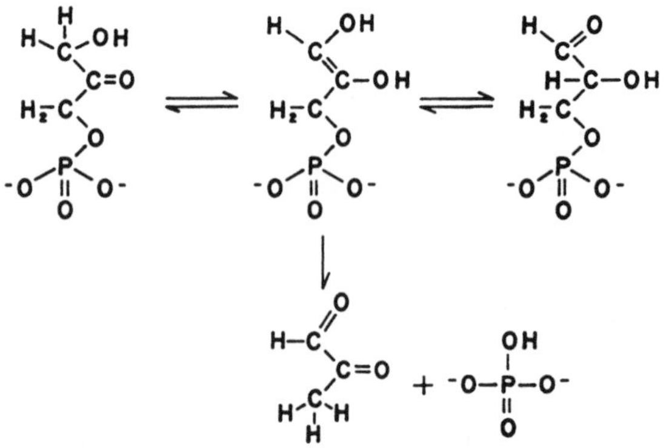

Figure 2.   The isomerization reaction catalysed by
triosephosphate isomerase.   The enzyme takes the ketone
dihydroxyacetone phosphate to the aldehyde D-glyceraldehyde-
3-phosphate.   Evidence for an enediol intermediate comes in
part from the side-reaction that also occurs: the enzyme
produces methyl glyoxal and inorganic phosphate.

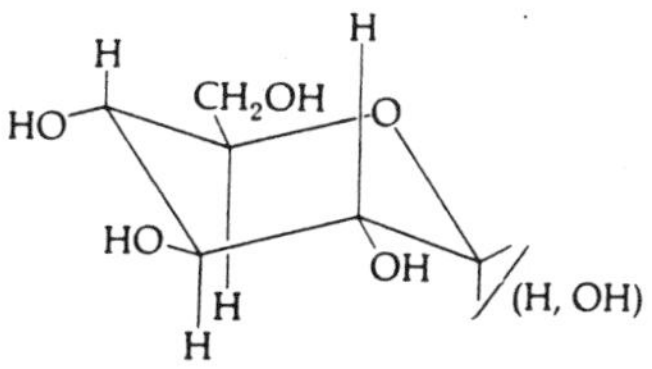

α- or β-D-Glucose
(α- or β-D-Glucopyranose)

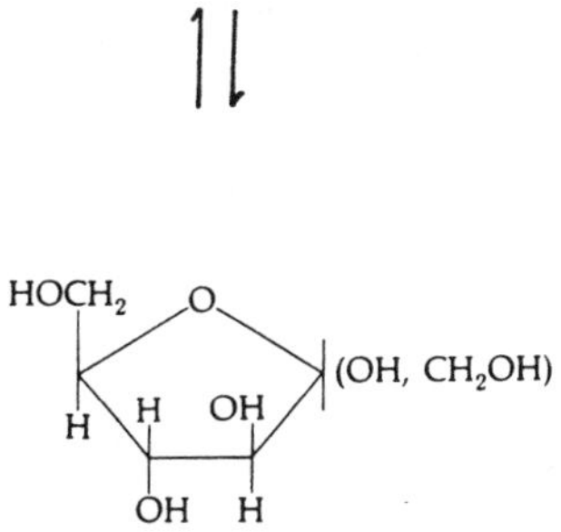

α- or β-D-Fructose
(α- or β-D-Fructofuranose)

Figure 3. The reaction catalysed by glucose isomerase. The enzyme takes the ketone fructose to the aldehyde glucose. The sugars exist in ring forms in solution, and there are two anomers for each. There is good evidence that glucose isomerase only acts on the alpha anomers.

binding or in the rate of catalysis, the free energy profile of
that mutant could be determined, and the specific microscopic
step(s) that were altered by the mutation could be identified.
Richard (1984) has determined that TIM accelerates the rate of
GAP to DHAP isomerization by almost 10 orders of magnitude over the
rate enhancement provided by a simple base catalyst such as the
acetate ion. Moreover, as indicated by the free energy profile,
the enzymatic reaction rate is very fast in physical-chemical
terms. kcat/Km (the pseudo first-order rate constant for the
reaction of enzyme with substrate) in the thermodynamically
favourable direction GAP to DHAP is 400,000,000 $M^{-1}s^{-1}$, which is
close to the expected diffusion-controlled limit. A Ferrari
indeed!
Glucose isomerase is also known in the biochemical literature
as xylose isomerase, and there is some evidence that xylose is the
physiological substrate. Nevertheless, we are concerned in this
paper with its action on glucose, and so those are the kinetic
values we shall report. (Even though the enzyme is more efficient
with xylose, the numbers are not very different from those for
glucose; it is like the difference in running your Fiat on high-
test vs. regular gasoline. It is still a Fiat.) The reaction is
the transformation of the alpha-anomer of glucose into the alpha-
anomer of fructose; there is NMR evidence that the beta-anomers,
even though predominant in solution, do not bind to the enzyme.
The turnover number for glucose at optimum pH is about 1 per
second, and the substrate is not very tightly bound. kcat/Km is
over 6 orders of magnitude lower than that for TIM, far from the
diffusion-controlled limit. Unlike TIM, the catalytic rate of GI
is not governed by a purely physical step. Chemistry is rate-
determining.
There are two complications with this comparison. Glucose
isomerase requires a divalent metal ion for catalysis, whereas TIM
uses no metals or cofactors. The physiological metal for GI is
thought to be magnesium. The second complication arises from the
different structural characteristics of the two substrates. DHAP
and GAP are open-chain sugars and have charged phosphate groups
available for binding, while glucose and fructose, which lack these
convenient "handles", exist chiefly in the closed form. Yet,
isomerization requires that the ring be open, so GI actually has a
more complex problem to face than it would appear on first
analysis.

The Second Lap: The Assumed Basic Chemical Mechanism

Elegant isotope labelling studies by Rose and coworkers (Rieder and
Rose, 1959; Rose, 1962) established the general mechanistic
features of the TIM reaction. Proton transfer is mediated by a
single enzymatic base, and the reaction proceeds via an
intermediate that is either a *cis* enediol phosphate (Figure 2) or
one of the two possible symmetrical enediolates. The evidence for
enzyme-mediated proton transfer is the catalysis by the enzyme of
loss of radioactive label from substrate to solvent water, or of
exchange-in of label from deuterated or tritiated water to

substrate. Chemical labelling by Offord, Waley, Knowles, and Hartmann (e.g., Waley *et al.*, 1970) has identified the base as the side-chain carboxylate of glutamic acid 165.

Knowles has pointed out that the pKa of the transferred hydrogen could be lowered by polarization of the adjacent carbonyl group (Webb and Knowles, 1974). Electron withdrawal to the oxygen atom would weaken the carbon-hydrogen bond and promote enolization. Two possible polarization mechanisms suggest themselves: hydrogen bonding to the carbonyl oxygen by a neutral donor, and electrostatic interaction by a cation, which may or may not also directly hydrogen-bond. Here at once a role for the magnesium ion in glucose isomerase suggests itself: the positive charge on the metal could act as an electrophile and facilitate base attack at C1 of the substrate. Use of highly directional coordination to a metal cation has the advantage of providing electrostatic stabilization for incipient negative charge development on the carbonyl oxygen, which is expected to occur in the endiolate-like transition state. These considerations apply whichever direction the reaction runs. And indeed, for TIM, there is direct evidence for polarization of the substrate carbonyl from infra red spectroscopy (Belasco and Knowles, 1980), although the relevant electrophile in the TIM case must be an amino acid.

There is only one problem with this scenario: it may be wrong for glucose isomerase. When the critical experiment of looking for exchange-in of radioactivity from solvent to product is done for this enzyme, no exchange is seen (Rose, 1981). The same holds for exchange-out of label from substrate into water: it does not occur for this enzyme. Thus, there is no direct evidence for the participation of an enzymic base, or for the existance of an enediol-like intermediate.

The Third Lap: The Structures of the Enzymes

Triose phosphate isomerase is a homodimer with an extensive, mostly hydrophobic subunit interface. Monomers have a strikingly symmetrical beta/alpha folding pattern that has come to be termed the "TIM barrel". The core of the monomer consists of eight strands of parallel twisted beta-pleated sheet, wrapped around the surface of an imaginary cylinder. Each strand is connected to the next, in the expected right-handed cross-over manner (Richardson, 1981), by one (or occasionally two) alpha helical segment. To a first approximation, the structure can be represented as (beta,alpha) x 8 (Figure 4). The connections between sheet and helix are not smooth, and short segments of polypeptide normally bridge the two regular secondary structure elements. In some cases, these segments are classical beta-turns, but often they are irregular in conformation and are simply termed "loops". Two of them are quite long (>7 residues) and deserve special attention. Residues 72 to 79 protrude from the surface of the monomer but are completely buried in the dimer; they form an interdigitating loop that leaves one monomer, forms extensive contacts with a pocket on the other monomer, and then returns (Figure 4). Although this loop does not generate all of the intersubunit contacts, it does form

most of them. The other long loop is comprised of residues 168 to
177. This loop sticks out into the solvent. Curiously, the amino
acid sequence of this loop is highly conserved throughout the
evolutionary history of the enzyme, from bacteria to people. Yet,
the apex of the loop is about 10 Å from the active site glutamate
165 and is even farther from the subunit interface, the only other
two regions of high amino acid sequence conservation in TIM (Alber
and Kawasaki, 1982), so it is hard to see immediately what its
function is.

The active site of TIM is a pocket containing Glu 165. This
pocket is located near the centre of the circular-like structure
shown in Figure 4, at the C-terminal end of the beta-sheet
cylinder, the end where all of the alpha helical segments begin.
Hol *et al.* (1978) have pointed out that the dipole moment of the
peptide bond gives rise to an appreciable macro dipole for an alpha
helix. The positive end of the helix dipole is the amino terminal
end, so the TIM active site is at the focus of the positive
electrostatic potential produced by the helices.

More than a dozen enzymes have now been found to have domains
that possess the characteristic TIM-barrel. Some of the others are
pyruvate kinase, KDPG aldolase, glycolate oxidase, Taka amylase,
muconate lactonizing enzyme, ribulose *bis*-phosphate carboxylase
oxygenase, tryptophan synthase alpha subunit (C. Hyde, personal
communication), enolase, muscle aldolase, flavocytochrome b2,
trimethylamine dehydrogenase, alpha amylase, and the two components
of the bifunctional enzyme phosphoribosyl-anthranilate
isomerase/indole-3-glycerolphosphate synthase. The TIM fold is the
most common structural motif in biochemistry, at least so far. And
glucose isomerase has it too (Figure 5). The GI polypeptide chain
fold is strikingly similar to that of TIM, with two exceptions.
The loop from residues 168-177 is missing in GI, and the
intersubunit loop has been replaced by a long C-terminal domain
that wraps around an adjacent subunit to form a dimer. Thus, the
monomer of GI is bigger than that of TIM (40,000 MW), and the dimer
interface is completely different. Glucose isomerase has a much
larger intersubunit contact region; in fact, it seems to be the
largest hydrophobic monomer-monomer interface yet observed. The
active site of GI is a deep pocket containing histidine 219,
glutamic acid 180, and aspartic acid 286. Any of these residues
could serve as the catalytic base in an enediol-type mechanism,
although one might expect that at least one of the two carboxylates
would be needed to bind the metal. Unfortunately, the crystal
structure of the native enzyme at pH 7 does not reveal which one,
for no metal ion is observed, even in the presence of high
concentrations of cobalt or magnesium. In the absence of
substrate, the cation is not tightly bound by Streptomyces
olivochromogenes GI.

The Fourth Lap: The Structures of the Enzyme-Substrate Complexes

The wonderful thing about both GI and TIM, from a structural
enzymologist's point of view, is that for these enzymes it is
actually possible to determine the structure of the productive

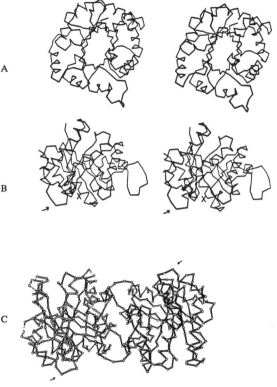

Figure 4. The structure of triose phosphate isomerase. **A)** Stereo view of one monomer down the axis of the eight-stranded alpha-beta barrell. **B)** Stereo view orthogonal to the first view. **C)** A view of one dimer looking down the two-fold axis relating each subunit. In both **B)** and **C)** the loop that moves when substrate binds is indicated by an arrow.

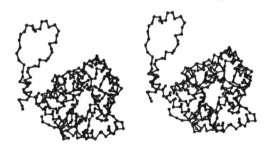

Figure 5. The structure of glucose isomerase. This is a stereo view of one subunit down the axis of the eight-stranded alpha-beta barrell.

enzyme-substrate complex by X-ray crystallography. That is not
possible for most enzymes. For a hydrolase, for example, an
attempt to do the crystal structure of a Michaelis complex at room
temperature by conventional crystallography would be futile:
substrate could be diffused into the solvent-filled channels in the
crystal, but it would rapidly be hydrolysed to products, which
would diffuse away (unless product binding was tight). Averaged
over the time required for data collection (days to a week or more)
the occupancy of the ES complex would be negligable. But TIM and
GI catalyse a simple single- substrate/single-product
equilibration: if substrate is soaked into the crystal, it will be
converted to product, but product is just the substrate for the
back reaction. So the crystalline enzyme system will settle to
equilibrium, and as long as the substrate concentration in the
mother liquor around the crystal is kept in excess of Km, the
thermodynamically-favoured complex will dominate what is observed
in the crystal. The free energy profile of Albery and Knowles
(1976a) indicates that, for TIM, the predominant form will be the
enzyme-DHAP complex. We do not have these data for the GI
reaction, so we must expect that at equilibrium we could see an
equally-occupied mixture of E-glucose and E-fructose. Whether the
resulting averaged structure could be interpretable will depend on
the resolution of the data as well as the similarity of the two
complexes conformationally. We prepared this complex
(TIM-DHAP) by diffusing 10 mM DHAP into a crystal of TIM mounted in
a flow cell (Petsko, 1985) on the diffractometer at -15C. Data
were collected to 3.5 Å resolution and a difference electron
density map was calculated using native amplitudes and phases
(Alber et al., 1981). The map showed the substrate bound in the
pocket containing Glu 165. The phosphate group, clearly identified
by its high electron density, lay nearest the solvent. However,
most dramatic was a large difference density feature indicating a
conformational change in the conserved loop, residues 168-177.
This loop had moved over 6 Å through space to fold down like a
giant flap or lid onto the phosphate end of the substrate, thus
closing off the active site (Figure 4).

This conformational change on substrate binding is consistent
with the fact that product release is rate-limiting for TIM: the
loop must move back out of the way to allow GAP to escape from the
active site pocket. If there is a disorder-to-order transition as
well, it may contribute directly to catalysis by raising the free
energy of the enzyme-substrate complex (Alber, 1981). We have
explored the role of the flexible loop by site-directed
mutagenesis. The yeast TPI gene was cloned and sequenced by Alber
and Kawasaki (1982), and has been expressed in E. coli (Petsko et
al., 1984; Davenport, 1985). Site-directed mutagenesis was carried
out by the two-primer oligonucleotide method of Zoller and Smith
(1983) using single-stranded bacteriophage M13 as a vector. We
elected to change Thr 172, which is the side-chain in the loop
nearest the contact point between the loop and the phosphate group
of the substrate, to aspartic acid on the assumption that charge
repulsion between the Asp carboxylate and substrate phosphate would
prevent closure of the loop. We also deleted the central five

residues of the loop genetically so that there would no longer be a flap to close over the substrate. We expected that both of these mutants of TIM would still catalyse isomerization but show increased methyl glyoxal production. Preliminary kinetic analysis of both mutants from crude E. coli extract shows that kcat/Km for the direction GAP to DHAP is reduced by approximately tenfold over that for the wild-type enzyme. Assuming that closure has indeed been prevented, the loop would appear to play a role in orienting as well as binding the substrate. We have not yet quantitated methyl glyoxal production for either mutant.

DHAP is bound in an extended conformation. No positively-charged residues make contact with the phosphate; it is held in place by hydrogen bonds from several glycine-containing loops, particularly 209-212 and 232-234. Main-chain hydrogen bonding to phosphate is a common mode of binding in proteins, especially those that do not carry out chemistry on the phosphate group (for an example, see Smith *et al.*, 1983). We presume that the negative charge on the phosphate is compensated by the positive helix dipoles that are oriented towards the active site. The catalytic sub-site consists of Glu 165, Cys 126, His 95, Ser 96, Glu 97, Asn 10, and Lys 12. Only Glu 165 and Cys 126 are on the side of the substrate where proton transfer occurs. The remainder of the residues interact with the substrate (or each other) on the carbonyl side of the sugar. The carboxylate group of Glu 165 is perfectly positioned for nucleophilic abstraction of the pro-R proton from C1 of DHAP and subsequent direct transfer to C-2. To test the importance of the position of this residue, Straus, *et al.* (1985) have carried out site-directed mutagenesis of the cloned gene for chicken TIM, and changed Glu 165 to Asp. The fundamental kinetic parameters kcat and Km have been determined in both directions for this mutant, as has the complete free energy profile (Raines *et al.*, 1986). Km is only slightly affected, but kcat is reduced by several orders of magnitude in both the forward and reverse directions. The free energy profile for the mutant shows that only the transition-state free energies have been seriously altered. Glu 165 to Asp substitution has slowed each of the enolization steps by a factor of about one thousand. We undertook to calculate the structure of the mutant enzyme in its complex with DHAP. Our starting point was the coordinate set for wild-type yeast TIM with substrate bound. The method of structure prediction was the minimum perturbation approach developed by Karplus and coworkers (Shih *et al.*, 1985). We replaced Glu 165 by Asp in the ES complex, using computer graphics to position the aspartate side-chain. We then cranked the two side-chain torsion angles of the new Asp 165 through all possible values in increments, keeping the rest of the protein fixed. At each point in the torsion angle scan, the interaction potential energy between Asp 165 and the surrounding protein atoms was computed. The resulting energy map was inspected for low energy regions and each of these low energy structures was then subjected to full energy minimization, with all atoms in a 7 Å sphere about the alpha carbon of the mutant residue allowed to move freely, while atoms outside this sphere were restrained with harmonic restraints. An adapted-basis Newton

Raphson minimizer was used. A variation of this procedure has been
used with success by Snow and Amzel (1986) to model immunoglobulin
variable regions.

The minimum perturbation approach yielded two minima separated
by large energy barriers. One minimum energy structure places the
side-chain carboxylate oxygens of Asp 165 over 5 Å from the nearest
substrate atom, an impossible position for catalysis. The other
structure, which is the lowest energy structure found in the
calculation, has one carboxylate oxygen 2.9 Å from C1 of DHAP, just
as observed in the wild-type TIM-DHAP crystal structure. But
although the distance of Asp 165 to the substrate in this model is
the same as the distance of the oxygen of Glu 165 to DHAP in the
wild-type ES complex, the orientation of the carboxylate group is
quite different in the mutant. Replacement of glu by asp is not a
structurally conservative mutation: it moves the bulky carboxylate
group closer to the surface of the protein. In the TIM active
site, this movement causes the carboxylate to collide with the
backbone of the protein around Gly 209. To relieve this steric
crowding the carboxylate must rotate (this is the minimum energy
position found), and when it does it can only reach the substrate
in a conformation in which the outer (anti) orbital of the oxygen
atom acts as the proton acceptor (Figure 6). In the wild-type TIM-
DHAP structure, where the longer side-chain of glutamate pushes the
carboxylate beyond the 209 loop, the syn orbital (the orbital on
the same side of the C-O bond as the C=O bond) is the proton
acceptor. Gandour (1981) has pointed out that the anti orbital is
10,000-fold less basic than the syn orbital. If that equilibrium
difference is used in the Bronsted formula together with a beta of
about 0.7, a rate reduction of 1,000-fold for proton transfer is
calculated for the mutant enzyme. This is the same value as
observed experimentally.

Although these calculations do not establish that the
difference in orbital usage is responsible for the reduced activity
of the Asp 165 mutant, they do provide a testable hypothesis. The
three-dimensional structure of the mutant enzyme, complexed with
substrate, will indicate whether the anti orbital is in fact the
only one available for proton transfer.

There are three residues that are in contact with the carbonyl
and hydroxyl oxygen atoms of the triose phosphates. One of these,
which is uncharged and may be purely involved in substrate binding,
is Asn 10. Mutation of this residue to valine or alanine would be
of interest. The other two residues may have more complex roles.
Lys 12 is positively charged at neutral pH and is close to the C2
oxygen of the substrate. We speculate that its role may be to
stabilize the transition state by charge-charge interaction. A
mutant TIM with glutamine replacing the lysine has been made but
not yet characterized: in crude cell extract it shows little or no
TIM activity. The positive charge on Lys 12 will also affect the
oxygen at C1, since electrostatic interactions remain strong at
reasonably long distances, and the dielectric of the active site
will be very low when the flexible loop is in the closed position,
so there should be little screening. His 95 is the most complex of
the putative electrophiles. It is hydrogen-bonded to the C1

A

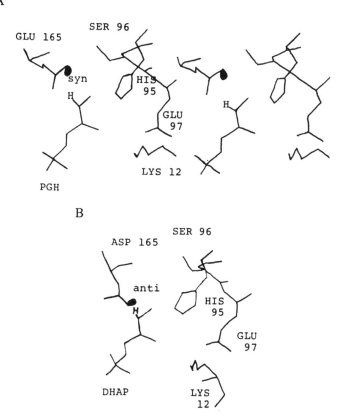

Figure 6. **A)** The active site of TIM in the crystallographically determined enzyme-substrate complex. Some of the important catalytic residues are indicated. Note that the active-site base, Glu 165, is positioned to use its more basic syn orbital for proton abstraction. **B)** The active site of TIM mutant E165D in the model-built enzyme-substrate complex. Note that the active-site base, Asp 165, is positioned to use its less basic anti orbital for proton abstraction.

substrate oxygen through its epsilon NH. If it has the normal
histidine pKa of about 6, it could function as an acid, protonating
the substrate carbonyl to form the cis-enediol intermediate (if His
95 does not do this, the proton needed to form the enediol may come
from water, or the intermediate may always be the charged
enediolate). The crystal structure is ambiguous on this point.
Protein crystallography cannot ordinarily detect protons, so the
ionization state of the histidine must be inferred from its
environment and interactions. In the refined native crystal
structures of yeast and chicken TIM, His 95 appears to be hydrogen-
bonded through its delta nitrogen to the main-chain -NH of residue
97 at the beginning of a short, irregular alpha helix. Since the
backbone amide must be protonated, the structure suggests that the
delta nitrogen of the histidine is unprotonated. Therefore, the
epsilon nitrogen must carry the proton, and the histidine, by this
analysis, is neutral. If it is, its two possible roles are as an
acid (though this is unlikely as on deprotonaton the histidine
would become anionic) or, more likely, purely as an electrophile.
Electrophilic catalysis, could be accomplished solely by the neutral
histidine hydrogen-bonding to the substrate oxygen at C1, but it is
also possible that the histidine could act as a relay for the
positive dipole of the short irregular helix. In that case, it
would also have a through-space electrostatic role.
        We have investigated the function of this residue by replacing
it with a side-chain that is uncharged and incapable of functioning
as an acid, namely, glutamine (Davenport, 1985; Nickbarg et al.,
1988). Glutamine is a better choice than asparagine because it
retains hydrogen bonding at a position comparable to that of the
epsilon nitrogen. If only hydrogen bonding to the substrate were
important, the glutamine mutant should be fully active. If acid
behavior is essential for catalysis, glutamine 95 would inactivate
the enzyme. If a through-space electrostatic affect is occuring at
this position, the mutant TIM might have reduced activity.
        His 95 to Gln TIM is an active enzyme. Kinetic measurements
indicate that Km is unchanged, but kcat in both directions is
reduced by a factor of about 200. This observation is in keeping
with the hypothesis that His 95 is not essential as an acid but
does act to stabilize the transition state electrostatically.
Support for this view comes from inhibition studies of the mutant
enzyme: simple competitive inhibitors are bound equally tightly by
wild-type TIM and the H95Q mutant, but the transition-state analog
inhibitor PGH binds to the mutant over 50-fold less well than to
the wild-type enzyme (Nickbarg et al., 1988). Unfortunately, label
exchange-in and exchange-out experiments, carried out by Elliot
Nickbarg and Jeremy Knowles at Harvard to determine the free-energy
profile of this mutant, show that it has undergone a subtle change
in mechanism. The data are complex, but the best interpretation of
them seems to be that, in the mutant enzyme, Glu 165 abstracts the
proton from C1 and then protonates the C2 carbonyl oxygen to form
the enediol intermediate (Nickbarg et al., 1988). It then abstracts
a proton from the C1 hydroxyl and delivers it to the C2 carbon to
form product! These data could be interpreted to indicate that
there must be direct proton donation to the substrate oxygen to

form the intermediate, and that His 95 normally fills that role. Alternatively, there could have been a conformational change in the mutant that allowed this two-base pathway to become favoured for steric reasons. Mutating His 95 has proven that an acidic residue is not necessary at that position, but it has not settled the question of the actual protonation state and role of His 95 in the normal enzyme. There is a caveat for all protein engineering in this result: it is dangerous to assume that simple mutations leave the catalytic mechanism unchanged.

Our findings on TIM, though incomplete, are consistent with the following picture:

1. The TIM-catalysed isomerization of DHAP to GAP proceeds via base-catalysed proton abstraction and formation of an enzyme-bound enediol or diolate intermediate. The organic chemistry analog of this reaction is the Lobry de Bruyn-Alberda van Ekenstein transformation, exemplified by the production of fructose when glucose is heated in base.

2. Desolvation of the active site maximizes all electrostatic effects by reducing the effective dielectric.

3. Glu 165 acts as the catalytic base. Steric desolvation of the active site increases the pKa of Glu 165 when substrate binds. The structure of the enzyme orients the carboxylate group so that proton abstraction is carried out by the more basic syn orbital.

4. The likely catalytic electrophiles are Asn 10, Lys 12 and His 95.

5. Acid catalysis by His 95 is not essential for isomerization.

6. Rather than a unique electrophile for each substrate oxygen, the enzyme seems to provide a positive electrostatic potential by means of a combination of side-chains and alpha helix dipoles. Thus, it is more accurate to speak of a catalytic surface than a specific site for electrophilic catalysis.

7. Substrate specificity is chiefly provided by helical dipole and backbone hydrogen bonding to the phosphate group.

8. The active site of triose phosphate isomerase is complementary, in both stereochemistry and charge configuration, to the transition state of the reaction it catalyses. This fact, combined with very efficient general base catalysis, is largely responsible for the high efficiency of TIM.

Glucose isomerase has not yet been investigated in anything like the same detail. In particular, the results from molecular biology are just beginning to come in. However, structural studies have been carried out on several enzyme-substrate complexes, and

although their results are still only at medium resolution, the
preliminary indications are that the GI mechanism is much more
complex.

Since GI is a single-substrate/single-product enzyme, the
strcuture of the GI-glucose-Mg adduct can be observed directly.
There are two alternative experimental methods: just soaking the
crystal in substrate solutions prior to mounting and data
collection, or continuously flowing substrate and metal over the
crystal. The former is an equilibrium experiment, but the latter
is a kinetic one. Continuous flow of glucose might be expected to
reveal the structure of the species that accumulates prior to the
rate-determining step of the reaction. Unfortunately, since the
reaction has not been dissected mechanistically, we have no idea
what that step is.

The crystal structure of the GI-glucose-Mg complex under
continuous flow conditions has been determined at 3 Å resolution.
The position of the bound metal atom has been confirmed by a
separate experiment in which the heavier cation manganese was
substituted for magnesium. The enzyme-substrate complex is a
glucose-metal-enzyme bridged system, with both protein and sugar
providing ligands to the magnesium atom. This result explains why
magnesium binds so weakly in the absence of substrate. The active
site glutamate and aspartate residues are both coordinated to the
metal, making them unavailable to serve as the catalytic base.
Glucose is bound in a compact manner, although at 3 Å resolution it
is impossible to determine if the ring has been opened. Histidine
286 is not positioned to function as the base in proton
abstraction: it appears to be on the wrong side of the sugar.
There are no other residues in the vicinity that can serve to
abstract the proton, and no electrophilic groups positioned for
polarization of the oxygens.

The mystery deepened when we examined the structure of the
enzyme-glucose complex in the absence of metals. The enzyme is
known to be catalytically inactive under these conditions. This
experiment was done in an equilibrium fashion, that is, by soaking
the demetallized GI crystal in a solution of glucose and then
mounting it in a sealed quartz capillary tube for data collection.
The 3 Å resolution structure of the complex revealed that the sugar
ring had been opened and the substrate was bound in a fully-
extended conformation. This result seemed to confirm an earlier
observation by one of us (G.K.F.), together with Mary F. Roberts of
Boston College, that the enzyme was able to catalyse the opening of
the ring. There was still no obvious candidate for a proton-
transfer base in this new conformation.

The mechanistic picture most consistent with these preliminary
data is a multi-step sequence in which sugar and metal bind to the
enzyme with the sugar in a closed, ring form coordinated to
magnesium via its C1 and C2 oxygen atoms. An enzymic base,
probably the imidazole side-chain of His 286, then catalyses the

opening of the ring. Subsequent steps are less clear structurally, but it is possible that a large rearrangement of the sugar then takes place, with an extended sugar conformation then binding, with metal, in the active site. In this scheme, the rate-limiting step is probably ring opening, as that would explain why the closed form was observed in the flow-cell experiment.

How is the actual isomerization catalysed? Failure to observe exchange-in or exchange-out of label, combined with the lack of an obvious basic amino acid side-chain in the right position, forces us to consider the possibility that the mechanism is fundamentally different from that of TIM. To return to the possibly overworked automotive analogy, the difference in top speed between the Ferrari and the Fiat is chiefly due to the differences in their engines, but both are still internal combustion engines of the same general principles. The mechanistic differences between GI and TIM appear to be more fundamental than that. It is almost as though one looked under the hood of one of the automobiles and saw, not an internal combustion engine at all, but a pair of squirrels in a cage. A race between such a car and a Ferrari would be unsporting indeed. TIM and GI may differ in a similarly radical way: the isomerization step of GI may not be a base-catalysed proton transfer via an enediol. It may be unfair to compare the speed of the two enzymes because GI may not be doing the same chemistry after all.

What chemistry is it doing? There is one other obvious mechanism for interconversion of a ketone and an aldehyde, a hydride transfer pathway. Such a mechanism would not lead to any exchange, since there is no hydride in solution to exchange with. Direct hydride transfer from C1 to C2 would require no enzymic base and would produce no intermediate. Direct hydride transfer would explain the requirement for a metal ion: in addition to providing binding for the sugar, the metal would polarize the sugar oxygen atoms and, in so doing, help generate the hydride ion. This mechanism would fit all of the observed data for GI. And it would be almost without enzymatic precedent.

There are, however, numerous organic precendents. The Cannizzaro reaction, in which two equivalents of a nonenolizable aldehyde such as bezaldehyde are reacted with hydroxide to form a primary alcohol and the salt of a carboxylic acid, is thought to involve hydride transfer to one aldehyde carbonyl from the carbonyl-addition product of the other aldehyde and hydroxide. The Leuckart reaction, formation of a tertiary amine from formic acid, a primary amine and either a ketone or an aldehyde, seems to procede via hydride transfer from formate to an iminium ion. And the Meerwein-Ponndorf-Verley-Oppenauer reaction, the reversible transfer of hydrogen between ketones and secondary alcohols in the presence of excess aluminum isopropoxide, is almost certainly a hydride-transfer reaction. This latter process is of particular interest to us because it requires a metal, just as GI does. The aluminum acts as a Lewis acid, coordinating the carbonyl oxygen and bringing the hydride donor (the carbon atom attached to the hydroxide of the alcohol) adjacent to it by simultaneously coordinating that oxygen as well. The magnesium or manganese in GI could be playing an identical role in an intramolecular hydride transfer. The mechanism of GI may have always been different from that of TIM because of the necessity of finding a way to bind a sugar correctly. The substrates for TIM have convenient handles: the phosphate group. TIM can use the phosphate to bind its substrates tightly and then do chemistry on a different part of the molecule. Glucose and fructose have no handles; the enzyme must use every available portion of the sugar to hold it in the active site, including the portion of the sugar where the isomerization is to take place. Once a metal ion was used to grab the C1 and C2 oxygane atoms, the chemistry of the reaction may have been unavoidable. A hydride transfer path was the lowest free-energy route to product with the strong Lewis acid attached to the substrate.

Structure can never prove mechanism. There is no direct evidence that GI uses a hydride transfer mechanism, and we do not wish to assert that it does. Our results, however, do suggest that alternatives to the traditional enediol mechanism should be considered for this enzyme, and that careful mechanistic studies should be carried out to evaluate the possibility that a hydride transfer could be involved. Until such studies have been completed, we believe that the race should be postponed. If the rate-determining step for GI really is ring-opening, it would be unsporting to match it against TIM, which faces no such problem. And it may also be impossible ever to engineer the TIM mechanism into GI, if the requirement of a metal atom to bind the sugar mandates a different mechanism for proton transfer. Nevertheless, comparison of these two enzymes has led to greater understanding, and appreciation, for both. A Fiat is not a Ferrari, but it is still a beautiful machine.

Literature Cited

1.   Alagona, G.; C. Ghio; Kollman, P.A.   J. Mol. Biol. 1986, 191, 23.
2.   Alber, T.   Ph.D. Thesis, Massachusetts Institute of Technology, Cambridge, 1981.
3.   Alber, T.; Kawasaki, G.   J. Molec. Appl. Gen. 1982, 1, 419.
4.   Alber, T.; Banner, D.W.; Bloomer, A.C.; Petsko, G.A.; Phillips, D.C.; Rivers, P.S.; Wilson, I.A.   Phil. Trans. Roy. Soc. Lond. 1981, B 293, 159.
5.   Albery, W.J.; Knowles, J.R.   Biochemistry 1976a, 15, 5627.
6.   Albery, W.J.; Knowles, J.R.   Biochemistry 1976b, 15, 5631.
7.   Belasco, J.G.; Knowles, J.R.   Biochemistry 1980, 19, 472.
8.   Campbell, I.D.; Jones, R.B.; Kiener, P.A.; Waley, S.G.   Biochem. J. 1979, 179, 607.
9.   Casal, J.I.; Ahern, T.J.; Davenport, Jr., R.C.; Petsko, G.A.; Klibanov, A.M.   Biochemistry 1987, 26, 1258.
10. Collins, K.D.   J. Biol. Chem. 1974, 249, 136.

11. Davenport, Jr., R.C. Ph.D. Thesis, Massachusetts Institute of Technology, Cambridge, 1985.
12. Farber, G.K.; Petsko, G.A.; Ringe, D. Protein Engineering 1987, 1, 459–466.
13. Gandour, R.D. Bioorganic Chem. 1981, 10, 169.
14. Hol, W.J.G.; Van Duijnen, P.T.; Berendsen, H.J. Nature, Lond. 1978, 273, 443.
15. Nickbarg, E.B.; Davenport, Jr., R.C.; Petsko, G.A.; Knowles, J.R. Biochemistry 1988, 27, 5948.
16. Petsko, G.A. Methods Enzym. 1985, 114, 141.
17. Petsko, G.A.; Davenport, Jr., R.C.; Frankel, D.; RajBhandary, U.L. Biochem. Soc. Trans. 1984, 12, 229.
18. Raines, R.T.; Straus, D.R.; Gilbert, W.; Knowles, J.R. Phil. Trans. Roy. Soc. Lond. 1986, A 317, 371.
19. Richard, J.P. J. Am. Chem. Soc. 1984, 106, 4926.
20. Richardson, J.S. Adv. Prot. Chem. 1981, 34, 168.
21. Rieder, S.V.; Rose, I.A. J. Biol. Chem. 1959, 234, 1007.
22. Rose, I.A. Brookhaven Symp. Biol. 1962, 15, 293.
23. Rose, I.A. Phil. Trans. Roy. Soc. Lond. 1981, B 293, 131.
24. Rose, I.A. Methods Enzymol. 1982, 87, 84.
25. Shih, H.H.-L.; Brady, J.; Karplus, M. Proc. Nat. Acad. Sci. USA 1985, 82, 1967.
26. Smith, W.W.; Pattridge, K.A.; Ludwig, M.L.; Petsko, G.A.; Tsernoglou, D.; Tanaka, M.; Yasunobu, K.T. J. Mol. Biol. 1983, 165, 737.
27. Snow, M.E.; Amzel, L.M. Proteins 1986, 1, 267.
28. Straus, D.; Raines, R.T.; Kawashima, E.; Knowles, J.R.; Glibert, W. Proc. Nat. Acad. Sci. USA 1985, 82, 2272.
29. Trentham, D.R.; McMurray, C.H.; Pogson, C.I. Biochem. J. 1969, 114, 19.
30. Waley, S.G.; Miller, J.C.; Rose, I.A.; O'Connell, E.L. Nature, Lond. 1970, 227, 181.
31. Webb, M.R.; Knowles, J.R. Biochem. J. 1974, 141, 589.
32. Webb, M.R.; Standring, D.N.; Knowles, J.R. Biochemistry 1977, 16, 2738.
33. Wolfenden, R.G. Nature, Lond. 1969, 223, 704.
34. Zoller, M.J.; Smith, M. Methods Enzymol. 1983, 100, 468.

RECEIVED January 3, 1989

Chapter 5

Computer-Automated Sequence Evaluation of Peptides

Application to the Study of Snake Venom Toxicity

Gilles Klopman and Ruben E. Venegas

Department of Chemistry, Case Western Reserve University,
Cleveland, OH 44106

A modified version of the Computer Automated Structure
Evaluation (CASE) program has been successfully
applied to the study of the neurotoxic and cytotoxic
activity of the snake venom toxins. The program
identified the sites that seem to be the most relevant
to the activity of these two classes of peptides. The
knowledge of the three dimensional structure of these
peptides together with the relevant fragments selected
by the CASE program helped to clarify the differences
between the activity of each type of toxin.

Traditional Quantitative Structure-Activity studies are pretty much
limited to the study of the biological activity of relatively small
Organic Molecules. We have introduced, some time ago, the CASE
program, a Computer Automated Structure Evaluation program that can
be used to identify molecular fragments directly responsible for the
biological activity of such organic molecules (1-10). With this
paper, we wish to introduce an expanded version of CASE, capable to
identify the relation between peptide sequences and biological
activity. The expectation is that such a program could help
delineate the activity of peptides and provide a better
understanding of the receptor site's geometry. For this initial
study we have selected a data base consisting of snake venom toxins
(11,12), for which extensive studies have been made and whose
tertiary structure has been well established (13).
    Snake venom toxins are usually classified into three
categories: short neurotoxins, long neurotoxins and cytotoxins.
Short neurotoxins contain 60-62 amino acid residues and 4 disulfide
bridges. Long neurotoxins have 60-62 amino acid residues and 5
disulfide bridges. Cytotoxins also contain 60-61 amino acid residues
and 4 disulfide bridges. It is known that short and long neurotoxins
act on postsynaptic nicotinic cholinergic receptors (13), but the
mode of action of cytotoxins is unclear.

0097-6156/89/0392-0052$06.00/0
© 1989 American Chemical Society

Elucidation of the active site of toxins would be of enormous importance for the understanding of both the mechanism of action of the toxins and of the structural organization of the receptor. A considerable amount of work has been done to that effect; this includes the study of many snake venom's sequences (11) and their three dimensional structures (14,15). The toxicity and binding of chemically modified toxins (11,16,17) have also been reported as well as that of smaller peptides with residual toxicity (18,19). In spite of all this work, the specific regions and the minimum number of functional amino acids needed to bind to the receptor and to produce toxicity have not been entirely clarified. Nevertheless, a number of conclusions have been reached from previous studies. Thus, from a comparison of neurotoxin sequences with that of similarly structured proteins but without toxic activity, the residues Trp-25, Arg-33, and Gly-34 (numeration according to Karlsson, ref. 11) were thought to be necessary for neurotoxicity (11). From chemical modifications studies (11,16), it was found that Trp-25, Asp-27, Arg-33, Gly-34, and Lys-49 seemed to be essential. X-ray studies of two neurotoxins showed that a few pairs of amino acids appeared to mimic the structure of acetylcholine (20). Finally, it was also observed that the four disulfide bridges appear to play an important part in maintaining the active conformation of the toxins and that complete reduction (21) or oxidation (22) terminate toxicity while denaturants such as urea have little or no effect on the toxicity of non-reduced toxin.

From a comparison of the primary structure of the neurotoxins, Karlsson (11) and Ryden et al. (12) observed that certain invariant amino acid positions in the structural chain are important for the general folding of the molecule, while others are important for the neurotoxic activity. The former are called structurally invariant residues, whereas the later are called functionally invariant residues.

Most previous studies are based on the assumption that the toxicity of snake toxins is induced by a narrowly defined active region. As a consequence, single amino acid residues were chemically modified and the effects of the modification assayed by in vivo toxicity tests (11,14,18). However, it was found that the derivatives modified at all those positions believed to be important still have significant activity. Instead, as has been previously shown by Karlsson (11), there is a gradual decrease of, but never a complete reduction in toxicity (affinity of binding).

A detailed analysis of these results seem to indicate that unlike most of the enzymes, there is not a single amino acid residue or small region in the toxin structure that is essential for biological function. Instead, the structure-function relationships of this important group of biologically active polypeptides may be governed by more global principles of organization.

Methodology

The CASE methodology has been modified to be usable for the evaluation of the amino acid sequences required for activity. The procedure calls for fragmentation of the peptide chain in fragments of 3 to 10 constituent units. These formerly consisted of heavy atoms with their hydrogens and, in the new context, are made up by small sequences of linked amino acids. For this purpose the molecular entry program (23), formerly KLN, has been modified so that each letter of the alphabet now represents an amino acid (see Table I). Each of these amino acid is only permitted one neighbor if it exists at the beginning or end of a chain and two neighbors if it exists within the bulk of the peptide. Furthermore, fragment inversion is not permitted anymore since, in contrast to ordinary molecules, peptide termini are not interchangeable. Once the fragments have been identified and collected along with a numerical representation of the biological activity of the peptides, the CASE analysis begins. Fragments coming from active peptides are labeled activating, while fragments arising from biologically inactive peptides are labeled as deactivating.

Table I. IUPAC Coding System[*]

Letter	Abbreviation	Amino Acid
A	Ala	ALANINE
R	Arg	ARGININE
N	Asn	ASPARAGINE
D	Asp	ASPARTIC ACID
B	Asx	ASPARTIC ACID/ASPARAGINE
C	Cys	CYSTEINE
Z	Glx	GLUTAMIC ACID/GLUTAMINE
Q	Gln	GLUTAMINE
E	Glu	GLUTAMIC ACID
G	Gly	GLYCINE
H	His	HISTIDINE
I	Ile	ISOLEUCINE
L	Leu	LEUCINE
K	Lys	LYSINE
M	Met	METHIONINE
F	Phe	PHENYLALANINE
P	Pro	PROLINE
S	Ser	SERINE
T	Thr	THREONINE
W	Trp	TRYPTOPHAN
Y	Tyr	TYROSINE
V	Val	VALINE

[*] The symbols used for amino acids are those recommended by the IUPAC-IUB Commission on Biochemical Nomenclature, as published in J. Biol. Chem. 1972, 247, 977.

The fragmentation of the peptide data base generates thousands of fragments consisting of short amino acid sequences. In order to establish which fragments are relevant to activity, a binomial distribution is assumed and any significant deviation from a random distribution of a fragment among the active and inactive categories indicates its possible contribution to the biological activity. At this point of the procedure the program is capable to distinguish between active and inactive toxins on the basis of the presence or absence of these fragments. Additionally, the program selects a subset of molecular fragments to be considered for multivariate linear regression. First, the program searches for a fragment which can effectively discriminate between active and inactive peptides. Subsequent fragments are then chosen to account for the remaining variance. The program executes a forward stepwise regression analysis on these independent variables to derive a quantitative estimate of each peptide's activity. The F partial statistic (95% confidence level) is applied to assure statistical validity of the incorporated variables. The measure of the activating/inactivating contribution made to the overall biological activity by the fragments is represented by the magnitude of the regression coefficients.

Once the analysis is completed, the program has the capability to evaluate the probability that unknown compounds have activity and to anticipate the extend of this activity.

Results

Short Neurotoxins. The 58 snake venom short neurotoxins submitted to analysis are presented in Table II. This data base, which contains 27 inactive and 30 active toxins, was built from data reported by Karlsson (11) and Dufton et al. (12).

F_I	: S S Q	F_{II}	: D H R G
F_{III}	: Synergistic presence of fragments T T K and R G T I I E R G C G C P		
F_{IV}	: W S D	F_V	: C P T V K
F_{VI}	: S C Y K K	F_{VII}	: W R D
F_{VIII}	: C N L		

Figure 1. The most important fragments selected by the CASE program from the short neurotoxins data base.

After the training set was entered in the computer, the program generated all the fragments believed to be related to the observed activities of each toxin. In this case, 20 fragments (10 inactivating and 10 activating) were selected as potential descriptors of the experimentally observed toxicity. Based on these, a stepwise regression analysis was performed. The activity of the toxins were represented as 0 indicating no activity, 1, indicating marginal activity and 2, substantial activity. Eight descriptors were selected to be of particular significance to the actual toxicity of the short neurotoxins. They are shown in Figure 1; the following Quantitative Structure Activity Relationship (QSAR) was generated:

Table II. The actual and predicted value of the short toxins
submitted to the CASE program

	Neurotoxins	Actual[*]	Calc.[*]
1	NAJA HAJE ANNULIFERA: CM-10	–	–
2	NAJA HAJE ANNULIFERA: CM-12	–	–
3	DENDROASPIS JAMESONI KAIMOSE: S5C10	–	–
4	DENDROASPIS JAMESONI KAIMOSE: S4C1	–	–
5	DENDROASPIS JAMESONI KAIMOSE: S4C4	–	–
6	DENDROASPIS JAMESONI KAIMOSE: S4C8	–	–
7	DENDROASPIS ANGUSTICEPS: C10S2C2	–	–
8	DENDROASPIS ANGUSTICEPS: C13S1C1	–	–
9	DENDROASPIS POLYLEPSIS: C	–	–
10	DENDROASPIS POLYLEPSIS: FS2	–	–
11	OPHIOPHAGUS HANNAH: DE-1	–	–
12	NAJA HAJE HAJE: CM-2	–	–
13	DENDROASPIS JAMISONI KAIMOSE: S2C4	–	–
14	DENDROASPIS ANGUSTICEPS: C8S2	–	–
15	DENDROASPIS ANGUSTICEPS: C9S3	–	–
16	NAJA MELANOLEUCA: S4C11	–	–
17	NAJA HAJE ANNULIFERA: CM-13B	–	–
18	NAJA HAJE HAJE: CM-11	–	–
19	NAJA NIVEA: CM-10	–	–
20	NAJA NAJA SIAMENSIS (KAOUTHIA): CM-9A	–	–
21	HEMACHATUS HEMACHATES: CM-1B	–	–
22	NAJA HAJE ANNULIFERA: CM-2A	–	–
23	NAJA HAJE ANNULIFERA: CM-3	–	–
24	DENDROASPIS VIRIDIS: TOXIN TA2	–	–
25	DENDROASPIS VIRIDIS: TOXIN 4.9.6	–	–
26	HEMACHATUS HAEMACHES: TOXIN 9B	–	–
27	DENDROASPIS ANGUSTICEPS: TOXIN TA1(F-VII)	–	–
28	NAJA NIVEA: B,(BETA)	++	++
29	NAJA MOSSAMBICA MOSSAMBICA: I	++	++
30	NAJA MOSSAMBICA MOSSAMBICA: III	++	++
31	NAJA HAJE HAJE: CM-10A	++	++
32	NAJA HAJE HAJE: CM-6	++	++
33	NAJA HAJE ANNULIFERA: A,(ALPHA)	++	++
34	NAJA HAJE ANNULIFERA: CM-14	++	++
35	NAJA MELANOLEUCA: D	++	++
36	NAJA NIGRICOLLIS: A,(ALPHA)	++	+++
37	NAJA NAJA ATRA: COBROTOXIN	++	++
38	NAJA NAJA OXIANA: II	++	++
39	HEMACHATUS HEMACHATES: II	++	+++
40	HEMACHATUS HEMACHATES: IV	++	++
41	DENDROASPIS VIRIDIS: 4.11.3	++	++
42	DENDROASPIS JAMESON: VN'I	++	++
43	DENDROASPIS POLYLEPIS	++	++
44	LATICAUDA SEMIFASCIATA: ERABUTOXIN A	++	++
45	LATICAUDA SEMIFASCIATA: ERABUTOXIN B	++	++
46	LATICAUDA SEMIFASCIATA: ERABUTOXIN C	++	++
47	LATICAUDA LATICAUDA: LATICOTOXIN A	++	++
48	LATICAUDA LATICAUDA: LATICOTOXIN A'	++	++
49	LATICAUDA COLUBRINA: II	++	++
50	LATICAUDA SCHISTOSA: 5	++	++
51	ENHYDRINA SCHISTOSA: 4	++	++
52	AIPYSURUS LAEVIS: A	++	+
53	AIPYSURUS LAEVIS: B	++	++
54	AIPYSURUS LAEVIS: C	++	+
55	HYDROPHIS CYANOCINCTUS: HYDROPHITOXIN A	++	++
56	HYDROPHIS ORNATUS: 75A	++	++
57	ASTROTIA STOKESII: A	++	++
58	ACANTHOPIS ANTARCTICUS: C	++	++

[*] – indicates inactivity, + indicates marginal activity
++, substantial activity and +++, extremely high activity.

$$\text{Activity} = 0.240 + 0.637\ F_I + 0.586\ F_{II} + 0.266\ F_{III}$$
$$+ 0.750\ F_{IV} + 0.358\ F_V + 0.533\ F_{VI} \qquad (1)$$
$$+ 0.917\ F_{VII} - 0.543\ F_{VIII}$$

Fragments I to VII are activating whereas Fragment VIII is deactivating. The F-test for regression is satisfied at the 0.05 confidence limit; $F_{(8,49,0.05)}=201.79$, with a correlation coefficient r^2 of 0.97 and a standard deviation of residuals of 0.217. The correlation is significant since the F-test is substantially better than required by our criteria to eliminate fortuitous correlations (24).

It can be seen from Table II that the predictions (using Equation 1) were quite satisfactory. All the inactives neurotoxins are accounted for correctly. Among the actives, two were predicted to be marginally active (52 and 54) and two extremely active (36 and 39). It has been observed that these two toxins (36 and 39) are indeed very potent (20).

We also submitted 6 short toxins that were found in the literature (25) after the training data base had been entered to the computer. Table III shows the results of the prediction for these neurotoxins; 4 out of the 6 compounds were correctly predicted to be active. The other two were predicted to be marginally active. To us, this indicates satisfactory predictive capability.

Table III. The actual and predicted values of the test compounds using Equation 1 *

	Neurotoxins	Actual	Calculated
1	D.j.kaimosae Toxin Vn-I1	++	++
2	L.colubrina c	++	+
3	L.colubrina d	++	+
4	L.laticaudata c	++	++
5	L.crockeri c	++	++
6	Hcyan Hyd B	++	++

* See footnote in Table II.

Cytotoxins. The 58 snake venom cytotoxins submitted to analysis are shown in Table IV. The data base, containing 35 inactive and 23 active toxins, was also build with data from the articles of Karlsson (11) and Dufton et al. (12). The same procedure as described for the short toxins was performed. 15 fragment were selected as potential descriptors of the toxicity of the cytotoxins and the stepwise regression analysis selected only 3 fragments as descriptors of their activity. The three fragments are shown in Figure 2. The following QSAR equation was generated:

$$\text{Activity} = 0.296 + 1.231\ F_I + 1.088\ F_{II} - 1.029\ F_{III} \qquad (2)$$

Table IV. The actual and calculated values of the Cytotoxins
submitted for analysis [*]

	Cytotoxins	Actual	Calc.
1	NAJA MELANOLEUCA: V"3	–	+
2	NAJA HAJE ANNULIFERA: CM–13A	–	+
3	HEMACHATUS HEMACHATES: 9B	–	–
4	HEMACHATUS HEMACHATES: 9BB	–	–
5	HEMACHATUS HEMACHATES: 11	–	–
6	HEMACHATUS HEMACHATES: 11A	–	–
7	HEMACHATUS HEMACHATES: 12A	–	–
8	NAJA NAJA: CM–XI	–	–
9	NAJA NAJA IIA	–	–
10	NAJA NAJA ATRA : CARDIOTOXIN	–	–
11	NAJA MELANOLEUCA : V"2	–	–
12	NAJA MELANOLEUCA : 3.22	–	–
13	HEMACHATUS HEMACHATES: 12B	–	–
14	DENDROASPIS JAMESONI KAIMOSE: S2C4	–	–
15	DENDEOASPIS ANGUSTICEPS: C8S2	–	–
16	NAJA HAJE HAJE: CM–2	–	–
17	DENDEOASPIS ANGUSTICEPS: C9S3	–	–
18	NAJA NIVEA : CM–10	–	–
19	NAJA NAJA SIAMENSIS: CM–9A	–	–
20	HEMACHATUS HEMACHATES: CM–1B	–	–
21	HEMACHATUS HEMACHATES: CM–2B	–	–
22	HEMACHATUS HEMACHATES: CM–1C	–	–
23	HEMACHATUS HEMACHATES: CM–12B	–	–
24	NAJA HAJE ANNULIFERA: CM–2A	–	–
25	ACANTHOPIS ANTARCTICUS: P2	–	–
26	ACANTHOPIS ANTARCTICUS: P3	–	–
27	ACANTHOPIS ANTARCTICUS: P5	–	–
28	ACANTHOPIS ANTARCTICUS: P6	–	–
29	PELAMIS PLATURUS: F6	–	–
30	PELAMIS PLATURUS: SO7	–	–
31	DENDROASPIS VIRIDIS: 4.11.3	–	–
32	DENDROASPIS JAMESONI: VNII	–	–
33	DENDROASPIS POLYLEPIS: ALPHA	–	–
34	NAJA HAJE ANNULIFERA: CM–13B	–	–
35	NAJA HAJE HAJE CM–11	–	–
36	NAJA NAJA NAJA: II COBRAMINE B	++	++
37	NAJA NAJA OXIANA	++	++
38	NAJA NAJA ATRA: II	++	++
39	NAJA NAJA NAJA: I COBRAMINE A	++	++
40	NAJA MELANOLEUCA: VII1	++	++
41	NAJA NAJA ATRA: I	++	++
42	NAJA HAJE ANNULIFERA: CM–4A	++	++
43	NAJA HAJE ANNULIFERA: CM–2A	++	++
44	NAJA HAJE ANNULIFERA: VII1	++	+
45	NAJA NIVEA: VII1	++	+
46	NAJA NIVEA: VII3	++	++
47	NAJA HAJE ANNULIFERA: CM–8	++	++
48	NAJA HAJE ANNULIFERA: CM–8A	++	++
49	NAJA HAJE ANNULIFERA: VII2	++	++
50	NAJA NIVEA: VII2	++	++
51	NAJA HAJE HAJE: CM–10B	++	++
52	NAJA NIGRICOLLIS: CARDIOTOXIN	++	++
53	NAJA MOSSAMBICA MOSSAMBICA: VII2	++	++
54	NAJA MOSSAMBICA MOSSAMBICA: VII3	++	++
55	HEMACHATUS HEMACHATES: 12B	++	+
56	NAJA HAJE ANNULIFERA: CM–13B	++	+
57	NAJA MELANOLEUCA: 3.20	++	+
58	NAJA MELANOLEUCA: CYTOTOXIN 2	++	+

[*] See footnote in Table II.

The correlation coefficient r^2 of 0.90 and a standard deviation of residuals of 0.479, together with a F-test value of F (3,54,0.05) = 154.56 seem to indicate that the equation is highly significant.

$$
\boxed{
\begin{aligned}
F_I &: P\ V\ K\ R\ G\ C\ I\ D\ V\ C\ P\ K \\
F_{II} &: C\ C\ N \qquad F_{III} : G\ C\ G
\end{aligned}
}
$$

Figure 2. The fragments selected by the CASE program from the Cytotoxins data base.

The predictions, using Equation 2, are displayed in Table IV. The results show that 17 out of the 23 active and 33 of the 35 inactive cytotoxins are predicted correctly. The remaining 6 actives and 2 inactives are predicted to have marginal activity. Thus, almost 90% of the variation of the data base can be explained with Equation 2.

Discussion

Short Neurotoxins. Figure 1 shows the fragments that were selected by the program for the QSAR equation. Figure 3 shows the primary structure of some of the snake venoms. In these, we have underlined the fragments that were selected by the QSAR equation as significant to activity.

RICYNHLGTKPPTTECTQEDSCYKNIWRNITEDNIRRGCGCFTPRGDMPGPYCCESDK**CNL**

MICHNQQ**SSQ**RPTIKTCPGETNCYKKRWR**DHRG**TIIERGCGCPSVKKGVGIYCCKTDKCNR

MECHNQQSSQPP**TTK**TCPGETNCYKKQWSD**HRGTIIERGCGCP**SVKKGVKINCCTTDRCNN

LECHNQQSSQPPTTKSCPGDTNCYNKR**WRD**HRGTIIERGCGC**PTVK**PGINLKCCTTDRCNN

MTCCNQQSSQPKTTTNCAES**SCYKKTWSD**HRGTRIERGCGCPQVKKGIKLECCHTNECNN

Figure 3. Examples of the relative positions of the most important fragments selected by the CASE program in some short neurotoxins.

Fragment I, SSQ, corresponding to the Ser-Ser-Gln amino acid sequence, is present in almost all the snake venoms except those from the snake of the family Elapinae (mambas). Fragment II, DHRG (Asp-His-Arg-Gly), contains two of the functionally invariant amino acids as defined by Karlsson. These are Arg and Gly. According to the QSAR equation, these are the two most important fragments. Fragment III represents the synergistic presence of the fragments TTK (Thr-Thr-Lys), and RGTIIERGCGCP (Arg-Gly-Thr-Ile-Ile-Arg-Gly-Cys-Gly-Cys-Pro). This descriptor is the least potent, according to the QSAR equation (Equation 1); its coefficient is very small. It should be noted that the RGTIIERGCGCP fragment contains two of the

functionally invariant (Arg-Gly) and four of the structurally
invariant (Gly-Cys, Gly-Cys) amino acids. Finally, it appears that
fragments 7 and 8 (WRD; Trp-Arg-Asp and WSD; Trp-Ser-Asp) are
similar and occupy similar locations in the peptide sequences. Thus
we conclude that Arg and Ser are interchangeable in this position
without any significant activity change.
    It is interesting to realize that many of these fragments
occupy the same positions that Osthoff et al. (26) identified as
surface accessible/inaccessible residues. In fact, five out of the
six activating fragments (I-V) contain surface accessible residues
only. On the other hand, the inactivating fragment (IV) has an
surface inaccessible residue. Fragment VI seems to be the only
exception, it contains a mixture of surface accessible and
inaccessible residues.
    The consideration of the relative location of the fragments
within the three dimensional structure of the peptide provide some
additional insight into the mechanism of action of these peptides.
Figure 4 shows the 3-dimensional structure of a typical short toxin
(12). It is based on the crystal structure of the short neurotoxin
erabutoxin b. We have indicated the positions of the fragments
relevant to activity with solid lines.
    The first and most important conclusion comes from the
observation that the two most important fragments(SSQ and DHRG) are
located at the extremities of loops 1 and 2 and that they face
each other controlling the entrance to the channel between them.
The other fragment (WSD/WRD) is connected to the DHRG fragment and
completes the outer loop of the toxin. These three fragments clearly
delineate a primary interaction site with the receptor. There is a
secondary region, apparently less important, but not necessary less
significant, that needs to be considered as well. It is the region
where the CPTVK fragment is located, i.e. in the third loop.
    One may speculate that the outer region, corresponding to the
fragments SSQ, DHRG, WSD/WRD is required in order for the peptide to
be able to attach to the receptor, while the inner region,
consisting of the CPTVK fragment could be linked to the toxic
activity. This is supported by the fact that the QSAR equation
(Equation 1) requires a minimum of three activating fragments in
order to yield an actual activity value of 1.9 or larger and accept
a peptide as active.

Cytotoxins. Figure 2 shows the fragments selected by the QSAR
equation for the activity of the cytotoxins. It can be seen that the
most important fragment related to the biological activity of the
cytotoxins is much larger that those identified as relevant to the
activity of the short neurotoxins. A consideration of the tertiary
structure of these cytotoxins is even more revealing as to the
difference between their activity and that of the short toxins.
    Figure 5 displays the backbone of a cytotoxin showing the
normal location of these fragments. The three dimensional structure
is extrapolated from the crystal structure of the short neurotoxin,
erabutoxin b (12). As in the case of the short neurotoxins, we have
drawn the different fragments with solid lines.
    It can easily be seen that the extremities of loops 1 and 2,
which appeared to be so important in the case of the short

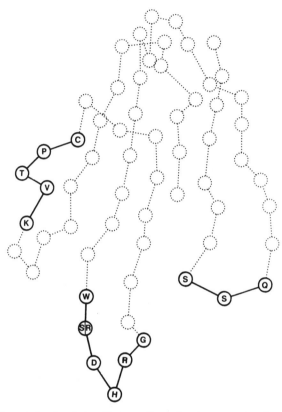

Figure 4. A typical backbone of a short neurotoxin. The most important fragments selected by the CASE program have been indicated with solid lines.

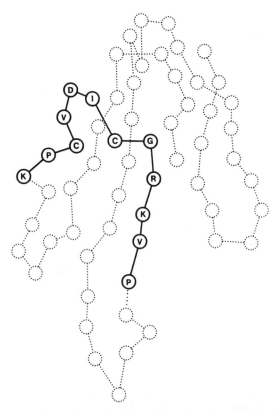

Figure 5. A typical backbone of a cytotoxin. The most important fragments selected by the CASE program have been indicated with solid lines.

neurotoxins, are not relevant anymore, thus suggesting that
different receptors are involved. It is now found that all the
relevant fragments are concentrated in the secondary region between
loops 2 and 3. Thus, while the folding of the cytotoxins is very
similar to that of the short neurotoxins, it is clear that the site
of activity is completely different and different strategies should
be used to either inhibit or simulate the activities of these two
classes of structurally related snake venom components.

Conclusions

The CASE analysis was able to identify the relevant sites of
activity of two series of peptides. From an evaluation of the
location of the relevant fragments, one can conclude that even
though both types of toxins have similar three dimensional
structure, the sites of neurotoxicity and cytotoxicity activity are
completely different and occur at totally different regions of the
peptides.
    These conclusions were made possible by the combined knowledge
of relevant fragments and the three dimensional structure of the
peptide. In the absence of a three dimensional structure, the
program would hardly be able to recognize the relative location of
relevant fragments in widely different peptides. This will strongly
limit the use of the CASE program in attempts to identify active
peptides of unknown three dimensional structure. On the other hand,
in those cases where the tertiary structure of the peptides is known
and constant, as it is here, the CASE analysis can help identify
relevant regions and gain insight into the nature of the receptor.

Acknowledgment

We wish to thank the Environmental Protection Agency and the Office
of Naval Research through its Selected Research Opportunities
Program (N0014-85-K-0090) for support this work.

Literature Cited

1. Klopman, G. and Rosenkranz, H. Mut. Res. 1984, 126, 227.
2. Klopman, G. and Contreras, R. Mol. Pharmacol. 1985, 27, 86.
3. Klopman, G., Kalos, A., and Rosenkranz H. Mol. Toxic. 1987, 1, 61.
4. Klopman, G. and Macina, O. J. Theor. Biol. 1985, 113, 637.
5. Klopman, G. and Frierson, M., and Rosenkranz, H. Environ. Mutagen. 1985, 7, 625.
6. Klopman, G. and Venegas, R. Acta Pharm. Jugosl. 1986, 36, 189.
7. Klopman, G. and Venegas, R. Pure & Appl. Chem. 1988, 60, 265.
8. Klopman, G., Contreras, R. and Waters, M. Mut. Res. 1985, 147, 343.
9. Klopman, G., Dimayuga, M. Mol. Pharmacol. 1988, 34, 218.
10. Klopman, G. J. Am. Chem. Soc. 1984, 106, 7315.
11. Karlsson, E. In Handbook of Experimental Pharmacology; Lee, C.Y. Ed.; Springer-Verlag: Berlin, Heidelberg, 1979; Vol. 52, pp. 159-212.
12. Dufton, M. and Hider, R. Crit. Rev. Biochem. 1981, 24, 113.

13. Ryden, L., Gabel, D. and Eaker, D. J. Peptide Protein Res. 1973, 5, 261.
14. Tsernoglou, D. and Petsko, G. FEBS Lett. 1976, 68, 1.
15. Low, B., Preston, H., Sato, A., Rosen, L., Searl, J., Rudko, A., and Richardson, J. Proc. Natl. Acad. Sci., USA. 1976, 73, 2991.
16. Walkinshaw, M., Saenger, W., and Maelicke, A. Proc. Natl. Acad. Sci. U.S.A. 1980, 77, 2400.
17. Menez, A. Pharmac. Ther. 1986, 30, 91.
18. Tu, A. Annu. Rev. Biochem. 1973, 42, 235.
19. Juillerat, M., Schwendimann, B., Hauert, J., Fulpius, B., and Bargetzi, J. J. Biol. Chem. 1982, 257, 2901.
20. Low, B. In Handbook of Experimental Pharmacology; Lee, C.Y. Ed.; Springer-Verlag: Berlin, Heidelberg, 1979; Vol. 52, pp. 213-257
21. Yang, C. Biochim. Biophys. Acta 1967, 359, 242.
22. Yang, C. Toxicon 1965, 3, 19.
23 Klopman, G. and McGonigal, M. J. Chem. Inf. Comput. Sci., 1981, 21, 48.
24. Klopman, G. and Kalos, A. J. Comp. Chem., 1985, 6, 492.
25. Endo, T., Nakanishi, M., Furukawa, S., Joubert, F., Tamiya, N. and Hayashi, K. Biochemistry. 1986, 23, 395.
26. Osthoff, G., Louw, A., and Reinecke, C. Toxicon. 1988, 26, 475.

RECEIVED November 14, 1988

Chapter 6

Application of Simulation and Theory to Biocatalysis and Biomimetics

Adel M. Naylor and William A. Goddard III

Arthur Amos Noyes Laboratory of Chemical Physics, California Institute of Technology, Pasadena, CA 91125

Examples are given for the role of simulation and theory in biocatalysis and biomimetics. Simulations on the novel Starburst Dendrimer polymers are used to suggest a design for encapsulating and delivering dopamine to the kidney for cardiovascular therapies. For Dihydrofolate Reductase (DHFR), the simulations (i) indicate why a particular mutation (Phe-31 to Tyr-31) causes a significant change in the catalytic rate, (ii) explain the high degree of kinetic similarity between two dissimilar forms of DHFR, and (iii) suggest that the stable form of the enzyme/substrate complex is *not* the reactive one.

A goal of our research efforts is to develop the theoretical tools useful in designing artificial biocatalytic systems for the production of fuels and chemical feedstocks. In the long term, one would envision the development of biocatalysts that could convert methane into more valuable (or more transportable) fuels or to convert syngas ($CO + H_2$) into various fuels and feedstocks. In the short term, we are focusing on systems capable of selective oxygenations or reductions. We would hope to develop artificial systems with the selectivity of cytochrome P-450 enzymes that play a role in selective oxidation of long chain alkanes and selective epoxidation of alkenes (1). Although selective, the various cytochrome P-450 enzymes involve complex assemblies (cofactors, co-enzymes) that would be difficult to reproduce and control in an artificial system (see Figure 1). Thus, we would hope to incorporate catalytic control procedures as effective as those in P-450, yet delete the excess baggage special to biological systems (e.g., cofactor, bulk protein necessary to ellicit stability and to create substrate binding pockets, etc.)

To that end we have focused our research on two aspects of this complex problem: (i) the design of artificial systems that possess precision sites capable of selectively encapsulating and delivering smaller molecules, and (ii) understanding the detailed structural and chemical aspects of enzyme active

0097–6156/89/0392–0065$06.75/0

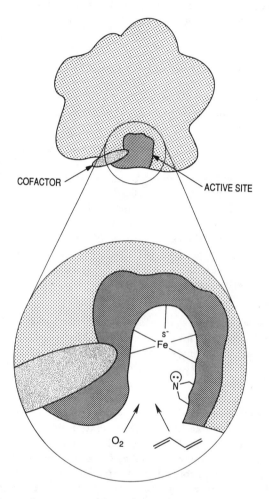

Figure 1. Schematic representation of cytochrome P-450 indicating the excess baggage carried by many biological catalysts.

sites involved in and affecting the important catalytic processes, i.e., substrate binding, product release, rate of catalysis.

Starburst Dendrimers :   Molecular Encapsulation

A recent synthetic development has led to a new class of polymers called "starburst dendrimers" (2) that provide the opportunity for design of precise encapsulation strategies. These novel materials (i) start with an initiator unit (termed the "core") that possesses multiple sites for monomer condensation and (ii) use monomer subunits terminating in functional groups that allow for regularized growth and multiple branching at the next generation. With the appropriate use of protecting groups and synthetic strategies, each generation of monomer condensation can be completed before embarking on a new one. Because of the unique chemical requirements for dendrimer formation, these polymers grow in a systematic manner, producing materials with a well-defined number of monomer subunits and a quantized number of terminal groups (Figure 2). With precise topology and chemical properties suitable for the encapsulation of specific target molecules that could be delivered to particular organs (by recognition of surface molecules), one could, in principle, change the monomer from generation to generation, developing onion-like molecules where every layer of the onion has a different chemical composition, thickness, or number of branching sites. Thus, one can imagine designing *and* synthesizing complex polymer structures where (i) internal layers are suitable for encapsulation of the desired molecule, (ii) outer layers are suitable for recognizing binding sites on the organ to which the target molecule is to be delivered, and (iii) intermediate layers protect the target molecule in the blood stream but release them (a) upon binding of the outer layer to recognition sites, (b) upon radiation with external light or charged particles or (c) upon change in acidity or solvent associated with the target organ.

β – Alanine Dendrimers. To illustrate this application, consider the β-alanine dendrimers where the core unit is ammonia (with three condensation sites) and the monomer unit is an amino amide (with two branch sites) as depicted below.

Core   Monomer

Experimentally it has been possible to develop complete dendrimers up through the tenth generation. However, no experimental structural data are available (these materials are fractal and do not crystallize). We have been carrying out molecular dynamics simulations on these β-alanine dendrimers up through generation 9 (3) using the molecular simulation facilities of **POLY-GRAF** (from Biodesign, Inc., Pasadena, CA 91101). These investigations indicate a dramatic change in the overall structural properties for the β-alanine systems as these polymers grow past generation 4. The early generation dendrimers

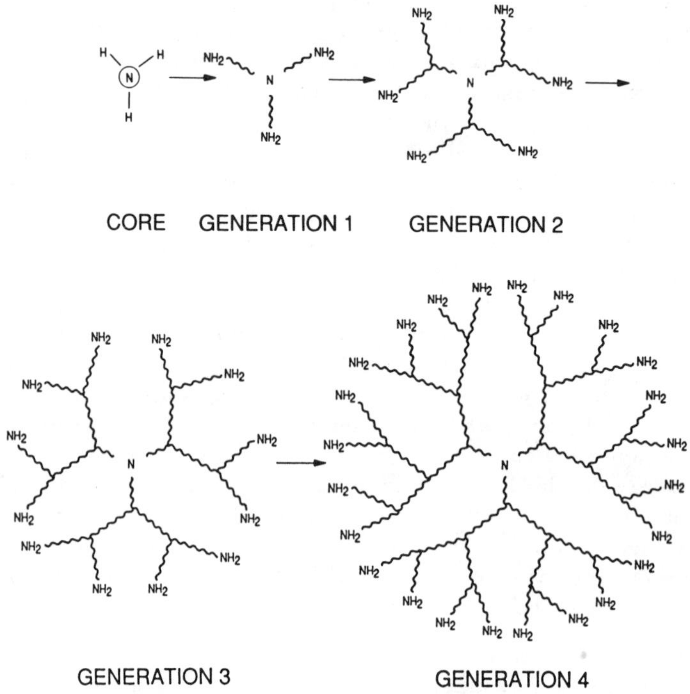

Figure 2. Cascade growth pattern for the β-alanine type dendrimers from the core ammonia unit up to generation 4.

(generations 1 through 3) possess very open and well-extended structures. These structures are hemispherical disks (with the core nitrogen responsible for the curvature) but there is no real inside to the polymer. This topology for the early generation systems is strikingly different from earlier proposals (4), but these hemispheric structures provide a simple interpretation of observed nuclear magnetic resonance relaxation times (Naylor, A. M.; Goddard III, W. A.; Keifer, G. E.; Tomalia, D. A. J. Am. Chem. Soc., in press 1988).

We find a distinct change in structural properties for those polymers above generation 5. The overall structure of the polymers is more sphere-like, with ample internal hollows connected by channels that run the length of the polymer assembly. These interior cavities should be suitable for sequestering guest molecules. Thus, in Figure 3, which limns a generation 6 dendrimer, we find an overall spherical structure containing a channel running through the interior of the polymer from one side to the other! To better illustrate the space available in the interior, we show in Figure 4 the solvent-accessible surface for the polymer (generation 6). [The solvent-accessible surface is constructed using the approach developed by Michael Connolly (University of California, San Diego) and is based on the definitions for molecular surfaces proffered by Frederic Richards (5). The molecular surfaces are composed of dots located in terms of a probe sphere (radius = 1.4 Å for water) rolling along the van der Waals spheres of the outer (accessible) atoms of the polymer.] Here we have used graphical slabbing to remove from view the front and rear portions of the image. The channels and cavities in this structure are representative of those found in the higher generation β-alanine dendrimers.

Dopamine – Sequestered Dendrimers. As an illustration of the dimensions of these channels and of how dendrimers might be used to sequester small molecules, we have used the molecular simulation capabilities of **POLYGRAF** to predict the optimum conformations for several dopamine 1 molecules

$$H_2N - CH_2 - CH_2 - \left\langle \bigcirc \right\rangle - OH$$

DOPAMINE OH

1

inside this starburst polymeric matrix. Dopamine was chosen because it is a good candidate for effective sequesterization in a β-alanine type dendrimer. Its size and shape are suitable for the cavities and channels found to exist in the higher generation β-alanine systems. From a chemical standpoint, dopamine possesses both the hydrogen bond donor and acceptor sites needed for favorable binding interactions to the polymer's carbonyl, amide, and amino substituents. We estimate that a generation 6 polymer should be capable of holding 15-20 molecules of dopamine. Figure 5 illustrates a dopamine/dendrimer complex with examples of the conformations adopted by the sequestered molecules and the polymeric material.

Pharmacologically, the ability (i) to selectively deliver dopamine to peripheral kidney receptors without eliciting complications due to the presence of dopamine receptors in the central nervous system (CNS) and (ii) to maintain a supply of nonmetabolized dopamine would be advantageous in cardiovascular hypertension therapy (6). The additional issues presented by this type of application include the dimensions of the dendrimer encapsulated dopamine and the targetting of the unit to the appropriate dopamine receptor sites.

The dimensions of the higher generation β-alanine dendrimers (see Figure 6 with the minimum diameter plotted as a function of generation) are such that these dopamine/dendrimer complexes would not readily cross the CNS blood-brain barrier.

In order to ensure the delivery to kidney dopamine receptors, we suggest modifying the terminal amine sites of the polymer with catechol fragments, as shown in 2

This leads to surface features resembling dopamine and may lead to selective binding at dopamine receptor sites (Figure 7). The polymer encapsulation matrix should protect the catecholamine from rapid metabolic inactivation.

These studies provide structural models that should be useful for analyzing the dopamine/dendrimer systems. The next step is to test the effectiveness of these modified materials for encapsulation of dopamine (and related materials) and to determine how effectively they are delivered to the kidney centers. As such experiments proceed, continuing simulation will be useful in providing a quantitative framework for understanding various results.

We expect that the judicious selection of a core unit, internal monomer subunits, and terminal monomer fragments will allow the design of dendrimers to complex with specific guest molecules and to deliver them to specific sites. It will, of course, be essential to develop synthetic schemes that allow for chemical control and fidelity.

Dihydrofolate Reductase :   Roles of Precise Structure in Catalysis

In designing new catalysts, it is essential to understand how the character of the active site (including cofactor) controls catalytic activity since one will want to modify this active site or cofactor. As a prototype for such studies, we have carried out a series of molecular simulations on the Dihydrofolate Reductase (DHFR) system.

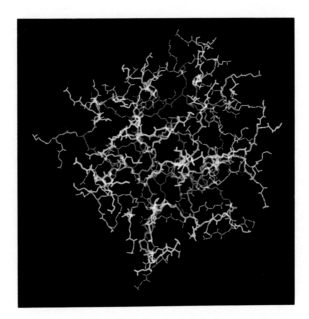

Figure 3. A representative structure for a generation 6 β-alanine dendrimer where generations 1 to 4 are colored red, generation 5 is shown in light blue, and generation 6 is yellow.

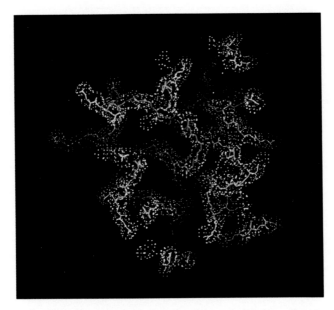

Figure 4. A view of a generation 6 dendrimer with its solvent-accessible surface displayed and clipped to reveal the nature of the internal cavities and channels found in the higher generation β-alanine dendrimers.

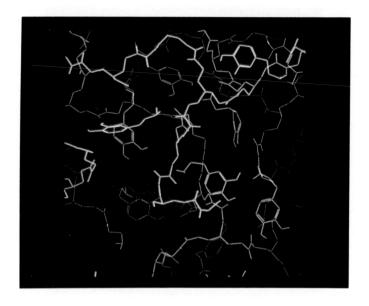

Figure 5. A view of various dopamine molecules (magenta) bound in the inner regions of a β-alanine dendrimer (generations 1 through 5 in light blue; generation 6 in yellow).

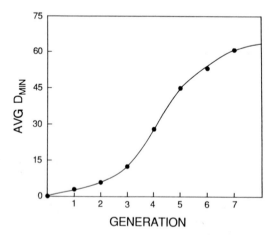

Figure 6. A plot of the β-alanine dendrimers "short" diameter (see text) as a function of generation. These diameters were calculated from our molecular simulations and based on the average of the smallest principal moment of inertia.

Introduction and Rationale. DHFR is an ideal system to study for a number of reasons. The catalytic properties of DHFR are such that under normal physiologic conditions and with the NADPH cofactor bound, 7,8-dihydrofolate (DHF) is reduced to 5,6,7,8-tetrahydrofolate (THF) (7). Thus DHFR plays an important role in cell metabolism by maintaining a supply of THF. THF is used by the cell as both a cofactor and in substrate quantities in the synthesis of deoxythymidine. By inhibiting the production of THF, deoxythymidine synthesis is curtailed, nucleic acid replication comes to a halt, and cell proliferation ceases. It is this biochemical cascade which supplies the pharmacological and chemotherapeutic applications of inhibitors to DHFR.

The abundant experimental data on DHFR provide both inspiration and detailed checks upon theoretical studies. The crystal structures of DHFR from two bacterial sources have been resolved, reported, and coordinates made available through the Brookhaven Data Base (8-10). The kinetic profiles of the enzyme under various conditions and, hence, mechanistic details have been determined (11,12). The recombinant DNA protocols for the successful study of site-directed mutants of DHFR have been reported (13-17).

DHF **3** is composed of (from left to right, below) a pterin ring, a bridging methylene unit, p-aminobenzoate, and a glutamate fragment.

DHF

3

THF

4

It is the N5-C6 double bond (circled, above) of 7,8-DHF that is reduced to 5,6,7,8-THF (4) by DHFR. Methotrexate (MTX), an important chemotherapy and anti-bacterial agent, is chemically quite similar to DHF (differences are circled).

MTX

5

MTX **5** contains the same benzglutamate fragment as DHF (but with a methylated amine) and a pteridine ring with an amino substitution at position 4. Indeed, we find similar binding sites for MTX and DHF on DHFR.

The crystal structure of the *E. coli* DHFR/MTX binary complex (9) reveals that the inhibitor binds in the active site in a kinked fashion (Figure 8). Asp-27 forms a salt-bridge to the bound pteridine ring while Phe-31 allows for the bend in the bound inhibitor. The remainder of the active site cavity surrounding the pterin ring is composed of amino acid residues that create a very hydrophobic environment.

Before embarking on designing improvements into the catalytic sequence, it is useful to know the detailed kinetics of the system. A profile of the steady-state kinetics of the *E. coli* form of DHFR was recently reported by Fierke, Johnson, and Benkovic (12). This study used stopped flow fluorescence and absorbance spectroscopies to measure the rates of ligand association and dissociation and the binding constants of key intermediates in the catalytic sequence, as diagrammed in Figure 9. This study revealed that the catalytic step, i.e., the N5-C6 double bond reduction, proceeds at a steady-state rate of 950 sec^{-1}, whereas the rate of THF product release was only 12.5 sec^{-1}, making it the rate-limiting step. Hence, any design modifications to increase the turnover of this system should focus first upon increasing the product off-rate.

A Synthetic Mutant : Phe $-$ 31 $\rightarrow$ Tyr $-$ 31. We now turn to using molecular simulation methods to examine some areas of the biocatalytic properties of DHFR that are not easily investigated experimentally. The general methods used for our studies incorporate computer graphics, molecular force fields, energy minimization, and molecular dynamics. **BIOGRAF** (from Biodesign, Inc., Pasadena, CA 91101) was the molecular simulation package used for these investigations. The AMBER force field was used for the calculations (18).

As an illustration of the use of simulations, we consider the effect on rate of a site mutation of DHFR. Benkovic *et al.* used recombinant-DNA techniques to synthesize the protein where Phe-31 was transformed into Tyr-31 (14). Preliminary experimental studies indicated a change in the pK_a of Asp-27 in this mutant form of the enzyme. Molecular simulations were run on both the wild-type enzyme and the Tyr-31 mutant to assess the structural changes produced by such a modification.

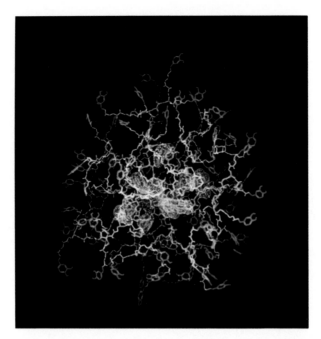

Figure 7. A catechol-modified, dopamine-loaded β-alanine dendrimer where the dopamines are displayed in magenta, generations 1 through 5 in light blue, generation 6 in yellow, and the catechol cap in red.

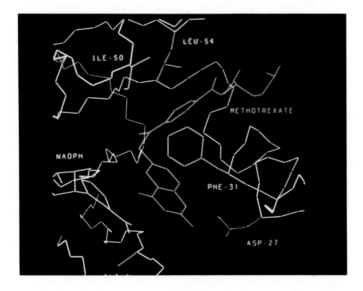

Figure 8. The active site of *E. coli* DHFR with MTX and NADPH bound.

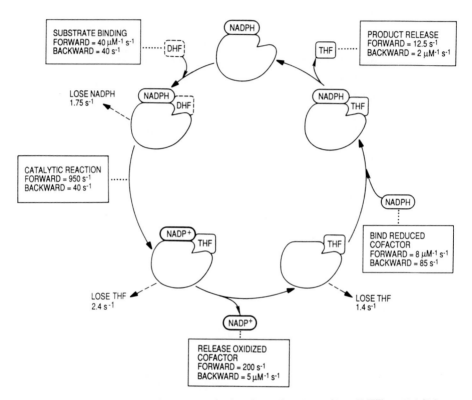

Figure 9. Steady-state kinetic cycle for the reduction of 7,8-DHF to 5,6,7,8-THF via DHFR.

The starting structure for our wild-type protein complex was based upon the crystallographic data, where the *L. casei* NADPH coordinates were used to model the cofactor into the *E. coli* system. To create the Tyr-31 mutant, the replace facility of **BIOGRAF** was used. For both series of simulations, a 10 Å solvent shell (containing experimental plus supplemental waters) surrounded the protein complexes. Counter ions were positioned near charged amino acid side chains to achieve electroneutral systems. The structures were then equilibrated via a sequence of molecular dynamics and energy minimization calculations.

Our calculations show that the pteridine ring is relatively undisturbed by the introduction of the Tyr hydroxyl group, yet the benz-glutamate portion of the bound substrate (or inhibitor) is markedly displaced (see Figure 10). We find that the mutant -OH group produces a 'bump' on the surface of the hydrophobic pocket near the benzyl group that disrupts the binding of the benz-glutamate fragment. This suggests that the product off-rate from the DHFR/NADPH/THF complex should be affected markedly by this substitution. Kinetic studies have verified that the product off-rate for the Tyr-31 form of *E. coli* DHFR is 50 times faster than that of wild-type protein (14)!

Natural Mutants : *E. coli* and *L. casei.* Consider now the question of how different one can make the active site *without* affecting the chemistry. The overall amino acid sequence homology between the *E. coli* and *L. casei* forms of DHFR is only 27%. However, as shown in Figure 11, a Gibbs free energy comparison of the steady-state data for the *E. coli* and the *L. casei* proteins shows that the reaction kinetics for these two forms of the enzyme are remarkably similar (19). In fact (using the ternary DHFR/NADPH/DHF complex as the energy reference), the energy differences between the two are, at every step, within 1 kcal/mol! Using the x-ray crystal structures and reorienting them so that the MTX of both complexes are superimposed (by docking one structure with respect to the other), we see that the conformation of MTX bound to the *E. coli* DHFR is very similar to that of MTX in the *L. casei* ternary crystal complex. The orientations of both the pteridine and the benzyl rings are identical for the two complexes and the backbone atoms of the glutamate substituent also align quite nicely. The discrepancy in these two forms of bound MTX occurs at the C-δ carboxylate group of the glutamate fragment, a position far removed from the catalytic site. A glance at the two different enzymes reveals that this difference in conformation is due to the positions of positively charged amino acid side chains on opposite sides of the opening for the active site (Arg-52 for the *E. coli* form and His-28 for the *L. casei* complex).

The results of docking the *L. casei* structure to the *E. coli* show that the overall folds for these two proteins are quite similar. Regions of secondary structural elements, i.e., α-helices and β-sheets, are conserved, while insertions and deletions in the amino acid sequences occur in loop regions located about the exterior regions of the enzyme. The structural domains of the DHF and NADPH binding sites are maintained. In the comparison of the DHF substrate

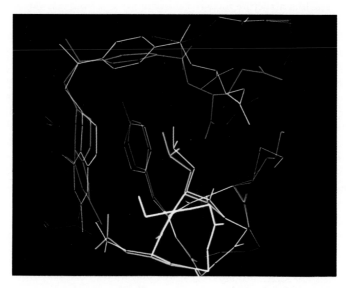

Figure 10. A comparison of MTX bound to wild-type DHFR (red MTX and Phe-31; blue active site residues) and Tyr-31 mutant protein (yellow MTX, Tyr-31, and active site residues).

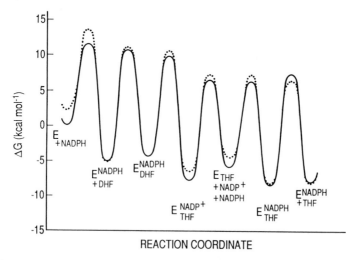

Figure 11. A Gibbs free energy plot of the kinetic profiles for *E. coli* (solid) and *L. casei* (dotted) DHFR (adapted from ref. 19).

binding pockets, one finds that nature, in some instances, substitutes like for like by using
(1) different aromatic side chains [as Trp-30 (*E. coli* ≡ *Ec*) → Tyr-29 (*L.casei* ≡ *Lc*), Tyr-100 (*Ec*) → Phe-103 (*Lc*), and Phe-153 (*Ec*) → Tyr-155 (*Lc*) indicate] or
(2) different aliphatic side chains [as Ile-5 (*Ec*) → Leu-4 (*Lc*), Leu-36 (*Ec*) → Val-35 (*Lc*), and Leu-112 (*Ec*) → Val-115 (*Lc*) demonstrate].
But there also are examples where aliphatic is substituted for aromatic (and vice versa) as with Ile-50 (*Ec*) → Phe-49 (*Lc*) and Tyr-111 (*Ec*) → Leu-114 (*Lc*). Similar substitution patterns are found in the NADPH cofactor binding site, where, in addition to those types described above, charged residues are maintained [i.e., His-45 (*Ec*) → Arg-44 (*Lc*) and Lys-76 (*Ec*) → His-77 (*Lc*)].

Using these superimposed structures with the MTX (from both crystal structures) and the NADPH (from the *L. casei* complex) as guides, the active site regions are identified for both enzymes. Here we define the active site to be those amino acids containing any atom within 7 Å of either of the bound substrates. Analyses of the residues in the active site region determine that the amino acid sequence homology in this portion of the protein is 35% (see Table I).

The two docked active site regions (with MTX bound) are shown in Figure 12. Examination of the docked active sites reveals that there are three general types of amino acid residues involved in the construction of the active site surface:
(1) amino acid residues conserved between the two bacterial forms of DHFR, e.g., Phe-31 (*Ec*) and Phe-30 (*Lc*);
(2) amino acid residues that differ between the two sequences and contribute chemically different side chains to the construction of the active site, e.g., Ile-50 (*Ec*) and Phe-49 (*Lc*); and
(3) amino acid residues that differ between the two sequences but contribute only chemically homologous main chain atoms to the construction of the active site, e.g., Ala-6 (*Ec*) and Trp-5 (*Lc*).
Thus, by modifying the definition of homology to also include those residues in the active site supplying only backbone atoms, one obtains a generalized 'chemical homology' of the active site. Indeed, the 'chemical homology' between the *E. coli* and the *L. casei* substrate binding pockets becomes 60% (19)!

A comparison of the solvent accessible surfaces [as described above; (5)] for these segments of the protein further substantiates these remarkable structural similarities. The surface areas mapped out for these regions agree within 93%. The solvent accessible sufaces for the MTX pteridine and the NADPH nicotinamide rings are essentially interchangeable for the two different sequences, as illustrated in Figure 13.

Hence, we see that nature creates essentially identical reactive surfaces for these bacterial DHFR systems from different amino acid building blocks (19) (Benkovic, S. J.; Adams, J. A.; Fierke, C. A.; Naylor, A. M. Pteridines, in press 1988). The components necessary for DHFR's ability to catalytically reduce the N5-C6 double bond of 7,8-DHF to 5,6,7,8-THF are conserved. The carboxylate group that supplies a proton to the pterin ring is present in both the *E. coli* and

Table I. Comparison[a] of DHFR Active Site Residues from *E. coli* and *L. casei*

Residue[b]	4	5	6	7	8	9	10	...	13	14	15	16	17	18
E. coli	L	i	A	**A**	L	A	V	...	V	i	**G**	M	e	n
L. casei	F	l	W	**A**	Q	N	R	...	L	l	**G**	K	d	g

19	20	21	22	23	24	25	26	27	28	29	30	31	32
a	m	**P**	**W**	n	L	**P**	A	**D**	L	a	w	**F**	k
h	l	**P**	**W**	h	L	**P**	D	**D**	L	h	y	**F**	r

33	34	35	36	...	42	43	44	45	46	47	48	49	50
r	n	**T**	l	...	m	**G**	**R**	h	**T**	**W**	**E**	**S**	i
a	q	**T**	v	...	v	**G**	**R**	r	**T**	**Y**	**E**	**S**	f

51		52	53	54	55	56	57	...	61	62	63	64	65
g	...	**R**	**P**	**L**	**P**	**G**	**R**	...	i	**L**	s	s	**Q**
p	k	**R**	**P**	**L**	**P**	E	**R**	...	v	**L**	t	h	**Q**

66	67	68	...	74	75	76	77	78	79	...	93	94	95
p	G	t	...	w	**V**	K	S	**V**	D	...	V	I	**G**
e	D	y	...	v	**V**	H	D	**V**	A	...	I	A	**G**

96	97	98	99	100	101	102	103	...	111	112	113	114	115
G	**G**	r	v	y	E	q	**F**	...	y	l	**T**	H	i
G	**A**	q	i	f	T	a	**F**	...	l	v	**T**	R	l

122	123	124	125	...	153
D	**T**	H	f	...	f
D	**T**	K	m	...	y

[a] Bold upper case indicates homologous, lower case indicates nonhomologous, and nonbold upper case indicates backbone chemical homology, as described in the text.

[b] Numbered for the *E. coli* form.

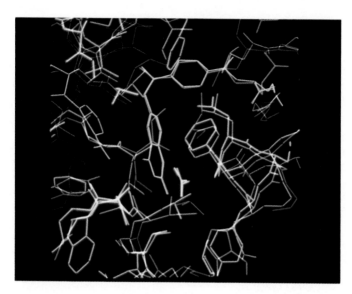

Figure 12. A comparison of the docked *E. coli* (red MTX and enzyme) and *L. casei* (yellow MTX and NADPH; blue enzyme) active sites. The conserved Phe's are shown to the right of the pteridine rings. The substituted side chains [Ile-50 (*Ec*) and Phe-49 (*Lc*)] appear in the 12 o'clock position above the benzyl ring. The chemically homologous main chain contributors [Ala-6 (*Ec*) and Trp-5 (*Lc*)] are shown in the 7 o'clock position.

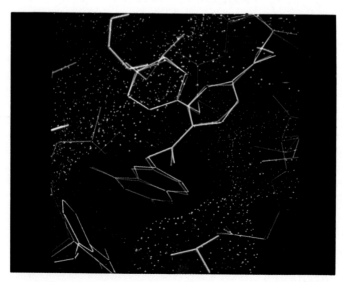

Figure 13. Dotted surface comparison showing the congruence of the *E. coli* (red) and *L. casei* (blue) active sites.

the *L. casei* sites as an Asp side chain. The hydrophobic pocket that surrounds the reactive pteridine moeity and prevents the aqueous environment from disturbing the catalytic process is formed by varied amino acids but maps out the same surface area and hydrophobic character. The hydride donating NADPH nicotinamide ring is positioned adjacent to the reactive center even though the NADPH binding sites are composed of different amino acid sequences.

Conformation of Bound Inhibitor. Another area under investigation focuses on the conformation(s) of the substrate and an inhibitor (MTX) bound to DHFR. The form of the DHFR/MTX complex is known from the crystallographic studies of Kraut *et al.* (8-10). However, the orientation of the bound pterin ring in the reactive DHFR/DHF is known to differ dramatically from the MTX crystal structure (20). Basically, these differences arise because there are two possible orientations of the pterin ring in the active site; one is flipped by 180° with respect to the other. Isotope labelling experiments on THF show that the reactive DHF must be bound in the conformation flipped from that observed by x-ray for MTX. In order to understand these differences, we ran simulation studies on altered forms of bound MTX and DHF to investigate the structural and energetic properties of these systems.

The starting structures for our binary DHFR/MTX calculations were based upon the crystallographic data. For the experimental form of bound MTX we used the coordinates as they were reported. For the pteridine-flipped form of bound MTX, termed MTX-flipped, we rotated about the C6-C9 and C9-N10 bonds of MTX to produce a starting conformation with the pteridine ring positioned in the active site but with its face flipped 180° (Figure 14). To be consistent with experiment, the bound MTX inhibitor was protonated at N1 (21). For both systems we used the experimentally determined solvent plus additional water to create a 10 Å solvent shell around the enzyme-inhibitor complex. Electroneutral systems were achieved by positioning the appropriately charged counter ions near to cationic and anionic side chains. The entire solvated protein and inhibitor systems were then equilibrated with a sequence of molecular dynamics and energy minimization calculations (using **BIOGRAF** and the AMBER force field).

These simulations indicate that the active site of DHFR can accommodate both forms of the bound MTX. After equilibration of both the experimental and the flipped forms, the carboxylate group of Asp-27 is found to be involved in a salt bridge with the pteridine ring of the inhibitor. The hydrophobic pocket surrounding the pterin ring has adjusted adequately to either conformation of the bound MTX. The energetic profiles indicate that the experimentally observed form of MTX bound to DHFR is ~3 kcal/mol lower in energy than the flipped form of the bound inhibitor.

Conformation of Bound Substrate. Now the question of the conformation of bound DHF substrate was addressed. Simulations were run on DHFR/DHF/NADPH ternary complexes to investigate both the structural and energetic requirements associated with the reactive and nonreactive forms of DHF (see Figure 14). As above, the crystallographic information available for

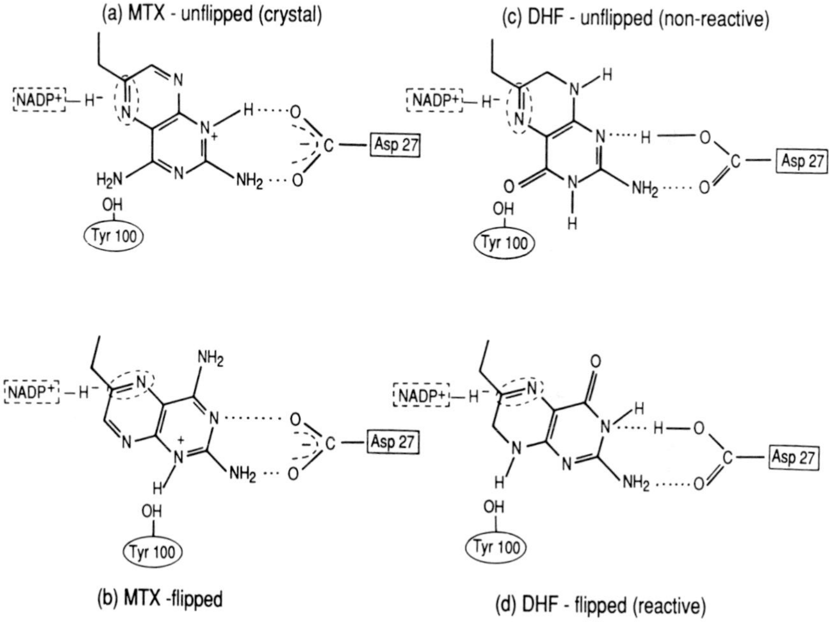

Figure 14. The orientations of the MTX and DHF pteridine rings in the active site of DHFR.

the *E. coli* binary and *L. casei* ternary complexes (with MTX) was used to generate starting structures for the molecular simulations. The coordinates for the *E.
coli* bound NADPH were modeled based upon those from the *L. casei* ternary
complex. The DHF units were positioned based upon the coordinates of the
MTX. For these simulations, the carboxylate group of Asp-27 was protonated
while the pterin ring of the substrate was not protonated at the N1 position.
Again, solvent and counterions were included and all atoms of the structures
were relaxed and equilibrated during the calculations.

The simulations indicate that there are two favorable conformations of
bound DHF in the active site of DHFR, each analogous to the favorable conformations of MTX. The amino acid side chains that create the hydrophobic
portion of the active site reposition themselves to allow for either form of the
pteridine ring. In the reactive orientation (termed DHF-flipped), the Asp-27
COOH prongs the C4 oxygen and the N3 sites. In the nonreactive conformation (termed DHF-unflipped), the carboxylate group straddles the N1 and the
N8 positions. The energetic results of the simulations find *the unflipped nonreactive form* (analogous to the x-ray form in MTX) of the pteridine ring *lower
in energy than the reactive form* by ~4 kcal/mol! This result seems to contradict experiment since no radio-labeled product resulting from DHF reduction
accommodates this orientation of bound substrate.

Closer examination of the active site regions reveals that the reducible C-N
bond of the pterin ring differs substantially with respect to the positions of the
NADPH nicotinamide rings. In the low energy nonreactive state, the NADPH
$C'4$ site is 4.1 Å from the carbon of the pteridine N5-C6 double bond, while in
the higher energy reactive form, this interatomic distance is reduced to only 3.2
Å! The shorter distance for hydride transfer during catalysis favors the reactive
conformation even though the energetics slightly favor the nonreactive form
of bound DHF. This information clearly suggests a kinetic mechanism for the
control of DHF reduction to THF via DHFR. Figure 15 depicts the relationship
between the NADPH nicotinamide ring and the reactive DHF substrate.

Wu and Houk have used ab initio calculations to propose a mechanism for
hydride transfer to the methyl iminium cation (22). Their results indicate that
H^- transfer proceeds via a syn transition state structure with a C-H-C angle
of 150-160° and a C-C interatomic distance of 2.6 Å (see Figure 16). What we
find for the reactive form of bound DHF and NADPH in an equilibrated ground
state is a pseudo-syn orientation of the reacting ring systems, a C-H-C angle
of 155°, and an equilibrium distance of 3.2 Å between the two carbon centers
(19). In contrast to the nonreactive conformer of DHF, simulations suggest that
the equilibrium distance between the two reacting carbons is 4.1 Å. The key
difference in character is the orientation of the pterin and nicotinamide rings.
In the productive conformation, the two-ring systems adopt positions that allow
for H^- transfer from the nicotinamide center to C6, while this relationship is
not accommodated by the nonreactive bound conformation of DHF.

In order to address the reaction rates of these species, we could monitor the
C-C distance as a function of time. Taking the probability distribution of C-C

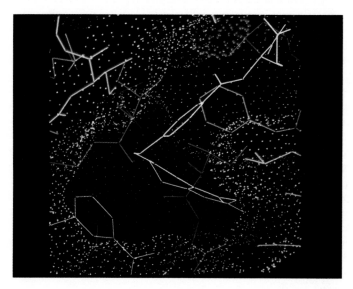

Figure 15. The catalytic pocket of DHFR showing the relationship between the NADPH nicotinamide ring (left) and the reactive DHF pteridine ring (right).

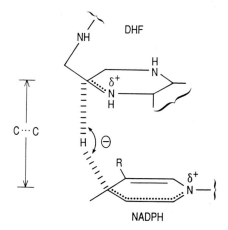

Figure 16. Proposed model for hydride transfer from NADPH to DHF (adapted from ref. 19). θ is the angle between the C4′ of NADP$^+$, the H$^-$ being transferred, and C6 of DHF.

with the reaction rate as a function of C-C distance, one should be able to predict relative reaction rates. However, qualitatively the large differences in equilibrium position certainly suggest a significant difference in rate. A test of this prediction would be to use NMR NOE experiments to examine conformation. We predict that over 90% of the bound complexes are the *non*reactive forms.

Summary

We have examined several systems chosen to illustrate the current role of theory and simulation in biomimetics and biocatalysis. It should be clear that the theory is not done in a vacuum (so to speak) but rather that the theory becomes interesting only for systems amenable to experimental analysis. However, the examples illustrate how the theory can provide new insights and deeper understanding of the experiments. As experience with such simulations accumulates and as predictions are made on more and more complex systems amenable to experiment, it will become increasingly feasible to use the theory on unknown systems. As the predictions on such unknown systems are tested with experiment and as the reliability of the predictions increases, these techniques will become true design tools for development of new biological systems.

Acknowledgments

This work was funded by a grant from the Department of Energy, Energy Conversion and Utilization Technologies. The DOE-ECUT program funded this work with the hope that development of simulation techniques would eventually have an impact on development of new, industrially useful processes for biotechnology and biocatalysis. We especially wish to acknowledge the foresight of Drs. Jim Eberhardt, Minoo Dastoor, and Jovan Moacanin in encouraging these efforts. The equipment used was also funded by the ONR/DARPA (Contract No. N00014-86-K-0735) and by a grant from the Division of Materials Research, Materials Research Groups, of the National Science Foundation (Grant No. DMR84-21119). We thank Professor Stephen J. Benkovic of the Pennsylvania State University and Dr. Donald A. Tomalia of The Dow Chemical Company for numerous helpful discussions and for materials in advance of publication.

Literature Cited

1. Cytochrome P − 450 : Structure, Mechanism, and Biochemistry; Ortiz de Montecellano, P. R., Ed.; Plenum Press: New York, 1986.
2. Tomalia, D. A.; Baker, H.; Dewald, J.; Hall, M.; Kallas, G.; Martin, S.; Roeck, J.; Ryder, J.; Smith, P. Macromolecules 1986, 19, 2466-2468.
3. Naylor, A. M.; Goddard III, W. A. Polymer Preprints 1988, 29, 215-216.
4. Tomalia, D. A.; Hall, M.; Hedstrand, D. M. J. Am. Chem. Soc. 1987, 109, 1601-1603.
5. Richards, F. Ann. Rev. Biophys. Bioeng. 1977, 6, 151-176.
6. Kebabian, J. W.; Agui, T.; van Oene, J. C.; Shigematsu, K.; Saavedra, J. M. Trends in Pharmacological Sciences 1986, 96-99.
7. Gready, J. E. Adv. Pharmacol. Chemother. 1980, 17, 37-102.

8. Matthews, D. A.; Alden, R. A.; Bolin, J. T.; Filman, D. J.; Freer, S. T.; Hamlin, R.; Hol, W. T. J.; Kisliuk, R. L.; Pastore, E. J.; Plante, L. T.; Xuong, N; Kraut, J. J.Biol.Chem. 1978, 253, 6946-6954.
9. Bolin, J. T.; Filman, D. J.; Matthews, D. A.; Hamlin, R. C.; Kraut, J. J. Biol. Chem. 1982, 257, 13650-13662.
10. Filman, D. J.; Bolin, J. T.; Matthews, D. A.; Kraut, J. J. Biol. Chem. 1982, 257, 13663-13672.
11. Stone, S. R.; Morrison, J. F. Biochemistry 1984, 23, 2753-2758.
12. Fierke, C. A.; Johnson, K. A.; Benkovic, S. J. Biochemistry 1987, 26, 4085-4092.
13. Villafranca, J. E.; Howell, E. E.; Voet, D. H.; Strobel, M. S.; Ogden, R. C.; Abelson, J. N.; Kraut, J. Science 1983, 222, 782-788.
14. Chen, J.-T.; Mayer, R. J.; Fierke, C. A.; Benkovic, S. J. J. Cellular Biochem. 1985, 29, 73-82.
15. Howell, E. E.; Villafranca, J. E.; Warren, M. S.; Oatley, S. J.; Kraut, J. Science 1986, 231, 1123-1128.
16. Taira, K.; Chen, J.-T.; Fierke, C. A.; Benkovic, S. J. Bull. Chem. Soc. Jpn. 1987, 60, 3025-3030.
17. Mayer, R. J.; Chen, J.-T.; Taira, K.; Fierke, C. A.; Benkovic, S. J. Proc. Natl. Acad. Sci. U.S.A. 1986, 83, 7718-7720.
18. Weiner, S. J.; Kollman, P. A.; Case, D. A.; Singh, U. C.; Ghio, C.; Alagona, G.; Profeta, Jr., S.; Weiner, P. J. Am. Chem. Soc. 1984, 106, 765-784.
19. Benkovic, S. J.; Fierke, C. A.; Naylor, A. M. Science 1988, 239, 1105-1110.
20. Charlton, P. A.; Young, D. W.; Birdsall, B.; Feeney, J.; Roberts, G. C. K. J. Chem. Soc., Chem. Commun. 1979, 922-924.
21. Cocco, L.; Temple, Jr., C.; Montgomery, J. A.; London, R. E.; Blakley, R. L. Biochem. Biophys. Res. Commun. 1981, 100, 413-419.
22. Wu, Y.-D.; Houk, K.N. J. Am. Chem. Soc. 1987, 109, 2226-2227.

RECEIVED November 4, 1988

WATER-RESTRICTED MEDIA

Chapter 7

Enzymatic Reactions in Reversed Micelles at Low Solubilized Water Concentrations

J. W. Shield, H. D. Ferguson, K. K. Gleason, and T. A. Hatton

Department of Chemical Engineering, Massachusetts Institute of Technology, Cambridge, MA 02139

α-Chymotrypsin has been used as a model enzyme to investigate dipeptide synthesis, hydrolysis kinetics, and substrate localization, in reversed micelles composed of cationic surfactants. Synthesis of the dipeptide N-benzoxycarbonyl-L-tyrosine glycinamide has been demonstrated with a non-optimized yield of 75%. Hydrolysis of a synthetic substrate, N-glutaryl-L-phenylalanine p-nitroanilide, is greatly enhanced in reversed micelles versus in aqueous solution, and does not demonstrate typical enzyme saturation kinetics. Reaction kinetics of a similar substrate, N-benzoyl-L-tyrosine p-nitroanilide, are not enhanced and do show enzyme saturation behavior. NMR free induction decay and spin-lattice relaxation measurements suggest that these differences are a result of different inter-actions of the substrates with the surfactant inter-face.

There are many potential advantages associated with conducting enzyme-catalyzed reactions in organic solvents, as opposed to traditional aqueous reaction media (1-2). A major benefit is the greater solubility and consequently higher concentrations some reactants and products have in an organic solvent. Secondly, the reaction equilibria for enzymatic reactions involving water can be manipulated to favor product synthesis in the low water environment of an organic solution; the low water environment also minimizes undesired hydrolysis side reactions. When substrate or product inhibition is a significant limitation, organic solvents can be used to partition the inhibiting molecule away from the enzyme. Furthermore, substrate specificity of enzymes can be different in organic solutions and can potentially be controlled by the choice of solvents.

Reversed micelles represent one technique of utilizing enzymes in organic solvents (3-5). Reversed micelles are thermodynamically stable, spherical, nanometer scale aggregates of amphiphilic

0097–6156/89/0392–0090$06.00/0

molecules solubilizing aqueous droplets in an organic solvent continuum. The hydrophilic head groups of the surfactant molecules surround the aqueous droplet or "water pool", while the hydrophobic surfactant tails protrude into the organic medium enveloping the micelle (Figure 1). Enzymes can be solubilized within the reversed micelle with retention of their catalytic activity. The parameter ω_o, defined as the ratio of the water concentration to the surfactant concentration, is an indication of the size of the reversed micelles.

This paper has two primary objectives. The first is to report on the use of an enzyme-containing reversed micellar medium for organic synthesis: specifically the formation of a model dipeptide. The feasibility of peptide synthesis in reversed micelles has been previously demonstrated (6). Small peptides are used in a variety of applications, such as artificial sweeteners, pesticides and pharmaceuticals. Since peptide bonds between an aromatic amino acid and a hydrophilic amino acid are of considerable interest (for instance in peptide analgesics), the synthesis of a tyrosine-glycine dipeptide was chosen for the model reaction.

The second objective is to examine the influence of reversed micellar solution parameters, including the interaction of substrates with the surfactant interface, on observed initial rate kinetics. This is of interest because a number of reports have indicated that enzymes in reversed micellar solutions exhibit an enhanced reactivity, or "super-activity" (7-9). As a model system, the hydrolysis reactions of synthetic substrates of α-chymotrypsin were studied in a reversed micellar solution. Nuclear magnetic resonance was used to examine the interactions between these substrates and the micellar environment.

Experimental

Materials. *N*-benzoxycarbonyl-L-tyrosine glycinamide (Z-Tyr-Gly-NH$_2$) and *N*-benzoxycarbonyl-L-tyrosine hexyl ester (Z-Tyr-OHx) were purchased from Bachem, Switzerland. *N*-benzoxycarbonyl-L-tyrosine methyl ester (Z-Tyr-OMe) was purchased from Chemical Dynamics, S. Plainfield, NJ. Glycinamide (Gly-NH$_2$), *N*-glutaryl-L-phenylalanine *p*-nitroanilide (GPANA) and *N*-benzoyl-L-tyrosine *p*-nitroanilide (BTPNA), bovine pancreatic α-chymotrypsin, and enzyme grade tris buffer were all obtained from Sigma, St. Louis, MO. Dodecyltrimethyl ammonium bromide (DTAB), also from Sigma, was recrystallized from diethyl ether and methanol. n-Hexanol and cetyltrimethyl ammonium bromide (CTAB) were from Fluka, Switzerland. n-Octane was from Aldrich, Milwaukee, WI. Analytical grade chloroform and n-heptane were from Mallinckrodt, Paris, KY and analytical grade methanol was from J.T. Baker, Phillipsburg, NJ. Deionized water was used throughout. Deuterated water, methanol, chloroform and octane from Aldrich were used as solvents in the NMR work.

Methods. Z-Tyr-Gly-NH$_2$ was synthesized from Z-Tyr-OMe and Gly-NH$_2$ in reversed micellar solutions containing 0.15 M DTAB as the surfactant in a 1:5 volume mixture of n-hexanol and n-octane. Hexanol acts as a cosurfactant and aids in solubilizing the Z-Tyr-OMe. Initial rate kinetic studies employed the hydrolysis of the synthetic substrates GPANA and BTPNA in reversed micelles of CTAB in a

1:1 volume mixture of chloroform and n-heptane. Owing to the limited commercial availability of deuterated n-heptane, deuterated n-octane was substituted in the NMR work. A control experiment showed that there was no effect on the observed reaction kinetics due to this substitution in the bulk organic continuum. Reversed micellar solutions were made by slow addition of 0.2 M tris pH=9.0 aqueous buffer to a dispersion of the CTAB surfactant in the organic solvent. Substrate solutions were made by adding the substrate directly to the reversed micellar solutions.

α-Chymotrypsin dissolved in 0.2 M tris buffer, pH=9.0, was injected into the substrate-containing reversed micellar organic solution to initiate the above reactions. Enzyme solutions were prepared fresh, stored on ice and used within four hours of preparation. Gentle agitation after addition of the aqueous α-chymotrypsin solution would produce an optically-transparent solution. For the dipeptide synthesis, 0.2 ml aliquots of the reaction mixture were periodically removed and the reaction stopped by the addition of 2 ml of methanol. Analysis was conducted on a Perkin-Elmer Series 4 HPLC using a C-18 column (Serva, Westbury, NY) and a gradient 0.1 M acetic acid/methanol elution scheme. Commercially available Z-Tyr-Gly-NH_2 and Z-Tyr-OHx were used as a standards.

Initial reaction rates were discerned spectrophotometrically at 410 nm by measuring the evolution of the chromophoric p-nitroaniline on a recording Perkin Elmer Lamda 3B spectrophotometer. Extinction coefficients were determined for every surfactant concentration and ω_0; they varied from 4000 to 6000 $ABS\text{-}M^{-1}\text{-}cm^{-1}$. Reaction mixtures and the spectrophotometer cell holder were maintained at 25°C.

Proton chemical shift values were obtained on a homebuilt 500 MHz nuclear magnetic spectrometer at a resolution of 0.003 ppm; spin-lattice relaxation times (T_1's) were determined using 1 to 4 repetitions of the standard inversion recovery 180°-τ-90° pulse sequence for eight τ values between 0.1 and 8 seconds. The T_1 values ranged from 2 to 5 seconds with a standard deviation of ±0.06 seconds. A delay of 30 seconds was used between repetitons to ensure that the protons had returned to equilibrium. To remove paramagnetic oxygen, samples were degassed by freezing, evacuating the head space and thawing for three cycles.

Owing to the limited aqueous solubility of GPANA and BTPNA, it was necessary to use water-miscible organic solvents to increase the substrate solubility in these solutions. For the initial reaction rate studies, GPANA was dissolved in 10% by volume methanol and BTPNA was dissolved in 20% by volume acetone. For the NMR studies, GPANA was dissolved in 10% by volume deuterated methanol and BTPNA was dissolved in 60% by volume deuterated methanol.

Results and Discussion

Dipeptide Formation. Figure 2 presents the time course of the dipeptide formation reaction. The limiting reactant, Z-Tyr-OMe, is depleted rapidly, being converted via nucleophilic attack of the glycinamide to the desired dipeptide product, Z-Tyr-Gly-NH_2; via trans-esterification to a transient intermediate, Z-Tyr-OHx; and via hydrolysis to the undesired side product Z-Tyr-OH. Dipeptide yield, based on the more expensive amino acid substrate, Z-Tyr-OMe, is 75% after 30 minutes using an enzyme concentration of 1 μM. Both the

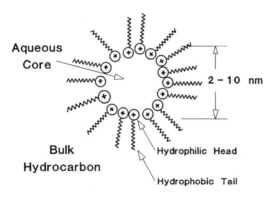

Figure 1.   Schematic representation of a CTAB reversed micelle.

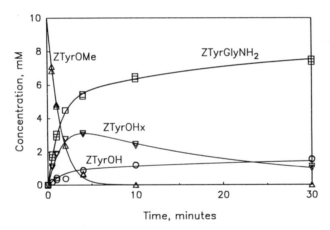

Figure 2.   Time course of the dipeptide synthesis of
Z-Tyr-Gly-NH$_2$.   Initial concentrations were [Z-Tyr-OMe] = 10 mM,
[Gly-NH$_2$] = 15mM.   [DTAB] = 0.15 M in 1:5 n-hexanol and n-octane.
ω_o = 6.5

yield and productivity obtained are comparable to similar reactions in other media (10).

Dipeptide formation in the reversed micellar medium is influenced by the localization and concentration of the various species in the reaction medium (Figure 3). α-Chymotrypsin is a hydrophilic protein and resides within the water pool of the reversed micelle. Glycinamide is a polar molecule and as such partitions into the reversed micellar water pools. Consequently, in the immediate environment of the enzyme, there is a locally high glycinamide concentration (ca. 0.8 M), accelerating the rate of dipeptide formation. The dipeptide product that is formed is hydrophobic and will partition away from the water pool, isolating it from back reaction and thus forcing the equilibrium towards synthesis.

The well-characterized mechanism of α-chymotrypsin-catalyzed hydrolysis of esters can be expanded to encompass transesterification and peptide bond synthesis. Such a kinetic model has been developed using the reaction scheme outlined in Figure 4. The highly reactive methyl ester substrate, Z-Tyr-OMe, is assumed to degrade irreversibly, while the desired dipeptide product and the acid byproduct form irreversibly. The third product, Z-Tyr-OHx, is a transient intermediate; thus the model provides for both its formation and subsequent degradation to either the dipeptide product or the free acid. Both esters are assumed to be in equilibrium with their Michaelis complexes, Z-Tyr-OMe-enzyme and Z-Tyr-OHx-enzyme, respectively. Best fit kinetic constants were found and are used to generate the concentration profiles shown in Figure 2. These kinetic constants qualitatively and often quantitatively describe the time course of the reaction conducted under a variety of other reaction conditions, including different hexanol, glycinamide, enzyme, and water concentrations (Ferguson, H. D., unpublished data.).

Kinetics of Model Substrates. In an effort to better understand enzymatic kinetics within reversed micelles, α-chymotrypsin hydrolysis of a model substrate, GPANA, was studied in CTAB reversed micelles. The hydrolysis kinetics of substrates by α-chymotrypsin is described by the Michaelis-Menten formulation

$$\text{rate} = \frac{d[P]}{dt} = \frac{k_{cat}[E][S]}{K_M + [S]} \tag{1}$$

In a reversed micellar system containing solubilized enzyme molecules, it is assumed that catalytically active enzyme molecules are only found within the reversed micelles. Furthermore there is no more than one enzyme molecule per reversed micelle, since the enzyme concentration is sufficiently small compared to the concentration of reversed micelles.

When considering enzyme kinetics in a reversed micellar system it is critical to recognize that there are two volumes upon which to base concentration dependent constants and variables, the total or observed reaction volume and the micellar or aqueous water pool volume (11). Additionally, the partitioning of the substrate between the bulk organic solvent mixture and the reversed micelles

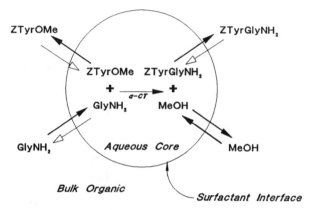

Figure 3. Schematic representation of the partitioning of reactants and products in Z-Tyr-Gly-NH₂ synthesis within reversed micelles. Filled arrows indicate direction of preferential partitioning.

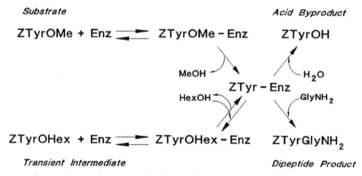

Figure 4. Reaction mechanism for Z-Tyr-Gly-NH₂ synthesis in DTAB, n-octane/n-hexanol reversed micelles.

is important. It can be characterized by a partition coefficient, P_S, defined as

$$P_S = \frac{[S]_{micelles}}{[S]_{bulk\ organic}} \tag{2}$$

If the substrate is preferentially soluble in the reversed micelles ($P_S \gg 1$), a comparison of the kinetic parameters observed for the overall system and the kinetic parameters intrinsic to the reversed micellar reaction medium gives

$$k_{cat,observed} = k_{cat,micelle} \tag{3}$$

and

$$K_{M,observed} = \phi \cdot K_{M,micelle} \tag{4}$$

where ϕ is the micelle volume fraction, and is directly proportional to both the micelle size and to the number of micelles. The parameter ω_0 is an indication of the micelle size, while the overall surfactant concentration is indicative of the number of micelles. Therefore, ϕ can be represented as

$$\phi = Constant \cdot \omega_0 \cdot [Surfactant] \tag{5}$$

The K_M dependence on ϕ has been shown for trypsin and N-benzoyl-D,L-arginine p-nitroanilide, but only when ω_0 was held constant (12).

The rate of α-chymotrypsin-catalyzed hydrolysis as a function of overall GPANA concentration in CTAB reversed micelles and in aqueous solution are shown in Figure 5. It is apparent that the reaction rate in the reversed micellar solution is on the order of 50 times more rapid than in the aqueous system. Furthermore, in the reversed micellar system there is no indication of enzyme saturation as the reaction is first order in substrate concentration. As enzyme saturation kinetics are not observed, it is impossible to differentiate between the parameters k_{cat} and K_M. Instead a second order bimolecular rate constant for both the micelle interior ($k_{micelle}$) and for what is experimentally observed ($k_{observed}$) is defined.

$$k_{micelle} = \frac{k_{cat,micelle}}{K_{M,micelle}} \quad and \quad k_{observed} = \frac{k_{cat,observed}}{K_{M,observed}} \tag{6}$$

In the case where $P_S \gg 1$, or the substrate is associated with the micelles not with the bulk organic solvent, Equations 3 and 4 become

$$k_{observed} = \frac{1}{\phi} \cdot k_{micelle} \tag{7}$$

Thus, if the intrinsic constant, $k_{micelle}$, is independent of the volume fraction of micelles, ϕ, $k_{observed}$ should be a linear function of $1/\phi$. Table I gives maximum solubility data for GPANA and BTPNA indicating that these substrates are associated with the reversed micelles and, consequently, should obey Equation 7. Results for GPANA in which ϕ was varied by changing the surfactant concentration, holding ω_o constant, show that this is indeed the case (Figure 6). The increase in the rate constant observed with decreasing ϕ is due to the reversed micelles ability to concentrate the hydrophilic substrate within the reversed micelles. However, when ϕ is varied by changing ω_o, holding the surfactant concentration constant, $k_{observed}$ is no longer proportional to $1/\phi$, but instead increases beyond what is predicted as ω_o is decreased (Figure 6). Therefore, other phenomenon, in addition to the concentration of substrate within the reversed micelles, must account for this rate enhancement at low ω_o.

A second synthetic substrate, BTPNA, was investigated to clarify if this rate enhancement in CTAB reversed micelles is observed for all substrates (Figure 7). Two major differences are observed: first, that there is no reaction rate enhancement in reversed micelles versus an aqueous based system, and second, that saturation kinetics are observed.

The observation that different substrates behave differently, and that there is an dependence on ω_o beyond that of ϕ, present the possibility that the specific localization of the substrate within the reversed micelle plays a role in determining the kinetics.

Table I.   Maximum solubility of substrates

Solution	GPANA	BTPNA
Aqueous	$< 1 \times 10^{-3}$ M	$< 1 \times 10^{-3}$ M
1:1 chloroform/heptane	2×10^{-5} M	$< 2 \times 10^{-5}$ M
Reversed micellar		
0.1 M CTAB	2.5×10^{-3} M	8×10^{-3} M
$\omega_o = 3$		

Substrate Localization.   To determine how the substrate molecules are associated with the surfactant interface layer, chemical shifts and spin-lattice relaxation rates for substrate molecule protons in reversed micellar and in aqueous solutions were measured. Both substrate molecules, GPANA and BTPNA, have three subunits: the phenylalanine or tyrosine aromatic ring, the p-nitro anilide, and the acyl group. Because each subunit has non-overlapping NMR spectral assignments, and assuming proton-proton dipolar coupling between the subunits is weak due to motional averaging, the spin-lattice relaxation behavior of protons on each of the three subunits can be considered separately. In fact, the relaxation rate, R, ($R=1/T_1$) for GPANA protons in aqueous solution varies from 0.29 to 1.39 s^{-1}, supporting this assumption. In addition, the p-nitro anilide protons of both GPANA and BTPNA in aqueous solution have $R=0.30\pm.05$ s^{-1}, demonstrating little change upon chemical substitution of the other two subunits. A faster spin-lattice relaxation rate of a given proton is indicative of increased rotational and translational motions occurring at the NMR frequency (500 MHz). Such an increase results when higher frequency motions are re-

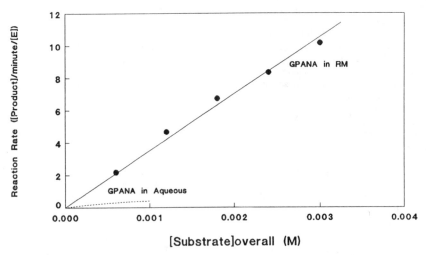

Figure 5.   Comparison of GPANA hydrolysis rates in aqueous
solution and CTAB reversed micelles.   [CTAB] = 0.1 M ω_o=3

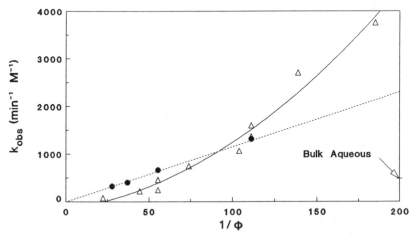

Figure 6.   Second order bimolecular rate constant for the
hydrolysis of GPANA by α-chymotrypsin in CTAB reversed micelles
as a function of $1/\phi$. ϕ = volume fraction of reversed micelles.
(•) ω_o=3, [CTAB] = .1, .2, .3, .4 M
(△) [CTAB]=.1 M, w_o=3, 4, 5, 5.4, 7, 10, 12, 25

stricted or new modes of low frequency motions are introduced. Restricted motion is the more probable effect in reversed micelles since the dimensions of the aqueous pool and the substrate are comparable and the largest increase in R occurs at the smallest ω_o. Also, since R changes differently for the various subunits, the concerted motion of the micelles is not the dominant effect.

The chemical shifts (δs) of substrate protons are different in reversed micellar media compared to aqueous solution. The chemical shift is a complex function of the environment around a proton, influenced by the solvent type, external electrostatic forces and the internal electronic structure of the molecule. A change in the chemical shift for substrate protons between an aqueous and reversed micellar solution is an indication of a change in the local electronic environment.

Table II details the changes in the chemical shift for protons on the three subunits of the substrate molecules for two different micelle sizes. The proton numbers refer to the identifications made in Figure 8. Table III shows the ratio of relaxation rates in reversed micelles to the relaxation rates in an aqueous system. These values have a standard deviation of ±0.05 units.

The protons on GPANA associated with the phenylalanine benzene ring (numbers 1 and 2) and those on BTPNA associated with the acyl group (numbers 5, and 6) have little or no change in their available motions in a reversed micellar environment versus in aqueous solution. Furthermore, these protons undergo small changes in their chemical shifts, indicating a minimal alteration in their local electronic environment. Thus the reversed micellar environment of these protons is similar to an aqueous environment, suggesting that these two subunits are in the water pool of the micelle.

In contrast, those protons on the other subunits of the substrate molecules do experience hinderance in the reversed micelles and undergo signifcant changes in their electronic environment. The p-nitro anilide protons (numbers 3 and 4) on both substrates have increased relaxation rates and proton 4 undergoes a large downfield chemical shift. Similar effects are seen in the GPANA protons associated with the acyl group composed of the glutaric acid (numbers 5 and 6) and in the BTPNA protons located near the hydroxyl on the tyrosine benzene ring (numbers 1 and 2).

Table II. Differences in Chemical Shifts
$\delta_{Reversed\ Micelles} - \delta_{Aqueous}$

Substrate Subunit	Proton Number	GPANA		BTPNA	
		$\delta_{\omega_o=5} - \delta_{Aq}$	$\delta_{\omega_o=10} - \delta_{Aq}$	$\delta_{\omega_o=5} - \delta_{Aq}$	$\delta_{\omega_o=10} - \delta_{Aq}$
amino acid	1	0.061	0.067	0.271	0.254
side group	2	0.273	0.252	0.242	0.222
p-nitro	3	0.172	0.169	0.125	0.125
anilide	4	0.650	0.630	0.484	0.464
acyl	5	0.285	0.273	0.048	0.086
group	6	0.428	0.298	-0.021	-0.027

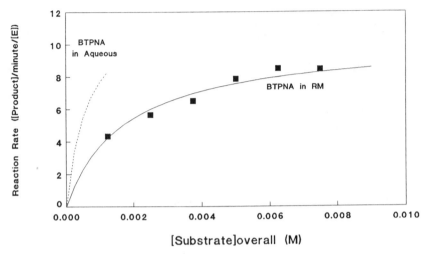

Figure 7.   Comparison of BTPNA hydrolysis rates in aqueous
solution and CTAB reversed micelles.   [CTAB] = 0.1 M ω_o=3

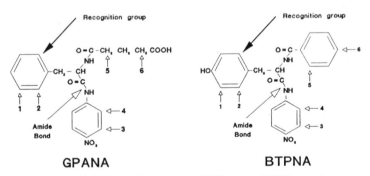

Figure 8.   Synthetic substrates GPANA and BTPNA.   Open arrows
indicate amide bond hydrolyzed by α-chymotrypsin.   Solid arrows
indicate hydrophobic recognition groups.   Numbers refer to
protons examined by NMR.

Table III. Ratios of Relaxation Rates

Substrate Subunit	Proton Number	GPANA		BTPNA	
		$\dfrac{R_{\omega_o=5}}{R_{Aq}}$	$\dfrac{R_{\omega_o=10}}{R_{Aq}}$	$\dfrac{R_{\omega_o=5}}{R_{Aq}}$	$\dfrac{R_{\omega_o=10}}{R_{Aq}}$
amino acid	1	1.04	1.00	2.14	1.83
side group	2	1.10	1.08	1.66	1.59
p-nitro	3	1.48	1.38	1.48	1.60
anilide	4	1.49	1.37	1.46	1.43
acyl	5	1.47	1.47	1.18	1.15
group	6	1.61	1.56	1.13	0.99

Consequently, these four subunits may be associated with the positively charged surfactant layer hindering their motion and inducing a downfield chemical shift. These substrate moieties could interact with the positively charged head groups of the surfactant, because the carboxylic acid carries a negative charge, the oxygens of the nitro group carry a fractional negative charge and the hydroxyl group is polar (Figure 9).

The configuration of the substrate within the reversed micelle may have significant implications for enzyme kinetics. In nature, α-chymotrypsin only hydrolyzes the peptide bond of polypeptides on the carboxylic acid end of aromatic amino acid residues. This selectivity arises because the aromatic portion of the amino acid fits into a recognition site next to the reactive site on the enzyme. The comparable amide bond on the synthetic substrates is noted with the open arrow in Figure 8. The aromatic ring that fits into the recognition site for GPANA and BTPNA comes from the amino acid side group in phenylalanine and tyrosine and are noted with solid arrows in Figure 8.

Can the localization of the substrate molecule within the reversed micellar environment explain why there are differences in reaction rate enhancement for different substrates? For the substrate GPANA there is a significant rate enhancement, more so than would be expected from a simple kinetic treatment due to concentration of the substrates in the reversed micelles. A similar substrate, BTPNA, does not show a rate enhancement; instead, the observed rate in reversed micelles is less than in an aqueous solution. For GPANA, the molecule interacts with the surfactant layer, in a manner exposing the recognition moiety and the amide bond to the center of the micelle, where the bond can be more easily recognized and hydrolyzed by the enzyme catalyst. For BTPNA, the recognition portion of the molecule interacts with the surfactant layer making it more difficult for the enzyme to hydrolyze the amide bond. It appears that the positioning and localization of substrate molecules within the reversed micelle has a profound effect on reaction rates. Further understanding of the factors influencing these effects would facilitate the design of enzyme-containing

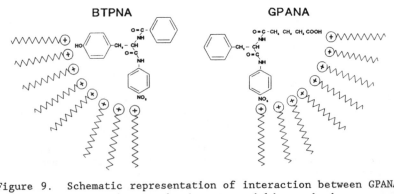

Figure 9.   Schematic representation of interaction between GPANA and BTPNA with surfactant head groups within cationic reversed micelles.

reversed micellar systems having the optimal selectivity and productivity for the reaction of interest.

Conclusions

Reversed micellar systems have certain attributes which can be exploited when considering enzymatically-based synthesis reactions. These systems can solubilize hydrophilic and hydrophobic reactants and, if the reactants interact with the surfactant layer, higher concentrations can be obtained than is possible in either an aqueous or an organic environment. Partitioning of reactants between the bulk organic portion of a reversed micellar solution and the micellar core can result in localized high concentrations of polar reactants. This can be used to promote desired reactions, such as the synthesis of dipeptides.

Observed reaction kinetics for some enzyme substrate systems solubilized within a reversed micellar solution are enhanced relative to those observed in aqueous solution. This enhancement can be due to simple concentration of the reactants within the micelles, but can also be influenced by the localization and orientation of the substrates being used.

Acknowledgments

The high field NMR experiments were performed at the NMR Facility for Biomolecular Research located at the F. Bitter National Magnet Laboratory, M.I.T. The NMR Facility is supported by Grant No. RR00995 from the Division of Research Resources of the NIH and by the National Science Foundation under Contract No. C-670.

This work was supported by Dow Chemical, an NSF Graduate Fellowship to H.D.F., and an NSF Presidential Young Investigator Award to T.A.H.

Literature Cited

1.   Martinek, K.; Semenov, A. N. Russ Chem Rev 1981, 50, 718-734
2.   Klibanov, A. M. Chemtech, June 1986, 354-359
3.   Martinek, K.; Levashov, A. V.; Klyachko, N.; Khmelnitski, Y. L.; Berezin, I. V. Eur. J. Biochem. 1986, 155, 453-468
4.   Shield, J. W.; Ferguson, H. D.; Bommarius, A. S.; Hatton, T. A. I&EC Fund. 1986, 25, 603-612
5.   Luisi, P. L.; Giomini, M.; Pileni, M. P.; Robinson, B. H. Biochim et Biophys Acta 1988, 947, 209-246
6.   Lüthi, P.; Luisi, P. L. JACS 1984, 106, 7285-7286
7.   Martinek, K.; Levashov, A. V.; Khmelnitsky, Yu. L.; Klyachko, N. L.; Berezin, I. V. Science 1982, 218, 889-891
8.   Barbaric, S.; Luisi, P. L. JACS 1981, 103, 4239-44
9.   Fletcher, P. D. I.; Rees, G. D.; Robinson, B. H.; Freedman. R. B. Biochim et Biophys Acta 1985, 832, 204-214
10.   Morihara, K.; Tatsushi, O. Biochem J. 1977, 163, 531-542
11.   Bonner, F. J.; Wolf, R.; Luisi, P. L. J. Solid-Phase Biochem 1980, 5, 255-268
12.   Martinek, K.; Levashov, A. V.; Klyachko, N. L.; Pantin, V. I.; Berezin, I. V. Biochim et Biophys Acta 1981, 657, 277-294

RECEIVED November 4, 1988

Chapter 8

Enzyme Structure and Function in Water-Restricted Environments

Electron Paramagnetic Resonance Studies in Organic Solvents and Reverse Micelles

Douglas S. Clark, Louise Creagh, Paul Skerker,
Mark Guinn, John Prausnitz, and Harvey Blanch

Department of Chemical Engineering, University of California,
Berkeley, CA 94720

Structure-function relationships were investigated for
two water-restricted enzyme systems: immobilized horse
liver alcohol dehydrogenase (LADH) in organic solvents
containing varying amounts of water, and tryptophanase
in reverse micelles of different water contents.
Electron paramagnetic resonance (EPR) spectroscopy and
spin-labelling techniques were used to probe the
effects of low water content on enzyme structure. The
oxidation of cinnamyl alcohol to cinnamaldehyde using
LADH was studied in various organic solvents. The
activity of the enzyme increased dramatically as small
amounts of water were added to each solvent; however,
the increase in activity could not be attributed to a
loosening up of the active-site conformation.
Tryptophan was produced from indole and serine using
tryptophanase in reverse micelles. The enzyme became
less flexible and the water became more rigid as
reverse micelle size decreased.

Recent research has demonstrated that enzymes can function in various
low-water environments (1-4), and that the properties of enzymes can
be favorably modified by nonaqueous solvents (5-7). Increased
substrate solubility, reversal of hydrolytic reactions, and improved
thermostability are among the practical advantages afforded by
nonaqueous solvents. However, the role of water in enzymatic
reactions at low water concentrations is not generally understood,
and there is some uncertainty regarding how much the conformation of
a protein changes as solvent water is removed (8,9). Nonaqueous
solvent systems therefore represent important media in which to
examine enzyme structure and function at the molecular level. Such
studies will prove valuable for the application of enzymes in low-

0097–6156/89/0392–0104$06.00/0
© 1989 American Chemical Society

water environments and should also provide fundamental insights into enzymatic reaction mechanisms and structure-function relationships. This paper describes preliminary results from studies of two water-restricted enzyme systems: immobilized horse liver alcohol dehydrogenase (LADH) in organic solvents containing various amounts of water, and tryptophanase in reverse micelles of different water contents. In each case, electron paramagnetic resonance (EPR) spectroscopy and spin labelling techniques were used to probe the effects of low water concentrations on enzyme structure. Advantages of EPR and spin labelling include their versatility (a wide range of spin labels can be purchased or synthesized and EPR spectroscopy can easily be applied to multiphase samples) and sensitivity to changes in the microstructure and internal dynamics of proteins. Moreover, the motion of spin labels can be quantified with the aid of computer simulations (10,11).

Immobilized LADH in Organic Solvents

Methods.   LADH (Sigma Chemical Co.) was immobilized to controlled-pore aminopropyl glass (Sigma, 75-100 Å nominal pore size) activated with glutaraldehyde at pH 7.5. The activated glass (750 mg) was rotated end over end in 30 ml of enzyme solution (25 mg LADH, 5 mg NAD^+ in 0.01 M phosphate buffer, pH 7.5) at room temperature for 3 hr. The immobilized enzyme was then washed with 500 ml of the phosphate buffer, and lyophilized from 5 ml of buffer containing 3 mg NAD^+. Immobilized LADH was assayed at room temperature in a variety of organic solvents containing 10 mM cinnamyl alcohol and 10 mM octanal (all organic solvents were dried initially over molecular sieves). Vials containing 10 mg of the immobilized enzyme in 4 ml of the reaction mixture were rotated at 60 rev/min, and 0.2 ml samples were withdrawn periodically. The samples were analyzed by HPLC (Hewlett Packard model HP-1090) and the formation of cinnamaldehyde was monitored at 300 nm. The thermal stability of immobilized enzyme in different solvents was determined by measuring the activity remaining after incubation in the solvent for 30 min at 80°C.

For EPR measurements, LADH was spin labeled with 4-(2-Iodoacetamido)-TEMPO (abbreviated as SL-1 and obtained from Aldrich Chemical Co.) prior to immobilization as described in reference 12. All spectra were collected at room temperature on a Bruker ER200D-SRC EPR spectrometer using a microwave power of 15.9 mW, a modulation amplitude of 1.0 G, and a scan range of 100 G.

Results and Discussion.   To examine the behavior of LADH in different organic solvents containing various amounts of water, the oxidation of cinnamyl alcohol to cinnamaldehyde was studied (cinnamyl alcohol oxidation by LADH in organic solvents was first reported by Deetz and Rozzell (13)). Reaction rates were measured in nearly anhydrous organic solvents and in solvents containing from 0.1 to 10% added water. The water content in the nearly anhydrous solvents ranged from 0.01 to 0.02%, as measured by Karl-Fischer titration. All rate data were obtained with enzyme immobilized to controlled pore glass and lyophilized from aqueous phosphate buffer of pH 7.5. Immobilized enzyme was used to prevent aggregation of the enzyme in the organics, which could lower the concentration of active enzyme and/or increase the likelihood of mass transfer limitations influencing the measured reaction rates.

The enzyme's activity in several nearly anhydrous solvents increased from total absence in acetonitrile to a maximum of 11 nmols (min-g support)$^{-1}$ in hexane, and in general the activity increased as the water solubility in the solvent decreased. This trend is believed to result from more extensive stripping of the essential hydration layer from the enzyme molecule by a more hydrophilic solvent like acetonitrile than by a less hydrophilic solvent like hexane (1). Furthermore, the activity of the enzyme increased dramatically as small amounts of water were added to each solvent. For example, the activity of immobilized LADH increased from 6.3 to 83 nmols (min-g support)$^{-1}$ when the water concentration in butyl acetate was increased from about 0.02% to 1.0%. It is of interest at this point to investigate more closely the role of water in these reactions and to examine the conformation of LADH in each of these solvent systems.

To this end, the spin labeling technique was used to probe the active site structure of LADH in various solvent systems. The spin label, SL-1, alkylated cysteine 46 (12), an amino acid in the active site of LADH that normally serves as a ligand to the catalytic zinc ion. LADH is a dimer, and each monomeric subunit contains one firmly-bound catalytic zinc ion. The position of enzyme-bound SL-1 was estimated by the spin label-spin probe technique (14,15). Cobalt (II) was employed as the spin probe, and the catalytic zinc in the enzyme's active site was replaced by Co^{2+} according to the procedure of Sytkowski and Vallee (16). The EPR spectrum of enzyme-bound SL-1 was then measured before and after replacement of the active-site zinc by cobalt; from the decrease in spectral amplitude the average nitroxide-metal distance was determined to be 4.8 ± 1.5 Å (17).

Shown in Figure 1 are the EPR spectra of spin-labeled LADH recorded in various solvents ranging from water to nearly anhydrous hexane, along with the spectrum of the completely dry, lyophilized enzyme. Also included are values of log P, a quantitative measure of the solvent's hydrophobicity (18), and the mean rotational correlation times (τ_R) of the spin label determined from spectral simulations (10,11). Since the EPR spectra are very sensitive to the spin label's motional dynamics and to the conformation of the surrounding protein (in general, spectra become broader and more asymmetric as the mean rotational correlation time of the spin label slows from about 10^{-10} to 10^{-7} sec), the spectra in Figure 1 indicate that the enzyme's active-site conformation became more rigid as the solvent became more hydrophobic. Indeed, the EPR spectrum of spin-labeled enzyme in hexane is virtually identical to the spectrum of lyophilized enzyme in the absence of solvent. However, increased rigidity appears to have had at most a secondary influence on the enzyme's activity. For example, the spectrum in anhydrous acetonitrile shows the greatest flexibility of all the organic-solvent spectra yet the enzyme had no activity in anhydrous acetonitrile. On the other hand, the spectrum in hexane reflects the most rigid conformation yet hexane afforded the highest activity of all the organic solvents.

Moreover, adding small amounts of water to the solvent had no apparent effect on the spin label's mobility, as evidenced by the spectra in Figure 2. EPR spectra recorded in butyl acetate with and without 1% water revealed that the active site conformation was unchanged by water addition even though the enzyme's activity was much higher when 1% water was present. Thus, the increase in activity upon water addition cannot be attributed to a loosening up of the active-site conformation. This result differs from a proposed model of the sequential hydration of dry lysozyme (19), in which restoration of enzyme activity followed a hydration-induced flexibility increase.

It is not possible at present to explain why water has such a pronounced effect on the reaction rates. Although structural differences were not detected as a function of water content, a structural role cannot be completely ruled out. Moreover, the reaction studied is quite complex and involves the oxidation of cinnamyl alcohol coupled with the reduction of octanal (to octanol) to regenerate NAD^+. The rate-determining step of this sequence is not obvious (hydride transfer or dissociation of the enzyme-octanol complex is a possibility (20), whereas the release of coenzyme is less likely since NAD(H) is expected to remain in the coenzyme binding site). Nonetheless, water apparently accelerated the rate-controlling step, possibly by modifying the electrostatic properties of the active site and/or by facilitating alcohol dissociation, yielding higher rates in solvents with lower affinities for water. Efforts to determine more about the mechanism of the water-induced rate enhancement are now in progress.

Finally, LADH exhibited a higher thermostability in organic solvents (Table 1), which is consistent with previous observations of enhanced enzyme thermostability in organic media (5). However, there was no correlation between structural rigidity, as measured by EPR spectroscopy, and stability against irreversible denaturation at 80°C. This result is relevant to the previous work of Zale and Klibanov (21), which demonstrated that a mechanism expected to stabilize an enzyme against reversible thermal unfolding (for example, increased structural rigidity) will not stabilize the enzyme against irreversible thermal inactivation unless the deactivation temperature is below the unfolding, or transition, temperature of the protein. Since a more rigid structure did not improve the thermostability of LADH at 80°C, either increased rigidity is not a stabilizer of LADH, or 80°C is above the transition temperature of LADH in organic solvents.

Tryptophanase in Reverse Micelles

Two-phase aqueous-organic systems permit enzymatic reactions involving hydrophobic substrates and/or products to be performed. The incorporation of enzymes into organic solvents with reverse micelles provides a promising technique for the synthesis of many organic compounds. The properties of reverse micelles have been

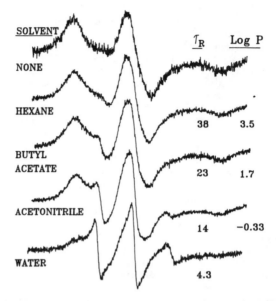

Figure 1.   EPR spectra of spin-labeled immobilized LADH in
            various solvents and in lyophilized form. The water
            content of each organic solvent ranged from 0.01 to
            0.02%. Rotational correlation times are given in
            nsec. Log P is the logarithm of the partition co-
            efficient of the solvent in an octanol-water mixture.

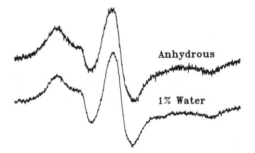

Figure 2.   EPR spectra of spin-labeled immobilized LADH in butyl
            acetate with and without 1% water.

reviewed recently by Luisi and Magid (22). Reports of enzymatic synthesis using reverse-micelle systems include tryptophan synthesis (3), peptide synthesis (23), triacylglycerol synthesis (24) and steroid conversion (25).

Reverse micelles are formed by the addition of a small volume of an aqueous solution to a surfactant-containing organic solvent. The surfactant molecules are orientated at the water-oil interface with the polar "head" groups in the aqueous phase and the nonpolar "tails" in the organic phase. Thus the reverse micelle can encapsulate an enzyme in the aqueous phase. The size of the reverse micelles can be controlled by varying the water-to-surfactant ratio, w_o.

The model system in this study involves the production of tryptophan from indole and serine using tryptophanase (Figure 3).

$$\text{L-serine + indole} \xrightarrow{\quad \text{tryptophanase} \quad} \text{L-tryptophan + } H_2O$$

This system exploits the advantages offered by reverse micelles. For example, indole is hydrophobic and inhibits tryptophanase at concentrations above 20 mM (3). The reverse-micelle system acts to keep the indole concentration in the aqueous environment of the enzyme low while the organic phase maintains a relatively high indole concentration.

Previous work on the use of a reverse-micelle system for the production of tryptophan reported kinetic data obtained under various conditions (3). Both the water-to-surfactant ratio and the cosurfactant used influenced tryptophan production. The present work reports results from EPR studies of the effect of these parameters on both the water and the enzyme in the reverse micelle. EPR spectra of $Mn(H_2O)_6^{2+}$ were recorded to investigate the state of the water in reverse micelles. A nitroxide spin label that reacts with lysine residues was employed to probe the microstructure of tryptophanase in reverse micelles of different w_o values.

Methods. The purification of crude tryptophanase purchased from Sigma Chemical Company is described elsewhere (3). The preparation of reverse micelles involved several steps and varied slightly depending on the type of experiment. The following describes reverse micelle preparation for kinetic experiments. Serine was first transferred to the organic phase by washing cyclohexane containing 5% v/v Aliquat-336 (tricaprylmethylammonium chloride, obtained from the Henkel Corporation) with an aqueous serine solution (0.20 M), thus exchanging serine for chloride as the anion associated with Aliquat in the organic phase. The aqueous solution was later analyzed to determine the amount of serine transferred to the organic phase. The non-ionic surfactant Brij-56 (Sigma), the cosurfactant 1-hexanol, and the substrate indole were then added to the organic phase at concentrations of 0.15 M, 3% v/v, and 0.10 M, respectively. Finally, an aqueous phase containing 3 mM dithiothreitol, 10 mM pyridoxal-5'-phosphate, and 0.1 M KCl and tryptophanase (freeze dried), pH 9, was added to the organic phase with a micropipette while gently stirring

Table 1. Thermal inactivation of immobilized LADH in water and in nearly anhydrous organic solvents

Solvent	τ_R (ns) of SL-1 in Active Site at 25°C	Percent Activity After 30 min at 80°C
Water	4.3	0.0
Butyl Acetate	23	58 ± 7
Heptane	38	54 ± 8

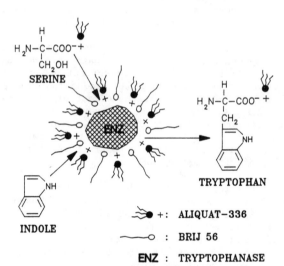

Figure 3.   Tryptophan synthesis in reverse micelles.

the solution. Reverse micelles for the EPR experiments were prepared without serine or indole.

Lysine-labelled tryptophanase was prepared by incubating the enzyme with 100-fold molar excess of 2,2,5,5-tetramethyl-3-pyrrolin-1-oxyl-3-carboxylic acid N-hydroxysuccinimide ester (Eastman Kodak Company) in 10 mM bis-tris-propane (Sigma), pH 8 (20% v/v i-propanol), for 24 hours at room temperature. Free spin label was subsequently removed by dialysis. The resulting lysine-labeled enzyme solution was used to make reverse micelles as described above.

The manganese EPR experiments were performed at room temperature without enzyme present. The aqueous phase consisted of a 0.5 mM solution of manganese(II) chloride. EPR spectra were recorded at X-band with a modulation amplitude of 10.0 G and a scan range of 2000 G.

Results and Discussion. Kinetic studies have shown that tryptophan production in reverse micelles is senstitive to w_0 and hence to micelle size (3). Figure 4 shows the effect of w_0 on tryptophan production. Tryptophanase exhibited its highest activity at a w_0 of about 20.

To determine if the properties of micellar water vary with the water content, the EPR spectrum of $MnCl_2$ dissolved in reverse micelles was recorded as a function of w_0. The results, shown in Figure 5, indicate that the spectrum of $Mn(H_2O)_6^{2+}$ was very sensitive to changes in w_0. As the water content decreased, the linewidths became increasingly broad, indicating a substantial change in the nature of the water. Such broadening in X-band spectra is consistent with an increase in the rotational correlation time of the manganous ion (26) and hence a more rigid water structure.

The effect of w_0 on the enzyme was examined by comparing the EPR spectra of lysine-labeled tryptophanase. Although the spin label is nonspecific, it can still provide molecular-level information about the enzyme under different conditions. EPR spectra of the spin-labeled enzyme in bulk water and in reverse micelles are shown in Figure 6. Much broader spectra were obtained in reverse micelles, and the calculated rotational correlation time of the attached label (10) increased with w_0. Thus, the enzyme-bound spin label became more constrained as the water content of the reverse micelle decreased. Since the rotational correlation time of the entire protein in bulk water calculated from the Stokes-Einstein equation is about 200 nsec, the motion of the spin label was still rapid relative to the tumbling rate of the enzyme. Therefore, broadening of the spectrum was apparently caused by a change in the local dynamics of tryptophanase rather than by a decrease in the enzyme's overall rotation rate. The tumbling rate of the enzyme could have decreased as well, however.

In summary, EPR has provided evidence that as the water content in reverse micelles decreases, the water becomes more rigid and the enzyme becomes less flexible. Kinetic studies have shown that there is an optimum water content for enzymatic activity. The link between this optimum and the state of both the water and the enzyme in the reverse micelle is the subject of ongoing research in this laboratory.

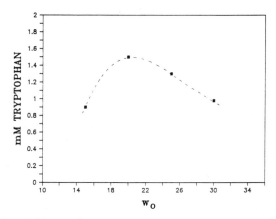

Figure 4.   Effect of water content on the amount of tryptophan
produced in 20 hrs. w_O is the molar water-to-
surfactant ratio.   Experimental conditions: 37°C,
pH 9, 0.15 M Brij,   0.05 M indole, 0.83 mg enzyme/ml
reactor (data from ref. 3).

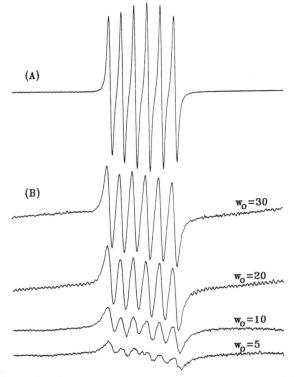

Figure 5.   X-band EPR spectra of $MnCl_2$ dissolved in (A) bulk
water and (B) reverse micelles.

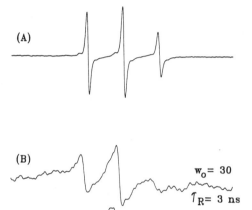

Figure 6.   EPR sprectra of lysine-labeled tryptophanase in (A) bulk water and (B) reverse micelles.

Literature Cited

1. Klibanov, A.M. Chemtech 1986, 16, 354.
2. Zaks, A.; Klibanov, A.M. Proc. Natl Acad. Sci. USA 1985, 82, 3192.
3. Eggers, D.K.; Blanch, H.W. Bioprocess Eng. 1988, 3, 83.
4. Randolph, T.W.; Clark, D.S.; Blanch, H.W.; Prausnitz, J.M. Science 1988, 239, 387.
5. Zaks, A.; Klibanov, A.M. Science 1984, 224, 1249.
6. Zaks, A.; Klibanov, A.M. J. Am. Chem. Soc. 1986, 108, 2767.
7. Randolph, T.W.; Blanch, H.W.; Prausnitz, J.M. AIChE J. in press.
8. Bello, J. Trends Biochem. Sci. 1985, Volume?, 110.
9. Baker, L.J.; Hansen, A.M.F.; Rao, P.B.; Bryan, W.P. Biopolymers 1983, 22, 1637.
10. Freed, J.H. In Spin Labeling: Theory and Applications; Berliner, L.J., Ed.; Academic: New York, 1976; Chapter 3.
11. Shiotani, M.; Sohma, J.; Freed, J.H.; Macromolecules 1983, 16, 1495.
12. Skerker, P.S.; Clark, D.S.; Biotechnol. Bioeng. 1988, in press.
13. Deetz, J.S.; Rozzell, J.D.; Trends Biotechnol. 1988, 6, 15.
14. Leigh, J.S., Jr. J. Chem. Phys. 1970, 52, 2608.
15. Dalton, L.A.; J.O. McIntyre, J.O.; Fleischer, S. Biochemistry 1987, 26, 2117.
16. Sytkowski, A.J.; Vallee, B.L. Biochemistry 1978, 17, 2850.
17. Clark, D.S.; Skerker, P.S.; Randolph, T.W.; Blanch, H.W.; Prausnitz, J.M. Ann. N.Y. Acad. Sci. in press.
18. Laane, C.; Boeren, S.; Vos, K.; Veeger, C. Biotechnol. Bioeng. 1987, 30, 81.
19. Finney, J.L.; Poole, P.L. Comments Mol. Cell. Biophys. 1984, 2, 129.
20. Fersht, A.; Enzyme Structure and Mechanism, Second Edition; W.H. Freeman: New York, 1885; p 396.
21. Zale, S.E.; Klibanov, A.M.; Biotechnol. Bioeng. 1983, 25, 2221.
22. Luisi, P.L.; Magid, L.J. CRC Crit. Rev. Biochem. 1986, 20, 409.
23. Luthi, P.; Luisi, P.L. J. Am. Chem. Soc. 1984, 106, 7285-86.
24. Morita, S.; Narita, H.; Matoba, T.; Kito, M. JAOCS 1984, 61, 1571.
25. Hilhorst, R.; Laane, C.; Veeger, C. FEBS Lett. 1983, 159, 225.
26. Reed, G.H.; Leigh, J.S. Jr.; Pearson, J.E. J. Chem. Phys. 1971, 55, 3311.

RECEIVED December 5, 1988

BIOMIMETICS

Chapter 9

Hydroxylation of C_2, C_3, and Cyclo-C_6 Hydrocarbons by Manganese Porphyrin and Nonporphyrin Catalysts

Richard H. Fish[1], Raymond H. Fong[1], Robert T. Price[1],
John B. Vincent[2], and George Christou[2]

[1]Lawrence Berkeley Laboratory, University of California,
Berkeley, CA 94720
[2]Department of Chemistry, Indiana University, Bloomington, IN 47405

Metal complexes that mimic the active site of monooxygenase enzymes and convert carbon-hydrogen bonds to carbon-hydroxyl in the presence of a monooxygen transfer reagents are called biomimetic catalysts. Studies concerning the activation of methane, ethane, propane, and cyclohexane to their respective alcohols with biomimetic catalysts that encompass manganese supramolecule porphyrins and open-faced porphyrins, manganese non-porphyrin tri and tetranuclear clusters, and a mononuclear manganese-substituted Keggin ion in the presence of monooxygen transfer reagent such as iodosylbenzene and t-butyl hydroperoxide will be discussed.

The use of biomimetic catalysts, that mimic monooxygenase enzymes such as cytochrome P-450 and methane monooxygenase by converting C-H to C-OH bonds in the presence of a monooxygen transfer reagent, is an area of intense research interest([1]). The monooxygenase enzyme, cytochrome P-450, has a metallo-porphyrin active site([2]), while methane monooxygenase has a metallo-non-porphyrin active site([3]). These two diverse monooxygenases also have different selectivities for hydrocarbon activation. For example, cytochrome P-450 will activate hydrocarbons greater than C_3, while methane monooxgenase will activate C_1-C_6 and possibly higher homologues.

While the focus of our research is to utimately activate methane to methanol, as is readily done by methane monooxygenase, we also want to understand what types of biomimics will activate higher homologues as well (C_2, C_3, and cycloC_6). In addition, the bond dissociation energies may play an important role in our ability to activate methane at ambient temperature, since methane has the highest C-H bond dissociation energy (kcal) of all alkanes, i.e., methane(104); ethane(98); propane(96); and cyclohexane (94).

Thus, we have evaluated several biomimetic catalysts, which encompass manganese supramolecule and open-faced porphyrins, manganese tri and tetranuclear clusters, and a mononuclear metal active site in a totally inorganic matrix, a manganese-substituted Keggin ion, with C_1-C_3 and cycloC_6 hydrocarbons in the presence of monooxygen transfer agents, iodosylbenzene and t-butyl hydroperoxide. We will also discuss solvent, catalyst lifetimes, and monooxygen transfer reagent as they effect the C-H activation reaction.

0097–6156/89/0392–0116$06.00/0

RESULTS AND DISCUSSION

MANGANESE SUPRAMOLECULE AND OPEN-FACED PORPHYRIN CATALYSTS, 1 AND 2.

Table I shows our results with C_1-C_3 and cycloC_6 hydrocarbons and manganese porphyrin catalysts **1** and **2** (Figure 1), with iodosylbenzene as the monooxygen transfer reagent, at room temperature in methylene chloride. It is evident that the supramolecule and open-faced porphyrin catalysts have similar reactivities with the hydrocarbons studied. Also, it is unfortunate that methane is not activated to methanol; however, ethane, propane, and cyclohexane are converted to their respective alcohols. Hence, we did not see any special reactivity with the supramolecule catalyst, **1**, and rationalize that too much flexibility in the "basket handles" does not provide the shape selectivity that we hoped for to gain a kinetic advantage with the difficult to react methane gas.

It is interesting to note that the corresponding iron complexes were less reactive than their manganese analogues, while catalysts lifetimes for **1** and **2** were on the order of 1-2 hr. Thus, both catalyst appear to undergo oxidative degradation and this reaction competes with the conversion of C-H to C-OH bonds. As well, the C-H activation results clearly show a trend of $C_6 > C_3 > C_2$ and follows the order of the bond dissociation energies([4]).

MANGANESE NON-PORPHYRIN CLUSTERS, 1-4

Table II shows the results with C_2, C_3, and cycloC_6 and manganese clusters **1-4** (Figure 1) with t-butyl hydroperoxide at room temperature in acetonitrile (methane did not react under the reaction conditions). The important observation of no catalyst decomposition upon continual addition of t-butyl hydroperoxide to again provide the initial turnover number is an extremely important characteristic of any biomimetic catalyst. It is interesting to note that this increase in catalyst lifetimes occurred in acetonitrile and not methylene chloride and shows the dramatic effect of a coordinating solvent. We did not see any indication of acetonitrile activation.

The Mn_4O_2 clusters were more active than the Mn_3O clusters and the Mn clusters also catalyzed t-butyl hydroperoxide decomposition (@ 1%) to acetone and methanol, which prevented reliable analysis of methane activation results. We could not compare the dinuclear manganese complexes to their tri and tetra analogues because of relative solubility differences; however, we were able to do this with several iron di and tetra clusters and found that the Fe_4O_2 clusters were more active with the hydrocarbons studied. Therefore, higher nuclearity or a variety of ligands may provide the shape selectivity we seek for ultimate methane activation with Mn and Fe clusters.

We also have attempted to inhibit these free radical reactions with 2,6-di-t-butyl-4-methylphenol and found no effect on the formation of cyclohexanol or cyclohexanone using catalyst **4**. This latter result strongly suggests that peroxyl, alkoxyl, or hydroxyl radicals are not intermediates in these reactions. The intermediacy of a putative oxo-manganese complex is further strengthened by the reaction of **1-4** with cyclohexene in the presence of TBHP or iodosylbenzene to provide cyclohexene epoxide and our proposed mechanism is shown in the Equation ([5]).

$$Mn_4O_2 + TBHP \longrightarrow Mn_2OMnOMn\overset{H}{O}OBu\text{-}t \longrightarrow Mn_2OMnOMn\text{-}O^{\cdot} + t\text{-}BuOH$$

$$Mn_2OMnOMn\text{-}O^{\cdot} + R\text{-}H \longrightarrow [\, Mn_2OMnOMn\text{-}OH \cdot R \,] \longrightarrow Mn_4O_2 + R\text{-}OH$$

Table I. Carbon-Hydrogen Activation of Hydrocarbons
Using Compounds **1** and **2** as Catalysts and
Iodosylbenzene as the Monooxygen Transfer Agent[a]

Hydrocarbon	Product (%)[b]		Turnover no.	
	1	**2**	**1**	**2**
CH_4	NPD [c]	NPD	—	—
CH_3CH_3	ethanol (1)	ethanol (2.7)	0.23	0.54
$CH_3CH_2CH_3$	isopropanol (9.6)[d]	isopropanol (13.5)[e]	2.1	2.8
	propanol (0.6)	propanol (1)		
$CycloC_6H_{12}$	cyclohexanol (72)	cyclohexanol (69.4)	16.7	14
	cyclohexanone (5.2)	cyclohexanone (1)		
	cyclohexyl chloride (4.5)	NPD		

a) Reactions of methane, ethane, and propane were run in a Parr
kinetic apparatus at room temperature for 24 h at 100-500 psi with a iodosylbenzene to
catalyst ratio of 20:1. Catalyst concentration was .0025 molar in methylene chloride.
The cyclohexane reactions were run at room temperature in Schlenk tubes with
substrate : iodosylbenzene: catalyst ratios of 1100:20:1 in methylene chloride.
Analysis and quantitation of products was obtained via capillary column GC analysis
with a 15m · .035 mm DB5 column.
b) Based on the mmoles of iodosylbenzene
c) No product detected
d) Ratio of 2^0 to 1^0 C-H bond reactivity on a per H basis is 45:1
e) Ratio is 42:1

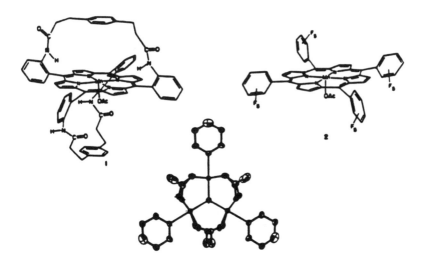

Mn₃O(O₂CCH₃)₆(py)₃   **[Mn₃O(O₂CCH₃)₆(py)₃](ClO₄)**

1   **2**

Mn₄O₂(O₂CPh)₇(bipy)₂   **[Mn₄O₂(O₂CPh)₇(bipy)₂](ClO₄)**

3   **4**

Manganese-Substituted Keggin Ion , MnPW₁₁O₃₉ ⁵⁻

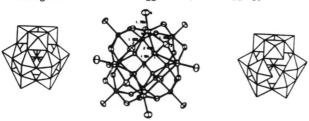

Figure 1: Structures of the manganese porphyrin and non-porphyrin catalysts.

Table II. Comparison of the C-H Bond Reactivity of C_2, C_3, and CycloC$_6$ Hydrocarbons with Mn_3-$4O_1$-$2L_xL_y$ Catalysts, 1-4, Using t-Butyl Hydroperoxide as the Monooxygen Transfer Reagent [a]

Hydrocarbon	Catalyst	Products(%)[b]	Turnover No.[c]
CH_3CH_3	1	ethanol(1)	2
	2	ethanol(<1)	<1
	3	ethanol(1)	2
	4	ethanol(<1)	1
$CH_3CH_2CH_3$	1	isopropanol(2)[d]	3
	2	isopropanol(<1)	<1
	3	isopropanol(5)	9
	4	isopropanol(3)	5
CycloC$_6$H$_{12}$	1	cyclohexanol(60) cyclohexanone(36)	121
	2	cyclohexanol(50) cyclohexanone(33)	114
	3	cyclohexanol(41) cyclohexanone(39)	126
	4	cyclohexanol(44) cyclohexanone(42)	127

[a] Reactions of ethane and propane were reacted in a Parr Kinetic Apparatus at partial pressures of 250 and 90 psi, respectively, at room temperature for 1-3h in acetonitrile. The ratio of t-butyl hydroperoxide (TBHP) to catalyst was 150:1, while the catalyst concentration was .0025M. The cyclohexane reactions were run in Schlenk flasks at room temperature for 1-3h with substrate : oxidant: catalyst ratio of 1100 : 150 : 1 and a catalyst concentration of .001M in acetonitrile. TBHP was added as a benzene solution.
[b] The analysis and quantitation was accomplished via capillary column GC and GC-MS analysis. Yields of alcohol and ketone were based on TBHP consumed (iodometric titration). The ketone yields are molar yields multiplied by 2, since two equivalents of TBHP are required to make one equivalent of ketone.
[c] Based on the mmoles of oxidizing equivalents/mmoles catalyst.
[d] Trace amounts of n-propanol (<<1%) were also formed(GC). As well, trace amounts of acetone were also found; however, a control experiment verified its formation from the Mn cluster-catalyzed decomposition of TBHP. Additionally, small amounts of isopropanol can also be oxidized to acetone under the reaction conditions.

MANGANESE SUBSTITUTED KEGGIN IONS, $MnPW_{11}O_{39}{}^{5-}$

Preliminary results with a manganese-substituted Keggin ion catalyst that has an extremely stable $PW_{11}O_{39}{}^{5-}$ backbone (Figure 1), shows some promise with small hydrocarbons(4). This catalyst can be heated to 65 °C for long periods without decomposition(6). An initial experiment with ethane and t-butyl hydroperoxide in benzene gave 2 turnovers of ethane to ethanol in three hr at 65 °C, while with propane the turnover number was 24 and provided isopropanol and n-propanol in a 5:1 ratio (Table III).

Unfortunately, methane did not provide methanol under these conditions. We are presently evaluating other metal-substituted Keggin ions as C-H activation catalysts for C_1-C_3 hydrocarbons.

Table III. Carbon-Hydrogen Activation of C1-C3 Hydrocarbons with a
Manganese-Substituted Keggin Ion Catalyst Using t-Butyl
Hydroperoxide as the Monooxygen Transfer Reagent in Benzene [a]

Hydrocarbon	Product (%)	Turnover Number
CH_4	-	-
CH_3CH_3	ethanol (2)	2
$CH_3CH_2CH_3$	isopropanol (30) n-propanol (6)	24

[a] Reactions of methane, ethane, and propane were reacted in a Parr Kinetic Apparatus at pressures of 500, 250, and 90 psi, respectively, at 65 °C in benzene. The t-butyl hydroperoxide (TBHP) / catalyst ratio was 177:1 with a catalyst concentration of 2.0×10^{-4} M. TBHP was added as a benzene solution. Yields were based on TBHP consumed (iodometric titration); ~ 75% in each case.

CONCLUSIONS

Although we have not as yet succeeded in our main goal of activating methane using iodosylbenzene or t-butyl hydroperoxide as monooxygen transfer agents, we have learned how to activate ethane and propane with several manganese mono, tri, and tetranuclear complexes. We hope to use these results as a foundation for the future utilization of oxygen gas as the monooxygen transfer reagent with iron cluster catalysts to give a system that mimics methane monooxygenase enzyme. In fact in a recently published paper, we reported on the synthesis and catalytic activity of a biomimic of methane monooxygenase enzyme, $Fe_2O(OAc)_2Cl_2(bipy)_2$, with t-butyl hydroperoxide or oxygen gas as the monooxygen transfer agents(7).

ACKNOWLEDGMENTS

The catalysis studies at LBL were supported by the Electric Power Research Institute under U. S. Department of Energy Contract No. DE-AC03-76SF00098, while the manganese cluster synthesis studies at IU were supported by NSF CHE 8507748. We wish to thank Linda Atherton of EPRI for support of the catalysis studies at LBL.

LITERATURE CITED

1. M.J. Nappa and C. A. Tolman, Inorg. Chem., 1985, **24,** 4711 and references therein.
2. F. P. Guengerich and T. L. MacDonald, Acc. Chem. Res., 1984, **17,** 9 and references therein.
3. R. C. Prince, G. N. George, J. C. Savas, S. P. Cramer, and R. N. Patel, Biochim. Biophys. Acta, 1988, **952,** 220 and references therein.
4. R. H. Fish, R. T. Price, and R. H. Fong (submitted for publication).
5. R. H. Fish, R. H. Fong, J. B. Vincent, and G. Christou J. C. S. Chem. Commun., 1988 , 1504.
6. M. Farji and C.L. Hill, J. C. S. Chem. Commun., 1987, 1487.
7. J. B. Vincent, J. C. Huffman, G. Christou, Q. Li, M. A. Nanny, D. Hendrickson, R. H. Fong, and R. H. Fish, J. Am. Chem. Soc, 1988, **110,** 6898.

RECEIVED November 11, 1988

Chapter 10

Biomimetic Catalytic Oxidation of Lignin Model Compounds

Robert DiCosimo[1] and Hsiao-Chiung Szabo

B.P. America Research and Development, Cleveland, OH 44128

The single-electron-transfer oxidation of
model compounds representative of the
arylglycerol β-aryl ether and 1,2-
diarylpropane linkages of lignin has been
examined by using Co(II), Mn(II), or
Co(II)/Mn(II) as catalysts. Catalytic
oxidation of 1-(3,4-dimethoxyphenyl)-2-(2-
methoxyphenoxy)propane-1,3-diol (DMMP) in 80%
acetic acid with 500 psi of 4% oxygen in
nitrogen and at 170 °C resulted predominantly
in products of Cα-Cβ bond cleavage when using
Co(II)/Mn(II) as catalyst. Cα-Cβ bond cleavage
of DMMP results from an initial single-
electron oxidation to produce an intermediate
aromatic radical cation; in the absence of
oxygen and catalyst, acid-catalyzed β-aryl
ether cleavage was the predominant reaction
pathway. Dihydroanisoin (DHA) and 1,2-bis(4-
methoxyphenyl)-propane-1,3-diol (BMPD) were
oxidized by stoichiometric quantities of
Co(III) to give solely products of Cα-Cβ bond
cleavage, but produced only acid-catalyzed
dehydration products under reaction conditions
necessary for catalytic oxidation.

The chemical bleaching of paper pulp is currently
performed using chlorine or chlorine dioxide, which for
kraft pulp results in the production of between 45 and
90 kg of organic waste/ton of pulp, containing 4-5 kg of
organically-bound chlorine/ton. (1,2) Bleaching of paper

[1]Current address: Central Research and Development Department, E. I. du Pont de Nemours
and Company, Experimental Station, Wilmington, DE 19880–0328

pulp whitens the pulp by removal of lignin or by
destroying the chromophores of lignin. Lignin is, after
cellulose, the principal constituent of higher plants,
and is a highly-branched, structurally intricate polymer
comprised of phenylpropanoid units.(3) The toxicity of
chemical bleaching effluents to fish and other aquatic
fauna has been known for some time,(4,5) and regulations
that will limit concentrations of polychlorinated
aromatics in waste streams will make alternatives to
the chemical bleaching of paper pulp with chlorine or
chlorine dioxide increasingly desirable. Lignin-
degrading enzymes are now being examined as biocatalysts
for the bleaching of paper pulp, as well as the pulping
of wood. "Ligninase" isolated from the white-rot fungi
Phanerochaete chrysosporium utilizes hydrogen peroxide
to generate an oxy-heme complex, which degrades lignin
by oxidizing the aryl groups of lignin or lignin model
compounds by a single electron transfer.(6-10) The
relatively stable radical cations that result decompose
via $C\alpha$-$C\beta$ bond cleavage (Figure 1).

One possible problem with using ligninase as a
biocatalyst for the degradation of lignin in paper pulp
is that the protein has an apparent molecular weight of
41,000,(10) and this may limit its ability to enter into
the high molecular weight cellulose-lignin polymer.
Faster rates of lignin degradation might be obtained
using much smaller "biomimetic" catalysts which function
via a similar mechanism.The autoxidation of
alkylbenzenes to aldehydes and carboxylic acids,
catalyzed by a number of different transition metals,
also proceeds by an initial electron transfer, resulting
in a one-electron reduction of the metal catalyst and
concomitant formation of a substrate radical cation
(Equations 1 and 2).(11)

$$M^{n+} + ArCH_3 \longrightarrow M^{(n-1)+} + [ArCH_3]^{\cdot+} \qquad (1)$$

$$[ArCH_3]^{\cdot+} \longrightarrow ArCH_2^{\cdot} + H^+ \qquad (2)$$

The ease of electron-transfer oxidation of aromatic
hydrocarbons to produce radical cations is directly
related to the ionization potential of these compounds,
with electron-donating substituents such as methoxyl
(almost every aryl group of lignin has one or two
methoxyl substituents) lowering the oxidation potential.
Examination of the ionization potentials for variously
substituted aromatic molecules(12) indicates that
oxidants such as Mn(III) and Co(III) should be quite
efficient in catalyzing the autoxidation of lignin and
lignin model compounds via a "biomimetic" mechanism that
parallels the oxidation of lignin by ligninase, and we

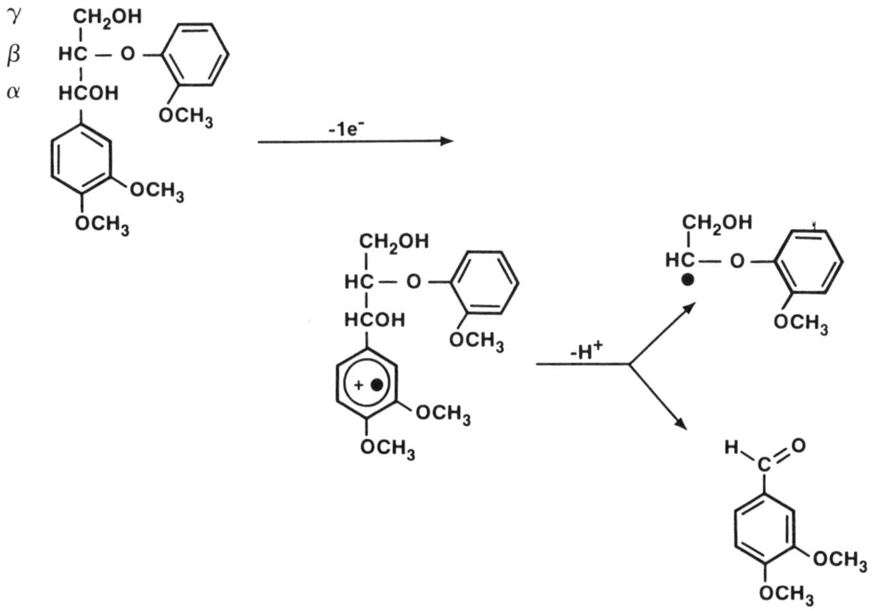

Figure 1. Cα-Cβ bond cleavage of a lignin model compound by oxidation via single-electron transfer. (Reproduced from Ref. 32.   Copyright 1988 ACS)

now report the results of a study of the autoxidation of
lignin model compounds by these catalyst systems.

Results and Discussion

The lignin model compounds whose oxidations have now
been examined by using autoxidation catalysts have all
previously been employed as lignin models in degradative
reactions using *Phanerochaete chrysosporium*, which
produces the enzyme ligninase, or in reactions that
examined the effect of kraft pulping or other chemical
or microbial oxidations on lignin model compounds.(13-
19) These model compounds represent the arylglycerol
β-aryl ether and 1,2-diarylpropane linkages of lignin,
which make up 30%-50% and ca. 7%, respectively, of the
major types of bonds connecting the phenylpropanoid
units of lignin.(3) Figure 2 depicts the four lignin
model compounds used in this study and the expected
products of the Cα-Cβ bond cleavage of these compounds
by their single-electron-transfer oxidation:
dihydroanisoin (DHA), 1,2-bis(4-methoxyphenyl)propane-
1,3-diol (BMPD), 1-(4-hydroxy-3-methoxyphenyl)-2-(2-
methoxyphenoxy)propane-1,3-diol (HMMP), and 1-(3,4-
dimethoxyphenyl)-2-(2-methoxyphenoxy)propane-1,3-diol
(DMMP).

Stoichiometric Oxidation of Lignin Model Compounds. The
stoichiometric oxidation of the lignin model compounds
DHA, BMPD, HMMP, and DMMP was first performed to
determine the ability of single-electron-transfer
oxidants such as Co(III) to produce Cα-Cβ bond cleavage
of the substrates (Table I). The diarylpropane model DHA
was completely oxidized to yield 2 equiv of
anisaldehyde. The diarylpropane BMPD produced at least
1 equiv of anisaldehyde; further oxidation of the Cβ
fragment (1-(4-methoxyphenyl)-1,2-ethanediol) produced
additional anisaldehyde. The arylglycerol β-aryl ether
model compounds HMMP and DMMP were also oxidized by
stoichiometric amounts of Co(III), but Cα-Cβ bond
cleavage was only observed for DMMP, which produced DBA
and guaiacol. Oxidation of HMMP by Co(III) in acetic
acid produced no products of Cα-Cβ bond cleavage, and no
other low-molecular weight (monomeric) products were
observed; it is likely that once oxidized to a
resonance-stabilized phenoxyl radical, dimerization to
biphenyl is the primary reaction pathway. The oxidation
of 2-methoxy-4-alkylphenols is known to result in ortho-
carbon coupling of two monomers to produce o,o'-
dihydroxybiphenyl, which are in turn subject to further
oxidation.(20)

Table I. Stoichiometric Oxidation of Lignin Model
Compounds by Co(III)

cmpd	[cmpd]:[Co]	solvent	T(^{o}C)	% conv.	% sel.
DHA	1: 0	AA	25	nr	--
DHA	1: 2	AA	25	100	100
DHA	1: 1	AA	25	53	94
DHA	1: 0	80% AA	25	66	0
DHA	1: 2	80% AA	25	100	62
BMPD	1: 0	AA	25	10	0
BMPD	1: 2	AA	25	100	97
BMPD	1: 2	AA	50	100	100
BMPD	1: 2	50% AA	50	88	54
HMMP	1: 0	AA	25	1	0
HMMP	1: 2	AA	25	88	0
HMMP	1: 0	50% AA	25	7	0
HMMP	1: 2	50% AA	25	73	0
DMMP	1: 0	AA	118	2	0
DMMP	1: 2	AA	118	99	67
DMMP	1: 0	50% AA	reflux	18	0
DMMP	1: 2	50% AA	reflux	40	38

[cmpd] = 1.0 mM, AA = acetic acid

Catalyst Regeneration Using Peracetic Acid. After
having used stoichiometric amounts of electron-transfer
oxidants for the oxidation of DHA, BMPD, and DMMP to Cα-
Cβ bond-cleavage products, the generation of catalytic
amounts of electron-transfer oxidants was first
demonstrated by using peracetic acid to oxidize Co(II)
to Co(III) in situ (Table II). Five equivalents of BMPD
were oxidized with 1 equiv of Co(III) in glacial acetic

Table II. Regeneration of Co(III) with Peracetic Acid

	Co(III)(mM)	CH_3CO_3H(mM)	% conv.	% sel.
BMPD	0.20	1.6	100	100
BMPD	0	1.0	87	30
DMMP	0.25	1.0	90	48
DMMP	0	1.0	8	0

[BMPD], [DMMP] = 1.0 mM, solvent = AA, 25 ^{o}C

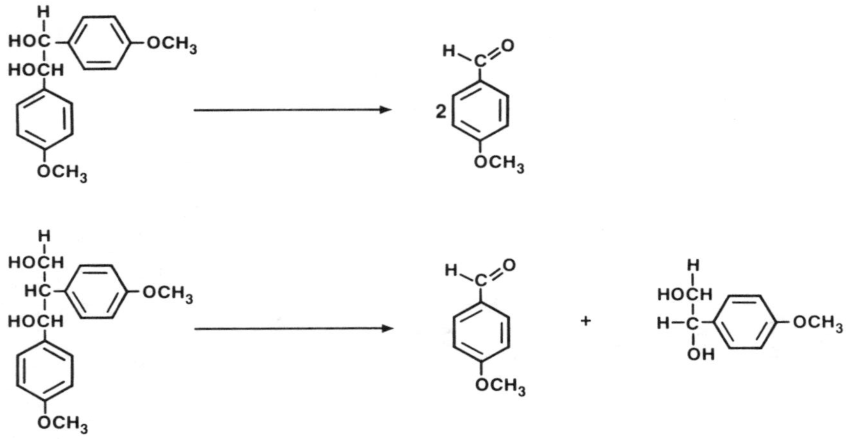

Figure 2. Model compounds representing 1,2-diarylpropane and arylglycerol β-aryl ether linkages of lignin. (Reproduced from Ref. 32. Copyright 1988 ACS). (Continued on next page.)

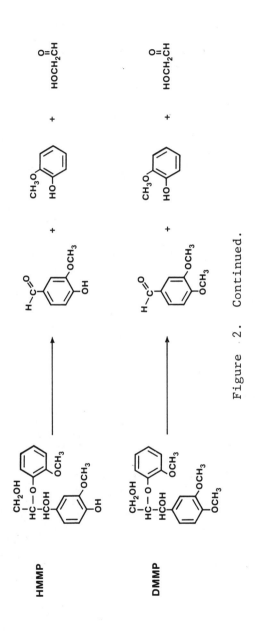

Figure 2. Continued.

acid at 25 °C by using 8 equiv of peracetic acid to
regenerate Co(III). Anisaldehyde was produced with 100%
selectivity at 100% conversion of BMPD. The reaction of
1 equiv of BMPD with 1 equiv of peracetic acid in the
absence of added catalyst gave only 30% selectivity to
anisaldehyde at 87% conversion. The catalytic oxidation
of DMMP using peracetic acid as the cooxidant was also
demonstrated: 4 equiv of DMMP was oxidized in the
presence of 1 equiv of cobalt(II) acetate by using 4
equiv of peracetic acid as the cooxidant. A 48%
selectivity to DMB at 90% conversion was obtained, and
three turnovers of Co(II) were achieved. DMMP is very
stable in the presence of peracetic acid under the same
conditions: a 92% recovery was obtained at 25 °C after 5
h. Because of the expense of using of stoichiometric
quantities of peracetic acid for lignin degradation, and
the large quantities of peracid that would be required
for the application of this type of catalytic oxidation
to a process such as paper pulp bleaching, an
alternative method of catalyst oxidation is desirable.
The most economical way to generate the desired
electron-transfer oxidants in situ would use oxygen as
the ultimate oxidant, and alkylperoxy or peroxyacid
intermediates formed during the reaction of oxygen with
the Cα-Cβ bond-cleavage products of lignin (in this
case, lignin model compounds) could reoxidize the
catalyst.

Acid-Catalyzed Dehydration of Lignin Model Compounds.
In addition to Cα-Cβ bond cleavage, both the
diarylethane- and diarylpropanediols and the
arylglycerol β-aryl ethers are subject to acid-
catalyzed dehydration reactions. DHA and BMPD could be
oxidized with stoichiometric amounts of Co(III) to give
good to excellent selectivity to Cα-Cβ bond-cleavage
products under reactions conditions that would otherwise
produce only the acid-catalyzed dehydration products
desoxyanisoin and trans-4,4'dimethoxystilbene,
respectively, but these same model compounds were not
stable at the higher reaction temperatures and pressures
(>150 °C, 500 psi 4% oxygen in nitrogen) required to
obtain catalytic reaction with oxygen and the Co(II),
Mn(II), or Mn(II)/Co(II) catalysts. HMMP was unsuitable
as a model compound since it did not undergo Cα-Cβ bond
cleavage when oxidized by Co(III). In contrast, the
arylglycerol β-aryl ether DMMP could be catalytically
oxidized to give predominantly Cα-Cβ bond-cleavage
products under the required high-temperature, high-
pressure reaction conditions, where in the absence of
catalyst and oxygen, acid-catalyzed dehydration and β-
aryl ether cleavage were also observed.(21)
      The stability of the lignin model compound DMMP
under the reaction conditions and in the solvents to be

used for catalytic oxidations was first determined in
the absence of added catalyst. After heating for 3 h at
170 °C and under 4% oxygen in nitrogen in glacial acetic
acid, no DMMP remained, and the products were the
diacetate   1-(3,4-dimethoxyphenyl)-2-(2-
methoxyphenoxy)propane-1,3-diol diacetate (DMPD, 66%
yield), the monoacetate 3-(3,4-dimethoxyphenyl)-3-
hydroxy-2-(2-methoxyphenoxy)propyl acetate (DHMA, 2.2%
yield)(where acetylation of the primary hydroxyl group
of DMMP has taken place), 3,4-dimethoxybenzaldehyde
(DMB, 7.6%), 3,4-dimethoxybenzoic acid (DBA, 9.9%), and
guaiacol (7.3%). A minor product also formed is the
monoacetate at the secondary hydroxyl group. In 80%
aqueous acetic acid, 5% DMMP remained, and DMPD (5.8%),
DHMA (12%), DMB (20%), dimethoxybenzaldehyde (DBA, 16%),
and guaiacol (35%) were produced; similar yields were
observed in 50% acetic acid, except for guaiacol (56%).
The production of DHMA and DMPD as byproducts was
observed in most reactions of DMMP with Co(II) or
Mn(II)/Co(II)(1:9), oxygen, and acetaldehyde (added as a
cooxidant for the generation of Mn(III)/Co(III), vide
infra). DMPD and DHMA were considered to be unreacted
starting material when determining conversions of DMMP
and selectivity to products.

Catalytic Oxidations. The effect of the addition of
oxygen and Co, Mn, and Mn/Co (1:9) oxidation catalysts
on the reaction of DMMP in 80% acetic acid at 170 °C is
illustrated by the examples listed in Table III.

Table III. Catalytic Oxidation of DMMP[a]

catalyst	reaction gas	conv. (%)	% selectivity		
			DMB	DBA	guaiacol
	N₂	92	4	6	77
	4% O₂ in N₂	77	26	21	49
Co(II)	4% O₂ in N₂	49	34	28	54
Mn(II	4% O₂ in N₂	89	41	33	0
Mn(II)/Co(II)	4% O₂ in N₂	79	29	42	9
Mn(II)/Co(II)	N₂	53	6	5	64

[a]Reactions were run for 3 h in 80% acetic acid at
170 °C and 500 psi of nitrogen or oxygen/nitrogen, using
10 mM DMP and 100 mM catalyst; Mn(II)/Co(II) ratio was
1:9. DMB = 3,4-dimethoxybenzaldehyde, DBA = 3,4-
dimethoxybenzoic acid.

Heating a 10 mM solution of DMMP in 80% acetic acid in
the absence of catalyst or oxygen results in acid-

catalyzed β-aryl ether cleavage to produce guaiacol and
3-(3,4-dimethoxyphenyl)-2-oxo-1-hydroxypropane,(21) with
very little Cα-Cβ bond cleavage. Adding oxygen but no
catalyst leads to an increase in Cα-Cβ bond cleavage and
decrease in β-aryl ether cleavage, while adding both
oxygen and catalyst produces the highest selectivities
(60-70% combined selectivities for DMB and DBA) to Cα-Cβ
bond cleavage. Running the reaction with catalyst but
no oxygen leads to acid-catalyzed β-aryl ether cleavage
as the predominant reaction pathway, but conversions
(related to the rate of reactions) are much lower than
in the absence of catalyst, indicating a possible
stabilization of DMMP to acid-catalyzed reactions by
chelation to the catalyst.

Acetaldehyde was added to the reaction mixtures as
a cooxidant for catalyst regeneration; acetaldehyde is
oxidized under these reaction conditions to peracetic
acid, which is capable of reoxidizing Co(II) to Co(III)
and Mn(II) to Mn(III).(22,23) Increasing the
concentration of acetaldehyde from 1.0 mM to 100 mM in
reaction mixtures containing DMMP (10 mM) and Mn/Co(100
mM) resulted in only a small increase in the conversion
of DMMP and the selectivity to DMB and DBA (Figure 3),
and a similar effect on conversion and selectivity was
obtained when using Mn(II) as catalyst. When using
Co(II) as catalyst, a marked increase in conversion was
observed between reactions run with no added
acetaldehyde and those containing 1-100 mM acetaldehyde.

Of the different catalyst used (Co(II), Mn(II),
and Mn(II)/Co(II) (1:9)), the mixed catalyst Mn/Co (1:9)
gave the best selectivities and conversions in the
presence of added acetaldehyde; a similar synergistic
effect when using Co(II) and Mn(II) for the autoxidation
of p-xylene has been previously reported.(24) Mn(II)
alone gave higher selectivity to Cα-Cβ bond-cleavage
products than Co(II), but the combination of
Mn(II)/Co(II)(1:9) generally resulted in the highest
conversion and selectivities to the desired products.
The catalytic oxidation of 10 mM DMMP using various
concentrations of Mn/Co (1:9) (0-500 mM) in 80% acetic
acid with 100 mM acetaldehyde at 170 °C and 500 psi 4%
oxygen in nitrogen was examined (Figure 4). Selectivity
to products of Cα-Cβ bond cleavage increased from 39%
with no added catalyst to 71% with 100 mM Mn/Co (1:9);
further increases in catalyst concentration only
produced moderate increases in selectivity at this
partial pressure of oxygen. Conversions of DMMP
remained fairly constant up to Mn/Co concentrations of
100 mM, but were slightly lower at higher
concentrations.

Increasing the concentration of DMMP while
maintaining the concentration of catalyst, acetaldehyde,
and oxygen constant resulted in a decrease in

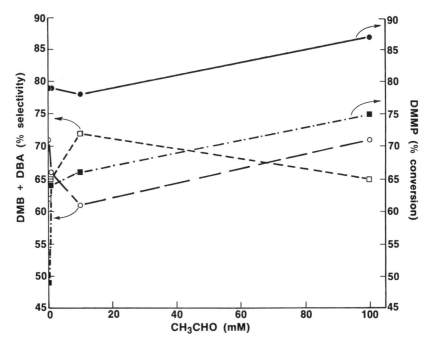

Figure 3. Selectivity to DMB and DBA and conversion of DMMP, as a function of acetaldehyde concentration. Reactions were performed by using 500 psi of 4% O_2 in nitrogen and either Mn(II)/Co(II) (1:9, 0.10 M; ●, conversion of DMMP; O, selectivity, to DMB and DBA) or Co(II) (0.10 M; ■, conversion; □, selectivity), in 80% acetic acid with DMMP (0.010 M) at 170 °C for 3 h. (Reproduced from Ref. 32. Copyright 1988 ACS)

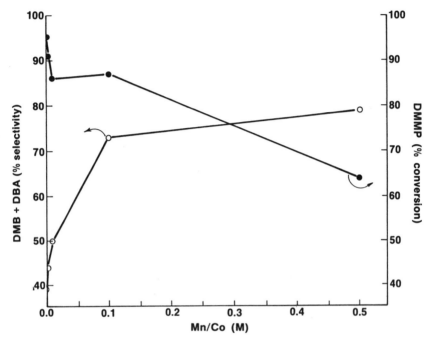

Figure 4. Selectivity to products of Cα–Cβ bond
cleavage (O) and conversion of DMMP (●) as a function
of catalyst concentration. Reactions were performed by
using 500 psi of 4% O_2 in nitrogen in 80% acetic acid
with DMMP (0.010 M) and acetaldehyde (0.10 M) at 170 ºC
for 3 h; Mn(II)/Co(II) = 1:9.(Reproduced from
Ref. 32. Copyright 1988 ACS)

selectivity to the Cα-Cβ bond-cleavage products DBA and DMB. A concomitant increase in the production of guaiacol was observed with increasing concentration of DMMP, indicating that the acid-catalyzed decomposition of DMMP becomes the predominant reaction pathway as the concentration of oxygen becomes limiting: increasing the partial pressure of oxygen in the reaction produces an increase in the selectivity to DBA and DMB at any given concentration of DMMP. The optimum ratio of reactants favoring Cα-Cβ cleavage in 80% acetic acid was 10 Mn/Co (1:9):10 acetaldehyde:1 DMMP using 10 mM DMMP and 8% oxygen in nitrogen; a 78% yield of DMB and an 18% yield of DBA at 100% conversion of DMMP were obtained. When the concentrations of all reactants except oxygen were increased at this same ratio, higher concentrations again gave lower selectivities to DMB and DBA. The rate of conversion of DMMP decreased slightly with increasing concentration of DMMP, all other reaction parameters being held constant.

The transition metal-catalyzed electron-transfer oxidation of DMMP requires oxygen for catalyst reoxidation. A blank check performed by heating a solution of 10:10:1 Mn/Co(1:9):acetaldehyde:DMMP(10 mM) in 80% acetic acid and at 500 psi of nitrogen and 170 °C for 3 h produced selectivities of 4% DMB and 11% DBA at 47% conversion, with a 64% selectivity to guaiacol; with no oxygen present, the predominant reaction of DMMP was acid-catalyzed dehydration and β-aryl ether cleavage. In contrast, the same reaction with 8% oxygen in nitrogen gave 63% selectivity to DMB and 21% selectivity to DBA at 100% conversion, and no guaiacol was observed. Similar results were obtained when using either Co(II) or Mn(II) alone as catalysts. The conversions of DMMP and yields of DMB, DBA, and guaiacol were approximately the same when solutions of DMMP were heated to 170 °C in either the presence or absence of added catalyst and/or acetaldehyde in the absence of oxygen.

Using a ratio of Mn(II)/Co(II):acetaldehyde:DMMP of 10:10:1 and 100 mM Mn/Co(1:9), running the reaction at 170 °C and 500 psi of 4% oxygen in nitrogen gave high selectivities to DMB and DBA at almost complete conversion of DMMP in glacial, 80%, and 50% aqueous acetic acid. In glacial acetic acid, the selectivity to DMB and DBA was 82% and 16%, respectively, at 97% conversion. In 80% acetic acid, the selectivity to DMB and DBA was 58% and 29%, respectively, at 99% conversion. In 50% acetic acid, the selectivity to DMB and DBA was 58% and 24%, respectively, at 100% conversion. These same reactions were examined at temperatures of 100 °C, 130 °C, and 150 °C. Low conversions (10-20%) were obtained when running reactions at 100 °C or 130 °C for 3-5 h; at 150 °C, DMMP

conversions increased to 50-60% at selectivities similar
to those obtained at 170 °C.

Conclusions

Under appropriate reaction conditions, i.e. high
catalyst and oxygen concentration and low DMMP
concentration, the catalytic oxidation of the lignin
model compound DMMP proceeds almost completely by Cα-Cβ
bond cleavage of the arylglycerol β-aryl ether.
Although DMMP undergoes autoxidation to produce some
products of Cα-Cβ bond cleavage in the presence of
oxygen alone, significant increases in Cα-Cβ bond
cleavage are produced by the addition of catalysts
capable of one electron-transfer oxidation of Cα-aryl
group. The mechanism of this catalytic oxidation mimics
the oxidation of the same lignin model compound by the
enzyme ligninase. The development of a "biomimetic"
catalyst for the oxidative degradation of lignin, which
does not depend on hydrogen peroxide for catalyst
reoxidation (as is found for ligninase and heme
proteins), would provide a distinct advantage for the
use of such systems over ligninase or other peroxide-
dependent microbial or enzymatic systems. It is
possible that hydroperoxy-lignin intermediates are
produced during the aerobic microbial degradation of
lignin, but because the heme is enzyme-bound, it is not
readily accessible to reoxidation by the hydroperoxy
intermediates; metal acetates such as cobalt(II) or
manganese(II) acetate should easily react with these
same hydroperoxy intermediates and be reoxidized. Also,
the microbial and enzyme systems are currently limited
to temperatures below 40 °C and are used in aqueous
systems at an optimum pH of 4.5-5.0, while the catalyst
systems that have already been developed for the
selective oxidation of alkylaromatics (such as p-xylene
to terephthalic acid), and which may be adapted to the
oxidative degradation of lignin, can be run in organic
or acidic or basic aqueous solvents at temperatures up
to 200 °C.
     One disadvantage of this "biomimetic" catalyst
system for lignin degradation is that only the
nonphenolic arylglycerol β-aryl ether DMMP was oxidized
via Cα-Cβ bond cleavage. Under the conditions for
catalytic oxidation employed, models of 1,2-
diarylpropane structures of lignin (DHA and BMPD) gave
primarily acid-catalyzed dehydration products, while the
phenolic arylglycerol β-aryl ether HMMP was oxidized but
did not produce products of Cα-Cβ bond cleavage. The
enzyme ligninase can oxidize these same diarylpropane
structures via Cα-Cβ bond cleavage, and as a substitute
for the chlorine bleaching of paper pulp for residual
lignin removal, the enzymatic reaction may produce

greater amounts of delignification than catalytic oxidation. However, both the studies of ligninase and biomimetic models of ligninase have focused primarily on reactions of arylglycerol β-aryl ethers, which are representative of the major type of structures found in lignin, but the structure of residual lignins remaining in paper pulps after cooking is not well-known.(25) Kraft cooking of pulp is believed to degrade β-aryl ether structures to styryl aryl ethers, diaryl ethers, and biphenyls, which are not easily degraded and are removed in a subsequent chemical bleaching step.(26,27) Rather than breaking carbon-carbon bonds for dissolution of residual lignin, oxidation by a biomimetic catalyst, or by ligninase itself, may result in further polymerization of the β-aryl ether degradation products. The treatment of kraft pulp with *P. chrysosporium* has been reported, and although treatment did not result in any bleaching, the remaining pulp was easier to bleach by conventional chlorine treatment due to degradation of some of the residual lignin.(28) An examination of the catalytic oxidation of residual lignin in paper pulp which utilizes oxygen and Mn/Co acetates in aqueous acetic acid needs to be performed before the efficacy of such a method can be judged in comparison to chlorine bleaching.

Experimental Section

General Remarks. Extreme caution should be taken when working with peroxides or peracids directly or when employing reaction conditions where peroxides or peracids will be generated in situ. No metal-ware (e.g. syringe needles) should be employed. Only all-glass reaction vessels, gas-tight syringes with Teflon luer-loc hubs, and Teflon syringe needles and cannulas were used. Dihydroanisoin (1,2-bis(4-methoxyphenyl)ethane-1,2-diol, DHA)(23) and 1,2-bis(4-methoxyphenyl)propane-1,3-diol (BMPD)(24) were prepared as previously described, whereas 1-(4-hydroxy-3-methoxyphenyl)2-(2-methoxyphenoxy)propane-1,3-diol (HMMP)and 1-(3,4-dimethoxyphenyl)-2-(2-methoxyphenoxy)-propane-1,3-diol (DMMP) were prepared according to slight variations of published procedures.(29,30) Cobalt(III) acetate was prepared by the ozonation of cobalt(II) acetate according to a reported procedure.(31) Reactions using oxygen/nitrogen mixtures at greater than atmospheric pressure were performed in Parr Model 4740 Hastelloy C high pressure reaction vessels equipped with glass liners and Teflon-coated stirring bars. Product selectivities were calculated on the basis of product yields and the amount of substrate reacted (conversion). Yields of products and recovered starting materials were determined quantitatively by HPLC.

Stoichiometric Oxidation of Lignin Model Compounds with
Cobalt(III) Acetate. In a typical procedure, a solution
of DMMP (6.8 mg, 0.018 mmol) and cobalt(III) acetate
(84.3%, 10.5 mg, 0.037 mmol) in 18 mL of glacial acetic
acid was heated to reflux in 20 min with stirring. One
hour later, the color turned from greenish black to
pink. The solution was cooled to room temperature and
veratrole (10.2 mg, 0.074 mmol) was added as an internal
standard for HPLC analysis. A 67% selectivity to DMB at
99% conversion of DMMP was obtained. For reactions
where cobalt(III) acetate still remained, an aqueous
solution of ferrous sulfate was added dropwise until the
color of the solution turned from green to pink; then
veratrole was added as internal standard.

Catalytic Oxidation of Lignin Model Compounds. In a
typical procedure, a Pyrex glass liner containing a
Teflon-coated magnetic stirring bar, DMMP (8.4 gm, 0.025
mmol), manganese(II) acetate (4.3 mg, 0.025 mmol),
cobalt(II) acetate (39.8 mg, 0.23 mmol), and
acetaldehyde (14 µL, 0.25 mmol) in 2.5 mL of 80% acetic
acid was placed in a 71-mL Parr Hastelloy C high
pressure reaction vessel (Model 4740). The reactor was
sealed, purged three times by pressurizing to 320 psi of
N_2 and then venting to atmospheric pressure, and then
charged with 336 psi of 4% O_2 in N_2). The reactor was
put in a heating block preheated at 170 °C and the
reaction mixture stirred for 3 h; at 170 °C, the reactor
pressure increased to 500 psi. The reactor was then
rapidly cooled to room temperature by placing it in an
ice/water bath and the vessel subsequently vented to
atmospheric pressure. Veratrole (11.2 mg, 0.081 mmol)
was added to the reaction mixture as an HPLC internal
standard and the mixture was analyzed to yield DMB
(37%), DBA (25%), and guaiacol (2.4%) at 87% conversion.

Literature Cited

1. Erickson, K. E.; Kolar, M. C.; Ljungquist, P.O.;
   Kringstad, K. P. Environ. Sci. Technol. 1985, 19,
   1219-1224.
2. Kringstad, K. P.; Lindstrom, K. Environ. Sci.
   Technol. 1984, 18, 236A-248A.
3. Sarkanen, K. V. In Lignins: Occurrence, Formation,
   Structure and Reactions; Sarkanen, K. V., Ludwig,
   C. H., Eds.; Wiley: New York, 1967; Chapters 3 and
   4.
4. Walden, C. C. Water Res. 1976, 10, 639-664
5. Dence, C. W.; Annergren, G. E. In The Bleaching of
   Pulp, 3rd rev.ed.; Singh, R. P., Ed.; TAPPI Press:
   1979; Chapter 3, pp 74-75.

6. Kuwahara, M.; Glenn, J. K.; Morgan, M. A.; Gold, M. H. FEBS Lett. 1984, 169, 247-250.
7. Kirk, T. K.; Mozuch, M. D.; Tien, M. Biochem. J. 1985, 226, 455-460.
8. Schoemaker, H. E.; Harvey, P. J.; Bowen, R. M.; Palmer, J. M. FEBS Lett. 1985, 183, 7-12.
9. Paterson, A.; Lundquist, K. Nature (London) 1985, 316, 575-576.
10. Farrell, R. L. Ann. N.Y. Acad. Sci. 1987, 501, 150-158.
11. Sheldon, R. A.; Kochi, J. K. Metal-Catalyzed Oxidations of Organic Compounds; Academic Press; New York, 1981; pp 122-133, 315-328.
12. Fukuzumi, S.; Kochi, J. K. J. Am. Chem. Soc. 1981, 103, 7240-7252.
13. Shimada, M.; Gold, M. H. Arch. Microbiol. 1983, 134, 299-302.
14. Kirk, T. K.; Nakatsubo, F. Biochim. Biophys. Acta 1983, 756, 376-384.
15. Oki, T.; Okubo, K.; Ishikawa, H. J. Jpn. Wood Res. Soc. 1974, 20, 549-557.
16. Adler, E.; Falkehag, I.; Marton, J.; Halvarson, H. Acta Chem. Scand. 1964, 18, 1313-1314.
17. Tien, M.; Kersten, P. I.; Kirk, T. K. Appl. Environ. Microbiol. 1987, 53, 242-245.
18. Huynh, V. B.; Paszczynski, A.; Olson, P.; Crawford, R. Arch. Biochim. Biophys. 1986, 250, 186-196.
19. Enoki, A.; Goldsby, G. P.; Gold, M. H. Arch. Microbiol. 1980, 125, 227-232.
20. Kratzl, K.; Gratzl, J.; Claus, P. Adv. Chem. 1966, 59, 157-176.
21. Adler, E.; Lundquist, K.; Miksche, G. E. Adv. Chem. Ser. 1966, 59, 22-35.
22.. Hendriks, C. F.; van Beeek, H. C. A.; Heertjes, P. M. Ind. Eng. Chem. Prod. Res. Dev. 1978, 17, 260-264.
23. Allen, G. C.; Aguilo, A. Adv. Chem. Ser. 1968, 76, 363-381.
24. Kurokawa, A.; Osaki, N.; Shigeyasu, M. J. Chem. Soc. Jpn. 1985, 207-213.
25. Gierer, J.; Wannstrom, S. Holzforschung 1984, 38, 181-184.
26. Gellerstedt, G.; Lindfors, E. L. Holzforschung 1984, 38, 151-158.
27. Gellerstedt, G.; Lindfors, E. L.; Lapierre, C.; Monties, B. Sven. Papperstidn. 1984, 87, R61-R67.
28. Kirk, T. K.; Yang, H. H. Biotechnol. Lett. 1981, 1, 374-51.
29. Hosoya, S.; Kanagawa, K.; Kaneko, H.; Nakano, J. Makuzai Gakkaishi 1980, 26, 118-121.

30. Vyas, G. N.; Shah, N. M. In <u>Organic Syntheses</u>;
     Rabjohn, N., Ed.; Wiley: New York, 1963; Collect.
     Vol. 4, p 836-838.
31. Tang, R.; Kochi, J. K. <u>J. Inorg. Nucl. Chem</u>. 1973,
     <u>35</u>, 3845-3856.
32. DiCosimo, R.; Szabo, H.-C. <u>J. Org. Chem</u>. 1988, <u>53</u>,
     1673-1679.

RECEIVED November 4, 1988

Chapter 11

Zeolite Catalysts as Enzyme Mimics

Toward Silicon-Based Life?

Norman Herron

Central Research and Development Department, E. I. du Pont de Nemours and Company, Wilmington, DE 19880–0328

The similarity between the rigid framework of a silico- aluminate zeolite having internal voids of molecular dimensions and the tertiary protein structure of an enzyme having a molecular sized substrate binding site has led to the development of 3 remarkable zeolite mimics of enzyme functions. A size encapsulated "ship-in-a-bottle" cobalt complex demonstrates oxygen binding behavior with evidence of cooperativity between the binding sites in an analogue of hemoglobin. Oxidizing systems which use zeolite supported Fe and Pd species to activate molecular oxygen at room temperature and pressure, demonstrate selectivities for hydrocarbon oxidation which are unrivaled in all but natural systems such as the cytochromes P450. Finally, semiconductor clusters arranged in a hyperlattice within zeolite frameworks display photoinduced electron transfer in analogy to the iron-sulfur proteins whose core structure they mimic.

The widespread use of their ion-exchange properties in the water-softening/detergent industry and their strong acid catalysis properties in petroleum-refining have made zeolites the workhorse materials in both applications. While this has attracted many researchers to the zeolite field, it has also had the effect of typecasting these remarkable materials into a limited number of chemical roles. The work reported below is a brief review of our own work here at Du Pont which attempts to dispel this stereotype by demonstrating that there are many remarkable similarities between zeolite structures and those of protein portions of natural

0097–6156/89/0392–0141$06.00/0

enzymes(1). By taking advantage of these similarities one can develop some exciting new catalysts which combine the attractive features of the robust, chemically inert zeolite with the tremendous selectivity and activity of enzymes.

What is a zeolite?(2) These materials possess open framework structures constructed of SiO_4 and AlO_4 tetrahedra linked through oxygen bridges. The open framework possesses pores and cavities of molecular dimensions 3-13Å making these the ultimate extrapolation of the quest for ever smaller reaction vessels. These "nano-bottles" are such that chemistry carried out inside them is itself affected by the confines in which it is being performed. One negative charge per aluminum is present on the framework and is compensated by loosely attached, and hence ion-exchangeable, cations. These cation-exchange sites allow the straight-forward introduction of active metal sites for catalysis (for a comprehensive discussion of ion-exchange and metal active sites in zeolites please see reference 2).

What is an enzyme? Let us hypothesize that the actual chemical trans-formation performed by a generic metallo-enzyme is carried out solely at the metal active site in a very non-selective catalytic reaction, typical of traditional homogeneous catalysis. However, nature demands much higher selectivity in her chemistry and so has constructed a very special environment in which to carry out this chemistry - the protein tertiary structure. The protein wraps around the active site performing several crucial functions a) protecting the active site from deleterious reactions such as self-destruction via bimolecular pathways b) sieving of substrate molecules so that only those capable of passing through the protein channels can gain access to the embedded prosthetic group. This can give the enzyme a high substrate-selectivity and c) providing a very stereochemically demanding void space in the vicinity of the active site where the substrate must reside during reaction. This leads to trans-formations at specific bonds within the substrate molecule. Presented in this fashion, the similarities between a metallo-enzyme and a metal ion containing zeolite become striking.

The following sections review 3 systems which we have developed to explore the generality of these concepts: mimics of hemoglobin, cytochrome P450 and of iron-sulfur ferredoxins. While the use of zeolites as enzyme mimics is an under-studied area it is certainly not new as evidence a previous volume in this series (1). The intent here is to emphasize the general concepts of zeolite biomimicry by highlighting the key results we have obtained. Interested readers are referred to the detailed publications referenced below for full experimental procedures and characterizational details.

Hemoglobin Analogue

Binding and transport of molecular oxygen is the first step in the respiratory chain and this function is performed in mammals by the iron proteins hemoglobin and myoglobin. Many synthetic models (3) and mimics(4) of this chemistry have been prepared using coordination complexes of iron, cobalt, manganese and other metal ions but all suffer from the same problems as the natural systems - namely autoxidation of the active sites with concurrent loss of oxygen binding behavior. Many of the autoxidation mechanisms identify oxo or peroxo dimer formation as the deleterious reaction(5).In addition to severely retarding this dimerization, the protein portion of hemoglobin also engenders a fascinating property known as cooperativity(6). Hemoglobin is a 4 subunit enzyme where each subunit has an iron oxygen binding site and these 4 sites interact such that binding of oxygen to the first subunit facilitates the binding of oxygen to the remaining 3 subunits of the tetramer.

Our synthetic mimic (7) consists of the well known oxygen binder cobalt salen (I) (8) constructed inside zeolite Y. This material is an example of the

SALEN I

"ship-in-a-bottle" (9) synthetic approach to encapsulated catalyst complexes in zeolites. Ion-exchange of cobalt(II) ions into the crystallite voids at a concentration of ~1Co per 2 supercages followed by sublimation of the flexible free ligand Salen into the same voids leads to assembly of the rigid complex . This complex involves square-planar coordination of the tetradentate salen ligand such that the complex has dimensions greater than the window size of the zeolite - once constructed inside the pores the complex is physically trapped on the basis of its size: a true ship-in-a- bottle (Figure 1). This complex as its pyridine adduct does indeed form an oxygen adduct as judged by the characteristic epr signal (Figure 1) generated upon exposure to dioxygen.

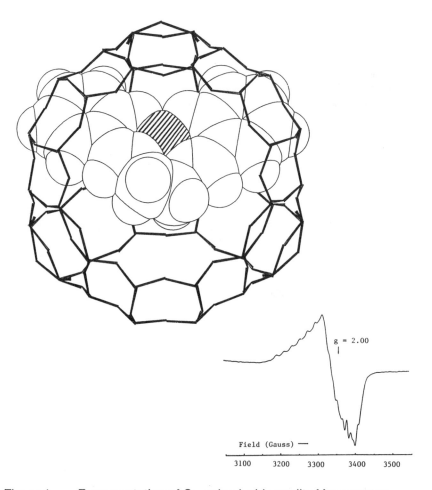

Figure 1.   Representation of Co-salen inside zeolite Y supercage. Zeolite framework has been reduced to stick bonds for clarity, Co atom is shaded. Inset shows epr spectrum of oxygen adduct at 298K and 760 torr oxygen.

Two of the remarkable features of this zeolite entrapped adduct are:

Firstly, compared to the same complex in free solution or as a crystalline solid, the zeolite encapsulated material displays quite remarkable stability towards autoxidation and peroxo-dimer formation(10). For example the half-life for the oxygen adduct epr signal at room temperature in air is ~4weeks when entrapped in the zeolite compared to several minutes in free solution (10) (in the crystalline Co-salen solid, peroxo-dimers are formed exclusively (10)). This is a manifestation of the extremely effective site-isolation achieved by entrapping the complexes inside the pores of the zeolite leading to elimination of the normal autoxidation mechanism.

Secondly, an examination of the thermodynamics of oxygen binding as plotted in a Hill plot (Figure 2) at 4 different temperatures shows evidence of a negative cooperativity between cobalt binding sites (slope<1) (11). This result means that binding of oxygen to the first few cobalt sites makes it progressively more difficult for subsequent oxygen to bind to other sites. This is the reverse of hemoglobin's behavior. The explanation is still unclear, but may well result from progressively more difficult oxygen binding as one progresses from the exterior to the interior of each zeolite crystallite. Binding of oxygen at the cobalt sites in the outermost cages of the crystallite is easiest but binding becomes more difficult as the oxygen has to diffuse toward the interior sites. A van't Hoff plot of the data reveals an enthalpy of binding of -11.4Kcal/mol and an entropy of -51e.u. which compare with values of -12.4Kcal/mol and -47e.u. for the same complex in pyridine solution(12). The lower oxygen binding constants inside the zeolite therefore appear to result from a reduced exothermicity consistent with the oxygen being bound at a restrictive site where the sterics of interaction of bound oxygen with the zeolite cavity walls are important.

This example demonstrates the ability of zeolites to reproduce the control (typical of enzyme proteins) of both the interactions between active sites and the thermodynamics of reactions at those active sites. The next example demonstrates the zeolite's ability to kinetically control product selectivity in an oxidation reaction typical of the monoxygenase enzymes.

Cytochrome P450 Analogue

Further on down the respiratory chain from hemoglobin lie the monoxygenase enzymes, cytochromes P450, which perform the function of selectively oxidizing organic materials to usable or excretable hydrophyllic compounds. Their unique ability to convert, for example, unactivated alkanes to alcohols with unusual selectivities using only molecular oxygen and a reducing cofactor (while in aqueous solution and at room temperature) has made these materials the envy of synthetic organic chemists. There have been numerous attempts to model the heme-iron active site of the enzymes(13) so as to reproduce some of their selectivity by including multiple bulky peripheral substituents upon the basic porphyrin nucleus. While these models have undoubtedly contributed tremendously to an understanding of the mechanistic features of the monoxygenases they have yet to demonstrate the phenomenal selectivities.

The enzyme cycle is represented in Figure 3, emphasizing only the redox and coordination at the iron center. If one accepts the tenet that the FeO^{3+} species is the active potent oxidant then the selectivity of the enzyme is dictated by how the protein sieves and directs substrates toward this indiscriminate oxidant. How does nature produce this oxidant? she takes molecular oxygen, two electrons and two protons and eliminates water!Our mimic(14) is designed to do the same thing except that we will take the two electrons and two protons together as molecular hydrogen and combine it with oxygen over Pd(0) to generate hydrogen peroxide. This hydrogen peroxide can then be reacted at an iron site to eliminate water and give the desired FeO^{3+} unit. If all of this is done inside the stereochemically demanding pores of a zeolite then any substrate which is simultaneously in those pores should suffer selective oxidation by the FeO^{3+} as directed by the zeolite framework.

The mimic is prepared by sequential ion-exchanges with iron(II) and Pd(II) tetrammine cations followed by calcinations and reduction of the Pd(II) to Pd(0) as previously described(14). A material with ~2wt% Fe(II) and 1wt% Pd(0) is used by immersing the dry zeolite solid in neat substrate alkane and then pressuring the reaction vessel with a 3:1 mixture of oxygen:hydrogen. After shaking this mixture at room temperature for 4 hours the products are analyzed by capillary GC. As a control to assess the intrinsic selectivity of such a Pd/Fe system in the absence of steric effects of the zeolite, catalysts prepared with amorphous silico-aluminate supports were run for comparison. In these cases all reactions must take place at the particle surface since there is no interior pore structure available. In addition, comparison of reaction selectivities of this catalysts with our zeolite materials allows us to ascertain that the Fe active sites must be actually inside (and not on the exterior surface) of the zeolite crystallites.

The first zeolite host explored was zeolite A which is a very selective

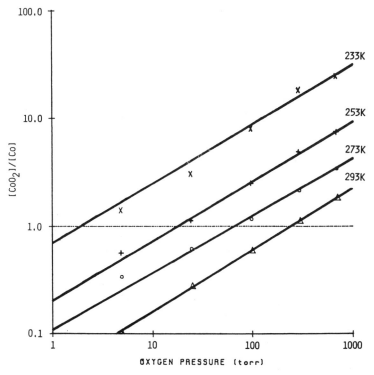

Figure 2.   Hill plot of oxygen binding to Co-salen.py in zeolite Y.

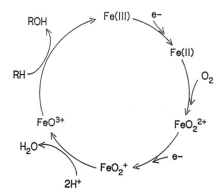

Figure 3.   Enzyme cycle of Cytochrome P450.

absorbent of linear alkanes to the exclusion of branched or cyclic hydrocarbons(15). It was therefore expected that extreme examples of substrate selectivity could be achieved in competitive oxidation of linear alkanes vs. cyclic alkanes.

Figure 4a confirms this expectation. While the selectivity for oxidation of n-octane in the presence of cyclohexane is slight (55:45) over the control silicoaluminate support, the selectivity over the A zeolite is tremendous (>200:1) in favor of the linear alkane.(plots are of total of all oxidation products from each substrate) This indicates that the zeolite is exerting its sieving effect and therefore the desired chemistry is occurring inside the zeolite pores. Indeed, not only is the chemistry occurring there but the vast majority of the octanol products are remaining there at the end of the reaction and can only be released for analysis by complete destruction of the framework using conc. sulfuric acid! This trapping of products is more than simple absorption since they are not released simply by displacement with a more polar molecule (eg. water) The production of secondary alcohols as part of the product mix means that the pores of the zeolite rapidly become filled with molecules which are too large to escape from the interior and remain trapped. These molecules then act as plugs for escape of even the linear alcohol products so that the entire zeolite interior becomes saturated with products and the catalytic activity is shut down.

The incredible substrate selectivity of this system pales in comparison to the regioselectivity displayed by the octane oxidation products! In Figure 4b the dramatic increase of products derived from terminal methyl group oxidation in the zeolite system is apparent (plots are normalized to a "per hydrogen" basis and represent the total of products (alcohols and ketones) at each position in the chain). Over the control catalyst the primary/ secondary oxidation ratio is 0.05 while in the zeolite A this ratio is 0.6. This selectivity for oxidation toward the end of the alkane chain probably arises from the very close fit between the alkane and the A pore size which essentially constrains it to have an extended "linear" conformation. It is therefore the methyl end groups which are the first to encounter and so be oxidized by the iron active sites which tend to be located in the six ring faces of the zeolite cage (illustrated schematically in Figure 5).

While the selectivities of this system are dramatic the activity is low (~1 turnover on Fe in a 4 hr. batch run) and the necessity of running all reactions in an explosion rated environment (because of the H_2/O_2 mixtures) combined with the need to dissolve away the zeolite to reclaim products make this a very impractical synthetic method for alkane

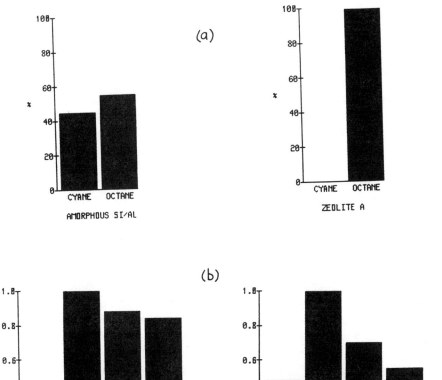

Figure 4.   Selectivity of alkane oxidation with Fe/Pd/A zeolite and
             H_2/O_2. a) substrate selectivity between n-octane and
             cyclohexane and b) regioselectivity of n-octane oxidation.

oxidation. These problems can each be addressed as follows. The low turnover and product trapping are really the same problem since we believe that it is the plugging of the pore system by products which leads to the shut down of the reaction since at that point no further substrate can get to the active sites - this is a familiar problem with zeolite catalysis (Herron, N. J. Coord. Chem, in press) and should be solved by two changes. 1) a larger pore system will permit egress of product secondary alcohols (at the obvious expense of lowered substrate selectivity) 2) a higher Si/Al ratio zeolite is more hydrophobic and at a ratio above ~20 begins to favor absorption of the reactant alkane over the product alcohols (at the expense of ion exchange sites). These criteria can be met by the ZSM-5 zeolite with its 10-ring channels and high Si/Al ratio. The inconvenience of using hydrogen/oxygen mixtures can be circumvented by using preformed hydrogen peroxide rather then making it in situ by combination over Pd(0). The ideal system is therefore a simple Fe ion-exchanged high silica ZSM-5 zeolite fed hydrogen peroxide (either aqueous or in organic solvents at low concentration). Oxidation of n-octane with this system does indeed lead to all products being recovered from the supernatant solution without zeolite dissolution and the system becoming truly catalytic with ~4 turnovers on Fe in 4 hours. Remarkably, the regioselectivity of the ZSM-5 system is even more pronounced for oxidation towards the terminus of the alkane chain with a primary/secondary oxidation ratio of 3.3. This material is now in the ballpark of a viable ω-hydroxylase mimic. This enzyme is capable of regioselective oxidation of terminal methyl groups of alkanes or linear carboxylic acids with a prim/sec oxidation ratio of ~10.

Iron-sulfur Protein Analogue

One of the essential cofactor enzymes in the cytochrome P450 network provides electrons to reduce iron and or oxygen to generate the active oxidant. These natural electron-transfer materials are typified by the iron-sulfur proteins(16). Work by Holm and others has modeled the basic iron-sulfur cores of these proteins and a variety of structure types have been modeled. One of these types, an iron-sulfur cubane like cluster consists of interpenetrating tetrahedra of iron and sulfide ions.

The fascination with using zeolites as very small reaction chambers for production of novel species which are not available in normal environments had led us to explore the possibility of synthesizing extremely small particles of semiconductor materials within the pores (Herron, N.; Wang, Y.; Stucky, G. D.; Eddy, M. M.; Cox, D. E.; Bein, T.;

Moller, K. <u>J. Am. Chem. Soc</u> in press.)(17). This is of interest from the standpoint that such small pieces of a bulk semiconductor lattice cannot fully develop the normal semi- conductor band structure and so reside in the so called size-quantized or quantum-confined regime. This is where the electron-hole pair of an excited semiconductor particle has a radius(18) larger than the actual particle size. The electron then behaves as a particle in a box and novel optical properties result. We decided, therefore, to look at preparation of CdS inside the zeolite cavities and then to explore the photo-oxidation chemistry of these species with absorbed olefins.

Cadmium ion-exchange of zeolite Y followed by calcination in flowing oxygen leads to materials having from 0 to 90% of the original sodium ions replaced by Cd. Treatment of the dry calcined zeolite with hydrogen sulfide gas (1atm) at 100°C generates the CdS clusters inside the zeolite pores(17). The quantum confinement effects are manifest in that the material is typically white or pale cream rather than the yellow-orange of bulk CdS. The actual structure of the CdS units in the zeolite is revealed by a detailed study of the powder x-ray diffractograms and EXAFS data. These techniques reveal the basic unit to be a cubane Cd_4S_4 cluster of interpenetrating Cd and S tetrahedra - (Figure 6) very reminiscent of the Fe_4S_4 cluster core discussed above. These clusters are located in the small sodalite cages of the framework and are strongly interacting with it through Cd-O bonds (Figure 6). What is particularly interesting is how these clusters begin to interact with one another as the loading density begins to rise above the percolation threshold of 15 vol%. At this point the absorption spectra begin to reveal a new absorption band and luminescence behavior starts to switch on as the three dimensionally interconnected array (cluster-cluster distance of ~6Å) of quantum dots begins to develop a semiconductor like band structure (Figure 6).

Since all of the CdS clusters reside in the sodalite cages of the zeolite Y framework, the larger supercages of the structure are still available for absorption of substrate molecules - in this case olefins for photo- oxidation via electron transfer. Colloidal CdS in free solution has been used for such oxidations previously(19) and in a competitive oxidation of styrene and 1,1-diphenylethylene we find that unconfined bulk CdS will effect oxidation in a ratio of 1:2 for these two olefins (irradiation at 365nm). In the zeolite confined system we find however that the ratio becomes 1:1 ie a slight shift in selectivity toward the smaller substrate as may be expected on the basis of size/diffusion effects. From the viewpoint of the enzyme mimic, we have here a system

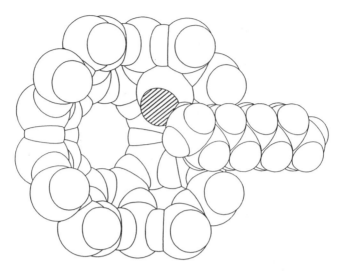

Figure 5.   Cutaway representation of n-octane proceeding through the 8-ring window of zeolite A towards the iron active site for oxidation. Cross hatched atom is the active oxygen on iron.

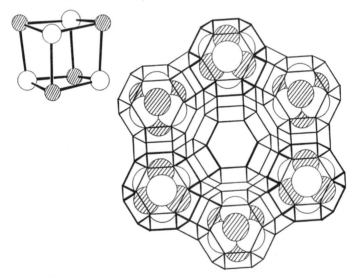

Figure 6.   CdS clusters in the sodalite cages of zeolite Y. The zeolite has been reduced to sticks connecting only the tetrahedral atoms for clarity. Inset shows the structure of an individual CdS cubane-like cluster. Cd atoms are cross hatched.

which mimics the core structure of iron sulfur proteins while also undergoing electron transfer (photo stimulated) with substrate molecules in analogy with these same proteins.

The future of this line of research lies not in the enzyme mimicry described above but more in the novel optical and especially non-linear optical properties of quantum confined semiconductor systems - the production of optical computer elements such as optical transistors, spatial light modulators and phase conjugate materials. From the biomimetic perspective we are moving in the direction of the silicon-based brain!

Conclusion

The above examples have demonstrated that viable enzyme mimics of hemoglobin, cytochrome P450 and iron-sulfur proteins can indeed be produced by making use of the analogy between protein tertiary structure and the pore structure of inorganic "Si-based" zeolite systems. These examples represent only the tip of a potentially enormous mountain of novel, robust and highly practical enzyme mimics. It only requires that biochemists view zeolites as sterically demanding supports for active sites and that zeolite chemists view zeolites as something other than acid catalysts or ion-exchangers. If that can be communicated by this and similar articles there may be considerable "life" left in these old rocks yet.

Acknowledgments

The technical assistance of J. B. Jensen, S. Harvey, J. D. Nicholson and J. E. Macdougall was invaluable while contributions of Drs. C. A. Tolman, Y. Wang, D. R. Corbin, R. D. Farlee, G. D. Stucky, M. M. Eddy, W. E. Farneth, T. Bein and K. Moller to various aspects of this work were likewise dramatic. The assistance of E. Jayne Allen in preparing this manuscript is greatly appreciated.

Literature Cited

1)   Dyer, A; Hayes, G. G.; Phillips, G. O.; Townsend, R. P. Molecular Sieves; ACS Adv. Chem. Ser., American Chemical Society: Washington, DC, 1973, No.121, 299.

2)   Breck, D. W. Zeolite Molecular Sieves; Wiley: New York, 1974.

3)   Collman, J. P.; Gagne, R. R.; Halbert, T. R.; Marchon, J. C.; Reed, C. A. J. Am. Chem. Soc. 1973, 95, 7868.

4)   see Jones, R. D.; Summerville, D. A.; Basolo, F. Chem. Revs., 1979, 79, 139.

5)   Alben, J. O.; Fuchsmau, W. H.; Beaudreau, C. A.; Caughey, W. S. Biochemistry, 1968, 7, 624.

6)   Baldwin, J. M. Brit. Med. Bull. 1976, 32, 213.

7)   Herron, N. Inorg. Chem. 1986, 25, 4717.

8)   Wilmarth, W. K.; Aranoff, S.; Calvin, M. J. Am. Chem.Soc. 1946, 68, 2263.

9)   This term was first coined in Herron, N.; Stucky, G. D.; Tolman, C. A. Inorg. Chim. Acta 1985, 100, 135.

10)   Floriani, C.; Calderazzo, F. J. Chem. Soc A 1969, 946.
      Ochiai, E. I. J. Inorg. Nucl. Chem. 1973, 35, 1727.
      Barkelew, C .H.; Calvin, M. J. Am. Chem. Soc. 1946, 68, 2257.

11)   Hill, A. V. J. Physiol. (London) 1910, 40, IV-VII.

12)   Tauzher, G.; Amiconi, G.; Antonini, E; Brunori, M.; Costa, G. Nature (London) New Biol. 1973, 241, 222.

13)   see for example Cook, B. R.; Reinert, T. J.; Suslick, K. S. J. Am. Chem. Soc. 1986, 108, 7281.

14)   Herron, N.; Tolman, C. A. J. Am. Chem. Soc. 1987, 109, 2837.

15)   Barrer, R. M. in Zeolite and Clay Minerals as Sorbents and Molecular Sieves, Academic Press: New York, 1978.

16)   Tsibris, J. C. M.; Woody, R. D. Coord. Chem. Revs 1970, 5, 417.
      Kimura, T. Structure and Bonding, 1968, 5, 1.

17)   Wang, Y.; Herron, N. J. Phys. Chem. 1987, 91, 257.

18)   Brus, L. E. J. Phys. Chem. 1986, 90, 2555.

19)   Fox, M. A. Acc. Chem. Res. 1983, 16, 314.

RECEIVED November 7, 1988

Chapter 12

Immobilization of Proteins and Enzymes onto Functionalized Polypropylene Surfaces by a Gaseous Plasma Modification Technique

R. Sipehia, J. Daka[1], A. S. Chawla[1], and T. M. S. Chang

Artificial Cells and Organs Research Centre, Faculty of Medicine, McGill University, Montreal, Quebec H3G 1Y6, Canada

Polypropylene membranes or beads were treated in gaseous plasma of anhydrous ammonia in order to add amino groups on to their surfaces. The presence of the amino groups was detected by FT-IR-ATR spectrometry. Through these amino groups in one batch of the samples, albumin was immobilized. The presence of immobilized albumin on the polymer surface was confirmed by FT-IR-ATR spectrometry. Glucose oxidase and peroxidase were immobilized individually onto two separate batches of polypropylene beads with amino groups on their surfaces. With the help of calibration curves, it was found that 40-55% of the immobilized enzymes were in the active form. Beads and membranes bearing enzymes and other proteins are important materials for biotechnology. This technique demonstrates that even inert polymers can be activated easily for attachment of these biomolecules.

Gaseous plasma generated by an electrical discharge at low pressure provides a unique and powerful method for the modification of surfaces of biomaterials without altering their bulk properties. This modification could be made by plasma polymerization wherein a thin, highly cross-linked and pin hole free film of filler free silicone polymer could be added onto a variety of substrate materials in order to prepare improved blood compatible surfaces (1). Alternatively, gaseous plasma could be used to add new chemical groups to a material surface which could then be used for attaching a variety of biomolecules. By anhydrous ammonia plasma, amino groups can be added to the surface of polypropylene membranes or to the surface of polypropylene beads. These amino groups can then be employed to bind albumin to polypropylene as was done in our previous work in which a quantitative measure of bound protein was

[1]Current address: Bureau of Radiation and Medical Devices, Health and Welfare Canada, Ottawa, Ontario K1A 0L2, Canada

0097–6156/89/0392–0155$06.00/0
© 1989 American Chemical Society

done using ^{125}I-labelled albumin (2,3). It was found that
immobilized albumin was strongly bound and had a higher surface
concentration of 275 $\mu g/cm^2$ compared with 28 $\mu g/cm^2$ obtained by a
chemical immobilization method (4). To show the versatility of the
plasma technique, we have extended the work to enzymes; glucose
oxidase and peroxidase, which were attached to two separate batches
of polypropylene beads.

In the present studies, a Fourier-transform infra-red
spectrometer in attenuated total reflectance mode (FT-IR-ATR) was
used to characterize the albuminated polymer membrane surface. FT-
IR-ATR is a powerful surface analysis technique in which a spectrum
of only a few micron thick surface layer is obtained. As albumin or
enzymes were attached only on the surfaces of polypropylene, FT-IR-
ATR technique was ideally suited for the their analysis.

MATERIALS AND METHODS

Glucose oxidase (from Aspergillus niger, specific activity 20
unit/mg), was purchased from Boehringer Mannheim Canada Ltd.
(Dorval, Quebec, Canada). Bovine albumin (Fraction V), peroxidase
(from Horseradish, specific activity 44 unit/mg) and O-dianisidine
dihydrochloride (purified crystals) were purchased from Sigma
Chemical Company (St. Louis, MO, USA). A 0.5M phosphate buffer at
pH 7.5 was used in these studies.

Anhydrous ammonia was purchased from Matheson Canada Ltd.,
Whitby, Ontario. The substrate materials used were polypropylene
membrane (Celgard-2400, Celanese Corp., Summit, NJ) and
polypropylene beads (Hercules Canada Ltd., Montreal, Quebec). The
Celgard-2400 was a 25.4 μm thick porous membrane with an effective
pore size of 0.02 μm with a 38% porosity. The beads as purchased
were slightly flattened spheres having a diameter of about 2.5-3 mm
and being about 3.5 mm thick. The membranes and the beads were
washed with distilled water, then with absolute ethanol in an
ultrasonic cleaner and were finally dried in a vacuum oven, at about
70° C. These substrate materials were ready for use as a control or
for further treatment. The further treatment involved the
attachment of NH_2 groups onto the surface of the substrate material
in an ammonia plasma reactor, perhaps by free-radical reaction, as
reported in our previous report (2).

The detailed discussions of the plasma reactor used has already
been given (5) Briefly, it was a cylindrical glass vessel of about
60 x 10 cm O.D. The radio frequency (RF) plasma generator (Tegal
Corp., Richmond, California) was capacitatively coupled to the
plasma reactor by placing flat strips of copper electrodes along the
outside circumference. The substrate polymer membrane was placed
7.5 cm downstream from the gas outlets.

In order to activate polypropylene beads, 40 beads were placed
inside a cylindrical container (28 x 8 cm O.D.) which was then
inserted in the plasma reactor. This container had an attached
glass rod (18 x 1 cm O.D.) the free end of which was coupled to an
electric motor by which the container, and hence polypropylene
beads, could be rotated inside the plasma reactor. The speed of
rotation was 3 rpm during the process of attachment of NH_2 groups
onto the surfaces of the beads.

The plasma reactor was evacuated using a rotary vacuum pump. The attachment of amino groups onto the surfaces of the membranes or beads was carried out at 0.4 mm Hg, because at this pressure, the attachment of NH_2 groups was found to be greatest (4). The 0.4 mm Hg pressure was maintained by anhydrous NH_3 feed. When the pressure inside the reactor had stabilized at 0.4 mm Hg a pulsed RF power of 30 W was applied. The times of power-on and power-off were equal. At the end of a 30-min reaction period, the plasma was switched off and the feed of anhydrous ammonia gas was stopped. The propylene beads were evacuated for an additional 30 min to remove the unreacted species. The beads exposed to ammonia gaseous plasma are referred to as PPB-NH_2. To characterize the surfaces of the control and the modified membranes, the FT-IR spectrometry (Nicolet 7000 Series) with an ATR attachment was used. KRS-5 reflection plate at an incident angle of $45°$ was employed for FT-IR-ATR work. Control or modified membrane samples were applied on both sides of the reflection plate. This allowed spectra of only few micron thick layer of the surfaces contacting the KRS-5 reflection plate to be obtained. Immobilization of albumin onto membrane having surface amino groups has been described (2,3).

Attachment of glucose oxidase to the amino groups on the polypropylene beads was carried out as follows: a 5-mL solution of glucose oxidase, containing 20 mg of enzyme in phosphate buffer, (0.5M, pH 7.5) was prepared. Thirty beads (PPB-NH_2) were soaked in this solution for one hour. After removing the beads, the concentration of the remaining enzyme solution was measured and was used in calculating the initial concentration of the enzyme on the bead surface.

The beads removed from enzyme solution were washed several times with phosphate buffer solution in order to remove loosely bound glucose oxidase. They were then soaked in the cross-linking solution of 1.5% glutaraldehyde in phosphate buffer for 2 h. The beads were removed from the cross-linking solution, washed with phosphate buffer and left in 0.13 M glycine for 24 h to eliminate the remaining free aldehyde groups on their surface. These polypropylene beads, with immobilized glucose oxidase, were referred to as GO-PPB.

The procedure used to prepare immobilized peroxidase was the same as described above for the glucose oxidase. The polypropylene beads with immobilized peroxidase on their surface were designated as P-PPB.

In order to determine the quantity of enzyme which had been covalently immobilized onto the beads, calibration curves relating enzyme activities to enzyme concentrations were prepared. Various concentrations of each enzyme (glucose oxidase and peroxidase) were employed in these calibrations. O-Dianisidine was used as an enzyme reactant. The appearance of absorbency due to the oxidation of O-dianisidine at 460 nm, by the catalytic activity of the enzymes, was followed with the help of the Bausch & Lomb, Double Beam, Spectronic 2000 spectrophotometer. The rate of reaction increased with the increased amount of enzyme employed.

RESULTS AND DISCUSSION

The FT-IR-ATR absorption spectrum of the control polypropylene
(untreated) is shown in Figure 1. It is a typical polypropylene
spectrum with absorption bands due to asymmetric and symmetric
stretching of CH_3 and CH_2 groups around 2900 cm^{-1}. The absorption
bands at 1460 and at 1380 cm^{-1} represent the asymmetric and
symmetric bending of CH_3 , respectively. Absorption bands at 2878
cm^{-1} (CH_3 stretching) and at 841 cm^{-1} (Methylene rocking modes)
suggest that the polypropylene membrane is of the isotactic form.

The FT-IR-ATR spectrum of the polypropylene membrane with amino
groups on its surface is shown in Figure 2. The spectrum shows the
appearance of a broad absorption bands between 3100 and 3600 cm^{-1}
representing asymmetric stretching for NH_2 groups. The absorption
band at about 1670 cm^{-1} represents the carbonyl stretching of an
amide group (the amide I band). The band at about 1550 cm^{-1}
represents the bending vibrations of $-NH_2$ group (the amide II
band). These bands suggest that residual oxygen in the plasma
reactor was taking part in the reactions to produce amide groups on
the polymer surface.

FT-IR-ATR spectra of the control membrane and of the
albuminated membrane are shown in Figures 3A and 3B, respectively.
Only a part of the spectra of interest are shown. The amide I band
of bovine albumin (highly α-helical) occur at 1658 cm^{-1} which is
due to C=O stretch. The amide II band appears at 1540 cm^{-1}
representing -NH bending.

The appearance of aminde I and amide II bands in the FT-IR-ATR
spectrum of the albuminated membranes (Figure 3B) confirms that
albumin is indeed immobilized. The above band did not appear in the
FT-IR-ATR spectrum of the control membrane (Figure 3A).

According to our activity- enzyme calibration curve, the total
amounts of the immobilized glucose oxidase and peroxidase on the
bead surface were found to be 52.0 $\mu g/cm^2$ and 43 $\mu g/cm^2$,
respectively. To assess the stability of enzyme-polypropylene
linkage (GO-PPB and P-PPB), the beads were washed with buffer for
up to six hours. The results of washing GO-PPB and P-PPB are shown
in Figure 4 and Figure 5, respectively. It can be seen from these
figures that after the initial removal of the physically adsorbed
enzymes, the concentrations of the enzymes tend to reach a steady
state. After washing with a buffer for six hours, the amounts of
glucose oxidase and peroxidase retained on the beads were found to
be 20.36 ug/cm^2 and 23.7 ug/cm^2 respectively on the basis of
calibration curves. Therefore, enzymes immobilized on polypropylene
beads using anhydrous ammonia plasma varied between 39-55% of the
original amounts. Control beads, which had no NH_2 groups on the
surface but were exposed to enzyme solutions showed no attachment of
the enzymes. This suggests that the NH_2 group is essential in the
binding of enzymes to the bead surfaces and the binding force
between the enzymes and the activated polypropylene support was
strong.

CONCLUSION

The results of the present ammonia plasma treatment show that a
polypropylene surface can be functionalized with NH_2 groups by the
ammonia plasma technique. The resultant polymer is fairly suitable

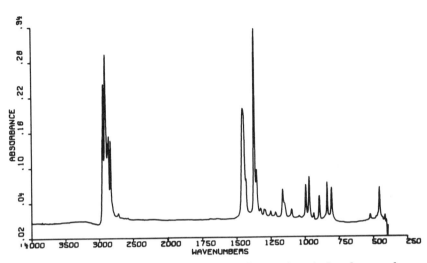

Figure 1. FT-IR absorption spectrum of an untreated polypropylene surface (control).

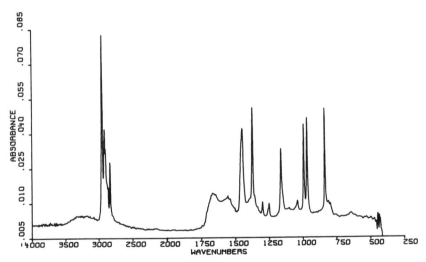

Figure 2. FT-IR spectrum of the polypropylene membrane with amino groups attached to its surface.

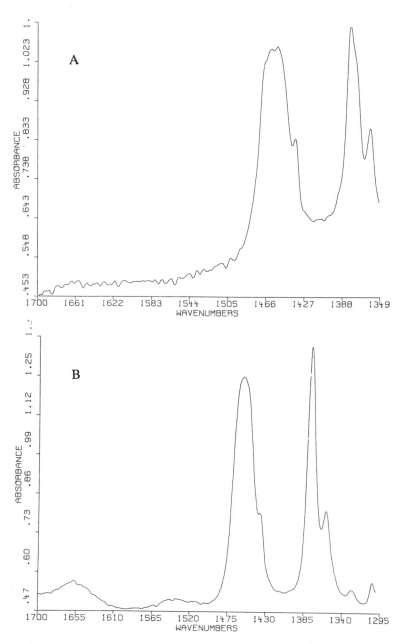

Figure 3.   Comparison of the FT-IR spectra of a control
             polypropylene membrane (A) with that of the albuminated
             polypropylene membrane (B).

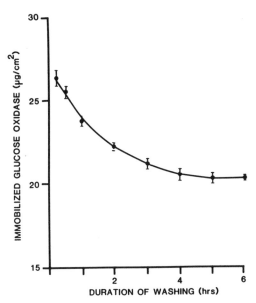

Figure 4. Concentration of immobilized glucose oxidase remaining on polypropylene beads (GO-PPB) after washing with phosphate buffer for various time intervals (n=3).

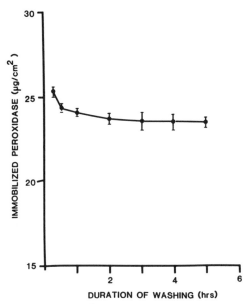

Figure 5. Concentration of immobilized peroxidase remaining on polypropylene beads (P-PPB) after washing with phosphate buffer for various time intervals (N=3).

for attachment of proteins, including those with catalytic
properties such as enzymes. Thus the immobilization of proteinious
antigens and antibodies to originally inert polypropylene can also
be achieved by this method.

ACKNOWLEDGMENT

The financial support provided by the Medical Research Council of
Canada, and the designation of grant support as a center of
excellence in science and technology by the Ministry of Higher
Education, Science and Technology of Quebec (to TMS Chang) is
appreciated.

REFERENCES

1. Chawla, A.S.; Sipehia, R.   J. Biomed. Mater. Res. 1984, 18, 537-545.
2. Sipehia, R.; Chawla, A.S.   Biomat., Med. Dev., Art. Org. 1982, 10, 229-   246.
3. Sipehia, R.; Chawla, A.S.; Chang, T.M.S.   Biomaterials 1986, 7, 471-473.
4. Hoffman, A.S.; Schmer, G.; Harris, C.; Kraft, W.G. Trans. Amer. Soc. Artif. Int. Organs 1972, 18, 10-16.
5. Chawla, A.S. Trans. Amer. Soc. Artif. Int. Organs 1979, 25, 287-293.

RECEIVED November 28, 1988

INDEXES

Author Index

Affiliation Index

Subject Index

Production by Rebecca Hunsicker
Indexing by Deborah H. Steiner

Elements typeset by Hot Type Ltd., Washington, DC
Printed and bound by Maple Press, York, PA

Recent ACS Books

Biotechnology and Materials Science: Chemistry for the Future
Edited by Mary L. Good
160 pp; clothbound; ISBN 0–8412–1472–7

Chemical Demonstrations: A Sourcebook for Teachers
Volume 1, Second Edition by Lee R. Summerlin and James L. Ealy, Jr.
192 pp; spiral bound; ISBN 0–8412–1481–6
Volume 2, Second Edition by Lee R. Summerlin, Christie L. Borgford, and Julie B. Ealy
229 pp; spiral bound; ISBN 0–8412–1535–9

The Language of Biotechnology: A Dictionary of Terms
By John M. Walker and Michael Cox
ACS Professional Reference Book; 256 pp;
clothbound, ISBN 0–8412–1489–1; paperback, ISBN 0–8412–1490–5

Cancer: The Outlaw Cell, Second Edition
Edited by Richard E. LaFond
274 pp; clothbound, ISBN 0–8412–1419–0; paperback, ISBN 0–8412–1420–4

Chemical Structure Software for Personal Computers
Edited by Daniel E. Meyer, Wendy A. Warr, and Richard A. Love
ACS Professional Reference Book; 107 pp;
clothbound, ISBN 0–8412–1538–3; paperback, ISBN 0–8412–1539–1

Practical Statistics for the Physical Sciences
By Larry L. Havlicek
ACS Professional Reference Book; 198 pp; clothbound; ISBN 0–8412–1453–0

The Basics of Technical Communicating
By B. Edward Cain
ACS Professional Reference Book; 198 pp; clothbound; ISBN 0–8412–1451–4

The ACS Style Guide: A Manual for Authors and Editors
Edited by Janet S. Dodd
264 pp; clothbound; ISBN 0–8412–0917–0

Personal Computers for Scientists: A Byte at a Time
By Glenn I. Ouchi
276 pp; clothbound; ISBN 0–8412–1000–4

Chemistry and Crime: From Sherlock Holmes to Today's Courtroom
Edited by Samuel M. Gerber
135 pp; clothbound; ISBN 0–8412–0784–4

For further information and a free catalog of ACS books, contact:
American Chemical Society
Distribution Office, Department 225
1155 16th Street, NW, Washington, DC 20036
Telephone 800–227–5558